DESKTOP PUBLISHING
BY DESIGN

EVERYONE'S GUIDE TO PAGEMAKER® 5

Praise for Desktop Publishing by Design:

"Desktop Publishing by Design is the best 'first book' on desktop publishing."

—*PC Week*

"If you work (or intend to work) with PageMaker, this text is an absolute must."

—*Computer Shopper*

"One of the most useful and attractive books we've seen on desktop publishing and design....Full of ideas and inspiration."

—*The New York Times*

"1993 Reader's Choice Award"

—*Publish*

"A treasure trove of useful, detailed examples and tips designed to help readers create desktop-published documents that get attention....An excellent reference work for anyone who is designing and creating documents with PageMaker. I loved it!"

Richard Landry,
Editor-in-Chief
—*PC World*

"If you're still looking for an overall introductory text in desktop publishing, this may well be the best yet....Microsoft Press simply doesn't seem to do anything but top-notch books. This is one more in a long string of high-quality texts that simply can't fail to satisfy....A splendid book."

—*Computing Now*

"The Strunk and White of desktop publishing....A brilliantly thought-out and classically executed work....For anyone already experimenting with desktop publishing, or contemplating doing so, it belongs in the most frequently used section of your library."

—*Woodstock Times*

DESKTOP PUBLISHING
BY DESIGN
EVERYONE'S GUIDE TO PAGEMAKER® 5

Blueprints for Page Layout

Using

Aldus® PageMaker®

on IBM® and

Apple® Macintosh®

Computers.

Includes

Hands-On Projects.

Ronnie Shushan

and

Don Wright

PUBLISHED BY
Microsoft Press
A Division of Microsoft Corporation
One Microsoft Way
Redmond, Washington 98052-6399

Library of Congress Cataloging-in-Publication Data

Shushan, Ronnie.
   Desktop publishing by design : Aldus Pagemaker edition / Ronnie
Shushan, Don Wright. -- 3rd ed.
     p.   cm.
   Includes index.
   ISBN 1-55615-566-2
   1. PageMaker (Computer file)   2. Desktop publishing. I. Wright,
Don. II. Title.
Z253.532.P33S58   1993
686.2'2544536--dc20   93-30326
                                              CIP

Printed and bound in the United States of America.

1 2 3 4 5 6 7 8 9   MLML   9 8 7 6 5 4

Distributed to the book trade in Canada by Macmillan of Canada, a division of Canada
Publishing Corporation.

Distributed to the book trade outside the United States and Canada by
Penguin Books Ltd.

Penguin Books Ltd., Harmondsworth, Middlesex, England
Penguin Books Australia Ltd., Ringwood, Victoria, Australia
Penguin Books N.Z. Ltd., 182-190 Wairau Road, Auckland 10, New Zealand

British Cataloging-in-Publication Data available.

Acquisitions Editor: Dean Holmes
Project Editor: Mary Ann Jones
Proofreader/Copy Editor: Jennifer Harris

To all the pioneers

scientists and artists
engineers and designers
programmers and publishers

who have shown the way

▶▶▶ CONTENTS ◀◀◀

PREFACE TO THE THIRD EDITION

In revising *Desktop Publishing by Design*, we found that the section addressing graphic design needed very little revision, and the PageMaker tutorials required almost a complete rewrite. The moral, which isn't very surprising, is that the principles of good design are timeless, while technology is in a constant state of change. To be sure, trends play an important role in our media-saturated culture. But even the most undisciplined of today's graphic styles are based on a traditional repertoire of visual principles.

The greatly expanded capabilities of PageMaker 5 presented two challenges for this revision. The first was how to make the tutorials useful to people who use PageMaker on very different levels. Many users will always prefer the visual, point-and-drag way of working that made PageMaker so popular in the first place, while others will want to master the mathematically precise manipulation made possible by the Control Palette. To address this, the tutorials often present parallel techniques side by side, so it's easy for you to focus on the technique that suits your style of working.

The second challenge was how to make the book more useful as a reference. The result is a new section called PageMaker Basics. In truth, it presents considerably more than the basics and is intended to serve both as an overview of PageMaker's capabilities and as a compendium of information that you're most likely to refer to in the course of a day's work.

The hands-on projects have been completely revised for PageMaker 5. The section on color has been greatly expanded to cover the program's increased color capabilities. And there's a new project focusing entirely on tabs, an essential tool of good typesetting that confounds a great many people.

One premise of this book that hasn't changed since the earlier editions is our belief that the computer is only a tool. Good design is not one of its default settings. PageMaker can enable you to draw a straight line and rotate it in tenth-of-a-degree increments, but it can't tell you how heavy to make the line or where to put it on the page. It places text in perfectly aligned columns, but it doesn't tell you how wide the columns should be or how much white space is needed to make the page appealing to read. It lets you experiment with as many typefaces as you can afford but requires your visual judgment to select and size the one that's right for your publication.

PageMaker is a wonderful tool, getting more powerful with each new release. But all the great features—color, typographic controls, mathematical manipulation of objects, rotation, zoom tools, and many more—are only an extension of your creativity. We hope this book will help you gain some of the skill, experience, and visual discrimination needed to use it well.

Ronnie Shushan
Don Wright

INTRODUCTION

▶ ▶ ▶ ▶ ▶

▶ ▶ ▶ ▶ ▶

T his book is about two dramatically different and complementary tools of communication: graphic design and electronic page assembly. The first is a tradition as old as recorded history, the second a technology unimaginable to most of us just a decade ago. In addition to changing the way we produce documents and publications of every kind, the combination of these tools is introducing more people than ever before to the art and technology of publishing.

Technology has always had an impact on visual communication, which is essentially what graphic design is. At every stage of the evolution of the communication arts—from prehistoric cave paintings to Gutenberg's movable type to today's computerized typesetting and imaging systems—technology has increased the potential for communication with audiences that are both broader and more specialized than before.

The computer is by all odds the most extraordinary of the technological clothing ever devised by man, since it is an extension of our central nervous system. Beside it the wheel is a mere hula-hoop.
—Marshall McLuhan

In the past, especially in the last half century or so during which graphic design as a commercial art has flourished, people entered the field through formal training in art schools and apprenticeships with experienced designers. The proliferation of desktop-publishing technology has attracted and, in some companies, required many people with no training in the visual arts to take responsibility for a wide range of printed material. Increased access to publishing tools has motivated many businesses to produce in-house publications that were previously done, in whole or in part, by outside contractors.

While expanding the number of people involved in printed communication, desktop typesetting and electronic page assembly has also radically changed the day-to-day operations of publishers, design studios, corporate art departments, and independent freelancers. Writers and editors who cannot draw a straight line find themselves assembling pages in electronic templates. Art directors used to specifying type on manuscripts are setting and manipulating it themselves. Production managers used to trafficking hard copy from one department to another are wrestling with the procedures of workgroup publishing.

Although they approach desktop publishing from different perspectives, people within both the business community and the publishing industry share a need for two different kinds of training. This book focuses on that need. It reviews the fundamental elements of graphic design for the many people without any training or experience in the visual arts who are suddenly responsible for producing—or who want to learn to produce—

business publications. And it provides hands-on tutorials for using Aldus PageMaker, the most popular electronic page layout program for both Macintosh and IBM-compatible computers.

There are very few rules in graphic design. A relatively subjective craft, it requires the designer to make one judgment after another based on such intangible criteria as "look" and "feel." Even if you have no inkling of the formal traditions and techniques taught in design schools, you have some personal experience with the elements designers work with—words, lines, colors, pictures.

On the other hand, there are hundreds and hundreds of rules for using Aldus PageMaker. Even with its user-friendly mouse, pull-down menus, and familiar drawing-board metaphor, PageMaker is not a program you just jump into and start producing pages with. It requires learning which commands to use and how to respond to dialog boxes and how the same commands in difference sequences produce different results. Sometimes the program appears to have a mind of its own. It can display your headline in one style when you know you specified another. It can refuse to place your graphic. It can appear to eat your text. It can tell you there's a bad hole record index detected by the line walker. (A bad what?)

One important quality common to designing printed pages and assembling them in PageMaker is that both tasks become intuitive as you gain experience. The variety of typefaces that intimidates a novice designer, for example, becomes a rich resource once you gain a feeling for the often subtle distinctions between them. The apparent mysteries of layout grids become time-saving production tools when you understand the simple principles that govern their use. Similarly, the endless rules that slow down the PageMaker rookie provide control and flexibility to the experienced user.

In a sense, this book tries to simulate experience both in graphic design and in using PageMaker. Section 1, "The Elements of Design," is a sort of primer of visual literacy as it relates to the printed page. It provides a vocabulary of graphic design in the context of desktop technology.

Section 2, "A PageMaker Portfolio" (and Chapter 3, "Creating a Grid," in Section 1) show sample pages from more than a hundred documents along with notes about design elements such as grid structure, type treatment, and use of art. Although these documents can't replace personal experience, they can provide the novice designer with a sense of the many different solutions to common design problems, and they can help you develop an eye for effective combinations. All the publications were created using PageMaker (along with other applications for word processing and graphics).

The third section, "PageMaker Basics," is an overview of the application. It's intended to provide an orientation to the program and to serve as a reference for features—such as the powerful new Control Palette and the much-improved printing functions—that aren't easily covered in a single hands-on project.

There are many techniques that can be applied in the search for visual solutions. Here are some of the most often used and easily identified:

Contrast	Harmony
Instability	Balance
Asymmetry	Symmetry
Irregularity	Regularity
Complexity	Simplicity
Fragmentation	Unity
Intricacy	Economy
Exaggeration	Understatement
Spontaneity	Predictability
Activeness	Stasis
Boldness	Subtlety
Accent	Neutrality
Transparency	Opacity
Variation	Consistency
Distortion	Accuracy
Depth	Flatness
Juxtaposition	Singularity
Randomness	Sequentiality
Sharpness	Diffusion
Episodicity	Repetition

—Donis A. Dondis,
A Primer of Visual Literacy

Think of buying a computer as like buying a car. A car just moves your body; your computer, though, is the chariot of your mind, carrying it through the whole universe. How much is your mind worth to you?
—Ted Nelson,
Computer Lib

The final section, "Hands-On Projects," provides actual experience. Here you'll find tutorials with step-by-step instructions for creating a variety of publications. The purpose is to help you learn and become more confident with PageMaker's tools and techniques by applying them to actual documents. PageMaker operates almost identically on the Macintosh and on IBM-compatibles, so you can do the projects on either type of computer. (Keystroke combinations are given for both types.)

The book was conceived to be used as a resource, rather than to be read from start to finish. If you want to start right in working with PageMaker, begin in Section 4. Or you might want to move back and forth between the overview in Section 3 and the hands-on exercises in Section 4. If you want to review publications of a particular kind, flip through Section 2. And if you want some grounding in design basics, start with Section 1. Even within each section, the chapters are organized so that you can begin at whatever point suits your needs and experience. If you stumble across an unfamiliar term, refer to the glossary at the back of the book.

We would like to acknowledge the contribution of the many designers who took the time to send us their work and talk about their experience with this marriage of art and technology. Thanks, also, to our friends and colleagues at Microsoft Press for their efforts in bringing this book from our studio to yours: to Dean Holmes for keeping watch, to Mary Ann Jones for managing the project at Microsoft and for her own editing, to Maureen Zimmerman for her editorial input, to Jennifer Harris for her very careful proofreading, to Becky Johnson for final production on the cover, and to all the others whose work goes on unbeknownst to us.

Thanks to the many people at Aldus who helped along the way: Freda Cook, Brad Stevens, David Salwitz, Dan Albertson, and especially Abbo Peterson for his tremendous effort in getting answers to a long list of technical questions. Thanks to everyone on the Aldus technical support team who particpated in that effort.

Visual communication of any kind, whether persuasive or informative, from billboards to birth announcements, should be seen as the embodiment of form and function: the integration of the beautiful and the useful.
—Paul Rand,
Thoughts on Design

Thanks to Bob Schaffel for clarifying issues of color production. To Jeff Milstein both for the delightful paper sculpture cards that add some whimsy to the color pages and for the use of his color printers. To Claudia Forest for 11th hour proofreading, copying, and compiling. To Megan Denver for answering dozens of SOS calls.

Thanks to Dan Martin at Sprintout for seeing us through the uncertainties of Linotronic output and for doing it quickly. And to Jeremy Stratton at ADMAC for guiding us through the uncharted waters of color separations in PageMaker 5. If we emphasize more than once the importance of having a good working relationship with service providers, it's because we value the expertise and good humor of the ones we've worked with.

And finally, thanks to Fred, who brings levity to even the longest days.

THE ELEMENTS OF DESIGN

CHAPTER 1

EFFECTIVE COMMUNICATION IN AN INFORMATION ENVIRONMENT

Past	Present	Future
Data	Information	Knowledge
Control	Access	Exploration
Calculation	Presentation	Communication

—Stuart Greene,
Apple Viewpoints

*T*he electronic age has given us an almost magical ability to store, retrieve, and analyze data. Whether you're making travel plans, checking the status of an insurance policy, or changing an assumption in a five-year plan, the computer can provide almost instantaneous answers to questions that only a decade ago might have remained unanswered for a day, a week, or even a month.

But the electronic age has not given us a paperless office. In fact, in a single year computers are said to churn out some 1200 pages of print for every man, woman, and child in the United States. Although they help us manage individual pieces of data, computers have increased our information overload.

In the midst of this overload, at a time when multimedia commands so much attention, it's useful to remember the fundamental power of print. Print is tangible; it has a life of its own. You can read it when you want, at your own pace, and keep it for future reference. And with desktop technology, you can produce more pages faster and cheaper than ever before.

But can you produce effective pages?

In the information environment, competition for the ever-shrinking attention span is fierce. We are saturated both as senders (too much to say, too little space) and as receivers (too much to read, too little time). The result is often information that is confusing, that you can't find when you need it, or that simply sits unread in a rotating stack of other communications that failed to deliver their messages. The cumulative result is an enormous amount of wasted effort and resources. The hidden costs, whether in sales or productivity or corporate image, are difficult to calculate.

The elements that make up a successful document—careful writing, thoughtful organization, effective design—grow out of an understanding of your message, your audience, and your resources. The publication checklist below can help guide you toward that understanding. The questions it raises force you to think through a great many variables and even some unpleasant realities. Some of the answers may raise more questions. The purpose of the checklist is to help you define your communication problem so that you can use graphic design as a way of solving it. We'll briefly consider each item on the checklist after a look at a few diverse examples of effective communication.

An erroneous conception of the graphic designer's function is to imagine that in order to produce a "good layout" all he need do is make a pleasing arrangement of miscellaneous elements. What is implied is that this may be accomplished simply by pushing these elements around until something happens. At best, this procedure involves the time-consuming uncertainties of trial and error, and at worst, an indifference to plan, order, or discipline.
—Paul Rand
Thoughts on Design

PUBLICATION CHECKLIST

- What is the purpose of your publication?

- Why is it needed?

- Who is the intended audience?

- What kind of information will your publication include?

- What kind of image do you want to project?

- Does the publication need to fit into a larger program or conform to a corporate style?

- What is the overall format?

- What kinds of art and photography—and how much—will be needed?

- What are the printing specifications?

- What will you use for camera-ready pages?

- How will the publication be reproduced?

- How will it be distributed?

- When is it needed?

- What is the budget?

The dramatically different documents reproduced on this and the following two pages illustrate the rich range of visual form that effective communication can take. Each of the four samples successfully solves a very different design problem, and their contrasting styles say a great deal about the different purpose and audience of each message.

A poster is one of the simplest and most direct forms of communication. It delivers a message that is as brief as it is bold. Although many posters rely heavily on graphics, this one is a reminder of the power of words.

The street language is well suited to the young audience; the rhythm of the words is in their own vernacular.

The typography follows the cadence of the words, so that the visual rhythm literally echoes the verbal message. Reverse type on a red background supports the jazzy rhythm and the serious message.

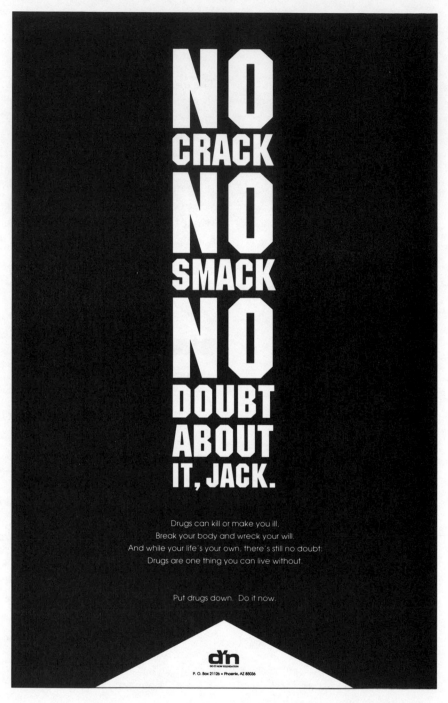

Design: Jim Parker (Phoenix, AZ)

Poster produced by the Do It Now Foundation.

Trim size: 12 by 19

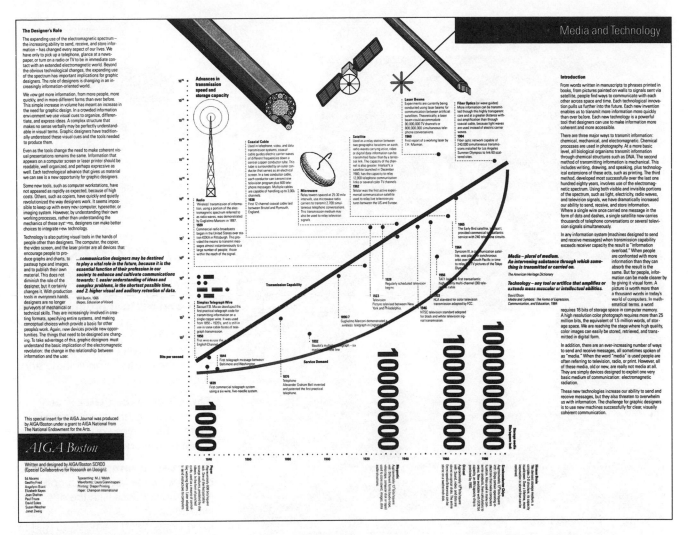

The carefully organized collection of information above is at the opposite end of the communications spectrum from the poster. The subject is media and technology; the audience is sophisticated (the document was designed as an insert for a graphic arts journal) and so is the delivery of information.

The chart encapsulates advances in transmission speed and storage capacity of media in the context of a time line. In addition to providing a great deal of information in a very small space, it cuts through the stereotypical image of charts as bland and linear.

Quotations inset between the running text and the chart provide a point of easy access in this complex page as well as another layer of historical context:

…communication designers may be destined to play a vital role in the future, because it is the essential function of their profession in our society to enhance and cultivate communications towards: 1. easier understanding of ideas and complex problems, in the shortest possible time, and 2. higher visual and auditory retention of data.
—Will Burtin, 1965

Design: Paul Souza, Ed Abrams, and Susan Wascher (Boston, MA)

Insert for the American Institute of Graphic Arts journal produced by AIGA/ Boston.

Trim size: 22 by 17

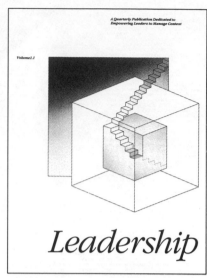

The conceptual illustration on the cover of this quarterly publication brings to bear the personal and subjective vision of the artist. It invites the reader to participate and engages the imagination.

The single-word title is very focused. It succinctly states the subject but leaves you curious as to how it will be addressed.

The overall image of the cover combines a feeling of accomplishment and success with the need for innovation and a sense of work yet to be done. Each element, as well as the whole, echoes the nature of leadership itself.

The dramatic photo composition on the cover of this PBS-series program guide has an emotional content that touches the reader in a way that straight typography cannot. The juxtaposition of a mushroom cloud against the outstretched hands of Gorbachev and Reagan evokes the terror and hope, the despair and optimism in the waning days of the Cold War. The photos also suggest the mix of historical and contemporary components in the series.

The title over the photos suggests that the series will be comprehensive. The wording is restrained and sets a tone that encourages the viewer to suspend moral judgments temporarily.

Design: Alison Kennedy (Boston, MA)

Program guide produced by WGBH and Central Independent Television.
Trim size: 8-1/2 by 11

Design: Weisz Yang Dunkelberger Inc. (Westport, CT)

Periodical published by Lefkoe & Associates, a management consulting and training organization.
Trim size: 9 by 12

What is the purpose of your publication?

Desktop technology can be used to produce documents as diverse as calling cards and four-color magazines. This book is concerned primarily with business documents, which usually fall into several categories. Identifying the category to which your document belongs (it may be more than one) can help you develop the right approach for the purpose.

Documents that persuade
Advertisements
Invitations
Fund raisers
Posters
Press releases
Promotional flyers
Prospectuses
Sales brochures

Documents that identify
Business cards
Certificates
Labels
Stationery

Documents that inform
Brochures
Bulletins
Curriculum listings
Fact sheets
Marketing plans
Product lists
Programs
Rate cards
Specification sheets

Periodicals that inform
Magazines
Newsletters
Newspapers
Reports

Documents that elicit response
Applications
Order forms
Surveys

Documents that provide reference
Calendars
Directories
Lists
Parts lists
Schedules
Timetables

Documents that give how-to information
Curriculum guides
Instruction manuals
Training guides

Why is your publication needed?

Desktop publishers get carried away with their tools. They...spend more time on the aesthetics of a document than the content of it.
—Boeing's DTP product manager, in an article in MacWEEK

One of the most important questions to ask yourself is why the reader needs or wants the information in your document. If you can zero in on that need, you can use it in your headlines and art to get the reader's attention. Keeping the reader's needs in mind also helps focus your writing.

In many cases the reader is at best indifferent and at worst resistant to the information you want to convey. If you acknowledge that indifference, you can try to devise some way of overcoming it. In the face of audience resistance, you might want to put extra effort and money into the cover. Or consider printing a strong opening sentence or two in large type on the cover to lure readers in. Puzzles, quizzes, and other involvement techniques can sometimes draw readers to a subject they might otherwise ignore. A headline that poses a bold question is a simpler version of this same approach and can work if your audience is likely to want to know the answer. (Readers can often be hooked by a question even if it's one they think they can answer.) Humor, where appropriate, can also cajole the audience into reading on. The technique depends on the publication, the audience, and the budget. But do try something. If you ignore audience indifference when you write and design a document, you can guarantee that it won't be read.

Who is your audience?

Unless you write like Stephen King or address a subject as important to your reader as his or her bank balance, you can't assume that your intended reader will actually read your document. You may have a target audience or even a captive audience, but you don't have a reader until you've involved that person through words or pictures or an overall impression. Identifying your audience helps you choose the techniques that engage readers. Are they colleagues? Customers? Potential investors? Clients? What style is appropriate? How much do they know about your subject? How much time are they likely to spend with your publication? What other information do they have on the subject? Is this their only source?

The business of reaching the audience is no different than before.
—Ben Bagdikian,
in a New York Times *interview about desktop publishing*

Think in terms of interaction rather than one-way communication. It doesn't hurt to think of yourself as an entertainer or a sales person anticipating your audience's reaction. Consider readers' responses so that you can adjust your approach.

As you develop your publication, put yourself in the readers' position:

- How quickly can they pick out the highlights? Most readers scan. They want a sense of what you have to say before they make a commitment to read on. They want the highlights before the details.

- Can they find the items that are relevant to their particular concerns? Many publications have a mix of information, with different subjects, themes, or types of material. In a company newsletter, for example, one employee may be interested in educational assistance while another is concerned with after-hours security. Understanding your readers' special interests helps you organize the material.

- How quickly can they read the text? Remember the problem of information overload. Your text should be clear and lean. Less is more in print.

- Can your readers understand the information? Have you assumed knowledge they don't have?

Instruction manuals and reference books require careful organization and graphic devices that help the reader to find what he or she needs. One study of computer documentation revealed that of all the questions phoned in to the technical support staff, 80 percent were covered in the manual; the users either couldn't find the answers quickly enough or didn't understand them.

What kind of information will be included?

Different kinds of publications have different elements. A brochure for a professional conference may require a program, a workshop schedule, brief biographies of the speakers, and a map. An advertisement may consist entirely of slogans, tag lines, and little pieces of information such as prices or an address. A press release needs the name of a person to contact for more information. A technical manual needs a glossary. Review the different kinds of information—text and visual—early on so that you'll have space for all the pieces and avoid oversights.

An awareness of the elements needed in your document also affects your format and pacing. For a newsletter with several short articles and small photographs, you might choose a four-column format, whereas a newsletter with one major article and a number of short, newsy items might work best in two unequal columns. You can't possibly make an intelligent decision about format until you have a fix on the kinds of information you'll be formatting.

What kind of image do you want to project?

The layout of the circus under canvas is more like the plan of the Acropolis than anything else; it is a beautiful organic arrangement established by the boss canvas man and the lot boss.... The concept of "appropriateness," this "how-it-should-be-ness," has equal value in the circus, in the making of a work of art, and in science.

—Charles Eames

Everything about a publication, from the style of the prose to the quality of the paper it's printed on, contributes to the image it conveys about the sender. And the single most important guideline in fashioning that image is appropriateness. The elements you select and the way you assemble and reproduce them become a matter not so much of good or bad design as of design that is appropriate for your purpose and audience. Even the crammed-full, poorly printed advertisements for discount department stores cannot be dismissed as "bad" design when put to the tests of appropriate and effective communication.

If you are promoting a financial service, you want prose that is well informed and authoritative and design and printing that is prosperous without being indulgent. A company that has had a bad year, on the other hand, wants to appear careful and restrained without creating concern about quality. And you want an entrepreneurial business plan to appear energetic, bold, and thorough all at the same time.

A travel brochure for a Caribbean cruise might use color photos to suggest escape, adventure, and celebration, and an ad for a new restaurant in the theater or art district might use words and decorative motifs to project a similar experience close to home.

As you consider the elements and design of your publication, write down a list of impressions you want to make. Formal. Informal. Friendly. Playful. Elegant. Stylish. Trendy. Classic. Adventurous. Conservative. Scholarly. Provocative. Diverse. Spirited. Generous. Concerned. How do you want your audience to perceive you?

Must your publication fit into a program or conform to a corporate style?

For a new program that requires continuity—say a series of health seminars, each with a promotional mailing before the event, a seminar program distributed at the event, and a follow-up questionnaire after the event—you'll want to develop a design that establishes an identity for the series and that can be followed for each event.

The issue of corporate identity has emerged as some companies have discovered that desktop publishing encourages more creativity than their image can handle. The logo begins appearing in different sizes and positions on the page. Documents from one department have a streamlined, stylized look, whereas documents from another use Victorian clip art. The corporate response is to establish formats and design standards so that different kinds of documents—order forms, product sheets, newsletters, reports, and so on—all have a consistent look. You may feel that having to adhere to these standards puts a damper on your style, but in fact it will probably free you to concentrate on the clarity and effectiveness of the elements within the established format.

What is the overall format?

Format includes everything from the organization of material to the page size to the underlying structure, or grid, of your layout. You rarely start a publication with an idea of what the format should be; rather, the format evolves out of the material and often changes as your understanding of the publication changes.

In developing your format, consider first the common elements in the publication. How many levels of headlines will you need? How will you separate items that appear on the same page?

Readers want what is important to be clearly laid out; they will not read anything that is troublesome to read.
—Jan Tschichold,
writing in 1935, cited in
Thirty Centuries of Graphic Design

Look at the formats of other publications, keep a file of what you like, and adapt those techniques to fit your needs. Professional designers do this all the time. Don't limit your file to the kinds of publications you will produce. You may never create an accordion-fold brochure, but some aspect of the format may help you solve a problem in your own publication.

Keep in mind that readers scan printed matter, and consider techniques to facilitate this:

- A strong visual framework will separate one item from another and indicate relative importance.

- Several short stories are almost always more accessible and inviting than one long one.

- Use sidebars or boxed copy to break the text into accessible chunks.

- Every headline and caption is a hook, a potential entry point for busy readers.

- Pay attention to the pacing: Balance text with visuals and offset "quick reads" with more demanding material.

- Use graphic devices to move the reader's eye from one place on the page to another, especially to key points or to little bits of information that you think are particularly interesting.

- Keep in mind also that many readers scan from back to front; can you get their attention in the middle of a story?

For magazines, newsletters, and other periodicals, develop your format with great care so that you can maintain a consistent style from one issue to the next. What departments and features will be included in every issue? Where will they appear?

What kinds of art or photography will be included?

We learn language by applying words to visual experiences, and we create visual images to illustrate verbal ideas. This interaction of word and image is the background for contemporary communication.
—Allen Hurlburt,
The Design Concept, 1981

You can produce professional, attractive documents without any art, but pictures unquestionably draw readers in more easily than words, and illustrations can greatly enhance your message. Art and photography can illustrate the text, provide additional information, create a mood, provoke questions in the reader's mind, and set the overall tone of a publication. Charts and graphs can squeeze a lot of facts into a small amount of space and be visually interesting at the same time. Even abstract geometric shapes can intrigue and invite and add movement to the page. Graphic devices such as borders, boxes, and tinted areas, along with icons such as arrows, bullets, and ballot boxes, all help create a strong sense of organization and move the reader from one part of the page to another. Consider these devices as ways to break up the text and make your pages more interesting, more accessible, and more informative. Keep in mind that you don't necessarily need a lot of art; often one or two strong images are more effective than half a dozen mediocre ones.

You will need to consider the amount and type of art to be used early on, because it will affect your format and will also generate loose odds and ends of text. Will you have captions? Numbers to identify figures? Sources for charts? Where will the art credits appear?

The art will affect the schedule too. Will you have the printer make conventional halftones or color separations from photos? Or will you scan the photos to place as digital images in the PageMaker file? Or will you have a service bureau do the scans? Each method requires a slightly different schedule. Conventional color separations can take anywhere from three days to two weeks, depending on your relationship with the printer and the extent of the color corrections needed.

What are the printing specifications?

Specifications—including page size, number of pages, type of binding, paper stock, quantity to be printed, and use of color, if any—are inextricably related to the overall format. Changing one often affects the other. Review your options early on with any outside vendors you plan to use (commercial printers, color separators, full-service copy centers); your specifications must be consistent with their capabilities and requirements.

If you've come to desktop publishing without any experience in working with printed materials, you'll encounter a new set of jargon as you move into printing and binding. It's just trade talk, and you'll pick it up in time. If your printer can print in four- and eight-page signatures as well as in sixteens, that might affect the number of pages you produce. If you can get a good price on an odd-size paper that works for your needs, you might want to adjust your page size. The binding you select may affect your page margins. For background on the fundamentals of commercial printing, buy a reference such as *Pocket Pal* (International Paper Company), which is a classic and inexpensive handbook for the graphic arts, or *Getting It Printed* (Coast to Coast Books), which is directed at novice publishers.

What will you use for camera-ready pages?

For some business documents, the 300-dots-per-inch output from a laser printer is sufficient for camera-ready pages. For others, you may want the higher resolution provided by an imagesetter, which prints up to 3556 dots per inch. Again, your decision here will affect your schedule and your budget.

When you plan to use high-resolution output, be sure to run test pages of your format early on. Rules, shades, and type weight are lighter at higher resolutions, and you may want to adjust your specs when you see the early tests. You'll want to work with the service bureau that will provide your output just as you do with your printer. You need to tell them what application (and version number) you used to create the file, which fonts are included, and whether there are linked graphics (such as digital photos or EPS graphics from an illustration file) that are required for printing. Knowledgeable personnel at good service bureaus are a valuable resource and can help you troubleshoot problems early on.

How will your document be reproduced?

For any but those jobs you consider routine, talk with the printer as early in the planning as possible.... Describe your needs and ask whether your piece can be printed practically. Consider suggestions about alternate papers, design changes, and other ideas about how to save time and money.... [But] remember that they want your business. By suggesting changes which take advantage of particular presses or papers, a printer may be shaping your job to fit that shop. Keep in mind that you are getting consultation and may not be ready to write specifications.

—*Mark Beach,*
Getting It Printed

As is the case with many aspects of publishing, the new technology has expanded the ways in which documents are reproduced. Will you use the office photocopy machine? A full-service copy center? A quick printer with offset presses and binderies? Or a commercial printer for higher-quality reproduction? Your printing needs will be determined by the number of copies, the quality desired, and your budget.

If you will be using commercial printers on a regular basis and you are new to publishing, try to develop a working relationship with local printers and learn more about that end of the business. Printing is a fine art but an inconsistent one; even highly experienced professionals fear the nasty surprises that can happen on press. Poor communication between publisher and printer can result in poor quality. Let your printer know what you expect. If you're not satisfied with the quality, follow up after you receive printed copies to find out what the problem was. Often the printer will blame it on the paper (which is rarely as good as you'd like it to be), or on the size of the run (it is difficult to maintain certain standards in large press runs, but the printer is supposed to have quality-control mechanisms to catch problems as they come up), or on some other plausible factors. But sometimes the problem could have been avoided. Perhaps your photograph was cut off because you didn't leave enough space between your art and the trim; next time you'll know to determine the tolerance and adjust your margins accordingly. By asking, you'll let the printer know you care about quality, and you may learn something.

How will it be distributed?

Whether your document is distributed through interoffice mail, given away in stores, or sent through the mail or some other delivery service, you want the purpose to be easily discernible. What is the reader's first impression? Is a person as likely to see the back cover first as the front? If the publication is folded, will the pacing of the words and images keep the recipients moving through the folds? If a flyer is to be tacked on a bulletin board, can the headline be read from a distance?

If your document will be mailed, it must conform to postal regulations for the appropriate mailing class. This may affect the size, the way the publication is folded, the placement of the mailing label, and the amount of space for the address if the publication is a self-mailer.

An early understanding of the restrictions and requirements of your distribution method can save you time and money and can affect certain decisions about your format as well.

When is it needed?

Regardless of your experience and that of your staff, expect productivity to drop in the beginning, as everyone learns the new system.... It will probably take at least three production cycles before you can get all the kinks out.... Many organizations continue to use traditional production methods in parallel with their new desktop systems, phasing in the new methods gradually. This means you won't see your cost savings right away, but you're not putting all your eggs in one new and untested basket.
—Janet Millenson,
writing in Publish *Magazine*

Schedules are a blessing and a curse. On the one hand there is the feeling that there's not enough time to do the job the way you'd like, but on the other hand everyone knows that any project will expand to fill the time available. Scheduling is especially sensitive when you are working with new technology. Desktop publishing is supposed to shave days off a project that would have taken a week, and weeks off one that would have taken a month. That can happen, but not the first week you have your system. You need time to learn, time to find out what you can and can't do with your particular configuration.

Most schedules are determined backwards, starting with when you want the document in your reader's hands. You then figure in the time required for distribution, printing, and other outside services, and finally you determine not how long you *need* to create the publication, but how long you *have*.

Schedules are a reality factor. The tighter the schedule, the simpler your format should be.

What is the budget?

Money is also a reality factor. It so affects everything about a publication that it's often the first consideration. We've put it last on the checklist, not out of disregard for its importance, but out of a belief that first you should think about what you want to do, and then you should look at what you can do. It's the nature of dreams to make us reach, and even when we can't grab hold of what we want, dreams often produce good ideas that can be scaled down to fit a budget. Take your budget and your schedule seriously, but don't let them be ever-present blinders.

CHAPTER 2

THE PRINCIPLES OF TYPOGRAPHY

Typographic arrangement should achieve for the reader what voice tone conveys to the listener.
—El Lissitzky

The ability to set type, modify it on-screen, compose it in pages, and then print the result in camera-ready form is the foundation of desktop publishing. This puts the fundamental building block of graphic design in the hands of anyone with a few thousand dollars. Suddenly, people who never much thought about the shapes of characters in the words they read have access to a rich typographic tradition, one developed over 500 years of practice. And seasoned designers used to telling typesetters what they want have to master the time-consuming subtleties themselves.

Typography at its most basic is simply the selection and arrangement of typefaces, sizes, and spacing on the printed page. But faced with the raw material for a page that isn't printed, the designer has a myriad of decisions to make. What typeface to use? How large to make it? How much space between the lines? How to distinguish paragraphs? How wide a column? How much contrast between headlines and body text? The answers to these and many other questions determine whether a page is inviting and easy to read—whether the eye can distinguish the relative importance of items and whether the overall appearance is both varied and unified.

In addition to the utilitarian functions implied in those questions, typography also gives a page a certain personality (formal or informal, modern or classic, ornate or sturdy) and an overall feeling (dense or open, light or dramatic). How do you choose from among the many typefaces available to project the desired image and to give your publication a distinctive and recognizable personality?

And then there are a host of subtleties and details that reveal whether the page is the work of an amateur or a pro. The spacing between individual characters, the way lines are hyphenated, the overall color of the type on the page are among the nuances that must be attended to.

As much as in any other area of graphic design, the answers to all these questions come largely from experience. Some of that experience we all have as readers. A great deal more can be gained by looking carefully at how type is styled in the whole range of printed materials. And finally, the computer makes it possible to discover the nuances of type through hands-on experimentation.

72 dots per inch (screen image)

300 dpi

1270 dpi

2540 dpi

There is a story, no doubt apocryphal, that a fifteenth-century scribe, upon examining one of Gutenberg's press sheets, exclaimed, "It's nice, but it's not calligraphy."

Computers have given us an invaluable control over typography, but they have also made possible a counterproductive versatility. We have so many typefaces available and so many special effects, we can change so readily from one size and style to another, that undisciplined typography can as easily fragment the message as help hold it together. Use the control to experiment, to find the right face and size and spacing for your purpose, but don't use the versatility to pack your pages with a half dozen or more styles that confuse more than they communicate.

The power to control typography from the desktop is all the more miraculous when you review the history of typesetting and see the progression from a craftsman's handling of each individual letter to a computer operator's ability to send electrical impulses around the world. In the fifteenth century, Johann Gutenberg liberated the printed word from the painstaking craft of handscripting with what now seems the almost equally painstaking craft of individually setting each metal character. With the introduction of linotype machines in the 1880s, keyboard operators could type in the text and the machine would cast an entire line in a single slug of hot metal. Phototypesetting eliminated the actual type altogether and produced text by projecting the images of characters on light-sensitive film or paper. Today's computer-driven laser printers have turned letters into patterns of dots and computer owners and operators into typographers.

This most recent "democratization" of typography has resulted in a wide range of quality in typeset material. The variables include the quality of the digital type itself, the resolution of the camera-ready output, and the intentions and experience of the person designing the type. The real miracle is the ability to choose the quality of type appropriate for your needs and budget.

The laser printer resolution of 300 dots per inch (dpi) is perfectly adequate as well as cost effective for many newsletters, reports, bulletins, price sheets, and a great many other documents. With the increasing affordability of 600-dpi printers, more manuals, brochures, and mid-range documents that used to be output on imagesetters can be done entirely on the desktop. The higher resolution of 1270 or 2540 or 3556 dots per inch is appropriate for many brochures, books, catalogs, technical manuals, magazines, and annual reports. High-quality, commercial typesetting is still available for advertising agencies, design studios, and publishers of fine books and magazines whose products require the cleanest, sharpest, most beautifully proportioned type.

This chapter is about the many ways of using type. It's intended to serve as a primer for those who are new to type design and as a summary of PageMaker's typographic capabilities for seasoned and novice designers alike. The main purpose is not to put forth rules you must remember but to suggest ways of looking at type on the printed page. As typographer Sumner Stone said in a *Publish* Magazine roundtable discussion on typography, "It's like learning how to appreciate different flavors of wine." Drink up.

A VISUAL GLOSSARY OF TYPOGRAPHY

The terminology used to describe type and its appearance on the printed page is a colorful and useful jargon. As with any specialized language, it enables people to communicate unambiguously, so that the instruction "align baseline of flush right caption with bottom of art" means the same thing to everyone involved in a job. But the language of typography also describes the subtlety and diversity among letterforms. This glossary is intended to display some of that richness in the process of setting forth basic definitions.

TYPEFACE

The name of a typeface refers to an entire family of letters of a particular design. (Historically, face referred to the surface of the metal type piece that received the ink and came into contact with the printing surface.) The faces shown on this spread are resident on most PostScript printers. Literally thousands of faces are available for desktop production today.

Avant Garde

ABCDEFGHIJKLMNOPQRSTUVWXYZ
abcdefghijklmnopqrstuvwxyz
1234567890!$,""?
ABCDEFGHIJKLMNOPQRSTUVWXYZ
abcdefghijklmnopqrstuvwxyz
1234567890!$,""?

Bookman

ABCDEFGHIJKLMNOPQRSTUVWXYZ
abcdefghijklmnopqrstuvwxyz
1234567890!$,""?
ABCDEFGHIJKLMNOPQRSTUVWXYZ
abcdefghijklmnopqrstuvwxyz
1234567890!$,""?

Courier

ABCDEFGHIJKLMNOPQRSTUVWXYZ
abcdefghijklmnopqrstuvwxyz
1234567890!$,""?
ABCDEFGHIJKLMNOPQRSTUVWXYZ
abcdefghijklmnopqrstuvwxyz
1234567890!$,""?

Helvetica	ABCDEFGHIJKLMNOPQRSTUVWXYZ abcdefghijklmnopqrstuvwxyz 1234567890!$,""? **ABCDEFGHIJKLMNOPQRSTUVWXYZ abcdefghijklmnopqrstuvwxyz 1234567890!$,""?**
New Century Schoolbook	ABCDEFGHIJKLMNOPQRSTUVWXYZ abcdefghijklmnopqrstuvwxyz 1234567890!$,""? **ABCDEFGHIJKLMNOPQRSTUVWXYZ abcdefghijklmnopqrstuvwxyz 1234567890!$,""?**
Palatino	ABCDEFGHIJKLMNOPQRSTUVWXYZ abcdefghijklmnopqrstuvwxyz 1234567890!$,""? **ABCDEFGHIJKLMNOPQRSTUVWXYZ abcdefghijklmnopqrstuvwxyz 1234567890!$,""?**
Times Roman	ABCDEFGHIJKLMNOPQRSTUVWXYZ abcdefghijklmnopqrstuvwxyz 1234567890!$,""? **ABCDEFGHIJKLMNOPQRSTUVWXYZ abcdefghijklmnopqrstuvwxyz 1234567890!$,""?**
Zapf Chancery	*ABCDEFGHIJKLMNOPQRSTUVWXYZ abcdefghijklmnopqrstuvwxyz 1234567890!$,""? ABCDEFGHIJKLMNOPQRSTUVWXYZ abcdefghijklmnopqrstuvwxyz 1234567890!$,""?*

For all of the variety found across thousands of typefaces, most of them can be grouped into three basic styles—serif, sans serif, and script. The samples shown on these two pages suggest the variation available in each style. These samples (and the ones throughout this chapter) are PostScript fonts from Adobe Systems.

Some legibility studies have found that serif typefaces are easier to read, the theory being that the serifs help move the eye from one letter to the next without the letters blurring together. On the other hand, sans serif typefaces are generally thought to be easier to read at very large and especially at very small sizes. It's difficult to make any hard-and-fast rules because legibility is affected not only by typeface but also by size, length of line, amount of leading, amount of white space on the page, and even by the quality of the paper.

SANS SERIF

Sans serif typefaces do not have finishing strokes at the end of the letterforms. The name comes from the French *sans*, meaning "without." Sans serif faces are also referred to as Gothic.

Helvetica   Futura   Univers

Avant Garde   Franklin Gothic

Eurostile   News Gothic   Optima

SCRIPT

Script faces simulate handwriting, with one letter connected to another visually if not physically.

Freestyle Script   Zapf Chancery

SERIF

Serifs are lines or curves projecting from the end of a letterform. Typefaces with these additional strokes are called serif faces. They are also referred to as Roman faces because the serifs derived from the marks made chiseling letters into Roman monuments. (Note that when describing serif faces, the word Roman is capitalized; when describing vertical letters as distinguished from italic ones, roman is lowercase.)

Palatino   Times Roman   Garamond

New Century Schoolbook   Caslon

Bookman   Century Old Style

Goudy Old Style   Glypha

Bodoni   American Typewriter

Trump Mediæval   Galliard

Lubalin Graph   New Baskerville

SIZE

Type is measured by its vertical height, in points. (There are 12 points to a pica and 6 picas to an inch.) But if you use a pica ruler to measure from the highest ascender to the lowest descender in any font, the result will be less than the size you've specified. That's because type size still allows for the shoulder above and below the letter in a piece of metal type, even though there's no metal in most typesetting today.

HeightHeightHeightHeightHeightHeight Height **Height**

6 pt 8 pt 10 pt   12 pt   14 point 18 point   36 point   72 point

WEIGHT

Weight refers to the density of letters, to the lightness or heaviness of the strokes. It is described as a continuum: light, regular, book, demi, bold, heavy, black, extra bold. Not all weights are available for all typefaces, and the continuum varies in some faces.

HELVETICA LIGHT   HELVETICA REGULAR
HELVETICA BOLD   **HELVETICA BLACK**

WIDTH

The horizontal measure of letters is described as condensed, normal, or expanded. Resident typefaces such as Times Roman and Helvetica are generally normal. You can condense and expand type in PageMaker using the Set Width option on the Type menu. Be careful, though, of extreme settings that distort the letterforms. If you want to use a condensed typeface for large amounts of body text, choose one that's available as a downloadable font rather than using the Set Width option.

CONDENSED   NORMAL   EXPANDED

SLANT

Slant is the angle of a type character, either vertical or inclined. Vertical type is called roman (in PageMaker, it is called Normal, and in some word-processing programs, Plain). Inclined type is called italic or oblique.

roman & *italic*

STYLE

In PageMaker, style refers to options such as bold, italic, and underline that you can choose as part of your type specifications. All the styles shown below are available in the Macintosh version of PageMaker; the outline and shadow styles are not available in the Windows version.

STYLE   **STYLE**   *STYLE*   <u>STYLE</u>
~~STYLE~~   STYLE   STYLE   STYLE

FAMILY

All the variations of a single typeface—the different weights, widths, slants, and styles—constitute a type family. Some families have more styles than others, providing for considerable type contrast within a document without the need to change typefaces. In addition to the Helvetica styles shown below, the family includes Compressed, Thin, Ultra Light, and Heavy variations. Some other families with many variations are Bodoni, Futura, Univers, and Stone.

Helvetica
Helvetica Italic
Helvetica Bold
Helvetica Bold Italic
Helvetica Condensed Light
Helvetica Condensed Light Oblique
Helvetica Condensed
Helvetica Condensed Oblique
Helvetica Condensed Bold
Helvetica Condensed Bold Oblique
Helvetica Condensed Black
Helvetica Condensed Black Oblique
Helvetica Light
Helvetica Light Oblique
Helvetica Black
Helvetica Black Oblique

ANATOMY

In designing, measuring, and identifying type, a precise vocabulary is essential. Here are the basics:

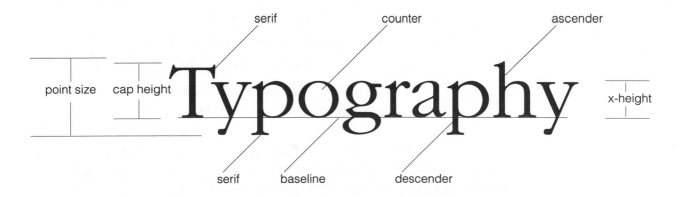

LEADING

The vertical space between lines of type is called leading (pronounced "led·ing"). It is measured in points and is expressed as the sum of the type size and the space between two lines. For example, 10-point type with 2 points between the lines is described as 10-point type on 12-point leading. It is written 10/12 and spoken "10 on 12." The term was originally used to describe the narrow metal strips inserted between lines of hand-set type.

Type with a generous amount of space between lines is said to have open leading; type with relatively little space between lines is said to be set tight. Type without any space between lines (such as the 10/10 and the 30/30 samples below) is said to be set solid. Leading that is less than the point size, as in the 30/26 sample, is called negative, or minus, leading; it is used primarily for large type sizes set in all caps.

10/10 Times Roman

These three type samples are all set in 10-point Times Roman. The first is set solid (10/10), the second is set tight (10/11), and the third (10/12) is set with PageMaker's automatic leading (120% of the point size).

10/11 Times Roman

These three type samples are all set in 10-point Times Roman. The first is set solid (10/10), the second is set tight (10/11), and the third (10/12) is set with PageMaker's automatic leading (120% of the point size).

10/12 Times Roman

These three type samples are all set in 10-point Times Roman. The first is set solid (10/10), the second is set tight (10/11), and the third (10/12) is set with PageMaker's automatic leading (120% of the point size).

30/26 Helvetica Condensed Black

THIS DISPLAY TYPE IS SET MINUS

30/30 Helvetica Condensed Black

THIS DISPLAY TYPE IS SET SOLID

30/34 Helvetica Condensed Black

THIS DISPLAY TYPE IS SET OPEN

LINE LENGTH

The length of a line of type is called the measure and is traditionally specified in picas. Fractions of picas are expressed as points (there are 12 points to a pica), not as decimals. So a column that is 10 and one-quarter picas wide is 10 picas 3 points, or 10p3.

Generally, the longer the line length the larger the type should be.

This is set to a 12p measure and can be easily read with a relatively small type size. This sample is 9/11.

This is set to a 20p measure and needs a larger type size for ease of reading. This sample is 10/12.

This is set to a 37p6 measure and needs a larger type size to be easily read. This measure is too wide for most running text and is best used for subheads, blurbs, and other short display type. This sample is set 13/15.

ALIGNMENT

Alignment refers to the shape of the type block relative to the margins. PageMaker offers five settings: align left, align center, align right, justify, and force justify. Body text is generally set flush left or justified, but justified type requires more attention to the spacing between letters and words, as you can see in the examples below.

Aligned left

The lines of text are even on the left edge (flush with the left margin) and uneven, or ragged, on the right. Flush left is the recommended alignment for body text in desktop publishing. It is easy to read and allows even word spacing.

Centered

Each line is centered; thus, both left and right margins are ragged. Centered text is often used for headlines and other display type, as well as for formal invitations and announcements.

Aligned right

The lines of text are even on the right and uneven on the left. This alignment is sometimes used for captions, display type, and advertising copy but is not recommended for body text. We are used to reading from left to right; if the left edge of the text is not well defined, the eye falters, and the text is more difficult to read.

Justified

The type is flush, or even, on both the right and the left margins. Because the normal space between letters and words is altered in order to justify text, justification sometimes results in uneven spacing, with "rivers" of white space running through the type. The narrower the measure, the more uneven the spacing is likely to be, as you can see by comparing these side-by-side examples.

Justified

The type is flush, or even, on both the right and the left margins. Because the normal space between letters and words is altered in order to justify text, justification sometimes results in uneven spacing, with "rivers" of white space running through the type. The narrower the measure, the more uneven the spacing is likely to be, as you can see by comparing these side-by-side examples.

Rag left and rag right

A less common setting is rag left and rag right. This is sometimes used for display type. It gives the page a poetic feeling without being formal. This setting cannot be achieved automatically: You must specify the indent for each individual line.

RULES

Rules are also typographic elements and are measured in points. Use PageMaker's Line command (on the Element menu) to specify the style and weight of rules. You can select a line style from the list, or you can specify custom rules from 0 through 800 points.

TYPE SPECIMEN SHEETS

Probably no two designers will agree on exactly which ten or fifteen faces to include in their own basic vocabularies, but they will almost always include a balanced selection of three or four faces from each broad type grouping—serif, sans serif, and slab serif—that they are likely to use 80 percent of the time for both headlines and body text. For example, my basic typographic vocabulary... includes Bodoni, Garamond, Century Old Style, Janson, Times Roman, Memphis, Cheltenham Old Style, Franklin Gothic, Futura, Helvetica, News Gothic, and Univers.

—Kit Hinrichs
Typewise

Designers have traditionally relied on specimen sheets to select and specify type in their publications. "Spec" sheets, as they are known, simply display typefaces in various sizes, weights, and styles so that you can judge the appropriateness of a particular face for the publication you're about to design, as well as the readability, color, and overall look of frequently used sizes. Spec sheets are also useful when you want to identify a typeface that you see and like in another publication.

Commercial typesetters generally supply spec sheets to their customers as a sort of catalog of what is available. You can also buy books of spec sheets, and some are now available specifically for electronic publishing.

You can also make your own spec sheets for the typefaces available on your own system or network. The time it takes will repay you generously every time you need to design a publication. In addition to providing you with a useful resource, making spec sheets is a good way to study the nuances of type.

The page at right shows one format for a spec sheet. Depending upon the kind of publication work you do, you may want to vary the components, with more or less display type, more or less running text, more or fewer small-size settings for captions, data, and so on. You may also want more variation in line length than our sample shows. Expand it to two pages, include character counts for various settings—in short, do whatever will be most useful to you. Once you have a format worked out and have set up one complete spec sheet as an electronic page, you can simply open a copy of that page for each typeface in your system, change the typeface, and then type over the identifying names for the new typeface. By using the same words and style for each sheet, you'll get a true comparison between the faces that are available to you.

In the sample, we've kerned the name of the typeface at the very top of the page, adding space between letters where needed so that none of the letters butt. You want to be able to see the shape of each letter when you use the spec sheets as an identification aid.

GARAMOND

Garamond Light
Garamond Light Italic
Garamond Bold
Garamond Bold Italic

ABCDEFGHIJKLMNOPQRSTUVWXYZ
abcdefghijklmnopqrstuvwxyz
1234567890!@#$%^&*( )+[ ] , ; " " ?

WALDEN BY HENRY DAVID THOREAU 12/14
WALDEN BY HENRY DAVID THOREAU

WALDEN BY HENRY DAVID THOREAU caps/sm caps
WALDEN BY HENRY DAVID THOREAU

Walden by Henry David Thoreau
Walden by Henry David Thoreau

14/16

When I wrote the following pages, I lived alone, in the woods, a mile from any neighbor, in a house which I had built myself, on the shore of Walden Pond.

9/11

I lived alone, in the woods, a mile from any neighbor, in a house which I had built myself, on the shore of Walden

I lived alone, in the woods, a mile from any neighbor, in a house which I had built myself, on the shore of

11/13

When I wrote
the following pages,
or rather
the bulk of them,
I lived alone, in the woods,
a mile from any neighbor,
on the shore of Walden Pond.

36

Aa Ee Gg Tt Ww
1234567890$?''

9/11

When I wrote the following pages, or rather the bulk of them, I lived alone, in the woods, a mile from any neighbor, in a house which I had built myself, on the shore of Walden Pond, in Concord, Massachusetts, and earned my living by the labor of my hands only. I lived there two years and two months. At present I am a sojourner in civilized life again.

I should not obtrude my affairs so much on the notice of my readers if very

W 72

10/12

When I wrote the following pages, or rather the bulk of them, I lived alone, in the woods, a mile from any neighbor, in a house which I had built myself, on the shore of Walden Pond, in Concord, Massachusetts, and earned my living by the labor of my hands only. I lived there two years and two months. At present I am a sojourner in civilized life again.

I should not obtrude my affairs so much on the notice of my readers if

11/13

When I wrote the following pages, or rather the bulk of them, I lived alone, in the woods, a mile from any neighbor, in a house which I had built myself, on the shore of Walden Pond, in Concord, Massachusetts, and earned my living by the labor of my hands only. I lived there two years and two months. At present I am a sojourner in civilized life again.

I should not obtrude my affairs so much on the notice of my

12/14

When I wrote the following pages, or rather the bulk of them, I lived alone, in the woods, a mile from any neighbor, in a house which I had built myself, on the shore of Walden Pond, in Concord, Massachusetts, and earned my living by the labor of my hands only. I lived there two years and two months. At present I am a sojourner in civilized life again.

I should not obtrude my affairs so much on the notice of

**Using key letters
to identify type**

When using spec sheets to identify type from other publications, look for key letters that tend to be distinctive, including the T, g, and M shown here (all 60 point). Numbers and question marks are also good indicators. You quickly learn to look for the shape of the serif (straight, triangular, rounded, or square), whether the bowls of the Ps and Rs and the tails of the g's are open or closed, the contrast between thick and thin parts of the letter, and so on.

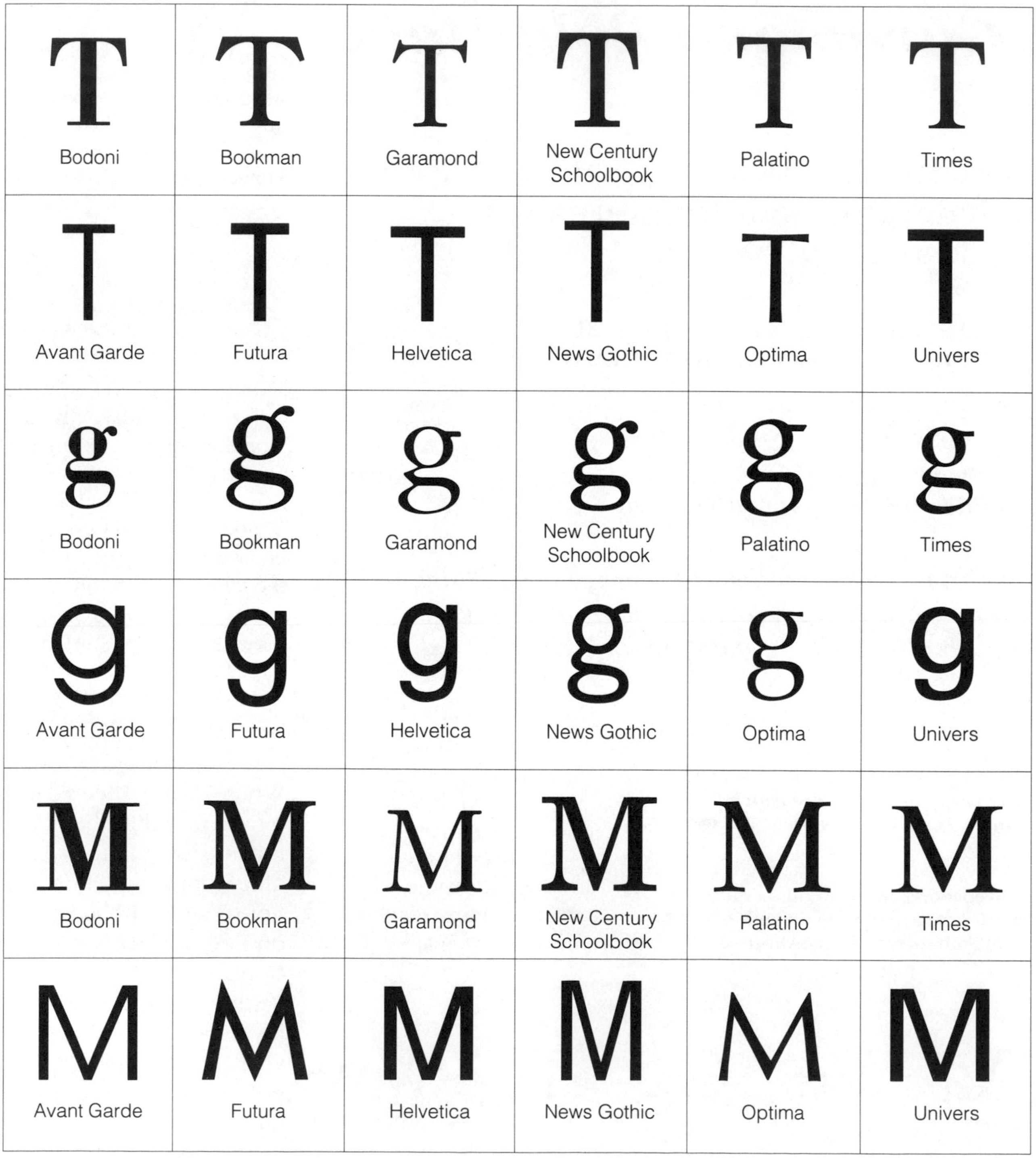

T	T	T	T	T	T
Bodoni	Bookman	Garamond	New Century Schoolbook	Palatino	Times
T	T	T	T	T	T
Avant Garde	Futura	Helvetica	News Gothic	Optima	Univers
g	g	g	g	g	g
Bodoni	Bookman	Garamond	New Century Schoolbook	Palatino	Times
g	g	g	g	g	g
Avant Garde	Futura	Helvetica	News Gothic	Optima	Univers
M	M	M	M	M	M
Bodoni	Bookman	Garamond	New Century Schoolbook	Palatino	Times
M	M	M	M	M	M
Avant Garde	Futura	Helvetica	News Gothic	Optima	Univers

The color of type

The addition of a second color (or several colors) can enhance the typographic design of a publication in many ways. But even when printed in black and white, type has a color on the printed page. Color in this sense means the overall tone, or texture, of the type; the lightness or darkness, which varies from one typeface and style to another; and also the evenness of the type as determined by the spacing. Spec sheets provide valuable guides to the color of different typefaces, which, as you can see in the samples below, vary considerably.

A large rose-tree stood near the entrance of the garden: the roses growing on it were white, but there were three gardeners at it, busily painting them red. Alice thought this a very curious thing, and she went nearer to watch....
—Futura Light

A large rose-tree stood near the entrance of the garden: the roses growing on it were white, but there were three gardeners at it, busily painting them red. Alice thought this a very curious thing, and she went nearer to...
—Goudy Old Style

A large rose-tree stood near the entrance of the garden: the roses growing on it were white, but there were three gardeners at it, busily painting them red. Alice thought this a very curious thing, and she went nearer to...
—Optima

A large rose-tree stood near the entrance of the garden: the roses growing on it were white, but there were three gardeners at it, busily painting them red. Alice thought this a very curious thing, and she went nearer...
—Palatino

A large rose-tree stood near the entrance of the garden: the roses growing on it were white, but there were three gardeners at it, busily painting them red. Alice thought this a very curious thing, and she went nearer to...
—Garamond

A large rose-tree stood near the entrance of the garden: the roses growing on it were white, but there were three gardeners at it, busily painting them red. Alice thought this a very curious thing...
—Avant Garde

A large rose-tree stood near the entrance of the garden: the roses growing on it were white, but there were three gardeners at it, busily painting them red. Alice thought this a very curious thing...
—Univers

A large rose-tree stood near the entrance of the garden: the roses growing on it were white, but there were three gardeners at it, busily painting them red. Alice thought this a very curious thing, and she went nearer...
—**Franklin Gothic Demi**

A large rose-tree stood near the entrance of the garden: the roses growing on it were white, but there were three gardeners at it, busily painting them red. Alice thought this a very curious thing, and she went nearer...
—Helvetica

A large rose-tree stood near the entrance of the garden: the roses growing on it were white, but there were three gardeners at it, busily painting them red. Alice thought this a very curious thing, and she went nearer to watch....
—**New Baskerville Bold**

A large rose-tree stood near the entrance of the garden: the roses growing on it were white, but there were three gardeners at it, busily painting them red. Alice thought this a very curious thing...
—**Souvenir Demi**

A large rose-tree stood near the entrance of the garden: the roses growing on it were white, but there were three gardeners at it, busily painting them red. Alice thought this a very curious thing...
—**Bookman Demi**

A large rose-tree stood near the entrance of the garden: the roses growing on it were white, but there were three gardeners at it, busily painting them red. Alice thought this a very curious thing, and she went nearer to watch....
—Glypha

A large rose-tree stood near the entrance of the garden: the roses growing on it were white, but there were three gardeners at it, busily painting them red. Alice thought this a very curious thing, and she went nearer to watch....
—**Century Old Style Bold**

A large rose-tree stood near the entrance of the garden: the roses growing on it were white, but there were three gardeners at it, busily painting them red. Alice thought this a very curious thing and she went ...
—**Am. Typewriter Bold**

A large rose-tree stood near the entrance of the garden: the roses growing on it were white, but there were three gardeners at it, busily painting them red. Alice thought this a very curious...
—**Futura Extra Bold**

The many personalities of type

Typefaces clothe words. And words clothe ideas and information.... Typefaces can do for words, and through words for ideas and information, what clothes can do for people. It isn't just the hat or tie or suit or dress you wear. It's the way you put it on...and its appropriateness to you and to the occasion that make the difference. And so it is with type. A type library is a kind of wardrobe with garments for many occasions. You use your judgment and taste to choose and combine them to best dress your words and ideas.
—U&lc, June 1980,
cited in an Adobe poster

Every typeface has its own personality, a look that makes it more or less suited for a particular type of publication. Confident, elegant, casual, bold, novel, romantic, friendly, stylish, nostaligic, classic, modern, delicate, crisp, sassy...the possibilities are endless. You have only to know the feeling you want, select an appropriate face, and then test it for legibility and effectiveness within your overall design.

The faces shown on these pages merely suggest the range available to today's desktop publisher. Having to choose from the many faces available can be intimidating to new designers. Begin by using a few faces and learning them well: how to achieve contrast through different styles and spacing within those families, which letter pairs require kerning, which counters fill in at small sizes, and so on.

Take note of typefaces you like in other publications and identify them using a type specimen book. Then gradually add new faces to your system, learning their unique subtleties as you did the few faces that you started with. As one designer cautioned in the same *Publish* roundtable on typography quoted earlier in this chapter, "There are only two kinds of typefaces: those you know how to use and those you don't."

GEOMETRY AND PRECISION
WHEN YOU WANT THE CUTTING EDGE

USE AVANT GARDE. IT'S MODERN WITHOUT BEING FORMAL AND GIVES A PAGE A VERY CRISP LOOK. IT SETS BEST IN ALL CAPS AND BENEFITS FROM KERNING SO THAT THE LETTERS SNUGGLE UP TIGHT AGAINST ONE ANOTHER.

A REPORT THAT SUGGESTS
The Writer Has Big Shoulders

would work well in Bookman. It's a sturdy, highly legible typeface, used in many newspapers and often described as a workhorse because it's so versatile. In both its light and bold faces, it has relatively little contrast between the thick and thin strokes.

WHEN YOU WANT TO KNOW THE SCORE

MACHINE IS THERE TO DELIVER IT IN A VERY BOLD WAY. IT IS A FACE WITH NO CURVES, ONLY ANGLES, AND IT SETS VERY CONDENSED. IT SHOULD BE USED FOR SHORT DISPLAY COPY ONLY AND NO SMALLER THAN 18 POINT (WHICH IS WHY THIS 9-POINT DESCRIPTION IS SET IN HELVETICA LIGHT RATHER THAN IN MACHINE). FOR BEST VISUAL RESULTS, MACHINE SHOULD BE KERNED. IN THE SAMPLE ABOVE, WE'VE KERNED TO TIGHTEN UP BOTH THE LETTER AND THE WORD SPACE.

This message demands your immediate attention...

so it is set in American Typewriter, which has the immediacy of a standard typewriter face but is more sophisticated. Type sets more economically, with more words per line, in this face than in true typewriter faces such as Courier.

If the plan is to GET ON THE FAST TRACK

try Lubalin Graph Demi. It's actually a serif version of Avant Garde with a square, Egyptian-style serif that is both modern and utilitarian. (Both Lubalin Graph Demi and Avant Garde were created by renowned designer Herb Lubalin.)

LIGHT AS THE ESSENCE OF SUNSHINE AND BOLD AS A MOONLESS NIGHT

is the broad personality of Futura. It's a classic typeface: Born of the machine age in the twenties, it continues to be a designer favorite. Its versatility ranges from advertising to editorial, from fashion to technology. It comes in a wide selection of weights and widths. An all-time favorite combination is Futura Light and Extra Bold, shown above. This text is Futura Light Condensed.

If the need is to be DRAMATIC AND SOPHISTICATED AT THE SAME TIME

then look no further than the Bodoni family. It is very urban, with a touch of the theatrical. This is especially true with Bodoni Poster, used above. This text is in Bodoni Bold.

THE ANNUAL MESSAGE FROM THE EXECUTIVE OFFICES

might well be set in Garamond. It's an extremely graceful, refined, and legible face that suggests the confidence that comes from success. The italic face is highly legible (many italic faces are not), as you can see from these few lines set in Garamond Light Italic.

The efficiency of type

The number of characters per line varies from one typeface to another, even when the same size type is specified. A typeface that has a relatively high character count per line is said to set efficiently (or tightly or economically) and is likely to look smaller than a less efficient typeface set in the same size.

To compare the efficiency of typefaces in your library, set a column of text in PageMaker, make multiple copies of it, and apply a different typeface to each copy. Traditional type charts (and some books on typography) provide tables for determining the character count of each face in various sizes and line lengths. These may not translate with 100 percent accuracy to your desktop system because there are subtle differences in the same typeface from one manufacturer to another. Still, they can be helpful for determining the relative efficiency of different faces when you're adding type to your library.

The words in these twelve blocks of text are exactly the same, and each text block is set 10/12. But the length varies from 10 to 15 lines because some typefaces set more economically than others, with more characters per line. Note also that the type in the shortest text block does not look the smallest. A condensed typeface with a large x-height sets tighter than a noncondensed face but still looks larger.

—Times Roman

The words in these twelve blocks of text are exactly the same, and each text block is set 10/12. But the length varies from 10 to 15 lines because some typefaces set more economically than others, with more characters per line. Note also that the type in the shortest text block does not look the smallest. A condensed typeface with a large x-height sets tighter than a noncondensed face but still looks larger.

—Garamond

The words in these twelve blocks of text are exactly the same, and each text block is set 10/12. But the length varies from 10 to 15 lines because some typefaces set more economically than others, with more characters per line. Note also that the type in the shortest text block does not look the smallest. A condensed typeface with a large x-height sets tighter than a noncondensed face but still looks larger.

—New Baskerville

The words in these twelve blocks of text are exactly the same, and each text block is set 10/12. But the length varies from 10 to 15 lines because some typefaces set more economically than others, with more characters per line. Note also that the type in the shortest text block does not look the smallest. A condensed typeface with a large x-height sets tighter than a noncondensed face but still looks larger.

—Helvetica Condensed Light

The words in these twelve blocks of text are exactly the same, and each text block is set 10/12. But the length varies from 10 to 15 lines because some typefaces set more economically than others, with more characters per line. Note also that the type in the shortest text block does not look the smallest. A condensed typeface with a large x-height sets tighter than a noncondensed face but still looks larger.

—Futura

The words in these twelve blocks of text are exactly the same, and each text block is set 10/12. But the length varies from 10 to 15 lines because some typefaces set more economically than others, with more characters per line. Note also that the type in the shortest text block does not look the smallest. A condensed typeface with a large x-height sets tighter than a noncondensed face but still looks larger.

—News Gothic

The samples on these two pages show the relative efficiency of a number of popular faces, with the serif faces across the top and the sans serif faces across the bottom. (All are from Adobe Systems.) In general, the more efficient faces have a smaller x-height; in addition to getting more characters per line, these faces require less lead because there is more built-in white space between the lines. Note the relatively small visual size and open lines of the New Baskerville setting, for example, compared to the larger, visually tighter look of Bookman or Avant Garde.

When efficiency is extremely important, consider using a condensed face with a large x-height. Note that the Helvetica Condensed Light sample looks larger than some of the others even though it sets the most economically.

The words in these twelve blocks of text are exactly the same, and each text block is set 10/12. But the length varies from 10 to 15 lines because some typefaces set more economically than others, with more characters per line. Note also that the type in the shortest text block does not look the smallest. A condensed typeface with a large x-height sets tighter than a noncondensed face but still looks larger.

—Palatino

The words in these twelve blocks of text are exactly the same, and each text block is set 10/12. But the length varies from 10 to 15 lines because some typefaces set more economically than others, with more characters per line. Note also that the type in the shortest text block does not look the smallest. A condensed typeface with a large x-height sets tighter than a noncondensed face but still looks larger.

—New Century Schoolbook

The words in these twelve blocks of text are exactly the same, and each text block is set 10/12. But the length varies from 10 to 15 lines because some typefaces set more economically than others, with more characters per line. Note also that the type in the shortest text block does not look the smallest. A condensed typeface with a large x-height sets tighter than a noncondensed face but still looks larger.

—Bookman

The words in these twelve blocks of text are exactly the same, and each text block is set 10/12. But the length varies from 10 to 15 lines because some typefaces set more economically than others, with more characters per line. Note also that the type in the shortest text block does not look the smallest. A condensed typeface with a large x-height sets tighter than a noncondensed face but still looks larger.

—Helvetica

The words in these twelve blocks of text are exactly the same, and each text block is set 10/12. But the length varies from 10 to 15 lines because some typefaces set more economically than others, with more characters per line. Note also that the type in the shortest text block does not look the smallest. A condensed typeface with a large x-height sets tighter than a noncondensed face but still looks larger.

—Univers

The words in these twelve blocks of text are exactly the same, and each text block is set 10/12. But the length varies from 10 to 15 lines because some typefaces set more economically than others, with more characters per line. Note also that the type in the shortest text block does not look the smallest. A condensed typeface with a large x-height sets tighter than a noncondensed face but still looks larger.

—Avant Garde

STYLING TYPE IN PAGEMAKER

[In type design] very small differences must be considered. The effect of using 9½-point type instead of 10-point type, a slightly longer or shorter line length, or 1 point more or less space between lines may seem inconsequential, but each small increment is repeated over and over.... Developing a sensitivity to the effects of these small choices is part of becoming a typographer.
        —Sumner Stone,
On Stone: The Art and Use of
Typography on the Personal Computer

It is very difficult to give general rules for specifying type. The variables are so numerous—the size of the page, the kind of reading material, how the text is broken up, the resolution of the output, the quality of the printing, and on and on and on.

In the absence of rules, good type design involves a multitude of subtle judgments. One way to develop your skills in this area is to examine printed material and note what, to your eye, does and doesn't work. Does the type get your attention? Is it easy to read? Does it help move your eye from one part of the page to another? Does it clarify the relationship between different items? Do special typographic effects further or hinder the communication? The more closely you look at type in other publications, the better you'll be able to evaluate your own type design.

The second way to learn about type is to experiment. Desktop typesetting facilitates experimentation to an unprecedented degree, which alone is likely to speed the learning curve of anyone coming into the field of graphic design today. Even a seasoned designer will try several settings before getting just the right relationship of display to body text, the balance of size, leading, and column width for the amount of text on a page, the desired contrast between sidebars and the main story. With commercial typesetting, both the cost and the turnaround time limit the ability to test different possibilities; when you work on the desktop, the time is your own (a mixed blessing, to be sure), and the cost of laser printouts is a few cents each.

Take advantage of this ability to experiment with **typeface, size, and leading.** In fact, "playing" with type styles is a good way to explore the mechanics of the program and the nuances of type design at the same time. To experiment with different type settings in the early stages of a project, use text in whatever stage it exists or create a text file of dummy type. You might want to create a *lorem ipsum* file, which looks like Latin but really isn't. (You'll see it in many of the sample documents we created for this book; take a few minutes to keyboard it into your word processor, and then you'll be able to place it as dummy text in your PageMaker layouts.) Some designers prefer using *lorem ipsum* to real text in the early stages because it encourages people to focus on the format and design rather than on reading the copy.

When you begin to develop the format for a project, try several settings of two or three different typefaces. The ability to specify both type and leading in increments of 0.1 point gives you tremendous flexibility. Vary the margins and the space between columns. Stretch the windowshade handles horizontally to see different line lengths. Try different headline treatments in relation to the body text—different sizes and styles, with different amounts of space between the headline and the text.

Learn early on to use PageMaker's **paragraph formatting** options to specify indents and space between paragraphs or between different text elements, such as headlines and body text. For many new users, the familiar typewriter functions of the Spacebar and the carriage return seem easier, but it is virtually impossible to maintain consistency using them, or to remember, when you compare different samples, how much space you inserted. When several people work on the same job, Spacebar and carriage-return spacing can wreak havoc. (See Project 2 for a detailed look at paragraph-formatting options.)

A lot of people have trouble setting **tabs** properly, and it's virtually impossible to get them right without learning to use the Indents/Tabs dialog box. (It's called Indents/Tabs because you can also set left, first-line, and right indents in this dialog box.) Don't even be tempted to use the Spacebar to set tabs; it simply won't work. (See Project 5 for hands-on practice with tabs.)

Learn to define and use a **style sheet.** It will save you more time than any other feature of the program. It will also help you maintain consistency throughout the publication and enable you to make global changes that would be a real headache to do manually. A style is simply the name you give to a collection of type attributes—typeface, size, leading, alignment, indents, and so on. You can apply all those attributes to a paragraph just by selecting the paragraph and clicking on the name of the style. It's much faster than going through two or three different dialog boxes to specify each attribute individually, and it's much easier than trying to remember, for example, the attributes for the chart headline on page 3 when you need to specify those same attributes for the chart headline on page 12. (See Project 4 for practice with style sheets.)

MEASURING TYPE

As mentioned previously, type is measured vertically, in points, and line lengths are measured in picas. If you haven't worked with points and picas before, you will soon appreciate the small unit of measure this system provides:

> 12 points = 1 pica
> 6 picas = 1 inch

To measure type in printed samples, you'll need a type gauge, a special ruler with several slots running for most of its length and various sizes (usually ranging from 5 or 6 to 15 points) marked along the sides of different slots. You can buy a type gauge in any art supply store; they're very inexpensive. (The most common type gauge is called a Haberule.)

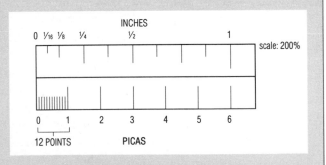

When using a traditional type gauge, keep in mind that the conversion from picas to inches is slightly different from that used on the computer: 6 picas (72 points) is 0.996 inch on a traditional type ruler; the conversion has been rounded off in electronic publishing software, where the 72-dots-per-inch resolution of many monitors converts so easily to 72 points to the inch.

LEADING METHODS

PageMaker has three different methods for distributing leading, the space between lines of type. To understand these options, you first need to understand the meaning of "slug" in typography.

When you drag over a line of type with the text tool, the highlighted area is analogous to a line of type cast in metal. The highlighted area is called the slug, and its height is equal to the amount of leading specified for the line.

The leading method you choose determines the position of the type within the slug. Some of PageMaker's typographic controls—such as paragraph rules and the position of subscripts and superscripts—are specified relative to the baseline of the text. To use these features, you have to know where that baseline is.

Proportional leading

Proportional leading *distributes two-thirds of the leading above the baseline and one-third below. This is PageMaker's default method, and so it's the one most frequently used. The difficulty is that when you need to know where the baseline is, you have to do a calculation. For example, in this line of 15/24 type, 16 points of the line slug is above the baseline, and 8 points is below.*

Baseline leading for type

Baseline leading *distributes all the leading above the baseline. This is the method used in traditional typography, and it enables you to control spacing without first having to calculate where the baseline falls. Note that the descenders of the "g," "y," and "p" drop below the line slug. When you cut and paste type with baseline leading, the descenders may appear clipped off. They'll print correctly, and they'll also look fine as soon as you redraw the screen.*

Top-of-caps leading

Top-of-caps *leading measures leading from the tallest ascender of the largest font in the line, even if that letter doesn't appear in the line. It's used much less frequently than either of the other methods. But in headlines with two or three lines, top-of-caps leading can enable you to control the space between lines without altering the position of the first line.*

Leading is a paragraph-level attribute, which means that the method you choose is applied to all the lines in a paragraph. To change the leading method for selected paragraphs, or to define the leading method for a paragraph style, you have to go through a nest of dialog boxes: Choose Paragraph from the Type menu; in the Paragraph Specs dialog box, choose Spacing; in the Spacing Attributes dialog box, select the leading method that you want.

Another PageMaker default to be aware of is Auto leading. When you specify a type size, PageMaker automatically changes the leading value to 120% of the type size value. You can change the percentage used for Auto leading (in the Spacing Attributes dialog box), but it's almost always better to specify a numeric value for the leading itself. That way, when you need to know what that value is (to style another text block similarly, or to determine the position of a paragraph rule or the spacing in a leading grid), you don't have to calculate what the leading is.

TYPOGRAPHIC REFINEMENTS

Even the simplest publication is likely to have some element of type that doesn't look quite right using the default setting: the line breaks in a headline, the shape of the right margin in flush left text, the two-word line that ends a paragraph at the top of a column. Part of what distinguishes professional from amateur typography is the fine-tuning of these details. In reviewing the typographic options available in Page-Maker, this section focuses primarily on the mechanics of the program. For a close look at the process of solving typographic problems in real documents, see the projects in Section 4.

Hyphenation

Hyphenation is an area of trade-offs. A line break in the middle of a word slows down reading. But disallowing hyphenation can be distracting, too: In justified text, it adds to uneven word spacing and letterspacing; in flush left text, it can create line lengths so uneven that they look odd. Use the Hyphenation command (on the Type menu) to control this aspect of your typography. Like Spacing, Hyphenation is a paragraph-level command and can be incorporated into the definition of a style.

Hyphenation Off Choose this option for headlines and other display type, in which hyphenation looks awkward and distracts from the impact.

Manual Only PageMaker will allow only those hyphens that you insert manually. To do so, set an insertion point where you want the hyphen, and then press Command-hyphen on a Mac, Ctrl-hyphen on a PC. These are called *discretionary hyphens* because PageMaker inserts them only if that word break occurs at the end of a line; if editing alters the line breaks, you won't end up with a hyphen in the middle of a line (as you would if you typed a hyphen without the Command- or Ctrl-key combination). Choose this option for captions and other text in which you would prefer not to allow hyphenation but want it available in case you can't make the text fit any other way.

Manual Plus Dictionary PageMaker first looks for manual hyphens, then for hyphens in the user dictionary, and then in its own dictionary to determine where to allow hyphenation.

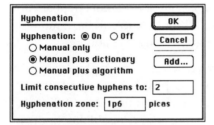

▲ ▲ ▲

Use the Hyphenation command (on the Type menu) to set hyphenation parameters for selected paragraphs or as part of a paragraph style.

In a narrow column like the one in this example, a soft rag (far right) gives the best appearance.

▼ ▼ ▼

Very hard rag (Hyphenation: Off)	Hard rag (Hyphenation Zone: 3)	Soft rag (Hyphenation Zone: 1)
The great error in Rip's composition was an insuperable aversion to all kinds of profitable labour. It could not be from the want of assiduity or perseverance; for he would sit on a wet rock, with a rod as long and heavy as a Tartar's lance, and fish all day without a murmur, even though he should not be encouraged by a single nibble.	The great error in Rip's composition was an insuperable aversion to all kinds of profitable labour. It could not be from the want of assiduity or perseverance; for he would sit on a wet rock, with a rod as long and heavy as a Tartar's lance, and fish all day without a murmur, even though he should not be encouraged by a single nibble.	The great error in Rip's composition was an insuperable aversion to all kinds of profitable labour. It could not be from the want of assiduity or perseverance; for he would sit on a wet rock, with a rod as long and heavy as a Tartar's lance, and fish all day without a murmur, even though he should not be encouraged by a single nibble.

TIP

Regardless of your hyphenation settings, you should review your pages and make some manual corrections, for both typographical and grammatical reasons. Occasionally you'll need to edit text to avoid a bad line break.

Manual Plus Algorithm After looking for manual and dictionary hyphens, PageMaker uses certain rules of logic to break words that aren't in its dictionary. These rules may not coincide with standard dictionary hyphenation, so proofread your text carefully if you use this method.

There are several other ways to control hyphenation.

Consecutive Hyphens Although the default setting for Limit Consecutive Hyphens is No Limit, good typesetting generally avoids hyphenation in more than two consecutive lines. To avoid having two consecutive lines hyphenated, type *1* in the box. To avoid having more than two consecutive lines hyphenated, type *2* in the text box.

Hyphenation Zone This determines how close to the end of an unjustified line PageMaker can insert a hyphen. In narrow columns, specify a small number (around 1 pica). This allows hyphens close to the end of the line, resulting in a softer rag in flush left text. But it also allows more hyphens after only two letters of a word. In wider columns, a harder rag (a Hyphenation Zone of 2 or 3 picas) with less hyphenation often looks better.

Ranked hyphenation PageMaker's dictionary ranks potential hyphenation points from best to third best. (See page 281 for how to edit the rankings.) The third-best ranking is used only in algorithm hyphenation.

To delete an undesirable hyphen Insert a discretionary hyphen (Command-hyphen or Ctrl-hyphen) immediately preceding the first character of the word, thus forcing the word to the next line. (Or edit the text to change the line break.) Use this technique when PageMaker hyphenates a proper noun or when a tight line of justified text ends in a hyphen.

To enter a nonbreaking hyphen When you don't want a line break in the middle of a hyphenated compound word, press Command-Option-hyphen on a Mac, Ctrl-Shift-hyphen on a PC (and ^~ in dialog boxes).

Nonbreaking spaces

When you press the Spacebar, PageMaker inserts a word space character. But there are four other space characters that you can use to gain greater control over the size of the space. They are called nonbreaking spaces because PageMaker will not break a line on either side of them.

A fixed space is the width of a word space for the specified font, but unlike a regular Spacebar character, a fixed space is nonbreaking. An em space is the width of the point size, an en is half that, and a thin space is half an en. So in 12-point type, an em is 12 points, an en is 6 points, and a thin space is 3 points. These space characters enable you to create consistent spaces without having to set tabs. And because they are based on point size, you can change the size of the space by changing the point size of the space character.

TIP

On some systems, the Ctrl-Shift-M key combination doesn't work. If that happens to you, call Aldus tech support. They will probably have figured out a solution by the time you read this.

Space	Macintosh	PC
em	Command-Shift-M	Ctrl-Shift-M
en	Command-Shift-N	Ctrl-Shift-N
thin	Command-Shift-T	Ctrl-Shift-T
fixed	Option-Spacebar	Ctrl-Shift-H

How to use We often use an en space between a boldface subhead and the body text following it, as in this paragraph. This eliminates the need for a colon and gives the text a cleaner appearance. And at some point sizes, we use thin spaces between periods for an ellipsis character; we just like the spacing better than the standard ellipsis character (Option-semicolon on a Mac, Alt-0133 on a PC).

> This is … an ellipsis character.
> This is . . . an ellipsis created with periods and thin spaces.

Use a fixed space between two words when you don't want to see a line break between them, such as the name of your company or the numeral following the word "Chapter." You can also use a fixed space when you need to kern the first or last character of a line beyond the text margin. See pages 41 and 407.

Widows and orphans

In traditional publishing, a widow is generally defined as one or two words that form the last line of a paragraph. PageMaker has no option for controlling these lines; you'll have to look for them yourself.

PageMaker does offer control for widows and orphans defined as follows: A widow is the first one, two, or three lines of a paragraph falling at the end of a column; an orphan is the last one, two, or three lines of a paragraph falling at the top of a column. If you specify 2 in the Widow Control option (in the Paragraph Specs dialog box), PageMaker will not allow the first one or two lines of a paragraph to fall at the bottom of a column but rather will force them to the top of the next column. Similarly, if you specify 3 in the Orphan Control option, PageMaker will not allow the last three lines of a paragraph to fall at the top of a column but rather will push a fourth line forward to keep them company, as it were.

A HANDFUL OF TYPOGRAPHIC CONVENTIONS

- **Space between sentences** It's difficult to get used to this if you've spent years pressing a typewriter Spacebar twice between sentences, but typesetting requires only one space after periods, question marks, exclamation points, and colons.

- **Dash** Type Option-Shift-hyphen on a Mac, Alt-0151 on a PC (with a PostScript printer) to get a long dash—also called an em dash—rather than typing two hyphens as you do on a typewriter.

For an en dash, used to indicate continuing or inclusive numbers as in 1994–97, press Option-hyphen on a Mac, Ctrl-equal sign on a PC.

- **Quotation marks** and **apostrophes** Each font has characters designed specifically as quotation marks and apostrophes ("/" and '), rather than the inch and foot marks ("/" and ') used on typewriters. To get these typeset characters whenever you type text in Page-Maker, choose Preferences from the File menu, click the Other button, and in the Other Preferences dialog box, click on Use Typographer's Quotes. Or use the keyboard combinations in the chart on page 46.

When you place text in PageMaker from a word-processing program, you can get typeset-style quotation marks automatically by selecting the Convert Quotes option in the Place dialog box.

In publications with continuous running text—a long report, for example—these controls can help you produce better-looking pages more efficiently. But in highly formatted publications, with art and display type, editing around the problem may be a better solution than the uneven column breaks created by automatically forcing lines forward and backward.

What's the big deal? Widows and orphans can have two unfortunate effects. They can interrupt the flow of text (a single line of a new paragraph at the bottom of a page). Or they can be eyesores (a very short line at the top of a column, which looks awful).

Fractions

6³/₈ — superscript
— subscript
▲ ▲ ▲

In a properly typeset fraction, the type aligns top and bottom.

Most fonts don't come with typographic fraction characters. By understanding how to create properly typeset fractions, you'll know how to fine-tune the specifications when you use PageMaker's Addition for automating the job.

Creating your own fractions

- Specify the numerator as a superscript (Command-Shift-equal sign on a Mac, Ctrl-Shift-backslash on a PC; or use the Case option in the Control Palette or in the Type dialog box).
- Type the slash as a fraction bar character (Option-Shift-1 on a Mac, Alt-0164—on the numeric keypad—in the Symbol font on a PC).
- Specify the denominator as a subscript (Command-Shift-hyphen on a Mac, Ctrl-backslash on a PC; or use the Case option).

Then select all three characters, bring up the Type Specs dialog box, click the Options button, and customize the superscript and subscript values. The following values work well for many typefaces and sizes, but you should check your printouts and adjust the specs as needed.

- Superscript/subscript size: 60% (specified as a percentage of the current point size, in increments as small as one-tenth of 1%)
- Superscript position: 30% (specified as a percentage of an em space shifted up from the baseline)
- Subscript position: 0% (specified as a percentage of an em space shifted up from the baseline)

You may need to kern around the slash for some numbers. If you have a lot of fractions, set the defaults for the Options dialog box to the superscript and subscript values that you want for your fractions. Or specify those values as part of any paragraph style that includes fractions in the text.

Formatting fractions with the fraction script

A script is a set of instructions that describes a series of actions. PageMaker includes two scripts for formatting fractions, one for fractions with a diagonal slash (½), and the other for fractions with a horizontal slash ($\frac{1}{2}$). To format the fractions: Type the fraction using standard keyboard characters (1/2), position the cursor *after* the denominator, choose Run Script from the Aldus Additions submenu (on the Utilities menu), and then select the fraction script you want to use from the Scripts folder in the PageMaker 5 folder. You have to repeat this procedure for every fraction in the document.

SPACING

PageMaker offers three basic options for adjusting the space within text.

- Kerning adjusts the space between individual pairs of letters by small increments relative to the point size of the text. It's used primarily in large type sizes to correct uneven spacing created by different shaped letters.

- Tracking adjusts the space across a range of text by a set amount. It's used primarily to lighten or darken the overall appearance of a text block, such as a headline.

- Word spacing and letterspacing adjustments are paragraph-level attributes, specified as a percentage of the normal word space or letterspace for that font size. It's the most useful adjustment for large amounts of body text, and it's particularly useful for creating optimum spacing in justified text.

Kerning

Kerning is the process of adjusting space between letter pairs for better overall balance. The shape of some letter pairs, such as Wo, Ya, and Tu, makes the space between the letters seem too big. The shape of other letters, such as Mi and Il, makes the letters seem too close together.

How much space to add or delete is a subjective visual judgment. When you kern, the goal is to achieve an optical balance of spacing across the entire line. One approach is to imagine pouring sand between the letters and then to add or delete space so that there would be a nearly equal volume of sand between each pair. Another approach is to visually isolate three letters to see whether the space on both sides of the center one is equal; you can quickly "scan" an entire headline this way.

PageMaker offers several tools for kerning text.

Automatic pair kerning uses the spacing adjustments specified in the font design, in increments as small as $\frac{1}{1000}$th of the point size. (This is finer than the increments available for manual kerning.) PageMaker's default is to apply automatic pair kerning to type larger than 12 points. To turn Auto Pair Kerning on and off and specify the point size above which it is applied, choose Paragraph from the Type menu, and in the Paragraph Specs dialog box, choose Spacing. This is a paragraph-level option and can be specified as part of a style definition.

It takes considerable time to compose large amounts of text with automatic pair kerning, so it is generally recommended for use only with display type. (That's why the default is set to larger than 12 points.) Also, there's a tremendous variation in the kerning that's built into individual font designs. Some fonts have over a thousand kerning pairs, some have two or three hundred, and some have none at all. And some kerning that is built in isn't very well adjusted. If you think body text

TIP

Use the zoom tool to enlarge
the page view of type that you want
to kern: Press Command-Spacebar
on a Mac, Ctrl-Spacebar on a PC.
Leave the keys pressed and when
you see a magnifying glass with a
plus sign in the center, click on the
type. To reduce the page view when
you finish kerning, press Command-
Option-Spacebar on the Mac,
Ctrl-Alt-Spacebar on the PC, and
click the zoom tool (this time with a
minus sign in the center) on the type.

in sizes of 12 points or smaller needs overall kerning, test a sample of
the text with a lower value for auto pair kerning; if the printouts solve
the spacing problems you have with the text, it may be worth the time
required to apply this overall.

Manual kerning is the process of specifying the amount of space to add
or delete between selected letter pairs, rather than relying on automatic
controls. If you ignore all the other options for adjusting spacing, learn
to pay attention to headlines and to manually kern letter pairs that
have odd gaps between them. (See pages 273 and 407 for a close look at
kerning headlines in real documents.)

All kerning adjustments are in units of an em, which is a space equal to the
point size of the type. For 100-point type, an em is 100 points wide; if you
decrease the space by $\frac{1}{100}$th of an em (the smallest increment available in
PageMaker for manual kerning), you remove 1 point of space between the
two letters. For 30-point type, an em is 30 points wide; if you decrease the
space by $\frac{1}{100}$th of an em, you remove 0.3 point of space.

To manually kern type, set an insertion point between the two letters
whose space you want to adjust, and use one of the Control Palette
techniques or keyboard combinations listed below.

Control Palette kerning

$-\frac{1}{100}$th of em (.01)	In the Control Palette kerning field, press the left nudge button once.
$-\frac{1}{10}$th of em (.1)	Hold down Command (Mac) or Ctrl (PC) while you press the left nudge button once.
$+\frac{1}{100}$th of em (.01)	In the kerning field, press the right nudge button once.
$+\frac{1}{10}$th of em (.1)	Hold down Command (Mac) or Ctrl (PC) while you press the right nudge button once.
To type a value	In the kerning text field, type a negative value to delete space and a position value to add space. Values can be as small as .01.

Keyboard kerning

$-\frac{1}{100}$th of em (.01)	Macintosh: Option-Delete[†] or Command-Shift-left arrow
	Windows: Ctrl-Shift-minus sign[*]
$-\frac{1}{25}$th of em (.04)	Macintosh: Command-Delete[†] or Command-left arrow
	Windows: Ctrl-Bksp or Ctrl-minus sign[*]
$+\frac{1}{100}$th of em (.01)	Macintosh: Option-Shift-Delete[†] or Com-Shift-right arrow
	Windows: Ctrl-Shift-plus sign[*]
$+\frac{1}{25}$th of em (.04)	Macintosh: Command-Shift-Delete[†] or Com-right arrow
	Windows: Ctrl-Shift-Bksp or Ctrl-plus sign[*]

[†] or Backspace key
[*] on the numeric keypad (with Num Lock off)

*Whichever technique you use for
manual kerning, the kerning value is
displayed in the Control Palette
kerning field. You can use this value
for text that repeats character pairs
you've already kerned.*

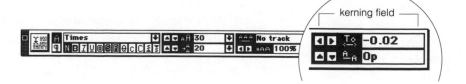
kerning field

TIP

In PageMaker, **kerning affects the space after a character.** So if you need to kern the first character of a line into the left margin, you can insert a fixed word space at the beginning of the line and kern between that space and the following character. Similarly, to kern the last character of a line beyond the right margin, add the fixed space to the end of the line and kern between that space and the preceding character. These techniques can be used to hang punctuation beyond the text so that it appears optically aligned.

Because kerning increments are so small, you'll want to kern at 400% or 800%. Even then you'll need to check the printouts carefully, and you can expect to go through three or four or even more printouts before you achieve overall balance. It's a very slow and exacting process.

Range kerning is used to manually kern a range of text, rather than simply a pair of letters. You select the text with the text tool and then use any of the Control Palette or keyboard techniques described on page 40. Range kerning is particularly useful when you need to shave a little space to make text fit or add a little to make it fill. But be careful not to overdo it, or you'll create text that has uneven color and may be difficult to read.

Expert Kerning is an Aldus Addition (on the Utilities menu) that evaluates every letter pair in selected text and inserts the appropriate manual kerning. It can be used with any PostScript Type 1 font installed on your computer.

To use this Addition, turn off Auto Pair Kerning for the selected text. With the text selected, choose Expert Kerning from the Aldus Additions submenu. In the Expert Kerning dialog box, specify Text, Display, or Poster, or type the font size of the master if you know it. For the kern strength, type a value from 0.00 through 2.00. The higher the value, the tighter the spacing.

Kern Edit, a stand-alone utility included with Macintosh PageMaker, enables you to modify a font's kerning pairs and save the modified font file so you can apply that kerning whenever you use the font, in PageMaker or any other application that allows kerning. You can edit existing kern pairs and create new ones as well. For designers who understand the nuances of typography and can invest the time required to edit the kerning tables for a font, this is a useful addition to PageMaker's typographic controls.

If you use this utility, be sure to include the modified screen font when you send files to a service bureau for high-resolution output.

Note how much better the headline on the right holds together, the result of tighter leading and manual kerning.

30/30 without kerning	30/20 with manual kerning
PAY ATTENTION TO HEADLINES	PAY ATTENTION TO HEADLINES

Tracking

Tracking adjusts character spacing uniformly across the selected text, according to five preset values ranging from Very Tight to Very Loose. (The default setting of No Track provides a sixth option.) Each track adjusts the letterspacing relative to the type size—the same tracking option is relatively tighter at larger type sizes than at smaller ones. But unlike kerning, which customizes the space between individual letter pairs, each tracking value applies exactly the same adjustment to the space between every pair of letters at that type size (including the Spacebar character and adjacent characters).

To apply a tracking value, select the range of text and choose one of the tracking options from the Control Palette's character view, from the Type menu, or from the Type Specs dialog box. You can also include tracking as part of a style definition. At small text sizes (especially at less than 8 point), Normal or Loose tracking can lighten the text and make it easier to read. In large display type, Tight tracking may make the words hold together better.

If you've condensed or expanded type using PageMaker's Set Width option, any tracking you apply is based on the adjusted width. For example, if you've condensed 40-point type to 80%, and you then apply a tracking value, the type is tracked as if it were 32-point type.

You can edit PageMaker's default tracks with the Edit Tracks command, available from the Aldus Additions submenu on the Utilities menu. This is subtle work, but if it suits your needs, keep in mind that PageMaker stores tracking information in a file called Tracking Values (on the Mac, where it is in the Aldus folder) and Trakvals.bin (on the

TIP

At very small sizes (generally less than 10 points) Normal tracking will increase the letterspacing over the default No Track setting. But at larger sizes (generally 10 point and above) Normal tracking will decrease the letterspacing over the default of No Track.

16-point type with different tracking values

No Track	Endless Typographic Details
Very Loose	Endless Typographic Details
Loose	Endless Typographic Details
Normal	Endless Typographic Details
Tight	Endless Typographic Details
Very Tight	Endless Typographic Details

Note that with No Track applied, large type appears disproportionately looser. With Tight tracking, the spacing in the larger type appears consistent with the spacing in the smaller type.

Top: No Track

Tracking

Bottom: Tight

Tracking

Tracking

Tracking

PC, where it is in the Aldus/Usenglsh directory). If you want to edit the tracking values for a given publication, but not for all publications, copy that tracking file to the same folder as the publication. When you use the Edit Tracks Addition, and when you print, PageMaker will look for this file first in the publication folder and then in the Aldus folder. Also, if you output your file at a service bureau, be sure to include the edited tracking file.

Spacing

Spacing attributes

Word space:			Letter space:		
Minimum	75	%	Minimum	-5	%
Desired	100	%	Desired	0	%
Maximum	150	%	Maximum	25	%

▲ ▲ ▲

The Spacing Attributes are designed to give you control over how Page-Maker justifies text, but they can also be used to alter the type color in flush left text.

When you want to adjust the spacing over large amounts of body text, use the Spacing Attributes dialog box. To access this dialog box, choose Paragraph, and in the Paragraph dialog box, choose Spacing. The values you specify are a percentage of the normal word spacing built into the font. This gives you considerable control over the spacing, without requiring as much composition time as automatic or expert kerning. Spacing is a paragraph-level attribute, and you can specify Spacing parameters as part of a style definition.

For both Word and Letter Space, there are Minimum, Desired, and Maximum settings. The value you specify for Desired spacing must be between the values specified for Minimum and Maximum. You can specify word spacing from 0% to 500% and letter spacing from –200% to 200%.

Don't assume that the default word spacing is the optimum setting. In most PostScript fonts, the width of the space character is half the width of a numeral. Many designers find the default word spacing too open, and they will begin by tightening the Desired Word Space to around 80% and fine-tune from there. Also, the range from Minimum to Maximum in the default values is fairly broad—75% through 150% for word spacing and –5% through 25% for letterspacing; adjusting the values for a tighter range often gives the type a more even texture.

On the other hand, open spacing can often be used to good effect. For example, the running heads in this book have the Desired Letter Space adjusted to 100% (the default is 0), doubling the space between letters. And when you set reverse type in black or colored boxes, opening the letterspace can make the text more legible. You'll see many examples of this in the Portfolio Section later in this book. When you alter the Desired Letter Space, the word spacing is adjusted proportionally (the result of the adjustment to the character preceding the word space and to the width of the Spacebar character itself).

For justified text, you'll need to experiment with different settings over a large block of text to determine the optimum spacing for the text size and column width. In doing this, it's helpful to understand the process by which PageMaker determines whether to fit a word on a line, push it to the next line, or hyphenate it.

The two main principles PageMaker uses in composing text are that it alters spacing before allowing hyphenation and that it squeezes space before expanding it. Specifically, PageMaker tries the following options in the order listed.

TIPS

To remove manual kerning With the text selected, press Command-Option-K on the Mac, Ctrl-Shift-0 (zero on the main keyboard) on the PC.

To remove tracking Select the text and press Command-Shift-Q on a Mac, Ctrl-Shift-Q on a PC.

To remove custom spacing attributes Select the text, display the Spacing Attributes dialog box (through the Paragraph command), and press Reset.

- Tighten the word space (up to the minimum value specified) to fill a line without hyphenation.

- Expand the word space (up to the maximum value) to push the last word to the next line.

- Hyphenate the last word to keep the spacing within the specified range.

- Adjust the letter space, first by tightening and then by expanding (within the specified range).

- As a last resort, use the maximum letter spacing and expand the word spacing as much as necessary to push the last word to the next line.

The example of justified type below is based on only a single paragraph, but it will give you an idea of how different values can affect the setting and how you rarely solve all the spacing problems without some manual fine-tuning. For the range kerning used in the third sample, we selected the text in line 7, which was too tight, and pressed Option-Shift-Delete (on a Mac) to add $\frac{1}{100}$th of an em to the letterspacing in that line. This forced the word "of" to the next line but left lines 7 and 8 with excessively open word spacing. We selected both lines and pressed Option-Shift-Delete three times. This opened the letterspace (and in doing so, removed some of the excess word space), making the overall color of the type more even. If you plan to use justified type, be prepared to spend time making these sorts of adjustments.

To find out where PageMaker has set lines tighter or looser than you've specified in the Spacing dialog box, turn on the Show Loose/Tight Lines option in the Preferences dialog box. PageMaker will highlight those lines on your screen display. You can then manually adjust those lines, either by kerning a range of selected text, by adjusting the hyphenation parameters, or by editing the text. If a lot of lines are highlighted, you probably need to change the design in some way—a wider column or a different type size, for example.

In justified type, you generally need to customize the Spacing Attributes and then use manual kerning to solve problems in individual lines. The order of the values for each setting follows the order in the Spacing dialog box: Minimum, Desired, and then Maximum.

Default spacing Word Space: 50/100/200 Letter Space: –5/0/25	Custom spacing Word Space: 50/85/150 Letter Space: –8/–3/15		Custom spacing as at left plus range kerning in lines 7 and 8
The ability to set type, to modify it on-screen, to compose it in pages, and then print the result in camera-ready form is the foundation of desktop publishing. Suddenly, the fundamental building block of graphic design is in the hands of anyone with a few thousand dollars.	The ability to set type, to modify it on-screen, to compose it in pages, and then print the result in camera-ready form is the foundation of desktop publishing. Suddenly, the fundamental building block of graphic design is in the hands of anyone with a few thousand dollars.	1 2 3 4 5 6 7 8 9 10	The ability to set type, to modify it on-screen, to compose it in pages, and then print the result in camera-ready form is the foundation of desktop publishing. Suddenly, the fundamental building block of graphic design is in the hands of anyone with a few thousand dollars.

KEYBOARD SHORTCUTS

Keyboard shortcuts for formatting text can save you time when you are testing different specifications. Here are some of the most useful:

Desired format	Macintosh	PC
Normal	Command-Shift-Sp	Ctrl-Shift-Sp or F5
Bold	Command-Shift-B	Ctrl-Shift-B or F6
Italic	Command-Shift-I	Ctrl-Shift-I or F7
Underline	Command-Shift-U	Ctrl-Shift-U
Strikethrough	Command-Shift-/	Ctrl-Shift-S
Outline	Command-Shift-D	NA
Shadow	Command-Shift-W	NA
Reverse	none	Ctrl-Shift-V
All caps	Command-Shift-K	Ctrl-Shift-K
Small caps	Command-Shift-H	none
Subscript	Command-Shift- –	Ctrl-\
Superscript	Command-Snift-+	Ctrl-Shift-\
Align left	Command-Shift-L	Ctrl-Shift-L
Align right	Command-Shift-R	Ctrl-Shift-R
Justify	Command-Shift-J	Ctrl-Shift-J
Center	Command-Shift-C	Ctrl-Shift-C
Force justify	Command-Shift-F	Ctrl-Shift-F
1 point larger	Option-Com-Shift->	Ctrl-Sh->
1 point smaller	Option-Com-Shift-<	Ctrl-Sh-<
1 graphic size larger*	Command-Shift->	Ctrl-> or F4
1 graphic size smaller*	Command-Shift-<	Ctrl-< or F3

* These "sizes" refer to the point sizes listed on the Size submenu.

TIP

When you **force justify** type, insert a fixed space between the words (Option-Spacebar on a Mac, Ctrl-Shift-H on a PC). This tells PageMaker to add space equally between letters and words in order to fill out the line. If you use a regular Spacebar character, PageMaker adds all the space between the words.

SPECIAL CHARACTERS & SYMBOLS

Both the Macintosh and the PC have extended character sets that enable you to incorporate special symbols—copyright and register marks, pound and yen signs, accents used in foreign languages, and so on—into your documents.

On the Macintosh, you can review the special characters by selecting the Key Caps desk accessory from the Apple menu. This displays a window with a typewriter keyboard and you can select the typeface whose characters you want to view from the Key Caps menu. To see the complete character set, alternately hold down the Option, Shift, and Command keys, and combinations of these keys. Note the keys needed to type the character you want when you return to the PageMaker layout.

On the PC, open the Character Map file (in the Program Manager's Accessory folder) to view a grid of all the characters for a specified typeface. Click on the character you need, and note the Keystroke displayed in the box at the lower right of the window. On the PC, you can also view character sets from within PageMaker: Open the Charset.pt5 file (in the PM5 directory). Follow the on-screen instructions for changing

TIP

Foreign-language characters
are simplified on the Mac because
some accents are separated from
the letters they modify. To enter an
accented character, type the key
combination for the accent, and then
type the letter. PageMaker enters the
sequence as a single character.

  ´   Option-e, then type letter
  `     Option-`, then type letter
  ¨   Option-u, then type letter
  ^   Option-i, then type letter
  ~   Option-n, then type letter

For a complete foreign-language
character set (using the Latin
alphabet), use the techniques
described beginning on page 45.

TIP

**If a special character fails to
print,** or if the wrong special
character prints, review the Print/
Options setting for Use Symbol Font
for Special Characters (Macintosh,
PostScript printers only). If the font
you're using includes the special
characters you need, do not check
this option. But if your font doesn't
include characters for the symbols,
turn this option on and PageMaker
will automatically substitute the
Symbol font.

the font. Then note the code for that character. To type the code, hold
down the Alt key and use the numeric keypad to type the number (preceded by 0 or 00 to result in a four-digit number).

Here are some commonly used characters. (A blank means that a special font is required for that character.) PC users note: All numbers in
Alt key combinations must be entered on the numeric keypad (with
Num Lock off). Typing Alt-0 plus the subsequent three-digit number
instructs PageMaker to remap the standard ASCII code to the ANSI
code used in Windows.

Character		Mac	PC
bullet	•	Op-8	Ctrl-Sh-8
cent sign	¢	Op-4	Alt-0162
copyright symbol	©	Op-G*	Ctrl-Sh-O
dagger	†	Op-T	Alt-0134
double dagger	‡	Op-Sh-7	Alt-0135
degree symbol	°	Op-Sh-8	Alt-0176
discretionary hyphen	-	Com-hyphen	Ctrl-hyphen
division sign	÷	Op-/	Alt-0247
ellipsis	…	Op-;	Alt-0133
em dash	—	Op-Sh-hyphen	Ctrl-Sh-=
em space		Com-Sh-M	Ctrl-Sh-M
en dash	–	Op-hyphen	Ctrl-=
en space		Com-Sh-N	Ctrl-Sh-N
fixed (nonbreaking) space		Op-Sp	Ctrl-Sh-H
forced line break		Sh-Return	Sh-Enter
fraction bar	/	Op-Sh-1	
infinity symbol	∞	Op-5	
inverted exclamation	¡	Op-1	Alt-0161
inverted question mark	¿	Op-Sh-/	Alt-0191
nonbreaking hyphen	-	Com-Op-hyphen	Ctrl-Sh-hyphen
nonbreaking slash	/	Com-Op-/	Ctrl-Sh-/
paragraph symbol	¶	Op-7	Ctrl-Sh-7
does-not-equal sign	≠	Op-=	
plus-or-minus sign	±	Op-Sh-=	Alt-0177
pound sign	£	Op-3	Alt-0163
registration symbol	®	Op-R*	Ctrl-Sh-G
section symbol	§	Op-6	Ctrl-Sh-6
square root, radical sign	√	Op-v	
thin space		Com-Sh-T	Ctrl-Sh-T
trademark symbol	™	Op-2*	Alt-0153
typographic open quotes	"	Op-[	Ctrl-Sh-[
typographic close quotes	"	Op-Sh-[	Ctrl-Sh-]
typog. single open quotes	'	Op-]	Ctrl-[
typog. single close quotes	'	Op-Sh-]	Ctrl-]
yen sign	¥	Op-Y	Alt-0165

* Mac only: If the font you're using doesn't have this
character, you can get both serif and sans serif from
the Symbol font using these combinations.

serif		sans serif	
®	Op-[	®	Op-Sh-zero
©	Op-Sh-[	©	Op-Sh-W
™	Op-]	™	Op-Sh-R

ZAPF DINGBATS

The Zapf Dingbats typeface provides useful typographic embellishments. It is resident on many PostScript printers and available as a downloadable font from Adobe. The characters are shown below with the key combinations used to produce them. PC users: For characters in columns 4, 5, and 6, you must hold down the Alt key and use the numeric keypad to type *0* and the three numbers listed.

Ch	Mac/PC
✁	Sh-1
✂	Sh-'
✃	Sh-3
✄	Sh-4
☎	Sh-5
✆	Sh-7
✇	'
✈	Sh-9
✉	Sh-0
☛	Sh-8
☞	Sh-=
✌	,
✍	-
✎	.
✏	/
✐	0
✑	1
✒	2
✓	3
✔	4
✕	5
✖	6
✗	7
✘	8
✙	9
✚	Sh-;
✛	;
✜	Sh - ,
✝	=
✞	Sh-.
✟	Sh-/
✠	Sh-2
✡	Sh-A
✢	Sh-B

Ch	Mac/PC
✣	Sh-C
✤	Sh-D
✥	Sh-E
✦	Sh-F
✧	Sh-G
★	Sh-H
✩	Sh-I
✪	Sh-J
✫	Sh-K
✬	Sh-L
✭	Sh-M
✮	Sh-N
✯	Sh-O
✰	Sh-P
✱	Sh-Q
✲	Sh-R
✳	Sh-S
✴	Sh-T
✵	Sh-U
✶	Sh-V
✷	Sh-W
✸	Sh-X
✹	Sh-Y
✺	Sh-Z
✻	[
✼	\
✽	]
✾	Sh-6
✿	Sh- -
❀	`
❁	a
❂	b
❃	c
❄	d

Ch	Mac/PC
❅	e
❆	f
❇	g
❈	h
❉	i
❊	j
❋	k
●	l
❍	m
■	n
❏	o
❐	p
❑	q
❒	r
▲	s
▼	t
◆	u
❖	v
◗	w
❘	x
❙	y
❚	z
❛	Sh-[
❜	Sh-\
❝	Sh-]
❞	Op-n (Mac) Alt-126 (PC)

Ch	Mac	PC
❡	Sh-Op-8	161
❢	Op-4	162
❣	Op-3	163
❤	Op-6	164
❥	Op-8	165
❦	Op-7	166
❧	Op-s	167
♣	Op-r	168
♦	Op-g	169
♥	Op-2	170
♠	Op-e	171
①	Op-u	172
②	Op-=	173
③	Sh-Op-'	174
④	Sh-Op-O	175
⑤	Op-5	176
⑥	Sh-Op-=	177
⑦	Op-,	178
⑧	Op-.	179
⑨	Op-y	180
⑩	Op-m	181
❶	Op-d	182
❷	Op-w	183
❸	Sh-Op-P	184
❹	Op-p	185
❺	Op-b	186
❻	Op-9	187
❼	Op-0	188
❽	Op-z	189
❾	Op-'	190
❿	Op-o	191

Ch	Mac	PC
➀	Sh-Op-/	192
➁	Op-1	193
➂	Op-l	194
➃	Op-v	195
➄	Op-f	196
➅	Op-x	197
➆	Op-j	198
➇	Op-\	199
➈	Sh-Op-\	200
➉	Op-;	201
➊	Op-Sp	202
➋	Op-` then Sh-A	203
➌	Op-n then Sh-A	204
➍	Op-n then Sh-0	205
➎	Sh-Op-Q	206
➏	Op-q	207
➐	Op- -	208
➑	Sh-Op- -	209
➒	Op-[	210
➓	Sh-Op-[	211
➔	Op-]	212
→	Sh-Op-]	213
↔	Op-/	214
↕	Sh-Op-V	215
➘	(PC only)	216
➙	Sh-Op-`	217
➚	Sh-Op-1	218
➛	Sh-Op-2	219
➜	Sh-Op-3	220
➝	Sh-Op-4	221
➞	Sh-Op-5	222

Ch	Mac	PC
➟	Sh-Op-6	223
➠	Sh-Op-7	224
➡	Sh-Op-9	225
➢	Sh-Op-0	226
➣	Sh-Op-W	227
➤	Sh-Op-E	228
➥	Sh-Op-R	229
➦	Sh-Op-T	230
➧	Sh-Op-Y	231
➨	Sh-Op-U	232
➩	Sh-Op-I	233
➪	Sh-Op-S	234
➫	Sh-Op-D	235
➬	Sh-Op-F	236
➭	Sh-Op-G	237
➮	Sh-Op-H	238
➯	Sh-Op-J	239
➱	Sh-Op-L	241
➲	Sh-Op-;	242
➳	Sh-Op-Z	243
➴	Sh-Op-X	244
➵	Sh-Op-B	245
➶	Sh-Op-N	246
➷	Sh-Op-M	247
➸	Sh-Op-,	248
➹	Sh-Op-.	249
➺	Op-H	250
➻	Op-K	251
➼	(PC only)	252
➽	(PC only)	253
➾	(PC only)	254

CHAPTER 3

CREATING A GRID: THE UNDERLYING STRUCTURE OF PAGE COMPOSITION

A major virtue of the grid system is the discipline it imposes on the untrained designer. As a teacher of publication design, I have found that it is only when the student divides and analyzes the space he is working with that he is able to achieve a cohesive design solution.
      —Allen Hurlburt, The Grid

There is nothing mysterious about a grid. It is simply an underlying structure that defines where to put things on the page. A letter typed on an old manual typewriter uses a grid; so does a handwritten list on a sheet of paper in which you note the names of items on the left and the costs on the right. Although grids used in publication design can be considerably more complex than that, they can also be that simple.

The grid itself is a series of nonprinting vertical and horizontal lines that divide the page. This technique has been the dominant approach to publication design for at least thirty years, primarily because it provides such an effective way of organizing the page and speeds up layout time considerably. A well-constructed grid can make a lot of decisions for you—where to place the headlines, text, and art and how to handle the many details that inevitably turn up. A grid gives a publication a planned, cohesive look and helps ensure consistency from one page to the next. It also sets visual ground rules that everyone involved in a publication can follow.

The grid system is perfectly matched to designing on computers, where the basic unit is a square pixel. It works on the same principle as modular furniture, storage units, and old-fashioned wooden building blocks. In fact, constructing and using a grid has the same tactile tidiness and infinite variety as playing with blocks.

Of course, not all graphic designers use the grid system in their work. Some use other formal techniques, such as perspective, and some use a more intuitive, more purely aesthetic approach to page design. In general, however, designers find it far easier to introduce diversity and visual interest to a formal grid than to impose order and balance on a free-form approach.

This chapter looks at the grids found in a wide variety of publications, some of them real, some of them hypothetical documents created for this book. (The real publications carry a credit identifying the designer and the purpose of the document; the hypothetical publications, which generally use a Latin *lorem ipsum* file for running text, do not carry that credit.) The chapter begins with simple one-column grids and proceeds to increasingly complex formats. By following the progression from simple to complex, you should get a good feel for how grids work and how to use them in your publications.

Because grids provide the underlying structure of the page, we've used them as a sort of lens for looking at the other elements of page composition—typography and art. Type size and leading are inextricably related to column width, as are the size and position of graphic elements. So although the organizing principle of this chapter is grids, you will also find information about styling type and working with art. Terms that may be unfamiliar to some readers, whether having to do with graphic design or electronic page assembly, are defined in the glossary.

Throughout the chapter there are blueprints for grids that you can adapt for your own needs. Each blueprint is based on one of the hypothetical documents; your own documents may have different elements. If you use a different typeface, it might look better a little smaller or a little larger than the one in the document on which the blueprint was based. If your headline is longer than the one in the sample, you might need to adjust the space between the head and the text. The blueprints are only guidelines; as you change one element, be sure to reevaluate the others to see if additional changes are needed.

Before moving on to the structure of the page, we'll look at the shape of the page and the elements that are often found on it.

THE ANATOMY OF A PAGE

Designing and assembling pages, whether by hand or on a computer, is more than a mechanical or electronic task. It's a way of looking at a page as having a certain size, shape, and proportion.

Look through the printed material around you and you'll see that most of the pages are 8.5 by 11 inches, the same size as the letters we read and the memos we send. It's the most efficient cut of paper, it stacks up in newsstand racks with other printed material, and it fits nicely in files. But it's the vertical, or portrait shape—more than the size—that feels so familiar.

Although the page itself is usually vertical, in multipage documents the reader sees two facing pages as a horizontal unit with the slight interruption of the gutter down the center. Take advantage of this wider, more expansive unit as you organize your material and design the actual pages. And think of consecutive pages as part of a three-dimensional whole that exists in time as the reader turns the pages.

In addition to its shape, the printed page has a vocabulary that enables editors, designers, layout artists, and printers to communicate unambiguously about a job. Turn the page for a visual glossary of terms you're likely to encounter in this book and elsewhere.

THE ANATOMY OF A PRINTED PAGE

Byline The author's name, which may appear after the headline or at the end of an article.

Overline (also called a kicker or eyebrow) A brief tag over the headline that categorizes the story.

Headline The title of an article.

Deck (also called a tag line) A line that gives more information about the story.

Stick-up cap An enlarged initial letter extending above the body text.

Bleed art A photo, drawing, or tint that runs off the edge of the page.

Picture window A rectangle that indicates the position and size of art to be stripped into the page.

Caption The text describing a photograph or illustration.

Body text The main text, also called running text.

Folio The page number.

Running foot A line across the bottom of the page that helps orient the reader within a document. Here it contains the folio and date.

Verso Left-hand page (literally, the reverse, with the right-hand page considered the front).

Alley The space between columns.

Wraparound text Copy that wraps around a graphic.

Subhead A phrase that identifies a subtopic.

Inside margin The space between the binding edge of the page and the text.

THE COMPANY BULLETIN

Cover story

The Headline Goes Here

Optional secondary lines follow the headline to guide the reader into the story.

by John Hamilton

Lorem ipsum dolor sit amet, consectetuer adipiscing elit, sed diam nonummy nibh euismod tincidunt ut laoreet dolore magna aliquam erat volutpat. Ut wisi enim ad minim veniam, quis nostrud exerci tation ullamcorper suscipit lobortis nisl ut aliquip ex ea commodo consequat.

Duis autem vel eum iriure dolor in hendrerit in vulputate velit esse molestie consequat, vel illum dolore eu feugiat nulla facilisis at vero eros et accumsan et iusto odio dignissim qui blandit praesent luptatum zzril delenit augue duis dolore te feugait nulla facilisi. Lorem ipsum dolor sit amet, consectetuer adipiscing elit, sed diam nonummy nibh euismod tincidunt ut laoreet dolore magna aliquam erat volutpat.

Ut wisi enim ad minim veniam, quis nostrud exerci tation ullamcorper suscipit lobortis nisl ut aliquip ex ea commodo consequat. Duis autem vel eum iriure dolor in hendrerit in vulputate velit esse molestie consequat, vel illum dolore eu feugiat nulla facilisis at vero eros et accumsan et iusto odio dignissim qui blandit praesent luptatum zzril delenit augue duis dolore te feugait nulla facilisi.

Nam liber tempor cum soluta nobis eleifend option congue nihil imperdiet doming id quod mazim placerat facer possim assum. Lorem ipsum dolor sit amet, consectetuer adipiscing elit, sed diam nonummy nibh euismod tincidunt ut laoreet dolore magna aliquam erat volutpat. Ut wisi enim ad minim veniam, quis nostrud exerci tation ullamcorper suscipit lobortis nisl ut aliquip ex ea commodo consequat. Duis autem vel eum iriure dolor in hendrerit in vulputate velit esse molestie conse-

quat, vel illum dolore eu feugiat nulla facilisis at vero eros et accumsan et iusto odio dignissim qui blandit praesent luptatum zzril delenit augue duis dolore te feugait nulla facilisi. Lorem ipsum dolor sit amet, consectetuer adipiscing elit, sed diam nonummy nibh euismod

Duis autem vel eum iriure

Ttincidunt ut laoreet dolore magna aliquam erat volutpat.Ut wisi enim ad minim veniam, quis nostrud exerci tation ullamcorper suscipit lobortis nisl ut aliquip ex ea commodo consequat. Duis autem vel eum iriure dolor in hendrerit in vulputate velit esse molestie consequat, vel illum dolore eu feugiat nulla facilisis at.

Vero eros et accumsan et iusto odio dignissim qui blandit praesent luptatum zzril delenit augue duis dolore te feugait nulla facilisi. Lorem ipsum dolor sit amet, consectetuer adipiscing elit, sed diam nonummy nibh euismod tincidunt ut laoreet dolore magna aliquam erat volutpat. Ut wisi enim ad minim veniam, quis nostrud exerci tation ullamcorper suscipit lobortis nisl ut aliquip ex ea commodo consequat. Duis autem vel eum iriure dolor in hendrerit in vulputate velit esse molestie consequat, vel illum dolore eu feugiat nulla facilisis at vero eros et accumsan et iusto odio dignissim qui blandit prae-

The caption helps entice the reader into the text of your story and also provides information about the art and photography.

8 JANUARY 1989

Sidebar A smaller story inside a larger one, boxed with its own headline to set it apart from the main text. (It can be positioned anywhere on the page.)

Breakout (also called a pull quote or blurb) A sentence or passage excerpted from the body copy and set in large type.

Top margin The distance from the top trim to the top of the text area. Running heads and feet and folios are often positioned in the top or bottom margin.

THE COMPANY BULLETIN

Running head A line of text across the top of the page that helps orient the reader within a document. It might include the document's title, author, chapter, subject of current page, or page number.

This display type is another technique to grab the reader's attention and pull him or her into the article.

Callout A label that identifies part of an illustration.

Sidebar heading is centered over the text in the sidebar

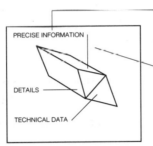

PRECISE INFORMATION

DETAILS

TECHNICAL DATA

Leader A rule that moves the eye from a callout to the part of the illustration it describes.

S equat, vel illum dolore eu feugiat nulla facilisis at vero eros et accumsan et iusto odio dignissim qui blandit praesent luptatum zzril delenit augue duis dolore te feugait nulla facilisi.

Lorem ipsum dolor sit amet, consectetuer adipiscing elit, sed diam nonummy nibh euismod tincidunt ut laoreet dolore magna aliquam erat volutpat. Ut wisi enim ad minim veniam, quis nostrud exerci tation ullamcorper suscipit lobortis nisl ut aliquip ex ea commodo consequat.

Duis autem vel eum iriure dolor in hendrerit in vulputate velit esse molestie consequat, vel illum dolore eu feugiat nulla facilisis at vero eros et accumsan et iusto odio dignissim qui blandit praesent luptatum zzril delenit augue duis dolore te feugait nulla facilisi. Lorem ipsum dolor sit amet, consectetuer adipiscing elit, sed diam.

Nonummy nibh euismod tincidunt ut laoreet dolore magna aliquam erat volutpat. Ut wisi enim ad minim veniam, quis nostrud exerci tation ullamcorper suscipit lobortis nisl ut aliquip ex ea commodo consequat.

The caption helps entice the reader into the text of your story and provides additional information about the art and photography.

✦ ✦ ✦

sent luptatum zzril delenit augue duis dolore te feugait nul ummy nibh euismod tincidunt ut laoreet dol magna aliquam erat volutpat.

Ut wisi enim ad minim veniam, quis nostrud exerci tation ullamcorper suscipit lobortis nisl ut aliquip ex ea commodo consequat. Duis autem vel eum iriure dolor in hendrerit in vulputate velit esse molestie consequat, vel illum dolore eu feugiat nulla facilisis at vero eros et accumsan et iusto odio dignissim qui blandit praesent luptatum zzril delenit augue duis dolore te feugait nulla facilisi. Lorem ipsum dolor sit amet, consectetuer adipiscing elit, sed diam nonummy nibh euismod tincidunt ut laoreet dolore magna aliquam erat volutpat. Ut wisi enim ad minim veniam, quis nostrud exerci tation ullamcorper suscipit lobortis nisl ut aliquip ex ea

Continued on page 11

Dingbat A decorative or symbolic device used to separate items on the page or denote items in a list.

Outside margin The space between the outside trim and the text.

Continued line (also called jumpline) A line of text indicating the page on which an article continues. Its counterpart on the continuation page is a carryover line identifying the story that is being continued.

Bottom margin The space between the bottom trim and the baseline of the last line of text.

Drop cap An enlarged initial letter that drops below the first line of body text.

Screen (also called tone) A tint, either a percentage of black or a second color, behind text or art.

Printing rule A rule that traps a screen or surrounds a text block or a piece of art.

Page trim The edge of the page. In commercial printing, the size of the page after it is cut during the binding process.

Gutter The space between two facing pages.

Recto Right-hand page.

ONE-COLUMN GRIDS

The fewer the columns, the easier a grid is to work with. A simple one-column format requires relatively little planning and allows you to place text quickly. When done well, this format has an unstudied, straightforward look in which the hand of the designer is relatively invisible. That lack of "fuss" suggests a serious purpose that is appropriate for business plans, reports, proposals, press releases, announcements, simple manuals, and various forms of internal communications. Even when you use a two-column grid for these types of documents, consider a one-column format for the opening page to create the feeling of a foreword. When you mix grids in this way, be sure to maintain consistent margins throughout.

The generous margins and leading and the frequent subheads make this page very open for a one-column format. The text is 10/16 Helvetica with an 8-pica left margin and a 7-pica right margin.

The sans serif Helvetica face used here has a straightforward look that is well suited to factual or practical information. By comparsion, the serif type in the sample on the facing page suggests a narrative, essay-like writing style.

The 6-point rules at the top and bottom give the page structure. Note that with an anchor such as this you can vary the depth of the text from one page to the next and still maintain continuity of page format.

The justified text balances the overall openness, creating a strong right margin that completes the definition of the image area. The page would not hold together nearly as well with ragged right text.

Charts and diagrams (not shown) run as half or full pages centered left to right.

Design: Wadlin & Erber (New Paltz, NY)

Page from a manual that addresses the subject of radon occurrence in homes for an audience of building inspectors, architects, and contractors.
Trim size: 8-1/2 by 11

REDUCING INDOOR RADON

UNIT I

RADON OCCURRENCE AND HEALTH EFFECTS

Introduction

Radon is a colorless, odorless, and tasteless gas produced by the normal decay of uranium and radium. It is a naturally occuring radioactive gas produced in most soil or rock which surrounds houses. As a result, all houses will have some radon. It is an inert gas, which means it tends to be chemically inactive. Since radon is not chemically bound or attached to other materials, it can move easily through all gas permeable materials.

Radioactive Decay

Radioactive decay is the disintegration of the nucleus of atoms in a radioactive element by spontaneous emission of charged particles, often accompanied by photon (gamma) emission. As these charged particles are released, new elements are formed. The radioactive decay chain for radon begins with **uranium** producing **radium**, which in turn produces **radon**. Each of these elements has a different "half-life" (the time required for half of the atoms of a radioactive element to decay). The "half-life" is important because its length determines the time available for decay products to be dispersed into the environment.

Types of Radiation

The three types of radiation are gamma, beta, and alpha.

Gamma radiation is photon "parcels of energy" which operate at much higher energy levels than visible light. These rays are relatively high in penetrating power. They can travel much more deeply into objects than alpha or beta particles, and can pass through the body.

Beta radiation involves an energized particle emitted from the nucleus of a radioactive atom. It has a negative charge, and has a mass equal to one electron. Beta particles have medium penetrating power, and can penetrate up to about 0.5 centimeter of surface tissue, or about a millimeter of lead.

1

The simpler grids are generally "quiet." They don't allow for as much variety in art and headline treatment as the multicolumn formats, but with the typefaces, rules, and other simple graphic devices available in electronic publishing, these pages can be effective and smart-looking.

Keep in mind that longer lines are more difficult to read than shorter ones because the eye has to travel farther from the end of one line to the beginning of the next. One-column pages risk becoming dense, dull, and uninviting. To compensate for this, use generous margins and space between lines and a relatively large typeface (10 to 13 points). Space between paragraphs also helps keep the page open.

The Past, Present and Future of Lotteries
People prefer to play on-line games

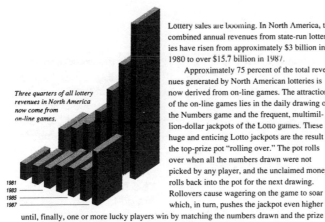

Three quarters of all lottery revenues in North America now come from on-line games.

Lottery sales are booming. In North America, the combined annual revenues from state-run lotteries have risen from approximately $3 billion in 1980 to over $15.7 billion in 1987.

Approximately 75 percent of the total revenues generated by North American lotteries is now derived from on-line games. The attraction of the on-line games lies in the daily drawing of the Numbers game and the frequent, multimillion-dollar jackpots of the Lotto games. These huge and enticing Lotto jackpots are the result of the top-prize pot "rolling over." The pot rolls over when all the numbers drawn were not picked by any player, and the unclaimed money rolls back into the pot for the next drawing. Rollovers cause wagering on the game to soar which, in turn, pushes the jackpot even higher until, finally, one or more lucky players win by matching the numbers drawn and the prize money is paid.

Outside of North America, those lottery jurisdictions that have added on-line technology to their operations have experienced great increases in revenues. For example, GTECH provided the first lottery-specific on-line system in Asia for Singapore Pools, Singapore's government-owned lottery company. The accompanying chart demonstrates the impact in sales gained by Singapore Pools after the GTECH network began operation.

In May 1986, Singapore Pools added on-line games. By the end of the year its sales had climbed 1600%, to average $8 million Singapore per week.

$8 million

on-line operations begin

months

The continuous running text in this sample requires a different treatment than the broken blocks of copy on the facing page. The inset art shortens the line length and makes the page more readable than it would be if the text were solid.

The margins are 6 picas top and bottom and 7 picas left and right.

The text is 12/16 Times Roman with a ragged right margin.

The headline treatment borrows editorial and typographic techniques used in magazines, with the contrasting style and size unified by the flush right alignment. The relationship of the two sizes is very nice here: The headline is 24-point Times Roman, and the tag line is 18-point Times Roman italic.

The chart and graph were created in Adobe Illustrator. The ability to create three-dimensional art for charts and graphs without having to be a technical illustrator is a great asset of desktop technology.

Design: Tom Ahern (Providence, RI)

Page from a capabilities brochure for GTECH, which provides on-line games for lottery networks.
Trim size: 8-1/2 by 11

Wide-margin one-column

A one-column grid with a wide margin is perhaps the most useful of all the designs in this book for internal reports, press releases, proposals, prospectuses, and other documents that have unadorned running text and need to be read fast. You may be tempted, with desktop publishing, to take something you used to distribute as a typewritten page and turn it into a multicolumn format, simply because you can. The danger is that you'll devote time to layout that would be better spent on content. As the hypothetical documents on the next three pages show, this simple one-column format can be smart, authoritative, and well planned. And though the line length is long, the white space provided by the wide margin gives the eye room to rest and makes the copy more inviting to read.

This format is especially well suited for single-sided documents that are either stapled or intended for three-ring binders. Use the left side of the page for the wide margin so that the space will look planned. (If you use the right side, it may look as though you ran out of copy and couldn't fill the page.) Although none are shown in these pages, headlines and subheads could extend into the margin for visual interest. So could short quotes, diagrams, and even small photos. When you want to make extensive use of the margin in this way, consider the "one + one-column" format discussed later in this section.

Extremely open leading facilitates quick scanning of a press release (on facing page), which usually commands less than a minute of the reader's time. The body text here is 11/20 Times Roman. With this much leading you probably would not want space between paragraphs; so you need an indent that is markedly wider than the space between lines. The indent in the sample shown is 3 picas for all paragraphs except the first.

The first paragraph is not indented. With flush left text, you rarely need to indent the opening paragraph or any paragraph that immediately follows a headline or a subhead. An indent would create an unnecessary visual gap at a place where the start of a new paragraph is obvious to the reader. To achieve this in running text where your paragraph indent is specified, for example, as 1 pica, you will need to select the opening paragraph and change its first line indent to 0.

The logo treatment can vary. The symbol could be flush with the left edge of the 6-point rule; a company name or logo could run across the top of the page, replacing the symbol and release line shown. (See the following page for an example.)

The headline should be short and straightforward. This is not the place to be clever.

The names of contacts for more information are positioned on a grid of two equal columns within the single-column format. The type is 9/12 Helvetica for contrast with the body text. If there is only one contact to list, position it in the right column of the two-column grid and move the "for immediate release" line to the left so that it is aligned left with the contact name.

The blueprint for this page appears on the following spread.

XYZ Corporation Announces New Plant Opening

For more information contact:

High Profile Publicity
Ann Millard
5432 Schoolhouse Road
Santa Monica, CA 92131
213-555-4664

XYZ Corporation
Marilyn Ferguson
1104 Beltway Drive
Los Angeles, CA 92111
213-555-3030

SANTA MONICA, CA. APRIL 10, 1989—Lorem ipsum dolor sit amet, consectetuer adipiscing elit, sed diam   nonummy nibh euismod tincidunt ut laoreet dolore magna aliquam erat volutpat. Ut wisi enim ad minim veniam, quis nostrud exerci tation ullamcorper suscipit lobortis nisl ut aliquip ex ea commodo consequat. Duis autem vel eum iriure dolor in hendrerit in vulputate velit esse molestie consequat, vel illum dolore eu feugiat nulla facilisis at vero eros et accumsan et iusto odio dignissim qui blandit praesent luptatum zzril delenit augue duis dolore te feugait nulla facilisi. Lorem ipsum dolor sit amet, consectetuer adipiscing elit, sed diam nonummy nibh euismod tincidunt ut laoreet dolore magna aliquam erat volutpat. Ut wisi enim ad minim veniam, quis nostrud exerci tation ullamcorper suscipit lobortis nisl ut aliquip ex ea commodo consequat.

Duis autem vel eum iriure dolor in hendrerit in vulputate velit esse molestie consequat, vel illum dolore eu feugiat nulla facilisis at vero eros et accumsan et iusto odio dignissim qui blandit praesent luptatum zzril delenit augue duis dolore te feugait nulla facilisi. Nam liber tempor cum soluta nobis eleifend option congue nihil imperdiet doming id quod mazim placerat facer possim assum. Lorem ipsum dolor sit amet, consectetuer adipiscing elit, sed diam nonummy nibh euismod tincidunt ut laoreet dolore magna aliquam erat volutpat. Ut wisi enim ad minim veniam, quis nostrud exerci tation ullamcorper suscipit lobortis nisl ut aliquip ex ea commodo consequat. Duis autem vel eum iriure dolor in hendrerit in vulputate velit esse molestie consequat, vel illum

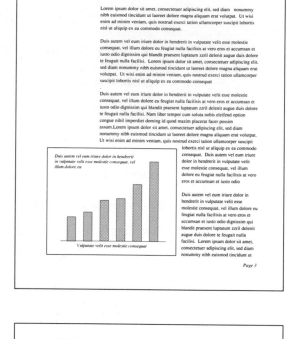

The basic grid for the documents on this page is the same as the one used for the press release. Tighter leading here (11/15 Times Roman) is balanced with a full line space (15 points) between paragraphs.

The business plan above has 6 picas between the left trim and the rule. The text block is 12 picas from the top trim.

Boldface subheads are the same size as the body text. Omitting paragraph space after the subheads visually connects each subhead to its respective text block.

The company name is 14-point Times Roman bold italic.

The caption is inset in the box around the art (a style commonly found in reports and business plans) and set in 10/12 Times Roman italic.

In the proposal at right, the art is the full column width with the caption (10/13 Times Roman italic) in the margin. Note the alignment of the date, folio, rules at the top and bottom of the page, and left margin of the caption. This alignment is important: It creates an implied border that gives structure to the page.

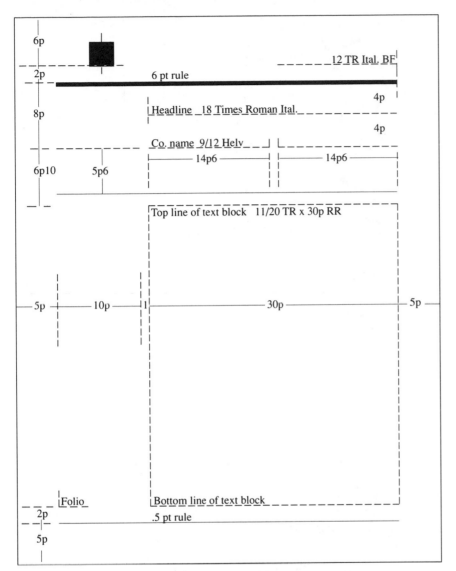

6p
2p
8p
6p10 5p6

12 TR Ital. BF

6 pt rule

Headline 18 Times Roman Ital. 4p

Co. name 9/12 Helv 4p

14p6 14p6

Top line of text block 11/20 TR x 30p RR

5p 10p 30p 5p

Folio Bottom line of text block
2p .5 pt rule
5p

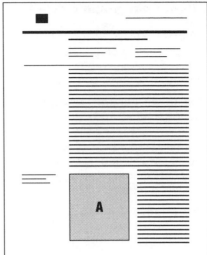

A

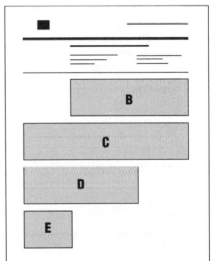

B

C

D

E

This blueprint shows the grid and type specifications for the press release on the preceding spread. The documents on the facing page use the same grid (except as noted in the annotations) but, for the most part, different type sizes.

A mixed grid structure is useful even in this simple format. Divide the text column into two equal units with a 1-pica space between. This creates two additional grid lines for placing small text and sizing art.

Blueprint measurements throughout the book are given in picas unless otherwise noted. The notation "x 30p" describes the measure, or length, of a text line. "RR" denotes a ragged right margin.

Guidelines for placing art on this grid

- Size all art to one of the following widths:
  A: 14p6—half the width of the text column with 1p between the art and the wraparound text
  B: 30 picas—the full width of the text column
  C: 41 picas—from the left edge of the 6-point rule to the right margin
  D: 25 picas—from the left edge of the 6-point rule to a point 1 pica short of the midpoint of the text column
  E: 10 picas—in the wide margin (if you have small mug shots)

- Avoid placing half-column art in the text column. Small charts and illustrations should be boxed with a 0.5- or 1-point rule to the sizes suggested.

- Placement is best at the bottom of the page, as shown in the examples at left. The top of the page is acceptable; the middle is not.

- For art that extends the full width of the column, the space between the text and the art should be equal to or greater than the leading.

- Place captions in the margin or inset them in a box around the art, as shown. Captions generally should be set one size smaller than the body text with tighter leading. Italic or a contrasting typeface is often used.

Attention to graphic detail makes the designer's hand more apparent in these documents than in the ones on the preceding pages. Both use a strong organization identity for external communication.

The large vertical headline fills the wide margin and establishes a distinctive style for a series of information sheets. Vertical type should always read upward unless the words themselves suggest downward motion.

The underlined headlines and bullets (which are gray) add variety to the simple page design.

Bulleted paragraphs with hanging indents are very effective when a message can be broken down into small chunks of information. The text immediately following the bullet should align exactly with subsequent lines.

The typeface is Palatino throughout.

IMAGESET :
First in Digital Graphic Design and Desktop Publishing

Services

GRAPHIC DESIGN SERVICES

■ ImageSet provides professional graphic design services for creating state-of-the-art computer graphics and page layouts for a variety of businesses, firms, and publications.

■ Brochures, newsletters, magazine covers, advertisements, menus, logos, annual reports, and corporate identity programs can be designed from start to finish by our graphic design department. If there is a special design problem, ImageSet will find a solution.

■ ImageSet offers electronic design templates that can be purchased and modified for a client's use. Design templates are preformatted designs that can be quickly adapted to just about any publication task (newsletters, flyers, price lists, etc.).

■ ImageSet offers graphic design consultation for companies and individuals using desktop publishing technology. ImageSet can provide graphic design consultancy to assist the client in designing templates for newsletters, brochures, logos, or even help develop a coherent corporate identity program which can be utilized for all the client's desktop publishing applications.

■ Should the need arise, ImageSet offers individual and group instruction on computer graphics and page layout programs.

DESKTOP PUBLISHING SERVICES

■ ImageSet offers an output service of high resolution print for individuals and organizations whose publishing tasks demand higher quality typeset than laser printer (300 dpi) resolution. To implement this service, ImageSet utilizes a Mergenthaler Linotype L100 commercial laser phototypesetting device.

*Design:
Mark Beale,
ImageSet Design
(Portland, OR)*

*One of a series of information sheets in the promotional literature for ImageSet Associates.
Size: 8-1/2 by 11*

A distinctive logo gives this simple page a unique personality. The descriptive line explains the otherwise cryptic name.

The black and gray border echoes the logo style and gives structure to what could have been an overly loose composition. Borders provide a simple and effective way to add graphic interest to a page.

Initial caps add variety to the text and help draw the reader into the page. Like the bullets in the sample above, the initial caps facilitate the "quick scan" nature of information presented in short paragraphs.

The typeface, Galliard throughout, has a calligraphic feeling that is more friendly than formal.

Stick Your Neck Out

Thanks for re-enlisting in the Giraffe Campaign

To show you how much we appreciate that, we've enclosed our official H.W.C.S.F.F.* telling the world that your membership in the Giraffe Project is in good standing and that you're entitled to all the rights and privileges thereof.

You'll also find an updated membership card, an *Instant Giraffe Citation* and a new campaign button — we're assuming that you, like so many other members, have been hit up for your old button by a friend or one of your kids.

People's faces do light up when they see Giraffe stuff — instead of letting them take yours, you can use the enclosed order form to get them their own buttons, mugs, shirts — and memberships. And don't forget to order more *Instant Giraffe Citations* yourself. Members who are using these report maximum satisfaction in being able to cite a Giraffe on-the-spot for meritorious action.

There will be exciting New Ideas and new "giraffenalia" in your upcoming year's worth of *Giraffe Gazettes.* We think you'll be surprised and delighted.

Keep scouting for new Giraffes and reporting your sightings to Giraffe Headquarters. We couldn't do the job without you.

And thanks again for your renewed vote of confidence in Giraffeness.

* *Handsome Wall Certificate Suitable For Framing*

*Design:
Scot Louis Gaznier
(Langley, WA)*

*Page acknowledging membership in the Giraffe Project, an organization that encourages people to "stick their neck out for the common good."
Size: 8-1/2 by 11*

Centering text inside a border
creates a more formal image. The style
of the border subtly changes the look
of a page. When you experiment with
the borders in PageMaker, use the
Custom Line option to try different line
weights for the double, triple, dotted,
and dashed lines. In the Custom Line
dialog box, note also that dotted and
dashed lines can print transparent or
opaque, a useful variable when you
have two or more colors.

**The justified text and the
centered headline** add to the
formality. Positioning the border
slightly off center keeps the design
from being quite so rigid.

On subsequent pages, the
border would be repeated and the
position of the first line of text would
remain constant, leaving the space
occupied by the headline open.

The 33-pica line length is the
widest of the one-column formats
shown in this section. The density of
the running text (11/15 New Century
Schoolbook) is maximum for a readable page, and you should avoid
paragraphs longer than the last one
shown here (11 lines).

The inset text helps relieve the
density of the long text lines.

This blueprint defines the
guidelines for the proposal above.

Charts, graphs, financials, and
other art should be centered horizontally within the text block, inset at
least 2 picas from the left and right
margins. Graphics of various sizes
can be accommodated, as shown
in the schematics at far right. If you
have data or art on several consecutive pages, placing them in the same
vertical position on the page suggests
care and planning. (It also takes a
little more time.)

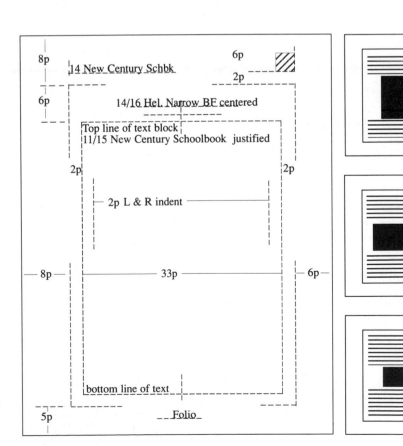

One-column grid with display heads

Many complex reports and proposals contain straight running text separated by subheads that recur throughout the document. The wide, one-column measure is ideal for the running text, and when the subheads are set fairly large and given plenty of white space and structural rules, the effect is well organized and easy to scan.

The highly structured report shown below contains a single topic on each page, with two recurring subheads placed in the same position on every page. You can adapt this format for a less structured document, placing the topic headline anywhere on the page with running text continuing from one page to the next as needed.

Bulleted text is used here to summarize the contents of each page. This technique works particularly well in long documents: The reader can make a horizontal pass through the pages for the highlights and then drop vertically into the running text for details. The ballot boxes are 11-point Zapf Dingbats.

The rules and generous white space (3 to 4 picas above each 0.5-point rule) provide a strong horizontal grid that facilitates scanning.

Art can be centered in the text column or inset on one side with the text wrapped around it, as shown in the schematics below.

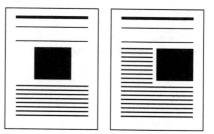

Tax Appeals
Providing Fair Hearings on Tax Disputes

Guiding Principles

- *Lorem ipsum dolor sit amet, consectetuer adipiscing elit, sed diam nonummy nibh euismod tincidunt ut laoreet dolore magna al.*
- *Ut wisi enim ad minim veniam, quis nostrud exerci tation ullamcorper suscipit lobortis nisl ut aliquip ex ea commodo consequat.*

Highlights of the Commission's Proposals

- **Duis autem vel eum iriure dolor in hendrerit in vulputate velit esse molestie consequat, vel illum dolore eu feugiat nulla facilisis at vero eros.**

Lorem ipsum dolor sit amet, consectetuer adipiscing elit, sed diam nonummy nibh euismod tincidunt ut laoreet dolore magna aliquam erat volutpat. Ut wisi enim ad minim veniam, quis nostrud exerci tation ullamcorper suscipit lobortis nisl ut aliquip ex ea commodo consequat. Duis autem vel eum iriure dolor in hendrerit in vulputate velit esse molestie consequat, vel illum dolore eu feugiat nulla facilisis at vero eros et accumsan et iusto odio dignissim qui blandit praesent luptatum zzril delenit augue duis dolore te feugait nulla facilisi. Lorem ipsum dolor sit amet, consectetuer adipiscing elit, sed diam nonummy nibh euismod tincidunt ut laoreet dolore magna aliquam erat volutpat. Ut wisi enim ad minim veniam, quis nostrud exerci tation ullamcorper suscipit lobortis nisl ut aliquip ex ea commodo consequat. Duis autem vel eum iriure dolor in hendrerit in vulputate velit esse molestie consequat, vel illum dolore eu feugiat nulla facilisis at vero eros et accumsan et iusto odio dignissim qui blandit praesent luptatum zzril delenit augue duis dolore te feugait nulla facilisi. Nam liber tempor cum soluta nobis eleifend option congue nihil imperdiet doming id quod mazim placerat facer possim assum. Lorem ipsum dolor sit amet, consectetuer adipiscing elit, sed diam nonummy nibh euismod tincidunt ut laoreet dolore magna aliquam erat volutpat.

- **Lorem ipsum dolor sit amet, consectetuer adipiscing elit, sed diam nonummy nibh euismd.**

Ut wisi enim ad minim veniam, quis nostrud exerci tation ullamcorper suscipit lobortis nisl ut aliquip ex ea commodo consequat. Duis autem vel eum iriure dolor in hendrerit in vulputate velit esse molestie consequat, vel illum dolore eu feugiat nulla facilisis at vero eros et accumsan et iusto odio dignissim qui blandit praesent luptatum zzril delenit augue duis dolore te feugait nulla facilisi. Lorem ipsum dolor sit amet, consectetuer adipiscing elit, sed diam nonummy nibh euismod tincidunt ut laoreet dolore magna aliquam erat volutpat. Ut wisi enim ad minim veniam, quis nostrud exerci tation ullamcorper suscipit lobortis nisl ut aliquip ex ea commodo consequat. Duis autem vel eum iriure dolor in hendrerit in vulpu.

5p
8 pt rule

24 Times Roman BF
8p 18 TR _ _ _ _ _ _ _ _ _ _ _ _

.5 pt rule

18 TR _ _ _ _ _

12/14.5 TR Ital.
10p   x 19p

.5 pt rule

1p Top line of text block

12/14.5 Times Roman x 39p RR

— 6p —   39p   — 6p —

Bottom line of text block

5p

One + one-column grid

The combination of one narrow and one wide column might be considered either a one- or a two-column grid. The narrow column isn't a true text column, but it is wide enough to use for different kinds of text, graphics, and display type without crowding.

Whether you set up this format as one or two columns on the screen may well depend on the length of the document: In a long document with a great deal of running text, setting up as one column enables you to "autoflow" the text; in a short document, setting up as two columns eliminates the need to "drag place" the text in the narrow column.

Whatever you call it and however you set it up, keep this format in mind. It's extremely useful for a wide variety of reports, newsletters, bulletins, and data sheets.

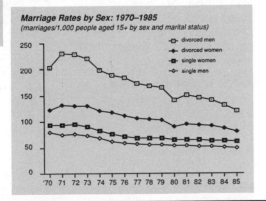

THE NUMBERS NEWS
6

A Publication of American Demographics
Martha Farnsworth Riche, Editor   Diane Crispell, Associate Editor

June 1988   Volume 8 Number

Will fewer couples tie the knot this June?

inside:

■ How are population projections tracking? (page 6)

■ Regions shift in per capita income (page 2)

■ Women's labor force patterns approach men's (page 3)

Divorced people are still more likely to marry than single people, but the gap is narrowing

Businesses that depend on married couples for a market need some hard rethinking: the marriage rate continues to decline, the number of unmarried couples continues to increase, and divorced people are waiting longer to remarry.

Final marriage statistics for 1985, produced by the National Center for Health Statistics, all point downward. Barbara Foley Wilson, who wrote the report ("Advance Report of Final Marriage Statistics, 1985"), said it was depressing to write: Marriages dropped substantially in every region, almost every month, in most states, and for every marital status group. To put these figures in context, remember that preliminary figures for 1986 and 1987 show the drop in the marriage rate continuing (*Numbers News*, Vol. 8, No. 5).

About two-thirds of the newly married were marrying for the first time; most of the rest had been divorced. However, as the chart shows, marriage rates are far higher for divorced persons: divorced men have higher marriage rates than divorced women, and single women have higher marriage rates than single men. Marriage rates have declined for all these groups since the early 1970s, falling by about one-third for single people to nearly one-half for divorced men.

Most people are now aware that young people are waiting longer to marry: the mean age at first marriage was 24.0 for women in 1985 and

Marriage Rates by Sex: 1970–1985
(marriages/1,000 people aged 15+ by sex and marital status)

□ divorced men
◆ divorced women
▣ single women
◇ single men

The Numbers News (ISSN 0732-1597) is published monthly. Copyright 1988 by American Demographics, Inc. All rights reserved. Reproduction without permission is prohibited. Subscription rate: $149 per year first class, subscribers outside the U.S., Canada and Mexico add $20. For subscription information or change of address contact American Demographics, P.O. Box 68, Ithaca, NY 14851. Telephone (607) 273-6343. Editor/Publisher: Martha Farnsworth Riche, Research Editor: Thomas Exter, Associate Editor: Diane Crispell, Conference Editor: Ellen Marsh, Research Assistant: Janet McClafferty, Production Manager: Stephanie Major, Marketing Director: Camilla Walter.

This newsletter uses the narrow column on the cover for headlines, contents listings, and story highlights. On inside pages the use is even more versatile, accommodating charts, graphs, news items, product notes, and conference listings.

The narrow column is 11p6, the wide column is 29 picas, and the space in between is 1 pica. The inside margins are 4p6, wide enough to accommodate the holes for a three-ring binder.

The tinted boxes run the full column measure without rules. Once you adopt this style, you should maintain it throughout. Text inside the boxes is indented 1 pica at both the left and right margins.

The logo uses the currently popular technique of enlarging the initial caps in an all cap name. Here the caps drop below the other letters, and tie in with the large issue number, a good device for quick reference and continuity.

The 2-point rules at the bottom of the page enclose publishing and masthead information. This type can be as small as 5 or 6 points.

Design: Carol Terrizzi (Ithaca, NY)

The Numbers News *is published monthly by American Demographics.*
Trim size: 8-1/2 by 11

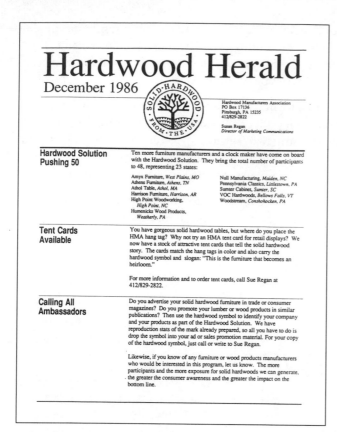

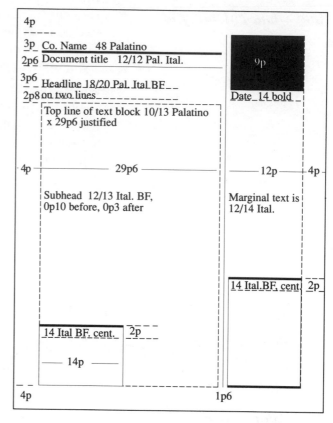

A deep space at the top of the page for the company identification, a narrow column for headlines and overhanging rules, and a wide column for body text create a very simple, effective format.

The text column is divided into two equal columns for listings. The address above the text area follows this grid.

The main headline and the running text are Times Roman; the headlines in the narrow column are Helvetica Narrow. Although Helvetica Narrow is considered a resident font in many laser printers, it is not a true PostScript font; the printer scales it from Helvetica. If you send a file to a service bureau for high-resolution output, you must tell them if you've used Helvetica Narrow so that they can load the scaling information into their printer.

The text column is 29 picas. The outside margins are 3 picas, and the top and bottom margins are 4 picas.

This blueprint matches the monthly report on the facing page. You can adapt the grid for either of the other publications shown in this section by reversing the narrow and wide columns and adjusting the margins.

The text is Palatino throughout.

The bold rules are 4 point; the lighter ones are 0.5 point.

The sales highlights box in the lower left has a 1-pica standoff for the text wraparound. The type in the sample is 12/14, with 1p3 left and right indents. The tab is set at 7p.

The type in the contents box is 10/11.5 italic with 1p3 left and right indents, a leadered tab at 9 picas, and 6 points after each listing.

The screens in both of the boxes are 10%.

You can use four art sizes, as shown above right. Another approach is to hang the art from a horizon line, as in the second schematic.

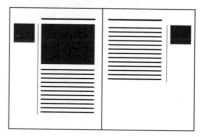

Design: Agnew Moyer Smith (Pittsburgh, PA)

The Hardwood Herald *is published by the Hardwood Manufacturers Association. Trim size: 8-1/2 by 11*

University Press

The Monthly Report on Sales, Promotion, and Product Development

March 1990

Political History and Economics Titles Continue to Boost Overseas Sales

Lorem ipsum dolor sit amet, consectetuer adipiscing elit, sed diam nonummy nibh euismod tincidunt ut laoreet dolore magna aliquam erat volutpat. Ut wisi enim ad minim veniam, quis nostrud exerci tation ullamcorper suscipit lobortis nisl ut aliquip ex ea commodo consequat. Duis autem vel eum iriure dolor in hendrerit in vulputate velit esse molestie consequat, vel illum dolore eu feugiat nulla facilisis at vero eros et accumsan et iusto odio dignissim qui blandit.

Praesent luptatum zzril delenit augue duis dolore te feugait nulla facilisi. Lorem ipsum dolor sit amet, consectetuer adipiscing elit, sed diam nonummy nibh euismod tincidunt ut laoreet dolore magna aliquam erat volutpat. Ut wisi enim ad minim veniam, quis nostrud exerci tation ullamcorper suscipit lobortis nisl ut aliquip ex ea commodo consequat.

Duis autem vel eum iriure dolor in hendrerit in vulputate velit esse molestie consequat, vel illum dolore eu feugiat nulla facilisis at vero eros et accumsan et iusto odio dignissim qui blandit praesent luptatum zzril delenit augue duis dolore te feugait nulla facilisi. Nam liber tempor cum soluta nobis eleifend option congue nihil imperdiet doming id quod mazim placerat facer possim assum. Lorem ipsum dolor sit amet, consectetuer adipiscing elit, sed diam nonummy nibh euismod tincidunt ut laoreet dolore magna aliquam erat volutpat.

London office to open this summer

Ut wisi enim ad minim veniam, quis nostrud exerci tation ullamcorper suscipit lobortis nisl ut aliquip ex ea commodo consequat. Duis autem vel eum iriure dolor in hendrerit in vulputate velit esse molestie consequat, vel illum dolore eu feugiat nulla facilisis at vero eros et accumsan et iusto odio dignissim qui blandit praesent luptatum zzril delenit augue duis dolore te feugait nulla facilisi. Lorem ipsum dolor sit amet, consectetuer adipiscing elit, sed diam nonummy nibh euismod tincidunt ut laoreet dolore magna aliquam erat volutpat.

Ut wisi enim ad minim veniam, quis nostrud exerci tation ullamcorper suscipit lobortis nisl ut aliquip ex ea commodo consequat. Duis autem vel eum iriure dolor in hendrerit in vulputate velit esse molestie consequat, vel illum dolore eu feugiat nulla facilisis at vero eros et accumsan et iusto odio dignissim qui blandit praesent luptatum zzril delenit augue duis dolore te feugait nulla facilisi. Lorem ipsum lobortis nisl ut aliquip ex ea commodo consequat. Duis autem vel eum iriure dolor elit, sed diam nonummy nibh euismod tincidunt ut laoreet dolore magna aliquam erat volutpat. Ut wisi enim ad minim veniam, quis nostrud exerci tation ullamcorper suscipit lobortis nisl ut aliquip ex ea commodo consequat.

Duis autem vel eum iriure dolor in hendrerit in vulputate velit esse molestie consequat, vel illum dolore eu feugiat nulla facilisis at vero eros et accumsan et

Overseas Sales	
FY 85	16, 365
FY 86	25,347
FY 87	36,897
FY 88	47,356
FY 89	59,000

University Press authors Jonathan Pritchard and Michelle Colibier are honored by the United States Library of Congress; see page 6.

TWO-COLUMN GRIDS

Two-column grids have a more designed and polished look than the one-column formats, yet they don't require a great deal of planning and can be assembled fairly quickly in PageMaker. They're useful for a wide variety of publications, including newsletters, brochures, annual reports, bulletins, menus, fact sheets, and catalog listings. When done well, they can range from honest simplicity to punchy straightforwardness. When done poorly, they can be boring or heavy-handed.

With two equal columns, the line length in an 8.5- by 11-inch page is usually between 16 and 21 picas, depending on the margins and the space between the columns. The type can drop down to 10/12 and still be quite readable. These factors make this format very economical in that you can fit quite a lot of text on a page. The greatest danger of the

Each editorial topic is contained on a single page, giving this brief annual report a simple, consistent, accessible style. The text does not have to fill out to the bottom margin. When your message can be broken down into one and two page units, this is a very effective format that is quite simple to produce.

The narrow margins (3 picas on the outside and bottom, 5 picas on the inside) work here because of the undersized page, the simple design, the open leading, and the white space at the top of the page. You wouldn't want margins any narrower than this, and without the compensating factors just mentioned wider margins would be essential.

The inset photos with wraparound text keep the running text from being too symmetrical. The depth of the photos varies according to the picture and the amount of text on the page. Photos can also run the full column width or extend halfway into the second column.

The body text is 10/14 Times Roman with 36-point initial caps. The headlines are 22 point.

Design: Carl A. Schuetz, Foxglove Communications (Baltimore, MD)

Pages from the annual report of the National Kidney Foundation of Maryland. Trim size: 7-1/2 by 10

two-column grid, however, is that you will try to fit in too much text and create pages that are dense and difficult to read. When in doubt, add an extra pica to the margins rather than to the text block.

With two columns you have more options in both the size and placement of headlines. You need to be careful, however, of the position of the heads—they shouldn't be too close to the top or the bottom of a column. (The very top of a column is, of course, okay). Also, take care that headlines in adjoining columns do not align with one another.

The off-center page created by a wide outer margin adds variety and sophistication to a two-column grid. This format is especially well suited to house organs.

A tight grid structure and well-defined image area is established by the extension of visual elements into the side and top margins and by the strong graphic treatment of the folios at the bottom of the page.

The graphic style of the breakout, folios, and logo and the headline treatment with bracket-style rules give the format a personal signature, as well as a consistency of visual style from one page to the next. The overall feeling is restrained without being bland.

Photos can be sized as shown here or, in the case of mug shots, used in half-column width with wrap-around text filling out the other half column. The rules around the photos crisp up the otherwise soft edges.

The text is Palatino throughout.

Design: Michael Waitsman,
Synthesis Concepts (Chicago, IL)
The Wildman Herald *is the national newsletter of Wildman, Harrold, Allen & Dixon, a law firm.*
Trim size: 8-1/2 by 11

Four wide-margin, two-column designs

Wide margins are the foundation for an open, two-column format that is very appealing and highly readable. All four documents in this section were designed using the grid in the blueprint on the following spread, but the kind of information, the intended audience, and the styles of the publications differ considerably.

The most varied and dynamic of the four designs (facing page) divides the vertical grid into horizontal story areas. This modular format requires more time and planning to execute than the others; you may have to adjust the depth of the text blocks several times to balance all the elements on the page.

The overall busyness of the design elements is appropriate here because it evokes the adventure of travel. You can create a more conservative look with this horizontal format by using a simpler nameplate and more uniform art styles. The format works for all-text documents, too, although to very different effect.

The nameplate at the top of the page uses the multiple headline style commonly found in newsstand magazines. Note the bold contents list and also the "Summer Specials" stamp, which is similar to the diagonal banner on many magazine covers. Deft handling of typography is critical in composing so many elements with varying emphases into a unified, readable whole.

The pictures use the grid effectively precisely because they break out of it. The mountains seem more expansive because they exceed the margins; the balloon seems to float off the page. The range of art styles, from realistic to schematic, adds to the feeling of adventure that a travel bulletin wants to project. The pictures are all from clip art files.

The type used throughout is Futura. The combination of Futura Light, Extra Bold, and Oblique in the headlines creates a colorful contrast without introducing another typeface. The unity of a single type family balances the complex nameplate treatment and the different styles of art.

Type specifications
Nameplate overline: 16-point Futura Light
Going: 96-point Light
Places: 36-point Futura Extra Bold Oblique
Contents: 14/14 Extra Bold
Lead story headline: 28/29 Light
Second story head: 18/18 Extra Bold
Body text: 10/12.5 Light

GOING PLACES

SUMMER SPECIALS

RIVERBOAT RACES
GRAND TETONS
GREAT BARRIER REEF

AROUND THE WORLD IN SO MANY WAYS

Lorem ipsum dolor sit amet, consectetuer adipiscing elit, sed diam nonummy nibh euismod tincidunt ut laoreet dolore magna aliquam erat volutpat. Ut wisi enim ad minim veniam, quis nostrud exerci tation ullamcorper suscipit lobortis nisl ut aliquip ex ea commodo Consequat. Duis

PLUS THE MANY ADVENTURES THAT AWAIT YOU CLOSE TO HOME

Autem vel velit esse molestie Consequat, vel illum dolore eu feugiat nulla facilisis at vero eros et accumsan et iusto odio dignissim qui blandit praesent luptatum zzril delenit augue duis dolore te feugait nulla facilisi. Lorem ipsum dolor sit amet, consectetuer adipiscing elit, sed diam nonummy nibh euismod tincidunt ut laoreet dolore magna aliquam erat volutpat. Ut wisi enim ad minim veniam, quis nostrud exerci tation ullamcorper suscipit lobortis nisl ut aliquip ex ea commodo consequat.

Duis autem vel eum iriure dolor in hendrerit in vulputate velit esse molestie consequat, vel illum dolore eu feugiat nulla facilisis at vero eros et accumsan et iusto odio dignissim qui blandit

praesent luptatum zzril delenit augue duis dolore te feugait nulla facilisi. Nam liber tempor cum soluta nobis eleifend option congue nihil imperdiet doming id quod mazim placerat facer pos assum.

Lorem ipsum dolor sit amet, consectetuer adipiscing elsed diam nonummy nibh euismod tincidunt ut laoreet magna aliquam erat volutpat. Ut wisi enim ad minveniam, quis nostrud exerci tation ullamcorper suscipit lobortis nisl ut aliquip ex ea commodo

The Symonton Foundation

What We've Accomplished

Lorem ipsum dolor sit amet, consectetuer adipiscing elit, sed diam nonumy nibh euismod tincidunt ut laoreet dolore magna aliquam erat volutpat. Ut wisi enim ad minim veniam, quis nostrud exerci tation ullamcorper suscipit lobortis nisl ut aliquip ex ea commodo consequa te feugait nulla facilisi.t.

The Centerville Nursing Home
Duis autem vel eum iriure dolor in hendrerit in vulputate velit esse molestie consequat, vel illum dolore eu feugiat nulla facilisis at vero eros et accumsan et iusto odio dignissim qui blandit praesent luptatum zzril delenit augue duis dolore te feugait nulla facilisi. Lorem ipsum dolor sit amet, consectetuer adipiscing elit, sed diam nonummy nibh euismod tin-

cidunt ut laoreet dolore magna aliquam erat volutpat. Ut wisi enim ad minim veniam, quis nostrud exerci tation ullamcorper suscipit lobortis nisl ut aliquip ex ea commodo consequat te feugait nulla

Duis autem vel eum iriure dolor in hendrerit in vulputate velit esse molestie consequat, vel illum dolore eu feugiat nulla facilisis at vero eros et accumsan et iusto odio dignissim qui blandit praesent luptatum zzril delenit augue duis dolore te feugait nulla facilisi. Nam liber tempor cum soluta nobis eleifend option congue nihil imperdiet doming id quod mazim placerat facer possim assum.

Job Training Program for Disadvantaged Youth
Lorem ipsum dolor sit amet, consectetuer adipiscing elit, sed diam nonummy nibh euismod tincidunt ut laoreet dolore magna aliquam erat volutpat. Ut wisi enim ad minim veniam, quis nostrud exerci tation ullamcorper suscipit lobortis nisl ut aliquip ex ea commodo consequat. Duis autem vel eum iriure dolor in hendrerit in vulputate velit esse molestie consequat, vel illum dolore eu feugiat nulla facilisis at vero eros et accumsan et iusto odio dignissim qui blandit praesent luptatum zzril delenit augue duis dolore te feugait nulla facilisi. Lorem ipsum dolor sit amet, consectetuer adipiscing elit, sed diam nonummy nibh euismod tincidunt ut laoreealiquam erat volut

The Symonton Foundation

What We Need to Do

Ut wisi enim ad minim veniam, quis nostrud exerci tation ullamcorper suscipit lobortis nisl ut aliquip ex ea commodo consequat. Duis autem vel eum iriure dolor in hendrerit in vulputate velit esse molestie consequat, vel illum dolore eu feugiat nulla facilisis at vero eros et accumsan et iusto odio dignissim qui blandit praesent luptatum zzril delenit augue duis dolore te feugait nulla facilisi.

Capital Fund
Lorem ipsum dolor sit amet, consectetuer adipiscing elit, sed diam nonummy nibh euismod tincidunt ut laoreet dolore magna aliquam erat volutpat. Ut wisi enim ad minim veniam, quis nostrud exerci tation ullamcorper suscipit lobortis nisl ut aliquip ex ea commodo consequat. Duis autem vel eum iriure dolor in hendrerit in vulputate velit esse molestie consequat, vel illum dolore eu feugiat nulla facilisis at vero eros et accumsan et iusto odio dignissim qui blandit praesent luptatum zzril delenit augue duis dolore te feugait nulla facilisi.

Lorem ipsum dolor sit amet, consectetuer adipiscing elit, sed diam nonummy nibh euismod tincidunt ut laoreealiquam eratorem Lorem ipsum dolor sit amet, consectetuer adipiscing elit, sed diam nonummy nibh euismod tincidunt ut laoreet dolore magna.

ipsum dolor sit amet, consectetuer adipiscing elit, sed diam nonummy nibh euismod tincidunt ut laoreet dolore magna aliquam erat volutpat. Ut wisi enim ad minim veniam, quis nostrud exerci tation ullamcorper suscipit lobortis nisl ut aliquip ex ea commodo consequat. Duis autem vel eum iriure dolor in hendrerit in vulputate velit esse molestie consequat, vel illum dolore eu feugiat nulla volutpat.orem ipsum dolor sit amet, consectetuer adipiscing elit, sed diam nonummy nibh euismod tincidunt ut laoreet dolore magna aliquam erat volutpat. Ut wisi enim ad minim veniam, quis nostrud exerci tation ullamcorper suscipit lobortis nisl ut aliquip ex ea commodo consequat. Duis autem vel eum iriure dolor in hendrerit in vulputate velit esse molestie consequat, vel illum dolore eu feugiat

Staff Expansion
Ut wisi enim ad minim veniam, quis nostrud exerci tation ullamcorper suscipit lobortis nisl ut aliquip ex ea commodo consequat. Duis autem vel eum iriure dolor in hendrerit in vulputate velit esse molestie consequat, vel illum dolore eu feugiat nulla facilisis at vero eros et accumsan et iusto odio dignissim qui blandit praesent luptatum zzril delenit augue duis dolore te feugait nulla facilisi. Lorem ipsum dolor sit amet, consectetuer adipiscing elit, sed diam nonummy nibh euismod tin

duis dolore te feugait nulla facilisi. Nam liber tempor cum soluta nobis eleifend option congue nihil imperdiet doming id quod mazim placerat facer possim assum. Lorem ipsum dolor sit amet, consectetuer adipiscing elit, sed diam nonummy nibh euismod tincidunt ut laoreet dolore magna aliquam erat volutpatillum .

This document shares the dignified simplicity found in the annual report reproduced at the beginning of the two-column grid section. It is designed to accommodate a subject head over a 0.5-point rule at the top of each page. If you omit that head, leave the rule in place.

The text seems to hang from the rule under the main headline. This strong structure provides consistency from page to page regardless of the column depth. The variable column depth gives you flexibility and speed when you assemble the pages on screen.

The banner, the main headline, and the rule below that headline extend 3 picas past the left text margin shown in the blueprint on the facing page. The banner is 2 picas deep with 14-point Garamond Bold type.

The main headlines are 30-point Bodoni Bold.

The body text is 10/13 Helvetica Light. The subheads are 10/12 Helvetica Black under 0.5-point rules.

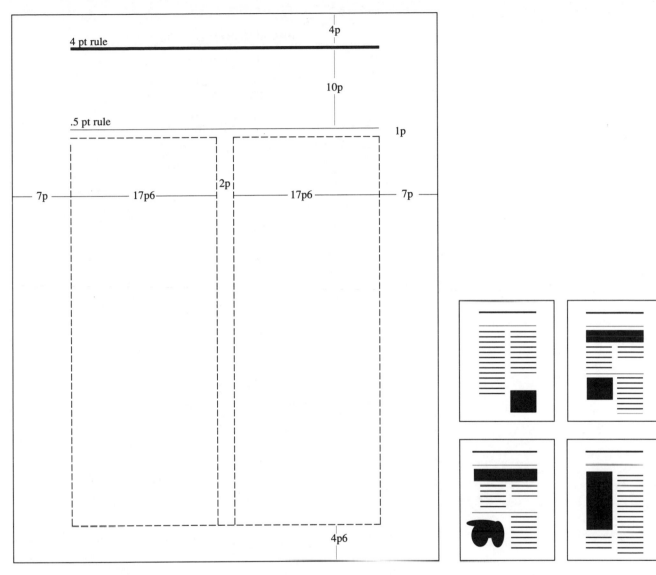

The blueprint above shows the basic grid for the documents on the previous two and following two pages.

The column width (17p6) is excellent for easy reading.

The generous margins require a generous space between columns.

The grid is centered on the page. If you shift the grid to one side for an off-center page, the wider margin can be used for annotations, notes, small pieces of art, and other marginalia.

A variation with a more structured nameplate and headline treatment is shown on the next spread.

Art can be placed on the grid as shown in the schematics or as shown in the sample pages.

1989 PROGRAM OF EVENTS

SCHOOL OF PHYSICAL SCIENCES

SOUTHEAST STATE UNIVERSITY
70TH SCIENTIFIC FORUM

MONDAY, MAY 8, 1989   FULTON AUDITORIUM

MORNING PROGRAM

7:45   Registration
Hendrerit in vulputate velit esse molestie
consequat, vel illum dolore eu feugiat.

7:45   Continental Breakfast
Nonummy nibh euismod tincidunt ut
laoreet dolore magna aliquam erat
volutpat. Ut wisi enim ad minim.

9:00   Introduction
Veniam, quis nostrud exerci tation ullamcorper suscipit lobortis nisl ut
aliquip ex ea commodo consequat.
Duis autem vel eum iriure dolor in.

10:00   Break
Hendrerit in vulputate velit esse
molestie consequat, vel illum dolore
eu feugiat nulla facilisis at vero eros et
accumsan et iusto odio dignissim qui.

10:30   Opening Address
Blandit praesent luptatum zzril delenit
augue duis dolore te feugait nulla
facilisi. Lorem ipsum dolor sit amet,
consectetuer adipiscing elit, sed diam.

12:00   Open House and Lunch
Nonummy nibh euismod tincidunt ut
laoreet dolore magna aliquam erat
volutpat. Ut wisi enim ad minim.

AFTERNOON PROGRAM

2:00   Overview of Seminars
Veniam, quis nostrud exerci tation
ullamcorper suscipit lobortis nisl ut
aliquip ex ea commodo consequat.

3:00   Faculty Roundtable
Duis autem vel eum iriure dolor in
hendrerit in vulputate velit esse
molestie consequat, vel illum dolore eu
feugiat nulla facilisis at vero eros et
accumsan et iusto odio dignissim qui
blandit praesent luptatum zzril delenit
augue duis dolore te feugait nulla
facilisi. Nam liber tempor cum soluta.

4:00   The Year in Review
Option congue nihil imperdiet doming
id quod mazim placerat facer possim
assum. Lorem ipsum dolor sit amet.,

4:30   Agenda for the Nineties
Consectetuer adipiscing elit, sed diam
nonummy nibh euismod tincidunt ut
laoreet dolore magna aliquam erat
volutpat. Ut wisi enim ad minim
veniam, quis nostrud exerci tation.

5:00   Discussion Period
UlLamcorper suscipit lobortis nisl ut
aliquip ex ea commodo consequat.
Duis autem vel eum iriure dolor in
hendrerit in vulputate velit esse.

EVENING PROGRAM

6:30   School of Chemistry Buffet
Consequat, vel illum dolore eu
feugiat nulla facilisis at vero eros et.

8:00   Class Reunion
Et iusto odio dignissim qui blandit
praesent luptatum zzril delenit augue
duis dolore te feugait nulla facilisi.
Lorem ipsum dolor sit amet, con.

Programs with many items briefly described, such as the one shown here, work very well in this two-column format. The column measure is wide enough to contain the agenda listings on single lines, but short enough so that the indented descriptions run over, creating visual separation between the headings.

A classic, traditional feeling appropriate for an academic program is created by the centered text in the open space at the top of the page and by the use of Garamond, a very refined and graceful typeface.

Nameplate type
1989 Program: 18-point Garamond
Top rule: 4 point
School of…: 12 point
Southeast State…: 18/21
Date and place: 10 point
Bottom rule: 0.5 point

The three subheads (Morning Program, etc.) are 10-point Garamond small caps. The double rules below them are from PageMaker's Lines menu. The rules under the agenda listings are 0.5 point, to match the weight of the double rules. You should maintain consistency in line weight throughout a page. The typeface underscore would be too heavy here.

The boldface time for each part of the program adds a different color to the type, which keeps the page from being too monotonous.

The program listings are 10/12 Garamond. The event after the time is tabbed to 3 picas from the left margin; the descriptive copy is set with a 3-pica left indent so that it is flush with the tabbed text.

The space between listings in the sample is specified as 1 pica paragraph space before each event heading and 4 points after it.

A newsletter style is adapted here for a sales department's monthly bulletin. The rules, bold heads with tag lines, and initial caps dress up and give a newsy image to what could be a pedestrian report.

The highly structured nameplate shows another way of using the open space at the top of the grid. (See the blueprint detail below right for specifications.)

The strong headline treatment requires white space around the various elements and makes separation of headlines in adjoining columns essential.

The initial caps are 60-point Helvetica Condensed Black. Often found in the editorial pages of magazines to highlight points of entry on a page, initial caps are generally underused in business publications. They are especially effective in complex pages such as this sample.

The wide, 3-pica paragraph indent is proportional to the initial cap. Be aware that very narrow letters (such as I) and very wide letters (M and W) will not conform to this proportion. The price of a truly professional document is editing to avoid these letters. Really.

The body text is 10/12 Bookman.

The illustration was created with PageMaker's drawing tools. The box around it uses a 2-point rule and a 10% shade. The headline is 10-point Helvetica Black Oblique, and the descriptive lines are 9/9 Helvetica Light with Helvetica Black numbers. The caption is 10/12 Bookman italic, centered.

The centered folio (10-point Helvetica Light) and the flush right continued line (9-point Helvetica Light Oblique) are aligned at their baselines 2 picas below the bottom margin.

THE GREAT OUTDOORS STORE

Month in Review

July 1989

BRISK START FOR CAMPING AND BACKPACKING EQUIPMENT

Fewer travelers abroad spurs sales in do it yourself activities.

orem ipsum dolor sit amet, consectetuer adipiscing elit, sed diam nonummy nibh euismod tincidunt ut laoreet dolore magna aliquam erat volutpat. Ut wisi enim ad minim veniam, quis nostrud exerci tation ullamcorper suscipit lobortis nisl ut aliquip ex ea commodo consequat. Duis autem vel eum iriure dolor in hendrerit in vulputate velit esse molestie consequat, vel illum dolore eu feugiat nulla facilisis at vero eros et accumsan et iusto odio dignissim qui blandit praesent luptatum zzril delenit augue duis dolore te feugait nulla facilisi.

Lorem ipsum dolor sit amet, consectetuer adipiscing elit, sed diam nonummy nibh euismod tincidunt ut laoreet dolore magna aliquam erat volutpat. Ut wisi enim ad minim veniam, quis nostrud exerci tation ullamcorper suscipit lobortis nisl ut aliquip ex ea commodo consequat.

Duis autem vel eum iriure dolor in hendrerit in vulputate velit esse molestie consequat, vel illum dolore eu feugiat nulla facilisis at vero eros et accumsan et iusto odio dignissim qui blandit praesent luptatum zzril delenit augue duis dolore te feugait nulla facilisi. Nam liber tempor cum soluta nobis eleifend option congue nihil imperdiet doming id quod mazim placerat facer possim assum.

Lorem ipsum dolor sit amet, consectetuer adipiscing elit, sed diam nonummy nibh euismod tincidunt ut laoreet dolore magna aliquam erat volutpat. Utwisi enim ad minim veniam, quis nostrud wisi enim ad minim veniam, quis nostrud exerci tation ex ea commodo

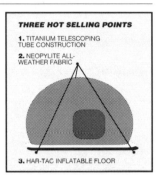

THREE HOT SELLING POINTS

1. TITANIUM TELESCOPING TUBE CONSTRUCTION

2. NEOPYLITE ALL-WEATHER FABRIC

3. HAR-TAC INFLATABLE FLOOR

The newly introduced two-person model X-2000-2 tent

WEATHERMAN PREDICTS ANOTHER HOT SUMMER. EXPECT BOOST IN WATER SPORTS GEAR

Jump in on the action in the new colorful inflatable water toys.

consequat. Duis autem vel eum iriure dolor in hendrerit in vulputate velit esse molestie consequat, vel illum dolore eu feugiat nulla facilisis at vero eros et accumsan et iusto odio dignissim qui blandit praesent luptatum zzril delenit augue duis dolore te feugait nulla facilisi.

Lorem ipsum dolor sit amet, consectetuer adipiscing elit, sed diam nonummy nibh euismod tincidunt ut laoreet dolore magna aliquam erat volut. Lorem ipsum dolor sit amet, consectetuer adipiscing elit, sed diam nonummy nibh euismod tincidunt ut laoreet dolore magna

1

Continued on page 3

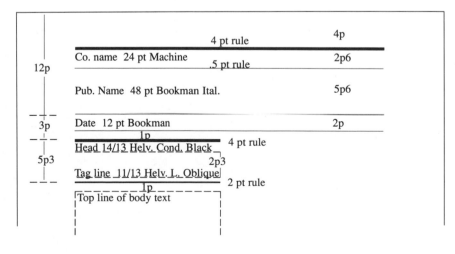

	4 pt rule	4p
Co. name 24 pt Machine	.5 pt rule	2p6
12p		
Pub. Name 48 pt Bookman Ital.		5p6
3p		
Date 12 pt Bookman		2p
1p		
Head 14/13 Helv. Cond. Black	4 pt rule	
5p3	2p3	
Tag line 11/13 Helv. L. Oblique		
1p	2 pt rule	
Top line of body text		

Wide-measure two-column grids

When you need to put a lot of running text or data on a page but still want a fairly simple format, consider a two-column grid with narrow margins and wide columns. You can see from the documents in this section—a newsletter, a catalog, an instruction sheet, and a journal—how adaptable this grid is to many different kinds of publications. Each of the examples uses this format in a completely different way and creates a very different image through typography and art.

A self-contained cover story emphasizes the importance of the topic, in this case a substantial contribution to a small boarding school.

The sidebar inset in the two-column grid is used here to quote the donor. The box is 14 picas wide with a 12p6 column measure. The use of a second color, blue, for the italic type draws the reader's attention to this statement.

Blue is also used in the banner, with reverse type, and for the display text.

The typeface on the cover is Galliard throughout.

A bolder, busier style for an inside story is created by the large headline, the recurrent subheads, and the bold rule around the photo. The banner, headline, and subheads print in blue.

The column width—22 picas—is the absolute maximum for running text on an 8.5- by 11-inch page. With a rule down the center of the page, you don't have to align the text in adjoining columns.

Other pages of the newsletter use a three-column grid, maintaining the banner, page frame, and rules

between columns for continuity. Mixing grids within a publication in this way accommodates a mix of short and long stories and different-size pictures and gives the publication a varied texture.

The body text is Galliard. The headlines are Helvetica Black Oblique.

Design: Scot Louis Gaznier (Langley, WA)

Pages from The Solebury School newsletter. Trim size: 8-1/2 by 11

The Newsletter

EDITOR: *Daniel Lusk* • ASSOCIATE EDITOR: *Jean Shaw Gaznier '53* • DESIGN: *Scot Louis Gaznier*

S P R I N G   1 9 8 8

Pledge to Build New Dorm Spurs Board to Consider Long-Range Capital Campaign

A RECENT PLEDGE of $250,000 for capital construction by Carol Chianese VanDuyne '52 has provided the impetus for the trustees of Solebury School to look into the feasibility of launching a full-scale campaign.

A feasibility study to explore options and create plans for faculty and student housing is going forward at this time, according to Bruce Bergquist, HEAD OF SCHOOL.

The study, authorized by the BOARD OF TRUSTEES at its January meeting, will consider three options with respect to improvement of present boys' living quarters: to renovate the existing facility, to rebuild the present dormitory, or to construct a new building in a different location on campus.

Bruce said that the Planning Committee has met frequently since the Board meeting, has selected an architect to act as consultant for the study, and is currently exploring options for location of a new building. It also is reviewing the feasibility of a new wing for the current dorm, which he said seems at this point a less likely option for providing the housing needed to meet both immediate and long-range goals for the school.

The Board also authorized preparation of a more formal long-range plan by administration and Board leadership. A written document is being created to clarify and project long-range goals for future development of the school — in essence to update and focus a long-range plan completed in 1985 by an ad hoc committee of students, faculty, administration and Board members.

When completed, the current study will provide schematics of a proposed new building, lay out a timetable for construction, and project costs.

Bruce anticipates completion of the study by April 15, in time for the Board to decide in May which of the options under consideration to include in a case statement

"I have made this decision because I believe in Solebury's future, and I feel fortunate and proud to be able to help the school reach its goals in such a substantial way. I also want this pledge to be used as an incentive for others to reach as deeply as they can into their own pockets and help. My two years at Solebury gave me more of a total education than any schools before or after that time. I want to make certain that students just like me continue to be able to have the Solebury experience. I am just as certain that all of you reading this have much to thank Solebury for. It helped us create our future as adults, and now it is time for us to repay that debt and help Solebury's future."

being prepared by Bruce and BOARD CHAIRMAN Bill Berkeley. The latter statement will present the case for a capital campaign for the school.

Balanced Budget

While the tenor of the Board's open session in January was cautious, dominated by realistic assessment and close examination, there was an obvious undercurrent of excitement. For the first time in a decade a Board faced the prospect of a balanced budget — a budget that not only projected realistic income figures and expenditures that do not exceed them; it also projected nominal salary increases and substantial reduction of indebtedness.

Members acknowledged a need to improve on the current rate of annual giving, citing a general caution on the part of donors that reflects current economic trends in the country. The Board targeted annual giving donations in the $5,000 – $10,000 range as critical to the continuing, improved health of the school.

Given a balanced budget for the coming fiscal year, and given long-range goals, the Board is considering major steps involving possible construction of new facilities in order to accomodate the proposed growth of the student body.

With Carol VanDuyne's pledge of $250,000 already a beginning for a capital campaign, the question now before the Board is whether the time is right for proceeding with a major fund drive that will accomodate the growth of the student body, enhance the quality of life for faculty, and in the process affect the growth of curriculum and programs and focus more clearly the character of the school.

The present challenge, said Bruce, "is to clarify our priorities and to act on them. We have come a long way, and we know what we want. Now we have some even harder decisions to make."

The Newsletter

CLEVE: SOMETHING EXTRA

CLEVE IS ONE of those talented part-time people there have been so many of in our little history. We tend to take them, once they are here, for granted. And, when they are specialists like Cleve Christie, we may not even know their names, much less meet them.

Cleve is easy to talk about because the numbers we can use are beautiful: 18 and 2, 22 and 1. Those are the season records, wins and losses of his Solebury boys varsity basketball team for the past two seasons.

Yet, while those are pretty numbers, they are far from being the whole story of Cleve's impact on his players or even on our school; they aren't even the interesting part.

Coaching our team is only one of the things Cleve does, and one might hurry to say that, while it may appear to be the shiny part, it is not a separate thing from the other parts of his life.

ROMEO AND JULIET'S

Dignified, tough, and generally soft-spoken, Cleve works for the Trenton Housing Authority and manages a number of public housing projects. That's a very important part of his life. Cleve lived with his grandmother on Southard Street, not far from where he took me for lunch — a cafe called Romeo and Juliet's. Cleve says the place was smaller when he was a kid and used to shovel snow for the people who owned it.

He recalls that he and his friends had one of the first basketball courts in the area. When a couple of houses were moved out of the neighborhood, they asked the township for some dirt to cover the bricks and refuse that were left behind. The Ewing Township trucks brought dirt and dumped it in huge piles and went away. Cleve says he organized the kids, got the lemonade, and together they spread out that dirt to make a court.

"When the township people saw our initiative," he recalls, "they came and put up baskets. Putting in time on the court kept me out of trouble."

LOFTY GOALS

Like many young kids, his idols were the basketball super stars of the day — Elgin Baylor, Jerry West, Bob Koosy — immortals of the game. "You set lofty goals, and if you

get halfway there, you're a lot farther than you might have been."

In high school, Cleve "lettered" in basketball and soccer, and continued to play basketball during the 4 1/2 years he was in the Air Force, stationed in Istanbul, Turkey. Twice he made the service all-star team. He returned then to Trenton, married, but left again to go back to school. He attended High Point College and graduated from Ashmore Business College in Thomasville, North Carolina.

Coaching grew quite naturally, he says, out of playing (he still plays in a couple of 30-and-older type leagues, "to get rid of hostilities," and to be with friends) and out of concern for kids.

Since 1970 he has coached in the Unlimited League, a part of the Trenton summer basketball program. His Merryman team has won the championship three times.

Besides coaching from 1984-1986 in the Pro-Am League in Camden — a development league for young professionals sponsored by the National Basketball Association (NBA) — Cleve coached for five years (1981–1986) in the Police Athletic League (PAL) for girls 12 years and under.

Cleve now directs the Summer Program. He says it "helps a lot of guys to get into college." NBA fans will recognize the names of John Battle of the Atlanta Hawks and Roy Hinson of the Philadelphia '76ers, both of whom are graduates of his summer program.

ROLE MODELS

Cleve is very conscious that he is a role model for kids and young people. "In the inner city, the only role models are the guys dealing drugs with their pockets bulging with money. I know it was tough when I came up — but not tough compared to now. I stay involved and give them some time; I have their ear."

For a time he was the director of an after-school pro-

The two-column grid is used in this book catalog to create an extremely open, well-organized, easily referenced format.

The long line length (maximum measure is 20p6) minimizes runover lines, so it's easy to pick out the title, author, and other details in each listing.

The small type size (8/11 Friz Quadrata) helps contain the lines, but the leading and white space are designed so that readability isn't compromised. This typeface has a good contrast of boldface to light-face that makes the book titles stand out. The use of boldface, roman, ital-ics, and all caps is handled carefully to delineate clearly what could have been a hodgepodge of details.

The hard left edge created by the type and the hairline rules contrasts with the openness of the very uneven right margin. Open at the top and the bottom, the page has a strong sense of verticality, which is emphasized by the weight of the category heads.

The headline type is Aachen Bold. The weight of the headlines is emphasized by the bold rules below. Note that in a two-line head the length of the bold rule is determined by the short second line; the hairline rule above the bold rule extends to the maximum measure.

The faceted sphere, with its mathematical precision and crystal-line structure, is appropriate for the scientific line of books being sold. The art was created using one of the generic solids in an early 3D rendering program and imported into PageMaker as a PICT file. Because tints print differently on LaserWriters and imagesetters (the final output was from an L300), the art was kept a little lighter and lower in contrast on-screen than was desired in the printed piece.

Design: John Odam (San Diego, CA)
Catalog from Academic Press, Harcourt Brace Jovanovich, Publishers.
Trim size: 24-3/4 by 11 inches, folded twice

PHYSICAL SCIENCES

THE REWIRING OF AMERICA
The Fiber Optics Revolution
C. David Chaffee
Atlantic Information Services, Inc., Washington, D.C.
1987, 256 pages, **$17.47** ($24.95)
ISBN: 0-12-166560-4

THE FOUNDATIONS OF MAGNETIC RECORDING
John C. Mallinson
Center for Magnetic Recording Research, University of California, San Diego
1987, 175 pages, **$20.97** ($29.95)
ISBN: 0-12-466625-6

ELECTRONS IN SOLIDS
An Introductory Survey
Second Edition
Richard H. Bube
Stanford University, California
1988, 328 pages, **$27.65** ($39.50)
ISBN: 0-12-138552-3

ENCYCLOPEDIA OF PHYSICAL SCIENCE AND TECHNOLOGY
edited by
Robert A. Meyers
TRW Electronics and Defense Sector, Redondo Beach, California
1987, 15-volume set, **$1750.00** ($2500.00)

HANDBOOK OF DIGITAL SIGNAL PROCESSING
ENGINEERING APPLICATIONS
edited by
Douglas F. Elliott
Rockwell International Corporation, Anaheim, California
1987, 999 pages, **$94.50** ($135.00)
ISBN: 0-12-237075-9

ISOTOPE CHRONOSTRATIGRAPHY
Theory and Methods
Douglas F. Williams and Ian Lerche
University of South Carolina, Columbia
W.E. Full
Wichita State University, Kansas
May 1988, 333 pages, **$34.97** ($49.95, tentative)
ISBN: 0-12-754560-3

HISTORICAL SEISMOGRAMS AND EARTHQUAKES OF THE WORLD
edited by
W.H.K. Lee
U.S. Geological Survey, Menlo Park, California
H. Meyers
National Oceanic and Atmospheric Administration Boulder, Colorado
K. Shimazaki
University of Tokyo, Japan
1988, 528 pages, **$31.50** ($45.00)
ISBN: 0-12-440870-2

COMPUTER SCIENCE

PROLOG FOR PROGRAMMERS
Feliks Kluźniak and Stanisław Szpakowicz
Warsaw University, Poland
With a contribution by Janusz S. Bień
Paperback Reprint: $17.47 ($24.95)/ISBN: 0-12-416521-4
1987, 320 pages
Casebound: $47.25 ($67.50)/ISBN: 0-12-416520-6
1985, 400 pages

INTRODUCTION TO COMMON LISP
Taiichi Yuasa and Masami Hagiya
Kyoto University, Japan
translated by
Richard Weyhrauch and Yasuko Kitajima
1987, 293 pages, **$20.97** ($29.95)
ISBN: 0-12-774860-1

U.S. and Canadian Customers
CALL TOLL FREE
1-800-321-5068
During normal working hours, weekdays only.
In Missouri, Alaska, or Hawaii
call 1-314-528-8110.
For detailed sales and discount information call our National Sales Desk at 1-619-699-6345

THE WRITER'S GUIDE TO DESKTOP PUBLISHING
Kathy Lang
Mayflower Computing Consultants, Looe, Cornwall, England
In Paperback: $13.97 ($19.95)/ISBN: 0-12-436275-3
1987, 184 pages

COLOR AND THE COMPUTER
edited by
H. John Durrett
Interactive Systems Laboratories, San Marcos, Texas
1987, 299 pages, **$41.30** ($59.00)
ISBN: 0-12-225210-1

PARALLEL COMPUTER VISION
edited by
Leonard Uhr
University of Wisconsin-Madison
1987, 320 pages, **$20.97** ($29.95)
ISBN: 0-12-706958-5

MATHEMATICS AND ECONOMICS

MATHEMATICS FOR DYNAMIC MODELING
Edward Beltrami
State University of New York at Stony Brook
1987, 277 pages, **$19.25** ($27.50)
ISBN: 0-12-085555-0

RANDOM SIGNAL ANALYSIS IN ENGINEERING SYSTEMS
John J. Komo
Clemson University, South Carolina
1987, 302 pages, **$27.97** ($39.95)
ISBN: 0-12-418660-2

ALGEBRAIC D-MODULES
A. Borel et al.
Princeton University, New Jersey
Volume 2 in the PERSPECTIVES IN MATHEMATICS Series
1987, 355 pages, **$23.10** ($33.00)
ISBN: 0-12-117740-8

THE BOOK OF SQUARES
Leonardo Pisano
(Fibonacci)
An annotated translation into Modern English by
L.E. Sigler
Bucknell University, Lewisburg, Pennsylvania
1987, 124 pages, **$13.97** ($19.95)
ISBN: 0-12-643130-2

INDUSTRIAL POLICY OF JAPAN
edited by
Ryutaro Komiya and Masahiro Okuno
University of Tokyo, Bunkyo-ku, Japan
Kotaro Suzumura
Hitotsubashi University, Kunitachi, Tokyo, Japan
Kazuo Sato
Rutgers University, Newark, New Jersey
March 1988, 590 pages, **$34.97** ($49.95, tentative)
ISBN: 0-12-418650-5

MACROECONOMIC THEORY
Second Edition
Thomas J. Sargent
University of Minnesota and Federal Reserve Bank, Minneapolis and Hoover Institution Stanford University, California
1987, 528 pages, **$31.15** ($44.50)
ISBN: 0-12-619751-2

AN INTRODUCTORY THEORY OF SECURITY MARKETS
J.D. Duffie
Stanford University, California
April 1988, 350 pages, **$27.65** ($39.50, tentative)
ISBN: 0-12-223345-X

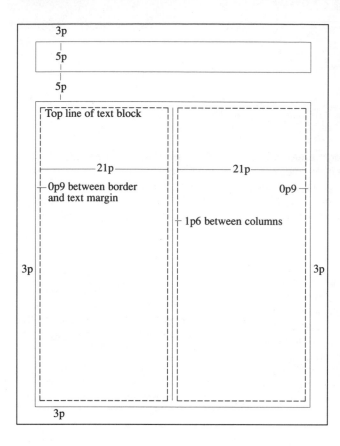

3p

5p

5p

Top line of text block

21p   21p

0p9 between border
and text margin   0p9

1p6 between columns

3p   3p

3p

The Journal of Contemporary Mythology

WINTER 1990

IN SEARCH OF
THE MODERN MYTH

By Raymond Chavoustier

orem ipsum dolor sit amet, consectetuer adipiscing elit, sed diam nonummy nibh euismod tincidunt ut laoreet dolore magna aliquam erat volutpat. Ut wisi enim ad minim veniam, quis nostrud exerci tation ullamcorper suscipit lobortis nisl ut aliquip ex ea commodo consequat hendrerit in velit esse molestie.

Duis autem vel eum iriure dolor in hendrerit in vulputate velit esse molestie consequat, vel illum dolore eu feugiat nulla facilisis at vero eros et accumsan et iusto odio dignissim qui blandit praesent luptatum zzril delenit augue duis dolore te feugait nulla facilisi.

Lorem ipsum dolor sit amet, consectetuer adipiscing elit, sed diam nonummy nibh euismod tincidunt ut laoreet dolore magna aliquam erat volutpat. Ut wisi enim ad minim veniam, quis nostrud exerci tation ullamcorper suscipit lobortis nisl ut aliquip ex ea commodo consequat. Duis autem vel eum iriure dolor in hendrerit in vulputate velit esse molestie consequat, vel illum dolore eu feugiat nulla facilisi. Nam liber tempor cum soluta nobis eleifend option. Ut wisi enim ad minim veniam, quis nostrud exerci

**We have not even to risk
the adventure alone,
for the heroes of all time have
gone before us.
The labyrinth is thoroughly
known. We have only to follow
the thread
of the hero path,
... and where we had thought
to be alone,
we will be with all the world.
—Joseph Campbell**

Congue nihil imperdiet doming id quod mazim placerat facer possim assum. Lorem ipsum dolor sit amet, consectetuer adipiscing elit, sed diam nonummy nibh euismod tincidunt ut laoreet dolore magna aliquam erat volutpat. Ut wisi enim ad minim veniam, quis nostrud exerci tation ullamcorper suscipit lobortis nisl ut aliquip ex ea commodo consequat.

Duis autem vel eum iriure dolor in hendrerit in vulputate velit esse molestie consequat, vel illum dolore eu feugiat nulla facilisis at vero eros et accumsan et iusto odio dignissim qui blandit praesent luptatum zzril delenit augue

gue duis dolore te feugait nulla facilisi. Lorem ipsum dolor sit amet, consectetuer adipiscing elit, sed diam nonummy nibh euismod tincidunt ut laoreet dolore magna aliquam erat qui blandit praesent luptatumvolutpatquis augue duis dolore tenostrud exerci.

Ut wisi enim ad minim veniam, quis nostrud exerci tation ullamcorper suscipit lobortis nisl ut aliquip ex ea commodo consequat. Duis autem vel eum iriure dolor in hendrerit in vulputate velit esse molestie consequat, vel illum dolore eu feugiat nulla facilisis at vero eros et accumsan et iusto odio dignissim qui blandit praesent luptatum zzril delenit augue duis dolore te feugait nulla facilisi hendrerit in vulputate velit esse molestie.

Lorem ipsum dolor sit amet, consectetuer adipiscing elit, sed diam nonummy nibh euismod tincidunt ut laoreet dolore magna aliquam erat volutpat. Ut wisi enim ad minim veniam, quis nostrud exerci tation ullamcorper suscipit lobortis nisl ut aliquip ex ea commodo consequat. Duis autem vel eum iriure dolor in hendrerit in vulputate velit esse molestie consequat, vel illum dolore eu feugiat nulla facilisis at vero eros et accumsan et iusto odio dignissim qui blandit praesent luptatum zzril delenit augue duis dolore te feugait nulla

facilisi.Lorem ipsum dolor sit amet, consectetuer adipiscing elit, sed diam nonummy nibh euismod tincidunt ut laoreet dolore magna aliquam erat volutpat. Ut wisi enim ad minim veniam, quis nostrud exerci tation ullamcorper suscipit lobortis nisl ut aliquip ex ea commodo consequat. Duis autem vel eum iriure dolor in hendrerit in vulputate velit esse molestie consequat.

Vel illum dolore eu feugiat nulla facilisis at vero eros et accumsan et iusto odio dignissim qui blandit praesent luptatum zzril delenit augue duis dolore te feugait nulla facilisi. Lorem ipsum dolor sit amet, consectetuer adipiscing elit, sed diam nonummy nibh euismod tincidunt ut

This blueprint was used for both documents on these two pages.

Equal margins on all four sides work best in this format. If you vary from that, do it decisively, as in a deep top margin, rather than subtly.

The depth of the panel at the top of the page and the space between the panel and the text block can vary depending on the elements to be included.

Art is best sized to the width of a single column. Small diagrams can be accommodated as shown in the instruction sheet at right. Art can also be inset in the text, like the quote in the page below.

The illustrations in the instruction sheet were drawn in a paint program for the purpose of position only. The printer would strip in the halftones to match the size and position in the layout.

Type specs for instruction sheet
Company name: 18-point Bookman with
    20-point caps
Headline: 16/15 Helvetica Black
Subheads: 12-point Helvetica Black
Text: 10/10 Helvetica Light with 6 points
    between paragraphs, Helvetica Black
    numbers, and a 1p4 hanging indent
Numbers in diagrams: 18-point Helvetica
    Black

The journal page at left is obviously designed for an audience predisposed to sustained reading.

The white box for the inset quote is the same width as the text columns. The 12-point rule anchors the quote so that it doesn't float in empty space. The type is 16/18 Helvetica Condensed Bold, centered, and contrasts with the classic feeling of the rest of the page.

The running text is Palatino. The initial cap is 96-point Zapf Chancery followed by a 5p6 indent.

ANTARCTICA

AUTOMATIC ICE MAKER INSTALLATION KIT
FOR TWO-DOOR SIDE-BY-SIDE REFRIGERATOR

IMPORTANT

The refrigerator must be level to ensure proper operation of the ice maker. See your owner's manual.

TOOLS YOU WILL NEED

Phillips head screwdriver
Drill with 1/4" bit
Adjustable open-end wrench
Needlenose pliers

PARTS LIST

1. Harness and fill-tube grommet.

2. Water supply unit with hose nut, rubber washer, water valve, and compression nuts.

3. Rectangular clip (4) for end assembly unit and split grommet (2).

4. Screws and nuts (See screw identification chart on page 3).

5. Fill spout.

6. Plastic fill tube for ice maker harness.

STEPS IN THIS PROCEDURE

Ut wisi enim ad minim veniam, quis nostrud exerci tation ullamcorper suscipit lobortis nisl ut aliquip ex ea commodo consequat. Duis autem vel eum iriure dolor in hendrerit in vulputate velit esse molestie consequat, vel illum dolore eu feugiat nulla facilisis

1. At vero eros et accumsan et iusto odio dignissim qui blandit praesent luptatum zzril delenit augue duis dolore te feugait

2. Nulla facilisihendrerit in vulputate velit esse molestie . Lorem ipsum dolor sit amet, consectetuer adipiscing elit, sed diam nonummy nibh euismod tincidunt ut laoreet dolore magna aliquam erat volutpat.

3. Ut wisi enim ad minim veniam, quis nostrud exerci tation ullamcorper suscipit lobortis nisl ut aliquip ex ea commodo consequat.

4. Duis autem vel eum iriure dolor in hendrerit in vulputate velit esse molestie consequat, vel illum dolore eu feugiat nulla facilisis at vero eros et accumsan et iusto odio dignissim qui blandit praesent luptatum zzril delenit augue

5. Duis dolore te feugait nulla facilisi.Lorem ipsum dolor sit amet, consectetuer adipiscing elit, sed diam nonummy nibh euismod tincidunt ut laoreet dolore magna

2

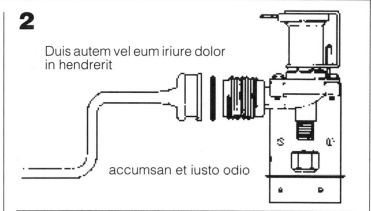

Duis autem vel eum iriure dolor in hendrerit

accumsan et iusto odio

3

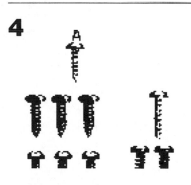

Ut wisi enim ad minim veniam, quis exerci tation

4

accumsan et iusto odio

5

Duis autem vel eum iriure dolor in hendrerit

1

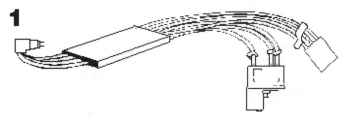

Ut wisi enim ad minim veniam, quis exerci tation

6

Nulla facilisihendrerit in vulpu

THREE-COLUMN GRIDS

The three-column grid is the most common format in publishing, widely used in magazines, newspapers, newsletters, catalogs, and annual reports. It is popular because it is so flexible, allowing you to place headlines, art, boxed copy, and other elements across any one, two, or even all three columns. This enables you to break the material into small chunks or modules, using various graphic devices to indicate the relative importance of items and relationships between them.

In the short line length, usually 12 to 14 picas, type sets efficiently in relatively small sizes (9- or 10-point type is frequently used for running

This informal, three-column format shows the value of simplicity. With the controls available in PageMaker, these pages are almost as easy to produce as a single-column typewritten document. A stapled, four-page statement of purpose, this was created when the organization first converted to desktop publishing. Three years later, they were printing the same information in an 11-by-17, three-color folder with computer-drawn art.

The horizontal rules provide a consistent structure that is balanced by open, ragged right type. The two-column heads, the angled, bit-mapped initial caps, and the playful art keep the three-column grid from feeling rigid and also suggest the personality of a foundation trying to reach young people.

The headline type is Bookman (with open spacing in the foundation's name). The running text is Avant Garde, a sans serif face with a large x-height. When generously leaded, as it is here, it is distinctive and inviting.

Lists of names work very well in the three-column format.

Design: Jim Parker (Phoenix, AZ)

Pages from a statement of purpose by the Do It Now Foundation.
Trim size: 8-1/2 by 11

text) that is still easy for readers to scan. The three-column grid also accommodates small pictures and large ones equally well, so that a really terrific photo can be given adequate space while a not-very-good mug shot can be kept appropriately sized to the width of a single column. This range enables you to use contrast as a design element in sizing art.

So why doesn't everyone use a three-column grid? One of the disadvantages of the format is that so many people do, and it can be difficult to devise a style that distinguishes your publication from all the others.

Page frames and column rules create a classic, three-column newsletter format. A second color, used for banners, breakouts, art, and sidebar tints, adds to the appeal.

Note the many devices used to vary the page composition: inset art, two-column tables and breakouts, sidebars that run the full page width in a two-column format

rather than a three-column one. Note also how the horizontal rules turn into the page on one or both sides of the center column; often, the facing page runs the horizontal rule across all three columns for contrast.

The shatter outline of the art (below left) contrasts sharply with the page structure. In general, irregularly shaped art helps keep a tight grid from being too rigid.

The reverse type in the banners is Avant Garde with open letter-spacing, which greatly improves the legibility of reverse type. The breakout is Avant Garde Italic, the headlines are Helvetica, and the running text is Times Roman.

Design: Jim Parker (Phoenix, AZ)

Pages from Newservice, *published by the Do It Now Foundation.*
Trim size: 8-1/2 by 11

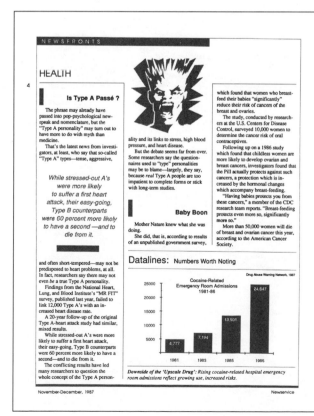

Modular verticals

The easiest way to lay out a three-column page is to run the text continuously in vertical columns. And one of the easiest ways to keep those verticals from being dull is through the use of tones. Whether shades of gray or a second color, tones can be used to separate, isolate, emphasize, or unify. Three different treatments are shown on these two pages.

The tones used in headline banners both unify and separate different elements on the page. The headline banners in this newsletter are 8-point rules (which print 60% black) on top of 20% black boxes, which vary in depth according the length of the headline. The two-line heads are centered in 3p9-deep boxes, the one-line heads in 3p-deep boxes. You can leave a master banner for each headline size on the pasteboard of your document and then make copies of them as needed.

The caption also prints in a 20% box. A three-line caption fits in the same 3p9 box as a two-line head.

Nashville, the type used for the publication name, is from Agfa Compugraphic. When Nashville is set tightly, its slab-serif style works well, and the word "NewsBeat" has been kerned to bring out that characteristic. The date, set in 9-point Futura, is set with 200% letterspace for additional contrast with the type above.

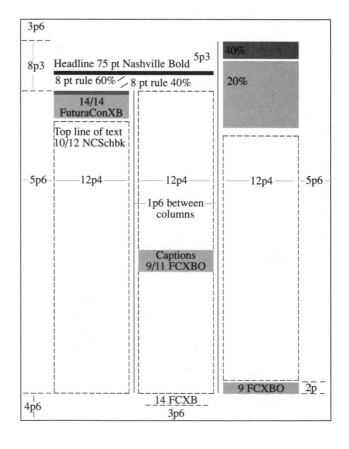

Art, headlines, and color tints are placed loosely in the grid to create a collage-like feeling in the first sample. The effect is casual and gives an inviting sense of the unexpected, which is relatively rare in three-column newsletters.

Color is a strong element in this design. The tone unifying the two related stories under a single headline is orange; it drops out to create a white border around the photos, which print over a blue tint. The two-column headline, initial caps, 8-point rules, and exclamation point also print in orange. The logo prints orange and blue.

The distinctive logo collages small sans serif type, boxed and angled, over the larger Roman-style title. An effective way to integrate the company and newsletter names, this device is relatively easy to execute if you have a good eye for proportioning type.

The Times Roman running text is set in relatively narrow columns surrounded by generous white space. For contrast, the display type is set in a bold Helvetica.

In the bottom sample, the tone is used behind secondary material—the issue highlights on the cover and sidebars on inside pages—rather than behind features.

The structured rules, justified text, and even column bottoms represent a completely different approach to page design than the previous sample. Each sets a style appropriate for its audience.

Design (top): Tom Ahern (Providence, RI)

Dateline *is published quarterly by*
GTECH Lottery.
Size: 8-1/2 by 11

Design (bottom): Kimberly Mancebo,
Robert Bryant Associates (Campbell, CA)

TeleVisual Market Strategies *is published by*
Telecommunications Productivity Center.
Size: 8-1/2 by 11

Introducing the horizontal

A true grid has a precise horizontal structure that is generally determined by the type specifications of the dominant text face so that a given number of lines will fit in each grid unit. The construction of the grid must also take into account the space between grid units. For example, if your type is 10/12, each grid unit and the space beween two units will be in multiples of 12 points, or 1 pica. If your type is 11/13, the grid units will be in multiples of 13 points, obviously a less convenient measurement to work with.

If you want to study an expertly used horizontal grid, see the Pitney Bowes publication toward the beginning of the Brochure section in Chapter 4.

Visual elements are sized to fit different combinations of these units, allowing for varied sizes and shapes which, because of their relationship to the underlying structure, are in proportion to one another and to the page as a whole. In some ways, the truly modular grid simplifies layout more than the mostly vertical structures apparent in many of the samples reproduced in this book. But an orthodox grid is also more difficult to construct. If you find the mathematically determined horizontal structure confusing or inhibiting, adopt a more informal approach to placing the elements vertically on the page.

The sample on the facing page is built on an 18-unit grid, with 3 vertical divisions and 6 horizontal ones. This schematic shows the placement of the sample's visual elements on the grid. You can see how the structure facilitates decision making by suggesting both size and placement; note also how the design overrides the grid when needed. Turn the page for additional diagrams, grid specifications, and another, very different design based on the same grid.

Type specifications
Overline: 10/12 Avant Garde reverse, centered, +200%
  letterspace
Publication name: 48-point Avant Garde, –20% letterspace
Story heads: 24/24 Bodoni Bold Italic
Body text: 10/12 Bodoni
Captions: 11/12 Bodoni Bold Italic

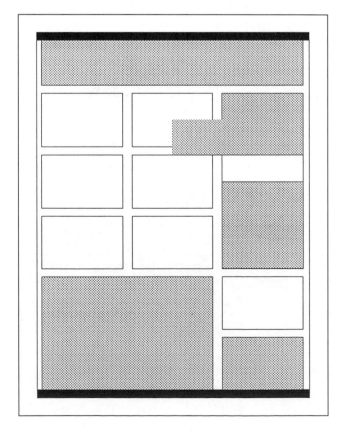

Triangle Hotel Trumpet

EAT, DRINK AND BE MERRY

Lorem ipsum dolor sit amet, consectetuer adipiscing elit, sed diam nonummy nibh euismod tincidunt ut laoreet dolore magna aliquam erat volutpat. Ut wisi enim ad minim veniam, quis nostrud exerci tation ullamcorper suscipit lobortis nisl ut aliquip ex ea commodo consequat.

Duis autem vel eum iriure dolor in hendrerit in vulputate velit esse molestie consequat, vel illum dolore eu feugiat nulla facilisis at vero eros et accumsan et iusto odio dignissim qui blandit praesent luptatum zzril delenit augue duis dolore te feugait nulla facilisi. Lorem ipsum dolor sit amet, consectetuer adipiscing elit, sed diam nonummy nibh euismod tincidunt ut laoreet dolore magna aliquam erat volutpat. Ut wisi enim ad minim veniam, quis nostrud exerci tation ullamcorper suscipit lobortis nisl ut aliquip ex ea commodo consequat.

Duis autem vel eum iriure dolor in hendrerit in vulputate velit esse molestie consequat, vel illum dolore eu feugiat nulla facil at vero eros et

accumsan et iusto etei odio dignissim qui blandit praesent luptatum zzril delenit augue duis dolore te. feugait nulla facilisi. Nam liber tempor

Sunday Jazz Brunch

FROM BIG BAND TO ROCK 'N ROLL

Duis autem vel eum iriure dolor in hendrerit in vulputate velit esse molestie consequat, vel illum dolore eu feugiat nulla facilisis at vero eros et accumsan et iusto odio dignissim qui blandit praesent luptatum zzril delenit augue duis dolore te feugait nulla facilisi.

Lorem ipsum dolor sit amet, consectetuer adipiscing elit, sed diam nonummy nibh euismod tincidunt ut laoreet dolore magna aliquam erat volutpat. Ut wisi enim ad minim veniam, quis nostrud exerci tation

ullamcorper suscipit lobortis nisl ut aliquip ex ea commodo consequat. Duis autem vel eum iriure dolor in hendrerit in vulputate velit esse

All-Night Buffet

molestie consequat. Lorem ipsum dolor sit amet, consectetuer adipiscing elit, sed diam nonummy nibh euismod tincidunt ut

Baoreet dolore magna aliquam erat volutpat. Ut wisi enim ad minim laoreet dolore magna aliquam erat veniam, quis nostrud eu feugiat nulla facilisis at vero eros et accumsan et

New Year's Gala in the Ballroom

Morning-After Room Service

This is a good place for the placement of a pull quote from the text

Lorem ipsum dolor sit amet, consectetuer adipiscing elit, sed diam nonummy nibh euismod tincidunt ut laoreet dolore magna aliquam erat volutpat. Ut wisi enim ad minim veniam, quis nostrud exerci tation ullamcorper suscipit lobortis nisl ut aliquip ex ea commodo consequat. Duis autem vel eum iriure dolor in hendrerit in vulputate velit esse molestie consequat, vel illum dolore eu feugiat nulla facilisis at vero eros et accumsan et iusto odio dignissim qui blandit praesent luptatum zzril delenit augue duis dolore te feugait nulla facilisi. Lorem ipsum dolor sit amet, consectetuer adipiscing elit,

in hendrerit in vulputate velit esse molestie consequat, vel illum dolore eu feugiat nulla facilisis at vero eros et accumsan et iusto odio dignissim qui blandit praesent luptatum zzril delenit augue duis dolore te feugait nulla facilisi. Nam liber tempor cum soluta nobis eleifend option

nostrud exerci tation ullamcorper suscipit lobortis nisl ut aliquip ex ea commodo consequat. Duis autem vel eum iriure dolor in hendrerit in vulputate velit esse molestie consequat, vel illum dolore eu feugiat nulla facilisis at vero eros et accumsan et iusto odio dignissim qui blandit prae-

nostrud exerci tation ullamcorper suscipit lobortis nisl ut aliquip ex ea commodo consequat. Duis autem vel eum iriure dolor in hendrerit in vulputate velit esse molestie consequat, vel illum dolore eu

sed diam nonummy nibh euismod tincidunt ut laoreet dolore magna aliquam erat volutpat. Ut wisi enim ad minim veniam, quis nostrud exerci tation ullamcorper suscipit lobortis nisl ut aliquip ex ea commodo consequat. Duis autem vel eum iriure dolor

congue nihil imperdiet doming id quod mazim placerat facer possim assum. Lorem ipsum dolor sit amet, consectetuer adipiscing elit, sed diam nonummy nibh euismod tincidunt ut laoreet dolore magna aliquam erat volutpat. Ut wisi enim ad minim veniam, quis

sent luptatum zzril delenit augue duis dolore te feugait nulla facilisi. Lorem ipsum dolor sit amet, consectetuer adipiscing elit, sed diam nonummy nibh euismod tincidunt ut laoreet dolore magna aliquam erat volutpat. Ut wisi enim ad minim veniam,

1　　2　　3

4

Page composition within an 18-unit grid such as the one discussed on these four pages can vary considerably. The page at left and schematic 1, above, show picture placement in which the horizontal and vertical structures are balanced. The second schematic shows a strong horizontal arrangement; the third, a strong vertical. In the fourth, one column is used only for head-lines, captions, and small photos, creating still another look.

Research Paper

Lorem ipsum dolor sit amet, consectetuer adipiscing elit, sed diam nonummy nibh euismod tincidunt ut laoreet dolore magna aliquam erat volutpat. Ut wisi enim ad minim veniam, quis nostrud exerci tation ullamcorper suscipit lobortis nisl ut aliquip ex ea commodo consequat.
　Duis autem vel eum iriure dolor in hendrerit in vulputate velit esse molestie consequat, vel illum dolore eu feugiat nulla facilisis at vero eros et accumsan et iusto odio dignissim qui blandit praesent luptatum zzril delenit augue duis dolore te feugait nulla facilisi.
　Lorem ipsum dolor sit amet, consectetuer adipiscing elit, sed diam nonummy nibh euismod tincidunt ut laoreet dolore magna aliquam erat volutpat. Ut wisi enim ad minim veniam, quis nostrud exerci tation ullamcorper suscipit lobortis nisl ut aliquip ex ea commodo consequat.
　Duis autem vel eum iriure dolor in hendrerit in vulputate velit esse molestie consequat, vel illum dolore eu feugiat nulla facilisis at vero eros et accumsan et iusto odio dignissim qui blandit praesent luptatum zzril delenit augue duis dolore te feugait nulla facilisi. Nam liber tempor cum soluta nobis eleifend option congue nihil imperdiet doming id quod mazim placerat facer possim assum.
　Lorem ipsum dolor sit amet, consectetuer adipiscing elit, sed diam nonummy nibh euismod tincidunt ut laoreet dolore magna ut aliquip ex ea commodo conse-quat.
　Lorem ipsum dolor sit amet iriure dsent luptatum zzril delenit augue duis dolore te feugait nulla

TEST RESULTS	Grp A	Grp B	Control
Uptatum zzril delenit augue	1,745	1,398	1,598
Dolore eu feugiat nulla	4,978	2,467	1,028
Tincidunt ut ladolore wisi enim	3,684	1,746	5,896
Tin vulputate velit esse	2,678	3,986	1,038
Dignissim qui blandit praesent	3,794	1,840	2,096
Uptatum zzril delenit augue	1,493	2,047	3,208
Dolore eu feugiat nulla	2,067	2,067	3,906
Total	**17,376**	**13,982**	**20,387**

NARRATIVE

Amet consectetuer adipiscing elit, suscipit lobortis nisl ut aliquip ex ea commodo consequat. Duis autem vel eum iriure dolor in hendrerit in vulputate velit esse molestie consequat, vel illum dolore eu feugiat nulla facilisis at Vero eros et

sectetuer adipiscing elit, sed diam nonummy nibh euismod tincidunt ut lcommodo consequat. Duis autem aoreet dolore magna aliquam erat volutpat. Ut wisi enim ad minim

continued on following page

FURTHER RESEARCH

Accumsan et iusto odio dignissim qui blandit praesent luptatum zzril delenit augue duis dolore te feugait nulla facilisi.
Lorem ipsum dolor sit amet, consectetuer adipiscing elit, sed

CONCLUSIONS

Diam nonummy nibh euismod tincidunt ut laoreet dolore magna aliquam erat volutpat. Ut wisi enim ad minim veniam, quis nostrud exerci tation ullamcorper suscipit lobortis nisl ut aliquip ex ea com-modo consequat. Duis facilisi.

Lorem ipsum dolor sit amet, tincidunt ut laoreet dolore magna aliquam erat volutpat. Ut wisi enim ad minim veniam, quis.

The sample at left uses the grid on the facing page to create hori-zontal divisions for text blocks. A text block can run any number of grid units and need not fill the entire unit. But regardless of the depth of the text, rules separating text blocks are placed at the midpoint of the space between two grid units.

The banner runs from the top margin to the midpoint of the space between the first two horizontal grid units. A hairline horizontal rule is placed midway between the last grid unit and the bottom margin.

The headline is 60-point Ameri-can Typewriter, reversed out of the 60% black banner.

The body text is 10/12 New Century Schoolbook.

Subheads are 12-point Helvetica Black, aligned at top with the top of a grid unit. The running text in these text blocks is 10/12 Helvetica Light. The text in the table is 10/24, creat-ing a full line space between each item so that this text aligns with running text in the adjacent column.

Grid units and type size are designed in relation to one another. The first detail here shows how 10/12 text fits in the grid units used in the samples on these two pages. For the sake of comparison, the second detail shows 10/14 text in the same 10/12 grid; you can see that with the increased leading, the grid no longer works. Both details are shown full size.

When constructing a horizontal grid, you can customize Page-Maker's vertical ruler with the leading value specified in points. (Use the Preferences command on the File menu.) With Snap to Rulers on, all guidelines, text, and graphics that you place on the page will align with ruler tick marks calibrated to the leading that you specified.

This grid was used for the samples in this section. Although all the units are of equal size, elements placed on the grid need not be. The grid is constructed as follows:

Margins: 3p top and bottom, 4p side
Columns: three, 1p6 space between
Horizontal grid units: 8p9 deep
  beginning at top margin, 1p6
  between units
Hairline vertical rules from top to
  bottom margin: 1p outside left and
  right margins and, where appropriate, between columns
Horizontal rules (Triangle Hotel
  sample on preceding spread):
  1p3 deep; top rule flush with top
  grid unit; bottom rule just below
  last grid unit

Note that the grid is slightly asymmetrical along the vertical axis. In the Triangle Hotel sample on the preceding spread, the 1p3-deep horizontal rule fills the space between the bottom grid unit and the bottom margin. In the Research Paper at left, a hairline rule visually fills the space at the bottom of the page. If you were to use this grid without horizontal rules to balance the space, you would probably want to shift the entire grid down 9 points to center it on the page.

Lorem ipsum dolor sit amet, consectetuer adipiscing elit, sed diam nonummy nibh euismod tincidunt ut laoreet dolore magna aliquam erat volutpat. Ut wisi enim ad minim veniam, quis nostrud exerci tation ullamcorper suscipit lobortis nisl ut aliquip ex ea commodo consequat.

Duis autem vel eum iriure dolor in hendrerit in vulputate velit esse molestie consequat, vel illum dolore eu feugiat nulla facilisis at vero eros et accumsan et iusto odio dignissim qui blandit praesent luptatum zzril delenit augue duis dolore te feugait nulla facilisi. Lorem ipsum dolor sit amet, consectetuer adipiscing elit, sed diam nonummy nibh euismod tincidunt ut duis laoreet dolore magna

1

Lorem ipsum dolor sit amet, consectetuer adipiscing elit, sed diam nonummy nibh euismod tincidunt ut laoreet dolore magna aliquam erat volutpat. Ut wisi enim ad minim veniam, quis nostrud exerci tation ullamcorper suscipit lobortis nisl ut aliquip ex ea commodo consequat.

Duis autem vel eum iriure dolor in hendrerit in vulputate velit esse molestie consequat, vel illum dolore eu feugiat nulla facilisis at vero eros et accumsan et iusto odio dignissim qui blandit praesent luptatum zzril delenit augue duis dolore te feugait nulla facilisi. Lorem ipsum dolor sit

2

A mixed grid

Varying the column width within a single page has many uses. It accommodates different kinds of material, allows for a varied page design, and can inspire you to organize the components of your document in a way that strengthens the intrinsic relationships and forms contrasts among them. In the sample shown below, the mixed grid is both functional and dramatic.

Sidebar vignettes set to a 13-pica measure are inset in a single wide column that provides the background narrative in this annual report. The sidebars, which run throughout the report, are human-interest stories. On other pages not shown, some sidebars are styled as two single columns that face each other across the gutter, others as two singles in the outer columns of facing pages.

The two different settings are unified by a single typeface (Goudy Old Style), generously leaded, yet they are styled for considerable contrast: The larger, roman type in the wide measure is justified and prints in warm brown; the smaller, italic type is ragged right and prints in black. The italic caption at the bottom of the page is set to the wide measure and prints in brown.

Design: Tom Lewis (San Diego, CA)
Page from the Medic Alert Annual Report.
Trim size: 8-1/2 by 11

Design (facing page): Edward Hughes, Edward Hughes Design (Evanston, IL)
Pages from the Roosevelt University Annual Report.
Trim Size: 8-1/4 by 11-5/8

REPORT TO THE READER

"My membership is like insurance coverage - the very best protection, and for a reasonable cost. I'm sure all the members feel as I do - grateful there is an organization called Medic Alert."

That's how one member described the secure feeling enjoyed by the more than 2.6 million people worldwide who wear the Medic Alert emblem. For 32 years, Medic Alert has warned health professionals about patients' special medical conditions, saving thousands of lives and sparing needless suffering. "As an EMT," another member wrote, "I know how much Medic Alert helps emergency personnel. If people would only realize how important it is for us to know their medical problems in an emergency maybe more would wear Medic Alert emblems."

In recent years, Medic Alert's emergency medical identification system has substan-tially improved operations management and product and service quality. The Foundation's quest for excel-lence is ongoing.

MEDIC ALERT'S NEW SERVICES This year, Medic Alert launched plans to di-versify into services that capi-talize on the Foundation's ability to manage an accu-rate, confidential medical data base. In August, in 1987, Medic Alert began

MEDIC ALERT PROTECTS TRANSPLANT RECIPIENT

Eleven years ago, a New Zealand school girl named Ann Crawford became ill with the flu. Unlike many flu victims for whom the malady is a fleeting annoyance, Ann suffered perma-nent lung damage. She fell prey to a series of infections that strained her breathing and weakened her heart.

In the years that followed, Ann en-dured a revolving door of hospital treatments. Her doctors experimented with megadose drug therapies to clear her frequent infections, but her lungs continued to worsen. Eight years

after her bout with the flu, Ann's health had become so fragile that few expected her to sur-vive the winter.

Only 19, Ann was not ready to give up. She had read up on the latest advances in thoracic surgery and transplant technology. She wondered, "Why not start all over again with a new heart and lungs?"

Ann's enthusiasm sparked support from the Lions Club in her area, which agreed to help finance the cost of her surgery. She traveled to the United Kingdom for the operation, and returned home with a new heart and lungs. Shortly after, she penned Pumps & Bellows, a detailed account of her illness and transplant operation.

This brave young woman from New Zealand, is breathing easier these days. But she will always require anti-rejection drugs to ensure that her body will not declare war on her new organs. In a medical emergency, responders need to know instantly of her transplant operation and drug regimen to administer proper treatment.

That is why Ann, like many others around the world, wears a Medic Alert emblem. After years of hospital stays and bed rest, the young New Zealander takes every precaution to protect her most treasured gift, a second chance at life.

From Evangeline: Thanks to Medic Alert my husband is alive today. He was in a very bad car accident. The paramedics saw his Medic Alert necklace and found his wallet card. His seat belt and his Medic Alert tag saved his life.

Asymmetrical three-column

Generally, asymmetrical three-column grids have two wide columns and one narrow one. This produces a slightly more interesting and an inherently more variable look than three equal columns, especially when you consider the possibilities that derive from combining two columns, whether two equal columns or one wide and one narrow.

The underlying structure is two 11-pica columns and one 18-pica column. When the wide column is combined with the inside narrow column, the resulting 31-pica measure provides additional flexibility in page composition.

The depth of the photographs remains constant from page to page, although the depth of the captions varies. Good photographs, well-printed, result in the rich blacks and grays evident here.

The captions are styled as display type, reversed out against the gray background.

The uneven bottoms of the three columns helps balance the tight structure created by the strong horizontal line across the top of the page, the strong left edge of the type columns (which is emphasized by the elongated page), and the tabbed folios that bleed off the bottom of the page.

Note that single-digit numbers are indented so that all numbers align right. This typographic refinement is all the more needed here with the hanging indent.

As precise as this format is, the pages are relatively easy to assemble. Having two standardized picture sizes minimizes art decisions, and the uneven bottoms speed up page assembly.

The slightly elongated page, elegant gray paper, and high-quality printing create an image that is both distinctive and consequential. Fine printing on excellent paper stock is essential to provide an even gray background throughout and to hold the crisp detail on the small, reverse-type numbers seen here and in reverse hairline rules used on tables (not shown).

Director **Geraldine Piorkowski** (left) and Associate Director **Rod Esbrook** (right) of Counseling & Testing and Career Planning & Placement Director **Arthur Eckberg** (center) will administer a three-year "Career Analysis & Placement Project" funded by the Irvin Stern Foundation.

Roosevelt University student **Kendy Kloepfer** met some of the requirements for a major in theatre by taking classes at the Lou Conte Dance Studio, home of the Hubbard Street Dance Company. Cooperative agreements with local institutions enable University students to earn degree credits while learning from experts unique to Chicago.

Two narrow outer columns and a wide center column create a somewhat specialized three-column grid. The layout implies that the center item is the most important one. In the pages shown here, the outer columns are used to present contrasting viewpoints on the same subject, an editorial approach that works particularly well in this format. The outer columns could also be used for quotes and other marginalia, resources related to the main story, brief listings, short profiles or news items, and so on.

The justified text in these pages adds to the formality of the subject matter and to the point-counterpoint approach of the editorial.

The blueprint gives dimensions and type specs for the nameplate on the cover. On subsequent pages, as in the one shown below left, the top

of the text block is 9p from the top trim, so that would be the dimension to use for the top margin on the page setup.

The word "Bulletin" is Bodoni Poster, condensed in FreeHand, placed in PageMaker, and cropped to clip off the bottom of the letters, which makes the type look as if it's emerging from behind the rule. You can now create the same effect in PageMaker. Use the Set Width option to condense the type, and then use the Group It Addition to turn the type into an EPS graphic, which enables you to use the cropping tool. (In order to use the Group It Addition, you must have at least two elements, so use a small white box or a reverse-type period.)

The Avant Garde ID lines on the cover and inside page were set with open letter and word spacing so that the "Educational Advancement" line fills the three-column measure.

The depth of the framed illustrations (in the center column on both pages) is a guideline only. The placement of visuals in the center column is best at the bottom of the page, although the top is also acceptable.

Space between art, captions, rules, and adjacent body text is often a difficult detail in page assembly unless you are working on a very precise grid. The closer any two elements are to each other, the more related they will seem to the reader. In these samples, note that the caption is closer to the picture frame below it than to the rule above, and the rule is closer to the caption than to the preceding text.

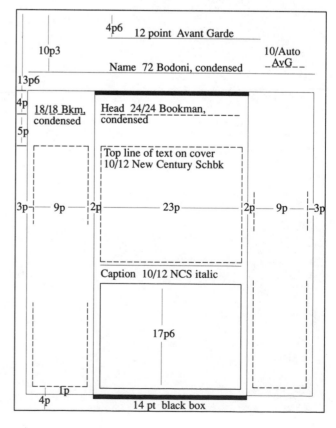

A S S O C I A T I O N

BULLETIN

TEACHERS
ADMINISTRATORS
COUNSELORS

PARENTS
SOCIAL WORKERS
PSYCHOLOGISTS

E D U C A T I O N A L   A D V A N C E M E N T   I N   A M E R I C A

A Case for Gradual Growth in Our Schools

Feugait nulla facilisi. Nam liber tempor cum soluta nobis eleifend option congue nihil imperdiet doming id

quod mazim placerat facer possim assum. Lorem ipsum dolor sit amet, consectetuer adipiscing elit, sed

Diam nonummy nibh euismod tincidunt ut laoreet dolore magna aliquam erat volutpatUt wisi enim ad minim veniam, quis nostrud exerci tation ullamcorper suscipit lobortis nisl ut aliquip ex ea commodo conse

A Primer for School Administrators in the Nineties

Torem ipsum dolor sit amet, consectetuer adipiscing elit, sed diam nonummy nibh euismod tincidunt ut laoreet dolore magna aliquam erat volutpat. Ut wisi enim ad minim veniam, quis nostrud exerci tation ullamcorper suscipit lobortis nisl ut aliquip ex ea commodo consequat.

Duis autem vel eum iriure dolor in hendrerit in vulputate velit esse molestie consequat, vel illum dolore eu feugiat nulla facilisis at vero eros et accumsan et iusto odio dignissim qui blandit praesent luptatum zzril delenit augue duis dolore te feugait nulla facilisi. Lorem ipsum dolor sit amet, consectetuer adipiscing elit, sed diam nonummy nibh euismod tincidunt ut laoreet dolore magna aliquam erat volutpat. Ut wisi enim ad minim veniam, quis nostrud exerci tation ullamcorper suscipit lobortis nisl ut aliquip ex ea commodo consequat.

Duis autem vel eum iriure dolor in hendrerit in vulputate velit esse molestie consequat, vel illum dolore eu feugiat nulla facilisis at vero eros et accumsan et iusto odio dignissim qui blandit praesent luptatum zzril delenit augue duis dolore te

Aliquip ex ea commodo consequat. Duis autem vel eum iriure dolor in hendrerit in vulputate velit esse mo

The Wisdom of Revolutionary Change in Education

Autem vel eum iriure dolor in hendrerit in vulputate velit esse molestie consequat, Vel illum dolore eu feugiat nulla facilisis at vero eros et accumsan et iusto odio dignissim qui blandit praesent luptatum zzril delenit augue duis dolore te feugait nulla facilisi.

Lorem ipsum dolor sit amet, consectetuer adipiscing elit, sed diam nonummy nibh euismod tincidunt ut laoreet dolore magna aliquam erat volutpat.

Narrow outer columns in a three-column grid are useful for publications as diverse as catalogs and technical journals.

In text-heavy publications, such as the one shown below, the narrow outer column can provide much-needed white space when reserved for art, captions, breakouts, and marginalia.

When you wrap ragged right text around a rectangular graphic, you get a much neater appearance if the graphic juts into the flush left margin.

The body text in the sample is 10/12 Galliard. The display type is Futura Condensed Extra Bold, set in 30-, 14-, and 10-point sizes. The captions are 10/12 Futura Heavy.

A classic catalog format on the facing page uses rules, art, white space, and the edge of text blocks to frame pictures. The art and text requirements dictate the size of the units, the only restraints being the vertical rules (and even those can be violated effectively).

The blueprint shows measurements for the sample below. To set up the format, specify 4p side margins and 3 columns with 1p6 space between; then drag the column guides to the measurements shown in the blueprint.

The grid for the catalog on the facing page is similar, but the left edge of the text is flush with the column rules, which drop out behind the text. This maintains the structure of the rules while providing maximum measure for copy. To construct this grid, position the vertical rules, including those in the page frames, at these intervals: 3p, 17p, 17p, 11p, 3p.

The type reinforces the impression of variety, with six different faces used. From top to bottom, they are Futura Condensed, Aachen Bold, Avant Garde, Palatino Italic, Franklin Gothic Heavy, and American Typewriter.

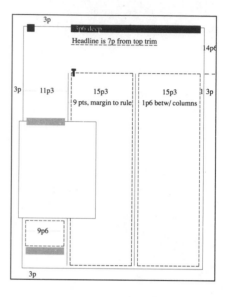

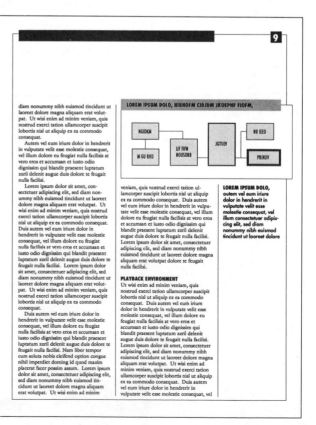

The Most Realistic Stuffed Animals You Ever Saw

LOREM IPSUM DOLOR SIT AMET, sectetuer adipiscing elit, sed diam nonummy nibh euismod tincidunt ut laoreet dolore magna aliquam erat volutpat. Ut wisi enim ad minim veniam, quis nostrud exerci tation ullamcorper suscipit lobortis nisl ut aliquip ex ea commodo consequat. Duis autem vel eum iriure dolor in hendrerit in vulputate velit esse molestie consequat, vel illum dolore eu feugiat nulla facilisis at vero eros et accumsan et iusto odio dignissim qui blandit praesent luptatum zzril delenit augue duis dolore te feugait nulla facilisi. Lorem ipsum dolor sit amet, consectetuer adipiscing elit, sed diam nonummy nibh euismod tincidunt ut laoreet dolore magna aliquam erat

UT WISI ENIM AD veniam, quis nostrud exerci tation ullamcorper suscipit lobortis nisl ut aliquip ex ea

UT WISI ENIM AD veniam, quis nostrud exerci tation ullamcorper suscipit

LOREM IPSUM DOLO, autem vel eum iriure dolor in hendrerit in vulputate velit esse molestie consequat, vel illum consectetuer ad-ipiscing elit, sed diam

FOUR-COLUMN GRIDS

Four-column grids are even more versatile than three-column formats. They provide an opportunity for varied page design within the same publication and for dramatic contrast among visual elements of different sizes. These grids are used frequently in magazines, newspapers,

Boxed sidebars work extremely well in a four-column setting, and can be sized with considerable variety depending on the number and depth of the columns used.

A half-page sidebar prints against a gray tone, with two narrow columns at the bottom combined to accommodate tables. Note that the box extends beyond the page frame, a technique you see frequently in graphic design today. Here those extra 9 points make it possible for the text set in the four-column format to run at the same 9-pica measure as the unboxed text. (Usually you lose a few points to the box.)

The "At a Glance" headline is used repeatedly over charts and graphs, which, with their captions, are self-contained items. A three-column treatment is shown, although other sizes are used as well.

The Times Roman running text is set 8/10 ragged right. Text this small really requires the narrow 9-pica column measure. Tables, captions, and headlines are set in a sans serif face for contrast.

Repeating headlines are inset between gray rules, with shorter rules on each end providing a spot of red that livens up the mostly text pages. The second color is repeated in charts and rules under initial caps.

Display type at the top of News Briefs pages, like the one shown below right, are tickertape-style previews of the stories on that page.

Design: Kimberly Mancebo, Robert Bryant Associates (Campbell, CA)

Pages from TeleVisual Market Strategies, *published ten times per year by Telecommunications Productivity Center. Trim size: 8-1/2 by 11*

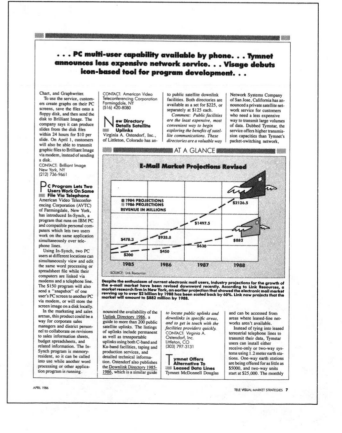

and newsletters. They are also well suited to reference material, directories, price sheets, and other documents that require collecting many small items on a page.

But four-column grids are also more demanding to work with and require more decisions throughout the design and production process. Inherent in their flexibility, also, is the need for balance, proportion, and a deft handling of detail.

Narrow columns also require special care with typography. The type size should be relatively small, to be in proportion to the column width, and so the face must be chosen for ease of readability. With relatively few words in a line, you need to watch for excessive hyphenation. Generally, you should avoid more than two hyphens in a row. Also, a narrow column accentuates the uneven spacing inherent in justified text, so choose that style with caution.

The ease of combining running text set to a two- and a four-column measure is a definite advantage of the four-column grid. As in the previous sample, serif and sans serif faces are used for contrast.

The bold 2-point rules and unusual folio and publication identification in the upper right corner add to the distinctive and contemporary look of the page.

The graphic combines bit-mapped, graduated-tone, and geometric art. A low-resolution scan of a photo was placed in PageMaker. The same digitized image was imported in FreeHand's template layer; the swimsuit was traced over the template in the drawing layer and filled with a graduated tone; the grid was drawn on a layer above that by cloning a square with a 2-point white line and no fill. The FreeHand art was saved as an EPS file and placed in PageMaker on top of the bit-mapped image. Using PageMaker's Text Wrap option, a graphic boundary was defined around the silhouette and the wraparound text was brought to the front layer to ensure that it printed over the white grid.

13

VERBUM 2.2

try, are losing a battle to stay alive against foreign clothing manufacturers. "Since 1980, 3,000 apparel/textile companies have closed their doors and 350,000 jobs have been lost. Of the $170 billion trade deficit, $20 billion is in the apparel industry.... In 1974, 80% of the shoes sold in this country were made in this country. Now more than 80% of the shoes are imports and footwear manufacturing in this country is practically dead." VanFossen was vice president of Corporate Information Services at Wolverine Worldwide, makers of Hush Puppies shoes, when he analyzed the company's declining competitiveness in marketplace would only be turned around with a fully automated factory. The design of the footwear in 3-D appeared to be the answer. "If I could design a shoe in 3-D, then I would have the data I needed to drive an automated factory," he concluded. "Everything you needed to know about price of material, what you had to do with it, how you had to stitch it together — I'd have all this information. That was what I was after."

In 1983 VanFossen started Computer Design Inc. in Grand Rapids, MI which was partially financed at that time by Wolverine. CDI installed their first system about five years ago at H.H. Cutler Co. of Grand Rapids, a childrens' wear company. Since then they have installed more than 50 systems in the U.S. and Europe. The CDI system is IBM PC-based, and the software starts at about $25,000. The designer can visualizes garment in 3-D on the screen and the program will automatically create 2-D flat pattern pieces. According to Jerry Johnson, vice president of Marketing at CDI, "On our CAD systems today designers can design fabrics, then wrap those fabrics onto a model to actually see how it would look. Change colors and try it again in minutes, not hours or days as it now takes to repaint or recolor fabric designs. Change necklines, sleeves, add pockets, take pockets away...all of these functions can be performed on our computer. These functions can greatly reduce product development time."

INTUITION AND INFORMATION IN FASHION DESIGN

Jackie Shapiro became one of the first fashion designers in the United States to explore the application of the computer with fashion design when she picked up her first Macintosh in 1984. She first used the computer to help develop her own line called "GARB", or Global Apparel Resource Bank, and even then she claimed that the computer was a vital part of her design process. "GARB has taken available technology and applied it...for designing clothing. To experiment and explore an infinite number of design solutions. To visualize...garments before making them. To coordinate one silhouette with another. To create, store and retrieve frequently used images: bodies, basics, prints, parts, stuff (garment treatments). To scale for measurements for pattern specification detail. To design labels, logos, illustrate...and to write this."

But using a computer alone does not make one a great de

CUSTOMERS LIKE TO DESIGN IT THEMSELVES

One Southern California store blends fashion design with a novel marketing approach. The store's name is Softwear Swimwear and they sell custom swimsuits "designed" on a computer.

Liz Norling and Gary Leeds opened a swimwear boutique which featured an unusual gimmick of allowing customers create their own sportswear. "Not necessarily a gimmick but a new twist." Liz corrected me. "In order to succeed in this day and age in retail, one needs a unique idea." The customer's image in a swimsuit would be scanned into a color computer program, and the customer could then select from 300 fabric patterns which can be projected on the scanned image of the sportswear on the computer monitor. That way the customer would know exactly what the swimsuit would look like before it's made.

Fashion trends change quickly, and this is one way for the customer to keep up with the fashion...or start his or her own trend.

"There are problems created by using the computer," acknowledged Norling. "We are working on a solution to the two dimensional look of the person on the screen. There is also a problem of confusing the customer with so many possibilities of color and fabric that it's hard for them to make a decision on which suit they want. We also tend to get into trouble by taking colors from the screen...and then finding out that we do not have the color in stock."

The customer can see three suits on the screen at one time to compare and evaluate which one looks best. The customer's image can also be saved in the computer and pulled up at a later time for design another suit. "This is a good feature" Norling says, "as the store's sales volume can be larger. If they like all three swimsuits they may buy all three! Overall, I think the addition of the computer system to our retail store is a great one as many customers are highly excited about designing their own clothing."

Design: John Odam (San Diego, CA)

Page from Verbum, *published quarterly. Trim size: 8-1/2 by 11*

The flexible size of art in a four-column grid is used to good advantage in this signage manual, where similarities and contrasts in visual details are the heart of the message. In the pages shown, note the possibilities for grouping photos as well as the variety of sizes.

Strong perspective lines in many of the photos lead your eye back into the distance. This depth illusion separates the photographs from the surface of the page. The severity of the grid structure, with the bolder-than-usual column rules, in turn enhances the perception of depth in the photos.

The vertical rules also delineate sections, as seen in the top page.

The text is Times Roman throughout, with italic captions set on a narrower measure with open leading for contrast to the running text. The white space makes it possible to run headlines the same size as body text so that they do not compete with typographic elements in the art.

Design: Denise Saulnier, Communication Design Group Limited (Halifax, Nova Scotia)

Pages from A Guide to Better Signs *published by the City of Halifax.*

Size: 8-1/2 by 11

Neon Signs

Fabrics

A fluorescent powder added to the glass tubing will produce yellow, green, rose and gold light. Very deep rich colours are produced by using coloured glass tubing to add to the colour of the gas.

When neon is used as a window sign, the glass tubing is attached to a sheet of clear acrylic which is suspended from the top of the window and is connected to the transformer by thin wires. Some sign makers prefer to enclose the entire neon sign in a clear acrylic box.

Certain gases (neon, argon, krypton, helium and xenon) contained in a glass vacuum tube will produce a coloured glow when an electrical current is passed through them. In the fabrication process, the glass tubing is heated and can be bent to virtually any shape. The air is removed from the tube and the gas inserted. A transformer is attached, which controls the transmission of electric current to the tube. Paint is used to cover areas of glass tubing which need to remain dark. Various gases produce different colours: neon is red-orange; argon is violet; argon and mercury together are blue; helium is gold; xenon is pale blue; krypton and argon together are purple.

Painted/printed: Fabrics such as cotton canvas, flag nylon, acrylic fabric and vinyl-coated polyester in a variety of colours can have lettering painted or silkscreen printed on and can then be sewn into flags, banners and awnings. Awnings are stretched across frames made of construction steel fixed to the building wall. Awnings can be manufactured to fit the building on which they will be installed and can be made in a wide variety of shapes.

Illuminated awnings use translucent vinyl-coated polyester to transmit light from shielded fluorescent or incandescent lights installed inside the awning. New finishes, materials and technologies have made this one of the most versatile

39

Chapter 6
Lighting techniques

Planning for the illumination of signs is an integral part of the sign design process. Signs, when well lit, can add liveliness to our streets. They create a mood of festivity, drama, excitement and warmth while contributing to the profile of our commercial districts at night.

One technique of sign illumination is to light the entire building front on which the sign is installed. In some cases there will be enough ambient light spilled on the building front from adjacent light sources to allow the sign to be read. (Street number signs can often be read because they are lit by street lights or lights over doorways.)

Decorative lamps can be installed on the exterior of buildings where they will create an atmosphere of warmth or excitement, highlight the architectural details of the building front, as well as lighting both the building's signs and the sidewalk area. Low wattage incandescent bulbs installed in rows or groups are another technique of providing general lighting for buildings and signs which were traditionally used on theatre marquees.

When lighting only the sign itself, spotlights are an efficient solution. Strong focus lights are used to illuminate the sign face from above, the sides or below. Care should be taken in placing spotlights in order to avoid reflection on the sign face. The spotlights should be shielded from the eyes of the viewers. Electrical cables attached to the spotlights should be hidden from sight, incorporated in the sign

support and fed into the building at a location as close to the sign as possible. Advance planning can usually ensure that there won't be unsightly electrical cables draping from the sign to the building or running along the building front.

Interior lit signs with opaque backgrounds and illuminated letters are a refined alternative to the typical electric back lit sign.

Metal faced channel letters with built in light sources mounted away from the walls, create a rather soft halo of light with the letters in silhouette.

Exposed neon lights can be formed to virtually any shape, and require very little maintenance.

The row of frosted glass globes lining the front of this restaurant, provides general lighting for customers and passers-by, while lighting the building's signs at the same time.

Above: Shielded spots light the fascia sign but protect the viewer from any glare.

Right: A projecting sign and a fascia sign are lit by a set of four spots. The electrical cable is fed along the sign support and then directly into the wall.

Above: Channel letters containing neon signs make an effective sign for both day and night.

The need to accommodate different kinds of editorial material often suggests the use of a four-column grid. The pages shown demonstrate the ease of combining two- and four-column settings.

The contents pages use the narrow measure for the short program descriptions on the left-hand page, and the wider measure for a tidy listing of the publication contents on the right. Contrasting column widths provide an immediate visual clue to the reader that these are different kinds of material. Art is sized to both column widths for variety and visual contrast, and the silhouetted dancing figures break the grid and float above it.

Note the implied horizon line that runs across all four pages, 11 picas from the top trim.

The short listings in the Program Highlights work especially well in narrow columns. The boldface dates are Helvetica Black, the listings are Garamond with boldface heads. Garamond is used for the contents page and running text in feature stories as well.

The music headline is Futura Condensed Extra Bold; the Program headline on the facing page is Futura Bold. Display typefaces with a variety of styles enable you to create subtle contrasts within the same type family.

Optical character recognition software (OCR) is a key component in the production cycle. The designer uses a DEST scanner with Publish Pac OCR software to capture text from typewritten copy that is provided by the client. They experience only about a 3 percent error, which the designer attributes to their using clean, double-spaced copy typed in a big, round face (they use Pica) and output on an impact printer. (With smaller faces and dot matrix output, the counters of letters tend to fill in, resulting in error rates as high as 20 percent.) The text is checked for spelling and typesetting conventions (single space after periods, and so on) in Microsoft Word and then formatted in PageMaker.

Design: Tom Suzuki (Falls Church, VA)

Pages from Worldnet *magazine, published bimonthly by the United States Information Agency.*
Trim size: 8-1/4 by 10-3/4

The cover and an inside flap show the contrasting but unified look in a folder that uses the four-column grid to combine two- and four-column settings.

The GTE logo on the cover is aligned left with the type. The underlying grid will almost always suggest an appropriate placement for loose items on the page.

The large, Palatino italic type on the cover shows off the calligraphic nature of this typeface.

The text in the narrow columns hugs the column rules, creating a very crisp left edge that emphasizes the verticality of the page. The loose ragged right margin makes the left edge seem stronger still in comparison.

The horizontal lines running through the map contrast with the strong verticality of the text above. Note the implied vertical edge of the map, aligned left with the second column of text. The map and rules print gray on the inside flap, with different colored dots denoting the locations listed. The cover map, surrounded by graduated tones of color that suggest the dimensionality of the earth, prints as green lines against white, with the background rules in gray.

Design: Weisz Yang Dunkelberger Inc. (Westport, CT)

Pages from The World of GTE, Year-End Highlights.

Trim size: 11 by 33-3/4, double gatefold

The World of GTE

GTE is one of the major corporations in the world, with annual sales and revenues exceeding $15.1 billion and assets of $27.4 billion. It has operations in 48 states and 33 countries. These facilities employ 160,000 people who work in three core businesses: telecommunications, lighting products and precision materials.

Argentina
Buenos Aires *Lighting*, P

Australia
Gosford *Lighting*, P
Queensland *Lighting*, P
Victoria *Precision Materials*, P

Austria
Grossenzerdorf *Lighting*, M

Belgium
Tienen *Lighting*, P
Tienen *Precision Materials*, P

Brazil
Santa Amaro *Precision Materials*, P
Sao Paulo *Lighting*, P
Vinhedo *Lighting*, P

Canada
Brockville, Ont. *Microtel Ltd.*, P*
Burnaby, B.C. *Microtel Ltd.*, P(2),L*
Drummondville, Que. *Lighting*, P
Montreal. Que. *Lighting*, P
Toronto, Ont. *Lighting*, P
Vancouver, B.C. *Microtel Ltd.*, P*
Windsor, Ont. *Precision Materials*, P(5)

Colombia
Bogota *Lighting*, P

Costa Rica
San Jose *Lighting*, P

Denmark
Hvidovre *Lighting*, M

Ecuador
Quito *Lighting*, M

France
Andrezieux-Boutheon *Precision Materials*, P
Barentin *Precision Materials*, P
La Fouillouse *Lighting*, P
Lyon *Lighting*, P
Nantes *Lighting*, P
Reims *Lighting*, P
St. Marcellin *Lighting*, P

Germany
Erlangen *Lighting*, P
Precision Materials, P
Sinsheim *Precision Materials*, P(3)

Greece
Athens *Lighting*, M

Haiti
Port au Prince *Precision Materials*, P

Hong Kong
Lighting, M
Precision Materials, M

Italy
Pero *Lighting*, M
Milan *Precision Materials*, P

Japan
Kahoku *Lighting*, P
Tokyo *Precision Materials*, M

Mexico
Juarez *Lighting*, P
Monterrey *Precision Materials*, P

Netherlands
Breda *Lighting*, P
Haarlem *Lighting*, P

Norway
Vestvollvn *Lighting*, M

Peru
Lima *Lighting*, M

Portugal
Lisbon *Lighting*, M

Singapore
Lighting, M

Spain
Madrid *Lighting*, M

Sweden
Stockholm *Lighting*, M

Switzerland
Geneva *Lighting*, M
Precision Materials, M

Taiwan
Taipei *Lighting*, M

Thailand
Bangkok *Lighting*, M

Trinidad
Mount Hope *Lighting*, M

United Kingdom
Charlestown *Lighting*, P
London *Lighting*, M
Malmesburg *Lighting*, P
Newhaven *Lighting*, P
Swansee *Precision Materials*, P

*Telecommunications plants operated by Microtel Ltd., a part of British Columbia Telephone Company.

Total GTE Employment by Country

Argentina, 340
Australia, 210
Austria, 16
Belgium, 870
Brazil, 1,260
Canada, 19,285
Colombia, 230
Costa Rica, 730
Denmark, 13
Dominican Republic, 2,765
Ecuador, 14
France, 1,525
Germany, 1,180
Greece, 6
Haiti, 950
Hong Kong, 270
Italy, 180
Japan, 385
Mexico, 345
Netherlands, 18
Norway, 11
Panama, 67
Peru, 12
Philippines, 150
Portugal, 10
Singapore, 6
Spain, 80
Sweden, 23
Switzerland, 75
Taiwan, 260
Thailand, 10
Trinidad, 5
United Kingdom, 1,460

Total: 32,761

GTE

One narrow + three wide columns for oversize pages

In a tabloid publication, the four-column grid provides a relatively wide measure for reading text, especially when one column is narrow as in the page shown here.

The body text is 10/13 New Baskerville, a graceful face with a light weight. It makes this oversize, mostly text page inviting and easy to read. The generous use of boldface in the running text emphasizes the "people" focus of the publication and facilitates scanning.

The display type is Helvetica Condensed Black.

The rules for the page frame and columns are a little bolder than is usually found, and the inside rules for the narrow columns run all the way to the page frame. The rigidity of that structure is balanced by white space and appropriately sized type. Note also how the initial caps interrupt the column rule.

The distinctive large folio reverses out of a box, which prints in a second color used also for the page frames, the initial caps in the headlines, and the ballot boxes signalling the end of each piece.

The bold, silhouette-style illustration, used throughout the publication, helps small images hold up on the oversize pages.

Design: Kate Dore, Dore Davis Design (Sacramento, CA)

Page from Communique, *published by Sacramento Association of Business Communicators.*
Trim size: 11 by 17

2

IABC Board

President
Robert L. Deen
Deen & Black
444-8014

First Vice President
Tracy Thompson
Carlson Associates
973-0600

Vice President/Programs
Tamra Weber
Deen & Black
444-8014

Vice President/ Professional Development
Mary Closson
The Packard Group
484-8709

Vice President/ Membership
Terri Lowe
Crocker Art Museum
449-8709

Vice President/ Communications
Pat Macht
AmeriGas/Cal Gas
686-3553

Vice President/ Academic Affairs
Jeff Aran
Sacramento Board of Realtors
922-7711

Treasurer
Diana Russell
Pacific Legal Foundation
444-0154

SYNERGY Chair
Della Gilleran
Della Gilleran Design
446-4616

Past President
Betsy Stone
Sutter Health
927-5211

Staff Secretary
Barbara Davis
Creative Consulting
424-8400

Delegates At Large:
Cindy Simonsen
Hanson Simonsen
451-2270

Rick Cabral
Connolly Development, Inc.
454-1416

Colleen Sotomura
The Sierra Foundation
635-4755

Newsletter Editors
Marisa Alcalay
Mercy San Juan Hospital
537-5245
Mary C. Towne
California Veterinary Medical Association
344-4985

Newsletter Design & Layout
Kate Dore
Dore Davis Design
920-3448

IABC Communiqué
January/February 1988

About Sacramento Communicators

Jolaine Collins, past president of the IABC Denver chapter and a recent addition to IABC Sacramento, will represent District 6 on the IABC Professionalism Committee. **Jan Emerson** has moved from Foundation Health Plan to a new position with the publications department at Sutter Health. **Dan Brown**, Group Director of Public Affairs for Aerojet General, will be the 1988 President of the new Sacramento chapter of the Public Relations Society of America.

IABC 1988 president **Robert Deen** and **Christi Black** have formed the partnership of Deen & Black, Communications and Public Affairs. Christi is the former executive director of the American River Parkway Foundation. They will be joined by IABC member **Tamra Weber**, former Communications Director for United Way, who will be an associate, and **Colleen Jang**, a recent CSU Chico communication graduate and member of the student IABC chapter. The new firm is located in an office building at 2212 K Street recently purchased by fellow IABC member **Della Gilleran** (who will chair SYNERGY in 1988).

Terri Lowe of the Crocker Art Museum is interested in volunteers to assist with Crocker's 1988 Bike-a-Thon fundraiser, scheduled for June. **Robert Deen** will chair the overall event, with IABC'ers **Jolaine Collins** and **Janice White**. Terri's number is 449-8709.

Stacey Eachus, former IABC Sacramento member who went to San Diego in June for a position with the National Cash Register Company, has returned to Sacramento in a public relations position with the California Association of Health Facilities.

The **CSU Chico** student chapter has expressed an interest in repeating the successful exchange program in which students were matched for a day with IABC Sacramento members to observe a typical work day.

The **Sacramento Communications Council** has been restructured as a quarterly meeting of the presidents of the dozen professional communications organizations involved, and will be chaired by the IABC president.

The **IABC's annual international conference** will finally be closer to home in 1988 — Anaheim. It should be an interesting one as the proposed IABC/PRSA merger comes to a head.

Mark your calendars now for upcoming **IABC Sacramento luncheons**, held the first Thursday of each month: Feb. 4, March 3, April 7, and May 5. ■

(Have something to contribute? Send information to Communicator Column, c/o editor, IABC Sacramento, P.O. Box 160481, Sacramento, Ca. 95816.)

Chapter Business

Meet the 1988 IABC Board of Directors

The IABC Sacramento Board of Directors serves on a calendar year basis. Being involved is an important part of the IABC experience, and members are encouraged to contact board members to find out more about the areas of activity outlined below.

Immediate Past President Betsy C. Stone will represent IABC Sacramento at the District level, and as circumstances dictate will speak for the chapter on the proposed IABC/PRSA merger. She is also responsible for organizing the District 6 conference for 1990 which Sacramento will host.

Robert L. Deen, the chapter president is responsible for group's overall direction and functioning.

1st Vice President Tracy Thompson oversees administrative matters and special projects at the president's direction.

Treasurer Diana Russell is responsible for the chapter's finances, including coordinating with the SYNERGY management team.

Vice President, Communications, Pat Macht is responsible for the chapter newsletter, all media relations (meeting notices, awards, etc.), and for any and all activities which relate to the chapter's image and visibility.

Vice President, Membership, Terri Lowe, directs membership recruiting efforts, including correspondence, planning, renewal program, roster, and special efforts as required.

Vice President, Programs, Tamra Weber, surveys the membership for their interests and selects luncheon speakers accordingly, coordinates arrangements, and ensures that monthly meeting notices go out in a timely manner.

Vice President, Academic Affairs, Jeff Aran serves as a liaison to local universities and coordinates with the IABC student chapter at CSU Chico.

Vice President, Professional Development, Mary Closson, develops seminars and programs to enhance members' professional skills and abilities, and conducts the annual membership survey.

Della Gilleran, 1988 SYNERGY Chair, is responsible for the overall direction and management of SYNERGY, Sacramento's coalition-based special event for the communications profession.

Delegates at Large: Rick Cabral, Cindy Simonsen, and Colleen Sotomura serve as at-large members of the board and take responsibility for special assignments as needed.

The board is responsible for the functioning and direction of the Chapter. Members are encouraged to discuss concerns or make suggestions to any board member at any time. ■

Plan On Being Active In 1988

The best way to meet new people, learn new skills and become a part of new groups is through active volunteerism.

Working together on projects gives you a chance to get to know people and for them to get to know you and your skills, capabilities and interests.

IABC/Sacramento encourages members to be involved in both IABC activities and general community activities. Consider your options:

The IABC chapter conducts ongoing efforts such as the scholarship and communications (including the newsletter). The board members responsible for these areas are listed in each issue of the newsletter, with their phone number, and all are interested in hearing from those who want to help.

Community involvement — IABC/Sacramento encourages members to accept leadership positions in community organizations such as United Way, KVIE, March of Dimes, etc. These members deserve and need the support of fellow chapter communicators and the chapter is often approached directly by organizations in need of volunteers.

To help you get involved, the chapter needs to know about your interest. Contact the appropriate board member directly, or let Chapter President Robert Deen know.

Make being an active volunteer part of your plan for self improvement in 1988! ■

Using the center columns

In this four-column grid, photos are enlarged to a two-column measure. The text in the narrow outer columns frames the pictures, and the generous white space provides an opportunity to dramatize the shape of the photos against the structure of the page.

The digitized photos, which are reproduced from a laser printout, need a layout in which the overall composition has more impact than the individual parts. Sizes and placements were chosen for dramatic contrast, with a passive close-up against an active middle shot on the cover and a dancing full-figure long shot against a close-up on the inside page.

The logotype gives the name "FLASH" a strong identity and emphasizes the action and boldness implied by the name. The typeface, Bodoni Poster, doesn't come with a true italic, but you can create the look of an oblique by using the skewing option in the Control Palette. (To skew text you must select it with the pointer tool.) Note that the serifs of the F and the H bleed off the left and right edges of the banner, which themselves have been stretched beyond the text margins.

Futura, used in the story headline and names of the models, is forever stylish. It has graced the cover of virtually every fashion magazine at one time or another. Placing the type on a 15-degree angle creates an additional dimension, a layer that seems to float above the rectilinear grid of the logo, text columns, rules, and photos. Keeping all the names and the headline on the same angle creates organized spontaneity rather than random movement.

MAY/JUNE 1988

MANNER continued from page 1

we can send them right away to clients here that are willing to use brand new people. That starts the ball rolling, and if things start to click right away, they stay in New York. If things don't happen immediately, we ask them to go to Europe and develop a strong book, learn how to really model, and then come back to New York. We deal with several agencies in Milan, Paris and Germany and we try to send models to the appropriate agency. Each individual model is different of course, and how much time each one would stay in Europe varies. It can take a couple of months or even a couple of years to get started. The truth of the matter is, if you are a real good model, you don't need a strong book, you need to have a look that works in New York. If you are a brand new model, and you have that look, you can start to work immediately. We are very lucky to have models like that.

If any men are interested in being with our agency

BILLY HAIRE

F L A S H

CHARLES WINSLOW

they should send a couple a pictures in the mail. Don't spend alot of money on pictures - snapshots will do - put your stats on the back, and send them in. You'll get an answer quickly, usually within a week after we receive them. We answer all mail that we get, but a warning, more than 99% of the people who send in pictures receive a "no."

If you are interested in modeling in New York, you should just take a deep breath, swallow, and come. You can go on and on and wonder and worry, but if you want to model you should come here and see everybody and find out what your chances are. But don't kid yourself. If the answer is "no" the answer is "no". Don't get the attitude of "Well, I'll show them!" The business is much too rough for that kind of attitude. Chances are you won't show them, they'll show you.

MANNER is located at
874 Broadway
New York, NY 10003
(212) 475-5001

9

Bodoni, used for the running text, is hard to beat for typographic elegance. Its alternating thicks and thins give this newsletter a distinctive look— fashionable but not trendy. The type just feels like Fred Astaire dancing. Bodoni needs open leading (10/13 was used) to take advantage of its tall ascenders and descenders without sacrificing legibility.

The logo treatment is adapted as a visual "prop" throughout the publication. On the page above, for example, it becomes a stage on which one of the models dances. The stylized lightning bolt from the logo provides an additional motif that can be used decoratively.

The photographs were scanned and then retouched in an image-editing program. In the Charles Winslow photo, for example, the background was removed to create a silhouette, and the neck area was lightened. Billy Haire's socks were given some tone (they were white in the original).

The images were balanced both for contrast and for light and dark using PageMaker's Image Control feature. The goal was to get enough contrast to be dramatic without letting the technique steal the show from the models themselves. Because laser printer proofs tend to print very heavy blacks, the darkness had to be carefully controlled.

The blueprint on the next page provides the basic grid structure for this and the following design, which conveys a very different image than the one shown here. For type specs for this design, refer to the commentary on these two pages, rather than the ones in the blueprint. Note also that the cover banner here has been stretched 2 picas beyond the side margins defined in the blueprint.

Design: Don Wright (Woodstock, NY)

Pages from Flash, *a bimonthly newsletter for models published by Nautilus Books, designed as a "Page Makeover" for* Publish *Magazine.*
Trim size: 8-1/2 by 11

The business report at right and on the facing page uses the same four-column grid as the fashion newsletter on the previous spread but to very different effect.

The report title in the nameplate is spaced to fill the banner. To achieve this effect, use the Force Justify alignment option. The slash is a hairline rule drawn with the perpendicular tool.

On page 2, the banner is 2p6 deep, with the same fonts and letter-spacing as the nameplate type but dropped down to 14 point. The top of the text block is 5p from the top of the banner.

The charts and graphs were created in PageMaker with 10-point Futura Light type.

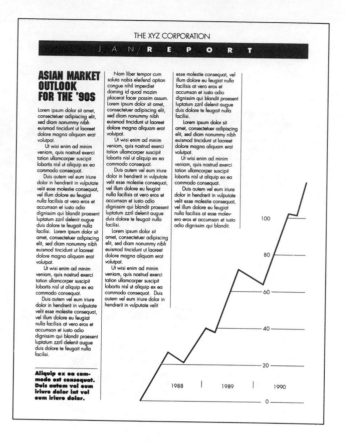

The blueprint shows the details for the sample on the facing page. The same column structure is used for the *Flash* newsletter on the preceding page.

The basic column width is 10p3. In addition to combining the center columns for art as shown in these samples, you could combine any two or three columns for variable art sizes or self-contained sidebars.

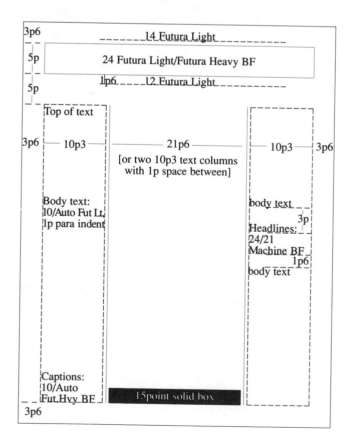

PRODUCTION LANDMARK FOR THE XYZ MACHINE: 100,000 UNITS

Lorem ipsum dolor sit amet, consectetuer adipiscing elit, sed diam nonummy nibh euismod tincidunt ut laoreet dolore magna aliquam erat volutpat. Ut wisi enim ad minim veniam, quis nostrud exerci tation ullamcorper suscipit lobortis nisl ut aliquip ex ea commodo consequat.

Duis autem vel eum iriure dolor in hendrerit in vulputate velit esse molestie consequat, vel illum dolore eu feugiat nulla facilisis at vero eros et accumsan et iusto odio dignissim qui blandit praesent luptatum zzril delenit augue duis dolore te feugait nulla facilisi.

Lorem ipsum dolor sit amet, consectetuer adipiscing elit, sed diam nonummy nibh euismod tincidunt ut laoreet dolore magna aliquam erat volutpat. Ut wisi enim ad minim veniam, quis nostrud exerci tation ullamcorper suscipit lobortis nisl ut aliquip ex ea commodo consequat. Duis autem vel eum iriure dolor in hendrerit in vulputate velit esse molestie consequat, vel illum dolore eu feugiat

Aliquip ex ea comimodo es consequat. Duis vel ex eat com modovel eumet.

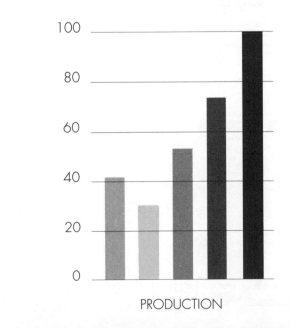

PRODUCTION

Aliquip ex ea commodo est consequat. Duis autem vel eum iriure dolor int vel eum iriure dolor.

nulla facilisis at vero eros et accumsan et iusto odio dignissim qui blandit praesent luptatum zzril delenit augue duis dolore te feugait nulla facilisi. Nam liber tempor cum soluta nobis eleifend option congue nihil imperdiet doming id quod mazim placerat facer possim assum.

DO YOU KNOW YOUR CUSTOMER?

Lorem ipsum dolor sit amet. Consectetuer adipiscing elitt. Sed diam nonummy nibh euismod tincidunt ut laoreet dolore magna aliquam erat volutpat. Ut wisi enim ad minim veniam, quis nostrud exerci tation ullamcorper suscipit lobortis nisl ut aliquip ex ea commodo consequat. Duis autem vel eum iriure dolor in hendrerit in

Vulputate velit esse molestie consequat, vel illum dolore eu feugiat nulla facilisis at vero eros et accumsan et iusto odio dignissim qui blandit praesent luptatum zzril delenit augue duis dolore te feugait nulla facilisi. Lorem ipsum dolor sit amet, consectetuer adipiscing elit, sed diam nonummy nibh euismod suscipit lobortis nisltincidunt ut laoreet dolore magna aliquam erat volutpat.

Within the four-column format you can balance strong vertical and horizontal material, as in the sample on the facing page. The image area for visuals in the first three horizontal units is almost square (9 by 9p3), a nice proportion in this grid, although other sizes are possible.

The layout in the *Safety Tips* page could be used as an expanded contents page, with the cover story in the text column and four different stories, briefly described with art from each, in the outer two columns. When using this technique, which is very effective, the cover art can be repeated inside or can be a detail from a piece of art that runs with the story.

The word "Safety" is 18-point Bookman italic. In order to inset it in the T of "Tips," we created a T with an elongated bar across the top by drawing a black box over the top of an I. In doing this, we encountered WYSIWYG problems: The manually created T aligned with the I on-screen but not on the printed page. We went through several trial-and-error adjustments before an incorrect on-screen image produced a correct printed page.

Events listings are well suited to the narrow measure, as shown in the sample flyer below left. And short introductory copy is still quite readable in one wide column.

The column specifications for the listings use the same measurements as the four-column format in the blueprint. The headline and listing specifications are shown in the details below.

The blueprint specifications are for the *Safety Tips* sample. You can divide the space in other ways to balance the vertical and horizontal divisions; the schematic below shows another possible arrangement. Don't forget white space as an element in the grid.

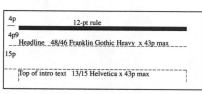

```
4p
         12-pt rule
4p9
     Headline   48/46 Franklin Gothic Heavy  x 43p max
15p

     Top of intro text   13/15 Helvetica x 43p max
```

```
Monday
June 13        2p    12 Fr Gothic Heavy
               2p    13 FGH reversed out of 2p banner
Madison        2p    13 FGH
                     12/13 Helv,  0p3 space after time
7:00 - 9:00 PM
Town Hall
245 Main Street
```

Public Hearings on Zoning and Land Use

The Green County Planning Commission will hold a series of public hearings on coordinating zoning ordinances and land use throughout the county. Green County is the first in New England to address these issues from a county-wide perspective and with a view toward the needs and future of the entire region. The public is encouraged to attend and to comment at the hearings. Written testimony can be brought to the hearings or sent to the commission's offices at the address listed below. The agenda will include:

- Natural resources in an age of changing supply and demand.
- The requirements of site review in the 1990's and beyond.
- Parks, recreation, and wilderness areas: new definitions for the future.
- Incentives for low-income housing.

Monday	Tuesday	Wednesday	Thursday
June 13	June 14	June 15	June 16
Madison	**Cooperstown**	**North River**	**Winchester**
7:00 - 9:00 PM	6:30 - 8:30 PM	7:00 - 9:00 PM	7:00 - 9:00 PM
Town Hall	Community Center	George Washington	Town Hall
245 Main Street	186 River Road	High Auditorium	45 Church Street
		Broadview and Elm	

GREEN COUNTY PLANNING BOARD
23 Center Street
Madison, New Hampshire
25876
307/466-8798

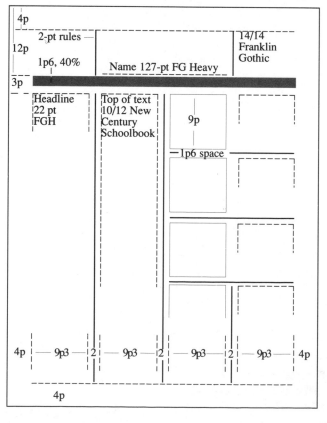

```
4p
12p    2-pt rules                                    14/14
                                                     Franklin
       1p6, 40%          Name 127-pt FG Heavy        Gothic
3p

       Headline     Top of text                9p
       22 pt        10/12 New
       FGH          Century
                    Schoolbook              1p6 space

4p — 9p3 — 2 — 9p3 — 2 — 9p3 — 2 — 9p3 — 4p
                      4p
```

Safety TIPS

from Timberline Power & Light Co.

Tools and Hazards of the Trade

L sectetuer sed adipiscing elite in sed utm diam nonummy nibh euismod tincidunt ut laoreet dolore magna aliquam erat volutpat. Ut wisi enim ad minim veniam, quis nostrud exerci tation dolor in ullamcorper suscipit lobortis nisl ut aliquip ex ea commodo feugiat consequat. Duis autem vel eum iriure dolor in hendrerit in vulputate velit esse molestie vero consequat, vel illum dolore eu feugiat nulla facilisis at vero eros et accumsan et iusto odio dignissim qui blandit.

Praesent luptatum zzril delenit augue duis dolore te feugait nulla facilisi. Lorem ipsum dolor sit amet,et zzril delenit consectetuer adipiscing elit, urt sed diam nonummy nibh euismod tincidunt ut laoreet dolore magna aliquam erat volutpat.

Ut wisi enim ad minim veniam, quis nostrud exerci tation ad minim ullamcorper suscipit lobortis nisl ut aliquip ex ea facilisi. Lorem ipsum commodo Duis autem vel eum iriure dolor iscingin hendrerit in vulputate velit esse molestie consequat, vel illum dolore eu feugiat nulla facilisis at vero eros et

Consequat duis aute vel eum iriure dolor in hendrerit in vulputate velit esse

Molestie consequal illum dolore eu feugiat nulla facilisis at vero eros et accumsan et iusto odio dignissim qui blandit praesent

Tatum zzril delenit augue duis dolore te feugait nulla facilisi. Nam liber tempor cum

Lorem ipsum dolor sit amet, consectetuer adipiscing elit, sed diam nonummy nibh euismod tincidunt ut laoreet dolore magna aliquam erat volutpat.

Ut wisi enim ad minim veniam, quis nostrud exerci tation ullamcorper suscipit

MIXED GRIDS

Grids with multiple and variable column widths can handle the widest range of elements, partly because the columns combine to produce so many different page arrangements. These grids allow for several different widths of text, which in turn allow for more contrast in type sizes and faces to distinguish components from one another. And of course the possibilities for picture placement are even more varied in size and scale than those of the text.

This type of grid is particularly useful in publications such as catalogs, which have many different kinds of elements that need to be distinguished from one another. The format also encourages browsing, with numerous headlines and art providing multiple entry points for busy readers.

Constructing this sort of grid requires a careful analysis of the material to determine the format. And executing the design requires a good eye for balance. This is "breaking the rules" territory and can backfire if you don't know what you're doing.

This five-column grid accommodates newsletter-style essays alongside catalog listings, with short quotes and 19th-century engravings adding verbal and visual personality to the pages. The result is lively, inviting, and well organized.

The variable column width is the key to the diverse page composition. From rule to rule, the narrow outer columns are 7 picas, the wider inner columns are 10p6. With 6-point margins between the text and rules, this creates four different measures for use in this publication:

- 6p (a single narrow column used for quotes)
- 9p6 (a single wider column used for product listings and for the continuation of essays from a previous page)
- 20p (two wide columns used for essays and product listings)
- 16p6 (one narrow and one wide column, used for listings).

In fact, additional combinations are available by combining three wide columns, one narrow and three wide, and, of course, all five columns.

Note the contrast in typeface among the different kinds of text. The essays are Palatino for both body text and headlines (which print blue), with Bodoni initial caps (also blue). The product listings are various weights of Futura. The category heads reverse out of 15-point blue banners; product titles, numbers, and prices also print blue.

The engravings are traditional clip art, photostatted and pasted onto camera-ready pages. Matching 19-century thematic art with contemporary subject matter provides a subtle visual humor, reinforced by placement which invariably breaks the grid.

The short quotes in the narrow columns include humor, anonymous aphorisms, and testimonials from satisfied customers.

*Design: Barbara Lee,
Folio Consulting (Englewood, NJ)*

Pages from the SuperLearning Newsletter/Catalog.
Trim size: 8-1/2 by 11

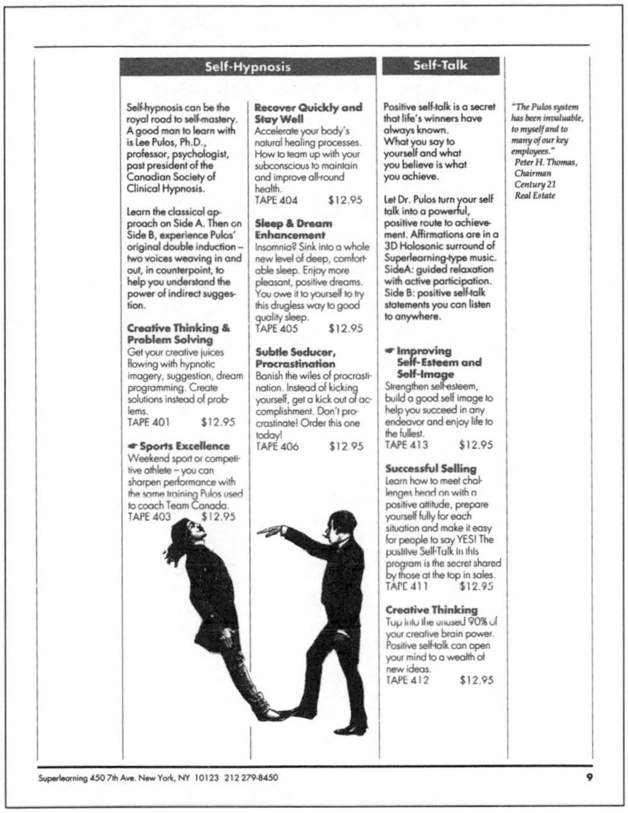

Self-Hypnosis

Self-hypnosis can be the royal road to self-mastery. A good man to learn with is Lee Pulos, Ph.D., professor, psychologist, past president of the Canadian Society of Clinical Hypnosis.

Learn the classical approach on Side A. Then on Side B, experience Pulos' original double induction – two voices weaving in and out, in counterpoint, to help you understand the power of indirect suggestion.

Creative Thinking & Problem Solving
Get your creative juices flowing with hypnotic imagery, suggestion, dream programming. Create solutions instead of problems.
TAPE 401 $12.95

☛ Sports Excellence
Weekend sport or competitive athlete – you can sharpen performance with the same training Pulos used to coach Team Canada.
TAPE 403 $12.95

Recover Quickly and Stay Well
Accelerate your body's natural healing processes. How to team up with your subconscious to maintain and improve all-round health.
TAPE 404 $12.95

Sleep & Dream Enhancement
Insomnia? Sink into a whole new level of deep, comfortable sleep. Enjoy more pleasant, positive dreams. You owe it to yourself to try this drugless way to good quality sleep.
TAPE 405 $12.95

Subtle Seducer, Procrastination
Banish the wiles of procrastination. Instead of kicking yourself, get a kick out of accomplishment. Don't procrastinate! Order this one today!
TAPE 406 $12.95

Self-Talk

Positive self-talk is a secret that life's winners have always known. What you say to yourself and what you believe is what you achieve.

Let Dr. Pulos turn your self talk into a powerful, positive route to achievement. Affirmations are in a 3D Holosonic surround of Superlearning-type music. SideA: guided relaxation with active participation. Side B: positive self-talk statements you can listen to anywhere.

☛ Improving Self-Esteem and Self-Image
Strengthen self-esteem, build a good self image to help you succeed in any endeavor and enjoy life to the fullest.
TAPE 413 $12.95

Successful Selling
Learn how to meet challenges head on with a positive attitude, prepare yourself fully for each situation and make it easy for people to say YES! The positive Self-Talk in this program is the secret shared by those at the top in sales.
TAPE 411 $12.95

Creative Thinking
Tap into the unused 90% of your creative brain power. Positive self-talk can open your mind to a wealth of new ideas.
TAPE 412 $12.95

"The Pulos system has been invaluable, to myself and to many of our key employees."
Peter H. Thomas, Chairman Century 21 Real Estate

Superlearning 450 7th Ave. New York, NY 10123 212 279-8450 9

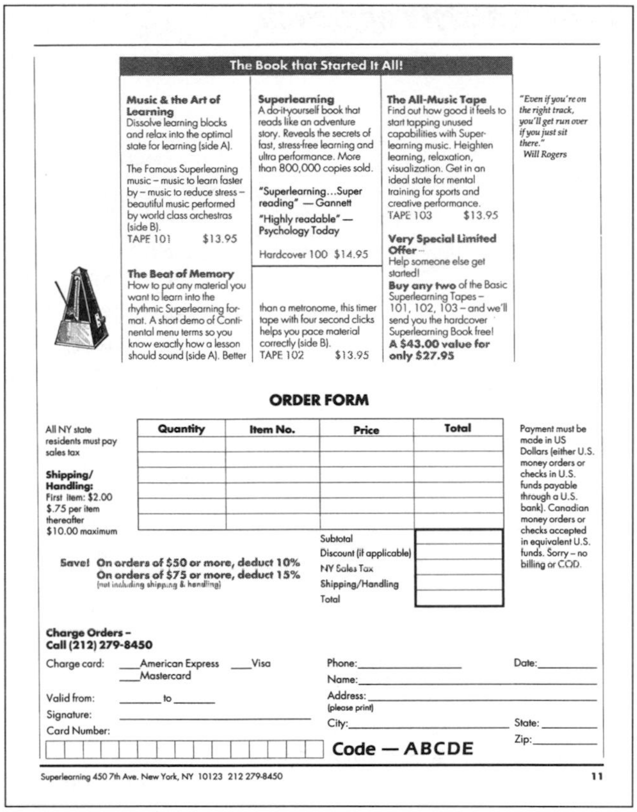

The Book that Started It All!

Music & the Art of Learning
Dissolve learning blocks and relax into the optimal state for learning (side A).

The Famous Superlearning music – music to learn faster by – music to reduce stress – beautiful music performed by world class orchestras (side B).
TAPE 101 $13.95

The Beat of Memory
How to put any material you want to learn into the rhythmic Superlearning format. A short demo of Continental menu terms so you know exactly how a lesson should sound (side A). Better than a metronome, this timer tape with four second clicks helps you pace material correctly (side B).
TAPE 102 $13.95

Superlearning
A do-it-yourself book that reads like an adventure story. Reveals the secrets of fast, stress-free learning and ultra performance. More than 800,000 copies sold.

"Superlearning...Super reading" — Gannett

"Highly readable" — Psychology Today

Hardcover 100 $14.95

The All-Music Tape
Find out how good it feels to start tapping unused capabilities with Superlearning music. Heighten learning, relaxation, visualization. Get in an ideal state for mental training for sports and creative performance.
TAPE 103 $13.95

Very Special Limited Offer –
Help someone else get started!
Buy any two of the Basic Superlearning Tapes – 101, 102, 103 – and we'll send you the hardcover Superlearning Book free!
A $43.00 value for only $27.95

"Even if you're on the right track, you'll get run over if you just sit there."
Will Rogers

ORDER FORM

All NY state residents must pay sales tax

Shipping/Handling:
First Item: $2.00
$.75 per item thereafter
$10.00 maximum

Quantity	Item No.	Price	Total

Subtotal
Discount (if applicable)
NY Sales Tax
Shipping/Handling
Total

Save! On orders of $50 or more, deduct 10%
On orders of $75 or more, deduct 15%
(not including shipping & handling)

Payment must be made in US Dollars (either U.S. money orders or checks in U.S. funds payable through a U.S. bank). Canadian money orders or checks accepted in equivalent U.S. funds. Sorry – no billing or COD.

Charge Orders – Call (212) 279-8450

Charge card: ___American Express ___Visa ___Mastercard

Valid from: _______ to _______

Signature: ______________________

Card Number:

Phone: ______________ Date: __________

Name: ______________________

Address: ______________________
(please print)

City: ______________ State: __________

Zip: __________

Code — ABCDE

Superlearning 450 7th Ave. New York, NY 10123 212 279-8450 11

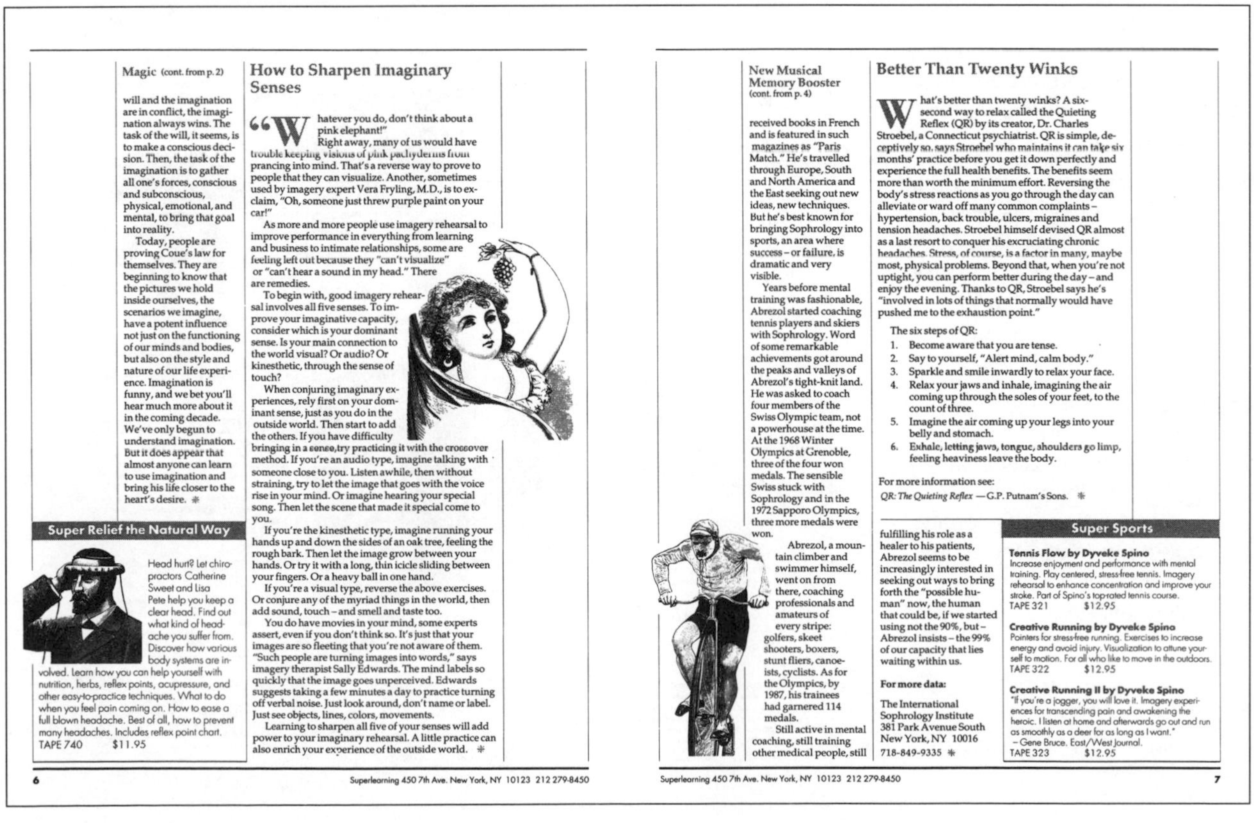

Magic (cont. from p. 2)

will and the imagination are in conflict, the imagination always wins. The task of the will, it seems, is to make a conscious decision. Then, the task of the imagination is to gather all one's forces, conscious and subconscious, physical, emotional, and mental, to bring that goal into reality.

Today, people are proving Coue's law for themselves. They are beginning to know that the pictures we hold inside ourselves, the scenarios we imagine, have a potent influence not just on the functioning of our minds and bodies, but also on the style and nature of our life experience. Imagination is funny, and we bet you'll hear much more about it in the coming decade. We've only begun to understand imagination. But it does appear that almost anyone can learn to use imagination and bring his life closer to the heart's desire. ✻

How to Sharpen Imaginary Senses

"Whatever you do, don't think about a pink elephant!"

Right away, many of us would have trouble keeping visions of pink pachyderms from prancing into mind. That's a reverse way to prove to people that they can visualize. Another, sometimes used by imagery expert Vera Fryling, M.D., is to exclaim, "Oh, someone just threw purple paint on your car!"

As more and more people use imagery rehearsal to improve performance in everything from learning and business to intimate relationships, some are feeling left out because they "can't visualize" or "can't hear a sound in my head." There are remedies.

To begin with, good imagery rehearsal involves all five senses. To improve your imaginative capacity, consider which is your dominant sense. Is your main connection to the world visual? Or audio? Or kinesthetic, through the sense of touch?

When conjuring imaginary experiences, rely first on your dominant sense, just as you do in the outside world. Then start to add the others. If you have difficulty bringing in a sense,try practicing it with the crossover method. If you're an audio type, imagine talking with someone close to you. Listen awhile, then without straining, try to let the image that goes with the voice rise in your mind. Or imagine hearing your special song. Then let the scene that made it special come to you.

If you're the kinesthetic type, imagine running your hands up and down the sides of an oak tree, feeling the rough bark. Then let the image grow between your hands. Or try it with a long, thin icicle sliding between your fingers. Or a heavy ball in one hand.

If you're a visual type, reverse the above exercises. Or conjure any of the myriad things in the world, then add sound, touch – and smell and taste too.

You do have movies in your mind, some experts assert, even if you don't think so. It's just that your images are so fleeting that you're not aware of them. "Such people are turning images into words," says imagery therapist Sally Edwards. The mind labels so quickly that the image goes unperceived. Edwards suggests taking a few minutes a day to practice turning off verbal noise. Just look around, don't name or label. Just see objects, lines, colors, movements.

Learning to sharpen all five of your senses will add power to your imaginary rehearsal. A little practice can also enrich your experience of the outside world. ✻

Super Relief the Natural Way

Head hurt? Let chiropractors Catherine Sweet and Lisa Pete help you keep a clear head. Find out what kind of headache you suffer from. Discover how various body systems are involved. Learn how you can help yourself with nutrition, herbs, reflex points, acupressure, and other easy-to-practice techniques. What to do when you feel pain coming on. How to ease a full blown headache. Best of all, how to prevent many headaches. Includes reflex point chart.
TAPE 740 $11.95

6 Superlearning 450 7th Ave. New York, NY 10123 212 279-8450

New Musical Memory Booster
(cont. from p. 4)

received books in French and is featured in such magazines as "Paris Match." He's travelled through Europe, South and North America and the East seeking out new ideas, new techniques. But he's best known for bringing Sophrology into sports, an area where success – or failure, is dramatic and very visible.

Years before mental training was fashionable, Abrezol started coaching tennis players and skiers with Sophrology. Word of some remarkable achievements got around the peaks and valleys of Abrezol's tight-knit land. He was asked to coach four members of the Swiss Olympic team, not a powerhouse at the time. At the 1968 Winter Olympics at Grenoble, three of the four won medals. The sensible Swiss stuck with Sophrology and in the 1972 Sapporo Olympics, three more medals were won.

Abrezol, a mountain climber and swimmer himself, went on from there, coaching professionals and amateurs of every stripe: golfers, skeet shooters, boxers, stunt fliers, canoeists, cyclists. As for the Olympics, by 1987, his trainees had garnered 114 medals.

Still active in mental coaching, still training other medical people, still fulfilling his role as a healer to his patients, Abrezol seems to be increasingly interested in seeking out ways to bring forth the "possible human" now, the human that could be, if we started using not the 90%, but – Abrezol insists – the 99% of our capacity that lies waiting within us.

For more data:

The International Sophrology Institute
381 Park Avenue South
New York, NY 10016
718-849-9335 ✻

Better Than Twenty Winks

What's better than twenty winks? A six-second way to relax called the Quieting Reflex (QR) by its creator, Dr. Charles Stroebel, a Connecticut psychiatrist. QR is simple, deceptively so, says Stroebel who maintains it can take six months' practice before you get it down perfectly and experience the full health benefits. The benefits seem more than worth the minimum effort. Reversing the body's stress reactions as you go through the day can alleviate or ward off many common complaints – hypertension, back trouble, ulcers, migraines and tension headaches. Stroebel himself devised QR almost as a last resort to conquer his excruciating chronic headaches. Stress, of course, is a factor in many, maybe most, physical problems. Beyond that, when you're not uptight, you can perform better during the day – and enjoy the evening. Thanks to QR, Stroebel says he's "involved in lots of things that normally would have pushed me to the exhaustion point."

The six steps of QR:

1. Become aware that you are tense.
2. Say to yourself, "Alert mind, calm body."
3. Sparkle and smile inwardly to relax your face.
4. Relax your jaws and inhale, imagining the air coming up through the soles of your feet, to the count of three.
5. Imagine the air coming up your legs into your belly and stomach.
6. Exhale, letting jaws, tongue, shoulders go limp, feeling heaviness leave the body.

For more information see:
QR: The Quieting Reflex — G.P. Putnam's Sons. ✻

Super Sports

Tennis Flow by Dyveke Spino
Increase enjoyment and performance with mental training. Play centered, stress-free tennis. Imagery rehearsal to enhance concentration and improve your stroke. Part of Spino's top-rated tennis course.
TAPE 321 $12.95

Creative Running by Dyveke Spino
Pointers for stress-free running. Exercises to increase energy and avoid injury. Visualization to attune yourself to motion. For all who like to move in the outdoors.
TAPE 322 $12.95

Creative Running II by Dyveke Spino
"If you're a jogger, you will love it. Imagery experiences for transcending pain and awakening the heroic. I listen at home and afterwards go out and run as smoothly as a deer for as long as I want."
– Gene Bruce. East/West Journal.
TAPE 323 $12.95

Superlearning 450 7th Ave. New York, NY 10123 212 279-8450 7

A collage-style approach

Within the basic three-column structure, this format allows the designer to nestle variable-width text blocks around art as needed. The large page size makes it possible to present several items on a single page, which reinforces the thematic organization of material and encourages browsing as well.

For this particular publication, the format solves the problem of placing a great many loose elements on the page—each of the items on the page shown includes the publishing information, the book cover, a brief one-paragraph review, text and art excerpted from the book being reviewed, and captions. The collage-style approach is a visual signature of the magazine from which this book spins off.

The underlying structure for this collage-style page is three 17-pica columns.

A pragmatic use of rules and boxes helps organize the disparate elements and separate one item from another. Boxes and silhouettes that overhang the rules create a dimensionality that lightens up the densely packed pages.

Design decisions are required for almost every text block in a grid used with this much flexibility. While most grids dictate the placement of elements on the page, this grid provides but a subtle understructure for the multitude of elements.

The type is from the Helvetica family, an ideal choice for its efficient word count and its legibility in small sizes as well as for the variety afforded within a single type family. The introduction of a second typeface to such a complex page could easily create chaos.

Design: Kathleen O'Neill

Pages from Signal, *a book created by* Whole Earth Review.
Trim size: 10-1/2 by 12-1/8

Playing with frames

This three + two-column format plays with rules to create frames within frames. The underlying grid is very symmetrical and modular, but the elements break through it and out of it in many different and sometimes subtly humorous ways. The resulting playfulness is especially useful in balancing the medical, scientific, and fundamentally difficult subject of aging.

Three 10-pica columns are used for the short items that make up this news section of a monthly magazine. Items whose headlines run across two or three columns take on more importance than those with single-column heads. The column width of the "featured" stories varies: two or three 10-pica columns, one 20-pica column, and two 14p6 columns are all used.

The narrow outer margins (4 picas from rule to rule) are used exclusively for captions. Brevity is essential in lines that rarely contain more than a single word.

The overall effect, which is very open and accessible, is achieved by sacrificing a considerable amount of text space. A distinct advantage of the format, not seen in the pages reproduced here, is that it creates a strong contrast when editorial and advertising pages face each other on the same spread.

Art almost invariably breaks out of the grid, creating a variety of depth illusions. Type, too, can appear to move through a three-dimensional page: The clipped-off bottoms of the Anti-Aging headline (left) make the type appear to be moving down through the box.

The body text is Helvetica with Futura headlines.

The paper is a heavy, noncoated, gray stock, which adds considerable bulk to a 36-page magazine. Blue and burgundy, used for banners, headlines, and tones behind the featured items, add color and reinforce the modular structure. Another similarly formatted section in the magazine uses green and purple.

Design: Regina Marsh (New York, NY)

Pages from Longevity, *published monthly by Omni International. Trim size: 8-1/4 by 10-3/4*

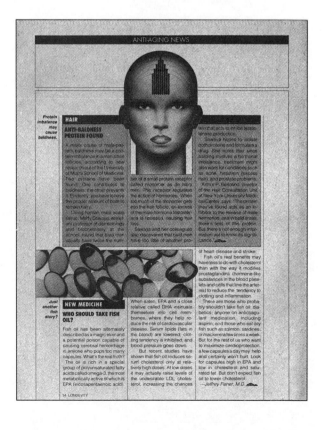

Variable column width

When you have variable-length components and want to contain each one within a single column, you can let the length of each item dictate the column width. Putting together such a page is a little like doing a jigsaw puzzle. This layout would be exceedingly expensive and time-consuming using traditional typesetting and pasteup. But the ability to stretch or shrink a text block in PageMaker gives you extraordinary on-screen control over the width and depth of each column. You assemble this kind of page from left to right and then make adjustments as needed.

The key to balancing all the elements on the page is to establish some horizontal constants in either text placement or illustration depth. In addition to unifying the page, these horizontal guidelines will help keep you from getting lost in a sea of choices.

A horizontal grid is used to balance the elements in variable-width columns on the two pages shown here. The headings for all items sit on a baseline 4p6 from the top of the page. The first line of body text sits on one of three baselines, all measured from the top trim: 11p, 27p6, or 39p.

The margins are 3 picas for the sides and bottom and 4 picas for the top.

The text is 10/12.5, with headlines in Helvetica Condensed Black and body text in Helvetica Condensed. Condensed sans serif faces are a good choice for short copy blocks in narrow columns.

The "Allsport" title is Helvetica Condensed Black, further condensed and rotated.

The rules are 1 point—heavier than usually found—in order to give more structure to the page.

ALLSPORT

Duis autem vel eum

Duis autem vel eum iriure dolor in esse hendrerit in vulputate velit esse molestie consequat, vel illum dolore eu feugiat nulla facilisis at vero eros et accumsan et iusto odio dignissim qui blandit praesent luptatum zzril delenit augue duis dolore te feugait nulla facilisi.

Lorem ipsum dolor sit amet, consectetuer adipiscing elit, sed diam nonummy nibh euismod tincidunt ut laoreet dolore magna aliquam erat volutpat. Ut wisi enim ad minim veniam, quis nostrud exerci tation ullamcorper suscipit lobortis nisl ut aliquip ex ea commodo consequat.

Duis autem vel eum iriure dolor in hendrerit in vulputate velit esse molestie consequat, vel illum dolore eu feugiat nulla facilisis at vero eros et accumsan et iusto odio dignissim qui blandit praesent luptatum zzril delenit augue duis dolore te feugait nulla facilisi. Nam liber tempor cum soluta nobis eleifend option congue nihil imperdiet doming id quod mazim placerat facer possim assum. Lorem ipsum dolor sit amet, consectetuer adipiscing elit, sed diam nonummy nibh euismod tincidunt ut laoreet dolore magna

Lorem ipsum dolor sit amet, consectetuer adipiscing elit, sed diam nonummy nibh euismod tincidunt ut laoreet dolore magna aliquam erat volutpat. Ut wisi enim ad minim veniam, quis nostrud exerci tation ullamcorper suscipit lobortis nisl ut aliquip ex ea commodo consequat.

Lorem ipsum

Aliquam erat esse volutpat. Ut wisi enim ad minim veniam, quis nostrud exerci tation ullamcorper suscipit lobortis nisl ut aliquip ex ea commodo consequat.

Duis autem vel eum iriure dolor in hendrerit in vulputate velit esse molestie consequat, vel illum dolore eu feugiat nulla facilisis at vero eros et accumsan et iusto odio dignissim qui

Duis autem vel eum iriure dolor in hendrerit in vulputate velit esse molestie lorem ipsum

Blandit praesent luptatum zzril delenit augue duis dolore te feugait nulla facilisi. Lorem ipsum dolor sit amet, consectetuer adipiscing elit, sed diam nonummy nibh euismod tincidunt ut laoreet dolore magna Lorem ipsum dolor sit amet, consectetuer adipiscing elit, sed diam nonummy nibh euismod tincidunt ut laoreet dolore magna aliquam erat

volutpat. Ut wisi enim ad minim veniam, quis nostrud exerci tation ullamcorper suscipit lobortis nisl ut aliquip ex ea commodo consequat.

Duis autem vel eum iriure dolor in hendrerit in vulputate velit esse molestie consequat, vel illum dolore eu feugiat nulla facilisis at vero eros et accumsan et iusto odio dignissim qui blandit praesent luptatum zzril delenit augue duis dolore te feugait nulla facilisi. Lorem ipsum dolor sit amet, con-

Ut wisi enim ades min ut wisi enim ad min

Sectetuer adipiscing elit, sed diam nonummy nibh euismod tincidunt ut laoreet dolore magna aliquam erat volutpat.

Ut wisi enim ad minim veniam, quis nostrud exerci tation ullamcorper suscipit lobortis nisl ut aliquip ex ea commodo consequat. Duis autem vel eum iriure dolor in hendrerit in.

Lorem ipsum dolor sit amet, consectetuer adipiscing elit, sed diam nonummy nibh euismod tincidunt ut laoreet dolore magna aliquam erat volutpat. Ut wisi enim ad minim veniam, quis nostrud exerci tation ullamcorper suscipit lobortis nisl ut aliquip ex ea commodo consequat.

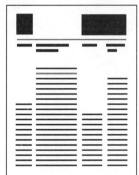

In the schematics above, the approach is to establish a horizon line for the headlines and for body text and then to hang copy from those lines in variable column widths. Art is sized to match the text width in each column, with variable heights but with a common baseline and a fixed amount of space between the bottom of the text and the top of the art.

The leftmost schematic shows the same approach in a vertically oriented page. Another approach is to have even bottoms and ragged tops, with art and headlines providing another horizontal constant at the top of the page.

Duis au

Vulputate velit esse molestie consequat, vel illum dolore eu feugiat nulla facilisis at vero eros et accumsan et iusto odio dignissim qui blandit praesent luptatum zzril delenit augue duis dolore te feugait nulla facilisi. Nam liber tempor cum soluta nobis eleifend option congue nihil imperdiet doming id quod mazim placerat facer possim assum.

Lorem ipsum dolor sit amet, consectetuer adipiscing elit, sed diam nonummy nibh euismod tincidunt ut laoreet dolore magna aliquam erat volutpat. Ut wisi enim ad minim veniam, quis nostrud exerci tation ullamcorper suscipit lobortis nisl ut aliquip ex ea commodo consequat. Duis

liriure dolor in hendrerit in vulput

Autem vel eum iriure dolor in hendrerit in vulputate velit esse molestie consequat, vel illum dolore eu feugiat nulla facilisis at vero eros et accumsan et

iusto odio dignissim qui blandit praesent luptatum zzril delenit augue duis dolore te feugait nulla facilisi. Lorem ipsu dolor sit amet consecteadipiscing elit, se.

quis nostrud exerci tation ullamcorper suscipit lobortis nisl ut aliquip ex ea c minUt wisi enim

Diam nonummy nibh euismod tincidunt ut laoreet dolore magna. Lorem ipsum dolor sit amet, consectetuer adipiscing elit, sed diam nonummy nibh euismod tincidunt ut laoreet dolore magna aliquam erat volutpat. Ut wisi enim ad minim veniam, quis nostrud exerci tation ullamcorper suscipit lobortis nisl ut aliquip ex ea commodo consequat.

Duis autem vel eum iriure dolor in hendrerit in vulputate velit esse molestie consequat, vel illum dolore eu feugiat nulla facilisis at vero eros et accumsan et iusto odio dignissim qui blandit praesent luptatum zzril delenit augue duis dolore te feugait nulla facilisi.

Lorem ipsum dolor sit amet, consectetuer adipiscing elit, sed diam nonummy nibh euismod tincidunt ut laoreet dolore magna aliquam erat volutpat. Ut wisi enim ad minim veniam, quis nostrud exerci tation ullamcorper suscipit lobortis nisl ut aliquip ex ea commodo consequat.Duis autem vel eum iriure dolor in hendrerit in vulputate velit esse molestie consequat, vel illum dolore eu

Feuga

Feugiat nulla facilisis at vero eros et accumsan et iusto odio dignissim qui blandit praesent.

Lorem ipsum dolor sit amet

luptatum zzril delenit augue duis dolore te feugait nulla facilisi. Nam liber tempor cum soluta nobis eleifend option congue nihil imperdiet doming id quod mazim placerat facer possim assum. Lorem ipsum dolor sit amet, consectetuer adipiscing elit, sed diam nonummy nibh euismod tincidunt ut laoreet dolore magna aliquam erat volutpat.

Ut wisi enim ad minim veniam, quis nostrud exerci tation ullamcorper suscipit lobortis nisl ut aliquip ex ea commodo consequat. Duis autem vel eum iriure dolor in hendrerit in vulputate velit esse molestie consequat, vel illum dolore eu feugiat nulla facilisis at vero eros et accumsan et iusto odio dignissim qui blandit praesent luptatum zzril delenit augue duis dolore te esse.

SECTION 2

A PAGEMAKER PORTFOLIO

CHAPTER 4

PROMOTIONS: FLYERS, POSTERS, FOLDERS, AND BROCHURES

Promotional literature is the most image-conscious of all publications. Here, more than anywhere else, the medium really is the message. That doesn't mean that the words don't count, but it does mean that the art, the graphic design, the texture of the paper, the color of the ink, and the overall production values make a first impression that it's difficult for the text to overcome if that impression is off the mark.

Of course, the image and production values that are appropriate vary tremendously. At one end of the spectrum, the category includes simple flyers that grass-roots organizations and small businesses leave under car windshield wipers; at the other end are slick four-color brochures distributed by large corporations to prospective clients. Both extremes, and everything in between, share the need to consider carefully the image they want to convey in order to produce the desired effect.

Promotional literature also presents a conceptual challenge that is rarely found in other kinds of business publications. If you can discover some unique perspective on your event, service, or product, you can turn that into an original and effective promotional idea. This is where catchy slogans, visual metaphors, and all the other tricks of Madison Avenue are used to good advantage. To be sure, if you're promoting a financial service or a funeral home, the style will be decidedly different than for a local eatery or theater group. But regardless of how frivolous or somber the concern, a fresh perspective on it will gain attention and set it apart from the competition.

FLYERS & POSTERS

You can look at flyers as modest posters, and posters as flyers on a grand scale. Although their budgets may differ dramatically, flyers and posters share the challenges inherent in any single-page promotion. To be effective, they have to deliver the strong graphic impression of a well-designed cover and the clear, concise information of a data sheet. Without the graphic appeal, the promotion will get lost amid all the other messages competing for the prospect's time and money; without the clear information, the flyer or poster becomes a piece of art, interesting to look at, perhaps, but probably not very effective.

Flyers and posters in this section

- *California Association of Midwives*—a photographic mandala for a fashion show fund-raiser
- *Student Recital*—the easy appeal of borders
- *Holiday Sale*—well-organized information
- *WGBH Brown Bag Lunches*—a simple format that works
- *A Walk in the Woods*—an illustrated theater announcement
- *AIGA poster*—the drama of life-size bit-mapped art
- *How to Design a Page*—and in doing so take advantage of all the technology

A scanned photo, copied and manipulated to create a mandala-like image, is a dynamic graphic element for flyers and posters that is relatively easy to create. The digitized image was rotated and flopped in MacPaint to create four versions oriented in different directions. Each version was saved as a separate file and imported into PageMaker, where the individual pieces were all composed into a single image.

The four corners created by the negative space of the art inside the 8-point-rule box provide an effective way to organize the type. The vertical rules add additional structure that keeps the type from floating in space.

The type and art print black against a shocking pink background, enhancing the playful feeling that sets the tone for the fashion show benefit.

The typeface is Garamond with a Futura Extra Bold headline.

Design: John Odam (San Diego, CA)
Flyer for a benefit auction for the California Association of Midwives. Trim size: 8-1/2 by 11

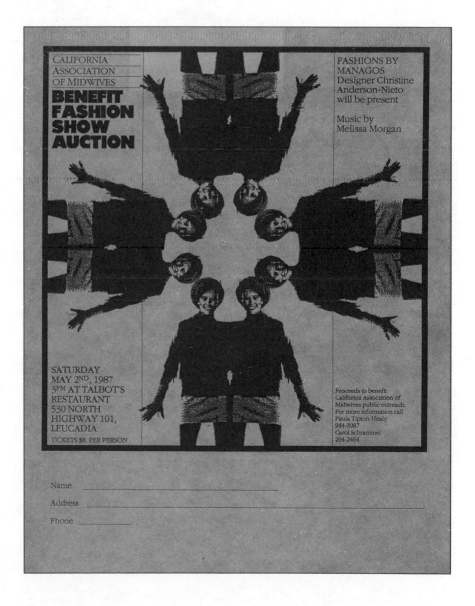

CALIFORNIA ASSOCIATION OF MIDWIVES
BENEFIT FASHION SHOW AUCTION

FASHIONS BY MANAGOS
Designer Christine Anderson-Nieto will be present

Music by Melissa Morgan

SATURDAY MAY 2ND, 1987 3PM AT TALBOT'S RESTAURANT 530 NORTH HIGHWAY 101, LEUCADIA
TICKETS $8. PER PERSON

Proceeds to benefit California Association of Midwives public outreach. For more information call Paula Tipton-Healy 944-3987 Carol Schrammel 264-2464

Name _____

Address _____

Phone _____

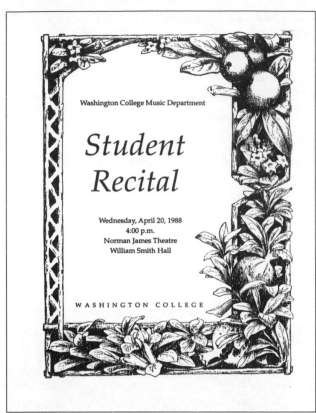

Borders from electronic or traditional clip art provide a quick, easy, and effective way to dress up a simple message. The one here is from *Victorian Pictorial Borders*, a book of public-domain art published by Dover Press. The designer simply photocopied the art to the desired size, ran out type on a laser printer, pasted the two together on an 8-1/2- by 11-inch page, and photocopied the result.

The large Palatino headline is easy to read. It combines modern and classical elegance in a style that works well with the floral border and is appropriate for the event.

When considering borders from the ever-expanding clip art universe, keep in mind that you can use and modify segments of them to bracket and separate text.

With desktop publishing, a small organization can take a hand-drawn sketch (shown at right) to a quick printer for an inexpensive printed page (shown above). Not too many years ago, the rough sketch served as the final promotion piece.

The information is organized with an eye toward line-for-line scanning and uses horizontal rules to reinforce that approach.

The type is Palatino throughout. Text set in all caps is generally difficult to read, but the choice works here for such a straightforward announcement of what, where, who, and when.

The illustration was drawn by hand and pasted manually onto the electronically composed page.

Design (above left): Diane Landskroener (Chestertown, MD)

Flyer for a recital at Washington College. Trim size: 8-1/2 by 11

Design (above right): Barbara Trupp; art production: Lisa Marks-Ellis, Synthesis Concepts (Chicago, IL)

Flyer for crafts sale. Trim size: 8-1/2 by 11

This simple format (above left), appropriately printed on brown kraft paper, announces events in a series of "brown bag lunch" lectures and demonstrations. The format establishes a strong identity for the series and is easy to execute for each event.

The shadowed box is a very simple attention-getting graphic. It is left in place on the template for the flyer so that only the type needs to be added for each new event.

The information above and below the boxed copy identifies the series and sponsor and is also a standing item in the template. It prints in red, so it looks stamped on.

The type is all from the Helvetica family.

A theater announcement (above right) features art based on the title of the play. The art originated as a charcoal drawing on very grainy paper. It was scanned at 72 dots per inch and resized proportionally in PageMaker, creating an image that has the feeling of a lithograph. Framing and centering the art in the formal layout increases its importance on the page.

The hairline border frames the page on three sides only. The dotted border around the coupon (from PageMaker's Lines menu) visually closes the bottom of the page and is an effective way to call attention to the coupon.

The typeface is Palatino, with contrast achieved through size, spacing, and placement. Note that in the two lines at the top of the page, the first line has open spacing and the second line normal spacing so that both are the same width as the art below. You can use the Force Justify alignment option to create this effect. (To do so, you have to define the text width as the width of the art.) Note also the proportions in the treatment of the rule between the title and the author.

Design (above left): Andrew Faulkner (Boston, MA)

Flyer for the WGBH brown bag lunches. Trim size: 8-1/2 by 11

Design (above right): John Odam and Doris Bittar (San Diego, CA)

Flyer for a benefit performance for The San Diego Chapter of Freeze/SANE. Trim size: 8-1/2 by 11

This poster for a lecture by two pioneers of electronic art speaks in the language of their subject: the new technology and its impact on graphic design.

A digitized image of the two lecturers is printed almost life-size. The reduction on this page does not do justice to the impact of the 17- by 22-inch poster. This bold enlargement of a digitized image gives the feeling of a glimpse into the future.

The art originated as a slide. It was digitized, saved in MacPaint format, and scaled in PageMaker. The oversize page was tiled and pasted together manually.

The text is handled in three panels that jut into the picture plane. A second color (orange) highlights the first name of each speaker and the date and sponsor of the event.

Folded twice, the poster also serves as a self-mailer.

Quoting from the poster: "New electronic formats, including the personal computer, CD's, and video imaging systems, have opened up vast new visual possibilities and have inexorably drawn our profession into a communications environment which is multi-media and interactive. The formerly separate disciplines of writing, visualization, and sound making are joined through these tools. Eric predicts a return to the designer as generalist—fluent in more than one discipline—and feels we need to readjust our notion of what constitutes adequate training for this broader role."

Design: Chris Pullman, WGBH Design (Boston, MA)

Poster for AIGA/Boston lecture by April Greiman and Eric Martin.
Trim size: 17 by 22

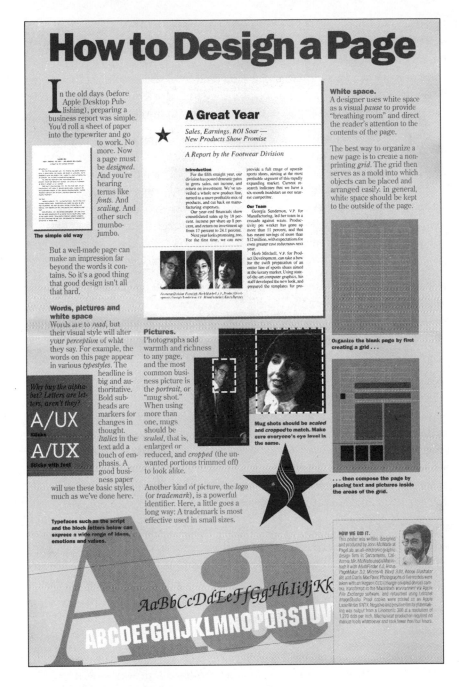

Design: John McWade, PageLab
(Sacramento, CA)

Poster produced for Apple Computer as
a takeaway promotion at Apple Business
Forums.
Trim size: 11 by 17

The subject is again technology and design. But while the poster on the opposite page uses dramatic art to get the attention of artists, here an organized, business-like format presents a brief lesson on design for business people being introduced to desktop publishing.

The design successfully incorporates the elements it describes— bold, authoritative headlines, subheads for easy reference, the use of an underlying grid, mug shots cropped and scaled to the same size—both in the poster itself and in the sample page centered under the headline.

Another contrast: Although the poster on the opposite page used a limited number of electronic tools to good effect, this one uses a great many of them. Photographs of live models were taken with a CCD (charge-coupled device) camera, transferred via Apple File Exchange to the Macintosh environment, and retouched using ImageStudio. (Photoshop wasn't around at the time.) Other software used included, in addition to PageMaker, Illustrator, MacPaint, and Microsoft Word. The designer bypassed the traditional mechanical and prepress work by supplying the printer with negative and positive film output from a Linotronic 300 at 1270 dots per inch. (At the time, the L300 could not print a tabloid-size page at 2540 dpi.)

FOLDERS

Folders provide a convenient format for promoting products, services, and events. The folded piece can be racked or mailed (either in a standard business envelope or as a self-mailer), and the fully open piece can be used as a poster. The format also works well for a series—educational literature and programs, for example; once you work out the format, you can make a template and reuse it for each piece in the series.

Having said all that, we must add that desktop technology has made the three-panel folder so ubiquitous that it has lost a great deal of its effectiveness. So if you're planning a folder, try to budget for a nonstandard page size (a 9-by-12 sheet folded three times has a distinctive edge over the standard letter-size sheet, though it will cost more to produce and won't fit in a standard business-size envelope). Give careful thought to the paper selection too: A heavier cover stock or good textured paper can make your promotion stand out from the flood of other folders we all receive.

The mechanics of a folded piece present unique conceptual and design opportunities. Try to use the panels to organize and build on a message, to visually lead readers from the cover through the inside flaps to the fully open piece. A folder, especially a large one, requires more effort of the reader than a booklet or brochure, so you need to motivate the reader to begin unfolding the piece to get to the message.

When planning the concept and layout, do a pencil sketch before you begin the electronic layout so that you can actually fold the piece and see it as the reader will. Once you have a pencil sketch in this form, it's easier to determine the most efficient way to create the electronic layout. For two-, three-, and four-panel folders, you can specify a page size equal to the individual panels and then use PageMaker's Build Booklet Addition to arrange the panels in printing spreads.

The mechanics of certain folds require that some panels be oriented sideways or upside down. Previously, this required manual pasteup. But with PageMaker's ability to rotate text and graphics, you should be able to create letter- and legal-size folders without any pasteup. Don't forget to indicate fold marks for the printer. For this purpose, insert dotted lines outside the image area on the camera-ready art.

Folders in this section

- *World Trade Institute*—a large-format program announcement
- *Slide Zone*—an accordion fold with a streamlined message
- *Drugs & Alcohol*—a strong, consistent format for an educational series
- *Transpac*—a star unfolds
- *Colligan's Stockton Inn*—warm, friendly, and as suitable for mailing as it is for posting
- *InFractions*—the spotlight on fashion
- *The Man Who Planted Trees*—a program for an in-store event
- *Family Programs*—a poster format for three months of museum events
- *Historic Hudson Valley*—tourist attractions in an 11-by-17 format

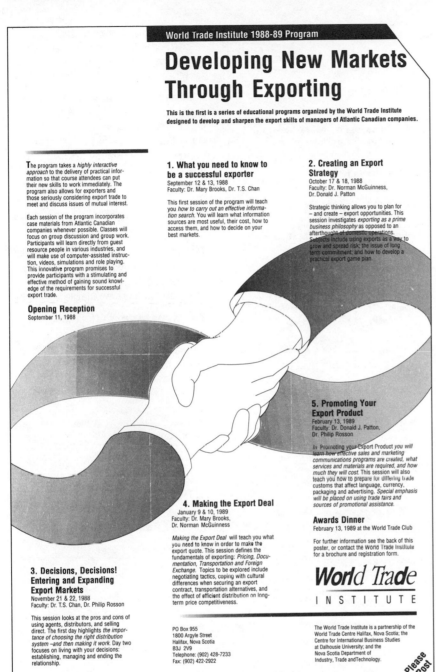

World Trade Institute 1988-89 Program

Developing New Markets Through Exporting

This is the first is a series of educational programs organized by the World Trade Institute designed to develop and sharpen the export skills of managers of Atlantic Canadian companies.

The program takes a *highly interactive approach* to the delivery of practical information so that course attendees can put their new skills to work immediately. The program also allows for exporters and those seriously considering export trade to meet and discuss issues of mutual interest.

Each session of the program incorporates case materials from Atlantic Canadian companies whenever possible. Classes will focus on group discussion and group work. Participants will learn directly from guest resource people in various industries, and will make use of computer-assisted instruction, videos, simulations and role playing. This innovative program promises to provide participants with a stimulating and effective method of gaining sound knowledge of the requirements for successful export trade.

Opening Reception
September 11, 1988

1. What you need to know to be a successful exporter
September 12 & 13, 1988
Faculty: Dr. Mary Brooks, Dr. T.S. Chan

This first session of the program will teach you *how to carry out an effective information search.* You will learn what information sources are most useful, their cost, how to access them, and how to decide on your best markets.

2. Creating an Export Strategy
October 17 & 18, 1988
Faculty: Dr. Norman McGuinness, Dr. Donald J. Patton

Strategic thinking allows you to plan for – and create – export opportunities. This session investigates *exporting as a prime business philosophy* as opposed to an afterthought of domestic operations. Subjects include using exports as a way to grow and spread risk; the issue of long term commitment; and how to develop a practical export game plan.

5. Promoting Your Export Product
February 13, 1989
Faculty: Dr. Donald J. Patton, Dr. Philip Rosson

In *Promoting your Export Product you will learn how effective sales and marketing communications programs are created, what services and materials are required, and how much they will cost.* This session will also teach you how to prepare for differing trade customs that affect language, currency, packaging and advertising. *Special emphasis will be placed on using trade fairs and sources of promotional assistance.*

Awards Dinner
February 13, 1989 at the World Trade Club

For further information see the back of this poster, or contact the World Trade Institute for a brochure and registration form.

4. Making the Export Deal
January 9 & 10, 1989
Faculty: Dr. Mary Brooks, Dr. Norman McGuinness

Making the Export Deal will teach you what you need to know in order to make the export quote. This session defines the fundamentals of exporting: *Pricing, Documentation, Transportation and Foreign Exchange.* Topics to be explored include negotiating tactics, coping with cultural differences when securing an export contract, transportation alternatives, and the effect of efficient distribution on long-term price competitiveness.

3. Decisions, Decisions! Entering and Expanding Export Markets
November 21 & 22, 1988
Faculty: Dr. T.S. Chan, Dr. Philip Rosson

This session looks at the pros and cons of using agents, distributors, and selling direct. The first day highlights *the importance of choosing the right distribution system –and then making it work.* Day two focuses on living with your decisions: establishing, managing and ending the relationship.

World Trade
I N S T I T U T E

PO Box 955
1800 Argyle Street
Halifax, Nova Scotia
B3J 2V9
Telephone: (902) 428-7233
Fax: (902) 422-2922

The World Trade Institute is a partnership of the World Trade Centre Halifax, Nova Scotia; the Centre for International Business Studies at Dalhousie University; and the Nova Scotia Department of Industry, Trade andTechnology.

Please Post

Design: Paul Hazell, Communication Design Group Limited (Halifax, Nova Scotia)

Folder for the World Trade Institute training programs.
Trim Size: 11 by 17, folded in half and then folded twice accordion style

Developing New Markets Through Exporting

A program designed
to develop and sharpen
the export skills of
managers of Atlantic
Canadian companies.

World Trade
I N S T I T U T E

1988-89 Program

The primary function of the cover of a folder is to get you to unfold it. And art that continues from one panel to another uses the physical properties of the format to achieve that purpose. In this sample, art bleeding off both sides of the cover leads the reader to the next panel (not shown), where the loops of the arms are completed. The fully open folder repeats the art.

The art was created in FreeHand and takes advantage of the program's graduated-tones feature, producing an airbrush-like effect.

The logo incorporates a subtly playful effect by transposing the sans serif d in "World" with the serif d in "Trade." Note also the spacing of the word "Institute" to match the length of the words above it.

The type is organized so that each panel contains a different text unit. This works particularly well for a program or series in which each event can be featured, as they are here. Numbering each event reinforces the organization.

The "Please Post" tab in the lower right is also visible in the half-folded position because of the cropped upper right corner.

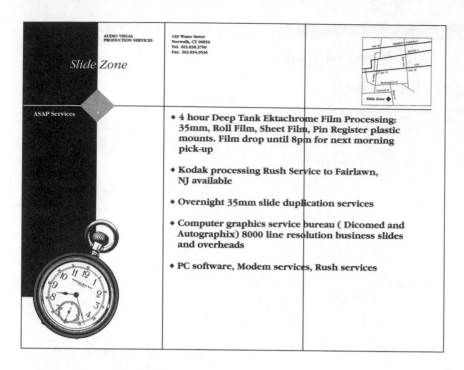

AUDIO VISUAL
PRODUCTION SERVICES

149 Water Street
Norwalk, CT 06854
Tel. 203.838.5700
Fax. 203.854.9536

Slide Zone

ASAP Services

◆ **4 hour Deep Tank Ektachrome Film Processing: 35mm, Roll Film, Sheet Film, Pin Register plastic mounts. Film drop until 8pm for next morning pick-up**

◆ **Kodak processing Rush Service to Fairlawn, NJ available**

◆ **Overnight 35mm slide duplication services**

◆ **Computer graphics service bureau (Dicomed and Autographix) 8000 line resolution business slides and overheads**

◆ **PC software, Modem services, Rush services**

The strong cover of this accordion-fold promotion opens to a single page handsome enough to tack up on the wall for reference.

The butting black-and-white panels, with the word "Slide" reversing out of the black, is the company logo. The negative-positive imagery is delightfully appropriate to the service—film and audio production. The diamond is repeated in the bulleted list and in the map, where it indicates the location of the business.

The clock dramatizes the focus of the folder, entitled ASAP Services. Bulleted copy specifies details for the rush services available.

The typeface is Garamond.

Design (above):
Weisz Yang Dunkelberger Inc.
(Westport, CT)

Folder from Slide Zone.
Trim size: 8-1/2 by 11, folded twice, accordion style

Rules, banners, geometric shapes, and initial caps provide organization and visual continuity for this series of educational pamphlets.

The display type is Avant Garde; the body text is Helvetica. The type prints in purple, and the rules and shapes print in rose. The colors vary from pamphlet to pamphlet.

Design (below): Jim Parker (Phoenix, AZ)
Drugs & Alcohol folder published by the Do It Now Foundation.
Trim size: 14 by 8-1/2, folded in half twice to create four panels

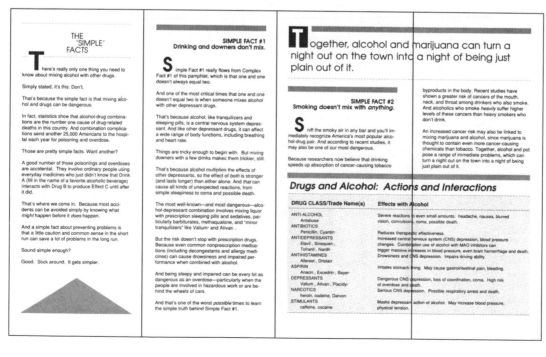

THE 'SIMPLE' FACTS

There's really only one thing you need to know about mixing alcohol with other drugs.

Simply stated, it's this: Don't.

That's because the simple fact is that mixing alcohol and drugs can be dangerous.

In fact, statistics show that alcohol-drug combinations are the number one cause of drug-related deaths in this country. And combination complications send another 25,000 Americans to the hospital each year for poisoning and overdose.

Those are pretty simple facts. Want another?

A good number of those poisonings and overdoses are accidental. They involve ordinary people using everyday medicines who just didn't know that Drink A (fill in the name of a favorite alcoholic beverage) interacts with Drug B to produce Effect C until after it did.

That's where we come in. Because most accidents can be avoided simply by knowing what *might* happen before it *does* happen.

And a simple fact about preventing problems is that a little caution and common sense in the short run can save a lot of problems in the long run.

Sound simple enough?

Good. Stick around. It gets simpler.

SIMPLE FACT #1
Drinking and downers don't mix.

Simple Fact #1 really flows from Complex Fact #1 of this pamphlet, which is that one and one doesn't always equal two.

And one of the most critical times that one and one doesn't equal two is when someone mixes alcohol with other depressant drugs.

That's because alcohol, like tranquilizers and sleeping pills, is a central nervous system depressant. And like other depressant drugs, it can affect a wide range of body functions, including breathing and heart rate.

Things are tricky enough to begin with. But mixing downers with a few drinks makes them trickier, still.

That's because alcohol *multiplies* the effects of other depressants, so the effect of *both* is stronger (and lasts longer) than either alone. And *that* can cause all kinds of unexpected reactions, from simple sleepiness to coma and possible death.

The most well-known—and most dangerous—alcohol-depressant combination involves mixing liquor with prescription sleeping pills and sedatives, particularly barbiturates, methaqualone, and "minor tranquilizers" like Valium· and Ativan· .

But the risk doesn't stop with prescription drugs. Because even common nonprescription medications (including decongestants and allergy medicines) can cause drowsiness and impaired performance when combined with alcohol.

And being sleepy and impaired can be every bit as dangerous as an overdose—particularly when the people are involved in hazardous work or are behind the wheels of cars.

And that's one of the worst *possible* times to learn the simple truth behind Simple Fact #1.

Together, alcohol and marijuana can turn a night out on the town into a night of being just plain out of it.

SIMPLE FACT #2
Smoking doesn't mix with *anything*.

Sniff the smoky air in any bar and you'll immediately recognize America's most popular alcohol-drug pair. And according to recent studies, it may also be one of our most dangerous.

Because researchers now believe that drinking speeds up absorption of cancer-causing tobacco

byproducts in the body. Recent studies have shown a greater risk of cancers of the mouth, neck, and throat among drinkers who also smoke. And alcoholics who smoke *heavily* suffer higher levels of these cancers than heavy smokers who don't drink.

An increased cancer risk may also be linked to mixing marijuana and alcohol, since marijuana is thought to contain even more cancer-causing chemicals than tobacco. Together, alcohol and pot pose a range of immediate problems, which can turn a night out on the town into a night of being just plain out of it.

Drugs and Alcohol: Actions and Interactions

DRUG CLASS/Trade Name(s)	Effects with Alcohol
ANTI-ALCOHOL	
Antabuse	Severe reactions to even small amounts: headache, nausea, blurred vision, convulsions, coma, possible death.
ANTIBIOTICS	
Penicillin, Cyantin	Reduces therapeutic effectiveness.
ANTIDEPRESSANTS	
Elavil , Sinequan , Tofranil , Nardil	Increased central nervous system (CNS) depression, blood pressure changes. Combination use of alcohol with MAO inhibitors can trigger massive increases in blood pressure, even brain hemorrhage and death.
ANTIHISTAMINES	
Allerest , Dristan	Drowsiness and CNS depression. Impairs driving ability.
ASPIRIN	
Anacin , Excedrin , Bayer	Irritates stomach lining. May cause gastrointestinal pain, bleeding.
DEPRESSANTS	
Valium , Ativan , Placidyl	Dangerous CNS depression, loss of coordination, coma. High risk of overdose and death.
NARCOTICS	
heroin, codeine, Darvon	Serious CNS depression. Possible respiratory arrest and death.
STIMULANTS	
caffeine, cocaine	Masks depressant action of alcohol. May increase blood pressure, physical tension.

This folder draws on the emotional connotations of the repeating image of the star; the red, white, and blue color scheme; and the corporate headquarters in the center of it all to solicit employee participation in the company's political action committee. The cover (not shown) sets the theme with an American flag in the same mixed-media art style as the panels shown.

The panels are integrated through the unfolding image of the star. When the panel seen on the far right, below, opens, the panel underneath it again completes the star. This is an effective use of the folder format to set a tone in the early panels before delivering specific information.

In the electronic layout, each panel was created as a separate 6-1/4- by 9-1/4-inch page and printed with crop marks.

The display text is 30/60 New Century Schoolbook with 72-point initial caps and letterspacing tightened to –8%. The left panel prints in blue, the right one in red. The two unseen panels on the fully open sheet contain running text set 10/12 in a two-column format.

Design: Partners by Design (N. Hollywood, CA); agency: Jonisch Communications (Los Angeles, CA)

Folder from the Transamerica Corporation Political Action Committee. Trim size: 24-15/16 by 9-1/4, folded three times

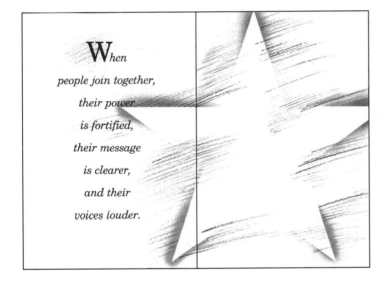

Designed for multiple use, this folder can be tacked up on bulletin boards fully open, while the folded piece functions as a self-mailer.

A warm, friendly, cheerful image is conveyed through the art style, typography, and newspaper-like composition. The flavor is just what you'd want from a country inn during the holiday season.

The typeface is New Century Schoolbook. It prints in green on a gray textured paper.

Borders and rules help organize the small items, which are set to different measures.

The art was created by hand and pasted onto camera-ready pages.

Each panel of this accordion-fold design (facing page, bottom) features a different clothes style. The panels were assembed on screen, two to a page, and two pages were pasted together for each four-panel side of the camera-ready art.

Silhouette photos work well for fashion because they highlight the shape of the clothes. The contrast between dark and light, front and back, and large and small adds to the casual liveliness of the composition. Although the larger photos share a common ground, the smaller ones bounce playfully around the page without regard for perspective. The interaction of the image with the background in a context that defies logic brings a fresh spatial energy to the page. Three additional styles, similarly formatted, are printed on the reverse side of the sheet.

The pattern through the center was created in PageMaker and echoes the subtler patten behind the logo. It's a decorative motif especially well suited for fashion literature.

The typeface is Goudy Old Style. Labeling is minimized to keep the spotlight on the clothes. The type and pattern print in teal blue with black accents.

Design (left):
Carla Bond Coutts
(Lahaska, PA)

Folder for
Colligan's
Stockton Inn.
Size: 8-1/2 by 14,
folded in half
twice

Design (facing
page, bottom):
Edward Hughes
(Evanston, IL)

Folder from
InFractions, Inc.
Trim size:
17-3/6 by 10-1/8,
folded three times
accordion style

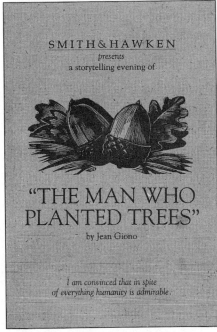

SMITH & HAWKEN
presents
a storytelling evening of

**"THE MAN WHO
PLANTED TREES"**
by Jean Giono

*I am convinced that in spite
of everything humanity is admirable.*

Growing Enterprises of Marin
is a non-profit organization funded through
various grants, which offers workshop
programs for mentally and developmentally
disabled adult citizens of Marin.

Using horticulture as their
focus, Growing Enterprises offers a unique
approach to sheltered employment by
introducing clients to all aspects of gardening
from greenhouse plant propagation to
landscape and grounds maintenance.
Currently enrolled in the program are 17
adults attending five days a week.

By encouraging the development
of work and social skills the goal of the
program is to enable clients to
eventually participate in an intergrated,
salaried work environment.

SMITH & HAWKEN
is pleased to present

**"THE MAN WHO
PLANTED TREES"**
performed by storyteller Ashley Ramsden
and cellist Hong Fang Zhou.

The Date:
Monday, May 23, 1988

The Time: 7:30 p.m.

The Place:
Outdoor Art Club
One East Blithedale Avenue
Mill Valley, California 94941

Donation: $4.00

Chamber music provided by Hong Fang Zaho, a noted cellist with
the Shanghai Symphony Orchestra and Ying Jiang, violinist,
concert master for the San Francisco Youth Orchestra.

Refreshments will be provided.

*The proceeds of this performance are going towards
Growing Enterprises of Marin.*

The traditional formality of centered type (above) is balanced by warm brown ink on oatmeal flecked paper.

The woodcut, a piece of art from the book featured at the event, was pasted in by hand.

The type is Goudy Old Style (except for the company logo, which is Palatino). The combination of bold, regular, and italic styles, the varied spacing, and the contrasting silhouettes of the different text blocks keep the centered alignment from becoming stiff or monotonous.

Design: Kathy Tomyris (Mill Valley, CA)

Program/announcement for an in-store performance.

Trim size: 11 by 8-1/2, folded once

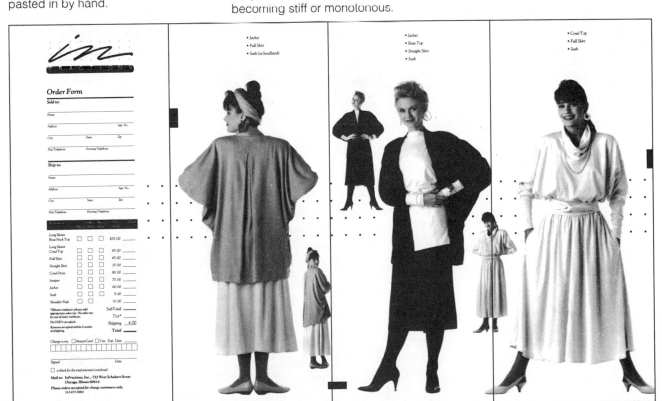

A quarterly program of events is designed as a poster, with different styles of art interspersed throughout the listings. Folded, the piece is suitable for self-mailing and is also easily racked in the museum lobby and bookstore.

The headline and names of months are Franklin Gothic Demi. The listings are in the Helvetica family.

The use of color and the space around each listing make it very easy to check out the programs on any given date. The main headline, banners at the top of each column, highlighted events, and dates print in red.

All elements—art, borders, and Macintosh-generated type—were manually pasted onto artboard to create camera-ready art for the oversize pages. In earlier versions of PageMaker, you couldn't create a page quite this large; but with Page-Maker 5.0, the maximum page size of 42 by 42 inches accommodates most publication needs.

Design: Ann Wassmann Gross (Chicago, IL)

Program from The Art Institute of Chicago. Trim size: 10-7/8 by 22-5/8, folded four times to create five panels

---

Family Programs · Fall '87

September

Sanat Şöleni: A Summer Festival of Turkish Arts
daily through September 7
12:00-3:00 Miniature Painting

Turkish Craft Demonstrations
through September 5
Tuesday, Thursday, Friday, and Saturday
12:30-2:30 Uğur Derman, Calligraphy
F. Çiçek Derman, Embroidery

Gallery Walks and Art Activities

Saturdays and Sundays, 2:00-4:00
Theme: Hispanic Arts in conjunction with the exhibition "Recent Developments in Latin American Drawing"
Saturday, September 12, 19, & 26
Sunday, September 13, 20, & 27

Artist Demonstration

Every Saturday and Sunday from 12:30-2:30
September: Carlos Cortez, Woodcut and linoleum-block printmaking

Arty Animals

Saturday, September 26   Age: 6 and older
Visit the Art Institute's galleries in the morning followed by a lunch break and tour of the Lincoln Park Zoo.

10:30-11:45	Gallery Walk: Animals in Art
11:45-1:00	Lunch on your own Provide your own transportation to zoo
1:00-2:30	Animal Walk: Lincoln Park Zoo
Cost:	$2.00 Member (adult or child) $3.00 Non-member (adult or child)

Name	# of children
Address	# of adults
City	State Zip Code
Telephone number	
Member	Non-member
$	
Amount enclosed	

Send check payable to *Museum Education*

Mail to: The Art Institute of Chicago
Department of Museum Education
Family Programs
Michigan Avenue at Adams Street
Chicago, IL 60603

October

Saturday, October 3
10:30-11:30 Early Birds: Once Upon a Time
1:00-2:00   Gallery Walk: American Art
2:00-4:00   Family Workshop: A Story in a Picture

Sunday, October 4
12:30-1:30   Early Birds: Once Upon a Time
12:30-1:30   Drawing in the Galleries
2:00-4:00   Family Workshop: A Story in a Picture

Saturday, October 10
10:30-11:30 Early Birds: Over and Under
1:00-2:00   Gallery Walk: That's What They Wore
2:00-4:00   Family Workshop: Weaving

Sunday, October 11
12:30-1:30   Early Birds: Over and Under
12:30-1:30   Drawing in the Galleries
2:00-4:00   Family Workshop: Weaving

Monday, October 12
1:00-3:00   Columbus Day Special: Family Workshop

Saturday, October 17
10:30-11:30 Early Birds: Animal Kingdom
1:00-2:00   Gallery Walk: Vase to Vase
2:00-4:00   Family Workshop: Symbolic Animals

Sunday, October 18
12:30-1:30   Early Birds: Animal Kingdom
12:30-1:30   Drawing in the Galleries
2:00-4:00   Family Workshop: Symbolic Animals

Saturday, October 24
10:30-11:30 Early Birds: Pablo's Palette
1:00-2:00   Gallery Walk: French Art
2:00-4:00   Family Workshop: The Eye of Picasso

Sunday, October 25
12:30-1:30   Early Birds: Pablo's Palette
12:30-1:30   Drawing in the Galleries
2:00-4:00   Family Workshop: The Eye of Picasso

Saturday, October 31
10:30-11:30 Early Birds: Tricks or Treats
1:00-2:00   Gallery Walk: Masks and Cover-ups
2:00-4:00   Family Workshop: 'Day of the Dead' Celebration

Artist Demonstration
Every Saturday and Sunday from 12:30-2:30
October: Noreen Czosnyka, The art of wall stenciling

Storytelling
Every Sunday from 2:00-3:00
October: Carmen Aguilar, Latin American folk tales

November

Sunday, November 1
12:30-1:30   Early Birds: Tricks or Treats
12:30-1:30   Drawing in the Galleries
2:00-4:00   Family Workshop: 'Day of the Dead' Celebration

Saturday, November 7
10:30-11:30 Early Birds: A Taste for Art
1:00-2:00   Gallery Walk: Portraits and Pictures
2:00-4:00   Family Workshop: The Delicious Still Life

Sunday, November 8
12:30-1:30   Early Birds: A Taste for Art
12:30-1:30   Drawing in the Galleries
2:00-4:00   Family Workshop: The Delicious Still Life

Saturday, November 14
10:30-11:30 Early Birds: Funny Food
1:00-2:00   Gallery Walk: Travel Plans
2:00-4:00   Family Workshop: Soft Sculpture

Sunday, November 15
12:30-1:30   Early Birds: Funny Food
12:30-1:30   Drawing in the Galleries
2:00-4:00   Family Workshop: Soft Sculpture

Saturday, November 21
10:30-11:30 Early Birds: Blue Plate Special
1:00-2:00   Gallery Walk: Art of Italy
2:00-4:00   Family Workshop: Designing Dishes

Sunday, November 22
12:30-1:30   Early Birds: Blue Plate Special
12:30-1:30   Drawing in the Galleries
2:00-4:00   Family Workshop: Designing Dishes

Friday, November 27
1:00-3:00   Special: "Day After Thanksgiving" Workshop

Saturday, November 28
10:30-11:30 Early Birds: Incredible Edibles
1:00-2:00   Gallery Walk: Animal Kingdom
2:00-4:00   Family Workshop: Edible Art

Sunday, November 29
12:30-1:30   Early Birds: Incredible Edibles
12:30-1:30   Drawing in the Galleries
2:00-4:00   Family Workshop: Edible Art

Artist Demonstration

Every Saturday and Sunday from 12:30-2:30
November: Lorraine Peltz, Still Life painting

Storytelling

Every Sunday from 2:00-3:00
November: Assorted tales by assorted tellers

Design: Wadlin & Erber (New Paltz, NY)

Folder published by Historic Hudson Valley. Trim size: 11 by 17, folded in half and then twice again

The elements needed to promote tourism work well in this 11-by 17-inch sheet, folded first in half and then in thirds.

The front cover, with its oval-shaped detail of an old engraving and centered format, suggests that this is the official guide to the region.

The tall orientation of the fully open sheet works well for a stylized map of the river valley. The river prints in blue, the surrounding valley in green. A detailed road map appears on the back cover (not shown).

A five-column format accommodates photos of different sizes and shapes to break up the text.

The photographs, all in color, were stripped in by the printer. Picture frames were positioned during electronic pasteup to facilitate the text wrap.

For the electronic layout, the designer set up a file of two 11-by-17 pages. LaserWriter proofs were tiled and pasted together so that the client could approve an actual-size, folded page proof before the designer ordered high-resolution output.

BROCHURES

Brochures provide a broader creative challenge than many other kinds of publications. Because they are generally one-shot efforts, intended for use over a relatively long period, more time, effort, planning, and money is often allocated to their development. The challenge, for writers and designers, is to come up with a theme or concept that is unique to the needs of that message for that audience at that particular time. The solution should *look* obvious once it is executed, although of course the conception and development of that absolutely right idea may have taken months of research, analysis, brainstorming, and rethinking of hypotheses, as well as many rounds of rough sketches and format changes along the way.

As the samples in this section demonstrate, there is considerable variety from one brochure to another and even within the pages of a single brochure. The styles are as diverse as the messages they convey; they range from straightforward simplicity to complex persuasion, from the stylishly new wave to the classically elegant, from the quietly dignified to the boisterously bold.

Even the size and shape of the page varies more in brochures than in other kinds of publications. This is partly because brochures are often produced in small press runs where the cost of paper isn't so critical, and partly because brochures often have generous budgets that can absorb the increased cost of a nonstandard paper size. As you'll see in some of the samples, an unusual size or an odd shape feels fresh to the eye just because it's different. Of course nonstandard sizes also give designers an opportunity to create unusual solutions to familiar problems and to play with the shape itself as part of the design motif. But unless the solution is a good one, the shape alone won't carry the message.

Brochures in this section

- *inFidelity: Keith Yates Audio*—stylishly active design
- *Clackamas Community College*—a strong, simple concept
- *Pitney Bowes Mail Management*—a lesson in variety
- *Westchester 2000*—structure and style from vertical headlines
- *Westinghouse Transportation Systems*—highly organized and accessible
- *Why Design?*—a five-column grid with punch
- *European Terracotta Sculpture*—quiet sophistication
- *Syracuse University College of Law*—markedly horizontal
- *Viva Tijuana shopping mall*—a large, bold, double gatefold
- *River Park Cooperative*—quiet quality in the shape of a square
- *Seybold Desktop Publishing Conference*—a stylish conference brochure
- *Subscription Programs*—compact information in an elegant format
- *Islam and the West*—the photographic story of a TV series
- *Sacramento Regional Foundation*—bit-mapped art and mug shots
- *Doane Raymond Accountants*—organized serendipity
- *Extending Desktop Publishing*—A showcase for technology and art

A sales brochure that calls itself a newsletter borrows editorial techniques from the newsletter format.

Each product is treated as a self-contained unit with its own design, and each spread has a different composition. The contrast and varied texture make each spread feel like a collage.

Two unifying elements balance the seemingly dominant diversity: an underlying four-column grid and a stylishly high-tech design that provides its own continuity.

Silhouette photos focus attention on and dramatize the product.

Computer-assembled gray tones of different values, such as the light gray of the first two letters of the logo against the darker gray of the banner, register perfectly. In traditional pasteup it would be virtually impossible to achieve a clean edge with overlapping gray tones.

*Design:
John McWade,
PageLab
(Sacramento, CA)*

Brochure published by Keith Yates Audio.

Size: 8-3/8 by 10-3/4

A simple concept, well executed, makes for a very effective four-color recruitment brochure for a small college.

The cover borrows techniques from advertising design, with large, centered display type expressing a single bold statement. When you use this technique, the statement had better be right on target for your audience. The inside pages answer the question implied on the cover.

Each spread follows an identical layout, creating a strong sense of continuity that orients readers very quickly to the information on the page. This would become monotonous in a longer publication. (Two additional spreads, not shown, do vary from this format, and a bind-in card provides a checklist of additional information the prospective student can request.)

The strong concept and controlled continuity of the layout require considerable planning. Creating and refining pencil sketches before you begin work on the computer can save a lot of time in this sort of project.

Each spread uses a different color scheme keyed to the box in the upper left corner. (The number in that box prints in reverse type.) On the right-hand page the color is repeated in the rule above the student quote and as a tone behind the boxed copy.

The bleed photos on the inside spreads heighten the strong horizontal axis created by the rule above them. Actually, there are elements that bleed on all four sides of the spread, setting up a visual tug of war that makes the pages very dynamic.

The principle of contrast is used very effectively here. The angled photos on the right-hand pages contrast with the crisp, clean rectangles that dominate the rest of the layout. These photos are also black and white, whereas the others are in color. And the two small photos play off against the one large one on each spread.

The typeface is Garamond throughout.
    Body text: 12/20
    Captions: 9/11 italic
    Numbers: 96 point
    Headline: 60 point condensed

Condensed Garamond was very "hot" in display typography at the time this brochure was produced. Few readers are aware on a conscious level that a particular font is in fashion, but there are subliminal effects to seeing a typeface that has a lot of media penetration. As is true with any kind of fashion, trends in typography change quickly.

Design:
Ralph Rawson
(Oregon City, OR)

A student recruitment brochure for Clackamas Community College.
Trim: 8-1/2 by 11

3. A price you can afford.

Tuition at CCC is $23 per credit hour, or $230 per term for a full-time student.* That's less than half the cost of tuition at a state university, and a fraction of what you'd pay at many private colleges. It adds up to a sensible, economical solution to the rising cost of a college education.

"Can I get financial aid?"

Last year, nearly half of CCC's full-time students received some kind of financial aid — an average of _____ student! The chances are good that _____ work study pro-

Chrissy Pagh
Freshman, Gladstone
"I chose Clackamas because I knew the quality of the classes was equal to a four-year school, without having to pay the money. I haven't had a teacher yet who hasn't been great. And because the classes are small, there's a lot more interaction and a lot more learning."

2. Courses that count.

Planning to transfer to a four-year institution?
All lower division college transfer courses at Clackamas Community College are fully accredited and transferable to any college or university in Oregon, and to public and private institutions throughout the _____ take your freshman and soph-_____ a junior to

Neale Frothingham
Sophomore, Oregon City
"Having been here for a year, and realizing how good the instruction is, I realize I made the best choice educationally that I ever could have made. The size of CCC definitely enhances the quality of education. It's very personal."

1. Teachers who care.

In class and _____
students get _____
Opportunities _____
theatre, spe _____
instrumenta _____
student ne _____
mural spo _____
20 specia _____
ranging _____
mountai _____

Clackamas Community College is a public two-year college with an annual enrollment of 2400 full-time and 8600 part-time students. The campus is located on 175 acres of forest and farm-land in the foothills of the Oregon Cascades, 20 miles southeast of downtown Portland.

Personal attention to your learning needs comes first at Clackamas Community College. Our classes are small (average size: 21 students). Our teachers can take the time to get to know you, to find out where you're going, and to help you get there. Our total commitment is to make your college experience a success.

At Clackamas, you can explore creative writing with an award-winning novelist, learn algebra with the man who wrote the textbook, or play in the band with some of Oregon's most sought after musicians. CCC's faculty includes nationally recognized experts on subjects ranging from computer-aided drafting to Middle Eastern history.

But our most important recognition comes from former CCC students. In surveys, letters, and interviews, they consistently say that the personal attention they got at Clackamas was a major reason for their success — in college and beyond.

CCC graduate Laura Onstott
(with chemistry instructor Margi Arighi)
"Margi made the class interesting, and fun, and always challenging. She always made me feel that I could succeed. By the end of that year, I knew I wanted to get a degree in chemistry." (Laura, now a senior at Reed College, was recently awarded a scholarship by the American Chemical Society.)

Everything you need to succeed.

CCC backs up your classroom experience with first-rate student support services, including:

❑ Program planning with CCC's expert team of counselors and advisors.

❑ Career planning and job placement assistance with the resources of CCC's Career & Job Development Center.

❑ Personal tutoring by CCC instructors and advanced students.

❑ The Computer Lab, with tutors on hand to help you build vital math and computer skills.

❑ And, if you're not yet ready for college level course-work, individualized instruction in basic reading, writing, math, and study skills (including high school completion programs).

Clackamas Community College is an equal opportunity, affirmative action institution.

An ambitious, high-budget production gives both the company and the designer an opportunity to dramatize their message. Although the resources to execute a brochure like this may be beyond your budget, the publication has elements you can incorporate in more a modest undertaking.

The story in this brochure is that managing mail is a complex business. The opening page (not shown) contains a single small photo of a row of rural mailboxes and begins, "There was a time when getting the mail out was pretty simple...." When you turn to the page shown below, the helter-skelter array symbolizes the choices, the pace, and the complexities of today's mail.

The words put the pictures into context, and the pictures dramatize the words. The story, as it unfolds on the next spread (not shown), is that increasingly complex mail systems require increasingly complex paperwork. But "Whatever you're sending, no matter where, we can show you how to get it there, how to prepare it for going, how to account for it after it's gone."

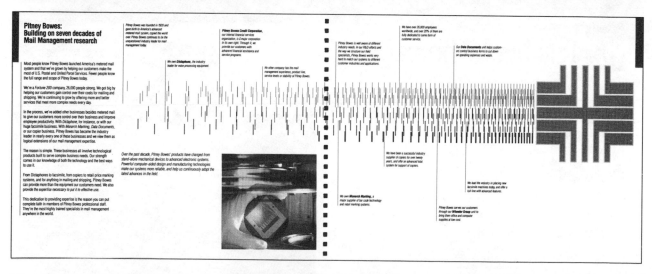

The direct statement of what Pitney Bowes is and what products it offers is presented as time-line-style captions to a piece of art that suggests the speed and intelligence of today's technology. The symbol on the far right is the company logo.

The information is broken down into accessible pieces. The very direct, well-written statement in the left column is only about 250 words long, with very short paragraphs. Each captionlike statement describes a different service or division of the company.

The strong, three-column grid is apparent when you compare the spread shown above to the one at right. The horizontal structure that runs across both is maintained throughout the 34 pages. This grid brings a feeling of order and control to pages that contain a wide variety of photos, charts, diagrams, documents, and other visuals.

The large photo in the spread below introduces a new service and adds yet another texture as you turn the pages.

Subtle graphic humor is seen throughout the brochure. A tortoise-and-hare metaphor is used in the diagram on this spread to compare the old and new meter refill service.

The typeface throughout the brochure is Helvetica Condensed for body text, Helvetica Condensed Black for headlines, and Helvetica Condensed Oblique for captions and for contrast with the opening text. The type treatment is kept simple to balance the diversity of the art and layout, with a crisp, modern, efficient look that is obviously appropriate to the subject.

Design: Weisz Yang Dunkelberger Inc. (Westport, CT)

Pitney Bowes brochure entitled Building on Seven Decades of Mail Management Expertise. *Trim size: 11-1/4 by 8-1/2*

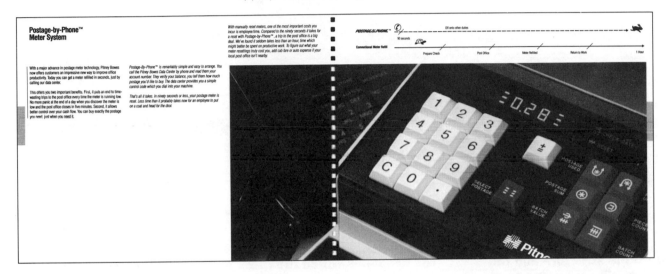

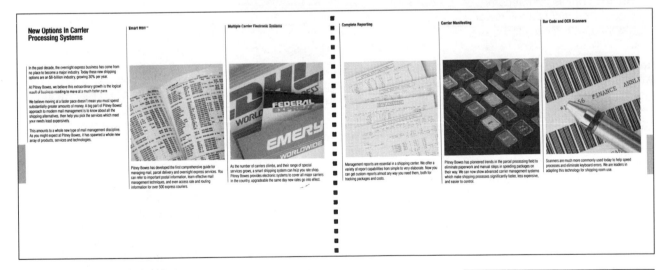

The structure of the grid is most apparent in the spread shown above. The sequence of photos with headings above and text below suggests a series of pigeonholes that echo the partitioning inherent in sorting mail. The grid reinforces an image in which nothing is accidental, everything is tightly choreographed.

The nine-unit grid used in this brochure is diagramed at right. It provides a useful structure for organizing a horizontal page.

The Challenge of Leadership

What will Westchester be like in the year 2000?

by Sidney P. Mudd
Chairman, Westchester 2000 Steering Committee

What will Westchester be like tomorrow and by the year 2000? Putting all guesses aside, we can be certain of our answer: it will be what we want it to be, if that is what we make it to be. There is a vast difference between wanting and making it happen, between just hoping that something will happen and working to make it happen. The degree to which we can shrink that difference will define the future of this lovely but troubled county to the year 2000 and beyond. Perhaps some examples will demonstrate.

Housing

The greatest need we have in Westchester is housing. We want it badly, for our children, our seniors, and for the employees that are sorely needed to keep our service, retail and business economies strong. The way to get it is perfectly clear. We need land, county land, city land, town and village land. We need lower costs of land per unit; we need rental units. To fill these needs means zoning changes, cluster homes, accessory apartments, the enlightened phase-out of rent control, subsidy where needed—all incentives to housing development.

We may have the means. Do we have the will?

Now the difference between wanting and making. Would we back government leaders, county and local, who seek the changes needed? Would we replace those unwilling to effect them? If we do, we could have the housing. If we won't, we'll never have it. Are there easy decisions to make and will everybody like them? Certainly not. We would all have to give a little. Are we big enough, strong enough, compassionate enough to make it happen? We'll see.

"It will be what we want it to be, if that is what we make it to be. There is a vast difference between wanting and making it happen."

Transportation

Our second greatest need in Westchester is transportation, both private and public. We know right now what the problems are and the solutions. The Hutchinson River Parkway, the Cross Westchester Expressway, the Route 35–202 corridor needs action; buses need lanes and appropriate parkway usage, more routes rather than fewer, commuters need parking, if ride-sharing is to grow and improved rail service is to draw more riders.

But how much do we want better transportation? Do we want it enough to make it happen? Would we support the decision-makers who must make the hard decisions? If we do, we'll have the transportation. If we don't, we won't have it. That's very clear. Again, we'll see.

A challenge met...A challenge ahead

Few counties, if any, have ever been studied with greater intensity, by a broader range of citizenry than ours has these past four years. Few counties, if any, are as naturally and humanly endowed. Few, if any, have more at stake in planning their future.

These four years have been well spent. They have defined the problems. They have recommended the solutions. The time for implementation is at hand. But, implementation depends on leadership. That is our present and continuing challenge. The challenge of leadership.

The first *Westchester 2000* report made 29 general recommendations. Twenty of these 29 recommendations require government action at local, county or state levels and often interaction among these levels. Nine recommendations could be implemented by the private sector alone. So the challenge of leadership falls, if unevenly, on both the public and the private sectors of our citizenry. There is much for all of us to do.

Who will lead us?

Who will provide the essential leadership in the public sector? Here we face an important fact: we have a county government and we have home rule. That is the way. The county executive and board of legislators are responsible for county leadership. Local elected officials are responsible for leadership under home rule. No one else is legally qualified. They either lead or fail to lead. Twenty recommendations challenge that leadership. Will we have it? We'll see.

Who will provide the essential leadership in the private sector? Here we face another important issue: We need more and stronger leadership from the business community of the county. They can make things happen in *Westchester 2000*, for which they generously supplied the original funding. Now is the time for private leadership. Will we have it? We'll see.

What can you do?

What can a private citizen of Westchester do? Some 800 have already done much these past four years. They have made the broad study, defined the needs and made the recommendations. Now it is the responsibility of each of us, young or old, privileged or not, black, white, hispanic to read this report, understand it is our future here at stake and resolve to elect, support and exhort the leadership without which this great county of ours can be in serious trouble.

What can business do?

If we are involved in business, regardless of position and certainly if we are among its leaders, we can examine the issues and study the recommendations. We can determine where the strength of our talent, the resources of our corporations can be put to best use for the future of our county. What a great difference that can make when it comes to getting things done. Will we have that private and corporate leadership? We'll see.

Will we meet the challenge?

The future of Westchester is in our hands. We know the problems. We know how to attack them. We know we must give a little to preserve and enhance what we have and hold dear. The challenge now is leadership. ■

1985 Initial Recommendations

A Blueprint for the Future

The initial *Westchester 2000* report, submitted by over 800 volunteers at a public conference in September 1985, identified the following major recommendations for improving the quality of life here in Westchester County.

1. Increase housing by reducing construction costs and lowering land costs.

2. Establish a non-profit economic development agency to sponsor new housing projects, especially in downtown areas.

3. Establish an organization that will publicize housing needs and the benefits of more housing.

4. Eliminate rent control, except where market rent rates can not be met by tenants.

5. Develop a housing program for people who are hard to house.

6. Create an education consortium that would promote support for schools, museums, and libraries.

7. Support higher state aid for the county's neediest school districts.

8. Use the economic development agency (see recommendation number two) to promote business development in downtown areas.

9. Organize a central contact for families requiring community health and social services.

10. Develop a council of social and health agencies to evaluate new programs pertaining to both areas.

11. Create a human rights commission to help people overcome violations of anti-discrimination laws.

12. Develop a countywide emergency telephone system.

13. Promote good health.

14. Promote ride-sharing.

15. Establish a county authority to provide adequate public parking.

16. Complete a municipal county planning process.

17. Develop a long-range plan to avoid water shortages.

18. Create a geographic information system to help translate data into maps.

19. Establish a council of chief elected officials to promote better regional planning.

20. Develop an intergovernmental relations commission to mediate intergovernmental disputes.

21. Establish a committee from within the intergovernmental commission to consider the reorganization of local government and school district boundaries.

22. Reassess property with protection of residential property as a whole from an increased share of total property taxes.

23. Redistribute some county taxes to impoverished communities.

24. Evaluate open land and take steps to preserve it.

25. Assign responsibility for preserving land to various levels of government.

26. Improve maintenance of our parks and upgrade recreational facilities.

27. Promote financial support for the arts and establish a children's museum.

28. Survey current performing arts facilities and determine whether a newer central facility is needed.

29. Develop a county tourism program.

Both the structure and the personality of this format come from the large vertical headlines and the bold rules with graduated gray tones.

The vertical headlines are New Century Schoolbook italic. They function as section heads and can be placed in any column except the far right one.

The banners with graduated gray tones were created in Cricket Draw. In the days before desktop technology, this effect had to be rendered by an airbrush artist, and then shot and stripped in as a separate halftone. Today's electronic drawing programs offer a variety of graduated tonal and screen effects that can be employed simply by clicking through a myriad of choices until you get the effect you want.

The headlines within the columns are Helvetica bold italic. The running text is New Century Schoolbook. The quotations inset in the running text are Helvetica italic.

The bottom rule and column rules provide enough structure for the page to allow ragged right and ragged bottom text.

All art and photos have a 1-point rule around them. This is a good technique for unifying photos of varying qualities throughout a publication.

The oversize pages were manually tiled in two sections of 8-1/2- by 11-inch pages printed in the landscape orientation on a LaserWriter. Tiling divides oversize pages into smaller blocks, or tiles, each of which prints on a separate sheet of paper. When tiling manually, you reposition the zero point to specify where each tile starts. In this publication, all of the top sections were printed first, with the zero point in the upper left corner of the page. Then the zero point was moved to the 8-inch point on the vertical ruler to print the bottom half of all the pages. The top and bottom tiles of each page were then manually pasted together at the best breaking point for that page.

Design: Gan Y. Wong (Hoboken, NJ)

Brochure published as a promotional supplement to the Gannett Westchester Newspapers.

Trim size: 11-1/2 by 13-3/4

Westinghouse Transportation
Systems and Support
Division

Overview

Westinghouse Electric Corporation has more than 100 years of
transportation experience as a leading supplier of electric propulsion
and automatic train control systems for mass transit applications.
Westinghouse also pioneered the development and application of
automated people mover technology with more operating systems
worldwide than any other company.

The purpose here is to organize simple material in a clean, orderly way. Doing that well makes a strong statement about the company's image.

The cover is a quick, businesslike summary of the brochure, an 11- by 17-inch sheet folded once.

The type is Helvetica Light, Helvetica Black, and Helvetica Black Oblique. The light, black, and condensed Helvetica faces provide a range of weights and styles within the same highly legible type family, which is why you see them frequently in this book and elsewhere.

The total measure of the two columns is the same on both pages, but on the left it's a narrow and a wide column, whereas on the right it's two equal columns.

Although this brochure is all text, you could easily introduce photos, charts, and diagrams into this format.

Design:
Agnew, Moyer, Smith
(Pittsburgh, PA)
Brochure for the
Westinghouse
Transportation
Systems and Support
Division.
Size: 8-1/2 by 11

Overview

Westinghouse Transportation Locations
The Westinghouse Transportation Systems and Support Division (WTSSD) is headquartered in suburban Pittsburgh, Pennsylvania and operates from two facilities:
- Allegheny County Airport Site (ACAS)
- Lebanon Church Site (LCS)

Total office and manufacturing space is nearly 271,000 square feet.

WTSSD has approximately 25 field locations in the United States, Canada, United Kingdom and Taiwan.

Employes
WTSSD employs about 800 personnel at its two locations near Pittsburgh, and about 125 at its various field sites.

People Mover Test Track
This automated facility, located at the LCS site, is 1570 feet long with a 10 percent grade for testing vehicle acceleration and deceleration, all vehicle operating systems, and includes a hydraulic guideway switch with a turn-out spur. Snow-making equipment enables the simulation of winter climate conditions.

Business Segments and Product Offerings

Original Equipment
AC and DC mass transit propulsion equipment, advanced automatic train controls (ATC), and complete automated people mover systems.

Mass transit propulsion equipment	*ATC system components*	*People mover systems*
• Air-operated cam	• Car-carried	• Airport
• Electrically-operated cam	• Wayside	• Downtown
• Solid-state thyristor chopper	• Station	• Commercial
• AC inverter	• Central	

After-Sales Customer Support
Parts, equipment, and services to operate and maintain mass transit and people mover systems. Designed to manage and maintain system configuration.

Customer support products and services
- Renewal parts and components
- Field engineering services
- Training programs
- Documentation
- Diagnostic services
- Reliability analyses

Mass Transit Contracts

Bay Area Rapid Transit in San Francisco, California
The first automated mass transit system began operation in 1972 with Westinghouse propulsion and ATC. The original 450-carset order represented the world's first production order for chopper control. In 1984, 120 additional carsets were ordered.

São Paulo Metro Transit System
First international application of automatic train control integrated with solid-state chopper-controlled propulsion; began operation in 1975.

Rio de Janeiro Metro Transit System
Microprocessors were applied to chopper propulsion for the first time; began operation in 1979.

Southeastern Pennsylvania Transit Authority System in Philadelphia, Pennsylvania
First chopper application to a light rail vehicle by Westinghouse; began operation in 1981.

Washington Metropolitan Area Transit Authority
Operating 300 cam-controlled cars with Westinghouse equipment since system start-up in 1976; add-on orders for 366 carsets of both cam and chopper propulsion were completed in 1987.

Vancouver Regional Transit System/BC Transit in Vancouver, British Columbia
First application of Westinghouse chopper propulsion to trolley buses. In 1982, 245 new buses began operation using Westinghouse equipment.

New York City Transit Authority
Over 3000 cars of the existing fleet are powered by Westinghouse cam propulsion systems. In 1987, Westinghouse received an order for 200 carsets of cam control equipment for the new R68A fleet.

Baltimore and Miami Metros
The first joint procurement project to obtain Urban Mass Transit Adminstration funding totalled 208 new cars and began operation in 1983. Baltimore has since ordered 28 additional carsets.

Niagara Frontier Transportation Authority in Buffalo, New York
Ordered 28 carsets of Westinghouse chopper propulsion equipment for its new light rail transit system; operation began in early 1985.

Massachusetts Bay Transportation Authority in Boston, Massachusetts
Awarded a 54-carset order in 1983 for Westinghouse to supply motors and gears with cam-controlled propulsion for the South Shore #2 heavy rail cars. One hundred carsets of light rail vehicle equipment with dual chopper control were also ordered at the same time.

Port Authority Trans Hudson in New York and New Jersey
Westinghouse has supplied PATH propulsion equipment since its inception, twenty-five years ago. A rehabilitation contract and a new car contract totalling 343 carsets of cam propulsion equipment were awarded in 1985.

Municipality of Metropolitan Seattle in Washington
Westinghouse is supplying 236 carsets of AC inverter propulsion for Seattle's new dual-mode trolley buses. This order represents the largest AC propulsion fleet in North America.

2

3

The organization of complex, multitiered information is the fundamental challenge in many publications. This tutorial about the effective use of electronic design addresses that very issue and uses the techniques it espouses. Information is broken into manageable "chunks," and the importance of different elements is made readily apparent through the use of headlines, rules, numbers, and color.

The handwritten annotations are red; the 6-point rules above headlines, the highlighted quote, and the marginal copy are green. Red and green spot color is also used in the diagrams.

The format combines different kinds of editorial material—running text, charts and diagrams, numbered points, quotes offset from the main text, and even handwritten annotations of typeset words. The mix of techniques gives readers different ways to enter the page. It must be carefully organized in order not to backfire.

The five-column grid uses an 8-pica measure with 1 pica between columns. The wider columns in the top spread are 17 picas wide (two of the five-column units plus the space between).

The typography adheres to the principles of simplicity and familiarity—Helvetica and Times Roman are used throughout.

The diagrams were created in Cricket Draw.

Design: Watzman + Keyes (Cambridge, MA)

Brochure entitled Why Design? *published by Watzman + Keyes Information Design. Trim size: 8-1/2 by 11*

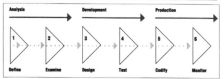

European Terracotta Sculpture

from the Arthur M. Sackler Collections

The Art Institute of Chicago / December 9, 1987 - March 6, 1988

end of the eighteenth century. Clodion's ex-
quisite terracotta statuettes (nos. 19 and 20)
captivated Rococo collectors. In his suite,
Neoclassical sculptors, such as Simon Louis
Boizot (no. 22) and Joseph Chinard (no. 23),
perfected his smooth, sensuous surfaces.
French artists also adopted the medium for
the portrait bust, enlivening this formal type
with the vivacity of touch possible in terracotta. Pajou, in his Bust of Corbin de Cordet
de Florensac (no. 24), achieves a sense of
motion and captures the sitter's alert gaze
with the flicker of a modeling tool through the
hair and incisions in the pupils. Such Rococo
portrait conventions were revived in the nine-
teenth century by Carrier-Belleuse (no. 29).
Nineteenth- and twentieth-century sculptors
flaunted the rugged surfaces of worked clay.
The brooding power of Rodin's Titans (no.
31) is emphasized by the retention of the
scumbled surfaces and blocky musculature
of the figures in their adaptation to the form
of a vase. Jagged, seemingly random gouges
in Vallmitjana's Wounded Bullfighter (no.
30) underline the violence of the subject. The
deliberate roughness of Martini's figural
studies expresses barely containable energy
(no. 33).
Changing attitudes toward terracotta over
the six centuries represented in this exhibition
are representative of similar developments
throughout the visual arts. One is the shift in
attitude toward the medium; it is less important to us today what materials are used by the
artist than how they are manipulated. Another
is our desire to see the traces of the artist's
encounter with the medium—our interest in
the process of creation as well as the finished
product. These beautiful studies and finished
works amply demonstrate the role of terracotta in the development of sculpture from the
Renaissance to the twentieth century.
This exhibition has been selected from over
one hundred examples in the Arthur M.

Sackler collections. In 1981-82 a larger exhibition of these holdings circulated to The
National Gallery of Art, Washington, D. C.,
The Metropolitan Museum of Art, New York,
and the Fogg Museum, Boston. It is a great
pity that Dr. Sackler's death last May pre-
vented him from the pleasure of seeing his
objects in this and other exhibitions from his
collections presented this year. We are most
grateful to the Sackler Foundation for continuing with plans for this show at such a difficult time and for its generous support for this
project. Dr. Lois Katz, Administrator of the
Sackler Foundation, has provided invaluable
advice and assistance.

Ian Wardropper
Associate Curator
European Decorative Arts and Sculpture

This exhibition was funded by The AMS Founda-
tion for the Arts, Sciences and Humanities,
Washington, D.C. and the Arthur M. Sackler
Foundation, Washington, D.C.
The Chicago exhibition was partially supported
by the John D. and Catherine T. MacArthur
Foundation Special Exhibitions Grant.

Jan Baptiste Van der Haegen
Flemish, 1688-c. 1740
Saint Joseph Holding the Christ Child, c. 1723
Terracotta statuette

Giuseppe Maria Mazza
Italian, 1653-1741
David Triumphant over Goliath, c. 1675/1725
Terracotta statuette

**The quiet, elegant sophisti-
cation** of this brochure projects an
image that is completely different
from any of the other documents in
this section. The style is entirely
appropriate for the subject of 17th-
and 18th-century terracotta
sculpture.

**The brochure is an 8-1/2- by
25-1/2-inch sheet folded twice**
to make six 8-1/2- by 11-inch pages.
Shown are the cover and the right-
hand page of the fully open brochure.

**Contrast is an effective
element** in this design. The
saturation of the full-bleed, sepia-
toned cover plays off against the
generous white space of the open
text pages as well as the silhouetted
shapes inside the brochure. The
reverse type in the cover banner is
set off like a plaque from the cover
art. Note the open letterspacing in
the brochure title, which improves
legibility of reverse type in relatively
small sizes.

The text is 9/14 Times Roman
italic in a 14-pica column. The use of
italic for running text is unusual
because it is generally difficult to
read. Here it adds to the traditional
elegance; the open leading and
surrounding white space compensate to improve readability.

The justified text is in keeping
with the formality of the design. The
hard edge of the right margin works
better with silhouette photos than a
ragged right margin would.

The silhouettes are enhanced
by other elements in the design. The
rules at the top of the page, from
which the text seems to hang, create
a free but defined space for the
shapes. The captions are set on a
half-column grid so as not to
interrupt that space.

*Design: Joseph Cochand,
The Art Institute of Chicago*

*Brochure for a show of European
terracotta sculpture at
The Art Institute of Chicago.
Trim size: 11 by 25-1/2, folded twice*

The unusually long page in the top sample uses rules to emphasize the horizontal format. This motif is established on the cover (not shown), where the four rules are broken only by a single photo that is centered horizontally and bleeds off the top of the page.

The placement of the initial cap and photo over the rules creates a three-dimensional effect, as if these elements float above the page.

The tab-style folio—reverse type in a gray box—is a popular device in today's graphic design.

The initial caps, 96 points, are also printed in gray.

The body text is 10/11 Palatino. That leading is fairly tight, but the 16-pica column width and the generous white space compensate to ensure readability.

The format is repeated on every page of the brochure. Only the depth of the photos varies.

Design (top):
Joanne Lenweaver,
Lenweaver Design
(Syracuse, NY)

Prospectus for
Syracuse University
College of Law.
Trim size:
12-3/16 by 7-5/8

THE FIRST YEAR LAW FIRM

Most American law schools prescribe a curriculum for first year students that has hardly changed at all since it was invented by Christopher Langdell at Harvard in the 1870's. That curriculum utilizes the Socratic teaching method in the traditional private law courses—contracts, torts, procedure, and property. The year is usually rounded out by such courses as constitutional law, criminal law, and legal writing.

Syracuse has not abandoned the features of this traditional curriculum that have rightly proved enduring. It is only that we believe today's beginning law student deserves more than this. Concerned that exclusive reliance on tradition does not provide enough individual attention to the development of basic lawyering skills, the Syracuse faculty has developed a first year program known as "Law Firm."

Organizing into small mock Law Firms, first year Syracuse students begin at once to see the real-world context in which legal problems arise and are resolved. Working together with their Law Firm associates, students develop legal writing, research, problem solving, and client counseling skills. Each Law Firm is directed by a faculty member who guides students through problems drawn from real law practice, integrated with materials covered in the traditional first year courses.

MAJOR PROGRAM AREAS CURRICULUM

The basic course of advanced law study at Syracuse is an innovative plan called the Major Program Areas Curriculum (MPAC). After the first year, each student selects a major program area that concentrates a portion of his or her study in one of four areas: business organizations and transactions; government and regulation; civil and criminal justice; or international law.

The goal of MPAC is not to force premature career choices or to develop narrow substantive specialties. Rather, its premise is that a good general legal education requires that some area of the law be studied in orderly sequence and in depth.

Rejecting the smorgasboard approach that has characterized much of American legal education in recent times, MPAC offers the Syracuse student an organized, in-depth study of the selected area during the final two years of law school. Integrating materials from disciplines beyond the law, MPAC assures that students not only become well-versed in their areas of current special interest, but that they develop the skills needed to explore the varieties of legal problems they may encounter in the future.

Everything about the design in the bottom sample is bold: the page size, the fold, the type size, and the colors (the background on the pages that unfold is green with orange, red, and magenta accents).

A double gatefold gives new meaning to the landscape-proportioned page. The pages shown below left unfold to a 36-inch-wide sheet (half of the foldout is shown on the right), allowing plenty of room for the artist's rendering of a shopping mall on the Mexican border.

The running text was set at 36 points and output on a LaserWriter. That output was shot down 50%, reducing the type size to 18 points and increasing the resolution from 300 to 600 dots per inch. This is a useful technique for improving the quality of type when you use laser proofs for camera-ready copy.

The display type is Bernhard Antique Bold Condensed. This font was not available for desktop computers at the time the brochure was created, so the designer pasted commercial type into position on the camera-ready pages.

The photos are a good scale for this design. Being relatively small, they make the large type seem even larger.

*Design (bottom):
Tom Lewis
(San Diego, CA)*

Brochure for a shopping mall called ¡Viva Tijuana! Trim size: 12 by 36 double gatefold

Como una pincelada de increíbles tonalidades. Naranjas, amarillos, verdes, rosas. ¡Viva Tijuana! hace que entre los visitantes renazcan ilusiones y se fortalezcan deseos escondidos. ¡Viva Tijuana! es alegre como el estallido de un cohetón de colores que se abre a la inmensidad de la noche.

Quien piensa en el "Old México", siente que el choque de lo moderno con lo antiguo produce efectos vivificantes, y no desperdicia la oportunidad de disfrutar en ¡Viva Tijuana! de la comodidad de un modernismo arquitectónico en un desarrollo sobre terreno que sabe historias viejas; es la fusión increíble del mañana con el ayer superado por la inteligencia del hombre moderno.

Around River Park

Conveniently located in Ulster County, 1-1/2 hours north of New York City, 1/2 hour from Stewart Airport, 15 minutes from the Mid-Hudson Bridge, 5 minutes from the NYS Thruway Exit 18 and the Village of New Paltz with express bus service to NYC and elsewhere.

River Park is just minutes from the Shawangunk Mountains where huge tracts of untouched wilderness include the Mohonk Preserve, a 5,400 acre publicly-accessible land preserve, and Minnewaska State Park covering over 12,000 acres. Numerous hiking trails and over forty miles of carriage roads provide perfect conditions for cross-country skiing, cycling and walking. Public facilities for golf and tennis are located in New Paltz.

New Paltz is famous for Huguenot Street, the oldest street of original homes in the U.S., and for SUNY New Paltz, with its vast educational and cultural facilities. The village boasts unique and interesting shops, diverse night life, and a highly respected public education system.

Area cultural groups and events include the Hudson Valley Philharmonic series, chamber music, concerts, summer theatre, art galleries, museums and open-air concerts.

River Park is surrounded by historic landmarks including the Mohonk Mountain House, West Point, and the Vanderbilt Estate.

The history surrounding River Park is rivaled only by natural and man-made wonders such as the nearby glacial lakes, Mohonk, Min-

newaska and Awosting, with their incredibly clear blue waters and jagged granite-faced shoreline. The cliff faces of the Shawangunk Mountains and old channels and locks from the D & H Canal provide many scenic and recreational possibilities.

The area's growing economic base is led by agriculture, IBM, Stewart Airport, SUNY New Paltz and a host of flourishing smaller businesses. All provide a stable and diverse job market.

An inspiring place, protected and private— River Park offers it all. Enjoy the unparalleled benefits of River Park Cooperative by calling 914-255-7904 . Select your homesite and then take a walk in the woods, or meadows , or wander down by the river...

The square shape of the page in the sample above is echoed in the logo, the photos, and the shape of the text block.

High-quality photos of nature set the tone for a real estate development with cooperatively owned wilderness and recreation facilities. The designer chose to let the single photo on the cover sell an image that the inside pages describe.

A coated ivory stock and good printing that holds details in the photos add to the image of quality.

The text is 10/11 Palatino. Again, this is relatively tight leading for body text. Here, the narrow 10-pica column width, the short paragraphs separated by more than a pica of space, and the wide margins ensure readability.

The conference brochure shown below has a highly structured page with banners, rules, boxes, and color tints used to enliven the otherwise straightforward text. The elements are precisely placed in relation to one another. The folio and the rule above it, for example, align with the date to the right and with the black box to the left of the text block.

The single 24-pica column works well on this small page size. On subsequent pages the wide margin is used for bold italic heads set larger than the body text.

The banner to the left of each contents listing is color-coded to the page number. The graduated color tones are picked up as background tints for the respective pages of the brochure; the tints are light enough to ensure legibility of surprinted type.

Conference Overview

The Seybold Desktop Publishing Conference is a Seybold Seminars Event

6922 Wildlife Road
Malibu, CA 90265
Telephone: (213) 457-5850
Telex: 6503066263
Fax: 457-4704

SEYBOLD
SEMINARS

The annual Seybold Desktop Publishing Conference has become the worldwide event-of-record for the burgeoning desktop publishing market, and a "must" occasion for both the publishing and the computer industries.

As the only major computer conference devoted to electronic publishing applications, the Seybold Conference combines a top-level three-day seminar with the world's premier exposition of computer-based publishing solutions. The 1988 Conference takes place September 14 - 17 at the Santa Clara Convention Center in the heart of Silicon Valley. The seminars run Wednesday through Friday, September 14 - 16. The exposition operates Thursday through Saturday, September 15 - 17.

You heard about the 1987 Conference. It brought "PostScript Mania" to the forefront with announcements of Display PostScript and Color PostScript, and the emergence of PostScript printer clones. Other highlights included the launch of desktop presentations, the introduction of "big system" capabilities on the desktop, debates on multi-user networked systems, some lively user sessions on exciting new applications, and a raft of new products.

The 1988 Conference is going to be even better. The market will see many more sophisticated and powerful products, and the collision between Macs, PCs and Unix workstations will be dramatic. Again, the Seybold Conference will be the most exciting (and most valuable) event of the year.

Subscription Series

John Singer Sargent

Kent Lydecker, Executive Director, Department of Museum Education

Tuesday evenings, February l0, l7, 24, and March 3, 6:00-7:00, repeated on Wednesday afternoons, February ll, l8, 25, and March 4, l:00-2:00

This series complements the *John Singer Sargent* exhibition, on view at the Art Institute February 7 to April l9. Kent Lydecker will present lecture I, II, and IV. Laurel Bradley, Director of Gallery 400, University of Illinois, Chicago, will present lecture III.
I   *American Artists Abroad: Sargent in the Expatriate Tradition*
II   *The Contemporary Scene: Sargent's Europe*
III *Sargent as a Portraitist*
IV   *The Unsung Sargent: The Boston Murals*

John Singer Sargent. *The Fountain, Villa Torlonia, Frascati,* l907. Oil on canvas. Friends of American Art Collection.

Four l-hour sessions. Member: $30. Public: $40 Student (with ID) $20. Single tickets sold only at the door on the day of the lecture. Member: $9.50. Public: $12. Student (with ID): $5.   Meet in Morton Hall.

From Mice to Magic: Film Animation

Moderator: Richard Peña, Director, Film Center, School of the Art Institute

Sunday afternoons, 2:00-3:30, March l5, 22, 29, and April 5

Screen animation is one of the oldest and most popular cinematic traditions — Mickey Mouse is at least as well known internationally as Charlie Chaplin or John Wayne — yet the history and development of the art of animation is usually treated at best as a footnote to film history. In this series, issues in the history of animation, along with exciting new developments in the field,

Betty Boop

will be discussed in lectures featuring the screening of relevant films.

I   *Animation in the Silent Cinema: The Pioneers — Emile Cohl, Windsor MacKay, and Lotte Reiniger* Donald Crafton, Professor, University of Wisconsin, Madison, and author of *Before Mickey*
II   *Animation in the Studio Era: Mickey Mouse, Betty Boop, and Popeye and Their Creators such as Tex Avery, Chuck Jones, Max Fleischer, and Walt Disney* Maryann Oshana, Northwestern University
III *The Techniques of Screen Animation: cels, pin-screen, sand, clay, puppets, and*

"direct animation." Stephanie Maxwell, Visiting Artist, School of the Art Institute, and prize-winning animator
IV   *Animation in the Eighties and Future Possibilities* Stephanie Maxwell

Four l -l/2 hour sessions. Member: $45. Public: $60. Student (with ID) $30. Single tickets sold only at the door on the day of the lecture. Member: $l4. Public: $l8. Student (with ID):$7.50. Meet in Fullerton Hall.

Baroque and Rococo Art and Architecture in Austria and Bavaria

Robert Eskridge, Lecturer, Department of Museum Education

Monday afternoons, April 6, l3, 20, and 27, l:00-2:00 repeated on Tuesday evenings, April 7, l4, 2l, and 28, 6:00-7:00 Throughout the l8th century a spring-like efflorescence of building and decoration shaped the cities and country villages of Austria and Bavaria. Situated between Italy and France, the region absorbed the best qualities of both to create the distinctive

J.M. Fischer and J.M. Feichtmayr. *Gilded Stucco Cartouche, Priory Church, Diessen, Bavaria.* l732-34.

monuments of the age. The series traces the Baroque and Rococo from its birth in Rome and Paris to its transformation in Central Europe.

I   *The Origins of Baroque and Rococo in Rome and Paris*
II   *The Baroque and Rococo in Austria*
III *The Bavarian Rococo Church*
IV   *Munich and Würzburg*

Four l-hour sessions. Member: $30. Public: $40. Student (with ID): $20. Single tickets sold only at the lecture. Member: $9.50 Public: $12. Student (with ID): $5.   Meet in Morton Hall.

Johann Bernhard and Joseph Emmanuel Fischer von Erlach. *Karlskirche, Vienna, Austria.* l7l6-33.

Design (facing page, top): *Wadlin & Erber (New Paltz, NY)*

Brochure for the River Park Cooperative. Trim size: 8 by 24, folded twice

Design (facing page, bottom): Weisz, Yang, Dunkelberger Inc. (Westport, CT)

Brochure for the Seybold Desktop Publishing Conference. Trim size: 6-3/4 by 8-3/8

Design (this page): Mary Grace Quinlan

Subscription programs brochure from The Art Institute of Chicago. Trim size: 10-3/4 by 9

The long vertical page of the brochure shown above is typical of museum programs. The shape fulfills two very different needs: In its vertical orientation, it is easily racked at information desks and museum stores; in its horizontal orientation, it's a self-mailer.

The two-column grid accommodates several self-contained items on a spread, with headlines in a second color (green here) for easy scanning. Variety on each spread increases the chance of getting the reader's interest.

The body text is 10/11 Garamond. The headlines are 11/13 Garamond bold italic.

Even though the photographs are small, the combination of the narrow page and narrow column width (11 picas) keeps them from looking like postage stamps. Art can also be sized to a two-column width.

This program guide for a TV series, *Islam and the West*, relies heavily on four-color photos to tell its story. The page composition varies considerably from spread to spread, depending on the size and placement of the pictures.

When selecting and placing several photos on a page or spread, keep in mind how they play against one another. When a visually literate eye is at work, as it is here, the photos work together to make a dynamic composition.

Contrast in subject, scale, direction, and color all contribute to the composition. It shows travel by land, travel by sea, and the gold coin that was the very reason for these century-old trade routes. The caravan moves back into the picture plane, the ship moves in a plane perpendicular to the caravan, and the movement of both contrasts with the still life of the coins. The vastness of the mountains makes the caravan seem small, and the coins smaller still. Consider also the visual forms themselves—the jagged mountains, the linear caravan, the circular coins, and the rickety lines of the ship.

The headline treatment at the top of each spread provides a strong unifying element given this varied compositon. The 3-point rule runs from one outer margin to the gutter, bleeding across the gutter (unless there is a full-bleed picture on one page of the spread).

The type is New Baskerville.

Design: Ira Friedlander (New York, NY)
Program guide for Islam and the West, *a television film series.*
Trim Size: 6 by 9

To this day caravans of camels still travel the Silk Route, long the only land link between East and West.
Left, Omani dhow.
Right, Islamic coins.

5. TRADE AND COMMERCE

Islam seeks never to separate everyday life from religion. A person's livelihood and his beliefs are linked and he is taught that social and economic justice—and charity—are worthy matters. Thus Islam has always supplied trade and commerce with a formidable religious base.

After the death of the Prophet, both the religion of Islam and Muslim political and economic domination spread with amazing rapidity. So, outward from the heartland of Islam they came—Muslims traders travelling up and down the coast of Africa, across the Sahara, over the Silk Route to China, through the Indian Ocean to the Orient.

The sea routes, which the Muslims controlled, were crucial for the economic life of the Islamic world, as well as for trade between the Far East and Europe. Accounts of travel by sea to distant lands captured the imagination of Islamic peoples and entered into their literature in stories such as 'Sinbad the Sailor' in The Thousand and One Nights.

Over the land routes, traders carried ideas along with spices, silk and paper from the East to the Islamic world and through it to the West. Traders also played a role in the transmission of technology, for example in bringing paper and papermaking from China.

The importance of travel in their lives led Muslims to develop geography on a global scale. Always in their journeys, they relied on a singularly important instrument, the astrolabe. The astrolabe gave these traders their bearings, and gave the West the tool with which to reach the New World. Columbus would have been lost without his astrolabe and maps plotted by Muslim traders. Prince Henry the Navigator depended not only on that device, he also had a Muslim pilot.

Everywhere they went, the Muslim traders brought the Quran, their book of guidance, as well as their science, their art, and their culture.

The cover art was derived from a piece of clip art that was digitized, saved in MacPaint format, and then enlarged in PageMaker. The effective, bit-mapped result bears little resemblance to the fine-line style of the original art. It prints burgundy on a tan background. The same art was reduced for use as a decorative element at the bottom of each page.

The "border within a border" page frame provides a space for the organization's name to run across the top of each inside page. The open letterspacing creates an effective and delicate treatment for a running head, but it needs to be anchored by a frame, such as the one in this brochure, or a rule, such as the ones under the running heads in this book. Note that the page frame is asymmetrical at the top and bottom, which keeps the design from being too rigid.

An underlying three-column grid used on text pages (not shown here) is carried through on the cover, where one column is used for the title and the other two combine to provide a wide column for art, and on the spread of photos, where the two inner columns on each page have been divided in half to accommodate small mug shots.

The photos were sized and cropped so that all the heads appear approximately the same size and with the same eye level. This technique, which is particularly important when you group mug shots in a linear fashion, gives equal importance to all the photos and helps minimize their varying reproduction quality. Imagine what a hodgepodge this page would be if all the heads were different sizes.

Design: John McWade, PageLab (Sacramento, CA)

Pages from the Sacramento Regional Foundation Yearbook.
Trim size: 11 by 8-1/2

Our Professionals
Our Firm

We measure our competence by your success in adapting to change - and helping you take full advantage of the opportunities change can bring.

At Doane Raymond, we make it our business to keep abreast of current developments. Your success in dealing with change and the opportunities it brings is a measure of our competence. The same philosophy applies to our own business. By using the latest methods and technologies we assure you, our client, of quality service at a fair price.

You need professionals with management knowledge and financial skills. Our investment in training and promoting bright, energetic individuals translates for you into professionals who possess sharp skills and a current, practical knowledge of the business world. Others recognize our leadership. Many of our partners and staff play leading and advisory roles in the accounting profession, business associations, government agencies, and community organizations.

Implementing the latest technologies to assure you of quality service at a fair price.

Such involvement and leadership is a great teacher. You, as our client, receive the benefits that a seasoned professional staff can bring to your activities. Solid auditing by our experienced staff yields dependable and practical advice. We respond quickly to your problems, bringing a diversity of experience.

Giving answers when you need them.

Communication is as crucial to you as it is to us. We talk with our clients. Whether it is a phone call, a meeting, or a report, our professionals know you must have answers. We provide those answers - when you need them.

Partners providing practical advice on your financial activities.

As a Doane Raymond client, you can expect a partner's attention whenever you need it. That same partner is an active member of your community; someone who understands the local business environment and can provide practical advice. In the city or town where you do business, we are there.

An accounting firm presents a clean, organized look in this brochure without being at all stuffy or staid.

The format is built around large photos on the left-hand page and two off-center text columns with smaller photos on the right-hand page. The large photos are nicely framed by a white background and are sized consistently from one spread to the next. The right-hand pages are solid tan, giving the appearance of a different paper stock. The smaller photos are the same size throughout the brochure and their placement bounces about the text columns.

The Bodoni text has very open leading. The italic captions print in blue, as do the subheads, initial caps, and rules that bleed off the top of the left-hand pages.

Captions stating the company's philosophy print in tan banners that match the color of the right-hand pages. The position of this tint block moves around from page to page, but it always overlaps the photo and the white border. This technique is currently a popular graphic device.

Design: Bill Westheuser, Communication Design Group Limited (Halifax, Nova Scotia)

Brochure from Doane Raymond Accountants.
Trim size: 8-1/2 by 11

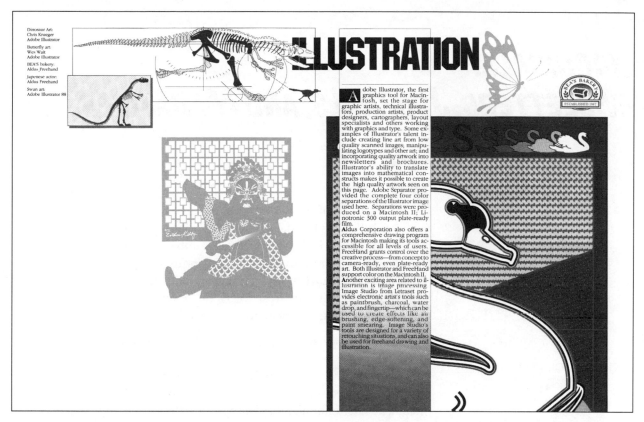

This brochure was produced by a commercial printer to showcase the art and technology of desktop publishing. The illustrations on the spread shown were created in Aldus FreeHand (the Japanese actor and bakery logo) and Adobe Illustrator (the dinosaur, the butterfly, and the transformation of an "S" into a swan).

The layout is built around columns of type, all the same measure but positioned on the page as free-form art objects. Each type column prints over a different graduated colored tone, which increases in darkness from top to bottom. The tones were created in Cricket Draw.

The art is placed around the type in different ways, depending on the individual pieces. In spite of the absence of a visible grid, the placement is always rectilinear, never haphazard. It takes considerable skill to make each spread function independently and still have a unifying visual style throughout the brochure.

Design: Wes Wait (Portland, OR)

Pages from Extending the Benefits of Desktop Publishing *produced by Dynagraphics.*
Trim size: 8-1/2 by 11

CHAPTER 5

PERIODICALS: NEWSLETTERS, JOURNALS, AND MAGAZINES

Regardless of subject, style, or frequency, the challenge common to all periodicals is to establish a strong identity that remains both familiar and fresh issue after issue. The subject, the tone, and the overall package and format should be unmistakably one's own, clearly established and consistently maintained over time. But within that familiar package, it's the fresh ideas, the unexpected images, the new ways of presenting recurring themes that keep readers interested.

Once the audience and editorial focus of a periodical is established, the foundation for the balancing act between the familiar and the new is the graphic format. This includes everything from logo and cover design to the treatment of feature stories and housekeeping details (mastheads, letters, calendars, and so on). Items that appear in every issue, such as contents listings, review columns, and news sections, should have a recognizable style and a relatively constant page position from one issue to the next. If there is advertising, the format must take into consideration where in the publication ads will appear, how to handle fractional ads, and how to distinguish clearly between ads and editorial items, especially when they appear on the same spread.

A format that works not only defines your image, it also determines how hard you'll work to produce each issue. A format consistent with your resources spells the difference between efficient and chaotic production. Desktop technology can streamline production tremendously, eliminating the days it used to take to turn manuscript into typeset galleys and to correct galleys as deadlines approached. The technology also gives editors and designers much greater control over the material through every step of the production cycle, allowing more refinement later in the process than was previously possible.

But established periodicals have established production systems. Converting to desktop publishing means that many functions previously performed by outside vendors are brought in-house to staffs that may already feel overworked. The technology continues to change the roles of editors, designers, production managers, and layout artists in ways that vary from one organization to another. If you are contemplating or are in the process of making the transition to desktop publishing, expect to spend six to twelve months evolving systems and roles. Talk with other people who have made the transition, and evaluate their experience within the context of your own product and the strengths and weaknesses of your staff. The benefits are ultimately everything they're alleged to be, but the transition can be quite a roller coaster.

NEWSLETTERS

Thousands and thousands of newsletters are published in this country. Whether for internal circulation or public relations, for marketing products or services, for raising money or raising consciousness, most newsletters exist to communicate specialized information to a targeted audience on a regular basis. It's essential to really understand your specialized audience and what you hope to accomplish through the newsletter. You should be able to define not just a general purpose but very specific benefits that your organization can measure as a result of publishing the newsletter.

Unlike magazines, which usually have a staff dedicated to creating and producing the publication, newsletters are often produced by people who perform other functions for an organization. It's very important to match the newsletter format to the time and resources you'll have to produce it. If you're starting a new newsletter or making the transition from traditional to electronic production, consider using a free-lance designer experienced in electronic publishing to create a format and electronic templates consistent with your needs and resources. This might give you a much smarter look than you could achieve with an in-house design and still yield the cost savings of in-house production.

Newsletters in this section

- *Newservice*—the appeal and accessibility of a modular format
- *Friends of Omega*—on composing photos on the page
- *Apple viewpoints*—a simple wide-and-narrow-column format
- *The Preston Report*—numbers as graphics
- *Nooz*—playfulness in a five-column tabloid
- *The Wire*—newspaper-style flair for a four-color in-house monthly
- *The Freeze Beacon*—magazine-style features in a newsletter format
- *Consumer Markets Abroad*—a format for charts and graphs
- *Perspectives*—a more open version of the two-and-a-half-column grid
- *Indications*—marketing analysis with dimensional art
- *O'Connor Quarterly*—a friendly and sophisticated people-publication
- *AmeriNews*—one approach to a tabloid format
- *Re:*—another approach to a tabloid format
- *Litigation News*—typographic variety for all-text pages
- *ThePage*—the impact of strong cover concepts

For hands-on instructions for creating newsletters, see Projects 4 and 6 in Section 4.

A highly organized, modular format takes editorial planning and attention to detail when you assemble the pages but is very appealing and easy to read.

The cover uses multiple "sell" devices to get the reader's attention: a strong bit-mapped photo and caption with a boldface leadin, a headline for a related story inset in the cover story, and a contents box.

The bold 15-point rules allow ample room for reverse type (Avant Garde, with extra letterspacing). The rules are printed in a second color that changes with each issue.

Art (below) **and pull quotes** (not shown) break the grid at the top of the page. Pull quotes are set short of a two-column measure and are bordered by a vertical rule on the left margin that descends into the text-block area. Pull quotes and rules, which print in the second color, are also placed inside columns to break up text in full-page stories.

Design: Jim Parker (Phoenix, AZ)

Pages from Newservice, published bimonthly by the Do It Now Foundation.
Size: 8-1/2 by 11

Newservice Cover (Page One)

D.I.N. PUBLICATIONS — VOL. 3 NO. 1

NEWSERVICE

PAGE • ONE

Making 'Safe' Sexy...

There's gold in them there ills.

At least that's how a growing number of companies see the new emphasis on "safe sex" practices that lower the risk of giving or getting the AIDS virus.

But How Safe Is 'Safe'? p. 7

With every day seemingly bringing a new hair-raising headline on who has—and who yet may get—the still-incurable disease (including a recent estimate by the World Health Organi-zation that the global population of AIDS victims will top 3 million by 1992), it hasn't taken long for entre-preneurs to smell the profit potential in the mounting fear of AIDS.

The biggest bene-ficiary of safe sex thus far has been the U.S. condom industry. Spurred on by Surgeon General C. Everett Koop's endorsement of condoms as "the best

Continues page 6

Sign of the Times: First there was sex, then there was safe sex, then there was making money off safe sex. Our 'Page One' report tells how—and how much.

Instant Workshop

Eureka!

It's the flash of inspiration when an idea is born. And while we'd all *like* to get to know the experience better, a new board game may just help.

Create winds through the four stages of creativity ("Focus," "Incuba-tion," "Aha!," and "Action"). In the process, player-"creators") respond to off-the-wall challenges like "Panto-mime ink coming out of the pen of the author you like most," and "Describe the sensation of walking on Jello."

Novel (not "correct") replies are rewarded with light bulb-shaped Idea tokens and (you guessed it) the player with the most tokens wins. But even *that* rule is up for grabs in *Create*.

In fact, the only firm rule is that there *aren't* any firm rules.

Which works out well, according to *Create's* creators, because that's the essence of the Eureka! experience.

For more information on *Create*, write: Creativity Research, P.O. Box 3325, Oakland, CA 94609.

INSIDE

PLUS: STUPID EDITOR TRICKS... READER MAIL...AND MORE!

Newservice   July-August, 1987

Page 2 — NEWSFRONTS

FITNESS

Brain Games: Jogging Creativity

Just when you thought you'd heard everything about the health benefits of jogging (and *still* can't always find a really good reason to get up and go), add one more to the list.

Regular running jogs the creative juices like few other activities, say psychologists after testing its effects on creativity.

In studies measuring creativity among college students, test group participants were enrolled in physical education classes that involved regular running, while others followed their normal, sit-around-and-study habits.

At semester's end, psychologists Joan Gondola of City University of New York and Bruce Tuckman of Florida State University re-tested their subjects. Results showed that runners not only improved on earlier creativ-ity-quotient scores but also outpaced nonrunners in creativity and original-ity.

Gondola and Tuckman say their results point up the continuing need for physical education programs in schools: "They are not frills, but

should be central to our learning and educational processes."

Zen and the Art of KickBoxing

What is the sound of one hand slapping an enemy into submission?

In traditional martial arts training, students wrestle with philosophical knots and questions of honor and ethics as much as each other. But quickie, value-free versions of traditional martial arts may actually increase levels of aggression, accord-ing to a Texas A & M researcher.

Comparing the benefits of training in traditional Tae Kwon Do, an age-old Korean body/mind philosophy and defensive art, with a Westernized technique emphasizing only self-defense, researcher Michael Trulson

found that delinquency-prone teens differed significantly at the end of six months.

Body/mind trainees demonstrated reduced anxiety, enhanced self-esteem, and lowered aggression while the body-only group showed increased levels of aggression, while lagging in all other areas.

A third group, given no training, exhibited no change.

Coffee Head

Just can't seem to wake up/settle down to work without one (or more) cups of coffee?

Millions of Americans jumpstart the day with their favorite caffeine-containing brew. Most say it in-creases their alertness level and helps them focus.

But experts now say that in some coffee drinkers, caffeine may actually reduce attention and impair work performance.

According to caffeine researcher Kristen Anderson of Colgate Univer-sity, coffee's attention-lifting power works best on simple tasks that require little concentration or thought.

But jobs requiring complex reasoning or quick decision-making seem to suffer when the mental wheels get greased with caffeine.

Personality plays one role in calcu-lating the benefits of drinking coffee. Anderson's studies show that extro-verts—outgoing individuals who tend to make quick, impulsive decisions—fare best following a jolt of java.

Introverts, who reach decisions after slowly mulling over the choices, slow down even more after a morning (or afternoon or evening) cup.

Newservice (ISSN 0739-4683) is published bimonthly by D.I.N. Publications, 2050 East University Drive, Phoenix, AZ 85034.

All contents © 1987 by D.I.N. Publications.

Newservice welcomes submissions from readers, but only those accompanied by SASE can be returned.

Subscriptions: $15 per year; $25/two years.

Postmaster: Please send change of address to **Newservice**, PO Box 21126, Phoenix, AZ 85036.

Editor: James D. Parker

Editorial Director: Christina Dye

Art Director: Anne Banks

Contributors: Jerrold S. Greenberg, Jennifer James, Sara Shannon Parker, Rita Robinson, Irwin Ross, Ph. D.

Customer Services: Jean Multer

Production: Sergio Gajardo, Vincent Ruziska, Gonzalo Sepulveda

July-August, 1987   Newservice

Page 3 — EDITOR'S COLUMN

Hip Deep in the Hoopla

We all see it every day, in the explosion of images and the prolif-eration of hype that's become the news:

Ollie North and Fawn Hall blur into Jim and Tammy Bakker, the "AIDS Crisis" dissolves into the "Cocaine Crisis," which segues into the "Urine Testing Crisis."

Hoopla gets mixed up with half-truths and half-truths with innuendo and hardly *anyone* can tell the innuen-does from the gossip.

That's why we're back.

Light years ago, when we originally thought this thing through, (yes, we *did* think it through, once), the idea behind the name and the justification for the concept was that **Newservice** would serve as a real *news service* for readers.

We knew that there wasn't much need for just another publication or for another editorial voice in an increas-ingly media-noisy world, so we set out to do something else: provide a filter and focus for a certain *type* of news.

And while we've stumbled and made our share of mistakes along the way, one thing we think wasn't faulty is our original notion that people really *do* need a means of boiling down the flood of information the modern world generates.

That's why we're happy to an-nounce that we're resuming bimonthly publication with this issue—because we think the need for a reliable infor-mation filter and hoopla detector has never been greater.

To get ourselves back onto a regular production schedule, we've had to make some minor concessions to reality, which we hope will ulti-mately mean a better and more useful publication.

So, if we look different this time around, it's for good reason. We've tinkered with our format, and come up with an editorial package that we think is both visually compelling and affordable.

We've opted for a more concise reporting style, one that gets the essence of a story across without requiring a free afternoon on your part to get through it.

And we've crammed as much honestly useful information into our pages as we could. We've done our best to strain out the pointless and silly (well, *most* of the pointless and silly, anyway), and filter *in* information that stands a chance of making a difference in your life—and the lives of the people you care about.

In short, we've made changes we hope will serve you as a reader and person to wade through the hoopla of everyday existence and discover more of the things in life that are truly worth knowing.

Let us know how we succeed.

See you in September.

LETTERS

Praise and Cons

To the Editor:

How dare you allow Ms. Porcelli ("Trouble-icious?" *Newservice*/4) to advise us to chew ice?

"Hold onto your new $500 porce-lain crowns," indeed. My dentist would go shrieking into the night if I admitted to him I chew ice.

May I rather recommend that one chew any number of whole food (pure) gums or gum substitutes available on the market. Granted, these are a little more expensive, but so what? Where I live, in the environs of the Black Hills of South Dakota, there are about three brands available through my favorite pure foods stores.

Another comment: I think your magazine is terrific. Who owns D.I.N. Publications? What does D.I.N. stand for?

Where have you been all my life?

Timothy P. Battey
Ellsworth AFB, SD 57706

The *D.I.N.* in our business title is an acronym for "Do It Now," which we take as the best of all possible re-sponses to "I'll quit tomorrow" or "I'll get around to it someday," or whatever happens to be one's own favorite excuse for not making one's life happen in the here-and-now.

It's taken from our full legal name, *Do It Now Foundation*.

As a non-profit organization, *Do It Now is a public corporation, chartered in California in 1968 and based in Phoenix, Arizona since 1972. We exist solely to provide substance abuse education materials and other informa-tional services.*

Where have we been all of your life? Right here, working—since 1968, anyway.

Where have you been all of ours?
—*Ed.*

Please address correspondence to **Newservice**, P.O. Box 21126, Phoenix, AZ 85036.

Newservice   July-August, 1987

The photographs available for most newsletters lack both the impact and the reproduction quality that would allow them to stand alone on the page. But when you group photos with an eye to both editorial content and the visual relationship that will be created between them, the whole can be greater than the sum of its parts.

Three photos often form an ideal combination. Two alone form only a one-on-one, back-and-forth relationship. Add a third, and you have a new and more dynamic chemistry. Four together will often start to pair off, and you're back with two's again. And visually, three photos can create an interesting triangular path for the reader's eye to follow.

In the example shown here, the photos promote summer workshops at a holistic learning center. The selection balances a single, silhouetted musician, a group seated casually at an outdoor seminar, and a third photo suggesting both the quiet time away from workshops and the recently improved wheelchair access on the campus.

When positioning photos on the page, consider where each picture will take the reader's eye, the relative size of the subjects, the lights and darks, and the horizon lines.

Three strong directions in these photos create visual energy that moves your eye from one picture to another. The silhouetted photo is looking away from the page; the lecturers standing in the group picture are looking into the page; and the figures shown from behind take your eye back into the page.

The people are captured in front views, back views, and profiles, and they are scaled differently in their individual environments. The uniformity of size generally recommended for head-and-shoulder portraits would make a group of casual photos such as this seem too static.

Silhouetting a photo, as in the top picture, can improve it by removing extraneous background images. The original photo in this instance included a group of people seated behind the subject; removing them focuses attention on the subject and also provides an interesting shape to work with. The free-form shape can be considerably larger than the other pictures without being out of balance. And you can rag the copy along the edge of the silhouette, which integrates the type and the photos. In this case, the photo was scanned in to produce a working on-screen image to help define the rag; a conventional halftone was stripped in by the printer.

Visual illusions can be part of the unseen structure in a group of images. In the bottom two pictures, the horizon lines seem to meet, so that for a moment they appear to create a single panorama; the space between them creates the effect of a window on the scene. Opening up the picture plane in this way creates a sense of perspective and gives dimension to the page.

Design: Don Wright (Woodstock, NY)

Pages from Friends of Omega Newsletter, *published by the Omega Institute. Trim size: 8-1/2 by 11*

Apple viewpoints

Apple News and Perspectives for the Developer Community

Published weekly by Apple Developer Services   September 12, 1988

Apple Integrated Systems Meets MIS Corporate Needs

Chuck Berger, Vice President, Apple Integrated Systems

In April of 1988, Apple made the decision to form Apple Integrated Systems. As the head of this new group at Apple, I'd like to take a few minutes to tell you about the reasoning behind the creation of Apple Integrated Systems—how we plan to accomplish our mission, and now it will affect you as a developer.

A lot has changed in the Macintosh® world over the past three and a half years. Macintosh has gone from a relatively simple machine to a broad product line including the Mac® II workstation. Additionally, we have gone from a handful of applications, peripherals, and virtually no communications capability to literally thousands of application options, complimented by powerful peripherals that have the ability for Macintosh to communicate in virtually any computing or communications environment.

> "...our customers view Macintosh *as the* workstation component of their emerging enterprise-wide communications and information systems."

As the capabilities and breadth of solutions that Macintosh offered grew, so did its popularity in the business marketplace. Macintosh has gone from being a relative unknown in the business world to being a strong niche player in the desktop publishing area, to finally being accepted as a general productivity tool throughout the business world.

While that has been great news for all of us, there is even better news ahead. The increased power of Macintosh and the broader range of solutions and applications we can offer, with the help of software and peripherals created by third-party developers, have led our customers to view Macintosh as *the* workstation component of their emerging enterprise-wide communications and information systems.

Continued on next page

NEWSBRIEFS

Special Events at AppleFest

Developer Services Suite
The Developer Services staff will host a hospitality suite at AppleFest® for those of you who would like to come by and talk with us, see demos of *The Information Exchange*, and get answers to your questions. We'll be in Room 106 in the San Francisco Civic Auditorium on Friday, September 16th from 3:00 to 5:00 P.M. Refreshments will be available.

Technical Forum
Bring your Apple® II and IIGS® technical issues with you to the San Francisco AppleFest this month. Apple II engineers, product managers, and writers are gathering each day to "talk tech" with you.
Place: *Brooks Hall, Room 314.*
Time: *Fri.-Sat. 1:30-2:30 P.M.*
    Sun. 1:00-2:00 P.M.
The forum is a special opportunity to discuss your technical questions, suggestions, and needs with the Apple II and IIGS development team. The technical focus will be on programming and hardware

Continued on next page

In this two-column format, the wide column is used for a single essay that continues from the cover to the two inside pages. The narrow column is used for short news items. A simple and effective format both editorially and graphically, it is also remarkably easy to execute.

Production takes less than two days. Unformatted word-processor files are sent from Apple to the art production house via AppleLink on Tuesday afternoon. By 10 A.M. Wednesday, copyedited, formatted text has been placed in an electronic dummy and faxed to Apple. Apple phones in corrections by 11, a revised page is faxed to Apple by 1 P.M., and additional corrections are phoned in if necessary. The courier picks up at 4 for delivery to the printer by 5. If you're tempted to say, "Yes, but that's Apple…," consider instead "Yes, keep it simple."

The condensed Garamond text face was made especially for Apple by Adobe. (Well, yes, that *is* Apple.…)

Design: The Compage Company (San Francisco, CA)

Cover of Apple viewpoints, *published biweekly by Apple Developer Services.*
Size: 8-1/2 by 11

The Preston Report

"RETIREMENT MADE EASY"   JUNE, 1987

Investing — the trick is to locate opportunities that will appreciate as hoped, diversify, and then monitor the results.

I submit the following for your consideration:

1. The ability to make consistently good investment returns over a period of time is **beyond the scope of the average person.**

2. Salesmen, stock brokers and financial planners offering products are ofttimes more concerned with their pockets than yours.

3. As in most fields of endeavor, if you want to excel, **follow and learn from those who have excelled** — this is especially true in investing. Look for those names that have already made fortunes for themselves, i.e., Warren Buffet, John Templeton, T. Rowe Price, etc. These will generally not be the people who publish investment and "timing" newsletters, work in large organizations, or make cold calls to obtain new businesses.

4. The better people in the investing field **eventually start their own funds or small money management boutiques.** They don't remain with large institutions (with a few exceptions — e.g., Peter Lynch of Fidelity Magellan).

5. The goal is to put as much of your money as possible in the hands of a "seasoned pro" — someone who's got his major mistakes and learning curve behind him.

6. **Keep it simple.** Timing services, technical jargon and fad investments (e.g., sector funds) are usually set up for the sponsor — they rarely stand the test of time. Again, study those who have made large fortunes over a prolonged period of time; the basics don't change.

At long last, the first issue. Blame tax reform and a busy, inclement winter in Connecticut. I hope the '86 tax bite wasn't too severe for most of you.

While thinking about this first issue of "The Preston Report," it seemed appropriate to discuss what seems to be the primary concern right now of many clients — investing.

P. T. Barnum perceptively noted "there's a sucker born every minute — and another one to take him."

THE BASICS $

ONE TURKEY HILL ROAD SOUTH, WESTPORT, CT 06880 203-226-3179   1

Bold headlines are assertive, while the American Typewriter face is friendly. The combination is just right for financial advice to retirees.

Introductory copy, set to a two-column measure and larger than the body text, helps draw readers into the page and effectively varies the basic three-column grid.

Large numbers (these are 32 point) make lists appealing and also function as graphic elements.

The three-layer dollar sign was created in Illustrator and stretched in PageMaker. The font is Bodoni, one of the few with a double downstroke in the dollar sign. The top sign has a 5-point white Stroke and a 30 percent black Fill; the middle one has a 6-point black Stroke to produce the outline; the bottom sign is solid black, set off to create a drop shadow.

Design: John Odam (San Diego, CA)

Design for The Preston Report, *created as a "Page Makeover" for* Publish *Magazine.*
Size: 8-1/2 by 11

Playfulness is the signature of this tabloid monthly newsletter. The typewriter look of Courier sets the casual tone, and every design element follows through in kind.

Mug shots don't have to be boring. The shapes used here only begin to suggest some ingenious ways to treat both casual and posed snapshots. The stars were created in MacDraw, and the other shapes in PageMaker. Photos were stripped in as halftones by the printer.

Letters as visual puns provide more play in the rebus-like graphic. The type was set in PageMaker. The eye was digitized from a photo that was cropped tight, saved in Paint format, and scaled in PageMaker. The bee was drawn in MacPaint.

The digitized courthouse art is treated as a vignette, with the edges gradually fading into the background of the page. (The effect was created in MacPaint from a scan of black-and-white art.)

The rotated photo provides an opportunity for an unusual caption treatment, with the names of those pictured angled into the photo.

For all the spontaneity in the treatment of graphic elements, the five-column grid provides the necessary understructure.

Design: Paul Souza (Boston, MA)

Pages from Nooz, *published quarterly by WGBH radio.*

Trim size: 11 by 17

4 THE WIRE MAY 1988 THE WIRE 5

News, events, awards, and issues reported from locations throughout North America.

AROUND CHAMPION

In celebration of their first place finish in the "Our Aim Is On Quality" competition, (l. to r.) Joseph Bellamy, Jaren Lee, Benjamin Griffin, and Fredrick Carter model their new jackets at the Waycross, Georgia, awards dinner.

MARTHA LANG

ALABAMA

Courtland — Two volunteer activities received donations from the Champion Fund for Community Service in the Timberlands Alabama region. The programs are Project Learning Tree, in which Donald Kimberly and Edward Lewis are volunteer teachers, and a youth baseball team on which Robert Pierce is serving as coach.

CONNECTICUT

Stamford — 235 new neighbors moved in on the fifth and sixth floors at One Champion Plaza last month. Arthur Andersen & Co., one of the world's largest accounting and consulting firms, has leased the space for ten years, with an option to extend its stay and to expand onto the fourth floor.

MAINE

Bucksport — As part of its ongoing involvement in its communities, Champion is helping non-profit developers build housing for people who cannot otherwise afford it. Champion is one of the two largest contributors to the Maine House-Raising Initiative, pledging $100,000 toward the program's $1.3 million goal. In addition to loans and grants to about 300 low-income families, the program will also provide technical assistance to home-builders.

• The high school football team will win a new scoreboard, if employees meet the Champion challenge. The company has agreed to pay half the cost of the scoreboard, and will match employee contributions.

• When Bucksport hosts a regional meeting of the Paper Industry Management Association this month, members of the professional group will tour the mill and see first hand its five major capital projects. The tour, set for May 13, climaxes one and a half days of presentations on change in the paper industry with a focus on the Bucksport facility.

MONTANA

Bonner — Another production record was set when the day crew on the No. 2 lathe turned out 132,900 linear feet of plywood. That computes to an average of 33,204 feet (3/8" basis) per hour.

Libby — The Champion Fund for Community Service has contributed $750 to the annual Libby Senior High School Party, to be held May 25. It also donated a truckload of firewood to be raffled off, with the proceeds also going to the celebration. The CFCS also gave $351 to the Kootenai Valley Roping Club for various repairs.

MAY 1988 $3.95

FORTUNE

	RANK	SALES BILLIONS	INCOME MILLIONS
GEORGIA-PACIFIC	44	$8.6	$458
IP	52	$7.8	$407
WEYERHAEUSER	58	$7.0	$447
KIMBERLY-CLARK	85	$4.9	$325
CHAMPION	90	$4.6	$382
JAMES RIVER	95	$4.5	$170

THE FORTUNE 100 PAPER COMPANIES

LAURIE SAPIA

In the Fortune 100 listing of top companies in the country, released in April by FORTUNE Magazine, Champion International ranked Number 90 in the United States, down from Number 86 last year, and Number Five in the paper industry.

THE WIRE

© 1988 King Features Syndicate, Inc. World rights reserved

Knowing how Champions love their hats, we're conducting a contest to find the best hats worn by employees and retirees.

To enter send a snapshot of yourself in your favorite hat. Entries must be postmarked no later than July 5, 1988. We'll judge entries based on how original, functional, inspiring, or just plain fun they are. Winners will be announced in the August issue. They will receive engraved trophies and, of course, their very own *WIRE* hats.

DIK BROWNE

• The Involvement program is showing real benefits, according to a recently completed audit of 287 completed Involvement projects. The accounting department reported that 86 projects helped cut costs or improve profitability, while 201 were safety-related or unauditable. The total cost of all projects for 1987 was $104,000, and they yielded savings of $387,000.

NEW YORK

Deferiet — A new woodyard crane is on the way. Having received approval from headquarters, management placed an order for a Manitowoc crane, which will cost about $500,000.

NORTH CAROLINA

Roanoke Rapids — Congratulations to Marshall Schneider, vice president and operations manager. Schneider was recently selected Industrialist of the Year for Halifax County, and also Eastern North Carolina Industrialist of the Year, by the Eastern North Carolina Industrial Council.

• John C. Brooks, commissioner of the state Department of Labor, presented a safety award to the mill, for the second consecutive year. The mill won the Certificate of Safety Achievement by maintaining an occupational injury and illness incidence rate at least 50 percent below the state's average for the industry.

OHIO

Knightsbridge — A review of the safety records of drivers in the corporate trucking area has identified 10 outstanding road drivers. Each of them has logged more than one million miles without an accident.

The Sartell mill was awarded this LeRoy Neiman print, "American Gold," an Olympic montage, by *Newsweek* magazine, which named Sartell "Mill of the Year." The award ceremony was held on April 18 under a tent outside the mill, where employees could attend the ceremony.

BRYAN PAGE

OREGON

Mapleton — In a special Arbor Day observance, Champion's John Rolin and Greg Miller helped plant trees and award prizes to the winners of the Mapleton Elementary School's poster contest, "What Trees Mean To Me." The two grand prize winners received $50 savings bonds. The contest was sponsored jointly by Champion, Davidson Industries, and The Gingerbread Village.

SOUTH CAROLINA

Newberry — As part of the Champion Fund for Community Service, the company donated $500 to the Ninety-Six Youth Sports Fund, where Tony Leopard is a volunteer; $500 to the Cross Hill Community Fire Department and Rescue Unit, for which Willie Charles Cook is a volunteer; and $500 to the Edgefield Dixie Youth, where Ricky Rhoden volunteers.

• Everyone's excited about this year's Bass Tournament, to be held on Champion Day, June 4. The turnout promises to be big, because the mill will be down for the day. Anglers will converge on Lake Greenwood, paying $12 each for a chance to win prize money for reeling in the biggest total catch, and for landing the biggest single bass. Sorry, bass.

TEXAS

Camden — Champion has hopped aboard the campaign to restore an historic caboose, as both forest products and timberlands contributed to the cause. The Texas Forestry Association Red Caboose No. 99, a real museum piece, was destroyed by fire two years ago. When no replacement could be found, the decision was made to restore the damaged caboose.

Huntsville — The 223 employees of Texas region timberlands have passed a major safety milestone. On April 4, they logged one million worker-hours without a lost time accident! Timberlands employees, who manage more than 1,000,000 acres in Texas, will be invited with their families to a celebration this month. They will also be celebrating two consecutive accident-free years — knock on wood.

• The Texas region planting team set a new record for production this season, planting 51,355 acres between November and March. About 40,000 acres were machine-planted, while the rest were hand-planted, using a total of 25,000,000 seedlings. They came almost entirely from the Livingston Nursery. This year's planting achieved higher quality, too, thanks to the Planting Quality Task Team's training program.

Lufkin — Texas Senator Phil Gramm visited the paper mill to see the results of the company's recent improvements, and to thank "one of our best corporate citizens" for investing in the community's economy. Champion has recently spent about $90 million to upgrade the mill, and has plans to invest more. Senator Gramm discussed his efforts to expand markets in the Caribbean for East Texas forest products.

Pasadena — Happy Birthday to the Champion Employees Federal Credit Union. Headquartered in Pasadena, it serves 3,351 members at Champion locations throughout Texas. The credit union turned 50 years old this year and has grown to manage assets of almost $12 million.

TO

CHAMPION UNITED WAY CAMPAIGN

	Employee Gifts		Corporate Gifts	
	1987	1988	1987	1988
Administrative Offices	$140,753	$128,413	$162,663	$147,742
Newsprint, Pulp & Kraft	$86,160	$99,918	$80,850	$108,600
Printing & Writing Papers DairyPak	$255,352	$248,791	$272,190	$310,926
Publication Papers	$132,488	$131,570	$97,536	$137,076
Forest Products	$81,525	$121,821	$109,875	$137,977
Total*	$696,278	$738,514	$703,114	$844,217

*Matching corporate-employee gifts on a dollar-for-dollar basis, begun this year, will be equal by 1990.

JOE LERTOLA

Champion's United Way contributions, pledged in 1987 for this year.

AROUND CHAMPION CORRESPONDENTS

DAIRYPAK
Mike Young, *Athens, GA*
David Hunter, *Belvidere, IL*
Lyle Lockard, *Clinton, IA*
Don Porterfield, *Ft. Worth, TX*
John Derosa, *Morristown, NJ*
Nona Schumacher, *Olmstead Falls, OH*

NATIONWIDE PAPERS
Michael Kouri, *Albuquerque, NM*
Donn Coleman, *Arlington, TX*
Wayman Winters, *Atlanta, GA*
James Hudson, *Baltimore, MD*
Floyd Poole, *Charlotte, NC*
W. R. Scholz, *Cincinnati, OH*
David Stall, *Denver, CO*
Terrence Payne, *Detroit, MI*
Gary Elliott, *Elk Grove, IL*
Billy Keith, *Houston, TX*
Wallace Burger, *Kansas City, MO*
Richard James, *Los Angeles, CA*
Joseph Okrublica, *Louisville, KY*
Henry Walker, *Memphis, TN*
Fred Michell, *Milwaukee, WI*
Ralph Erickson, *Minneapolis, MN*
Joseph A. Sadowski, *St. Louis, MO*
Thomas Marler, *San Antonio, TX*
William Patterson, *San Francisco, CA*
George Likins, *Springfield, MO*
Jack Luker, *Topeka, KS*

NEWSPRINT, PULP AND KRAFT
Chuck Grotsky, *Columbus, OH*
Diana Hill, *Lufkin, TX*
Charles Norrell, *McKinney, TX*
Richard Sloane, *Plano, TX*
Sue Tamburrino, *Quinnesec, MI*
Carolyn Blythe, *Roanoke Rapids, NC*
Richard Romine, *Sheldon, TX*
Sue Stenson, *Walden, NY*

PRINTING & WRITING PAPERS
Charles Curtis, *Canton, NC*
Maria Eckl, *Courtland, AL*
Kevin Williams, *Hamilton, OH*
Janet Webb, *Pensacola, FL*
Mack Howey, *Waynesville, NC*

PUBLICATIONS PAPERS
Joe Bigl, *Bucksport, ME*
Luke Galloway, *Deferiet, NY*
Tony Woerner, *Sartell, MN*

TECHNICAL CENTER
Tom Neider

TIMBERLANDS
Allen Deaby, *Bangor, ME*
Carolyn Bragdon, *Bucksport, ME*
Rita Coan, *Courtland, AL*
John Barfield, *Deferiet, NY*
Tom McCarty, *Greenville, SC*
Myrna Waggoner, *Huntsville, TX*
John Norman, *Jacksonville, FL*
Judy Callovi, *Kingsford, MI*
Dennis Elder, *Milltown, MT*
Jennifer Johnston, *Pensacola, FL*
Carl Lynch, *Roanoke Rapids, NC*
Patrick Hackley, *New Hampshire/Vermont*

WOOD PRODUCTS
Jann Norrell, *Abbeville, AL*
Ed Roberts, *Bonner, MT*
Jim Rich, *Camden/Corrigan, TX*
Robin Shepard, *Citronelle, AL*
John Doane, *Costigan, ME*
David Burton, *Klickitat, WA*
Dan Miller, *Libby, MT*
Chuck Wofford, *Lumber City/Swainsboro, GA*
Dennis Elder, *Missoula, MT*
James Little, *Roseburg, OR*
Beverly Herbert, *Silverstreet, SC*
Martha Lang, *Waycross, GA*
Roland Bales, *Whitehouse, FL*

CORPORATE
Janet Madden, *Hamilton, OH*
Flora Kueppers, *Stamford, CT*

This house organ for an international corporation is formatted as a monthly newspaper. The spread shown, a standing feature in every issue, reports "news, events, awards, and issues...from locations throughout North America."

The art is as varied as you'll find in any publication, with charts, photos, paintings, line art, and even a magazine cover contributing to a very spirited page.

The five-column format provides several advantages for a feature with so many pieces. Art can be sized anywhere from one to three columns wide and placed in overlapping columns to make an already lively spread even more dynamic. Narrow columns accommodate the numerous subheads without eating up too much space and give sufficient depth to items that are only 25 to 50 words long. These short text blocks would look like captions in a wider margin.

The cover features a different employee each issue, in the context of his or her committment to some community organization. The typographic treatment of the "Snapshot" text reinforces the informal, personal approach of this cover concept. Depending on the photo, the orientation may be horizontal (as shown here) or vertical.

Design: Weisz Yang Dunkelberger Inc. (Westport, CT)

Pages from THE WIRE, *published monthly by Champion International Corporation. Trim size: 11 by 15*

VOLUME II NO.4 FALL 1987

NAVY WHISTLEBLOWER SPEAKS OUT See Page 6

THE BEACON

Quarterly Newsletter of SANE/FREEZE of San Diego

INF TREATY

An Open Letter to Reagan and Gorbachev

Our organization congratulates both of you for your leadership and courage in bringing about a tentative agreement to eliminate all intermediate nuclear missiles in Europe and Asia. For many years we have been campaigning vigorously to reduce the threat of nuclear war. Now you have heard us!

We look to you, Mr. Reagan, to use your considerable influence with those members of the Senate who oppose arms control to help bring about the ratification of the INF Treaty. We further urge you to do your utmost to oppose any amendments that might defeat its purpose.

We look to you, Mr. Gorbachev, to continue your initiatives to improve the relations between our countries. Allay the fears that your large military forces create in Western Europe by bringing about balanced reductions in offensive conventional weapons. Help to avert a conventional arms buildup to offset the loss of nuclear weapons.

And we ask that neither of you lose sight of the fact that, while an agreement to reduce one particularly provocative and dangerous type of nuclear weapon is greatly welcomed, it will not in itself end the arms race. Nor will it repair the damage done by the scuttling of other arms limitation treaties. Significant though the agreement may be, it will reduce the total world nuclear arsenal only by a slight amount.

Finally, since it is the stated goal of both nations to reduce all nuclear weapons by at least 50%, let us call an immediate bilateral halt to the testing, production and deployment of any further nuclear weapons systems. It makes no sense to eliminate some weapons with one hand while creating many more with the other.

Signed, San Diego SANE/FREEZE

MEET THE PRESIDENT

Rev Coffin's Vision for SANE/FREEZE

The following is an edited version of the article by Kathleen Hendrix of the Los Angeles Times which appeared in that paper October 15, 1987. Our Executive Director, David Carpenter, attended the meeting with Rev. Coffin who, when he saw the Beacon, raved about its content and professionalism.

It was a hot night, ending one of several days in which the air refused to budge, and the meeting of the (Southern California regional) chapter of SANE/Freeze was slow to come to order. The 20 or so wilted people gathered in the community room of an apartment building in Hollywood, mixed themselves instant coffee, spread out notices of other meetings ... and waited for the Rev. William Sloane Coffin, Jr., to arrive.

In he came, looking rumpled and slightly paunchy, shirt open at the throat and sleeves rolled up. He appeared undaunted by the heat, ... and with a friendly grin in place, strode across the room relaxed and affable, clapping back at the people who stood to applaud him."It's neat," he told the group, "to get a chance to see what's going on." For many in that room, it was, in return, a chance to meet the legend, and their new national president.

Coffin became a household word during the '60's, when as chaplain at Yale he became a civil rights and anti-Vietnam War activist, joining freedom rides, marching in the South, collecting draft cards with Dr. Benjamin Spock, speaking out and getting arrested over and over again.

Coffin did not start his life this way. Born to wealth, his family founded the W. & J. Sloane furniture business. He first considered a career as a concert pianist, and then a diplomat. He was an Army liaison officer to the French and Soviet armies during World War II, and a CIA officer in West Germany during the Korean War, training anti-communist Russians for work within the Soviet Union. Finally, he said only half-jokingly ..., he lost the battle to stay out of the ministry. World War II had raised too many of the right questions.

Last July, saying the timing in history was right, Coffin announced he would step down as senior minister of New York City's Riverside Church at the end of 1987 to become the first president of SANE/Freeze. In creating the position of President, over that of the co-directors of the newly merged groups, the SANE/Freeze ... board announced it was looking for someone to "articulate the vision." If there is one thing Bill Coffin can do, it is articulate the vision. And shape it. It is not without reason that he calls his new job with the secular organization "a full-time peace and justice ministry." . . . As he defines it, the SANE/Freeze (people) join him in a "disarmament and development" organization, concerned with

Continued on page 10

1

A tightly structured nameplate, along with the headline and folio treatments, creates a strong identity for this newsletter. The lighthouse incorporated into the logo is a recognizable local landmark. The banner with reverse type at the top of the cover highlights the feature article shown in the spread below.

A scanned photo on the cover is treated as a posterlike portrait of the subject, producing a more effective result than trying to make a bit-mapped image look like a halftone.

A magazine-style feature provides a change of pace, editorially and visually, from the modular format elsewhere in the newsletter. The bit-mapped art ironically conjures up the image of video games in a story that is all too much anchored in the real world. The art was created in MacPaint and stretched across the two pages in PageMaker.

The typeface is Palatino. Varying the size and measure of individual headlines creates emphasis without the need to change the typeface.

Design:
John Odam
(San Diego, CA)

Pages from The Freeze Beacon, *published quarterly by San Diegans for a Bilateral Nuclear Weapons Freeze.*
Size: 8-1/2 by 11

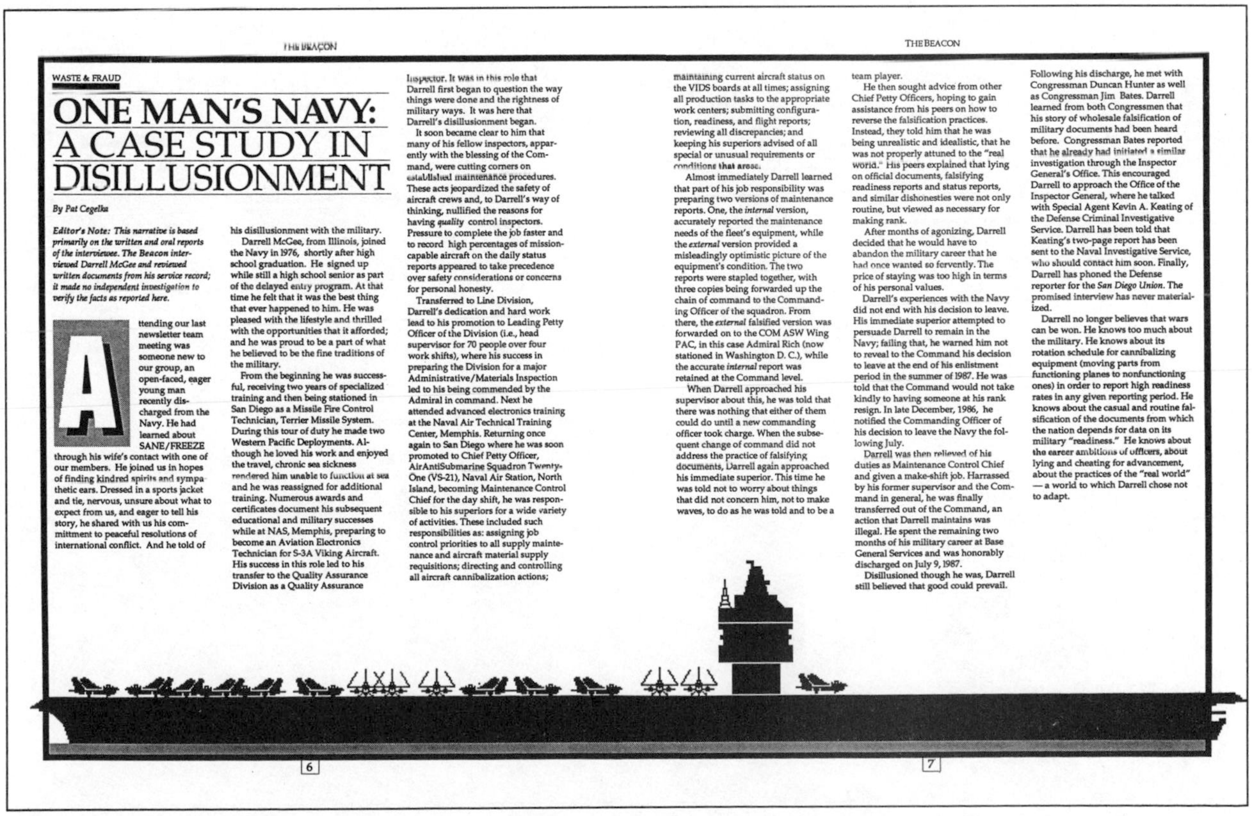

THE BEACON

WASTE & FRAUD

ONE MAN'S NAVY: A CASE STUDY IN DISILLUSIONMENT

By Pat Cegelka

Editor's Note: This narrative is based primarily on the written and oral reports of the interviewee. The Beacon interviewed Darrell McGee and reviewed written documents from his service record; it made no independent investigation to verify the facts as reported here.

Attending our last newsletter team meeting was someone new to our group, an open-faced, eager young man recently discharged from the Navy. He had learned about SANE/FREEZE through his wife's contact with one of our members. He joined us in hopes of finding kindred spirits and sympathetic ears. Dressed in a sports jacket and tie, nervous, unsure about what to expect from us, and eager to tell his story, he shared with us his committment to peaceful resolutions of international conflict. And he told of his disillusionment with the military.

Darrell McGee, from Illinois, joined the Navy in 1976, shortly after high school graduation. He signed up while still a high school senior as part of the delayed entry program. At that time he felt that it was the best thing that ever happened to him. He was pleased with the lifestyle and thrilled with the opportunities that it afforded; and he was proud to be a part of what he believed to be the fine traditions of the military.

From the beginning he was successful, receiving two years of specialized training and then being stationed in San Diego as a Missile Fire Control Technician, Terrier Missile System. During this tour of duty he made two Western Pacific Deployments. Although he loved his work and enjoyed the travel, chronic sea sickness rendered him unable to function at sea and he was reassigned for additional training. Numerous awards and certificates document his subsequent educational and military successes while at NAS, Memphis, preparing to become an Aviation Electronics Technician for S-3A Viking Aircraft. His success in this role led to his transfer to the Quality Assurance Division as a Quality Assurance Inspector. It was in this role that Darrell first began to question the way things were done and the rightness of military ways. It was here that Darrell's disillusionment began.

It soon became clear to him that many of his fellow inspectors, apparently with the blessing of the Command, were cutting corners on established maintenance procedures. These acts jeopardized the safety of aircraft crews and, to Darrell's way of thinking, nullified the reasons for having *quality* control inspectors. Pressure to complete the job faster and to record high percentages of mission-capable aircraft on the daily status reports appeared to take precedence over safety considerations or concerns for personal honesty.

Transferred to Line Division, Darrell's dedication and hard work lead to his promotion to Leading Petty Officer of the Division (i.e., head supervisor for 70 people over four work shifts), where his success in preparing the Division for a major Administrative/Materials Inspection led to his being commended by the Admiral in command. Next he attended advanced electronics training at the Naval Air Technical Training Center, Memphis. Returning once again to San Diego where he was soon promoted to Chief Petty Officer, AirAntiSubmarine Squadron Twenty-One (VS-21), Naval Air Station, North Island, becoming Maintenance Control Chief for the day shift, he was responsible to his superiors for a wide variety of activities. These included such responsibilities as: assigning job control priorities to all supply maintenance and aircraft material supply requisitions; directing and controlling all aircraft cannibalization actions; maintaining current aircraft status on the VIDS boards at all times; assigning all production tasks to the appropriate work centers; submitting configuration, readiness, and flight reports; reviewing all discrepancies; and keeping his superiors advised of all special or unusual requirements or conditions that arose.

Almost immediately Darrell learned that part of his job responsibility was preparing two versions of maintenance reports. One, the *internal* version, accurately reported the maintenance needs of the fleet's equipment, while the *external* version provided a misleadingly optimistic picture of the equipment's condition. The two reports were stapled together, with three copies being forwarded up the chain of command to the Commanding Officer of the squadron. From there, the *external* falsified version was forwarded on to the COM ASW Wing PAC, in this case Admiral Rich (now stationed in Washington D. C.), while the accurate *internal* report was retained at the Command level.

When Darrell approached his supervisor about this, he was told that there was nothing that either of them could do until a new commanding officer took charge. When the subsequent change of command did not address the practice of falsifying documents, Darrell again approached his immediate superior. This time he was told not to worry about things that did not concern him, not to make waves, to do as he was told and to be a team player.

He then sought advice from other Chief Petty Officers, hoping to gain assistance from his peers on how to reverse the falsification practices. Instead, they told him that he was being unrealistic and idealistic, that he was not properly attuned to the "real world." His peers explained that lying on official documents, falsifying readiness reports and status reports, and similar dishonesties were not only routine, but viewed as necessary for making rank.

After months of agonizing, Darrell decided that he would have to abandon the military career that he had once wanted so fervently. The price of staying was too high in terms of his personal values.

Darrell's experiences with the Navy did not end with his decision to leave. His immediate superior attempted to persuade Darrell to remain in the Navy; failing that, he warned him not to reveal to the Command his decision to leave at the end of his enlistment period in the summer of 1987. He was told that the Command would not take kindly to having someone at his rank resign. In late December, 1986, he notified the Commanding Officer of his decision to leave the Navy the following July.

Darrell was then relieved of his duties as Maintenance Control Chief and given a make-shift job. Harrassed by his former supervisor and the Command in general, he was finally transferred out of the Command, an action that Darrell maintains was illegal. He spent the remaining two months of his military career at Base General Services and was honorably discharged on July 9, 1987.

Disillusioned though he was, Darrell still believed that good could prevail. Following his discharge, he met with Congressman Duncan Hunter as well as Congressman Jim Bates. Darrell learned from both Congressmen that his story of wholesale falsification of military documents had been heard before. Congressman Bates reported that he already had initiated a similar investigation through the Inspector General's Office. This encouraged Darrell to approach the Office of the Inspector General, where he talked with Special Agent Kevin A. Keating of the Defense Criminal Investigative Service. Darrell has been told that Keating's two-page report has been sent to the Naval Investigative Service, who should contact him soon. Finally, Darrell has phoned the Defense reporter for the *San Diego Union*. The promised interview has never materialized.

Darrell no longer believes that wars can be won. He knows too much about the military. He knows about its rotation schedule for cannibalizing equipment (moving parts from functioning planes to nonfunctioning ones) in order to report high readiness rates in any given reporting period. He knows about the casual and routine falsification of the documents from which the nation depends for data on its military "readiness." He knows about the career ambitions of officers, about lying and cheating for advancement, about the practices of the "real world" — a world to which Darrell chose not to adapt.

6 7

A two-and-a-half-column format is ideal for accommodating charts, graphs, and tables of different sizes. The narrow column works well for headlines and pull quotes, too. The running text always begins at the top of the page, and the charts are positioned flush with the bottom margin. Occasionally graphics are positioned one above the other. Given the diversity of the visuals, this consistent placement brings order to pages that might otherwise feel haphazard.

Hairline rules create a half-page frame; a second half-frame brackets the main text block. This motif is adapted for the charts, where the headline and the half-frame are inside a box and alternate from the left to right side. This device might appear contrived in some publications, but it is both functional and subtly decorative here.

Tables are created in Microsoft Word and placed in PageMaker following what the managing editor describes as the Golden Rules of Tabs: Use only one tab for each column of data. (If you need more space between two columns, reset the tabs; do not insert two tabs to increase the space). Do not use the Spacebar to adjust space between columns. Be sure to specify left, right, or center alignment. And work in the word-processing program at the same column width you will use in your page layout.

Charts are created in Cricket Graph. Maps are drawn by hand and stripped in by the printer.

Design: Carol Terrizzi (Ithaca, NY)

Pages from Consumer Markets Abroad, *published monthly by American Demographics.*
Trim size: 8-1/2 by 11

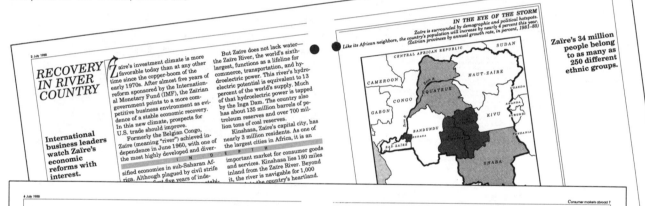

2 July 1988   Consumer markets abroad 3

RECOVERY IN RIVER COUNTRY

International business leaders watch Zaïre's economic reforms with interest.

Zaïre's investment climate is more favorable today than at any other time since the copper-boom of the early 1970s. After almost five years of reform sponsored by the International Monetary Fund (IMF), the Zaïrian government points to a more competitive business environment as evidence of a stable economic recovery. In this new climate, prospects for U.S. trade should improve.

Formerly the Belgian Congo, Zaïre (meaning "river") achieved independence in June 1960, with one of the most highly developed and diversified economies in sub-Saharan Africa. Although plagued by civil strife...

But Zaïre does not lack water—the Zaïre River, the world's sixth-largest, functions as a lifeline for commerce, transportation, and hydroelectric power. This river's hydroelectric potential is equivalent to 13 percent of the world's supply. Much of that hydroelectric power is tapped by the Inga Dam. The country also has about 135 million barrels of petroleum reserves and over 700 million tons of coal reserves.

Kinshasa, Zaïre's capital city, has nearly 3 million residents. As one of the largest cities in Africa, it is an important market for consumer goods and services. Kinshasa lies 180 miles inland from the Zaïre River. Beyond it, the river is navigable for 1,000...

IN THE EYE OF THE STORM

Zaïre is surrounded by demographic and political hotspots. Like its African neighbors, the country's population will increase by nearly 4 percent this year. (Zaïrian provinces by annual growth rate, in percent, 1981–85)

Zaïre's 34 million people belong to as many as 250 different ethnic groups.

6 July 1988   Consumer markets abroad 7

MANAGING GROWTH
Both urban and rural population growth should slow early in the next century. (Annual rate of population growth in urban and rural areas, in percent, 1980–2025)

REFORM'S REWARDS

The Zaïrian government had few choices but to reform under the IMF program in 1982, when the country's foreign-debt burden had reached about US$5 billion. But reform went beyond the rescheduling of debt. Other initiatives included devaluing the national currency (the zaïre), establishing market rates of exchange for most prices and interest rates, liberalizing trade (including customs duties and administrative procedures for export manufacturers), and reorganizing government-owned enterprises known as *parastatals*. In addition, the government improved tax collection and limited public spending and employment.

These reforms produced immediate results. Inflation fell from 76 percent in 1983 to 30 percent in 1985. The government turned an operating budget deficit that was 6 percent of GDP in 1982 into a 1 percent surplus in 1985.

Because the government eliminated exchange and price controls, the black market has shrunk and more profits now accrue to legitimate traders and small farmers. Local supplies reach their markets on a more regular basis.

The periodic shortages that were common in Zaïre now occur less frequently. Both foreign and domestic goods are more plentiful than in the 1970s. Fiscal controls ensure that key industries like mining receive the foreign exchange and local currency they need to operate, thus providing steady jobs for Zaïre's industrial workers.

But these successes have not eliminated Zaïre's debt problem. Not long ago, 50 percent of the government's annual budget was required to meet debt-repayment schedules. From the early days of the austerity program in 1983 through October 1986, Zaïre paid Western financial institutions and governments nearly US$1 billion more than it received in loans, grants, and foreign assistance.

SAFE RETURNS

Because the Zaïrian government recognizes that foreign investment is key in keeping the economic momentum alive, it established a new investment code in April 1986. That code offers numerous tax advantages to foreign businesses, some of which vary by location of the enterprise, number of jobs generated, type of industrial activity, training and promotion of local staff, export orientation, and value added to local resources. Most benefits under the new investment code last for five years, but some last longer, especially for mining ventures. Zaïre guarantees the repatriation of profits to foreign investors.

In addition to a new investment code, the country recently signed a bilateral investment treaty with the United States. That treaty provides additional protection to foreign investors in the areas of transfer of profits, employment of expatriate technical and managerial personnel, and dispute settlement. In 1986, Zaïre became a member of the World Bank's Multilateral Investment Guarantee Agency, which insures foreign investors against the possibilities of currency manipulation and expropriation.

ROOM TO GROW

The Zaïrian government hopes to channel foreign investment into the sectors in which the country has a natural advantage, such as timber, floriculture, and aquaculture. The government considers more than half of Zaïre's estimated 250 million acres of forests—containing over 100 varieties of lumber-producing trees—"exploitable." These forests contain types of wood that don't exist anywhere else in the world, such as African mahogany. Forestry experts predict that Zaïre could become the leading supplier of African hardwood by the mid-1990s.

Unlike the majority of African land, Zaïre's land is extremely fertile. The eastern provinces are ideal for growing perishable products—such as strawberries and fresh-cut flowers—for an expanding export market. Low labor costs, a well-run national airline for transporting cargo (Air Zaïre), and multiple growing seasons position the country favorably in these highly competitive markets.

SOURCES

Statistics on Zaïre are hard to find. While the country took a census in...

URBAN SHIFT
The share of Zaïrian urbanites to the total population will shift from one-quarter to two-thirds by 2025. (Population of Zaïre, in thousands, and percent urban and rural, 1985 and projected 2025)

1985	
Total population	34,672
Percent share	*100.0%*
Urban population	8,668
Urban share	*25.0%*
Rural population	26,004
Rural share	*75.0%*
2025	
Total population	90,097
Percent share	*100.0%*
Urban population	57,717
Urban share	*64.1%*
Rural population	32,380
Rural share	*35.9%*

Source: National Census of Zaïre 1985; World Demographic Estimates and Projections 1950–2025, United Nations, New York, 1988, p. 176.

Source: World Demographic Estimates and Projections, 1950–2025, United Nations, New York, 1988, p. 176.

FARM TO FACTORY
Despite high unemployment, many Zaïrian workers are moving from farming into industry and services. (Labor force by sector, in percent, 1965 and 1980)

1965 — Services 9%, Industry 9%, Agriculture 82%

1980 — Services 16%, Industry 13%, Agriculture 72%

Source: Robert A. Wesser, Jr. & Associates.

WHO WORKS?
Work will cluster around middle age for Zaïrian men and women in the next century. (Labor force participation by sex and age group, in percent, 1985 and projected 2025)

Age group	1985 Women	1985 Men	2025 Women	2025 Men
Total	28.1%	50.2%	29.8%	51.3%
10–14	19.2	30.0	0.4	2.0
15–19	36.8	61.4	26.3	46.4
20–24	42.6	86.6	53.2	83.8
25–29	46.9	96.0	54.3	95.1
30–34	50.9	96.7	55.7	96.7
35–39	53.3	96.8	58.1	96.6
40–44	56.5	96.5	60.3	96.0
45–49	55.9	95.9	58.2	94.6
50–54	54.0	94.6	55.3	91.6
55–59	52.7	92.1	36.2	84.9
60–64	45.5	85.4	23.4	65.2
65 and older	28.9	66.2	9.7	28.6

Source: World Demographic Estimates and Projections 1960–2025, United Nations, New York, 1988, p. 177.

Perspectives

Vol. 3 No. 2 Spring, 1988

Reporting on legislative and political issues

Outlook for AIDS testing looks up, six bills propose eliminating ban

"California now is the only state that forbids AIDS antibody or HIV testing."

The California Legislature's long standing claim to fame is its volume of bills introduced each session. This year is no exception. By the Feb. 19 deadline for new bills, over 7,500 bills were introduced, of which 147 addressed AIDS. These legislative proposals range in subject matter from confidentiality laws, to extensions of HIV testing to provisions for research and education.

Of greatest interest to TLC are six bills that would repeal the prohibition (contained in AB 403, passed in 1985) against antibody testing of insurance applicants for exposure to the AIDS virus. California now is the only state that forbids AIDS antibody or HIV testing. Each measure proposes to authorize health care service plans, nonprofit hospital service plans and/or life and disability insurers to establish mandatory and uniform minimum requirements for assessing AIDS risks for purposes of determining insurability. Specifically, these are: AB 2900 (Johnston, Isenberg); AB 3305 (Johnston); AB 3421 (McClintock); AB 3538 (Johnson); AB 4036 (Mojonnier); and AB 4450 (Peace).

From a political perspective, both AB 2900

Continued on page 2

INSIDE PERSPECTIVES

Single premium life:

Congress has mixed view of issue, while industry juggles positions

Threatening serious consequences for the life insurance industry, the confusion continues to grow over the issue of taxation of single premium policies. During March, the House and Senate each held separate subcommittee hearings on single premium and other investment-oriented life insurance products. The general consensus at the conclusion of the hearings was that it seemed unlikely that the current law will be retained without changes.

Due to marketing practices of some companies, many members of Congress view single-premium policies as "tax loopholes." The likelihood of changing the current law is further enhanced by the life insurance industry's disagreement on an accepted industry-wide position. Major life insurance trade associations are advocating different positions or approaches to the problem.

View from the Hill

Continued on page 2

The two-and-a-half-column format has a very different look when the text is broken up with banners, boxed copy, and illustrations.

Note the absence of rules to separate columns and define the image area. With the wide margin and generous space around headlines, the text block provides sufficient definition. A format with more tightly packed pages would need rules to delineate the elements.

The wide margin is used for quotes, a contents listing, and photos (not shown) that extend an additional 2-1/2 picas into the first text column.

Crimson banners with reverse Garamond type are used for department-style headlines.

The headlines and marginal quotes are Helvetica. The running text is Garamond.

The type prints in blue on bone-colored stock. Boxed copy prints over lavender or light blue tints. A blue tone prints over photos as well.

Design: Partners by Design (N. Hollywood, CA); Agency: Jonisch Communications (Los Angeles, CA)

Pages from Perspectives, published quarterly by the Transamerica Life Companies. Size: 8-1/2 by 11

PAC Talk

Political pundit offers view of presidential races

"Despite the fact that Americans are in the mood for a change, there simply isn't enough momentum for the Democrats to get back in the White House."

Described as the "nation's hot new political pundit," political analyst William Schneider set the stage for his observations of the presidential primary campaigns with a few personal definitions before offering any commentary or opinion at the TALCPAC 200 Club breakfast.

"A pundit is someone who comes on to the field of battle after the fighting stops and then shoots the wounded," he explained. "The primary is the 'killing ground' where they try to kill off the candidates. But this year, they all refuse to die!"

Of course, since that Feb. 19 breakfast, the field of presidential candidates has dwindled considerably. In any event, Schneider's perceptions of the 1988 presidential campaigns provided 200 Club members with new and often amusing insights to the primary season.

"For the Democrats to get back to the White House, they must have an issue like the Depression or Watergate," Schneider said. "But so far they only have the stock market crash and 'Iran-gate'. Despite the fact that Americans are in the mood for a change, there simply isn't enough momentum for the Democrats to get back in the White House," he added.

Schneider conceded that all the candidates from both parties were really competent, but pointed out that "there is not a vision between them."

In his comments on various candidates, Schneider quipped that Massachusetts Governor Michael S. Dukakis attracts the "Masterpiece Theatre audience in politics." Dukakis is "addicted to good government" and is "committed to process," he said.

Suggesting that the Massachusetts governor will use Harvard's Kennedy School of Government to fill key management posts, Schneider remarked that with Dukakis in the White House we would have "government by case study."

He described Illinois Senator Paul Simon as the "Orville Redenbacher" of the Democratic party, explaining that Simon "appeals to the constituency that longs for Mario Cuomo to run." Schneider painted a vivid picture of traditional Democratic fundamentalists as those who "cry and cheer when someone gives a revival speech."

As for the Republicans, he called Kansas Sen. Bob Dole a "superb deal maker."

Schneider also accurately predicted that Vice President Bush would nearly capture the GOP nomination on Super Tuesday (March 8). He reasoned that President Reagan had a strong base in the South, which would help Bush. "But Dole lacked the money, the base and the momentum going into the Southern primary to win," Schneider remarked.

Schneider also commented briefly on the vice presidency, calling it "the last cookie on the plate. No one ever wants it, but someone always takes it. If Bush offers George Deukmejian the vice presidency, Duke will take it," stated Schneider.

Presidential Politics

Who has what it takes?

The presidential primary season enters the last stretch of the campaigns with the final primaries in California, New Jersey, Montana, New Mexico and North Dakota.

Vice President George Bush captured enough delegate votes in the Pennsylvania primary to win the Republican nomination. Now, he is watching the Democratic candidates scramble for delegates as he starts to plan strategy for the November election.

Democratic front runner, Massachusetts Governor Michael Dukakis is still short of the 2,081 delegates needed to secure his party's nomination on the first ballot. Even a big win in California or New Jersey on June 7 won't give Dukakis all the delegates he needs. So, he and his staff are busy seeking commitments from delegates from who are uncommitted or whose candidates have withdrawn.

He also must consider the 645 "super delegates." This is a category created by the Democratic Party's new rules. The party awards 15 percent of the convention seats to Democratic officeholders and party leaders.

Although Dukakis has 30 percent more delegates than the Rev. Jesse Jackson, who ranks second in delegate count, he cannot afford to alienate voters committed to other Democratic candidates. Whoever leaves Atlanta with the Democratic nomination will need to unite the party in order to win in November.

June 1988 ballot propositions

Two initiatives call for careful consideration

California voters will be faced with a dozen statewide propositions on their ballots this June. These initiatives cover a broad range of policy issues from earthquake safety and wildlife protection to technical revisions to the state's constitutional spending limits. Of the 12 initiatives, four are bond issues.

Two initiatives, however, are particularly noteworthy on campaign finance reform . The following is a brief description of both.

Between 1976 and 1986, the cost of running for office in California Legislature has skyrocketed. In 1976, 226 candidates ran for 100 seats (80 Assembly; 20 Senate). Each candidate spent an average of $33,933 to run for office. In 1986, the average spent by 192 candidates for the same offices spent an average of $176,195, an increase of 519 percent.

Proposition 68, sponsored by Common Cause and the League of Women Voters, is an attempt to deal with some of the problems of campaign finance. In short, it limits the amount of funds that can be contributed during any one calendar year and election; it prohibits fund raising during nonelection years; it prohibits transfers of campaign money between candidates; and it establishes a limited form of public financing through a voluntary check-off system on the state income tax form. This measure also limits the amount of money legislative candidates can spend, contribute or loan.

Proposition 73, the second campaign funding initiative on the ballot, is not as complicated as Proposition 68. Sponsored by a bipartisan group of legislators, this measure specifically prohibits both public financing for political campaigns and the transfer of funds between candidates. It limits political contributions from individuals, political committees and parties. This measure also limits the honoraria elected officials can accept during a calendar year.

Historical Perspective

Convention Trivia

The Democrats hold the record for the longest nominating convention and most ballots. In 1924, the convention stretched 17 days and 103 ballots before the Democrats selected John W. Davis of West Virginia to run against President Calvin Coolidge.

Keeping numbers straight on initiative process

"Since...1911, 200 initiatives have been up for votes over the past 77 years."

Since California voters approved the initiative and referendum process in 1911, 200 initiatives have been up for votes over the past 77 years. Of these, 54, or 28 percent, have been approved.

The initiative process has proven to be a powerful voice of the public in affecting change throughout the state, and even across the nation. For example, in 1978 the Tax Limitation Measure, commonly known as Proposition 13, put a cap on property taxes. Since then, other states have copied California's lead on this issue.

Until 1982, the slate of ballot measures for each election began numbering with 1. However, this became increasingly confusing with controversial issues. Proposition 13 was a tax-cutting measure in 1978, but a water conservation proposal in 1982 had the same number.

In 1983, the Legislature passed a law requiring ballot measures to be number consecutively beginning with the November 1982 elections and continuing for 20 years.

This year the June ballot measure will begin with number 66. In 2002, initiatives will begin renumbering with number 1.

Ballot Measures 66 77 88 Through June 7

4

5

A serious, analytical image appropriate for a marketing news-letter is established through the continuous running text and the dimensional, diagrammatic art.

The narrow side margins (2 picas 6 points) allow for wide, 14-pica text columns, about the maximum width in a three-column grid. The density of the text is balanced by white space from a deep, 12-pica top margin, the floating art, and the open leading in the breakouts.

The dimensional "Market Power Grid," abstracted from the cover illustration (not shown), is picked up also as a design motif at the start of each section. The tinted square in each icon is keyed either to the larger grid on the page shown or to a similar grid on another page. The grid was created in Illustrator.

A second color is used for the art, headlines, and breakouts. This helps break up the text and allows for small subheads without loss of emphasis.

The leaders and the narrow-measure callouts emphasize the vertical structure of the grid and keep the page clean and crisp. The small Helvetica type for the callouts contrasts with the larger Times Roman used for running text and breakouts.

The bold initial cap, floating above a gray tinted box, draws the reader's eye to the beginning of the text. This is particularly effective in a page that otherwise lacks any dramatic contrasts.

Design: Marla Schay and Micah Zimring, Watzman + Keyes (Cambridge, MA)

Pages from Indications, *published bimonthly by Index Group, Inc. Trim size: 25-1/2 by 11, folded twice*

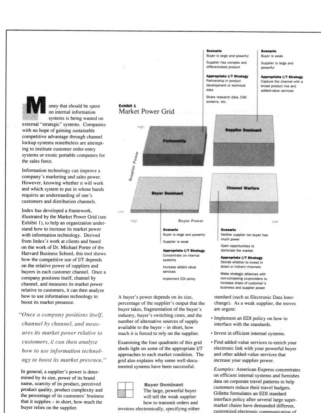

This newsletter achieves a completely different style within the three-column format than does the publication on the facing page. Here, rules and banners separating stories provide a clearly visible page structure, whereas the continuous narrative in the preceding publication is designed with a less apparent, though equally tight, framework. Compare also the justified text of this publication with the ragged right of the preceding one, and the paragraph indents here with the flush left first lines and open paragraph spacing shown on the facing page. Note, too, that the photos here are angled to break out of the grid, while the dimensional art on the facing page is positioned to emphasize the grid.

The angled snapshots over blue shadows loosen up the tightly structured page and also convey a warm, people-oriented image.

Goudy Old Style, used throughout, is a delicate typeface that is handled here with considerable sophistication. Note the open spacing of the all-caps category heads, which set elegantly against the gray banners above each story; the graceful initial caps, which print blue; and the alignment of text in adjacent columns, which adds to the crispness of the justified text. The delicacy of this typeface also makes it relatively forgiving of the uneven spacing often found in justified type.

Design: Kimberly Mancebo, Castro Benson Bryant Mancebo (Campbell, CA)

Pages from the O'Connor Foundation Quarterly. Trim size: 8-1/2 by 11

COMMUNITY OUTREACH

O'Connor Reaches Out to Kids as it Co-Sponsors Children's Discovery Museum Groundbreaking

Why did dozens of O'Connor Hospital employees spend an entire Saturday of their own free time volunteering at the Children's Discovery Museum Groundbreaking?

To help kids learn about health care. They manned interactive learning centers where they showed kids how to splint arms, listen through stethoscopes, navigate wheelchairs, read x-rays, and walk on crutches.

Not only did O'Connor employees participate in the Groundbreaking activities, but they also hope to establish long-term involvement after the Museum opens next year. ⬛

ADMINISTRATIVE DIRECTOR of Radiology Carol Yanz explains how x-rays give an "inside out" view of people.

PATIENT CARE

Monte Villa's Self Discovery Helps Troubled Youths

Located in a serene setting in Morgan Hill, O'Connor's Monte Villa Hospital (MVH) offers confidential adolescent psychiatric programs and chemical dependency services.

The Self Discovery program is committed to affirming life and respecting the dignity of adolescents and their families. The program offers troubled youths a chance to feel better about themselves, to understand their feelings and needs, to discover that they are likeable, and to feel accepted.

When a person comes to Monte Villa Hospital for care, he or she undergoes full medical and neuropsychological evaluations. Group and individual counseling promotes healing of specific physical, spiritual, familial, social, educational and emotional problems. Follow-up care is an integral part of the program. Accredited schooling is also available. For details, call Susan Titus at 408/779-4151. ⬛

NOBODY SAID ADOLESCENCE WOULD BE EASY, but for some teens it is absolutely overwhelming. Compassionate counselors help these youths find their way. The symbol was created by the teenagers at MVH and is used on T-shirts and binders as a reminder of the importance of their efforts in Self Discovery.

PHYSICIAN PROFILE

Golden Gloves Champion Dr. Calcagno Practices 50 Years at O'Connor

Imagine combining the slam bang vigor of a Golden Gloves boxing champion, the gentle sensitivity of a community volunteer, and the sophisticated intelligence of a physician. Put them all together and you've got the fascinating Dr. Joseph Calcagno, general practitioner at O'Connor for nearly half a century.

From the time Dr. Calcagno was old enough to walk, he gleefully tagged along with his dad to local boxing competitions, dreaming of the day when he, too, would win a title. The day came during pre-med school at Santa Clara University when he "left-and-right-hooked" his way through eliminations to win a 1934 Golden Gloves award in the Lightweight Division. That victory still remains one of the special moments in his life.

When he graduated from medical school in 1939, he joined World War II's War in the Pacific. "I spent the whole six years on the islands in field hospital MASH units," he says. "We were the envy of the soldiers, not only because we got Coca-Cola and fresh milk and meat from Army pilots as fringe benefits, but because we had 30 nurses to work with!"

By 1946, he was home again and opened a medical practice on Race Street. Soon after, his passion for boxing came back into focus, this time not as a participant, but as a licensed ringside physician for the California State Athletic Commission. As such, he has been the attending doctor at boxing and wrestling matches on the average of every other weekend for 46 years, with as many as 3-4 dozen matches in a single weekend. He examines

> **"I**n 1946, he opened a medical practice on Race Street, across from the O'Connor Sanitarium. He's been there ever since."

all competing boxers and wrestlers—both amateur and professional—about an hour before each match and treats them immediately after they compete.

"Most injuries are minor face, eye and lip cuts," he explains, "but occasionally the officials or I will stop a fight if we see someone taking a beating, and submit a record to the California Athletic Commission."

As the only boxing/wrestling attending physician in the Santa Clara Valley, he ends up performing annual physicals on at least five professional boxers, wrestlers, officials or judges on any given weekday. They all need Dr. Calcagno's "stamp of approval" to retain their state licences.

A 20-year Volunteer for PAL
As a firm believer in community service, Dr. Calcagno extends his passion for these sports into volunteer work, having regularly donated his time to the boxers and wrestlers of the Police Athletic League (PAL) since the organization was founded in 1968.

Dr. Calcagno is one of those rare individuals who has been able to integrate his professional skills into the healing arts into a hobby which he adores.

"I feel very lucky," he says, "My hobby has become my work. What more could a person ask for?" ⬛

DR. CALCAGNO (photo left) now works beneath a wall filled with awards from his four decades of volunteerism. (Right) Barely into his twenties, Santa Clara University student Dr. Calcagno wins a Golden Gloves title.

The two true tabloids on this page use the 11-by-17 page in similar ways but to different effect. Both rely heavily on white space and display type to make the oversize page accessible.

The three + one-column format (above) creates a half-frame of white space around the image area.

Photos, captions, and a statement of goals break into the white space without filling it.

The logo prints in red ("Ameri") and blue ("News"). The red is picked up in the banners with reverse type and in the rule at the bottom of the page. The blue is picked up in the initial cap, the two-column inset text, and the tint in the contents box. Red and blue are crisp, bold colors that liven up a mostly text page.

The two-column format (above right) is unusual for a tabloid, but the wide margin, used only for pull quotes and blurbs, and the space around the bold headlines make it work.

The nameplate banner is repeated in a smaller size on inside pages, providing strong identity.

A second color, crimson, is used for the alternating thick and thin rules, initial caps, display text inset in the running text, and company identification in the lower left.

The type is Helvetica Black for headlines and blurbs inset in running text, and Bookman for running text, captions, and marginal quotes.

Design (above left): Kate Dore, Dore Davis Design (Sacramento, CA)

Cover of AmeriNews, the inhouse newsletter of AmeriGas–Cal Gas. Trim size: 11 by 17

Design (above right): Mary Reed, ImageSet Design (Portland, ME)

Cover of Re:, a commercial/industrial real estate newsletter published by The MacBride Dunham Group. Trim size: 11 by 17

An all-text, newspaper-style page can be made engaging and attractive. Rules, initial caps, white space, and a second color all support the structural device of using story headlines to divide the page into text units with varying sizes and shapes. The effect is infinitely more appealing to readers than columns of type that simply march down the page. The approach here is conservative—and appropriately so for a bar association newsletter; the same devices, however, can be used to create many other styles.

The top of the image area is dropped so as not to crowd the page. The resulting white space creates a strong horizon line.

The body text is Times Roman, and the subheads are Times Roman bold italic.

The headlines and folios are Caslon Extra Bold. The logo and the initial caps are set in Novarese.

The headlines are centered between brown rules, with a 2-point rule above and a 1-point rule below.

The initial caps print over a box with a horizontal-line fill and no outside rule (this fill also prints brown). Note the careful alignment of the baseline of the initial cap with the bottom rule in the box and the even spacing between the thin-line rule of the fill and the 1-point rule above. When you rely on typographic devices for the look of a page, these details are critical.

Design: Michael Waitsman, Synthesis Concepts (Chicago, IL)

Pages from Litigation News, *published by the American Bar Association. Trim size: 10-3/4 by 13-7/8*

The cover-story concept, seen frequently in magazines, has unusual impact when used effectively in a newsletter. At their best, newsletters have an intimacy with their readers (the result of a shared special interest) and a timeliness that even magazines lack in today's fast-paced communications. So a newsletter cover story implicitly announces, "Here's a problem that many of you are grappling with, and here's what we know about it." Anyone who works with PageMaker can see the immediate appeal of the cover stories shown on the facing page, from a newsletter that aptly describes itself as "a visual guide to using the Macintosh and PageMaker in desktop publishing."

The visual continuity in the covers of this newsletter also seems closer to the world of magazines than to that of newsletters. Newsletters typically achieve their cover identity through a familiar grid and typographic treatment. Here, the cover design varies quite a bit from one issue to the next depending on the subject. But the strong nameplate treatment, the unsual shape of the page, and the always-on-target theme provide their own very effective and unmistakable identity.

The grid is basically one wide column with a wide margin used for captions, art, and marginalia. One advantage of this format, especially in a narrow page such as this, is that you can easily break the grid and use the whole page.

Design: David Doty, PageWorks (Chicago, IL)

Pages from ThePage, *published monthly by PageWorks.*
Trim size: 7 by 11

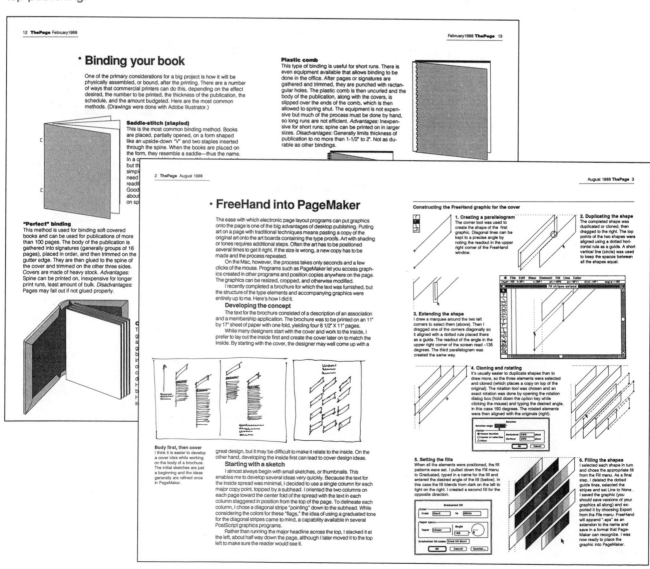

October 1987
A visual guide to
using the Macintosh
in desktop publishing

ThePage10

High resolution reproduction

Which sections of the object below have been reproduced on
a Linotron and which on a LaserWriter?

May 1988
A visual guide to
using the Macintosh
in desktop publishing

ThePage17

Design Ideas for newsletters

NEWSLETTER DESIGN

EpiGram

Nameplate, flag, banner, logo, or masthead?

What do you call that splash of type across the top of a newsletter or magazine? It is often referred to as the masthead. That's actually the one thing it is not. The masthead of a publication is the listing of the staff, generally found on the inside pages.

The most appropriate term is banner, or banner head but nameplate is also widely used. The term logo is less appropriate unless the design is also a symbol representing an organization.

Inside...
Newsletter ideas, publications of interest, the Bettmann Archive, putting photos on the page, ThunderScan into PageMaker, more clip art, and EmDash fonts (this page is set in ArchiText by EmDash).

Create a unique look for your newsletter

Newsletters are one of the forces propelling the desktop publishing revolution. They are seen as a quick way to gain a foothold in the publishing business. Design a newsletter for your client or boss and you're all set, right? What could be easier?

Newsletters are more complex than they appear. With choices of type, numbers of columns, use of photographs or art, handling of running heads, and all the little details of design, there is much to consider before arriving at a final solution.

More important, however, is that the above elements combine to form a unique and unified whole. On the next six pages are six fictional newsletter designs. Use them as idea starters to help structure your own design efforts.

February 1988
A visual guide to
using the Macintosh
in desktop publishing

ThePage14

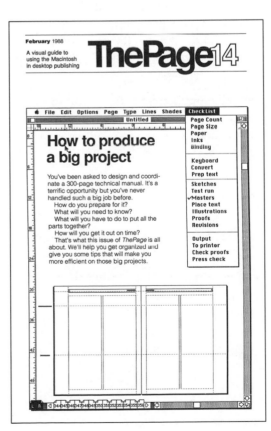

How to produce a big project

You've been asked to design and coordinate a 300-page technical manual. It's a terrific opportunity but you've never handled such a big job before.

How do you prepare for it?

What will you need to know?

What will you have to do to put all the parts together?

How will you get it out on time?

That's what this issue of *ThePage* is all about. We'll help you get organized and give you some tips that will make you more efficient on those big projects.

June 1988
A visual guide to
using the Macintosh
in desktop publishing

ThePage18

The graphics evolution

Aldus FreeHand represents another step in the evolution of graphics programs. It competes head-on with Adobe Illustrator and Cricket Draw, yet offers several interesting advances in technology. Michael Waiteman discusses the strengths and shortcomings of this new program and offers some thoughts on the future of Macintosh illustration programs.

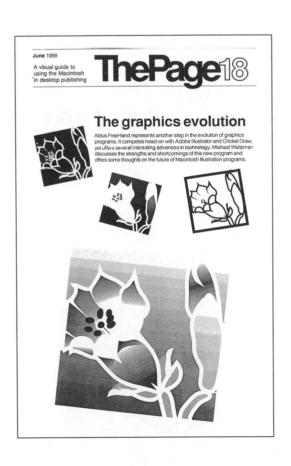

JOURNALS & MAGAZINES

The complexity of the magazine format, with its variety of editorial material in any given issue and the need to juggle several issues at once, makes the collaborative effort between editors and graphic designers one of the key elements of success. Editors who think visually and designers who get involved in the content of the material produce stories that are dynamic and attention-getting, with innovative approaches to even the most familiar ideas. The editor's job isn't over when the manuscript moves from word processor to page layout, and the designer doesn't wait for the manuscript to begin his or her work. Both work together to develop, shape, present, and refine each idea throughout the production cycle. Although desktop publishing is changing the nature of that collaboration, in some ways it presents the greatest opportunities for those editors and designers who don't see their functions as limited to either words or pictures.

Another unique challenge in producing magazines is the opportunity to use the dimension of time that is implicit in the magazine format. Each department and feature story is developed as a self-contained unit, but when you bind them together they become pieces of a whole. Play with that dimension as you make up the order of items in the magazine. Move from a picture story to an article with sustained reading text, from a story with black-and-white photographs to one that uses color illustration, from an idea that is light and accessible to one that is provocative and demanding. Even though few people read magazines from front to back, offering contrast from one story to the next creates an interesting texture and an attention-getting pace. Besides, using that dimension is fun and keeps your job interesting. The more you work with the flow and the pacing, the more they become a useful guide both in early planning and last-minute problem solving.

One of the great dangers in magazine publishing is that your approach will become stale. Don't confuse a consistent format with overreliance on formula. The degree to which you are inspired in producing each issue is probably a good measure of how that issue will be received by readers.

Journals and magazines in this section

- *Washington College Magazine* —a good format for feature articles in an alumni magazine
- *Back Talk Journal*—sophisticated type and photography in a small-format journal
- *American Demographics*—a format designed to introduce data, and some good filler ideas
- *Business North Carolina*—lessons learned from the redesign of a regional business magazine
- *HeartCorps*—a stylish, upbeat design for an audience of heart patients

K arl and Irma Miller nurture the College's students as lovingly as the Hynson-Ringgold gardens. Young adults who know the elderly couple say they have an uncanny ability to bridge the generation gap.

A B O U T   T O W N

Karl And Irma Miller: Tillers Of Good Will

by Sue De Pasquale '87
Photographs by J.M. Fragomeni '88

Karl and Irma Miller are matter-of-fact when it comes to ... about their gardening projects in ...

At 84 and 81, they see nothing unusual about a workload that keeps them bending, hoeing, digging and watering for hours upon hours nearly every day of the week. But ask people half their ... a quarter—who know ...

P I E C E S   O F   T H E   P A S T

Colonel Brown And The Dancing Duo

by P.J. Wingate '33

Although Washington College has been promoting the arts and sciences for over 200 years, it is not well known for its contributions to the performing arts. Nevertheless, a Washington College graduate played a vital role in creating the most celebrated dance team in the history of the theatre—Fred Astaire and Ginger Rogers.

This alumnus was Hiram S. Brown, Class of 1900, and later president of the movie firm RKO, which produced the first Astaire-Rogers film, "Flying Down to Rio," and subsequently made millions of dollars from a series of movies by this most gifted pair of dancers. Colonel Brown, as he was known throughout most of his adult life, was no longer president of RKO when most of those later movies were produced, but it took no great foresight for Brown's successors to see that they had an artistic diamond necklace and a financial gold mine in the dance team of Ginger Rogers and Fred Astaire.

Both Rogers and Astaire had played in Broadway shows before they made their first movie together, and had also played minor roles in the movies, but neither was even close to being called a movie star when Hiram Brown brought them together in 1933. The best that could be said for them then was that they were featured players. The listed stars for "Flying Down to Rio" were Gene Raymond and Dolores Del Rio, both of whom have long since vanished into the mists of obscurity along with the plot of the movie itself.

Not so for Rogers and Astaire. They shot up into the theatrical sky like rockets, propelled by their own incomparable talents and the enchanting tunes by Vincent Youmans who provided the music they danced to: "The Carioca," "Orchids in the Moonlight," "Music Makes Me," and the title song, "Flying Down to Rio." In all subsequent movies which they made together, Ginger Rogers and Fred Astaire were the stars, and their dancing became artistic treasures which will be preserved for centuries to come.

The story of this famous dance team is too well known to be repeated here.

PHOTO: CULVER PICTURES

18   19

This alumni publication used to be a tabloid. After converting to desktop production, the magazine saved enough money on typesetting and pasteup to upgrade the tabloid to the glossy format shown here.

The style of feature articles defines a magazine's personality as much as any other element. Here, good photos given lots of space, graceful Palatino italic headlines, upsized introductions set on a two-column measure, and plenty of white space define an accessible style that opens every feature article. Subsequent pages of features follow the three-column format with photographs sized one, two, or three columns wide. This consistent style greatly speeds up layout and production time because so many decisions are already made.

The understated style works fine for a captive audience, which an alumni magazine such as this enjoys. A magazine with paid circulation has to work harder at varying its style and using catchy headlines to sell readers on each story.

Design: Meredith Davies (Chestertown, MD)

Pages from Washington College Magazine, *published quarterly. Trim size: 8-1/2 by 11*

B A C K   P A I N

A Legal Perspective

SEE YOU IN
COURT

A *Back Talk* interview with John E. Collins, counsel for the plaintiff.

Back injury accounts for one in five injuries in the workplace. It cripples not only employees, but also corporate profits, as employers are left to carry the burden of low productivity and ever-increasing insurance premiums from workers' compensation carriers.

After injury, it's often left to attorneys to argue accountability. Accordingly, *Back Talk* asked one, "Who's to blame?"

John E. Collins has practiced civil and criminal law in Dallas for more than 20 years. He notes that he is board-certified in the specialty of Personal Injury Trial Law, and is a past president of the Texas Trial Lawyers Association and the Association of Trial Lawyers of America. Currently, 85 percent of his firm's business is in the field of personal injury claims, half of which is back injury.

Collins provides a lawyer's perspective on the problem of back injury — and some free counsel to those employers and insurance companies interested in lowering the cost of back injury permanently:

EDITOR: Each year in the United States, it's believed that back injuries cost $16 billion in disability and lost productivity. Indeed, one-third of all compensation

At odds with back-injured employees? A personal injury attorney tells how to lower a company's risk of litigation.

costs are related to low back pain. Depending on who one talks to, different people are accountable for the problem. Let's address the medical system first. In Texas, for example, an injured worker chooses the health care provider, not the company. Is that a positive or negative aspect of the system?

COLLINS: It's clearly positive. Before the workers' compensation law was amended, workers were very suspicious about going to a doctor of someone else's choosing. That created hostility between the patient and the health care provider.

EDITOR: On the other hand, is there inherent risk that the person will access the health care system through the wrong portal of entry, and thereby lower the chance of recovery?

COLLINS: Free choice will always have risk.

EDITOR: In your experience, how many people get sidetracked with a questionable medical provider?

COLLINS: Not many. Less than 10 percent. Most people will go to great lengths to obtain the best possible medical treatment.

EDITOR: In general, do you think doctors do a good enough job in identifying those people who might be classified as "malingerers," i.e., those trying to fake injury for disability payment.

COLLINS: I don't see many of those people. Most of the time, when I turn down a case, it's often that the injury is not serious enough to warrant my involvement — like a back strain. The employee is off only a couple weeks. These people usually want to consult an attorney just to ensure that, long-term, they'll have access to medical care for their injury.

Unfortunately, some employers and insurance companies make it a habit to harass people with back injuries, and to run them off after they return to work. And that makes for more problems.

EDITOR: What percent of the disability suits brought nationwide have little substance?

COLLINS: Not many. I don't want to take a case to the courthouse that's of doubtful merit. Ninety-nine percent of that type of work

Full-bleed photos, used frequently in this journal, have power and impact that you just don't get with photos that are contained on the page. The cover image provides a silhouette that is enviably appropriate for a clinic specializing in back pain.

Good printing on a heavy, coated paper stock brings out the best in the design and photos. The rich blacks contrast with the warm gray/brown used as a second color in the cover type, running heads, bold rules, pull quotes, and boxes for reverse-type initial caps.

The type selection contrasts the clean lines of Helvetica Black with the tall, thin shape of Garamond. The banner centered under the running head works because the two words above it have the same number of letters. The initial cap/small cap style of the subhead and running foot adds additional detail to the sophisticated typography.

Design: Bob Reznik (Plano, TX)

Pages from Back Talk Journal, published annually by the Texas Back Institute. Trim size: 7-1/2 by 11

WHAT IS A WORKING WOMAN?

If you think only half of women work, think again.

◆

by Horst H. Stipp

Whether a woman works outside the home or not is a vital piece of information for marketers who target women. Most rely on the standard published figures—52 percent of women aged 16 and older were working in 1986, for example.

New research indicates that this figure may be way off the mark. In fact, among a target group dear to the hearts of marketers—women aged 18 to 49—about 90 percent can be considered part of the labor force. The "typical housewife" has become rare indeed.

How can the standard statistics understate women's work patterns so dramatically? They overlook the fact that women enter and exit the labor force frequently. Both men and women occasionally change jobs, get laid off, or go to school. But many women also

Horst H. Stipp is the director of Social Research at NBC.

stop working for a while after they have a baby, when they get married, and for other reasons. Overall, women enter and exit the labor force much more frequently than men. As a result, a large percentage of women are both working and not working over a relatively short period of time. Many of today's non-working women will be tomorrow's working women and vice versa. Most important, the attitudes of women with discontinuous work patterns are similar to those of women who are in the work force continuously.

THE PATTERN

The frequency with which women exit and reenter the labor force today is much less than it was 10 or 20 years ago. Nevertheless, demographers Suzanne Bianchi and Daphne Spain find that "women's participation in the labor force over the life course still remains more discontinuous than men's as women continue to exit and reenter the

---

A magazine that is chock-full of charts, graphs, tables, and just about every other form of statistical data works doubly hard to open each story as a general-interest feature. Bold headlines, hand-tinted photographs framed by heavy rules, and lots of white space provide lively hooks and a respite from the data prevalent elsewhere. The upsized introductory blurbs explain or provide context for the headline.

Effective fillers are the hot spots of many magazines. Fillers are simply standing items of varying length that you can plug in wherever space allows (or requires). A good concept for a filler is a fresh, timely, fascinating, or quirky angle on the magazine's subject matter. It's right on target even when it seems to come out of left field. A good filler is generally a quick read and may well be the first thing some readers look for when they pick up the magazine. The Demo Memo filler (above right) runs several times in each issue of *American Demographics*. It's easy to recognize and, for less than a minute of your time, is almost guaranteed to deliver some fascinating fact. The Lincoln Sample (below right) is, by definition, a limited-run filler: It follows a photographer's route from the Atlantic to the Pacific coast, with a picture of the road ahead taken every nine miles, exactly. Editorial techniques such as these keep magazines lively and changing and also provide flexibility in production.

DEMO MEMO

Percent change in college enrollment in foreign languages, 1960–1986:

Japanese 1,282%
Chinese 839%
Spanish 130%
German .... −17%

Statistical Abstract of the United States 1988, Bureau of the Census

26 **THE LINCOLN SAMPLE, STOP NUMBER 26.** 3,060 miles to go. Adams Co., Rt. 30, a few miles past Hubcap City. I am entering Gettysburg, home of The Address, but the sign says we're in Marlboro Country. Beyond the cowboy is the Penn Eagle Motel where I'm spending the night. The owners are from India and it's suppertime—the lobby smells like curry. I made 20 stops today—that's 180 miles. 00225

Design: Michael Rider (Ithaca, NY)
Pages from American Demographics, *published monthly.*
Trim size: 8-3/8 by 11

When this regional business magazine approached a redesign, the staff focused on four goals: to capture the contrast of old and new that typified the audience; to sharpen the spotlight on people; to create a simple format that would free the small staff to focus on content rather than layout; and to convert the magazine to desktop publishing.

The audience combined the deep-rooted traditions of the North Carolina mountains and agricultural areas with the high-tech innovations of businesses and universities in the state's Golden Triangle. Understanding the unique character of one's audience enables a magazine to use that character as a building block in the publication's design.

The typography in the logo captures the contrast inherent in the audience. The word "Business," set in Futura Extra Bold Oblique, is bold, contemporary, and aggressive. The words "North Carolina," set in the genteel, soft, and almost lyrical Palatino, add a quiet, reserved, and sophisticated counterpoint.

The spotlight on people was part of the magazine's editorial image all along. But the redesign process gives you the opportunity to look with fresh eyes at what you are already doing, as well as the opportunity to redefine your goals and determine how best to reach them. In this case, the new understanding led to a change from covers that varied in their subjects and art styles to photographic covers featuring a single business leader in his or her natural enviroment.

The emphasis on good, varied photographs continues on the inside pages. Concentrating on a consistent visual approach and finding a small group of photographers who understand and can deliver the magazine's photographic style frees the art director from having to start at square one with every story.

A table of contents should be highly organized, graphically interesting, and uncompromisingly utilitarian—all at the same time.

The numbers in the contents listings are 24-point Futura Extra Bold Oblique. They are graphic as well as functional elements on the page. As is the case with headline type, numbers set in large sizes require careful kerning to achieve the even spacing seen here.

The rules are 18 point, with 9-point Futura Extra Bold reverse type in all caps.

The descriptive lines are the 10/13 Palatino used for body text inside the magazine.

Art picked up from inside the magazine makes the contents page visually interesting and is selected both to highlight important stories and to arouse curiosity. If you use the art at the same size as it appears elsewhere in the magazine (even if it's just a detail from a larger picture), you avoid the cost of additional color separations.

FEATURE

BUSINESS IS LOOKING UP FOR GENERAL AVIATION

*When it comes to flying for business or pleasure,
the sky's not the limit.*

By J.A.C. Dunn

The little plane circles the airport once, a tiny moving X in the cloudless eastern Carolina sky. Its single engine makes a barely audible hum. It disappears briefly beyond the woods, then suddenly reappears just over the trees surrounding the airport and lands on the longer of Warren Field's two runways. Taxiing to the front of the low, brick terminal building, it swings around to face the broad expanse of rough grass between the tarmac. The pilot cuts the engine, steps out of the cockpit and strolls across the apron and through the double glass doors of the terminal lobby.

"Morning," he says, genially, at large. Salesman, you think. He has a little sandy mustache and very alert eyes. Pointing at a tired-looking, twin-engine plane at one side of the apron, he asks, "That airplane out there. What is it? Does it fly?"

"That's an old DC-4," says Joe Leggitt, the airport manager. He's a stocky, muscular young man with a smiling, sunburned face. He used to be a commercial fisherman. He wears a khaki jumpsuit befitting the all-purpose manager of an all purpose rural airport, but behind the counter he is barefoot. Warren Field is not a stuffy establishment. Authorities, he tells the pilot, impounded the plane after a drug raid last spring. It has been grounded ever since.

"You don't see many of those around any more," the visitor says reverently. He leans against a counter and lights a cigarette. "I was flying over and noticed it, and I thought, 'I have to find out about *that*.' I'm just flying around, looking at the country. I have an appointment in Baltimore this afternoon. I don't want to get there too soon."

He introduces himself: Richard Leachman of Cessna Finance Corp. in Raleigh. Aircraft finance. It fit with the blue blazer, gray slacks, white button-down shirt, necktie and polished loafers. An airplane nowadays is often a corporate asset, not a Sunday toy, and its pilot, rather than a flying playboy nicknamed Ace, is likely to wear a business suit with a briefcase as his co-pilot. The Aircraft Owners and Pilots Association describes the average general aviator as 44 years old, the owner of a house and two cars, married with two children, a licensed, instrument-rated pilot who flies a single-engine, fixed-gear aircraft 116 hours a year and likes to fish.

Despite its apparent imprecision, the term "general aviation" is very specific. It embraces all flight except commercial airlines and the military. It doesn't grab the headlines, the way Piedmont's recent merger with USAir or the opening of a regional airline hub does, but its statistics are astonishing. The nation's general

Charles (left) and Winfield Causey were farming with their father in 1963. But they got bitten by the flying bug and turned from furrows to runways.

MAURY FAGGART

FEATURE

Phyllis Gallup replaced one plane wrecked by a student, who walked away from the crash. "All she said was, 'Oh, my hair must be a mess,' " Gallup says.

MAURY FAGGART

was a licensed pilot before he was 21. In 1921, he flew from London to China solo. The Winston-Salem airport bears his name.

But it was only after World War II that airports, and aircraft to use them, began to take off in North Carolina. The stimulus was a liberal sprinkling of leftover military airfields, most of them in the eastern part of the state. The airports at Wilson, Rocky Mount (now closed), Lumberton, Kinston, New Bern, Beaufort-Morehead City, Washington, Manteo and Edenton were all originally military fields.

Most were used for training. Warren Field had T-6 trainers based on it, and the original runways are still in use, although their 45-year-old concrete pavement is showing signs of wear. The 82nd Airborne Division flew troop-carrying gliders at Maxton, and pilots took basic flight training at Horace Williams Field in Chapel Hill. When the present Raleigh-Durham Airport replaced Raleigh Municipal, it was called Raleigh-Durham Army Air Base until transferred to civilian hands after the war.

Several airports are still used by the military, such as McCall Field in Aberdeen and Oak Grove at New Bern. Thirty miles southeast of Elizabeth City is Harvey's Point, a small airfield deliberately kept small because the Central Intelligence Agency operates it. Some of the participants in the Bay of Pigs invasion were trained there.

During the 1950s, the economic value of general aviation began to take off. In 1958, the Federal Aviation Act provided the first federal funds for airport development. Nearly 20 North Carolina airports received improvement money until 1970.

In 1965, Gov. Dan Moore created the position of aviation specialist in what was then the Department of Conservation and Development to help communities attract

new business by providing a place for companies to park their planes. The state established an airport aid program with $127,000 in 1967, though this money could not be used to improve airports that had scheduled commercial service. The fund was increased to $150,000 a year in 1971.

The airport aid fund was increased to $2 million in 1973, when the reorganization of state government placed the aviation specialist in the Department of Transportation. Half the money went to airports with commercial service. The fund was increased to $3 million in 1974 and the distinction between commercial and general-aviation airports removed.

The federal deregulation of commercial airlines brought about this change. Before deregulation, airlines were subsidized, sometimes by as much as $60 per passenger per stop at an airport, to enable airlines to serve relatively low-traffic places, such as Elizabeth City. Airport managements charged the airlines for airport improvements, which the airlines paid for from their subsidies.

After deregulation, it became harder to maintain and improve airports because airline subsidy money was gone. But most communities found it worth their while to

A plane is a time machine, says the N.C. Division of Aviation's Willard Plentl. He wants every industrial area of the state to have an airport within a half-hour drive.

MAURY FAGGART

Design:
R. Kimble Walker
(Charlotte, NC)

Pages from
Business North Carolina,
published monthly.
Trim size: 8-1/4 by 10-7/8

A strong, simple format enables the small staff to produce a quality magazine that competes for readers' time with big-budget national business magazines. By minimizing the choices for each story, the editor and art director can concentrate on substance rather than form.

The 72-point Futura Extra Bold initial cap with an 18-point bold rule continues the visual motif from the cover. Rules over photos print in a different color for each feature. This bold, crisp look helps tie together editorial pages in a magazine fractured by small-space ads.

The body text, 10/13 Palatino in two 16-pica ragged right columns, sets about one-third fewer words than the more typical 9/10 justified text found in many magazines. The open text was another result of the redesign, and the editors feel that less has proved to be more.

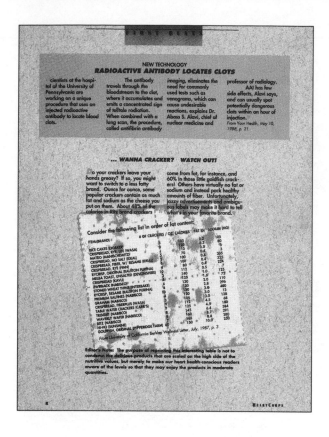

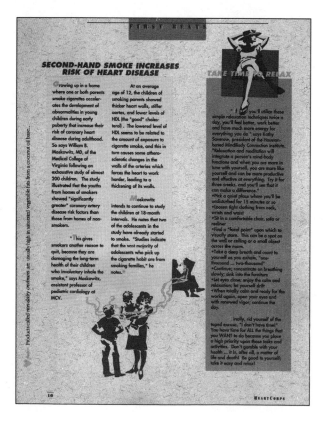

A stylish, varied, and active design gives an upbeat image to this magazine for heart patients. The pages are full of tips, techniques, charts, and other information highlighted through a visual repertoire that includes initial caps, large numerals, and frequent use of sidebars.

Department pages such as the ones shown at left break from the traditional columnar format by having each item treated almost as if it were an index card. The shape of the text block, as well as the type size, leading, and column width, vary from item to item, but the single typeface (Futura) and the textured background unify these pages.

Dimensionality is another signature of this design. Note the use of the cracker as a self-referential background for a chart, with type surprinting at the top and bottom. And in the page shown below left, the first text block appears to be sandwiched between art in the foreground and background; in the second item, the art is woven under the headline and over the text.

The headline type for feature stories (shown on the facing page) is Bodoni Poster, condensed to different degrees for each story depending on the length of the headline and the layout of the page. This provides the benefits of a unified typeface with many variations. Bodoni Poster works unusually well with this treatment because it maintains its distinctive relationship of thick and thin strokes. Many typefaces deviate too much from the original design when condensed.

The text wraparound (facing page, bottom) adds graphic interest to the page and also minimizes the text lost to a fairly large illustration. This technique can be prohibitively expensive using commercial typesetting. Desktop publishing makes it affordable, though it may require a lot of fine-tuning to avoid bad line breaks and achieve even spacing.

Design: Tom Lewis (San Diego, CA)

Pages from Heartcorps, *published bimonthly. Size: 8-1/4 by 10-3/4*

ROPE JUMPING
TOO GOOD TO PASS UP?

BY KEN SOLIS, MD

An often re-peated adage states, "The best exer-cise is the exercise which you do." There are four essential questions which you must ask yourself to define if an exercise is one that you will likely do *on a regular basis and for an indefinite period of time*: 1) Is it right for your body? 2) Is it easily accessible? 3) Will it give the results you are looking for? and 4) Do you enjoy it?

Perhaps surprisingly, rope jumping is one form of aerobic exercise which nicely fits the bill for many people, even recovered heart pa-tients. Now, even without the help of telepathy, I know that a good number of you readers have already been struck with the "but ... too" disease: "I'd love to try it, *but*

I'm *too* uncoordinated to jump rope" - or - "it sounds like fun, *but* it'd be *too* hard on my knees" - or - "it's *too* hard on my wind, and it's *too* boring." In fact, rope jumping is one of the most user-friendly, safe, ver-satile and productive exer-cises available. Unfortu-nately, it is also one of the most misunderstood. So before we write off rope jumping to highly-tuned pu-gilists and energetic school children, let's see if rope jumping is an exercise which you just might want to do.

ARE YOU READY FOR IT?

First ask your physi-cian if your heart is ready for moderate to vigorous exer-cise. Rope jumping is not recommended for the early phases of cardiac rehabilita-tion since the heart rate response is less predictable

RATED PERCEIVED EXERTION (RPE) SCALE

0	Nothing at all
0.5	Extremely weak
1	Very Weak
2	Weak
3	Moderate
4	Somewhat strong
5	Strong
6	
7	Very strong
8	
9	Extremely strong
10	Maximal

FIGURE 1. On a scale of 1 to 10, exercise intensity is guided by using your own internal "sense" of how hard you are working. Exert-ing yourself in the range of 3 to 5 correlates well to the "target heart rate.

(reference: Borg, G.V., *Medicine and Science in Sports and Exercise*, 14:377-87, 1982.)

28   HEARTCORPS

TIPS TO GET YOU THROUGH THE HOLIDAYS

BY LEE LIPSKER, PH.D.

Sugar plum fairies, chestnuts roasting on an open fire, colorful wrapping paper, friends and relatives gath-ered together, ... the holiday period of November through December evokes images which are nearly universal. It seems that most everyone is caught up in the spirit and mood of the season. Just think of the gusto with which we proclaim, "Happy Thanksgiving! ... Happy Hanukah! ... Merry Christmas! ... Happy New Year!" Unfortunately, this two or three month period of the year is often a time of anxiety, stress, and depression for persons with heart disease and their immediate family members.

Depression is a commonly reported problem for those who have experienced myo-cardial infarction (MI), coronary bypass sur-gery, angioplasty, or other heart-related illnesses. In fact, the research literature suggests that between 55% and 90% of all heart attack victims experience significant signs of de-pression as long as one year after the attack. In most cases, the depression and accompa-

1 TALK ABOUT IT. Part of the nature of depression is the ten-dency to believe that your difficulties are so unique that no one else could possibly under-stand. After all, you certainly wouldn't want to "burden" someone else with your problems! Nothing could be further from the truth. The many issues discussed here are so common that they are nearly as universal as are the mistletoe and colored lights. Surely everyone has experi-enced the disappointment felt when our expectations have not been met. Can any one of us honestly say that we have not been disillusioned by the over-commercialization of the holidays - at least for a little while? More significantly, most of your friends and family have had moments of depression. We all know what it is like to be "down."

Many of the issues that are involved in depres-sion are of interest to the people that are closest to us. The variety of emotions that often accompany heart disease need attention. Your physician may be interested in your feelings for several reasons, not the least of which is the possibility of side-effects from prescribed medication. The holidays are often a period of increased spirituality - the perfect time to call on your pastor or rabbi. Or as described below, the holiday time might be the right time to get involved in a support group.

Talking to someone about your problems can have many beneficial effects. First, by articulating our feelings we get to hear for ourselves just what is bothering us. Once the issues are on the table, we can call on many of our own resources to deal with them. With our thoughts laid out for us, we can identify the ones that are rational and have some basis in truth. Talking about what is bothering us also opens the door for help. It is often enough just to remind ourselves that some-one will listen to us and care about how we feel. When we share our pain, discomfort, fear or sadness, we allow others to demonstrate their love and caring for us. In the sharing process, good ideas for solutions or understanding are generated by the parties involved.

2 GET INVOLVED. Few things contribute to our psychological well-being as greatly as knowing that we're important and needed. The holiday time presents us with a myriad of opportunities to become active in projects that can add immeasurably to our self-esteem. From volunteer-ing on the children's ward at the local hospital to address-ing and stuffing envelopes at the area American Heart Association or American Red Cross office - there are unlimited places and programs in which you can direct some energy.

This form of involvement accomplishes

WALKING...
TAKING YOUR EXERCISE IN STRIDE

BY BILL BUSH, EDITOR-IN-CHIEF

A good brisk walk, several times a week, can strengthen the heart.

One of the most important steps in restor-ing heart health can be many steps taken in quick succession -- a brisk walk. The remarkable benefits of regular walking for cardiac re-habilitation have been acknowledged by virtually all cardiolo-gists, who cite their own clinical experi-ence and the growing body of long-term research.

Many heart patients wonder how something as easy as walking can have such a big impact on their physical condi-tion. The simple truth is, a good brisk walk, several times a week can strengthen the heart. Adhering to a regular walking pro-gram may also have a favorable effect on blood pressure, serum cholesterol level, weight control, and psychological attitude. You may be thinking, "Can just simple walking regularly do all that?" and the answer is a resound-ing "Yes!"

While it is known and reported

that high-intensity, "power" walking de-livers great fitness benefits; low-intensity walking, "a brisk walk around the block" will return substantial health benefits as well, especially if done regularly and frequently. This is especially welcome news for the thou-sands who have come to believe that heart attack re-covery and heart health can only be gained through heavy-duty exercise. The "no pain, no gain" body-building adage simply doesn't hold true for cardiac rehab.

Dr. Neil Gor-don, at the Institute for Aerobics Research in Dallas, Texas, starts every patient with a walking program. Ac-cording to Gordon, "Walking is the ideal exercise for heart at-tack patients." He rec-ommends walking for cardiac patients be-cause it tends not to

promote the injuries common to jogging, like shin splints, muscle and tendon pulls and joint inflam-mation. "Often heart patients are older and ill-pre-pared to

suffer the jarring and compres-sion that go with other types of exercise," says Dr. Gordon. "Walk-ing is a nat-ural move-ment for the body

and , therefore, it is very low impact but can be very aerobic if done properly."

Patients at Gordon's clinic are tested to determine optimum exertion levels for the course of their cardiac

ILLUSTRATION: JOHN CARLYLE

rehabilitation. Using a treadmill, Gordon gradually increases speed and elevation to a point where the pa-tient is substantially taxed and approach-ing problems -- 70% to 85% of that level of exertion is determined to be the patient's "symptom-limited maximum heart rate." Gordon's exercise pre-scription, which all patients must have before undertaking any type of strenuous program, is typically a regimen calling for walking sessions lasting 20 to 40 minutes, three to five times a week at

the rate determined by the stress test.

Dr. Gordon, in our interview, empha-sized that the "symp-tom-limited maximum heart rate" is quite dif-ferent from the "target heart rate" training guidelines that have thousands of fitness-devoted Americans regularly checking their pulses during and after exercise. (See page 24.)

The American Heart Association and American College of Sports Medicine rec-ommend an exertion level measured at 60-75% of the maximum heart rate, sus-tained for 30 minutes at least three times a week. They assert that exercise above 75% may be too strenuous unless in excellent physical con-dition; and exercise below 60% gives the heart and lungs little physical condi-tioning.

Brisk walking - - about four to five miles per hour, can elevate heart rates into the ideal conditioning range. But even walk-ing at three and one-half miles per hour may be too taxing for those on the mend from a heart attack.

Fortunately, there is an increasing body of knowledge through research that suggests substantial health benefits can be achieved at exercise levels far below the 60% to 75% target zone. "Walking for 45 minutes a day is wonderful, even without ever reaching your target heart rate zone," says Dr. Bob Hopper of the Cardiac Health & Diagnostic Center in Long Beach, California. Hopper, an exercise physiolo-gist, makes a key dis-tinction between *health* and *fitness* : the data suggests physical activity is related to lower heart disease risk, not necessarily fitness. A good physi-cal fitness program will achieve heart healthy benefits, but walking and never achieving your target heart rate is also very good."

Hopper says moderate activity equal to expending about 2000 calories a week will reduce the risk of heart disease, but not necessarily improve fitness. He admits that his is a minority "but growing" opinion on the value of moderate exercise for heart health. However, he argues that nationally, adherence to more rigorous fitness pro-grams have been dismal, especially in older age groups. "The fitness craze has been a failure," says Hopper. "Only a small percentage of Ameri-cans, one study says about 6.5%, reach the American College of Sports Medicine guide-lines of 30 minutes at the target heart rate, three times a week."

Hopper strongly believes in the ACSM guidelines, but takes a more pragmatic view when dealing with cardiac rehab patients. "We talk with our cardiac patients and find out that they have not been able to stay with a fitness pro-gram. For the long term, its better to get heart patients on a

Generally, the more deeply an exercise makes you breath, the more it burns calories and body fat...

22   HEARTCORPS   SEPTEMBER/OCTOBER 1988   23

CHAPTER 6

DATA: CATALOGS, DATA SHEETS, FINANCIALS, AND FORMS

Publications with large amounts of data rely heavily on careful organization and deft styling of typography. Some require clear delineation and consistent handling of repetitive elements, such as product names, prices, and descriptive listings; others require formats that can accommodate different kinds of elements, such as continuous narrative interspersed with tables, charts, and graphs.

Before settling on an approach, you'll need to analyze the material and experiment with different typographic styles. The ability to experiment on the desktop is a decided advantage when you are designing these publications, and you can save time by testing small samples of data before styling the entire document. In testing the type style and tab positions for tables, be sure to include both the maximum and minimum number and length of elements you have to accommodate, so that you can see the balance of the two in any format.

CATALOGS & DATA SHEETS

When you have to pack a lot of text into a small space, you will generally enhance the appeal and overall readability if you choose a small, tightly leaded, condensed type style and maximize the space around the text. Larger sizes surrounded by less white space result in pages that are dark and unrelievedly dense. Use rules and borders to aid organization and to change the color of the page. Even in publications without a second color, rules with contrasting weights can add much-needed graphic variety as well as organizational clarity.

Catalogs and data sheets in this section

- *Tables Specification Guide*—diverse elements in a landscape format
- *Books on Black Culture*—art to liven up straightforward catalog listings
- *Beverly Hills Motoring Accessories*—boxes, banners, and more boxes and banners
- *The Concept Technical Manual*—technical illustrations for ski clothes
- *Teaching Tools*—a highly structured catalog of educational software
- *School of Visual Arts*—a little style to dress up straightforward listings
- *Clackamas Community College catalog*—a format that accommodates many different kinds of listings
- *Portland State Quarterly*—adventurous typography in a college newspaper format

- *The Huck Lockbolt Fastener Design Guide*—technical illustrations in a utilitarian format
- *Triad Keyboard*—easy-to-scan text and life-size photos
- *Maxtor Data Sheets*—high-quality, high-tech still lifes
- *Infrared Optics Cleaning Kit*—handsome simplicity
- *Smith & Hawken product assembly sheets*—an easily implemented format consistent with the company look
- *Questor Inlets*—leadered callouts and a functional use of color

The horizontal format provides more flexibility than a vertical page in organizing the many options available for items in this catalog.

The master pages include the rules, logo, headlines, and black box on the top page, and the rules and bar coding on the bottom page. In addition to simplifying electronic page assembly, this uniformity brings visual order to a complex document. It also makes it easy for readers to find information about any given product because similar information appears on the same place on every page. If a master item is not used on an actual page, it is masked over with a No Lines-Paper Fill box and that slot appears blank.

The line drawing of each item prints as a white line in a black box. This technique dramatically highlights the subject of each page, making it the dominant item amid the many other kinds of information. The drawings were created in MacDraft, saved as PICT files, and sized proportionally in PageMaker.

For the data on the bottom page, pencil roughs were used to determine the number and depth of items for each table in the catalog. Several templates were then made, with a different configuration of rules on the master page of each one. The text for all pages using the same configuration was created in a single Microsoft Word file and placed in PageMaker. Planning pays off by eliminating the need to redraw rules on every page and by making it possible to refine the tabs in PageMaker for an entire file, representing many catalog pages at one time.

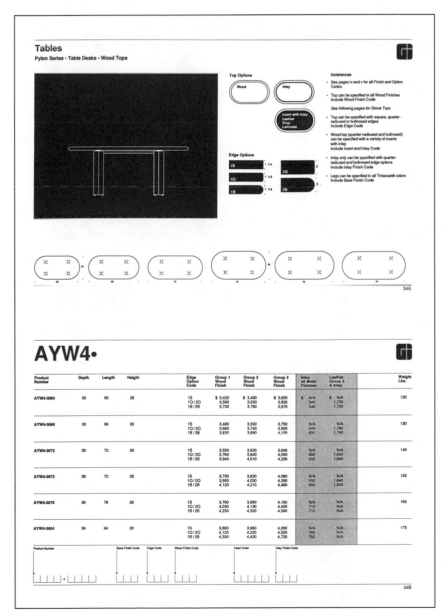

Design: Manfred Petri (Atlanta, GA)

Pages from Tables Specification Guide and Price List, *from Geiger International. Trim size: 11-7/8 by 8-3/8*

The bold banner across the top of each page and the striking silhouettes of the African art give this book catalog a distinctive personality that is obviously appropriate to the theme of black culture.

The two text columns are boxed in with rules. The outer column is consistently used for art, which is photocopied (with permission) from one of the books in the catalog and pasted into position on the camera-ready pages. When a category of books does not require the two text columns on a page, additional art is used as filler.

The typeface for the book listings is Helvetica. The use of boldface caps to set off the titles, regular caps for the authors, and space between this highlighted information and the descriptive listings is handled consistently throughout and makes the catalog easy to use. The type overall is relatively dark, a result of using laser printer output for camera-ready copy. That darkness works here with the art style and format.

The category heads are Times Roman, reversed out of the black banners at the top of each page.

Design: Lisa Menders (Royal Oak, MI)

Pages from Books on Black Culture, *a mail-order catalog published by the book end in Southfield, MI.*
Trim size: 8-3/8 by 11

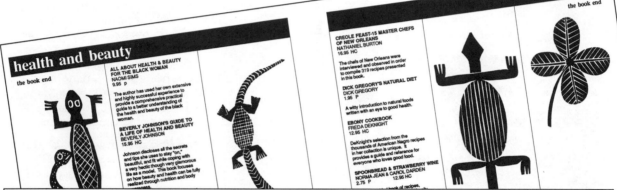

health and beauty
the book end

ALL ABOUT HEALTH & BEAUTY FOR THE BLACK WOMAN
NAOMI SIMS
9.95 P

The author has used her own extensive and highly successful experience to provide a comprehensive practical guide to a better understanding of the health and beauty of the black woman.

BEVERLY JOHNSON'S GUIDE TO A LIFE OF HEALTH AND BEAUTY
BEVERLY JOHNSON
15.95 HC

Johnson discloses all the secrets and tips she uses to stay "on," beautiful, and fit while coping with a very hectic though very glamorous life as a model. This book focuses on how beauty and health can be fully realized through nutrition and body resiliences.

cooking
the book end

CREOLE FEAST-15 MASTER CHEFS OF NEW ORLEANS
NATHANIEL BURTON
16.95 HC

The chefs of New Orleans were interviewed and observed in order to compile 319 recipes presented in this book.

DICK GREGORY'S NATURAL DIET
DICK GREGORY
1.95 P

A witty introduction to natural foods written with an eye to good health.

EBONY COOKBOOK
FREDA DEKNIGHT
12.95 HC

DeKnight's selection from the thousands of American Negro recipes in her collection is unique. It provides a guide and reference for everyone who loves good food.

SPOONBREAD & STRAWBERRY WINE
NORMA JEAN & CAROL DARDEN
2.75 P   12.95 HC

... book of recipes.

biography
the book end

GOOD MORNING BLUES-AUTOBIOGRAPHY OF COUNT BASIE
ALBERT MURRAY
10.95 P

Gives the fascinating life and times of Count Basie, one of the pre-eminent figures in jazz history. Tales of his childhood days to his fame, and his influence on the music world.

GROWING-UP IN A RURAL SETTING
DAVID FIELDS
6.50 P

This book deals with the author's growing up in the rural south, and his leaving the south for the north; and the personal problems he had to overcome in order to maintain his dignity and sanity.

HARRIET TUBMAN-THE MOSES OF HER PEOPLE
SARAH BRADFORD
4.95 P

An exact, unaltered and unabridged, reprint of Bradford's memorable biography of Harriet Tubman.

HARRIET TUBMAN-THE ROAD TO FREEDOM
RAE BAINS
1.95 P

Young person's biography beautifully illustrated telling the tale of Harriet Tubman and her passage to freedom.

HEART OF A WOMAN
MAYA ANGELOU
3.95 P

One of the most remarkable personal narratives of our age. Maya Angelou describes her later years as a singer and dancer, journeys to New York City. Maya speaks with an intimate awareness of the heart within us all. (Fourth of five volumes)

HIT AND RUN-THE JIMI HENDRIX STORY
JERRY HOPKINS
8.95 P

The intimate shocking story of Jimi Hendrix who electrified audiences everywhere. Revealed are his personal battles with sex, drugs and people.

HORNES - AN AMERICAN FAMILY
GAIL LUMET BUCKLEY
18.95 HC

Lena Horne's daughter gives us an intimate look into "America's historic family secret", the black bourgeoisie. In words and pictures kept by family and friends, Buckley brings this fascinating story to life.

I KNOW WHY THE CAGED BIRD SINGS
MAYA ANGELOU
3.95 P

An autobiographical narrative examining black life in a rural community during the 1930's. Her portrait is a Biblical study of life in the midst of death. (first of five volumes)

I WONDER AS I WANDER
LANGSTON HUGHES
9.95 P

The Big Sea was the first volume of Hughes's autobiography. This is the second volume. Personal history intertwined with narratives of his travels. Written with bounce and zest.

I'M GONNA MAKE YOU LOVE ME
JAMES HASKINS
2.75 P

As much as a life story, this is a book about the music business and especially about Motown and the recording industry. A fascinating and dazzling account of Diana Ross's life and rise to stardom.

I, TINA: MY LIFE STORY
TINA TURNER
16.95 HC

One of the most sensational life stories in show business, encompassing the lowest lows and the highest highs. The story of a true survivor, she tells it the way it is.

JACKIE ROBINSON-FIRST OF THE CHOSEN FEW
JOSEPH NAZEL, JR.
2.25 P

The life story of the first black man to play in the major league. Covers his early baseball years to his later career as a successful businessman and civil rights activist.

biography
the book end

JAMES BROWN:GODFATHER OF SOUL
JAMES BROWN
18.95 HC

In his own words, Brown tells of his rise from a world of poverty and segregation to one of wealth, musical pre-eminence, even political influence. More than a revealing celebrity memoir, his autobiography is a spectacular performance.

JAMES VAN DER ZEE-PICTURE TAKIN' MAN
JIM HASKINS
8.95 P

Based on numerous interviews with James Van DerZee and liberally illustrated with some of his best work, this is an intimate portrait of a gifted artist who recorded more than half century of black history.

JESSE JACKSON AND THE POLITICS OF RACE
THOMAS LANDEES
17.95 HC

Here is Jesse Jackson's life story, from his unusual childhood to his quest for the presidency. Includes the momentous story of America's civil rights movement and its recent move toward black separatism.

JESSE JACKSON: AMERICA'S DAVID
BARBARA REYNOLDS
11.95 P

One of the most objective, thoroughly researched and documented writings on Jesse Jackson. An important book for everyone.

JOHN COLTRANE
BILL COLE
10.95 P

A biography of the late jazz great John Coltrane, his contribution to American music and some of the forces that shaped his life.

JUST MAHALIA BABY-MAHALIA JACKSON STORY
LAURRAINE GOREAU
13.95 P

A fast-paced and richly detailed biography of the great queen of gospel, Mahalia Jackson. It brings life not only to Mahalia but to an entire ethos for people who will never be able to have any other contact with it.

KAFFIR BOY
MARK MATHABANE
19.95 HC

The true story of a black youth's coming of age under apartheid in South Africa. A descriptive and enlightening story of human struggle in South Africa.

KING REMEMBERED
FLIP SCHULKE
7.95 P

An extraordinary tribute to one of the most influential leaders of our time. Based on exclusive interviews of Dr. King's closest friends and features the most comprehensive single collection of still photographs of King's life and times.

LADY SINGS THE BLUES
BILLIE HOLIDAY
5.95 P

Billie Holiday tells her own story of her turbulent adolescence in Harlem during the 1920s, the excitement of working in New York City's famous jazz clubs with the musicians who brought jazz to the forefront of American culture, and her own dazzling rise to the top.

LANGSTON HUGHES-BEFORE & BEYOND HARLEM
FAITH BERRY
12.95 P

The first full-length portrait of Langston Hughes, one of the finest poets of our times. Berry concentrates on the writer's life and career from his formative years through his involvement in the Harlem Renaissance; she traces his place in the society and in literary and political worlds.

LAY BARE THE HEART
JAMES FARMER
8.95 P

The story of James Farmer's life revealing the mammoth struggle of the civil rights movement. This book captures the inspiring strengths and human weaknesses of the movement.

LEADERSHIP, LOVE & AGGRESSION
ALLISON DAVID
15.95 HC

A brilliant psychobiographical study of the four most important American Negro leaders. Davis brings to this study of the ego-development of four great men both psychological insights and profound knowledge of social anthropology.

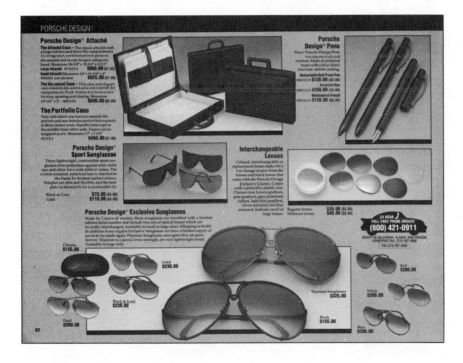

Boxes and banners are used throughout to organize the many elements on each page.

Black banners along the top function as tabs, with product categories in reverse type.

Photos are framed by 0.5-point rules on three sides; the 8-point rule at the bottom of each frame provides a solid base for each photo. This is particularly effective when the product is a car and also gives the catalog a distinctive style. Note the varied directions of the cars in the top row of photos.

Small objects are carefully arranged as still lifes to best display shape, texture, and different views and styles of the same product. The pattern of objects repeated on the page plays with color and shape to provide visual interest. Grouping small objects in one photo saves space as well as photo expenses.

Silhouette photos that extend beyond the picture frames have more dimensionality than photos that are contained. This technique provides variety within the basic format and maximizes the use of space where needed.

Text prints on a gray background. The boldface Helvetica headlines and prices are offset from the descriptive text, which is set smaller in Palatino.

Design: Bob Lee, Lee & Porter Design (Los Angeles, CA)

Pages from a catalog published by Beverly Hills Motoring Accessories. Trim size: 11 by 8-1/2

Simple technical diagrams
with leadered callouts tell the story in this wholesale catalog of ski clothes. Why diagrams? Because here the message is warmth, freedom of movement, and protection from impact and sliding hazards, rather than the fabric and fashion angle typically captured in photographs.

Careful alignment of elements
provides structure within a free-form design. A formal grid would have restricted the size of art and placement of callouts. The distinctive logo treatment, the art and callout style, and the typeface provide visual consistency from page to page.

The typeface is Bodoni, with Helvetica Black used for boldface emphasis in headlines. The ragged right margin suits the casual style and short line length of the callouts. As much as possible, leaders extend from the justified left margin, the top or the bottom, rather than the ragged right.

This highly structured format
positions the product in the same place on every page. The position of the headlines, lists of features, screen details from the programs, system requirements, and other elements also remain constant, making it very easy to find any piece of information for any product.

The headline and other boldface type is American Typewriter and matches the type on the packaging.

The row of triangles under each product name is a right-leadered tab. The leader is customized with a Zapf Dingbat and a character space (the keystroke for the Dingbat is unshifted t). You can define a style for a customized leader; then, each time you want to add it to the document, simply position the cursor, apply the style, and insert the tab.

The triangles in the upper right of each page function as product category tabs. Each category uses a different color for that triangle, for the line of small triangles, and for the quote under each product.

Design (top):
Oscar Anderson,
Weingart/Anderson
(Chicago, IL)
Page from the
Concept Technical
Manual, *published*
by Apparel
Technology.
Size: 8-1/2 by 11

Design (bottom):
Partners by Design
(N. Hollywood, CA)
Pages from the
Davidson Educa-
tional Software
catalog.
Size: 5-1/2 by 8-1/2

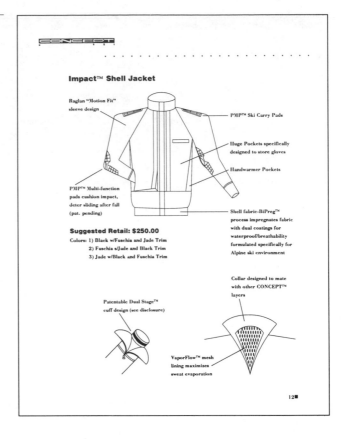

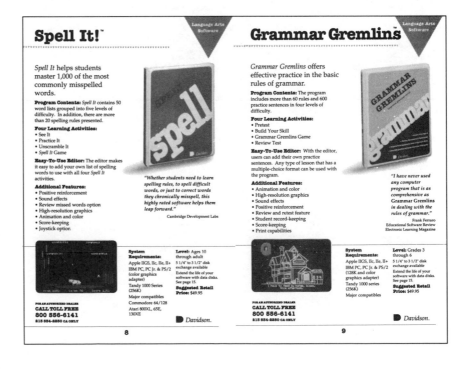

90 JOURNALISM AND PUBLIC RELATIONS

JOURNALISM AND PUBLIC RELATIONS

WRITING AND EDITING are the primary skills needed for a career in journalism and public relations. Learning to think and write clearly are skills that ean be taught. And when the quality of thinking is drawn from intelligence, personal style follows.

Our society becomes increasingly complicated and with that awareness comes the need for skilled professionals who understand how to communicate creatively, to persuade and to present a point of view with clarity.

Journalism today no longer means working only for newspapers. Journalists work on staff and freelance for magazines, radio stations, television local stations, networks and cable stations.

Public relations experts also work on staff and freelance for individual corporations — almost every large company needs a public relations division — educational institutions, in all broadcast media, as well as with specialized public relations firms. As a writer learning or reacquainting yourself with the essentials of style can be the beginning of a new career with a focus. A working knowledge of the press, understanding how to write press releases or copy, and editing can be important regardless of where you focus your writing talent. The more skills and the more flexibility you have as a writer the more valuable you will be in applied writing in journalism and public relations.

Class hours: 7:00 pm to 9:40 pm unless otherwise indicated. Add registration fee (non-refundable) of $20.00 when registering for these courses.

TE109A
Freelance Magazine Writing: Making the Right Moves for Success
Mon - 2 Credits - $250.00
Creative careers need professional guidance. This is a course for writers who need to know how the marketplace operates. We will examine how to: query editors, make contacts, exploit research resources, gear an article to the appropriate magazine, negotiate fees and expenses. Drawing on your own editorial interests and enthusiams, you will learn how to produce winning story proposals, getting actual assignments from real magazines. Guest lecturers will include accomplished writers and editors. A certain passion for the printed word, rather than any publishing experience, is the course's only prerequisite.
David Abrahamson, Writer, Journalist. B.A., Johns Hopkins University; M. Journalism, University of California; Oxford University. Formerly, Managing Editor, "Car and Driver." Publications include: "The New York Times Magazine," "Science '86," "New York," "Playboy," "Backpacker."

TE205A
Editing Workshop
Thurs - 2 Credits - $250.00
Copy editors are the unsung heroes of the publishing world. Their work clears what was muddled, simplifies the complex, and imposes stylistic order. Good copy editors are in great demand for newspapers, magazines and book publishers. Learn how to handle the copy - the hard, sweaty part - and write headlines, the fun part.
Jack Robbins, Copy Editor, Business Week. Formerly, Editor, McGraw-Hill; Reporter, "The New York Post."

TE207A
How to Promote Practically Anything — Including Yourself
Thurs - 2 Credits - $250.00
This is a course in personal public relations. You will be shown how to put together your own press package for your company or yourself. Topics will include: working knowledge of the press; release writing; fundamentals of public speaking; projecting your own image.
Marilyn McCrudden, President, McCruddon and Sullivan Communications. B.A., University of Minnesota. Clients include: Grafton Street Irish Imports; Parke Bernet Galleries; Delmonico's Hotel; Carson, Lundin & Thorson, P.C., Architects; Scandinavian Airlines; Hearst Publications. Publications: "Who's Who in American Women."

Open leading and a two-column measure (left) add importance to the introduction for each new section of this course catalog without requiring the space of a full page.

Small pieces of art, which print in green, are sprinkled throughout the catalog to help break up the text.

Quotes from instructors and experts in the field (below right) are also used to break up the text. Although the type is smaller than that usually found in blurbs, the open leading, the border, and the green initial cap combine to make this an effective graphic element.

The typography for course listings is a 2-point rule, a Futura Heavy course number, a Futura Bold course title, italic for schedule/credit/fee data, and Century Old Style for running text with the instructor's name in boldface.

The triangle borders use the same Zapf Dingbat technique as the educational catalog on the facing page but without a character space.

Design: School of Visual Arts Press (New York, NY)

Pages from the catalog for The School of Visual Arts. Trim size: 7-1/4 by 10-3/4

68 PHOTOGRAPHY

process their own film outside class.
William L. Broecker, Photographer. B.A., University of Michigan; M.A., Michigan State University. Editor: *ICP Encyclopedia of Photography; Leica Manual 15th ed.*; Associate Technical Director, *Encyclopedia of Practical Photography*. Publications: "Popular Photography," "Invitation To Photography," "35mm Photography," "Color Photography Annual," "Exposure," "Infinity."

PROFESSIONAL

The following courses are offered to advanced students of photography and working photographers who are able to maintain the pace of classes that take for granted basic technical skills and experience. These professional level courses focus on portfolio development in the different photographic specializations. Critical analysis of all aspects of the photograph from concept through to finished prints/chromes is offered. At this stage self-initiated work is essential and the personal aesthetic is further refined.

¶ If you are interested in learning new techniques or exploring unfamiliar advancements in technology, there are a number of courses for you to consider.
¶ If you are dissatisfied with the results your current portfolio is getting, a professional course offering critical analysis may be helpful.

PC300A
Advanced Printing
Tues - 2 Credits - $250.00
Lab Fee, $20.00
A course designed for the intermediate and advanced student who is interested in approaching printing as a fine art. Each print will be tailored to the photograph itself. Students should come to the first class session ready to print. Prerequisites: PC205, Basic Photography II, and PC256, Black and White Printing, or presentation of your portfolio at the first session.
Bob Brooks, Photographer, Printer. Has worked in many studios including those of Irving Penn and Bob Adelman. One-Person Exhibition: Plaza Caribe. Group Exhibitions: Floating Foundation of Photography; The People Yes Show, Central Park. Clients: Xerox Corporation, Playtex, Coca-Cola, Fischbach Gallery. Publications: "U.S. Camera," "The Visual Dialogue," "Art News."

PC307A
Photojournalism
Thurs - 2 Credits - $250.00
A survey of practical photojournalism as it exists at wire services and newspapers. The training of perception and the use of the camera as a reporting tool are stressed. Topics to be discussed include: journalism for the photographer; personal vision vs. professional credibility; new technology and how it will affect you; paying the rent as a freelancer; how words can make your camera lie; the use and abuse of photography in public relations; portfolio critique and preparation. Students must have access to their own or commercial darkroom.
Edward Hart, Picture Editor, United Press International, New York City Bureau. B.A., Long Island University. Formerly, Writer/Producer, UPI Television Service. Member: National Press Photographers Association, Society of Professional Journalists, Reporters Committee for Freedom of the Press.

PC316A
Advanced Studio Photography
Mon - 2 Credits - $250.00
Model and Equipment Fees, $35.00
(Limited to twenty students)
A course designed for the advanced student who has successfully completed PC221, Basic Studio Photography, or equivalent. The first two weeks will be devoted to still-life, shot with the 4" x 5" view camera using Polaroid film. (Students must supply their own Polaroid film Type 52). The remainder of the course will be devoted to 35mm or 2 1/4" x 2 1/4" format. Controlled lighting, using strobe to establish mood rather than just illuminate, will be the theme of all assignments. The student will shoot still-life, fashion, beauty and nudes.
Len DeLessio, Photographer. B.F.A., School of Visual Arts. Publications: "Business Week," "Cosmopolitan," "New York," "Parents," "People," "Penthouse," "Viva," "Time," "Elle," "Working Woman." Clients include: American Optical, Binney & Smith/Crayola, Chesebrough Ponds, Fujinon Optical, Andrew Geller Shoes, General Foods - Gaines Dog Food, Mercedes-Benz, Parke-Davis, Perry Ellis, Pierre Cardin Fragrances, P&G - Cascade, Tide, Highpoint, R.J. Reynolds -

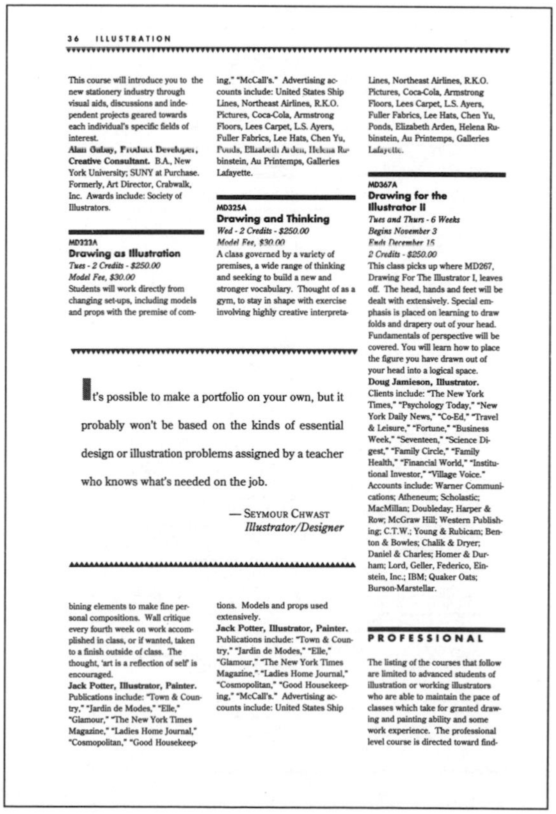

36 ILLUSTRATION

This course will introduce you to the new stationery industry through visual aids, discussions and independent projects geared towards each individual's specific fields of interest.
Alan Gabay, Product Developer, Creative Consultant. B.A., New York University; SUNY at Purchase. Formerly, Art Director, Crabwalk, Inc. Awards include: Society of Illustrators.

MD323A
Drawing as Illustration
Tues - 2 Credits - $250.00
Model Fee, $30.00
Students will work directly from changing set-ups, including models and props with the premise of combining elements to make fine personal compositions. Wall critique every fourth week on work accomplished in class, or if wanted, taken to a finish outside of class. The thought, 'art is a reflection of self' is encouraged.
Jack Potter, Illustrator, Painter. Publications include: "Town & Country," "Jardin de Modes," "Elle," "Glamour," "The New York Times Magazine," "Ladies Home Journal," "Cosmopolitan," "Good Housekeeping," "McCall's." Advertising accounts include: United States Ship Lines, Northeast Airlines, R.K.O. Pictures, Coca-Cola, Armstrong Floors, Lees Carpet, L.S. Ayers, Fuller Fabrics, Lee Hats, Chen Yu, Ponds, Elizabeth Arden, Helena Rubinstein, Au Printemps, Galleries Lafayette.

MD325A
Drawing and Thinking
Wed - 2 Credits - $250.00
Model Fee, $30.00
A class governed by a variety of premises, a wide range of thinking and seeking to build a new and stronger vocabulary. Thought of as a gym, to stay in shape with exercise involving highly creative interpretations. Models and props used extensively.
Jack Potter, Illustrator, Painter. Publications include: "Town & Country," "Jardin de Modes," "Elle," "Glamour," "The New York Times Magazine," "Ladies Home Journal," "Cosmopolitan," "Good Housekeeping," "McCall's." Advertising accounts include: United States Ship Lines, Northeast Airlines, R.K.O. Pictures, Coca-Cola, Armstrong Floors, Lees Carpet, L.S. Ayers, Fuller Fabrics, Lee Hats, Chen Yu, Ponds, Elizabeth Arden, Helena Rubinstein, Au Printemps, Galleries Lafayette.

It's possible to make a portfolio on your own, but it probably won't be based on the kinds of essential design or illustration problems assigned by a teacher who knows what's needed on the job.

— SEYMOUR CHWAST
Illustrator/Designer

MD367A
Drawing for the Illustrator II
Tues and Thurs - 6 Weeks
Begins November 3
Ends December 15
2 Credits - $250.00
This class picks up where MD267, Drawing For The Illustrator I, leaves off. The head, hands and feet will be dealt with extensively. Special emphasis is placed on learning to draw folds and drapery out of your head. Fundamentals of perspective will be covered. You will learn how to place the figure you have drawn out of your head into a logical space.
Doug Jamieson, Illustrator. Clients include: "The New York Times," "Psychology Today," "New York Daily News," "Co-Ed," "Travel & Leisure," "Fortune," "Business Week," "Seventeen," "Science Digest," "Family Circle," "Family Health," "Financial World," "Institutional Investor," "Village Voice." Accounts include: Warner Communications; Atheneum; Scholastic; MacMillan; Doubleday; Harper & Row; McGraw Hill; Western Publishing; C.T.W.; Young & Rubicam; Benton & Bowles; Chalik & Dryer; Daniel & Charles; Homer & Durham; Lord, Geller, Federico, Einstein, Inc.; IBM; Quaker Oats; Burson-Marstellar.

PROFESSIONAL

The listing of the courses that follow are limited to advanced students of illustration or working illustrators who are able to maintain the pace of classes which take for granted drawing and painting ability and some work experience. The professional level course is directed toward find-

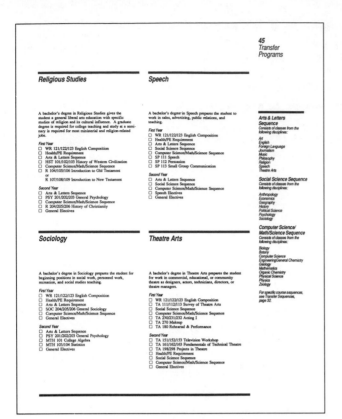

The format for this catalog accommodates several different kinds of listings, three of which are shown here. The distinctive treatment of the top and bottom margins and the consistency of the type style unify the different components of the catalog.

The heavy rules are 4 point.

The typeface makes good use of the contrast between Helvetica Narrow and Times Roman.

Design: Lisa Wilcox and Bill Symes (Oregon City, OR)

Pages from the Clackamas Community College catalog. Trim size: 8-3/8 by 10-3/4

A highly styled newspaper format (below) sets a dynamic tone for the "Course Highlights" section in the opening pages of this continuing education catalog.

The type styling in the spread below illustrates how you can achieve a great deal of variety through an adventurous use of the two most familiar typefaces. The Helvetica family is used for display and Times Roman for running text. Note, though, the contrasting leading and column widths, the letterspacing, reverse type, wrap-around text, type on tints, dotted rules, initial caps, and boxed copy. Each text block is treated as a pattern of type that is distinct from every other text block on the spread.

The same four-column grid ties together the opening pages and the course information (above left). In the course listings, the outer column is used to list the schedule, credit, and fees for the courses described on that page. Where needed, the outer two columns can be used for this purpose.

Design:
Jonathan Maier
(Portland, OR)

Pages from the Portland State University Quarterly Bulletin for Continuing Education.
Trim size:
11-1/4 by 13-9/16

James Burke,
British Television
Writer and Producer

The Huck Lockbolt Fastening System

The Huck Fastening System consists of three separate components that function as a single operating unit.

1 Fastener: LGP shear-type fasteners and GP tension-type fasteners are available in a wide range of diameters and grip lengths, and a variety of materials and finishes.

2 Nose Assembly: Nose assemblies provide a link between the fastener and the installation tool. Each is designed to install a specific fastener type and diameter. They can be easily attached to and removed from installation tools.

3 Installation Tool: Huck tooling is available in three configurations:

1. Pneumatic hand-held systems which are powered by 90-100 psi air pressure.

2. Hydraulic hand-held systems which are powered by Huck POWERIG® Hydraulic units.

3. Automated Drivmatic drill riveter systems which can be mounted on drill riveter lower rams.

Pin Position and Swage Gage part numbers are listed for each fastener diameter and type. These gages are designed to inspect installed fastener grip and collar swage. For instructions for use, refer to Boeing standard BAC 5004-2.

The Model 2702 Hydraulic Installation Tool coupled with the Model 940 POWERIG Hydraulic Unit. A combination that's light weight and maneuverable.

Head   Annular Locking Grooves   Collar

Shank   Breakneck   Pintail

The Lockbolt Pin consists of a head, shank, annular locking grooves, breakneck, and pintail. (note: locking grooves are not helical threads)

The Collar is smooth bore (inside diameter and outside diameter), is symmetrically double-ended, and can be installed in either direction.

A real production workhorse, the Model 225 Pneumatic Installation Tool, like all our tools, is factory tested to offer years of dependable service.

Huck offers a wide variety of nose assemblies to meet the requirements of any application.

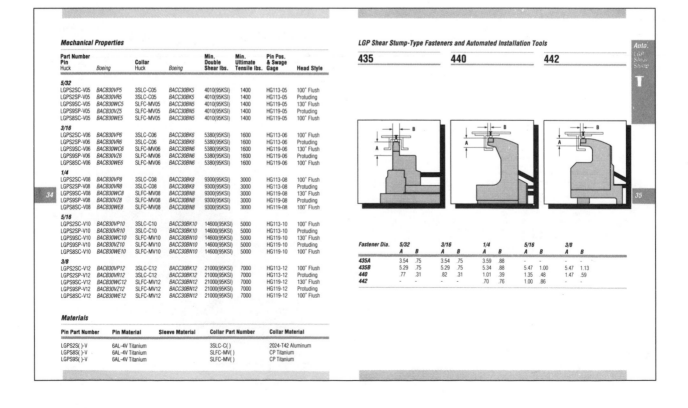

Mechanical Properties

Part Number Pin Huck	Boeing	Collar Huck	Boeing	Min. Double Shear lbs.	Min. Ultimate Tensile lbs.	Pin Pos. & Swage Gage	Head Style
5/32							
LGPS2SC-V05	BACB30VP5	3SLC-C05	BACC30BK5	4010(95KSI)	1400	HG113-05	100° Flush
LGPS2SP-V05	BACB30VR5	3SLC-C05	BACC30BK5	4010(95KSI)	1400	HG113-05	Protuding
LGPS9SC-V05	BACB30WC5	SLFC-MV05	BACC30BN5	4010(95KSI)	1400	HG119-05	130° Flush
LGPS9SP-V05	BACB30VZ5	SLFC-MV05	BACC30BN5	4010(95KSI)	1400	HG119-05	Protuding
LGPS8SC-V05	BACB30WE5	SLFC-MV05	BACC30BN5	4010(95KSI)	1400	HG119-05	100° Flush
3/16							
LGPS2SC-V06	BACB30VP6	3SLC-C06	BACC30BK6	5380(95KSI)	1600	HG113-06	100° Flush
LGPS2SP-V06	BACB30VR6	3SLC-C06	BACC30BK6	5380(95KSI)	1600	HG113-06	Protuding
LGPS9SC-V06	BACB30WC6	SLFC-MV06	BACC30BN6	5380(95KSI)	1600	HG119-06	130° Flush
LGPS9SP-V06	BACB30VZ6	SLFC-MV06	BACC30BN6	5380(95KSI)	1600	HG119-06	Protuding
LGPS8SC-V06	BACB30WE6	SLFC-MV06	BACC30BN6	5380(95KSI)	1600	HG119-06	100° Flush
1/4							
LGPS2SC-V08	BACB30VP8	3SLC-C08	BACC30BK8	9300(95KSI)	3000	HG113-08	100° Flush
LGPS2SP-V08	BACB30VR8	3SLC-C08	BACC30BK8	9300(95KSI)	3000	HG113-08	Protuding
LGPS9SC-V08	BACB30WC8	SLFC-MV08	BACC30BN8	9300(95KSI)	3000	HG119-08	130° Flush
LGPS9SP-V08	BACB30VZ8	SLFC-MV08	BACC30BN8	9300(95KSI)	3000	HG119-08	Protuding
LGPS8SC-V08	BACB30WE8	SLFC-MV08	BACC30BN8	9300(95KSI)	3000	HG119-08	100° Flush
5/16							
LGPS2SC-V10	BACB30VP10	3SLC-C10	BACC30BK10	14600(95KSI)	5000	HG113-10	100° Flush
LGPS2SP-V10	BACB30VR10	3SLC-C10	BACC30BK10	14600(95KSI)	5000	HG113-10	Protuding
LGPS9SC-V10	BACB30WC10	SLFC-MV10	BACC30BN10	14600(95KSI)	5000	HG119-10	130° Flush
LGPS9SP-V10	BACB30VZ10	SLFC-MV10	BACC30BN10	14600(95KSI)	5000	HG119-10	Protuding
LGPS8SC-V10	BACB30WE10	SLFC-MV10	BACC30BN10	14600(95KSI)	5000	HG119-10	100° Flush
3/8							
LGPS2SC-V12	BACB30VP12	3SLC-C12	BACC30BK12	21000(95KSI)	7000	HG113-12	100° Flush
LGPS2SP-V12	BACB30VR12	3SLC-C12	BACC30BK12	21000(95KSI)	7000	HG113-12	Protuding
LGPS9SC-V12	BACB30WC12	SLFC-MV12	BACC30BN12	21000(95KSI)	7000	HG119-12	130° Flush
LGPS9SP-V12	BACB30VZ12	SLFC-MV12	BACC30BN12	21000(95KSI)	7000	HG119-12	Protuding
LGPS8SC-V12	BACB30WE12	SLFC-MV12	BACC30BN12	21000(95KSI)	7000	HG119-12	100° Flush

Materials

Pin Part Number	Pin Material	Sleeve Material	Collar Part Number	Collar Material
LGPS2S( )-V	6AL-4V Titanium		3SLC-C( )	2024-T42 Aluminum
LGPS8S( )-V	6AL-4V Titanium		SLFC-MV( )	CP Titanium
LGPS9S( )-V	6AL-4V Titanium		SLFC-MV( )	CP Titanium

LGP Shear Stump-Type Fasteners and Automated Installation Tools

435   **440**   **442**

Fastener Dia.	5/32		3/16		1/4		5/16		3/8	
	A	B	A	B	A	B	A	B	A	B
435A	3.54	.75	3.54	.75	3.59	.88	-	-	-	-
435B	5.29	.75	5.29	.75	5.34	.88	5.47	1.00	5.47	1.13
440	.77	.31	.82	.31	1.01	.39	1.35	.48	1.47	.59
442	-	-	-	-	.70	.76	1.00	.86	-	-

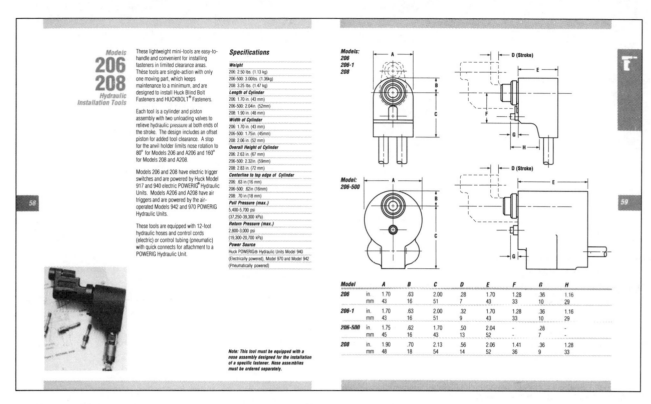

Utility informs every aspect of the design of this technical manual for selecting and using fasteners and fastener installation tools. The manageable size, the spiral binding, the tabbed section dividers, and the careful handling of the many different kinds of material on virtually every spread show consistently high production values.

The three-column format accommodates a wide range of recurring elements—descriptive text, product photos, technical drawings, and specification tables—with generous white space being an integral part of the design.

The introduction to the fastening system (facing page, top) sets the style with dramatically silhouetted product shots complemented by an exceptionally well-rendered technical illustration. The parts on the right-hand page seem to float above the page, a dimensional illusion not often found in technical manuals and specifications. The designer used scanned photos to work out the size and position of images on the page; the printer created and stripped in traditional halftones.

The typography throughout is Helvetica Condensed and Helvetica Condensed Bold. Both faces are used in roman and oblique for additional contrast where needed. The Helvetica Condensed family (available as downloadable fonts from Adobe Systems) is unequalled for combining economy of space and maximum readability.

Red is used as an accent color for rules, product headlines, and boxes. The tabbed section dividers are printed on laminated stock that matches the color of the printed ink exactly.

The black shadows behind boxed illustrations (facing page, bottom) highlight the illustrations and separate them from one another. This device makes it possible to run as many as six of these illustrations on a page with a great deal of text and very little white space.

The technical illustrations were created in Adobe Illustrator.

Design: Steven Bliss (Kingston, NY)

Pages from the Lockbolt Fastener Design Guide, *produced by the Huck Manufacturing Company.*
Trim size: 7-3/4 by 9-1/8

Quick and easy scanning is the goal of this format, an 11- by 17-sheet printed on both sides and folded in half.

Bold headlines and subheads, very open leading, and a graphic element to denote itemized text are all designed to move the reader through the copy quickly. This highly utilitarian approach is intended to suggest that the product will be similarly streamlined and easy to use.

The body text is 10/18 Palatino. The headline is 16/18 Helvetica Black, and the subheads are 12/18 Helvetica Black.

Life-size photos deliver impact. Here they create the illusion that there are windows cut into the paper and that you are looking through them to read the keys.

Design: Kimberly Mancebo (Campbell, CA)

Data sheet for Triad Systems Corporation. Trim size: 11 by 17, folded in half

---

Triad's New Easy Keys Are Designed With You In Mind

The keys are grouped the way you'll use them. And each key is labelled with a name that makes sense, so you don't have to memorize abstract "F-key" codes or obscure combinations.

Here Are a Few of The Keys to the Best Point-of-Sale Program In Your Industry

▶ Our ten-key numerical keypad makes SKU entry quick, easy and accurate for any clerk.

▶ The CHARGE key automatically sets the correct discounts, pricing and tax for your charge customers. The right price is given to the right customer.

▶ Clerks can receive payments quickly at Point-of-Sale, just by using the ROA key.

▶ Clerks can cash checks and process paid-outs quickly

and efficiently, using the PAID OUT and NO SALE keys. And you get a complete report, by clerk and by terminal. So everyone's cash drawer balances at day's end — or you'll know why.

▶ The VOID key captures information about voids — of single items and of entire

transactions — by clerk and by terminal. You get the register control you need.

▶ The TOTAL key keeps everything totally up-to-date: inventory quantities, item sales history, customer accounts. Daily reports recap sales and gross profits for the day.

Contractor Point-of-Sale Brings You These Additional Keys To Success

▶ Clerks can create quotes in minutes — and save them for

later retrieval — just by using the QUOTE key.

▶ As soon as a customer approves a quote, clerks can retrieve it and create an order from it, using the ORDER key. Without ever re-posting ordered merchandise.

▶ You can invoice orders automatically, using the INVOICE key. The customer's account balance and available credit are updated instantly. Automatically. Every time.

The New Easy Keys Are Your Key To Back-office Efficiency, Too

▶ Need help? It's at your fingertips, anytime you need

it, using the HELP key.

▶ Feeling disoriented? Hit the HOME key. You're instantly back at the top of the screen.

▶ Want to see it all on paper? The RUN key starts any

report, any time you want a hard copy.

▶ And the END key takes you back to the hub of your system, the Main Menu.

These two-sided data sheets have the ingredients needed to position an expensive product: a high-quality still life photograph on the front and carefully organized, detailed information on the back.

The tactile quality of the heavy, coated stock used for the data sheets adds measurably to the first impression. Production values are a key element of the image conveyed in sales literature.

The format is maintained for every product in the series: The photo bleeds off the right edge of the paper, the product name prints in reverse type in the banner that bleeds off the top, and the company logo is at the bottom, aligned with the left edge of the photo. Each product is photographed against two sheets of overlapping paper, which add texture and color to the image. The top sheet is gray; the bottom sheet is an accent color that changes from one product sheet to the next, a technique that unifies and distinguishes at the same time.

The layout of the back of the sheet is dictated by the information and changes as needed from one product to another. The margins, typographic style, and logo placement remain consistent throughout the series. Boldface heads, generous space between columns, and bulleted lists with hanging indents all contribute to the clarity of the information and the ease with which it is accessed.

Design: Judy Butler, Barbara Jacobsohn, and Teri Baptiste (San Jose, CA)

Data sheets from the Maxtor Corporation. Trim size: 8-1/2 by 11

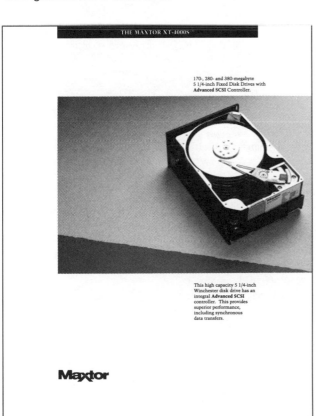

THE MAXTOR XT-4000S

170-, 280- and 380-megabyte 5 1/4-inch Fixed Disk Drives with **Advanced SCSI** Controller.

This high capacity 5 1/4-inch Winchester disk drive has an integral **Advanced SCSI** controller. This provides superior performance, including synchronous data transfers.

Maxtor

This data sheet is not as slick as the one on the preceding page, but the handsome format, careful product display, and well-organized typography still evoke confidence in the product.

The three-column grid is given a strong horizontal structure through the use of horizontal rules.

The top rule and the company logo print in red, adding a spot of color that contrasts with the overall quietness of the page.

The contents of the kit are itemized in a bulleted list with hanging indents. The typography, Helvetica Black and Helvetica Light, is simple, nicely spaced, and easy to read.

A simple format with well-rendered line drawings (facing page, top left and bottom) is used for all the assembly and care sheets shipped with products from this large mail-order business.

The rules, logo, column guides, and footlines are standing items in the electronic templates, and a text placeholder is left in position for the product name. For each new product, the actual name is typed over the placeholder (maintaining the text specifications and placement), and text is placed in position. The bottom sample is a half-page size, printed two to a sheet and then trimmed.

Before the conversion to desktop publishing, there was no standard format for these information sheets. According to one of the designers, it took only a few hours to go from no standards to an easy-to-implement design that was consistent with the corporate look.

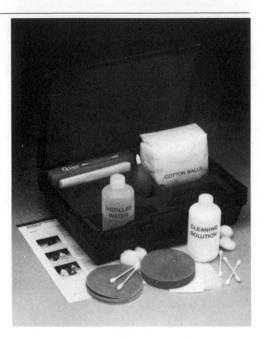

Design (above): Agnew Moyer Smith (Pittsburgh, PA)

Data sheet for an infrared optics cleaning kit from Two-Six Incorporated.
Trim size: 8-1/2 by 11

Design (facing page, top left and bottom): Kathy Tomyris and Deborah Paulson (Mill Valley, CA)

Product sheets from Smith & Hawken.
Trim size: (top) 8-1/2 by 11; (bottom) 5-1/2 by 8-1/2, printed two to a sheet

S M I T H & H A W K E N
Adirondack Chairs

#2093 Cedar Adirondack   #2090 Painted Chair
#2094 Cedar Footrest   #2091 Painted Footrest
#2095 Cedar Table   #2092 Painted Table

Your Adirondack Chair will arrive packed in one box. When you are ready to assemble it, unpack and carefully lay the Chair parts on a clean, flat, padded surface such as a carpeted floor or the cardboard box the Chair was shipped in. Carefully examine the contents.

ADIRONDACK CHAIR
CHAIR PARTS: Two Arms with front Legs attached, Seat, and Back
HARDWARE: Six sets of 1-1/4" carriage bolts with washers and nuts, Two cap nuts and washers for the hanger bolts attached to the seat.
TOOLS REQUIRED: Crescent wrench or 3/8" wrench

As you assemble the Chair, do not drive in the carriage bolts. Slide in the bolt, slip on the washer and then thread on the nut. As you tighten the nut, use the wrench to draw the bolts up tight. When each bolt is tight, the square end under the bolt head will seat and prevent the bolt from turning. You might also apply a small amount of beeswax or parafin to the bolts to ensure that it will be easy to disassemble the Chair.

CHAIR ASSEMBLY
1. With the seat lying flat on the floor, attach the Chair back onto the hanger bolts mounted at the back of the seat. Be sure that the back is pulled flush to the seat and the fit is smooth. Loosely secure with a washer and cap nut on each side. You should not tighten any of the hardware until the Chair has been completely assembled.

2. Turn the Chair on its side and line up the two holes drilled in the leg portion of the arm/leg assembly with the corresponding holes on the forward side of the seat. Placing the nut and washer on the inside, use two carriage bolts to loosely attach.

3. On the same side, line up the back of the arm with the hole drilled in the arm support attached across the back of the Chair. You may have to press down slightly on the arm in order to line up these holes, but as long as you have left the other carriage bolts loose, there will be enough flexibility in the Chair for the arm to fit.

4. Turn the Chair over and repeat the arm/leg assembly for the other side.

5. Now begin to tighten the carriage bolts. Tighten each a little bit at a time rather than tightening each all at once.

ADIRONDACK FOOTREST
FOOTREST PARTS: Footrest, two Legs, and four sets of 2" carriage bolts with nuts and washers.

ASSEMBLY: Attach the legs to the inside of the Footrest frame and use two carriage bolts on each side to secure. Tighten firmly.

ADIRONDACK TABLE
TABLE PARTS: Table top, four Legs and eight sets of 2" carriage bolts with nuts and washers.

ASSEMBLY: The four legs attach to the outside of the table top with two carriage bolts each. Tighten firmly.

CARE FOR YOUR ADIRONDACK
We recommend that you store your furniture indoors over the winter months, especially in harsh climates.

The Cedar Adirondack requires no specific care. The wood will gradually weather to a soft grey when placed outdoors. If you prefer a finished chair, a UV resistant exterior varnish can be applied on an annual basis.

The Painted Adirondack is finished with a durable Linear Polyurethane paint. If you should wish to repaint the Chair, we recommend that you use a high quality enamel paint.

25 Corte Madera, Mill Valley, California 94941   Customer Service (415) 383-6292

Questor Inlets

The Standard Questor Inlet

To Questor (Path A)

In-line Filter

Heated Enclosure

To Vent (Path B)

Flow-by Tee

To Vent

Heated Capillary Transfer Line

Flange Heater

Questor Analyzer

All Questors are equipped with a 16-position rotary valve suitable for sampling from positive pressure sources and from compressed gas cylinders. The gas lines connected to the valve have two possible flow paths:

Sample Source Selected for Analysis (Path A)

Sample passes through final filter to valve common. At flow-by tee, the majority of the sample flows to the vent. A small and constant flow of sample passes through the capillary transfer line to the Questor Analyzer.

Sample Source Not Selected (Path B)

To insure fresh stream at the valve at all times, samples not selected flow through the valve to vent. This means that the delay times to transfer gases from your reactor to Questor are minimized. Calibration gases are normally dead-ended to conserve gas.

S M I T H & H A W K E N
Caring for your Teak Planter

The Teak Planters and Window Boxes can be left exposed to the weather all year round. The wood will gradually weather to a soft, silver gray as the oil in the exposed wood dries. This is the preferred method of non-maintenance. If you prefer an unweathered appearance, you may choose to maintain the golden color of the teak by applying teak or tung oil every 6-8 months. When doing so, apply the oil sparingly and rub in well, leaving no oil on the surface to soak in. The planter should be kept moisture free while the oil is drying, about two days.

As the wood weathers, checks may appear in the exposed ends and finials of the planters. This is the opening of the wood grain due to variations in the temperature and humidity. Checking does not effect the structural integrity or strength of the planter.

Please call if you have any questions or need more information.

25 Corte Madera, Mill Valley, CA 94941   (415) 383-6292

Design (top right): Agnew Moyer Smith (Pittsburgh, PA)

Data sheet for the Questor Inlet system from the Extrel Corporation. Size: 8-1/2 by 11

A narrow column for the product photo and text (above) leaves plenty of space for the technical illustration and leadered callouts.

All the leaders are parallel to one another and the callouts align left for a highly organized presentation.

Yellow is used as a functional second color to indicate the flow of gases.

Three typefaces are used for contrast: Futura Heavy for the boldface, Times Roman for the running text, and Univers Light for the callouts.

FINANCIALS

The financials in this section are from annual reports, where a narrative story, tabular data, and charts and graphs often must coexist between the same covers. In some reports the financials are quarantined in the back. The greater challenge—one that results in a more impressive presentation—is to devise a format that allows you to integrate the financial data into the body of the report.

Annual reports are very image-conscious documents. The style of presentation is obviously related to the size of the organization and the health of the bottom line. But whether yours is a growing company with increased earnings or a modest organization with a not-so-great year, the typographic organization discussed in the introduction to this chapter and in the introduction to the Catalog section is the first building block for financial presentations.

Financials in this section

- *MasterCard*—slick, dramatic photos with a life-sized twist
- *College Auxiliary Service*—mug shots that put a face on numbers
- *Psicor*—tabular data and bar chart highlights
- *Medic Alert*—elegant typography in an integrated format
- *Spencer Foundation*—contrasting type for grant summaries

A lavish annual report such as the one on the facing page reflects the bullishness of a good year. For modest or declining earnings, you'd expect a more conservative presentation.

A photo of the product itself is used to chart growth in comparison to the competition. The life-size photos dramatize the product, especially when juxtaposed against smaller-scale photos of the competition.

The financials in the bottom spread shown give the big picture—cards in circulation, merchant outlets, gross dollar volume—against a dramatic black background in which the earth revolves. The image of the earth reinforces the message of global growth set forth in the table at the top of the page.

Straightforward charts become dramatic when each bar prints in a different color, as they do here, against a black background.

Design: The Will Hopkins Group (New York, NY)

Pages from the annual report of MasterCard International, Inc. Trim size: 8-1/2 by 11

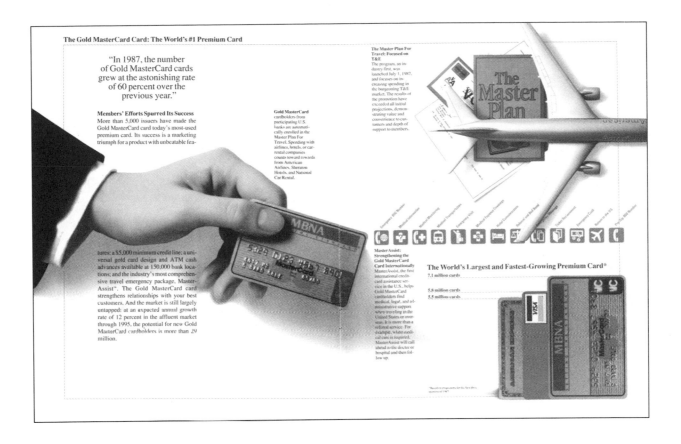

The Gold MasterCard Card: The World's #1 Premium Card

"In 1987, the number of Gold MasterCard cards grew at the astonishing rate of 60 percent over the previous year."

Members' Efforts Spurred Its Success
More than 5,000 issuers have made the Gold MasterCard card today's most-used premium card. Its success is a marketing triumph for a product with unbeatable features: a $5,000 minimum credit line; a universal gold card design and ATM cash advances available at 150,000 bank locations; and the industry's most comprehensive travel emergency package, Master-Assist™. The Gold MasterCard card strengthens relationships with your best customers. And the market is still largely untapped: at an expected annual growth rate of 12 percent in the affluent market through 1995, the potential for new Gold MasterCard cardholders is more than 29 million.

Gold MasterCard cardholders from participating U.S. banks are automatically enrolled in the Master Plan For Travel. Spending with airlines, hotels, or car-rental companies counts toward rewards from American Airlines, Sheraton Hotels, and National Car Rental.

The Master Plan For Travel: Focused on T&E
The program, an industry first, was launched July 1, 1987, and focuses on increasing spending in the burgeoning T&E market. The results of the promotion have exceeded all initial projections, demonstrating value and convenience to customers and depth of support to members.

Master Assist: Strengthening the Gold MasterCard Card Internationally
MasterAssist, the first international credit-card assistance service in the U.S., helps Gold MasterCard cardholders find medical, legal, and administrative support when traveling in the United States or overseas. It is more than a referral service. For example, when medical care is required, MasterAssist will call ahead to the doctor or hospital and then follow up.

The World's Largest and Fastest-Growing Premium Card*

7.1 million cards

5.8 million cards
5.5 million cards

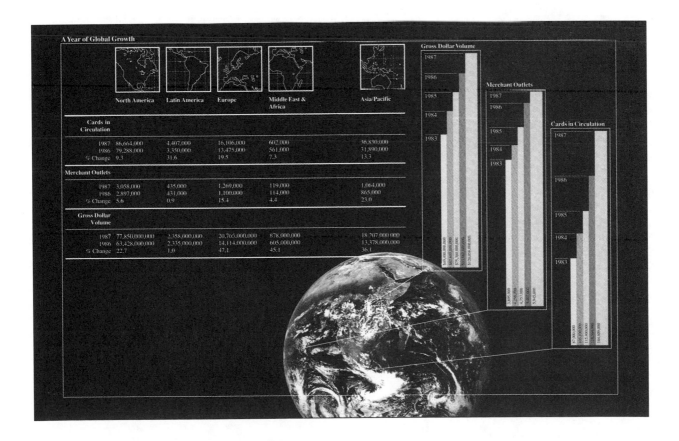

A Year of Global Growth

	North America	Latin America	Europe	Middle East & Africa	Asia/Pacific
Cards in Circulation					
1987	86,664,000	4,407,000	16,106,000	602,000	36,830,000
1986	79,288,000	3,350,000	13,475,000	561,000	31,890,000
% Change	9.3	31.6	19.5	7.3	13.3
Merchant Outlets					
1987	3,058,000	435,000	1,269,000	119,000	1,064,000
1986	2,897,000	431,000	1,100,000	114,000	865,000
% Change	5.6	0.9	15.4	4.4	23.0
Gross Dollar Volume					
1987	77,850,000,000	2,358,000,000	20,765,000,000	878,000,000	18,207,000,000
1986	63,428,000,000	2,335,000,000	14,114,000,000	605,000,000	13,378,000,000
% Change	22.7	1.0	47.1	45.1	36.1

Gross Dollar Volume
1987
1986
1985
1984
1983

Merchant Outlets
1987
1986
1985
1984
1983

Cards in Circulation
1987
1986
1985
1984
1983

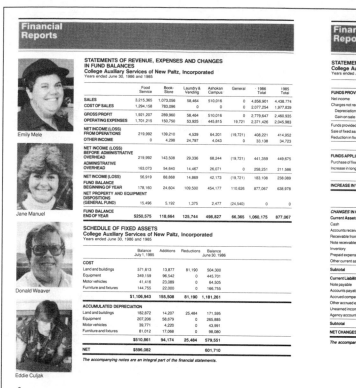

Financial Reports

STATEMENTS OF REVENUE, EXPENSES AND CHANGES IN FUND BALANCES
College Auxiliary Services of New Paltz, Incorporated
Years ended June 30, 1986 and 1985

	Food Service	Book-Store	Laundry & Vending	Ashokan Campus	General	1986 Total	1985 Total
SALES	3,215,365	1,073,056	58,464	510,016	0	4,856,901	4,438,774
COST OF SALES	1,294,158	783,096	0	0	0	2,077,254	1,977,839
GROSS PROFIT	1,921,207	289,960	58,464	510,016	0	2,779,647	2,460,935
OPERATING EXPENSES	1,701,215	150,750	53,925	445,815	19,721	2,371,426	2,045,983
NET INCOME (LOSS) FROM OPERATIONS	219,992	139,210	4,539	64,201	(19,721)	408,221	414,952
OTHER INCOME	0	4,298	24,797	4,043	0	33,138	34,723
NET INCOME (LOSS) BEFORE ADMINISTRATIVE OVERHEAD	219,992	143,508	29,336	68,244	(19,721)	441,359	449,675
ADMINISTRATIVE OVERHEAD	163,073	54,640	14,467	26,071	0	258,251	211,586
NET INCOME (LOSS)	56,919	88,868	14,869	42,173	(19,721)	183,108	238,089
FUND BALANCE BEGINNING OF YEAR	178,160	24,604	109,500	454,177	110,626	877,067	638,978
NET PROPERTY AND EQUIPMENT DISPOSITIONS (GENERAL FUND)	15,496	5,192	1,375	2,477	(24,540)	0	0
FUND BALANCE END OF YEAR	250,575	118,664	125,744	498,827	66,365	1,060,175	877,067

SCHEDULE OF FIXED ASSETS
College Auxiliary Services of New Paltz, Incorporated
Years ended June 30, 1986 and 1985

	Balance July 1, 1985	Additions	Reductions	Balance June 30, 1986
COST				
Land and buildings	571,613	13,877	81,190	504,300
Equipment	349,159	96,542	0	445,701
Motor vehicles	41,416	23,089	0	64,505
Furniture and fixtures	144,755	22,000	0	166,755
	1,106,943	155,508	81,190	1,181,261
ACCUMULATED DEPRECIATION				
Land and buildings	182,872	14,207	25,484	171,595
Equipment	207,206	58,679	0	265,885
Motor vehicles	39,771	4,220	0	43,991
Furniture and fixtures	81,012	17,068	0	98,080
	510,861	94,174	25,484	579,551
NET	596,082			601,710

The accompanying notes are an integral part of the financial statements.

Emily Mele
Jane Manuel
Donald Weaver
Eddie Culjak

6

Financial Reports

STATEMENT OF CHANGES IN FINANCIAL POSITION
College Auxiliary Services of New Paltz, Incorporated
Years ended June 30, 1986 and 1985

	1986	1985
FUNDS PROVIDED		
Net income	183,110	238,089
Charges not requiring expenditures of funds		
Depreciation	196,420	195,363
Gain on sale of assets	(53,653)	0
Funds provided by operations	325,877	433,452
Sale of fixed assets	109,359	0
Reduction in fixed assets	0	1,169
	435,236	434,621
FUNDS APPLIED		
Purchase of fixed assets	254,378	207,010
Increase in long-term notes receivable	120,541	0
	374,919	207,010
INCREASE IN WORKING CAPITAL	60,317	227,611

CHANGES IN COMPONENTS OF WORKING CAPITAL	1986	1985
Current Assets		
Cash	(85,189)	(132,608)
Accounts receivable-trade	36,643	59,222
Receivable from State	130,755	203,065
Note receivable	3,853	0
Inventory	65,520	49,763
Prepaid expenses	(13,377)	16,779
Other current assets	(9,449)	(5,769)
Subtotal	128,756	190,452
Current Liabilities		
Note payable	0	(2,633)
Accounts payable	88,763	(29,762)
Accrued compensation	15,228	1,123
Other accrued expenses	46,359	(7,038)
Unearned income	3,930	(19,150)
Agency accounts	(85,841)	20,301
Subtotal	68,439	(37,159)
NET CHANGES	60,317	227,611

The accompanying notes are an integral part of the financial statements.

Carmela Bellomo
Mary Anne Boylan
Jennifer Clune
Teresa Gordon

7

Photos in the narrow outer margins throughout the report above emphasize that this college auxiliary service is a people business. The mug-shot format enables the publication to serve three very different purposes—annual report, morale booster for current employees, and recruiting tool for managerial-level positions.

Contrasting bold and regular Helvetica with light and bold rules helps organize the tables. The tables were set in Microsoft Word and the tabs in PageMaker. The crimson banner at the top of each page provides accent color.

A conservative approach to financial highlights (right) combines straightforward tables and bar charts. Color rules set off the main headline and the income and balance sheet category heads.

The typeface is Futura. The charts print in tones of red and blue.

Design (above): Wadlin & Erber (New Paltz, NY)

Spread from a report for the College Auxiliary Services at The College of New Paltz, State University of New York. Size: 8-1/2 by 11

Design (right): Lisa Menders (Royal Oak, MI)

Page from the Psicor, Inc. Annual Report. Size: 8-1/2 by 11

Financial Highlights

All amounts are in thousands, except per share data.

Income Statement Data:	1982	1983	1984	1985	1986
Revenue	$5,822	$10,151	$13,546	$16,324	$21,162
Expenses					
Operating supplies	1,442	3,489	4,630	5,113	6,379
Salaries and related expenses	2,232	2,837	4,092	5,829	7,892
General and administrative	903	1,151	1,819	2,215	2,746
Depreciation and amortization	696	891	1,003	1,174	1,362
Insurance	94	109	125	98	485
Total expenses	5,367	8,477	11,669	14,429	18,864
Operating income	455	1,674	1,877	1,895	2,298
Other expense—net	615	820	740	520	450
Income (loss) before income taxes	(160)	854	1,137	1,375	1,848
Provision for income taxes	0	62	438	537	665
Net income (loss)	$ (160)	$ 792	$ 699	$ 838	$ 1,183
Earnings (loss) per share (1)	$ (.06)	$ .29	$ .25	$ .30	$ .38
Number of shares used in computation (1)	2,700	2,750	2,779	2,838	3,121

Balance Sheet Data:	1982	1983	1984	1985	1986
Working capital (deficiency)	$ (834)	$ (378)	$ 80	$ 262	$ 5,428
Total assets	5,838	6,652	6,313	8,402	14,200
Total long-term debt	2,991	2,147	1,570	1,636	365
Shareholders' equity	524	1,316	2,014	2,853	10,690

(1) See "Earnings Per Share" at Note 1 of Notes to Financial Statements.

SOURCES OF REVENUE AND HOW THEY WERE SPENT   19

Financial Highlights . . . The Medic Alert Foundation International accounts for all membership fees, contributions and other revenues with utmost care. These pages were prepared under the direction of Robert C. Johnson, Treasurer, to highlight the financial activity for the twelve month period ended September 30, 1987. A complete, audited financial statement is available on request.

Fund Balance Summary . . . All fund balances for this period increased $1,179,960 because support and revenue exceeded expenditures. All Foundation funds totaled $4,163,018, of which $2,206,916 is invested in the headquarters building. Fund balances are used for working funds and have been designated to cover the cost of updating the Foundation's membership services computer system.

WHAT WE RECEIVED . . .

Total support and revenue for the 12 months was derived from several sources:

Membership Fees - The number of new members was the same as the previous year. However, reorders increased 10% and updates increased by 14%. The volume of gold and silver emblems is also increasing. As a result, membership fees increased 6%.

Contributions - Contributions by our membership for the support of Medic Alert continued to increase. All solicitations were made by mail to members only. Contributions amounted to 42% of the Foundation's total support and revenue.

Other Revenue - Reimbursement from foreign affiliates for support of international membership expansion increased during the year. Earnings on investment increased because the Foundation held longer investment balances.

SUPPORT AND REVENUE

	For Twelve months 9/30/87	Compared to prior 12 month period
Member's Fees	$3,769,278	up 6%
Contributions	3,023,234	up 26%
Other Revenues	379,152	up 60%
Total Support and Revenue	7,171,664	up 13%

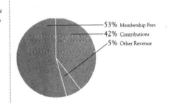

- 53% Membership Fees
- 42% Contributions
- 5% Other Revenue

EXPENSES

	For Twelve months 9/30/87	Percent of Expenditures
Membership Services	$4,096,091	69%
Professional Education Volunteer Training & Public Information	447,860	7%
International Development	221,511	4%
Total Services	$4,765,462	80%
Management & General	546,505	9%
Fund Raising	652,487	11%
TOTAL EXPENSES	$5,964,454	100%

FUND BALANCES

Beginning of Period (10/1/86)	$3,328,254
Support & Revenue	7,171,664
Expenditure and Charges to Funds	<5,991,704>
End of Period (9/30/87)	$4,508,214

- 69% Member Services
- 11% Fund Raising
- 9% Management & General
- 7% Professional Education & Training; Public Relations
- 4% International Development

WHAT WE SPENT...

Membership Services - The cost of establishing new members' medical records and maintaining and updating members' records.

Professional Education, Volunteer Training and Public Information - Costs of continuing education of professionals, volunteers and the public to the vital information and lifesaving potential of Medic Alert services.

Fund Raising - Fund raising expenses increased by only 1%, while contributions increased by 26% and substantially increased the number of members and donors to the Foundation.

Management and General - These costs declined slightly, primarily due to one time costs charged in the previous year.

Grantee	Unpaid Balance 9/1/86	Authorized During the Fiscal Year	Payments During the Fiscal Year	Unpaid Balance 9/1/87
Summary of Grants				
California State University, Fresno Fresno, California Ernst L. Moerk, language teaching/learning in the home ($49,800 in 1986)	$ 26,000	$ —	$ 26,000	$ —
University of California, Berkeley Berkeley, California David L. Kirp, school and community response to children with AIDS	—	102,100	34,600	67,500
University of California, Berkeley Berkeley, California Martin Trow and Sheldon Rothblatt, two centuries of British and American higher education ($195,250 in 1985)	155,750	—	42,500	113,250
University of California, Berkeley Berkeley, California Aaron Wildavsky, cultural theory: foundations, applications, implications	—	146,700	83,100	63,600
University of California, Irvine Irvine, California Ellen Greenberger and Wendy A. Goldberg, impacts of parental employment on the socialization of children	—	7,494	7,494	—
University of California, Irvine Irvine, California Jean Lave, context, cognition, and activity in the lived-in world	—	21,000	21,000	—
University of California, Los Angeles Los Angeles, California Burton R. Clark, research organization and training of advanced scholars	—	340,050	—	340,050
University of California, Los Angeles Los Angeles, California Linda M. Perkins, race, uplift, education, and black women	—	50,700	39,200	11,500
University of California, Los Angeles Los Angeles, California Kathryn Kish Sklar, Florence Kelley and the women's world of reform	—	59,100	—	59,100

44

Design (above):
Tom Lewis
(San Diego, CA)
Pages from the Medic Alert annual report.
Size: 8-1/2 by 11

Design (left):
Edward Hughes
(Evanston, IL)
Pages from The Spencer Foundation Annual Report.
Size: 7-1/4 by 10

Data for revenues and expenses in the report above is accompanied by sidebars with explanatory notes and comparisons to previous years' data.

The format throughout the report combines a single column of running text with one- or two-column text sidebars. On pages without financials, the sidebars focus on human interest stories, such as the volunteer of the year, and special events, such as a video documentary about the foundation.

The elegantly styled typography, with its use of large and small caps, is Goudy Old Style. The running text and financial data print in gray-brown; the sidebar and running head print in black.

Contrasting type makes this summary of grants (left) easy to follow. The boldface is Franklin Gothic Heavy; the regular and italic faces are Goudy Old Style. Italic text and chart headings print in crimson.

FORMS

The goal of a form is decidedly simple: It should be easy to read, easy to complete, and easy to retrieve data from, all of which is easier said than done. Once you think you've got it right, try testing your form on some typical subjects. Chances are they'll question something you thought was obvious or enter information in the wrong place. Of course, there's no way to account for the range of attention, or inattention, respondents will bring to the forms you create. But the goal of designing an effective form is to try to make it is simple as possible.

A company with a long tradition of graphic design excellence turns forms into a minimalist art. Intended for internal use, these forms assume more information on the user's part than would be appropriate in a form to be circulated outside the company.

The black panels with reverse type give the forms a dramatic and sophisticated style. The shadow in the company logo adds to the effect.

An unruled, 10% gray panel sets off the "needed" and "used" dates to be filled in for each item on the billing form. Gray should be used cautiously in spaces where the respondent must write.

Design: Mary Salvadore (Boston, MA)
Forms from WGBH Television.
Trim size: 8-1/2 by 11

Camera Billing Form

WGBH

| | | | Pos. Stat | Reverse | Film Neg. | Film Pos. | Halftone | Cont. Tone | Color-Key |
| | | | needed used | needed used | needed used | needed used | needed used | needed used | needed used |

Name   Project Code   Schedule No.

Traffic/Archive Recycled Tape Credit Form: 915

WGBH

Dept./Project

Date Submitted

Intended Date of Recycling

Request Reference Number

Unit Manager

The intended date of recycling asks you to name a date upon which the tape in question may be destroyed.

Credits for recycled tape may be applied to *existing* projects only. Some materials authorized for recycling may not meet even minimum quality standards. In such cases a lesser than standard amount of credit – or none – may be issued. All recycled tape credits must be used during the current fiscal year.

This recycling authorization form must be signed below by an appropriate department head, producer, post-production supervisor, and/or unit manager associated with *the tape to be recycled.*

	Quantity	Archive/Traffic Numbers	Project Code to be Credited
2 Inch Videotape			
1 Inch Videotape			
3/4 Inch Cassette			
Beta/VHS			

The undersigned accepts full responsibility for the destruction/recycling of all materials listed with the understanding that the materials will be destroyed/recycled on or after the indicated intended date of recycling.

Authorized Signature

Forms in this section

- *Billing and Traffic*—an artful style for internal use
- *Employee Information*—a lesson in good spacing
- *Math Learning Center*—the boxed-in approach
- *Proposal Evaluation*—ruled space for narrative responses
- *Subscription Card*—with an electronic picture of the product
- *Application for Admission*—adapting a publication's grid for a form
- *InFractions*—a triplicate sales receipt

Employee Information

Basic Information • *Required for all Actions*

| Action (*circle*) | Hire | Separation | Personal | Pay Rate | LOA | Job Change | Other |

Last Name | First Name | Middle Initial

Effective Date | Employee Number | Dept./Location

Personal

Street | City

State | Zip Code | Telephone

Birth Date | Social Security No.

| Sex (*circle*) | Male | Female | Race (*circle*) | White | Asian | Am. Indian | Black | Hispanic | Other |

Salaried Personnel Only • Attach Voided Original Check for Direct Deposit Services

Insurance

Marital Status

Spouse Name | Birth Date

Dependent Name | Birth Date

Dependent Name | Birth Date

Dependent Name | Birth Date

Life Beneficiary | Relation

Leave of Absence

Start Date | Anticipated Return Date

Reason for Leave

Pay Rate • *Do Not Fax Pay Information*

| Previous Pay Rate | New Pay Rate | Pay Type (*circle*) Hourly | Salary |

Job Change

Previous Position/Level | New Position/Level

Previous Department | New Department

Separation of Employment

| Type of Separation (*circle*) | Resignation | Discharge | Other |

Vacation Pay Due | Severance Pay Due

Explanation • Comments

Authorization / Date

Originator | Senior Management

Human Resources | Payroll

A banner incorporating the company logo, used here and in the forms on the facing page, is a useful device for maintaining a consistent image in forms and other communications.

Ruled gray panels direct the eye to different categories of questions in this employee information form. The distance between the top and bottom of each panel is the same as the distance between all the other rules on the page.

The typeface is Helvetica bold and regular throughout, with italic used to distinguish special instructions (such as the word "circle" when two or more options are given).

Design: Manfred Petri (Atlanta, GA)
Employee Information form from Geiger International.
Trim size: 8-1/2 by 11

Order Form

Math and the Mind's Eye

Math Learning Center
P.O. Box 3226, Salem, OR 97302
(503) 370-8130

Bill To _____

Ship To _____

Phone _____

P.O. # _____ Cash Enclosed _____ Charge _____

(Term net 30 days)

Quantity	Catalog #	Description	Unit Price	Total
	ME 1	Unit I **Seeing Mathematical Relationships** available Dec 1, 1987 The Handshake Problem, Cube Patterns, Pattern Block Trains and Perimeters, Diagrams and Sketches	$3.50	
	ME 2	Unit II **Visualizing Number Concepts** available Feb 1, 1988 Basic Operations, Odd and Even Numbers, Factors and Primes, Averaging, Greatest Common Divisors, Least Common Multiples	$5.00	
	ME 3	Unit III **Modeling Whole Numbers** available Oct 1, 1987 Grouping and Numeration, Linear Measure and Dimension, Arithmetic with Number Pieces, Base 10 Numeration, Base 10 Addition and Subtraction, Number Piece Rectangles, Base 10 Multiplication, Base 10 Division	$6.50	
	ME 4	Unit IV **Modeling Rationals** available Apr 1, 1988 Egg Carton Fractions, Fractions on a Line, Fraction Bars, Addition and Subtraction with Fraction Bars, Multiplication and Division with Fraction Bars, Introduction to Decimals, Decimal Addition and Subtraction, Decimal Length and Area, Decimal Multiplication and Division, Fraction Operations Via Area: Addition and Subtraction, Fraction Operations Via Area: Multiplication, Fraction Operations Via Area: Division	$9.75	
	ME 5	Unit V **Looking at Geometry** available Nov 1, 1987 Geoboard Figures, Geoboard Areas, Area of Silhouettes, Geoboard Triangles, Geoboard Squares, Pythagorean Theorem, Geoboard Perimeters, An Introduction to Surface Area and Volume, Shape and Surface Area, Areas of Irregular Shapes	$7.50	

All orders for less than $20, except for school purchase orders, must be prepaid.	**Total for Materials**	
All Canadian orders must be paid in U.S. dollars.	**No shipping charges to U.S. destinations by Postal Service**	
Prices are effective October 1, 1987 and subject to change without notice.	Canadian orders please write for shipping costs	
We do not accept credit cards	**TOTAL**	

☐ Check here if you do not have the 1988 Math Learning Center catalog and want a copy.

THE CENTER FOR FIELD RESEARCH
PROPOSAL EVALUATION

Name of Applicant _____ Title of Proposal _____

SIGNIFICANCE OF RESEARCH:
To whom, to what, and in what ways, would this research be significant?

_____
_____
_____

CONCEPTUALIZATION:
Are the research objectives well defined with respect to their scholarly, educational, and public contexts?

_____
_____
_____

METHODOLOGY:
Is the methodology appropriate and adequate to the research objectives?

_____
_____

VOLUNTEER ASSIGNMENTS:
Are the assignments for non-specialists useful and valuable, both to the project's objectives and to those participants?

_____
_____
_____

copyright 1987 Earthwatch

Boxed information (above) provides a highly organized, easy-to-follow order form.

When a form requires more than a few words for each answer (above right), ruling the space generally improves the legibility of the responses.

The typeface is Times Roman throughout, but the styling of headlines as small and large caps makes it look distinctive and contrasts nicely with the italicized questions below. The type prints in blue on a gray background.

Reproducing a page from a publication is an effective marketing technique for subscription cards and other circulation and sales promotions.

The page reproduced on the card below is an Encapsulated PostScript file created from the original electronic document of that page; the EPS file was then placed on the order form as a single piece of art.

Design (above left):
Jonathan Maier (Portland, OR)

Order form for educational materials from the Math Learning Center.
Trim size: 8-1/2 by 11

Design (above):
Earthwatch (Watertown, MA)

Form used to evaluate field research proposals by this nonprofit scientific research organization.
Trim size: 8-1/2 by 11

Design (left): Consumer Markets Abroad

Bind-in subscription card from Consumer Markets Abroad.
Trim size: 7-3/4 by 4-1/4

It's time to get your own subscription.

Make sure you see *Consumer Markets Abroad* on time every month. Start your own subscription to *Consumer Markets Abroad*, the newsletter of worldwide consumer trends and lifestyles by returning this postage-free card. **Send no money now.** We will send you a risk-free issue and bill you $189 for a one-year subscription. If you decide not to subscribe, simply write cancel on the invoice, send it back, and keep the free issue. Your subscription includes another eleven issues plus, for your twelfth issue, *Trends and Opportunities Abroad, 1988,* a 200 page softbound reference guide to overseas markets.

Name _____
Company _____
Title _____
Street _____
City/State/Zip _____
Phone _____

CMA/N87

Consumer Markets Abroad is a publication of American Demographics, Inc., a subsidiary of Dow Jones, Inc.

120
Application for
Admission

Application for Admission

Date

Applying for entrance in ❏ Summer ❏ Fall ❏ Winter ❏ Spring   19 _____

Social Security number

Name
Last   First   Initial

Date of birth
Month   Day   Year

Address
Street

City   State   Zip

Phone number
Day   Evening

State resident ❏ Yes (living in Oregon currently and for preceding 90 days)
❏ No

District resident ❏ Yes (Clackamas County except for Sandy Union High and Lake Oswego School Districts)
❏ No

Course of study
Please include program title and code (see back of form).

High school last
attended
Name   State

Date of high school
graduation or GED
Month   Day   Year

Sex ❏ Male   ❏ Female

Ethnic data (optional)
❏ White, non-Hispanic   ❏ Asian or Pacific Islander
❏ Black, non-Hispanic   ❏ American Indian or Alaskan Native
❏ Hispanic   ❏ Handicapped, needing special assistance*

*the Handicap Resource Center coordinates special assistance such as notetakers and sign language interpreters. If you need assistance, check this box and the HRC will contact you. Response is voluntary and will not influence admission to the college.

In case of emergency,
please notify
Name   Home phone   Work phone

Direct application to Office of Admissions
Clackamas Community College
19600 South Molalla Avenue
Oregon City, OR 97045

Clackamas Community College supports equal education opportunity regardless of sex, race, national origin, age, marital status, handicap or religion.

An application bound into a college catalog uses the catalog grid to create a clear and smart-looking form.

The running head, the 2-point rules at the top and bottom margins, the headline and text style, and the use of the narrow outer column are design elements from the catalog format, shown on pages 126–127.

The shadowed ballot boxes for options to be checked by the respondent are Zapf Dingbats. (The keystroke for this character is an unshifted o.)

Design: Lisa Wilcox and Bill Symes (Oregon City, OR)

Admission application from the Clackamas Community College catalog. Trim size: 8-3/8 by 10-3/4

---

732 West Schubert
Chicago, IL 60614
312.477.5063

Sales Receipt

Sold to:
Name
Address   Apt. No.
City   State   Zip
Day Telephone   Evening Telephone

Ship to:
Name
Address   Apt. No.
City   State   Zip
Day Telephone   Evening Telephone

Office Use Only/Order Number

Date

Style No.	Description	Color Blk.	U/W	Blu.	Total Quantity	Price Each	Total
101	Long Sleeve Boat Neck Top	❏	❏	❏		$35.00	
103	Long Sleeve Cowl Top	❏	❏	❏		45.00	
204	Pants	❏	❏	❏		35.00	
205	Full Skirt	❏	❏	❏		45.00	
206	Straight Skirt	❏	❏	❏		35.00	
308	Cowl Dress	❏	❏	❏		80.00	
309	Jumper	❏	❏	❏		75.00	
410	Jacket	❏	❏	❏		60.00	
511	Sash	❏	❏	❏		9.00	
	Shoulder Pads	❏	❏			10.00	

Signed   Date   Sub Total
Charge to my ❏ MasterCard ❏ Visa   Exp. Date   Tax
                                                        Shipping
❏ a check for the total amount is enclosed. No COD's accepted   Total

Preprinted triplicate sales forms speed up order writing and help ensure completeness and clarity as well. If you compare this form to the sales promotion for the same company (on page 121), you'll see how the combination of a strong logo and consistent type styling create a distinct and consistent image for a company of any size.

Design: Edward Hughes (Evanston, IL)

Order form from InFractions Inc.

Trim size: 5-1/2 by 8-1/2

SECTION 3

PAGEMAKER BASICS

SECTION 3

PAGEMAKER BASICS & BEYOND

This overview of PageMaker is intended to provide an orientation to the program and to serve as a reference for features that aren't easily covered in a single hands-on project. We encourage you to read through it with your hands on the keyboard and mouse. Try out the drawing tools in the Toolbox, type some text and experiment with the different formatting options in the Control Palette, use the nudge buttons to see the fine control they provide. The more you explore here, the faster your learning curve will be when you produce publications in the Projects section.

Having said that, we must add that if you are a newcomer to PageMaker, it's difficult to understand some of the basics until you've actually put them to use creating a document. Don't worry about what you don't get. Just familiarize yourself with the big picture, and use this section for reference later.

And of course you don't have to read this section all at once. In fact, our recommendation is that you read a few sections, then try a few projects, then come back and read a few more sections, and so on. The order of the information in this section corresponds (roughly) to the tasks required to produce the documents in the following section, so a back-and-forth approach should work very well.

BEGINNER'S NOTE: GETTING SET UP TO READ THIS SECTION WITH YOUR HANDS ON THE KEYBOARD AND MOUSE

1. Launch PageMaker.

   Open the folder that contains your Aldus PageMaker files and double-click on the PageMaker 5.0 application icon.

2. Open a new document by selecting New from the File menu.

   Move the pointer to the File menu, hold down the mouse button, drag to highlight the word "New," and release the mouse button. This brings up the Page Setup dialog box.

3. Click OK to use the default specifications in the Page Setup dialog box.

   The specifications that PageMaker automatically uses unless you specify otherwise are called defaults, and for reviewing the basics, the default settings are fine.

4. Use this page as a sort of scratch pad to practice the tools and features described. When the page is full and you want a clean slate, choose Insert Pages from the Layout menu, and okay the default setting of adding 2 new pages.

THE PUBLICATION WINDOW

PageMaker gives you two very different ways of viewing and working on a publication: the layout view and the story view.

When you open a document, PageMaker automatically displays the layout view, which is where you do most of your work. This view resembles an electronic pasteup board on which you format and position all the elements on the page. The magic is that you can see on-screen how your page is shaping up: the relationship of headlines to body text, the size of the pictures, how crowded or open the page appears. You can almost literally grab hold of objects and drag them around the page, as if they were pieces of paper on a table.

If you select Edit Story from the Edit menu, PageMaker displays the story view. Note that there's a blinking cursor—you can just start typing. You can type and edit text in both views, but when you want to type or edit long chunks of text, it's faster to do so in the story view, where you work in one continuous window (similar to that in a word-processing program), rather than moving from one publication page to another as you do in layout view.

For most of the projects in this book, you'll work in the layout view. For a detailed look at the story view, see Project 2.

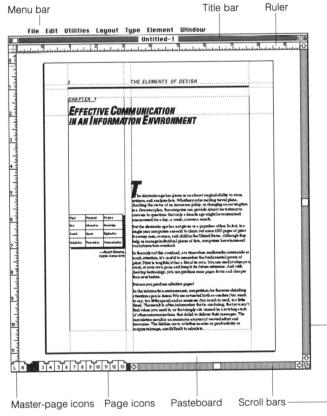

▲ ▲ ▲

The layout view.

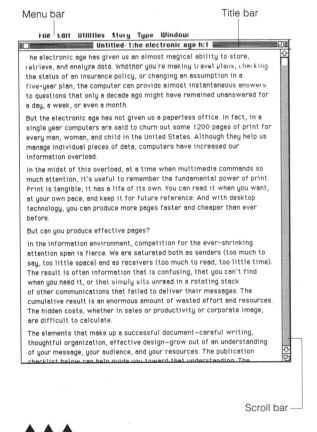

▲ ▲ ▲

The story view of the main text in the same publication.

The Pasteboard

The pasteboard is the area surrounding the page, the on-screen equivalent of the drawing board. Items on the pasteboard display outside all the pages of a publication, but they do not print.

Think of the pasteboard as a work surface on which you can store items that you'll need from time to time when working on the publication. These might include:

- Printing items that you'll use on some, but not all, pages of the publication, such as a banner treatment or a breakout box.

- Spacing guides to measure distances between items such as photographs and captions.

- Text and graphics that you're not yet ready to move into position or that you've cut from one page and want to insert elsewhere.

In long documents, the pasteboard can become hopelessly cluttered. To minimize the chaos, keep the following technique in mind. If any part of a pasteboard item (including a selection handle) overlaps any portion of a page, that item is considered part of the page and appears on the pasteboard only for that page. You can use this overlapping technique to attach pasteboard items to individual pages so that they won't appear on the other pages. Note: Any portion of an item that overlaps the page will print, so be sure to remove these items before printing your camera-ready pages.

MENU COMMANDS

The design cues for PageMaker's menu commands are much the same as those in other Macintosh and Microsoft Windows software.

Commands that are followed by an ellipsis, such as New, Print, and Type Specs, display dialog boxes through which you select options and type in specifications. Many dialog boxes have buttons that bring up additional dialog boxes.

Commands that are followed by a solid, right-pointing arrow indicate submenus, also referred to as pop-up or pull-down menus. Pointing to one of these commands and holding down the mouse button displays another menu, which you can scroll to choose the desired option or specification. On the Layout menu, for example, there's a submenu for options relating to Guides and Rulers. And on the Element menu, there's one submenu for Line weights and another for Fill options (shades of gray and patterns).

You'll also find pull-down menus within some dialog boxes and in the Control Palette. These are usually indicated by a shadow behind the text box on the Mac, and by a down-pointing arrow next to the text box on the PC. To reveal the submenu, you move the pointer to the text box or the arrow, hold down the mouse button, and drag over the submenu to select the option that you want. For example, if you display the Type Specs dialog box (from the Type menu), you can display a submenu of all the fonts installed in your system.

A toggle command is one that you click on and off by selecting that command from the menu (such as Rulers on the Guides and Rulers submenu under Layout) or from the various palettes listed on the Window menu. A

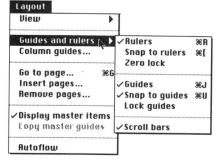

▲ ▲ ▲

Menu commands with arrows display submenus. Those with ellipses display dialog boxes. A command that is checked is turned on; select the command again to turn it off. A gray command is currently unavailable.

TIP

For novice Mac or Windows users When we say to select an option from a menu, move the pointer to that menu, hold down the mouse button, and drag the pointer down the menu to the desired option; when the option is highlighted, release the mouse button. Dragging the pointer down a menu is also called scrolling down the menu. (PC users: If you have a two-button mouse, use the left mouse button to drag and select. Use the right mouse button when you want to lock a displayed menu in view until you make a selection.)

Clicking and dragging are different. In order to drag, you must move the mouse to position the pointer and then hold down the mouse button *while* you move the mouse to drag. But when you click, you move the mouse to position the pointer, and when the pointer is in the right spot, you quickly press and release.

check mark before the command indicates that the command is active, or displayed; no check mark means it is inactive, or hidden. Similar to these are commands that are on (and checked) until you choose another command in the same category (such as page magnifications, listed on the View submenu, and weights, listed on the Line submenu under Element).

When a command is gray, it currently does not apply to anything on the page and cannot be selected. For example, the Cut and Copy commands are gray if there is nothing selected at the time. If the command you want to use is gray, you can generally make it accessible by selecting the text or object you want to apply that command to. Exceptions: Commands such as Find, Change, and Spelling (on the Utilities menu) are always gray when you're working in layout view because these functions are available only in PageMaker's story view.

Keyboard shortcuts are listed on the menus for many commands. If you're a beginner, it's great not to have to remember keyboard commands, to simply point, click, and drag. But eventually you'll want to speed up your work by learning commands for frequently used procedures. We'll give keyboard shortcuts throughout the project instructions, and you can refer to the menu abbreviations for them as well.

PC users note: You can also use the underlined letters on menu options to get to submenu options. For example, say you can't remember the keyboard shortcut for turning Guides on and off. Guides is a layout function, and when you scroll the Layout menu, you'll see that the "a" in Guides and Rulers is underlined; so type *a* to display the Guides and Rulers submenu. Now you'll see that the "G" in Guides is underlined, so type *G* to turn the Guides command on or off. The keys for the underlined letters can be used only when the menu is displayed; they're not the same as the keyboard shortcuts that follow menu options, which you can use without even displaying the menu.

THE TOOLBOX

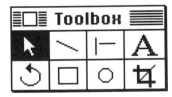

▲▲▲

To select a tool, click on its icon in the Toolbox. As you select one tool and then another, note that the on-screen pointer turns into different shapes, depending on the tool.

The Toolbox (also called the Tool Palette) is a movable window with tools for typing and editing text, drawing simple graphics such as rules and boxes, and moving and manipulating objects on the page. We almost always work with the Toolbox displayed, but if you work on a small monitor, you'll want to learn the keyboard shortcut for displaying and hiding the Toolbox.

To display the Toolbox Select Toolbox from the Window menu.

To close the Toolbox Click the box in the upper left corner (called the close box on a Mac, the Control menu box on a PC). Or choose Toolbox from the Window menu.

Keyboard shortcut for displaying and closing the Toolbox: Command-6 on a Mac, Ctrl-6 on a PC.

To move the Toolbox Point to its title bar and drag it to a new location on the screen.

To use a tool after it's selected You must click somewhere in the publication window to tell PageMaker where you want to use the tool. When you click with the text tool, that's called setting an insertion point. When you use the drawing tools, the pointer turns into a crossbar; position the crossbar where you want to begin the object, hold down the mouse button, and drag the crossbar in the direction you want the object to extend.

To draw perfect circles and squares, hold down the Shift key when you draw with the ellipse and rectangle tools. Holding down the Shift key when you draw with the diagonal line tool constrains the lines to 45° angles, just as if you were drawing with the perpendicular line tool.

To toggle back and forth between an active tool and the pointer   Press Command-Spacebar on a Mac, F9 on a PC. This is handy when you want to repeatedly draw a graphic and then move it or type short text blocks and reposition them on the page.

Name	Toolbox icon	On-screen icon	Purpose	Tool selection shortcut
Pointer tool	▶	▶	select objects to move or manipulate	Shift-F1 (Mac) F9 (PC)
Diagonal line tool	\	+	draw lines at any angle	Shift-F2
Perpendicular tool	|—	+	draw lines in 45° increments	Shift-F3
Text tool	**A**	I	type, select, and edit text	Shift-F4
Rotation tool	↺	✳	freely rotate text or graphics	Shift-F5
Rectangle tool	☐	+	draw squares and rectangles	Shift-F6
Ellipse tool	○	+	draw circles and ellipses	Shift-F7
Cropping tool	⌗	⌗	crop graphics	Shift-F8

SELECTING OBJECTS

Before you can move or manipulate an object in any way, you must select it. This rule—which has no exceptions—holds whether you use the pointer, a dialog box option, or the Control Palette to make the change. You simply cannot do anything to an object on the page before you tell PageMaker which object you want to work on.

Generally you select the object with the pointer tool. Even though you use the drawing tools to create boxes and rules and so on, when you want to resize or otherwise manipulate the graphic, you must select it with the pointer tool. Exceptions: To edit text, you select with the text tool; to manually crop a graphic, you select with the cropping tool; to manually rotate an object, you select with the rotation tool.

To select a single object   Click once on the object with the pointer tool.

To select several objects   Hold down the Shift key while you click on each of the objects.

To select two or more adjacent objects in one move   Position the pointer tool at any corner of the group of objects, hold down the mouse button, and drag

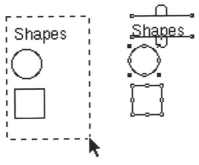

▲ ▲ ▲

To select several objects, *drag the pointer around them (left). When you release the mouse button, all the objects that were fully enclosed in the selection rectangle will be selected (right).*

the pointer to define a box around all the objects you want to select. This is called drawing a marquee or dragging a selection box around the objects.

To select everything on the visible page or spread With the pointer tool active, choose Select All from the Edit menu, or press Command-A on a Mac, Ctrl-A on a PC. Note: This selects everything on the pasteboard as well as on the page (even items that aren't visible at the current page view).

To deselect an object Click in any blank area of the page or on the Toolbox. To deselect one of a group of selected objects, hold down the Shift key and click on the object you want to deselect. You can use this deselect technique when you want to select most, but not all, of the objects in an area. Draw a marquee around the group to select everything, and then hold down the Shift key and click on each object you don't want selected.

To group multiple selected objects so that you can manipulate all of them as a unit, use the PS Group It Addition. See page 419 for details.

Selection handles

When you select a graphic, PageMaker displays eight little rectangular handles around the graphic. You can then manipulate the graphic either by using the appropriate tool from the Toolbox or by typing values or using the nudge buttons in the Control Palette, which we'll explore shortly.

> **To move the graphic** Point to any edge between the handles and drag. Or type new values for the *x-y* coordinates in the Control Palette.

> **To resize the graphic** Point to any handle and drag in the direction you want to resize. Or type new values for height and width in the Control Palette.

> **To resize the graphic proportionally** Hold down the Shift key while you drag. Or click on the proportional scaling option in the Control Palette before typing a new height or width value.

When you select a text block with the pointer, PageMaker displays what are called windowshade handles above and below the text block.

> **To move the text block** Point anywhere inside the selected text block or on the top or bottom windowshade, and drag the text to a new position on the page. Or type new values for the Control Palette *x-y* coordinates.

> **To make the text block narrower or wider** Point to any corner handle and drag in the desired direction.

For a comparison of using the text tool and the pointer tool to work with text, see page 266. For a detailed discussion of text blocks, see page 336.

TIP

To keep an object selected when you switch between a drawing or manipulation (rotation or cropping) tool and the pointer, hold down the Shift key while you click on the tool.

SELECTING TEXT

When you want to edit or format text, use the text tool to select it.

To select a range of text Choose from one of the following techniques:

- Drag over the text with the text tool.

- Set an insertion point at the beginning of the text you want to select, hold down the Shift key, and set another insertion point at the end of the text you want to select. All the text between the two insertion points will be selected.

TIP

The paragraph marker is an invisible character that PageMaker inserts every time you press Return or Enter to indicate a new paragraph. When you select text by dragging over it, often you don't select the invisible paragraph marker. And when you delete that paragraph, the paragraph marker (and the space it defines) remains on the page. This doesn't sound like a big deal, but you'd be surprised how often it causes problems. When you triple-click on a paragraph to select it, PageMaker automatically includes the paragraph marker in the selection.

TIP

When you're editing text in Page-Maker, there are places where it's difficult to determine on-screen whether you have the **correct letterspacing and word spacing.** Sometimes it looks as if there's a space in the middle of a word when in fact there isn't; and sometimes it looks as if there's no space between two words when in fact there is. A quick way to check is to use the arrow keys. With the text tool, set an insertion point in the text in question. If one click on the arrow key moves the cursor past the next letter, there's no space; if it takes two clicks, there is a space.

This technique is especially useful when you want to select a range of text that spans more than two facing pages.

- Use the Shift key in conjunction with the arrow keys and the numeric keypad, as described shortly.

To select all the text in a story Set an insertion point anywhere in the story and choose Select All from the Edit menu (Command-A on a Mac, Ctrl-A on a PC).

This technique is useful if you want to change type specs or apply a style to an entire story or if you want to delete an entire file. It selects all the text in a story, even if some of the text is not yet placed on the page.

To click-select Remember these timesavers:

- Double-click on a word to select the word and the space following it.

- Triple-click on a paragraph to select the paragraph and the paragraph marker following it.

Using the keyboard to move through text

When you edit text, use the arrow keys and the numeric keypad to move quickly through and select text without so much clicking and dragging.

The arrow keys are very intuitive.

- Press an arrow key to move the cursor right or left one character or up or down one line.

- Hold down Command on a Mac, Ctrl on a PC, and press the up or down arrow key to move one paragraph.

- Hold down Shift and press the appropriate arrow key to select text in that direction.

The numeric keypad As with the arrow keys, pressing Shift in combination with a key on the numeric keypad selects the text in the following directions:

1:	To the end of the line, and after that to the end of the next line
7:	To the beginning of the line, and after that to the beginning of the previous line
Command (or Ctrl)-1:	Forward one sentence
Command (or Ctrl)-7:	Back one sentence
2:	Down one line
8:	Up one line
3:	Down one screen or to the end of the text block, depending on the page view
9:	Up one screen or to the top of the text block, depending on the page view
4:	To the previous character
6:	To the next character
Command (or Ctrl)-4:	To the previous word
Command (or Ctrl)-6:	To the next word
Command (or Ctrl)-8:	Up one paragraph
Command (or Ctrl)-2:	Down one paragraph

THE CONTROL PALETTE

With the Control Palette you can apply most text-formatting features without ever opening a dialog box, and you can manipulate objects with mathematical precision. The Control Palette simplifies many functions for beginners and gives advanced users tools that are more precise than ever.

You'll get hands-on practice working with the Control Palette in many of the projects. But because it's such a pivotal feature, we want to collect a lot of information about it in one place for easy reference.

Three Views of the Palette

The Control Palette is exceedingly smart. The options it displays change depending on the tool and object selected. One view displays options for formatting text as individual characters, a second view displays options for formatting text as paragraphs, and a third view displays options for manipulating objects.

Certain principles apply in all three views of the Palette.

Changing and applying settings

There are several ways to change settings using the Control Palette.

- When you click a button or select an option from a menu, PageMaker applies that attribute immediately to the selected text or object.

- When you type a name or a value for an option, you must apply the change by clicking the Apply button, on the left side of the Palette, or by pressing Return or Enter.

- In the text views, pressing the Tab key moves to the next option and also applies a change made by typing a number or name.

Selecting values in the Control Palette

When you want to type a new value in the Control Palette, select the current value by dragging over it or by double-clicking on it.

Note: In some Control Palette fields, double-clicking selects the measurement specification, and in other fields, it doesn't. When you want to override the current unit of measure (to specify picas, for example, when the Control Palette is displayed in inches), you must include the current measurement specification in your selection. Turn the page for more on controlling the measurement system displayed in the Control Palette.

> **TIP**
>
> **If you type the wrong value** in the Control Palette, or if you get an error message that you typed an invalid number, press Escape *before* clicking on another option. This restores the previous value.

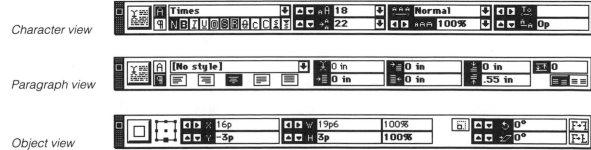

Character view

Paragraph view

Object view

Controlling the Control Palette

To display (or hide) the Control Palette Use the Control Palette command on the Element menu. Or press Command-apostrophe on a Mac, and Ctrl-apostrophe on a PC.

To move the Control Palette Position the pointer in the vertical bar on the left edge of the Control Palette window, hold down the mouse button, and drag the window to a new location.

To display text-formatting attributes Select the text tool when the Control Palette is displayed.

To display character-formatting attributes Click on the A icon in the Control Palette. These attributes include typeface, size, leading, boldface, italic, and so on.

To display paragraph-formatting attributes Click on the ¶ icon in the Control Palette. These attributes include alignment, indents, and paragraph styles, which are collections of attributes that you define for use again and again.

To toggle between the character and paragraph views Press Command-Shift-accent grave (`) on a Mac, Ctrl-Shift-accent grave (`) on a PC. (That's the key above the Tab key.)

To display options for manipulating objects Use the pointer tool to select the object you want to manipulate. The Control Palette will display options that allow you to position, size, crop, rotate, and skew the object with mathematical precision.

To move from one option to another Press the Tab key. To move backward, press Shift-Tab.

The active option is highlighted or indicated by a bar above or below (if it's a button).

To display a Control Palette field in a different unit of measure Select that field and press Command-Option-M on a Mac, Shift-F11 on a PC.

To "power-nudge" Hold down the Command (Mac) or Ctrl (PC) key while you click a nudge button, thus increasing the nudge amount by a factor of ten.

To activate and deactivate the Control Palette Press Command-accent grave (`) on a Mac, Ctrl-accent grave (`) on a PC. (Again, that's the key above the Tab key on most keyboards.)

Note that there's one key sequence for displaying the Control Palette and another for activating it. It's an important distinction, which you may not appreciate until you find that numbers you think you're typing in the Control Palette end up in the publication window and text you think you're typing in the publication window ends up in the Control Palette. That's because even though the Control Palette is displayed, it's not always active.

When the Control Palette is active, keystrokes affect the Control Palette. When the Control Palette is inactive, keystrokes affect the publication window. (The Control Palette is active when the vertical bar on the left edge is darkened. On a color monitor, the vertical bar displays in color.)

You can always activate either the Palette or the publication window by clicking in it. But when you're typing and don't want to take your hands off the keyboard, this keyboard shortcut for activating and deactivating the Control Palette is extremely useful. Note also the following distinctions when using the Return and Enter keys to apply changes typed in the Control Palette.

To apply a change typed in the Control Palette and keep the Control Palette active Press Shift-Return on the Mac, Shift-Enter on the PC. Your next keystroke affects the Control Palette.

To apply a change and make the document window active Press Return on the Mac, Enter on the PC. Your next keystroke affects the document.

A light gray or white bar on the left end of the window indicates that the **Control Palette is inactive.** *Keystrokes affect the publication window.*

A dark gray or color bar on the left end of the window indicates that the **Control Palette is active.** *Keystrokes affect the Palette window.*

Changing the Unit of Measure

PageMaker displays Control Palette values using the measurement system specified for the publication. (See page 210 for more about measurement systems.) To see a measurement displayed in a value other than the default, select the value, and then press Command-Option-M on a Mac, Shift-F11 on a PC. Each time you press that key combination, PageMaker cycles to the next unit of measure available for that option. Note: Not all units of measure are available for every option. Type size and leading, for example, are always measured in points, never in inches.

When typing numeric values, you can override the default unit of measure by typing the abbreviation for the unit of measure you want to specify. See page 210 for a list of the abbreviations.

Nudge Buttons

Some Control Palette fields have nudge buttons, little arrows that you click to manipulate text or graphics in small increments. Click up- and right-pointing arrows to increase the value displayed, click down- and left-pointing arrows to decrease the value. Holding down Command (on a Mac) or Ctrl (on a PC) while you click a nudge button is called a **power nudge** because it increases the nudge amount, usually by a factor of ten.

For example, the nudge amount for type size is 0.1 point. So if your type size is 10 point and you click the up nudge button, the type size increases to 10.1. And if you hold down the Command or Ctrl key while you click the up nudge button, the type size increases to 11 point.

The default values for nudge buttons are listed in the descriptions of the various options on the following pages. Where indicated, you can change the default value through the Preferences command on the File menu. But for other options, the nudge amount is fixed; kerning values, for example, are always specified as either 0.1 em or 0.01 em.

When setting the nudge preferences, note the Use Snap To Constraints option. If you turn on this option and you turn on either Snap to Guides or Snap to Rulers on the Guides and Rulers submenu (on the Layout menu), changes you make by entering a new value in the Control Palette or by clicking a nudge button are constrained by ruler tick marks and ruler guides. See "Snap To commands" on page 211.

Use the Preferences command (on the File menu) to change horizontal and vertical nudge increments for the size, position and baseline offset fields.

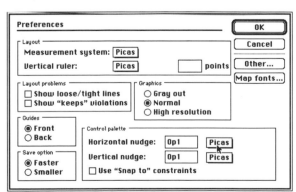

The Character View

If you've worked in a word-processing program with a formatting ribbon, you're already familiar with many of the text features of the Control Palette. The formatting ribbon in Microsoft Word, for example, includes some of the options found in both the character and paragraph views of the Control Palette.

If you select text with the text tool and then specify new text attributes, PageMaker applies the new attributes to the selected text. If you click the text tool to set an insertion point and then specify new attributes, Page-Maker applies those attributes to the text typed following that insertion point. If you specify new attributes before selecting text or setting an insertion point, PageMaker applies that formatting to all text that you subsequently type in that publication.

 Apply button Click this button (or press Tab, Return, or Enter) to apply changes made by typing a name or number in a Control Palette option box.

 View buttons Click one of these buttons to select the character or the paragraph view option. In the detail at left, the character view button is selected.

 **Font** Display the submenu to select a typeface, or type the name of the font you want. (Actually, you don't have to type the entire name; after you've typed enough letters that are unique to that font name, PageMaker displays the full name in the box.)

 **Type-style, case, and position buttons** Click the buttons to turn attributes on and off. A black box indicates an attribute is on, a gray one indicates it is off.

[N] Normal (roman). Click this button to clear all other selected type styles.

[B] Bold. Note: If you have typefaces from large families, such as Helvetica Condensed and Futura, be sure you know the effects of using type-style options. For example, does clicking Bold give you Helvetica Condensed Bold or Helvetica Condensed Black?

[I] Italic.

The character view See Project 1 for hands-on practice.

▼ ▼ ▼

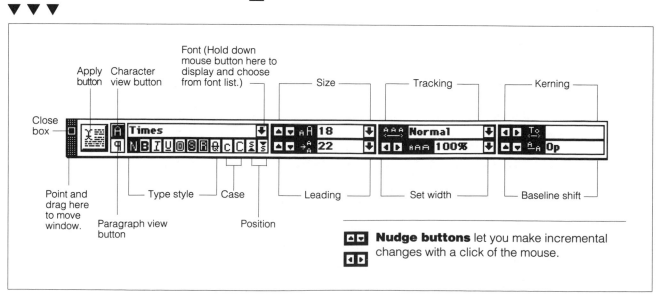

Close box

Apply button | Character view button | Font (Hold down mouse button here to display and choose from font list.) | Size | Tracking | Kerning

Point and drag here to move window. | Paragraph view button | Type style | Case | Position | Leading | Set width | Baseline shift

Nudge buttons let you make incremental changes with a click of the mouse.

TIP

If you **use the Tab key to move
around the Control Palette,**
you can then use the right and left
arrow keys to move forward and
backward in the options within a
field (such as type style or alignment); you can also press the Spacebar to turn a selected option on or
off. These shortcuts don't work if you
select a field by clicking on it or
dragging over it.

☑ Underline.

☑ Outline (Mac only).

☑ Shadow (Mac only).

☑ Reverse (white on black or colored type).

☑ Strikethrough.

☑☑ Small caps (left) and large caps (right).

☑☑ Superscript (left) and subscript (right).

Type size Type a value in the box, or select one from the submenu.

    Nudge: 0.1 point

    Command-Nudge or Ctrl-Nudge: 1 point

    Allowable values: 4 to 650 points, in tenth-of-a-point increments

Leading Type a value in the box, or select one from the submenu.

    Nudge: 0.1 point (can be changed by specifying a new value for
    Vertical Nudge in the Preferences dialog box)

    Command-Nudge or Ctrl-Nudge: 1 point

    Allowable values: 0 to 1300 points, in tenth-of-a-point increments

    Note: If Auto leading is specified in the Type Specs dialog box, chang-
    ing the type size will automatically change the leading. See page 34 for
    a discussion of PageMaker's leading options.

Tracking To set selected text tighter or looser than the default, select an
option from the list or type a name in the box. See page 42 for more information about tracking.

Set width To expand or condense the horizontal width of the characters,
specify a value in the box, or select one from the list. Values greater than
100% expand the type so it is wider than in the original design; values less
than 100% condense the type so it is narrower.

    Nudge: 1%

    Command-Nudge or Ctrl-Nudge: 10%

    Allowable values: 5–250%

Kerning To adjust the space between letters in selected text, enter a value
in the box. See page 39 for more information on kerning.

    Nudge: 0.01 em

    Command-Nudge or Ctrl-Nudge: 0.1 em

    Allowable values: –1 em to 1 em

Baseline shift To shift the baseline of selected text relative to the line slug,
type a value in the box. (See page 34 for a discussion of line slugs.)
Unshifted text has a value of 0.

    Nudge: 0.01 inches, or the value specified for Vertical Nudge in the
    Preferences dialog box

    Allowable values: –1600 to 1600 points

The Paragraph View

You can apply paragraph-formatting attributes to a single paragraph by setting the insertion point anywhere in the paragraph; you don't have to select the whole paragraph. To apply paragraph attributes to multiple paragraphs, you must select at least part of each paragraph.

Apply button Click this button (or press Tab, Return, or Enter) to apply changes made by typing a name or number in a Control Palette option box.

View buttons Click one of these buttons to select the character or the paragraph view. In the detail at left, the paragraph view is highlighted.

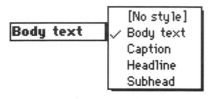

Paragraph style Paragraph styles are collections of text-formatting attributes that you define under a given name. One easy way to define a style: Format some text with the desired attributes, and when you like the way the text looks, type a name for the style in this Control Palette text box. To apply a style to text, select the text and choose a name from the Style pull-down menu in the Control Palette. See Project 4 for a detailed explanation of other ways to define and use styles.

Alignment icons Click on the appropriate icon to specify left, right, centered, justified, or force-justified alignment. (See page 23 for a description of various alignment options.) When you use the Tab key to move to the alignment icons, you can then press the right and left arrow keys to move forward and backward among the alignment options, and you can press the Spacebar to turn a selected option on or off.

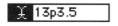

Cursor-position indicator As you type, PageMaker tracks the position of the cursor along the horizontal ruler, with 0 being the left margin. You can't specify a cursor position in this box, but the information displayed is useful in setting indents. See page 408 for a hands-on exercise.

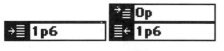

Indent options Type a value to specify the left, first-line, or right indent. In each field, note the position of the arrow relative to the text; that indicates which indent is specified in which field.

Space Before and Space After Type a value to specify the amount of space before or after the selected paragraphs. Again note the arrow positions.

Align-to-grid option When you want baselines of adjacent columns to align, click on the align-to-grid option.

Grid-size option When align to grid is turned on, you generally type the leading value of your body text in this box. See Project 6, page 384, for more about leading grids.

The paragraph view *See Project 2 for hands-on practice.*

▼ ▼ ▼

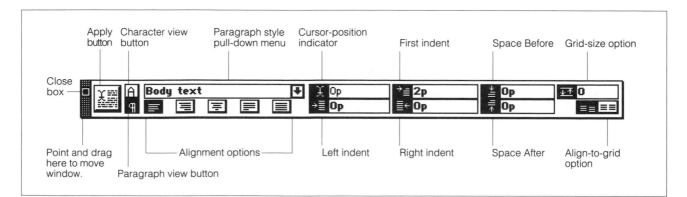

The Object View

When you select an object with the pointer tool, or when any tool other than the text tool is active, the Control Palette displays options for numerically tracking and manipulating objects on the page. Depending on what you're doing at the time, these options may include moving, resizing, rotating, reflecting, skewing, and cropping the object. The PageMaker manual calls this the layout view, but we think of it as the object view because you use it to manipulate objects. (And when you select text with the pointer tool, you can manipulate the text block as an object.)

The great thing about PageMaker is that you have the choice of manipulating objects visually, by dragging with the pointer tool; or mathematically, by typing values in the Control Palette. And of course you can combine the two approaches: You can use the pointer tool to move or size an object, for example, while getting numeric feedback as the values in the Control Palette change.

To specify values in the Control Palette

Select the object you want to manipulate and use one of the following three techniques. Then click Apply, or press Return or Enter.

Enter a new value Select the current Control Palette value (by dragging over it or by double-clicking on it) and type a new one. You can override the current unit of measure by typing the abbreviation for the measurement system you want to use. (See page 210 for the abbreviations.)

Select the value . . .   type a new value, and press Apply.

Use arithmetic Set an insertion point after the existing Control Palette value, and type an arithmetic expression (plus, minus, times, or divided by). This is a great way to divide a box in half, or by a fifth, or . . .

Type an arithmetic expression . . .   and press Apply.

Note: Although you can generally override the unit of measure specified for the publication, you cannot mix measurement systems in arithmetic expressions. For example, if the width value is 3 inches, you can't type *+2p*. If you want to add an increment of 2 picas, select that value and press Command-Option-M on a Mac, Shift-F11 on a PC; each time you press those keys, the selected value cycles to the next unit of measurement. When the measurements are displayed in picas, you can type *+2p*.

Click a nudge button to increase or decrease the value by incremental amounts. The nudge amount is generally specified in the Preferences dialog box. (See the description of each option for details.)

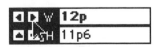 

Before clicking the nudge button one time . . .   and after.

TIP

When the Control Palette is not active, you can move objects by the nudge amount using the arrow keys. To power-nudge the object, press Command or Ctrl plus an arrow key.

Apply button Click this button (or press Return or Enter) to apply changes made by typing a number in an option box. In the object view, the appearance of the Apply button changes depending on the kind of object selected or the task being performed. (The Apply buttons in the adjacent screen details indicate, left to right, a selected TIFF, a selected EPS, and dragging column guides.) If no object is selected, the button displays the icon for the currently active tool.

The Proxy The handles on the Proxy represent the corners, edges, and center of the selected object. The selected handle is called the *reference point*, and it determines how PageMaker applies changes you make using the Control Palette. See the sidebar on the following spread for a detailed look at the Proxy.

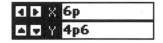

Position The position field displays the x (horizontal) and y (vertical) values corresponding to the active reference point on the Proxy for the selected object. If no object is selected, the values correspond to the position of the pointer. Positive values indicate a position to the right or below the zero point; negative values indicate a position to the left or above the zero point.

As you'll see in the Proxy sidebar, the reference point works differently for the position field than for the other Control Palette options. When you type a new value in the position field, if the reference point displays as a solid box, PageMaker moves the object so that the reference point is at the new position. But if the reference point displays as an arrow, PageMaker resizes the object so that the reference point is at the new position. Note that in both cases, the reference point moves.

Nudge: determined by the values specified in the Preferences dialog box. The default is 0.01 inch, 0p1.

Command-Nudge or Ctrl-Nudge: the default value times ten.

Allowable values: any value that positions the object entirely within the pasteboard and that maintains horizontal and vertical dimensions greater than zero.

The object view *See Projects 3, 6, 7, and 8 for hands-on practice.*

▼ ▼ ▼

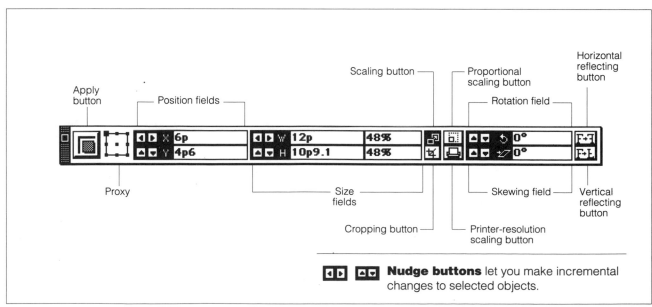

 Nudge buttons let you make incremental changes to selected objects.

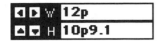

Size The *W* value corresponds to the width and the *H* value corresponds to the height of the selected object. When you select a rule, PageMaker displays a single value designated as *L* (length).

Nudge: determined by the values specified in the Preferences dialog box. The default is 0.01 inch, 0p1.

Command-Nudge or Ctrl-Nudge: the default value times ten.

Allowable values: Maximum size of a graphic is 45.51 inches. Maximum size of a text block is 22.75 inches. (This assumes a page size large enough to contain those elements: Any value you type must position the entire object within the pasteboard and must create a horizontal and vertical dimension greater than zero.)

Percentage scaling This field displays the percentage that the original object has been enlarged or reduced. To enlarge the selected object, type a value greater than 100. To reduce the object, type a value less than 100.

When you resize imported graphics, PageMaker remembers the scaling percentage. But when you resize PageMaker-drawn graphics, the scaling percentage relative to the original size is displayed only until you deselect the object. If you subsequently select the object, the scaling percentage displays as 100%.

Allowable values: any value that positions the item within the pasteboard and that maintains horizontal and vertical dimensions greater than zero.

Scaling

Cropping

Scaling and cropping buttons Only one of these buttons can be active at a time. If you work on a small screen and frequently hide your Toolbox, you can use these buttons to toggle between the pointer tool to resize a graphic and the cropping tool to crop it. If you use the Tab key to move to either of these buttons, once one of them is active pressing any arrow key on your keyboard toggles to the other. ("Active" is indicated by a bar above or below the button.)

On   Off

Proportional-scaling button To resize an object without changing its proportions, turn this option on. (It's the equivalent of holding down the Shift key while you drag on an object's handle to resize it.) If you change the width, either by typing a new value for *W* or for the percentage, the value for height will automatically change as well. If you want to change an object's height and width independently, turn this option off.

Curiously, the default setting is proportional scaling off. But once you turn proportional scaling on to resize a graphic, it remains on for all subsequent graphics in that publication unless you turn it off.

On   Off

Printer-resolution scaling When you resize monochrome bit-mapped images (but not grayscale), turn this option on so that PageMaker will constrain the resizing to the resolution of your target printer, thus avoiding moiré patterns. The target printer is the one you'll use for final, camera-ready output, which may not be the same as the printer you use for proofing. You specify Target Printer Resolution as a number of dots per inch, in the Page Setup dialog box. See page 372 for a side-by-side comparison of resizing an image with and without this option turned on.

Note: PageMaker gives priority to printer resolution over proportional scaling. So if you turn on both options, PageMaker scales the object to the next size that fits the target printer resolution.

Text continues following the sidebar on pages 206–7.

THE PROXY

The handles on the Control Palette's Proxy represent the corners, edges, and center of the selected object. The selected handle is called the **reference point,** and it determines how PageMaker applies changes you make using the Control Palette.

To orient yourself to the way reference points work, draw a rectangle. While it is selected, note that the x-y coordinates in the Control Palette correspond to the active reference point. If you click on a different reference point, the x-y coordinates change. Any changes you specify in the Control Palette are made from the active reference point.

Once you get comfortable with reference points (and we strongly recommend that you do), they can save you a lot of time. For example, if one corner or side of a graphic is correctly positioned in the layout and you want to resize the image, setting the proper reference point before resizing can prevent having to reposition after resizing. But if you don't pay attention to the reference point, you'll often have to reposition objects whenever you make any other kind of change to them using the Control Palette. And that's an annoying waste of time.

To set the reference point for a selected object, click on one of the handles in the Proxy. Or, if you click directly on a handle on the object itself, the corresponding handle on the Proxy is automatically selected. *Keyboard shortcut:* When you use the Tab key to move through the Control Palette to the Proxy, you can use the arrow keys to move from one handle to another. And when Num Lock on the numeric keypad is on, you can select a reference point by pressing the number key on the keypad that corresponds to the position in the Proxy. If you try each technique, you'll see that keyboard shortcuts are very intuitive and easy to remember.

The reference point can display as a solid box or as an arrow.

A reference point that displays as a solid box is a **stationary reference point.** When you make changes in the Control Palette, the corresponding point on the selected object remains stationary. The changes are made as if you used the pointer tool to drag the handle opposite the reference point. Exception: When you specify changes in

the position field, and the reference point displays as a solid box, PageMaker moves the handle corresponding to the reference point to the new location.

A reference point that displays as an arrow is a **moving reference point.** When you make changes in the Control Palette, it's as if you used the pointer tool to drag the handle on the selected object that corresponds to the active reference point.

To change from one kind of reference point to the other, click on a solid box to turn it into an arrow; click on an arrow to turn it into a solid box. Or when you use the Tab key to activate the Proxy, press the Spacebar to move back and forth between a solid box and an arrow.

Although reference points may seem confusing at first, there are just a few simple rules—and a couple of exceptions—required to master them.

- When the reference point displays as a solid box, the corresponding handle on the selected object remains stationary. When the reference point displays as an arrow, the corresponding handle on the selected object moves according to changes made in the Control Palette. (Exception: the position field.) See screen details on the facing page.

- When the reference point is a corner handle or the handle that represents the center of the object, you can specify both vertical and horizontal changes in the Control Palette. When the reference point is a center handle on any side of the Proxy, changes are constrained to either the horizontal or vertical direction.

  If you're unable to select the field that you want to change, you probably need to change the active reference point. For example, if the reference point is the top center handle, you can select the y and H fields, but not the x and y fields. And if the reference point is the left center handle, you can select the x and W fields, but not the y and H fields.

- When you select multiple objects, the handles on the Proxy correspond to the outermost handles on the selected objects. You can change the position and rotation of multiple selected objects, but to resize or skew them as a unit, you must use the PS Group It Addition (see page 419).

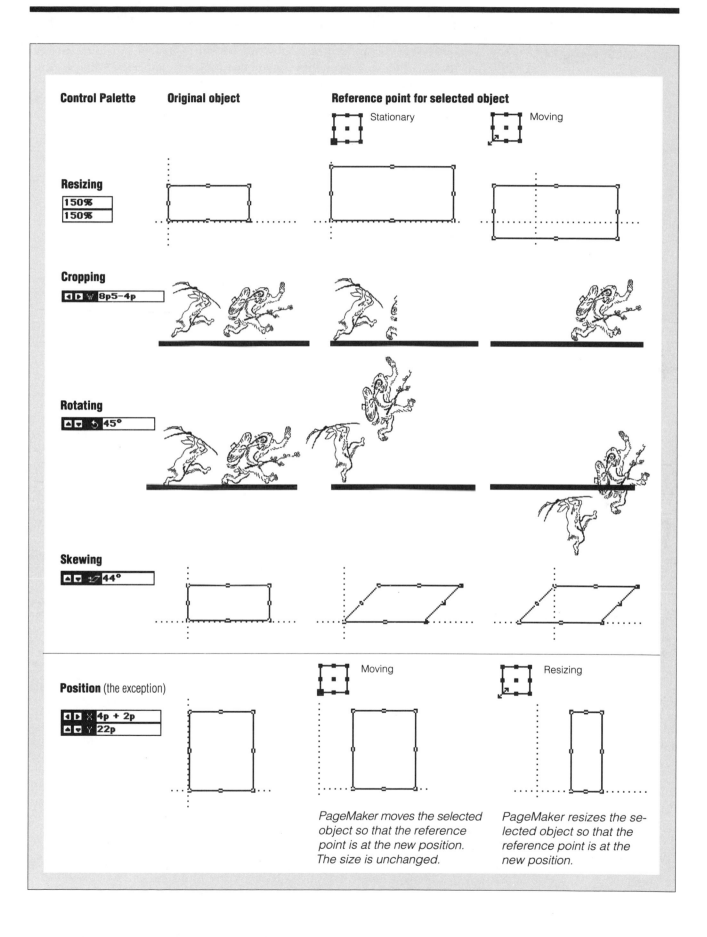

Control Palette **Original object** **Reference point for selected object**

Stationary   Moving

Resizing
150%
150%

Cropping
◄ ► W 8p5–4p

Rotating
▲ ▼ ↻ 45°

Skewing
▲ ▼ ∠ 44°

Position (the exception)
◄ ► X 4p + 2p
▲ ▼ Y 22p

Moving   Resizing

PageMaker moves the selected object so that the reference point is at the new position. The size is unchanged.

PageMaker resizes the selected object so that the reference point is at the new position.

Rotation Although you can rotate objects manually using the rotation tool in the Toolbox, we find the movement difficult to control. So when we rotate objects, we almost always do so by typing a value in the rotation box in the Control Palette. Type a positive number to rotate the object counterclockwise; type a negative number to rotate the object clockwise.

When you rotate an object, the Proxy rotates as well.

> Nudge: 0.1 degree
>
> Command-Nudge or Ctrl-Nudge: 1 degree
>
> Allowable values: –360 to 360 degrees, accurate to 0.01 degree

Skewing Type a positive number to skew an object horizontally to the right; type a negative number to the skew toward the left.

> Nudge: 0.1 degree
>
> Command-Nudge or Ctrl-Nudge: 1 degree
>
> Allowable values: –85 to 85 degrees, accurate to 0.01 degree

Reflecting To flip an object horizontally, click the top button; to flip vertically, click the bottom button. When you reflect an object, the active reference point in the Proxy is reflected as well. Note that when you reflect an object horizontally, PageMaker adds 180 degrees to the rotation value.

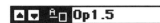

Baseline offset This option is displayed only when you use the pointer tool to select an inline graphic. A setting of 0 aligns the baseline of the graphic with the baseline of the surrounding text. See pages 374–78 for a detailed look at inline graphics.

> Nudge: determined by the value specified for Vertical Nudge in the Preferences dialog box
>
> Command-Nudge or Ctrl-Nudge: the default times ten
>
> Allowable values: 0 to the height of the selected inline graphic

HANDS-ON THE CONTROL PALETTE

See the Projects section for the following hands-on exercises with the Control Palette's object view.

Change the active reference point: page 289

Quick measuring technique: page 295

Align objects by typing a value: page 296

Align objects using the nudge buttons: page 297

Size a PageMaker-drawn graphic: page 305

Use arithmetic in the Control Palette: page 322

Rotate a text block: pages 324–25

Maintain consistent space between objects: page 334

Rotate, reflect, and skew objects: pages 370–71

Use the printer-resolution scaling option: page 372

Adjust the baseline of an inline graphic: page 377

Determine scaling for art being stripped in by a commercial printer: page 400

Crop a photo: page 402

Draw and align identical circles: page 413

Draw concentric circles: page 418

MEASUREMENTS

PageMaker gives you flexibility with the way measurements are displayed and entered in the Control Palette and in dialog boxes. Here are the basics.

Rulers

It is almost always useful to work with the rulers visible—they are indispensable for placing items where you want them on the page. **To display rulers, press** Command-R on a Mac, Ctrl-R on a PC. Or scroll the Layout menu to display the Guides and Rules submenu, and then choose Rulers.

The increments shown on the rulers depend on the page view and monitor. The larger the page view and the larger the monitor, the finer the increments shown. At 50% page view on our 13-inch monitor, the ruler tick marks are at 6-point increments, whereas at 200% and 400%, the tick marks are at 1-point increments. At 50% page view on our 16- and 24-inch monitors, the tick marks are at 3-point intervals, and at 200% and 400%, the tick marks are at 1-point increments.

The zero point

Note this distinction between the zero point and the zero-point marker.

The zero point *is where the zeros on the horizontal and vertical rulers meet.*

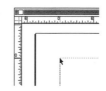

The zero-point marker *is where the rulers meet.*

When you move the mouse around the publication window, hairline markers move on both rulers to define the position of the pointer on the screen relative to the zero point. And Control Palette values are also displayed relative to the current zero point.

To move the zero point Drag the zero-point marker to a new position.

To reset the zero point to the default position Double-click on the zero-point marker.

> For single-sided pages, the default is the upper left corner of the page. For facing pages, the default is in the top center, between the two pages.

TO ADD FILES AFTER YOU'VE INSTALLED PAGEMAKER

If you need to add a print driver, import filter, or any other individual file, follow this procedure:

On a PC Insert disk 1 from PageMaker 5.0. Choose Run from the File menu, and in the Run dialog box, type *A:\Aldsetup* (assuming the disk is in drive A), and click OK. In the Aldus Setup Window, select the kind of file you want to install (for example, Filters), and click Setup. In the directory box, type the location where the new file should be installed, and click OK. PageMaker displays a dialog box where you can select the name of the specific

file you want to install. PageMaker will tell you which disk to insert and will then decompress and install the file.

On a Mac Locate the disk with the file you want to install. (You might have to insert several disks to do so.) If the file is compressed (indicated by a down arrow at the top of the file icon), double-click on the icon. PageMaker's Installer copies a decompressed version to the location that you specify. If the file isn't compressed, drag the icon to copy it to the appropriate location on your hard drive.

Units of measure: picas, inches, and more

The Preferences command on the File menu lets you specify whether you want the rulers displayed in inches or picas (or millimeters or ciceros). Picas are the traditional measuring system for the graphic arts.

> 1 inch = 6 picas
> 1 pica = 12 points (see page 33 for more on points and picas)

The pica system is used to measure type, leading between lines, and space between graphics and other elements on the page. But we generally think of page size in inches; and we also size art in inches, a tradition resulting from the fact that the proportion wheels used to size art give results in inches, not picas.

PageMaker has an extremely useful feature that allows you to **override the current unit of measure** within dialog boxes, such as Page Setup or Column Guides, and in the Control Palette. You simply type a one-character abbreviation for the measurement you want to use. This enables you to open a new document with, for example, an 8.5- by 11-inch page size and 3-pica margins all around without converting either measure and also without closing the dialog box to change the Preferences. If the current measure in the Preferences dialog box is set to inches, simply type *8.5* and *11* in the Page Size boxes and *3p* in the Margin boxes.

The abbreviations are logical and easy to remember. (Do not insert a space before or after the abbreviation.)

To change a measurement to	Type
Inches	*i* after the number
Picas	*p* after the number
Points	*0p* before the number
Picas and points	*p* between the numbers
Millimeters	*m* after the number

In the Control Palette, you can display any field in a unit of measure other than the one specified. Select that field and press Command-Option-M on a Mac, Shift-F11 on a PC. Each time you press the key combination, the display cycles to the next unit of measure.

In the project instructions, we freely mix measurement systems, using whichever is most useful for the space or object being measured. This leaves it up to you to type the abbreviation or change the Preferences.

ACCURACY IN PAGEMAKER

The Control Palette values are said to be accurate to ½0th of a point, a unit endearingly referred to as a twip. This equals ¹⁄₁₄₄₀th of an inch. Values entered in the Control Palette are rounded to the nearest twip.

Using the rulers, the finest increment you can measure is ¼th of a point. So the Control Palette can increase your accuracy over the rulers by a factor of five. When specifying percentages, PageMaker is accurate to ¹⁄₁₀th of a percent.

The PageMaker manual says that the Snap To commands enable you to position elements with an accuracy of ¹⁄₂₈₈₀th of an inch. (See the facing page for more on the Snap To commands.)

For the most precise work, you should use the Control Palette. Once you get used to working with it, it's also faster than performing the same operation manually with the pointer. But when you're working on the fly with the pointer tool, and you use the Snap To commands, the accuracy is still excellent.

Fractional measurements

In PageMaker's dialog boxes and in the Control Palette, fractions of inches are expressed as decimals, fractions of picas are expressed as points, and fractions of points are expressed as decimals. Thus, you'll find measurements such as these:

> 8.5 by 11 inches
> 7 picas 6 points (noted in PageMaker as 7p6)
> 9.5 points (noted in PageMaker as 0p9.5)

Remember that there are 12 points in a pica. When calculating measurements, be careful not to confuse fractions of picas expressed as decimals with points. For example, if you used a calculator to divide 11 picas in half, you'd get 5.5 picas. Properly translated into points, that's 5 picas 6 points, or 5p6. To convert a fraction of a pica into points, multiply the fraction by 12. Say you want to divide a 7-pica measure into three units: 7 ÷ 3 = 2.33 picas; 0.33 × 12 = 3.96. So one-third of 7 picas is actually 2 picas 3.96 points, or 2p3.96. These fractional differences may seem insignificant, but if they are not accurately worked out, they can throw off your layout as they accumulate and leave you feeling incredibly frustrated.

Snap To commands

Snap to Rulers and Snap to Guides are two toggle commands on the Guides and Rulers submenu (under Layout). These commands turn rulers or guides into magnets. When you turn on Snap to Rulers, any item that you place, move, or draw is pulled to the nearest tick mark visible on the ruler. When you turn on Snap to Guides, any item that you place, move, or draw is pulled to the nearest margin, column, or ruler guide.

Turn on Snap to Rulers when you
- Pull in ruler guides or place text blocks or graphics that you want aligned to a specific tick mark on the ruler
- Work with a leading grid

Turn off Snap to Rulers when you
- Pull in ruler guides that you want to align with a graphic or text block already on the page
- Want to align text or graphics with an existing guide that might not be on a ruler tick mark

Turn on Snap to Guides when you
- Place text in columns
- Want to align existing graphics with existing guides

Turn off Snap to Guides when you
- Position graphics or text blocks near, but not directly on, the guides

You can also constrain changes you make in the Control Palette to guidelines and ruler tick marks, but it's a little difficult to understand exactly how this works. In the Preferences dialog box, in the section for the Control Palette, turn on Use Snap To Constraints. This has no effect, however, unless you also turn on one of the Snap To commands on the Guides and Rulers submenu. If you turn on Snap to Rulers, Control Palette changes that you make by typing a new number or clicking a nudge button are constrained to ruler tick marks. Similarly, if you turn on Snap to Guides, any Control Palette change that would move an item within three pixels of a guideline causes PageMaker to snap the item to the guideline.

Although you can use either inches or picas as the unit of measure in PageMaker, fractions of inches must be specified as decimals. We find the following conversions useful to have on hand.

Inches	Decimals	Points	Picas
1/32	0.03125		
1/16	0.0625	4.5	
3/32	0.09375	6.75	
1/8	0.125	9	
5/32	0.15625	11.25	
3/16	0.1875	13.5	1p1.5
7/32	0.21875	15.75	1p3.75
1/4	0.250	18	1p6
9/32	0.28125	20.25	1p8.25
5/16	0.3125	22.50	1p10.5
11/32	0.34375	24.75	2p0.75
3/8	0.375	27	2p3
13/32	0.40625	29.25	2p5.25
7/16	0.4375	31.50	2p7.50
15/32	0.46875	33.75	2p9.75
1/2	0.50	36	3p
17/32	0.53125	38.25	3p2.25
9/16	0.5625	40.50	3p4.5
19/32	0.59375	42.75	3p6.75
5/8	0.625	45	3p9
21/32	0.65625	47.25	3p11.25
11/16	0.6875	49.50	4p1.5
23/32	0.71875	51.75	4p3.75
3/4	0.750	54	4p6
25/32	0.78125	56.25	4p8.25
13/16	0.8125	58.50	4p10.5
27/32	0.84375	60.75	5p0.75
7/8	0.875	63	5p3
29/32	0.90625	65.25	5p5.25
15/16	0.9375	67.50	5p7.50
31/32	0.96875	69.75	5p9.75
1	1	72	6p

PAGE VIEW AND CHANGING PAGES

The View submenu (under Layout) lists eight different page views available in PageMaker. At larger page views, you see less of the page in greater detail, and the ruler tick marks are displayed in finer increments. At smaller page views, you see more of the page but less detail.

The view you choose depends on the size of your monitor and the precision (and perfection) you require for what you're doing at the time. Generally, you edit text at Actual Size or 200%, depending on the legibility of the screen font. You check overall page composition at Fit in Window so that you can see the entire page or spread at once. And you check critical alignments at 200% or 400%.

The option Show Pasteboard reduces the page so that you can see the entire pasteboard surrounding it. This view is useful when you want to place a large piece of art or a text block on the pasteboard before moving it onto the page. Also, when you clean up your pages at the end of a job, use this view to check the pasteboard and discard duplicate or outdated items you might have left there. Occasionally, one of those items should have been included in the publication, so checking at this view can also prevent omissions.

Because of the many variables in system configuration, we've generally left it to you to determine the page view as you work on the projects.

You can change the page view by scrolling the View submenu, but that's pretty slow. And since you need to change page views frequently when working in PageMaker, you'll save considerable time by learning a variety of techniques.

*To display the **magnifier tool** for enlarging the page view, press Command-Spacebar on the Mac, Ctrl-Spacebar on the PC.*

Using the magnifier tool to change page views

Use the keyboard commands at left to display a magnifier, or zoom, tool. (You must continue pressing the keys to keep the magnifier in view.) You can click the magnifier in the part of the page you want center-screen at the next largest page view. Or you can use the magnifier to draw a selection box around the area you want enlarged as much as possible while still fitting in the publication window.

Using this second technique, you can enlarge part of a page up to 800%, even though that view isn't shown on the View submenu.

To zoom out, *or reduce the page view, press Command-Option-Spacebar on the Mac, Ctrl-Alt-Spacebar on the PC.*

Keyboard shortcuts for changing page view

The keyboard shortcuts listed on the View submenu are easy to remember, but the result of using them can be confusing because it varies depending on what you're doing at the time.

- Select the object or objects that you want to work on before pressing the keyboard shortcut so that those elements will be centered in the window at the new page view.

- If nothing is selected, the first time you choose a page view other than Fit in Window, the center of the page will be centered in the window at the new page view. This generally results in having to scroll around the page to get to the area you want to work on. And that wastes time.

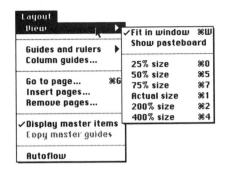

▲ ▲ ▲

You can change page views by se-lecting a new option from the View submenu, but there are faster ways.

- If you're returning to a previous page view and nothing is selected, the page position will be as it was the last time you used that page view. Keep this in mind when you move back and forth between an enlarged view for detail work and Fit in Window to see your changes in the context of the page or spread.

Page view	Macintosh shortcut	PC shortcut
Fit in Window	Command-W	Ctrl-W
Show Pasteboard	Shift-Command-W	Shift-Ctrl-W
25%	Command-0 (zero)	Ctrl-0 (zero)
50%	Command-5	Ctrl-5
75%	Command-7	Ctrl-7
Actual Size	Command-1	Ctrl-1
200%	Command-2	Ctrl-2
400%	Command-4	Ctrl-4

To zoom to a specific part of the screen at a different page view

Use these shortcuts to control what part of the screen you see when you change views. This minimizes the time spent scrolling around the screen at the new page view.

To move to this view	Mac shortcut	PC shortcut
Actual Size	Command-Option-click on point you want center-screen.	2-button mouse: Click right mouse button on point you want center-screen.
		1-button mouse: Ctrl-Alt-click on point you want center-screen.
200%	Command-Option-Shift-click on point you want center-screen.	2-button mouse: Shift-click right mouse button on point you want center-screen.
		1-button mouse: Ctrl-Alt-Shift-click on point you want center-screen.

Other shortcuts

To get the grabber hand On a Macintosh, hold down the Option key, click the mouse button, and drag. On a PC, hold down the Alt key, click the left mouse button, and drag. Use the grabber hand to scroll around the screen at the current page view.

To move to the next page or spread Press Command-Tab on a Mac, F12 on a PC. If you press the keys repeatedly, you can move through several spreads without seeing them displayed. See the related tip at left.

To move to the previous page Press Command-Shift-Tab on a Mac, F11 on a PC.

To display the next page or spread at Fit in Window Press Shift when you click on the page icon.

To move to a specific page, including one whose icon is not displayed
Choose Go to Page on the Layout menu, type a number in the Page Number text box, and press Return or Enter. Using keyboard shortcuts, you can move in and out of this dialog box without ever displaying it on-screen! Try it: Press Command-G or Ctrl-G; then immediately, without even looking up from the keyboard, type the number of the page you want to go to;

TIP

When you move from a publication page to a master page, you can return to that same publication page by pressing Command-Tab on a Mac, F12 on a PC.

then press Return or Enter. When you're making corrections in a long document, this is much faster than clicking on page icons.

To display hidden page icons in long documents Click the arrow on either side of the page icons that are displayed to see icons for lower- and higher-numbered pages. (Better yet, use the previous Go to Page shortcut.)

To change page views for all pages in the publication Hold down the Option key on a Mac, Alt on a PC, and select the desired magnification from the View submenu. This is particularly useful when you want to check an entire document at Fit in Window before printing.

To view all the pages in sequence Use the previous tip to specify the page view you want for all the pages. Then hold down the Shift key and choose Go to Page from the Page menu. PageMaker will display pages one after another, beginning with the first page or spread in the file. To stop the show, click the mouse button or press Esc.

TOOLS FOR BUILDING PAGES

One of the ways in which all good computer software saves you time is by using electronic memory to take some of the burden off the considerably less perfect human memory. PageMaker has several major features that fall into this category. You'll get detailed explanations and hands-on practice with all of them in the Projects section, but no section on PageMaker basics would be complete without an overview of these important tools.

Master Pages

Master pages are like a blueprint for all the other pages of the publication. Every new document that you create automatically has master pages—they're indicated by the L and R icons at the lower left of the publication window. Those pages are empty when you start, but anything you put on a master page appears on every other page of a document.

For example, say you want to create a publication with four equal columns. When you create the new document, page 1 is visible. If you choose column guides and specify 4 columns with 1 pica space between, Page-Maker will create 4 equal columns between the margins on page 1. But when you turn to page 2, you'll be back to the single column that is the default setup for all PageMaker documents.

If, on the other hand, you click on the master-page icons and specify 4 columns in the Column Guides dialog box, every page in the publication will display column guides in exactly the same place. Not only does this save you the time of creating columns on every page, but it ensures consistency from one page to the next.

Master pages can include a nonprinting layout grid (column and ruler guides that define where to place text and graphics), text and graphics that will appear on most pages in the publication (page frames, rules between columns, report or issue dates, and so on), and page-number markers (which tell PageMaker where and in what type style to insert page numbers).

For hands-on practice creating master pages, see Project 4. For a complete discussion of master pages, see pages 306–7 in that project. For details on automatic page numbering, see the tip on page 305.

PAGEMAKER'S NONPRINTING GUIDES

PageMaker has three types of guides that appear on-screen but do not print—called, logically enough, nonprinting guides. Each of the three looks different on the screen, has slightly different functions, and is set up and manipulated in slightly different ways.

▲ ▲ ▲

Margin guides *define the top, bottom, and sides of the image area of the page. Their position is specified in the Page Setup dialog box when you open a new document, and you can change them at any time by returning to that dialog box.*

▲ ▲ ▲

Column guides *control the alignment of text and graphics. PageMaker's default is one column, defined by the margin guides. The side margins look heavier than the top and bottom ones because they are actually column guides on top of margin guides. When you drag a column guide off the margin guide, the margin guide remains in its original position.*

▲ ▲ ▲

To specify two or more columns *and the space between them, use the Column Guides command on the Layout menu. (See page 304 for how to create unequal columns.) Note that the column guides do not extend beyond the top and bottom margins.*

▶ ▶ ▶

*Use the pointer to pull in **ruler guides** from the vertical and horizontal rulers as needed. In this sample page, ruler guides are used to align elements such as the bottom of the initial cap box and the baselines of adjacent text, and the tops of adjacent picture frames. Ruler guides extend to the page trim; you can use them to align elements that fall outside the margins, such as a folio. When a ruler guide is on top of both a margin guide and a column guide, as it is on the far right of this page, it looks like a solid rule on-screen, but it will not print.*

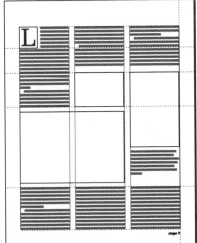

TIPS

To begin with a blank page, with no margin guides, specify all margins as 0 in the Page Setup dialog box.

To divide a page into several equal vertical units, use the Column Guides command to do the arithmetic. Simply specify the number of units you want as the number of columns and specify 0 as the space in between. Bring in ruler guides over the column guides, and then return to the Column Guides dialog box to specify the number of columns for text.

Style Sheets

Learning how to define and use style sheets will save you more time than any other feature in PageMaker. We'll say that more than once in these pages because we know many people who shy away from styles, thinking it's an advanced feature that will be difficult to learn.

We'll look at styles in great detail in Project 4 (pages 311–19). But here we want to give just a brief overview to convince you of their value.

A style is simply a collection of text-formatting attributes. Most of the text formatting that you can do from the Control Palette or from the Type menu can be incorporated into a style definition. When you apply that style to a paragraph, the paragraph takes on all the formatting attributes that are part of the style.

All the styles that you define for a publication are known as the style sheet. The style names are listed in several places: on a pull-down menu in the Control Palette's paragraph view, as a movable Style Palette window that you can hide and display from the Window menu, and on the Style pull-down menu toward the bottom of the Type menu.

To apply a style to a paragraph, you simply set an insertion point anywhere in the paragraph and click on the style name.

The body text you're reading right now, for example, is 10/12 Palatino, flush left, Space After 0p6, Desired Word Space 80%, Desired Letterspace 4%, Limit Consecutive Hyphens to 2, Hyphenation Zone 1. By defining a body text style, we can apply all those attributes to a paragraph with one click of the mouse, rather than having to go into four dialog boxes to individually specify the text, paragraph, spacing, and hyphenation attributes. The time saving is enormous.

If you want to change a style after you're halfway through laying out a 60-page report, no problem. You simply redefine the style, and PageMaker automatically reformats all the text to which you've already applied that style. It's another enormous time saving. In fact, if you had to go back over the 30 pages you'd already done and reformat all the text manually, you might not make the change. And if you did take on that task, chances are you'd miss some of the paragraphs and end up with inconsistent formatting.

TIP

Note the distinction between Page-Maker's type styles and paragraph styles. **Type styles** are variations on a typeface—bold, italic, reverse, and so on; they can be applied to individual characters. **Paragraph styles** are the named collections of type attributes that you define on your style sheet. They're called paragraph styles because they apply to whole paragraphs, rather than to selected characters within a paragraph.

Templates

Templates are publication designs that you reuse over and over. Any publication that you create repeatedly using the same basic design should be set up as a template. If you send an announcement for a monthly meeting, produce a series of educational folders, publish a newsletter, or design a book series, you should develop a template for the basic design.

You'll get hands-on practice creating and using a template in Project 4. You'll set up the layout grid on the master pages and define the style sheet for the publication. Then you'll create the items that always appear on the same page and in the same position in each issue: the logotype and issue date on page 1, the department heads on pages 2 and 3, the mailing label on page 4. When you save the publication, you choose Template in the Save As dialog box. Each time you open the template in the future, Page-Maker opens an untitled copy. If you want to open the template itself to revise it, in the Open dialog box, choose Original.

PageMaker 5.0 ships with templates that provide the page setup and basic design for a wide range of documents: a calendar, an envelope, an invoice, a disk label, two brochures, two newsletters, a CD liner, CD notes, and more. To save disk space, these are included as scripts, rather than as actual publication templates.

You don't need to know anything about scripting to use the templates. Just choose Open Template from the Aldus Additions submenu, on the Utilities menu. In the Open Template dialog box, choose the template you want from the list. PC users note: To use this feature, you must have installed the Windows 3.1 default TrueType fonts Arial and Times New Roman.

If you want to save disk space, you can create your own template scripts. These are text-only files with the extension atg. To view these files to get a feeling for how they are written, use your word processor to open a few of the files for the templates that ship with PageMaker. On the Mac, follow this path: System/Aldus/Additions/Templates. On the PC, follow this path: Aldus/USEnglsh/Additions/Template.

Placing Text and Graphics from Other Applications

From the very first version of PageMaker, one feature that made desktop publishing possible is the ability to bring into the layout text and graphics created in other applications. The importing capabilities have expanded considerably since then, but in many ways, this feature is still the heart of the matter. The layout is just a shell where all the pieces come together. Often most of the pieces are created outside of PageMaker.

There are several ways to bring text and graphics into PageMaker.

- **Place command** (File menu) This is the original and still most frequently used method. The Place dialog box enables you to scroll through your folders or directories and choose the text or graphic file that you want to bring into the layout. PageMaker provides import filters for the formats used by a great many text and graphics applications. You must install these import filters when you install PageMaker in order for PageMaker to recognize the text and graphic files. For a detailed look at placing text, see pages 268–269 and 331. For a detailed look at placing graphics, see pages 331-33.

- **OLE (object linking and embedding)** This is a new way of sharing data among programs, found primarily in Windows-based applications. It's useful with programs that support OLE but do not support export formats recognized by PageMaker. It's similar to pasting, but it creates a link between PageMaker and the source file or application that can be useful when you make revisions. (See page 223 for a detailed discussion of linking.) If you use these techniques with text, PageMaker displays a graphics icon. The text will print, but you cannot display, format, or edit it in PageMaker.

  For *object-linking*, simply copy the object in the source application, and then choose Paste Link from PageMaker's Edit menu. A Paste Link button is also available in the Paste Special dialog box (also accessed from the Edit menu).

  For *object-embedding*, you don't even have to save a source document. While working in PageMaker, choose Insert Object (from the Edit menu). In the dialog box, choose the type of object you want to create.

PageMaker launches that source program; you create the object and choose Update (or an equivalent command) from the File menu in that program; and the object is automatically inserted into PageMaker. If you want to revise the object later, select the object in PageMaker, and choose the command from the bottom of the Edit menu (which will include the name of the application used to create the object). PageMaker launches that application, with the object in a document window.

- **Pasting from the Clipboard** When you copy to the Clipboard, the copy may include information for different text or graphic formats. If you choose the Paste command in PageMaker, PageMaker chooses the format that best preserves the appearance of the original document, and that gives you the maximum ability to edit or manipulate the object in PageMaker. When you choose Paste Special, PageMaker displays a list of those available formats, and you can choose the one you want. (They're listed in descending order of how much control you have over the element when you paste it in PageMaker.)

- **Publish and Subscribe** (Mac only) One advantage of this technique is that you see a preview of the file before you import it. Say you create a logo in FreeHand. Using Publish and Subscribe, you save (but do not export) the FreeHand logo and then choose Create Publisher from the Editions submenu. In the dialog box, you name the file, choose the location on your hard drive, and specify the format (EPS or PICT). Use the Publisher Options to specify whether you want the file updated On Save (automatically) or Manually. In PageMaker, you choose Subscribe To from the Editions submenu (on the Edit menu). The dialog box displays a preview of the published file, and if that's the file you want, you click Subscribe. Position the loaded icon just as if you were placing it.

LAYERS

In PageMaker, as in other object-oriented programs, every element on the page is an object and every object is on a separate layer. It's as if each element you create or place is on a piece of clear acetate, and all the pieces of acetate are stacked on top of one another.

When objects don't touch, the layers are of no concern to you; it doesn't really matter what's on the top or the bottom. But when items overlap, such as white text in a black box, the layers become very important. If the black box gets on top, you won't see the text that's reversed out of it.

When you have several overlapping objects, it's sometimes difficult to select the one you want to manipulate. Sometimes even though you can see an object, you click and click and click and keep selecting the object above it in the stacking order. Keep in mind the following techniques.

The Command-click or Ctrl-click method To select an object that is behind another object, select the top object; then press Command (on a Mac) or Ctrl (on a PC) and click again. Each time you click, PageMaker selects the next object down in the stacking order.

To select an object that is hidden behind another object: Select the top object (left). While it is still selected, hold down the Command (Mac) or Ctrl (PC) key, and click again; PageMaker displays the handles for the second item in the stack (center). Choose Bring to Front (Element menu), or press Command-F or Ctrl-F.

▶ ▶ ▶

The selection rectangle method Use the pointer tool to draw a selection box around all the objects. Then hold down the Shift key and one by one click on a handle of each object that you want to deselect, until only the object you want to manipulate is selected.

To change the stacking order You can also select an object with the pointer and choose either the Bring to Front or the Send to Back command from the Element menu (Command-F or Ctrl-F and Command-B or Ctrl-B). Using these commands brings objects to the very top or the very bottom of the stacking order; all the objects in the middle shift accordingly. Of course, sometimes in order to select the object that you want to move to the front or back, you have to use the Command-click or Ctrl-click technique described above for moving through the stacking order.

Guides (margins, ruler guides, and column guides) are also part of the stacking order. By default, guides are in front. So if you draw a rule over a guide and later want to change the weight of that rule, you may have trouble selecting the rule because it's behind the guide. Use any of the techniques just described to select objects that are behind guidelines.

You can also change the Guides setting through the Preferences command on the File menu. In the dialog box, under Guides, just click Front or Back. We generally like the Guides in the back, so we change the default by opening the Preferences dialog box when there is no PageMaker document open and selecting Back. Then every time you open a new document, the Guides will be in the back.

If you have trouble selecting an object, chances are the handles from some other object are on top of whatever you're trying to select. Text handles sometimes extend beyond the text; likewise the selection box defined by the handles around a graphic may be bigger than the actual graphic. Sometimes there are handles that seem to have nothing inside them, which may turn out to be reverse type or a white box or rule. Even a paragraph space that gets left behind when you delete text will show up between text handles.

To diagnose the situation, choose a page view that lets you see the entire page, and then with the pointer tool selected, choose Select All from the Edit menu or press Command-A on a Mac, Ctrl-A on a PC. With all the selection handles displayed, you'll be able to see what's overlapping the object you're trying to select.

When you move a text block or graphic, it is automatically brought to the front. When you move a group of objects, the objects retain their stacking order relative to one another but the whole group moves to the front.

When you draw a selection rectangle, only those items that are entirely enclosed within the selection area will be selected. The screen detail at right shows how to select frogs that are behind the text block without selecting the text block itself.

► ► ►

I've seen him set Dan'l Webster down here on this floor—Dan'l Webster was the name of the frog—and sing out, 'Flies, Dan'l, flies!' and quicker'n you could wink he'd spring straight up and snake a fly off'n the counter there, and flop down on the floor again as solid as a gob of mud, and fall to scratching the side of his head with his hind foot as indifferent as if he hadn't no idea he'd been doin' any more'n any frog might do. Smiley was monstrous proud of his frog, and well he might be, for fellers that had traveled and been everywheres all said he laid over any frog that ever *they* see.

SAVING YOUR WORK

The keyboard shortcut for saving—Command-S or Ctrl-S—is easy to remember and takes much less time than redoing lost work. A general rule of thumb is to save every 15 to 20 minutes or whenever you've done something you'd really hate to redo. In the projects, we've generally left it to you to save according to your own habit.

After you've saved a publication for the first time, PageMaker automatically performs a mini-save whenever you move to a new page or spread, insert or delete a page, change the page setup, use the Clipboard, switch between layout and story view, or click OK in the Define Styles dialog box.

The compacting function of Save As

When you save a document with the Save command, changes made since the last save are appended to the end of the file. So even if you delete text or graphics, the document might continue to grow in size. When you save a document using the Save As command from the File menu, the file is compacted, actually eliminating from memory the discarded elements from previous versions. We've often seen files reduced by 300 to 400 KB after doing a Save As.

So when you've made substantial changes in a document, and when you're saving a document before closing it, and before you send a file to a service bureau for output, use the Save As command to compress the file. Try performing a Save As to speed up response time and for general trouble-shooting too. If you want to keep the same name (we generally do when compressing files), just click OK (or press Return or Enter) when the Save As dialog box comes on-screen. You'll get another box asking whether you want to replace the existing document with that name; click Yes.

You can instruct PageMaker to make every Save a Save As. From the Save options at the bottom of the Preferences dialog box, choose Smaller. However, we prefer to leave the setting at Faster for routine saves and then do a Save As at the end of a work session before closing the file.

UNDOING CHANGES

It's great to be able to experiment, to try out different approaches, whether you're sizing a graphic, formatting text, or pulling all the pieces together in the page layout. And when you don't like the result, it's a relief to be able to return to what you had before you started fooling around. Page-Maker has several options that enable you to undo your work when you don't like what you've done.

Undo Choose this command from the Edit menu (or press Command-Z on a Mac, Ctrl-Z on a PC) to reverse the most recent action. If the command is gray, the action isn't one that can be undone. For example, you can't undo changes in paragraph styles, text formatting, line weight, or fill options.

Remove Transformation Choose this command (from the Element menu) to undo all rotation, skewing, and reflecting applied to the selected object.

Revert Choose this Command (from the File menu) to undo all changes made since you last saved the document. Hold down the Shift key while you choose Revert to undo all changes made since the last mini-save.

DEFAULTS

We've referred several times to defaults, which are simply preset values or options that PageMaker uses unless you specify otherwise. Whenever you find yourself having to make the same change over and over—a typeface, a line weight, the unit of measure—it's time to change the default.

Like most programs, PageMaker has application defaults and publication defaults. Application defaults apply to all new documents; publication defaults apply only to the current document. You can change and override both kinds of defaults, but it does save time to set them to the choices that you use most frequently.

You can change **application defaults** *after* you've launched PageMaker but *before* you've opened a document. For example, PageMaker's default unit of measure is inches, so unless you specify otherwise, your ruler increments will be measured in inches. If you work in picas and points more frequently than inches, you'll want to change the application default to picas. Before opening a new document, choose Preferences from the File menu, and select Picas from the submenu for both the Measurement System and the Vertical Ruler. All new documents will then use picas for their unit of measure.

You can change the application default for any menu command that is black, rather than gray, when there is no document open in PageMaker. When you change an application default, the new value will apply to all new publications you open; existing publications will not be affected.

You specify **publication defaults** after a PageMaker document is open. To change a publication default, choose the pointer tool, be sure no text or graphic is selected, and select the specifications you want to set as the current publication default.

If, to continue the example used earlier, you have inches as your application default and you open a new document and change the unit of measure to picas, the ruler increments will be picas for that publication but not for subsequent ones. You can change the publication defaults at any time while the document is open.

At those times when PageMaker seems to have a mind of its own, insisting on one typeface or line style when you continue to select another, try changing the publication defaults to the specifications you want. For example, the default line weight is 1 point. If the rules in your publication are hairline, specify that as the default so that you don't have to change the line weight of every line or graphic that you draw.

The project instructions generally assume that you are working with PageMaker's original defaults. If you've changed any of the application defaults, your screen may look different from what is described in a particular project.

If you want to **restore PageMaker's original defaults,** simply throw out the PM 5 Defaults file. If you work on a Macintosh, delete or rename the file named PM5.0 Defaults (in the Preferences folder in your System folder). If you use the PC version, delete or rename PM5.cnf (in Aldus/USEnglsh). The next time you open PageMaker, the program will automatically create a new, unaltered default file.

FONTS

How you install and enable fonts varies depending on the computer platform (Mac or PC), the printer (PostScript or non-PostScript), the kind of fonts you use (PostScript, TrueType, Intellifonts, and so on), and whether you use a type management utility (such as Adobe Type Manager or FontMinder). You'll need to refer to the font or type management documentation for the procedure appropriate for your setup.

When you print on a PostScript printer, or on a non-PostScript printer using a type management utility such as ATM, you need to install two different versions of the font: a screen font, which is the bit-mapped version used for screen display, and a printer font, which is a scalable outline that produces smooth characters in printing.

Be aware that only PostScript and TrueType fonts support the full range of sizes and manipulation available in PageMaker. Other scalable fonts (including Intellifonts and Bitstream Speedo) support the full range of sizes but not 360-degree rotation, reflection, or skewing. Nonscalable fonts (including Bitstream Fontware and fonts used by the HP LaserJet II) print only at the sizes you have installed, and they cannot be transformed. If you transform fonts in the last two groups, PageMaker prints a low-resolution screen version of the font.

If you open a PageMaker file that includes fonts not currently installed in your system, PageMaker warns you by displaying the Panose Font Matching Results dialog box. If you frequently open and close fonts on your system, move files from one computer to another, or share files with clients, colleagues, or customers, you will at some point see this dialog box.

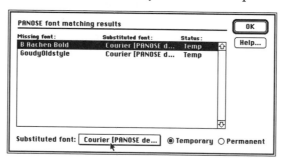

By default, PageMaker substitutes Courier for the missing font. To choose a different substitute: Select the name of the missing font, and scroll the Substituted Font pull-down menu to choose from among the installed fonts.

When you substitute a font, the missing font is listed on the Type menu, followed by the name of the substituted fonts in brackets. When you use Adobe's SuperATM to simulate a missing font, the font name is followed by a diamond.

To customize font-matching settings, choose Preferences from the File menu, and in the Preferences dialog box, choose Map Fonts. Use this dialog box to choose the default font for substitutions. Click the Spellings button to review and edit the different font spellings used for files shared by Macintosh and PC PageMaker. Click the Exceptions button to specify a font that should always be substituted for a particular missing font in all future publications that you open.

TIP

On the PC, to print TrueType fonts to PostScript printers, you must set the fonts to print as Adobe Type 1 fonts. From the Program Manager, follow this path: Main/Control Panel/Printers. In the Printers dialog box, choose Setup, then Options, and then Advanced. For the TrueType Fonts Send to Printer As option, select Adobe Type 1 from the pull-down list.

TIP

Font substitution—whether through the Panose dialog box or Adobe's SuperATM (which simulates missing fonts rather than choosing substitutes for them)—should be used as an alert to a problem that needs to be fixed, not as the solution to that problem. No designer who has given any thought to type design would accept a font substitution. If it is necessary that you do accept one for final output, carefully review all the type specs and make adjustments for the substituted font.

LINKS

The idea of links is much simpler than it sounds at first. The basic concept is that there is an electronic link between a PageMaker document and the original source files for text and graphics that you've placed in that document. PageMaker knows the name of that source file and its location on your hard drive.

Part of the complication comes from the fact that links work a little differently depending on how you import files from other applications. Most of the discussion on the following pages pertains to files that are imported using the Place command, which is the method most people use most of the time. If you come across a reference to other methods with nomenclature you've never heard of (such as OLE or Publish and Subscribe) and want to learn more about those methods, see pages 217–18. Otherwise, just ignore the information.

Another complication comes from the fact that PageMaker provides considerable flexibility in how you manage links. But this requires reading about a half-dozen features to find the one or two that you want to use.

> **TIP**
>
> You can **update an imported file without using the Links feature.** Select the object you want to update, choose Place, and in the Place dialog box, scroll through your folders to select the name of the updated source file. Then click the Replacing Graphic button, and press Return or Enter. PageMaker updates the layout with the new version of the graphic. You can use this technique to update text, as well; see page 269.

If you're a novice at page layout, creating fairly simple pages, you can probably get by without any attention to links. What's simple? Documents in which all the text revisions are made in the PageMaker layout (rather than in the original word-processing file), documents with no art, or with only simple black-and-white line art or art that will be stripped in conventionally by a commercial printer.

But if your pages include art that is revised after being placed in the PageMaker layout, using the link to the originating file can save you time. And for halftones and complex graphics with large file sizes, maintaining the link is essential to printing the file correctly.

Using Links for Revision Control

Revisions are inherent in the publishing process. And computers seduce us into going back again and again to tweak yet another detail. Some of those changes are made directly in the page layout. But frequently art, photos, and text that have been placed in PageMaker are later revised in the applications in which they were created. When you update the link to the source file, PageMaker replaces the earlier version with the current one.

> **Link options: Defaults**   [**OK**]
>
> **Text:**   [Cancel]
> ☒ Store copy in publication
> ☐ Update automatically
> ☐ Alert before updating
>
> **Graphics:**
> ☒ Store copy in publication
> ☐ Update automatically
> ☐ Alert before updating

▲ ▲ ▲

*Use the **Link Options dialog box** to define whether PageMaker should automatically update the PageMaker object whenever the original source file is revised.*

Specify how linked objects should be handled

You define how you want linked files to be stored and updated in your publication through the Link Options command on the Element menu. The dialog box gives you the following options:

Store Copy in Publication PageMaker stores a complete copy of the external source file in the layout, so there is no need for a link to an external file.

Update Automatically If the external copy has been modified, the internal linked copy will automatically be updated the next time you open the file. This is wonderfully convenient but also a little dangerous. In a workgroup situation, for example, you'd want to be sure that the person who made the changes intended them to be incorporated; he or she might have been exploring some refinement that didn't work out or that isn't yet finished.

TIP

Can't remember the name of a graphic that you need to revise? Select the graphic and choose Link Info (from the Element menu). The name of the graphic is at the top of the Link Info dialog box. (In the dialog box shown below, the name of the selected graphic is logo/color.eps.) The location of the graphic on your hard drive is listed in the top line on the right side of the dialog box.

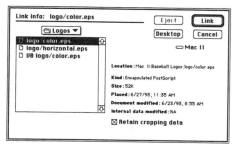

▲ ▲ ▲

The Link Info dialog box (opened from the Element menu) gives you a file history of the selected object. If the link is out of date or broken, scroll through your folders or directories to select the current file and click on Link, or double-click on the filename. PageMaker replaces the current publication copy with the updated one selected through this dialog box.

Alert Before Updating If you choose this option in conjunction with Update Automatically, PageMaker displays an alert message for you to respond to before updating the PageMaker copy of the graphic. Having been alerted that a change has been made, the layout person can check with the person responsible for the source file to see whether the layout should be updated.

You can set the Link Options for the entire publication or for individual elements in the publication.

- To set the defaults for the entire publication, choose Link Options from the Element menu when no text or graphic is selected.

- To set the options for an individual text or graphic file, either use the Link Options command when that element is selected or use the Link Options button in the Links dialog box when that element is highlighted in the document list.

Note: If you use Publish and Subscribe (Macintosh System 7 only) to import text or graphics into PageMaker, you can specify Automatic or Manual updating through the Subscriber Options dialog box (on the Editions submenu on the Edit menu).

Manually update a single item

Select any element, and choose Link Info (from the Element menu) to get a file history for that element or to update the link.

The file history includes the location on your hard drive, the kind of file and its size, the date and time you placed the file in the current publication, the date and time the external file was last modified, and the date and time the internal copy of the file was modified. Choose Retain Cropping Data to have PageMaker apply the current cropping to the updated file.

If you need to update the link, scroll through your folders or directories to find the current copy of the source file, and click on the Link button. Or just double-click on the name of the source file.

Manually update several items

If you know several elements need to be updated, choose Links (from the File menu) to speed up the process. (See page 226 for a detailed description of this dialog box.) From the list of linked documents, select the name of an element that has been revised, and click the Update button. Repeat this for every element whose revision is ready to be incorporated into the layout. When you okay the dialog box, PageMaker will replace all the outdated elements that you selected with the revised versions.

If you have a great many linked elements, and if some of them have similar names, the long list in this dialog box can be intimidating. In this case, use the Link Info dialog box as described above for manually updating a single selected graphic.

Use another application to update an object

If you're doing both layout and graphics, the Edit Original command (from the Edit menu) will be one of your favorite features. Say you're moving through the layout and you see that the illustration on page 3

TIP

Keyboard shortcuts for the Edit Original command Select the object you want to edit, hold down the Option key on a Mac, the Alt key on a PC, and double-click on the object. Or just double-click on an OLE object. To edit the object in an application other than the one used to create it, add the Shift key to the procedure.

needs some work. Select that graphic with the pointer tool, and choose Edit Original. PageMaker launches the application used to create that graphic and opens the graphic file. Make the changes needed, save the file, and return to the PageMaker layout. When you update the link (or if you have automatic updates scheduled, the next time you open the layout file), PageMaker replaces the old graphic with the updated version. You can use this feature with text also, but you'll lose any changes to the text made in PageMaker, including formatting.

Be aware of certain variations and restrictions on the way this feature works.

- If the selected graphic wasn't created on your computer, or if you've moved or deleted the application used to create the graphic, you'll see a dialog box that says the application used to create the document is missing or the program was not found. If you have another application that can be used, you can launch that application through this dialog box.

- If, on the other hand, you get a message saying the file was not found, it probably means that the link for the selected graphic is not up to date. (If you change the name of a source file or its location on your hard drive, the link is broken.) Update the link (through the Link Info dialog box under Element), and then choose Edit Original again.

- If you know that the graphic is not associated with an application, hold down the Shift key when you choose Edit Original. This automatically displays the Choose Editor dialog box, from which you can launch the appropriate application.

Links and the Clipboard

When you copy text or graphics from other programs and paste them into a PageMaker document, the copy you paste has no link to an external file. But if you use the Paste Link command (on the Edit menu) to paste an OLE object, you can establish a link.

When you cut or copy a graphic or text range in PageMaker and paste it elsewhere in that same document or in another document, PageMaker will transfer any existing link information. When you add a PageMaker object to a Library, existing links travel with the object.

Unlinking objects

When you have automatic updates specified and you don't want a particular object to be updated, you can break the link to the source file. In the Links dialog box, select the name of the object, click Unlink, and then click OK. If you want to reestablish the link later, you have to select the object, choose Link Info (from the Element menu), and scroll through your folders to select the name of the source file.

How links get broken

Several everyday tasks can break the link between PageMaker and the source file: renaming the file or the directory it is stored in, deleting the file, or moving the file to a different location on your hard drive. When you open a file with a broken link or try to print a page from it, PageMaker displays a warning (see screen detail at left). If you need links for revision management or for printing, you will need to reestablish these broken links.

When you open a publication that includes an object with a broken link and that link is required for printing, PageMaker displays the Cannot Find dialog box. To reestablish the link, scroll through your folders to locate the source file, highlight the filename, and then click Link (or just double-click on the filename). Clicking Ignore accepts the broken link; clicking Ignore All accepts broken links for all graphics in the publication. If you do choose Ignore, the file may not print properly.

▼ ▼ ▼

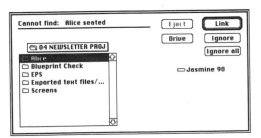

When you update a link

When you update a link, PageMaker replaces the source file currently in the publication with the updated version. Any resizing, rotating, skewing, reflecting, and text wrap applied to the earlier version carries over to the updated version. To retain cropping, choose Retain Cropping Data in the Link Info dialog box. Any image control specifications that you may have made to an object within PageMaker are lost when you update the link.

LINK STATUS SUMMARY

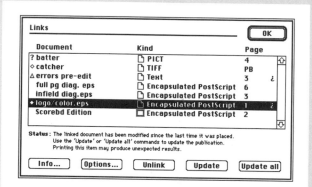

PageMaker constantly tracks the status of the link between the external source file and the copy of that file in the PageMaker document. To see a list of all linked files and their status, choose Links from the File menu (Command-equal sign on a Mac, Ctrl-Shift-D on a PC).

In the Links dialog box, PageMaker lists the name of each source file, the kind of file (image, text, EPS, PICT, and so on), and the page location in the PageMaker document (PB stands for pasteboard, LM and RM for left and right master pages). Icons to the left of the filename or to the right of the page number indicate the status of each document. When you select a filename from the Document list, the status of that file is described in the Status field below the list box.

Mac icon	PC icon	Status	Action to take
No icon	No icon	Link is up to date.	None needed.
◇	–	Source file has been modified, and the linked internal file is not scheduled for automatic update.	Click the Update button in the Links dialog box to update the file, or use the Place command to replace the existing element with the updated one.
◆	+	Source file has been modified since it was imported in the publication and is scheduled for automatic update.	If a complete copy is not stored in the layout, click Update in this dialog box. If a copy is stored in the publication, PageMaker will update it when you print or reopen the layout file or when you click Update in this dialog box.
(PC only)	X	The object is linked to a file stored outside the publication, and that file has been modified since it was imported.	To update the file, click Update in this dialog box. (On the PC, the difference between X and + is that + indicates a copy is stored in the publication and X indicates it is stored outside the publication.)
?	?	The link has been broken; PageMaker cannot find the external source file.	You've probably moved or renamed either the publication file or the external source file. To reestablish the link, choose the Info button; in the Link Info dialog box, scroll to find the appropriate external source file, select it, and click Link.
△	!	Both the linked file and the internal Page-Maker file have been modified.	If both sets of changes are needed in the PageMaker file, you'll have to compile them manually. You want to avoid this situation.
¿	¿	The object will not print at high resolution.	Check the Status field for details.
NA	NA	The item was pasted without links or is OLE-embedded.	None. All information about the object is stored in the publication file.

Maintaining Links for Printing

Alert when storing graphics over: [256] kBytes

▲ ▲ ▲

If a graphic file is larger than the value specified for this option in the Other Preferences dialog box, the link to the original source file is required for printing.

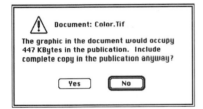

▲ ▲ ▲

When you place a graphic larger than the threshold specified in the Other Preferences dialog box, PageMaker displays this warning. Clicking No keeps your files small because PageMaker places a low-resolution copy in the document file and links that copy to the external source file.

For some graphics, a complete copy is stored in the publication, with all the information needed for printing. But for others—such as complex illustrations and halftone photos—PageMaker stores a low-resolution copy of the graphic in the publication. When you print the publication, Page-Maker reads the data from the linked source file and applies any sizing, cropping, and other image manipulation done in the page layout to the high-res original.

Whether PageMaker stores a complete graphic or a low-res copy of it in the publication is determined in the Other Preferences dialog box. If the graphic file is smaller than the value specified for Alert When Storing Graphics Over, a complete copy is automatically stored in the publication. But if the graphic file is larger than the value specified (the default value is 256 KB), when you place the graphic, PageMaker alerts you to the size of the file and asks whether you want to include a complete copy in the publication.

If you respond Yes, the publication file will include all the information needed to both display and print the graphic at high resolutions. The downside is that this increases the size of your PageMaker file and slows it down. If you respond No in the message box, PageMaker stores a low-resolution screen version of the graphic in the publication file and creates a link to the original source file.

When you send a publication to a service bureau for camera-ready print-outs (or when you copy your files for output on any printer that's not net-worked to your workstation), it's essential to send these linked graphics along with the PageMaker publication. Otherwise, the graphics will not print properly.

There's an easy way to facilitate copying linked files:

- Create a folder or directory for the service bureau files.
- Do a Save As of the PageMaker file to bring up the Save As dialog box.
- In the Save As dialog box, select the Files Required for Remote Printing option. Choose the service bureau directory as the destination for the files saved.
- PageMaker will copy the publication file, and any linked files required for printing, to the selected directory. You can then copy the files from that directory to disks to send to the service bureau.

There's another Save As option, available in both Macintosh and PC Page-Maker, called Copy All Linked Files. If you select this option, PageMaker will copy both the PageMaker file and any external source files linked to the publication, whether or not the linked files are required for printing. This is useful when you need to transfer files from one workstation or location to another, and you want to have all the source files available.

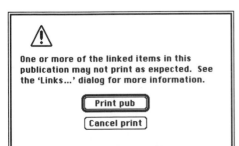

PageMaker displays yet another warning when you print a document that includes an element with a broken link. It displays this warning even if the element that may not print correctly isn't on any of the pages specified to print.

◀ ◀ ◀

PRINTING

When you plan a publication, one of the first considerations should be what printer you'll use to output your camera-ready pages. Will you use your desktop printer, with 300- or 600-dots-per-inch resolution, or will you send the files to a service bureau for output from an imagesetter at resolutions of 1270 dots per inch and higher? The more dots per inch, the sharper the printed page will be. And the decision determines certain specifications that you make in PageMaker when you set up the new publication file. (See the sidebar on the facing page.)

Most people who come to publication work through desktop technologies assume that they'll use their desktop printer for camera-ready pages. And most people who come to desktop publishing from traditional publication work assume that they'll send their files to a service bureau for high-resolution output.

If you fall into the first group, you may not be aware that for anywhere from six to ten dollars per page, you can improve the quality tremendously by using a service bureau. On an important job with only a few pages (letterhead, business card, promotional folder), doing so doesn't add much expense, although it does take a little extra effort and will add a day or two to the schedule. If you fall into the second group, you're seeing 600-dpi printers become quite affordable, and perhaps you're reluctantly acknowledging that with today's tighter budgets, the resolution is adequate for some jobs.

So before looking at PageMaker's printing options, consider the samples on the following spread, which illustrate the ways different kinds of elements are reproduced at different resolutions. Although there are differences from one manufacturer's printer to another at the same resolution, the comparisons should help you determine which resolution is appropriate for a particular job. Note especially the variation in tints, the relative smoothness of the art, and the sharpness of type at very large and very small sizes.

For many flyers, reports, price lists, and other fast-turnaround, short-shelf-life documents, 300-dpi output is both adequate and efficient. But for publications that include tints (gray or color), digital halftones, and detailed graphics, resolutions above 1000 dpi provide the crisp, smooth output required for quality work.

Whereas personal laser printers transfer and fuse toner to paper, imagesetters use a light-sensitive photographic process to print on resin-coated paper or film. The ability to go directly to film further increases the sharpness of the final image because it eliminates one generation of duplication that would be required at the printer. This can save you money as well. Keep in mind, though, that with film you can't paste in a last-minute correction by hand the way you do with paper or repro; you have to reprint the entire page.

Because they print on rolls rather than sheets, imagesetters can also print larger page sizes than desktop printers can. The actual size varies from one imagesetter to another, but currently you can expect to print color pages a little larger than 13 by 18 inches and still get crop marks and registration marks; for black-and-white pages, you can generally get pages a little larger than 11 by 35 inches (sometimes even longer), again, with printer's marks.

TIP

If you use a laser printer for final pages, use these techniques to improve the image quality:

• Use high-quality paper with a smooth, white finish.

• Experiment with different density settings on your printer. Lighter is generally better, because everything darkens up on press.

• For undersize pages, you can increase the effective resolution by using the Scaling option to enlarge the printed page and asking the printer to photographically reduce the page before making plates.

• Some toner cartridges simply produce sharper copies than others do. When you get a good one, save it for masters. Cartridges that are very new or very old produce the most uneven coverage and generally should not be used to print camera-ready pages.

SETTING UP AND SPECIFYING YOUR PRINTER

To print from PageMaker, you need the correct print drivers. If you use a PostScript printer, you also need the PPD (PostScript printer description) file for your printer and for any other printer that you occasionally print on, such as the imagesetter at your service bureau.

The files you need come with PageMaker 5.0. If you didn't install them when you installed PageMaker, you can add them at any time. (See page 209 for how to add files after you've installed PageMaker.)

Once you're working in PageMaker, there are two dialog boxes in which you specify printer information: first in Page Setup (displayed when you create a new publication) and again in the Print dialog box. This works a little differently on the Mac and the PC.

In Macintosh PageMaker

Setting up If you work on a PostScript printer, select the Chooser from the Apple menu. Select the PSPrinter icon—that's the new PostScript printer driver version 8.0. (If you don't see that icon in the Chooser, install it now; it's on disk 5 of the PageMaker 5.0 disks, in the Extensions folder.) Select your printer from the list at the right side of the dialog box. Then click Setup, and in the dialog box that is displayed, click Select PPD; then scroll the list of PPDs to select the name of the printer you usually print from. (The PPDs are in the folder Printer Descriptions; it's in the Extensions folder in your System folder under System 7, or in the System folder under System 6.) Before closing the Chooser, turn on Background Printing so that you don't have to wait for a print job to be completed before resuming work.

In PageMaker In the *Page Setup dialog box*, for the Target Printer Resolution, specify the dots per inch for the printer you'll use for final output. If you proof on a 300-dpi printer but will print your camera-ready pages at 1270 from an imagesetter, specify 1270. PageMaker uses this information when resizing monochrome bit-mapped images. (See page 372 for details.)

In the *Print dialog box*, the Print To field displays the name of the printer you've selected in the Chooser. If you print on a PostScript printer, there's also a field labeled *Type*; the PPD you selected in the Chooser is displayed by default. To change the PPD, scroll the submenu to select the one you want.

In Windows PageMaker

Setting up If you print on a PostScript printer, you should use the Windows PostScript printer driver, version 3.1. If you print on a non-PostScript printer, you should use the Microsoft Universal printer driver, version 3.1. Both drivers are on disk 6 of your PageMaker installation disks.

For both types of printers, in the Program Manager, open the Main directory and double-click on the Control Panel icon; in the Control Panel window, click on the Printers icon. Review the list box for the default and installed printers on your system. If the printer driver you need isn't installed, click Add and select your printer from the List of Printers box.

In PageMaker In the *Page Setup dialog box*, scroll the Compose to Printer submenu to select the name of the printer that you'll use for your camera-ready output, even if that's different from the printer you'll use for proofs. If you're printing the file at a service bureau, you need to know which imagesetter they use (and which version) so that you can choose that printer driver from the list. (If their printer driver doesn't appear on the list, you'll need to install it now.)

The printer you select here determines what fonts and font sizes are available, as well as the image area of the printed page. (Some printers require a margin around the edge of the page beyond which they cannot print.)

For the Target Printer Resolution, specify the dots per inch for the printer you'll use for final output. If you proof on a 300-dpi desktop printer but will print your camera-ready pages at 1270 from an imagesetter, specify 1270 in this box. PageMaker uses this information when resizing monochrome bit-mapped images. (See page 372 for details.)

In the *Print dialog box*, the Print To field displays the name of the printer selected as the default in the Windows Printers Control Panel. If that's not the same as the printer you are currently using, change it now by scrolling the Print To pull-down menu to select another name.

If you print on a PostScript printer, there's also a field labeled *Type*; scroll that submenu to select the PPD (PostScript printer description) for the printer listed in the Print To field.

**Laser Writer NTX
at 300 dots per inch**

Display: 80-pt Galliard Italic; *Type In Gray:* 80-pt Futura Extra Bold, specified in PageMaker in 10% increments from 10 to 80% Black. *This caption:* 6.5/8 Galliard roman and italic; *sans-serif captions:* 7-pt FuturaLight and Futra Extra Bold.

Hairline rule

.5 pt rule

1 pt rule

Bit-mapped clip art

Encapsulated PostScript art imported from FreeHand.

Digital halftone printed at 53 lines per inch

**LaserWriter Pro 630
at 600 dots per inch**

Display: 80-pt Galliard Italic; *Type In Gray:* 80-pt Futura Extra Bold, specified in PageMaker in 10% increments from 10 to 80% Black. *This caption:* 6.5/8 Galliard roman and italic; *sans-serif captions:* 7-pt FuturaLight and Futra Extra Bold.

Hairline rule

.5 pt rule

1 pt rule

Bit-mapped clip art

Encapsulated PostScript art imported from FreeHand.

Digital halftone printed at 120 lines per inch

Linotronic 300
at 1270 dots per inch output to paper

Display
TYPE IN GRAY

Display: 80-pt Galliard Italic; *Type In Gray:* 80-pt Futura Extra Bold, specified in PageMaker in 10% increments from 10 to 80% Black. *This caption:* 6.5/8 Galliard roman and italic; *sans-serif captions:* 7-pt FuturaLight and Futra Extra Bold.

Hairline rule

.5 pt rule

1 pt rule

Bit-mapped clip art

Encapsulated PostScript art imported from FreeHand.

Dion Ogust

Digital halftone printed at 120 lines per inch

Linotronic 300
at 2540 dpi output to film

Display
TYPE IN GRAY

Display: 80-pt Galliard Italic; *Type In Gray:* 80-pt Futura Extra Bold, specified in PageMaker in 10% increments from 10 to 80% Black. *This caption:* 6.5/8 Galliard roman and italic; *sans-serif captions:* 7-pt FuturaLight and Futra Extra Bold.

Hairline rule

.5 pt rule

1 pt rule

Bit-mapped clip art

Encapsulated PostScript art imported from FreeHand.

Dion Ogust

Digital halftone printed at 120 lines per inch

Changing Printers from Proof Pages to Camera-Ready Pages

If you proof your pages on a desktop printer and print camera-ready output at a service bureau, you must pay attention to a number of variables and requirements in order to get the results you want.

Specify the printer used for final output This is explained in detail on the facing page.

Test your type specs at the final resolution In a job of any importance, you should run test pages at the service bureau that will provide your high-resolution output. The test should include samples of the various type specifications used in the publication (headline styles, body text, captions, and so on). If you will be using rules, gray tints behind boxes, a special effect with halftones, whatever, include a representation of those elements so that you can evaluate how they look at the high resolution. Tints, rules, and type generally print lighter at high resolution. Type that looks too dark or too tight on a 300-dpi laser-printed page might look just fine at 1270. For our tests, we usually run a few complete pages and then compile a lot of loose elements on a few additional pages to keep the cost down.

Troubleshoot your electronic production techniques For longer publications, use your test pages to troubleshoot your production techniques. Are you importing art from a drawing program that you've never used before? Include a test image to be sure the format in which you saved or exported the source file prints correctly from the imagesetter. Do your pages include Encapsulated PostScript files made from another Page-Maker document? Testing one such file will tell you whether you're making the EPS files correctly. The problems with conflicting fonts are not as common as they were a couple of years ago, but there's always potential for incompatibility between your fonts and the service bureau's.

TIP

We can't emphasize enough the value of developing a **good working relationship with a service bureau.** It will save you time and probably money too. Let them know in advance that you'll be sending files. Ask how they want the files prepared, and don't hesitate to open a dialog box on-screen with your service bureau contact on the other end of the telephone. Be sure to fill out their work order form completely and to label all disks or cartridges that you send them. And pay special attention to fonts and linked files, as described on this and the following page.

Do not assume that whatever can be successfully printed on your desktop printer can be successfully printed on a high-resolution imagesetter. The compatibility between output devices with varying resolutions is sometimes mysteriously imperfect.

Quite apart from the different systems and fonts that may reside on your computer and that of your service bureau, a high-resolution printer has to process and print considerably more information than your laser printer does. A 300-dpi printer has to manage only 90,000 dots per square inch, but an imagesetter printing at 1270 dpi must process over a million and a half dots per square inch; at 2540 dpi, the number jumps to almost six and a half million. The difference between those numbers and the information they represent accounts for a great deal of machine time (if your service center bills you for pages that take longer than a specified time to print) and more than a few glitches.

Compile a font list To print a PageMaker file, the computer driving the printer must have both the screen font and the printer font for every typeface used in the file. If you stumbled over that sentence, understand that most fonts used in publication work have two parts: the screen font is a bit-mapped version used for screen display; the printer font is a scalable outline used for printing. Each part is kept in a different file, and both files must be installed on the computer in order for the font to print correctly.

You generally don't have to think about this with your printer because you select fonts according to what is installed. But when you send a file to a service bureau, it becomes a critical issue. If the correct fonts aren't available, PageMaker will substitute another font, and you'll need to reprint the job with the correct fonts.

So when you send a file to a service bureau, you must include a list of every font used in the publication. Include the name of the vendor for each font too. (If you're using Bitstream's Garamond, the service bureau has to use Bitstream's Garamond; Adobe's Garamond won't do.) Then check with the service bureau to be sure they have all the fonts in your file. For each font they don't have, you'll have to send them both the printer font and the screen font. (Most font licensing agreements allow this "loaning" of fonts for high-resolution output.)

Warning: It's very dangerous to rely on memory when you make a font list. A really good service bureau will alert you to the missing fonts before they print the file. But even if you escape without to having to rerun the file, you lose time at the back end of the job when time (and energy) is in short supply.

One way to ensure that you compile a complete and accurate font list is to choose **Display Pub Info** from the Aldus Additions list (Utilities menu). Unfortunately, the way this Addition compiles its list is by listing every font installed in your system with a Y(es) or N(o) designation to indicate whether the font is included in the publication. We have a great many fonts on our system and prefer the faster, streamlined approach of **Checklist**, a third-party utility that lists only fonts included in the document and provides a number of other useful features (including a list of linked files required for printing).

More often than we'd like to admit, this check reveals fonts we didn't know were in the document. There are all kinds of reasons this happens. For example, sometimes when you change type specs a word space or new paragraph character gets left out of the selection. Even though you don't see it, the invisible character remains behind, with whatever type formatting was originally applied to it. And the font for such invisible characters shows up on the font list.

If your font-checking utility reveals fonts that are (but shouldn't be) in the document, use the Find command in the Story Editor to search by Attribute for the font you need to change. See page 284 for how to do this.

Both the Display Pub Info Addition and Checklist enable you to save the font information for a file and open it in a word-processing program. For complex files with a lot of fonts, you can just print this font info from the text document and include it with your work order for the service bureau.

Include linked files As described in detail on page 227, for graphics with large file sizes (generally over 256 KB, unless you change the default), PageMaker stores a low-res copy of the file in your publication and reads the data from the original source file when you print. So in order for these linked files to print correctly, the original source file must be available when you print at a service bureau. Use the Copy Files Required for Remote Printing option, in the Save As dialog box, to ensure that PageMaker copies all the necessary files to a folder designated for your service bureau.

TIP

Many service bureaus that provide high-resolution output base their page rate on a maximum printing time, such as 8 minutes per page. Anything beyond that time is charged as overtime. **To minimize overtime charges,** keep your pages clean: Eliminate items from the pasteboard; avoid unnecessary masks; do final graphics editing (cropping, rotating, and so on) in a graphics program, rather than in PageMaker; and do a Save As to compress the file before sending it for output. Some service bureaus offer a discount if you send them a PostScript file of your PageMaker document. See page 238 for details on that procedure.

The Print Dialog Box Displays

The Print dialog box (accessed from the File menu) has a series of buttons down the right side. These buttons, and the options they display, vary a little depending on your printer. Unlike in most other dialog boxes, selecting a button here changes the options displayed without actually opening another dialog box. So you don't have to move through a maze of dialog boxes to get from one set of options to another. One click gets you to any of the displays, as well as to Print or Cancel.

The effects of Print, Cancel, and Reset

Print This prints your file using the current specifications and saves those specs so that they're displayed the next time you open the Print dialog box. To save your specifications without printing, click Print and then, in the box that shows the printing status, click Cancel.

Cancel This undoes all changes you've made since opening the dialog box and closes the Print dialog box without printing.

Reset This undoes all changes you've made in the current Print display. Changes made in other Print displays are retained. To undo changes made in all the displays since opening the dialog box, press Option while you click Reset on the Mac, and press Shift while you click Reset on the PC.

Print/Document display

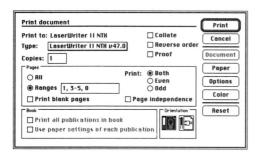

Print To and **Type** See the sidebar "Setting Up Your Printer," on page 229, for a discussion of these options.

Copies Specify the number of printed copies you want by typing any number from 1 through 32,000. (Does anyone print anything close to 32,000 copies on their desktop printers?) If you're unable to print multiple copies on your printer, try selecting the Collate option as well.

Collate Turn on this option when you print multiple copies and want PageMaker to print all pages of one copy before beginning another.

Reverse Order Some printers print the first page first, some print the last page first. Turn on this option to reverse your printer's normal order.

Proof When you want to check the text and don't need to see graphics, turn on this option to speed up printing. PageMaker prints a box where each imported graphic appears in the layout.

Pages You can choose to print all the pages in the document, a specified range of pages, only the even pages, only the odd pages, both even and odd pages, blank pages or not. See the tip at left. This flexibility in printing is a terrific time (and paper) saver. Bravo Aldus!

Page Independence (PostScript printers only.) Choose this option if you are printing to a file that you'll open in a page-imposition or other prepress program. It tells PageMaker to store font information with each page.

Print All Publications in Book When you use the Book command (on the File menu) to link different publications together in a book list, you can check this option if you want to print all the files. PageMaker will use the print settings specified in the current publication, with these exceptions:

PageMaker preserves the Orientation specified for each publication.

If you specify a range in the current publication, PageMaker prints the range specified for each individual publication. And if you use the

TIP

In the Ranges field, you can specify **discontinuous pages.** If you have revisions on pages 2, 3, 4, and 7, type *2, 3-4, 7* in that text field. Type a hyphen before a number to print all the pages up to that number. (Type *-7, 10* to print all the pages from the beginning of the file up through page 7 and page 10.) PageMaker ignores spacing and will warn you if a typo results in a character other than a number, a hyphen, or a comma or if you type a number that falls outside the pages in the publication.

PostScript options in the Print Options dialog box display (PostScript printers only), PageMaker prints the entire book to disk.

Use Paper Settings of Each Publication Choose this option to print the book list using the Size and Source settings specified for each publication.

Orientation By default, PageMaker selects the icon for the same orientation—Tall or Wide—specified in the Page Setup dialog box. And that's generally what you want.

Print/Paper display

This button appears only if you use a PostScript printer. On non-PostScript printers, the Paper button is replaced by a Setup button that displays a dialog box specific to the printer selected in the Print To field. Some of the Setup options are similar to the Paper options described in the following text. Other Paper options (Scale, Tile, and Duplex) are available through the Options button on non-PostScript printers. For any options available in the printer-specific Setup box and in the PageMaker Print dialog box displays, the PageMaker specifications override the printer-specific ones.

Size Note this distinction: The Page Size specified in the Page Setup dialog box is the actual size of your publication. The Paper Size specified in the Print dialog box is the size of the paper in the printer you are using. Sometimes they're the same, but sometimes they're not.

The pull-down menu for this field lists only those paper sizes included in the PPD file for the printer specified in the Print To field. Note that when you select a page size, the paper dimensions are displayed.

Source From the pull-down menu select the desired paper-bin option. PageMaker displays only options included in the PPD for the current printer.

Print Area The dimensions displayed give the area of the paper that you can actually print on. Note (in the screen detail at left) that the Print Area is smaller than the Paper Size. That's because most desktop printers cannot print to the edge of the paper; a required margin of about 0.125 to 0.5 inch is common. If you want to bleed an image off the edge of the paper, you generally print on an imagesetter.

If you want printer's marks or page information (date, filename, and so on), the print area displayed here must be larger than the page size of your publication. Or you can choose Reduce to Fit, and PageMaker will reduce the page just enough to fit the additional information in the imageable area of the paper.

On non-PostScript printers (which do not display this field), use the following technique to determine the Print Area. Open a PageMaker publication with the page size the same as the paper size in your printer. Draw a shaded box a little larger than the page on all four sides. The printed size of the box defines the imageable area for your printer.

Center Page in Print Area If your printer offsets the printed page asymmetrically from the edge of the paper (some, but not many, do), choose this option to have the image centered.

Tile Use this option to print publications larger than the paper size in your printer. See page 414 for hands-on practice with this feature.

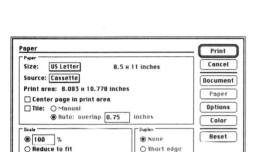

TIP

If you need to print **double-sided pages** on your desktop printer and don't have Duplex capabilities, use the Even/Odd Pages option in the Print/Document display. First print the odd-numbered pages, and then run the pages through again to print the even-numbered pages. Let the pages cool for a few minutes before the second pass through the printer. Be sure to test beforehand whether the pages should be flipped or rotated for the second pass. (It varies depending on the printer.)

Scale To reduce or enlarge your publication when printing, you can specify a percentage from 5% through 1600%, in increments of 0.1%.

Reduce to Fit Choose this option to reduce the publication (including printer's marks) to fit the selected paper size.

Thumbnails Choose this option to print miniature pages of your publication. The number per page (from 1 through 1000) determines the size of the thumbnails. Thumbnails are great for reviewing the layout and pacing of your publication and for keeping track of loose ends and reminders.

Duplex Use this option to print on both sides of the page. (If your printer doesn't have this capability, this option is gray.) Choose Short Edge or Long Edge to correspond to the binding edge of the paper in the document.

Print/Options display

Graphics (PostScript printers only.) These options determine how PageMaker prints TIFF graphics. See page 396 for a detailed explanation.

Markings When you use either of the following options (and they are both extremely useful) your paper size must be larger than your page size by the amounts specified in the following table:

Additional Space Required for Markings

Option	Vertical	Horizontal
Printer's Marks	0.75 inch	0.75 inch
Page Information	0.5 inch	none
Both	0.875 inch	0.75 inch

Printer's Marks Use this option to print crop marks, which the commercial printer uses to cut excess paper beyond the trim size specified for your publication. When you output files on a imagesetter, you must specify crop marks because the paper is larger than the page size.

Choosing this option also prints registration marks, density-control bars, and a color-control strip on every composite page or color separation. See page 454 for a discussion of these marks.

Page Information Choose this option to print the date, filename, page number, and spot or process color name at the bottom of each sheet of paper or film.

Send Data (Macintosh PostScript printers only.) To speed up data transmission to the printer, choose Faster. PageMaker will send the images in binary format. If you get a transmission or timeout error using Faster, choose Normal.

Include PostScript Error Handler (PostScript printers only.) Choose this option if you want PageMaker to print an error message on the page on which the error occurs. The text and graphics on the page still won't print, but at least you'll have some clue as to why not. When you send files to a service bureau, check with them before including this option. They may use their own custom error handler.

Write PostScript to File This option sounds more complicated to use than it is. In fact, it's very similar to exporting files in EPS format from graphics programs such as FreeHand and Illustrator. Part of what intimidates people about it is the phrase "Write PostScript to File," which suggests

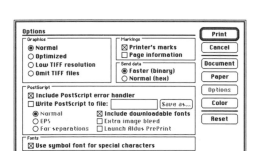

TIP

When a print job fails on a PostScript printer, PageMaker leaves a temporary file on your hard drive. The temp files can be huge—they contain the actual PostScript code required to print the publication, including all the image and EPS data—so remember to get rid of them. On the Mac, the files are in the Rescued Items folder in the Trash, so just empty the Trash. On the PC, the files (named Pm....tmp) are in the directory named in the "set temp" line in the Autoexec.bat file. Before deleting temp files, you should exit Windows to MS-DOS.

you might have to know something about programming—not the case at all. It's also sometimes called "printing (or saving) the file to disk," because what you're doing, essentially, is creating a file that includes all the necessary printing information—including fonts, linked graphics, pages to be printed, printer's marks, and so on. See the sidebar on page 238 for details.

Use Symbol Font for Special Characters (Macintosh PostScript printers only.) If the fonts used in your publication include characters for symbols such as ®, ©, ™, °, ±, , and so on, leave this option unchecked. If your fonts don't include characters for such symbols and you need them in your document, turn on this option. PageMaker will substitute the symbol font character in order to print these symbols. See pages 45–46 for more information on special characters.

Print/Color display

You need to understand the basics of color printing to prepare and print color files correctly. And we'll look at that in detail in Project 9. Most color publications are separated at a service bureau, directly to film.

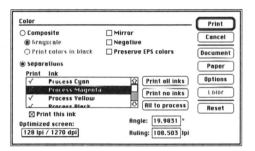

Composite Choose one of the followings options to print all the colors on a single page, rather than as color separations.

Color/Grayscale The option displayed (Color or Grayscale) depends on the printer selected for Type in the Print dialog box. Choose Color to print a color composite (for example, on a QMS color printer). Choose Grayscale when you're printing a composite on a black-and-white printer and you want PageMaker to simulate color intensity using shades of gray. (For example, red will print darker than pink.)

Print Colors in Black Choose this option to proof your color pages in black and white. PageMaker prints all solid colors as black and all tints of colors as a percentage of black. For example, if your pages include Pantone 185 (a fire-engine red) and a 20% tint of that same color, the Pantone 185 will print as black, and the 20% tint of that color will print as 20% black.

Separations Choose this option to print each ink on a separate piece of paper or film. For details about using this option, as well as Screen, Angle, Ruling, and the associated buttons, see pages 452–54.

The following options are available on PostScript printers only.

Mirror Always ask your commercial printer how to print color separations: emulsion side up or down? negative or positive? right-reading or wrong-reading? The following table will tell you how to get the desired result in PageMaker:

	Right-reading		Wrong-reading	
Emulsion	Up	Down	Up	Down
Set Mirror to	Off	On	On	Off

Negative Choose this option to print separations (paper or film) as negatives. If you want to print positives, turn this option off.

Preserve EPS Colors If you edited imported EPS colors in PageMaker and want to print the graphics using the colors specified in the original program, choose this option. If you want to print the graphics with the edited colors, leave this option unchecked.

WHEN AND HOW TO MAKE POSTSCRIPT FILES

When to use this option

- If your service bureau prefers to receive Post-Script files rather than the native PageMaker document. To print the file, they don't have to open it in PageMaker or worry about what fonts you've used. You, however, must be sure to choose all the right specs—page range, printer's marks, and so on—because any errors are your responsibility. Other service bureaus prefer the control they have when working with native PageMaker files. Always check with your service bureau before making the PostScript file, and review all options with them.

- If you're working on a system that doesn't have a printer or if you need to print a file from a system that doesn't have PageMaker installed. To print the PostScript file on the remote system, use a PostScript downloading utility such as Laser Writer Utility on the Mac, or copy the file to a printer port in Windows.

- If you want to use a page from your publication as a piece of art in another publication. For example, you might want to use a book cover as a graphic in an ad for the book.

- If you want to open or print the file in a postprocessing program, such as TrapWise or PrePrint.

How to use this option

1. If you're making a Normal PostScript file or one For Separations (as described in step 5), the printer specified for Type (in the Print/Document display) should be the printer that will be used for final output. If you're using a service bureau, scroll the list to select the name and version of their imagesetter. (If the Type option doesn't appear when you select the Document button, you may not be using the correct PostScript printer driver. See page 229.) If you work on a PC, the printer specified in the Print To field should match the printer selected for Compose To in the Page Setup dialog box.

2. Specify the printing options as you would for a file that you're printing normally: the page ranges, paper size, how graphics are printed, whether you want printer's marks, and so on.

3. Choose Write PostScript to File in the Print/Options display. Note that the Print button changes to a Save button.

4. Review the default filename and location.

   PageMaker uses the publication name plus an extension that identifies the kind of PostScript file you specify in step 5. Change that if you wish by typing a new name. The default location is the folder or directory in which the application is stored. You'll probably prefer to store it with your publication files. To change the location, click Save As on a Mac or Browse on a PC to scroll through your folders or directories to choose a new location.

5. Specify the type of PostScript file you want.

   Normal Use this option if you are printing the file at a service bureau or other remote printer. The default filename adds a ps extension to the filename (for example, Ad2.ps).

   EPS Use this option to include the page as a graphic in another publication or to trap color separations in a prepress program. The default filename is an abbreviated document name plus a page number followed by an eps extension (for example, News_4.eps).

   For Separations Choose this option to create an OPI (open prepress interface)-compatible file, for separation through a postprocessing program such as Aldus PrePrint (see pages 450–51). The default filename adds a sep extension to the publication name (for example, Ad2.sep).

6. Specify these other options if appropriate.

   Include Downloadable Fonts Choose this option if the printer being used to print the PostScript file does not have all the fonts used in the publication. Always check with your service bureau before checking this option.

   Extra Image Bleed Choose this option if your file contains an image that bleeds off the page and you'll be using a postprocessing program.

   Launch Aldus PrePrint Choose this option if you are creating a PostScript sep file and want to open that file in PrePrint immediately.

7. Choose Save.

PRINTER STYLES ADDITION

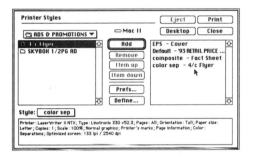

▲ ▲ ▲

To add a publication to the printing queue, *scroll through your folders or directories to select the filename, and then click Add. The box on the right lists all the files in the print queue. (The designation to the left of each filename is the printer style applied to that file.)*

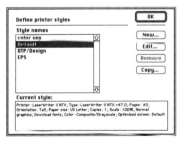

▲ ▲ ▲

When you click the Define button in the Printer Styles dialog box, Page-Maker displays the Define Printer Styles dialog box shown here. Click New to name a new style; when you okay the name, PageMaker displays the default Print dialog box, where you select the print settings that you want for the current style.

Be sure to try the Printer Styles Addition. You can use it to queue several documents for batch printing, with custom settings for each file, and begin printing just before you leave for lunch. You can also define print dialog box settings as part of a printing style that you then apply to documents in the printing queue.

To create and print a queue of documents Choose Printer Styles from the Aldus Additions submenu. In the Printer Styles dialog box, scroll through your folders or directories to select the name of the file you want to add to the queue, and then click Add. (Or just double-click on the filename.)

To make changes in the printing queue, select a filename from the queue list on the right side of the dialog box and click the appropriate button: Item Up and Item Down rearrange the order of the queue, and Remove does just what it says.

To specify custom print settings, such as page range, color separation specs, and so on, for a particular file: Double-click on the filename in the queue list to bring up the Print dialog box, from which you can access the options described on the previous pages in this section.

To define printer styles In the Printer Styles dialog box, click Define, which brings up the Define Styles dialog box, where you click New. This brings up a dialog box in which you type a name for the style. When you click OK, PageMaker displays the Print dialog box, from which you select the various settings that you want for that style. When you finish, click OK, and you'll be back in the Define Styles dialog box, with the name of the style you just defined added to the Style Name list and a description of the style at the bottom of the screen. From here, you can create another new printing style, edit or remove existing ones, or use the Copy button to create a new style based on an existing one. Or click Close to return to the Printer Style dialog box.

To apply printer styles In the Printer Styles dialog box, the Style pull-down menu lists all the printer styles you've defined. To apply a style, choose a publication from the File Name list, select a style from the pull-down list, and then click Add. The name of the printer style is listed before the filename in the Queued Print Job list. If you forget to select a printer style before adding a name to the list, just select the name on the list, and choose a new style from the pull-down menu.

Note: You cannot save a print queue. When you close the Printer Styles dialog box, the print queue is removed from memory. But the printer styles that you defined are saved and appear on the Style pull-down menu the next time you use this Addition.

If a publication is open when you print using this Addition, its print settings will be modified to those assigned to it in the Printer Styles dialog box. If you don't want this to happen, either save the file before printing with Printer Styles and then close without saving again, or use Printer Styles when the document is not open.

It would be terrific if you could choose a previously defined printer style directly from the Print dialog box in an active publication. Alas, not yet.

HANDS-ON PROJECTS

INTRODUCTION TO THE PROJECTS

*The projects in this section are struc-
tured so that beginners can start
right in on Project 1 without any prior
experience in creating PageMaker
documents. The instructions do assume, however, that your computer
is up and running, that PageMaker is
installed, that you can locate files on
your hard disk, and that you know
how to print from your workstation.*

The purpose of these projects is to provide experience with PageMaker's
tools and techniques in the context of creating real publications. Reading
about a technique in a manual is quite different from applying that technique in a layout that has both editorial and graphic requirements. Manuals describe how to use a technique when nothing else on the page gets in
the way; in real life, something almost always gets in the way, or doesn't
fit, or ends up in the wrong place. We didn't have to contrive situations
that would give you experience with the problem solving and graphic
refinement required to use PageMaker well; the situations came up naturally in the course of creating the project documents, just as they do in
real-life publications.

By taking the time to work through the projects, you'll not only build
knowledge of specific techniques, but perhaps even more important,
you'll begin to understand the program's internal logic. It's this understanding that enables you, eventually, to figure out why the program
responds in certain ways and how to work around apparent limitations.

If you find that you can use one of the project formats as a prototype for
your own publication, that's fine. The point, however, is not so much to
say that a classified ad should look like the one in Project 2 or that a newsletter should look like the one in Project 4, but to help you understand the
basic techniques and develop a certain manual dexterity so that you can
use those techniques for effects that require some precision.

One of the wisest and most universally acknowledged pieces of advice in
the world of computers is to learn a few programs and to learn them well.
With that in mind, we've exploited PageMaker's text and graphics tools
as much as possible, more so than one might actually do in real-life work.
Certain parts of the projects could be done faster or more effectively in a
word-processing program, others in a graphics program. Doing them in
PageMaker will help you master the tools and techniques available—and
perhaps have some fun in the process.

THE PROJECTS AT A GLANCE

The first five projects are arranged in order of complexity. Each one assumes that you are familiar with techniques used in the previous project. If you are a beginner, you should do those five projects in sequence (although Project 5 could be done before Projects 3 and 4). After that, you should have no problem skipping around among the other projects.

Each project includes a list of techniques covered in that project. Use these lists to help you choose the projects you want to work through.

Project 1   A Simple Certificate for PageMaker Novices

This project guides you through the basic procedures of setting up a new PageMaker document, using the rulers, moving around the publication window, changing the page view, typing text in PageMaker, and using PageMaker's tools to create circles, rectangles, and lines.

Project 2   Placing and Copyfitting Text in a Small Ad

This project provides an introduction to placing text from a word-processor file in PageMaker. It will also give you practice in formatting text using the type and paragraph specifications. And it looks at the techniques you can use to make a given amount of copy fit the space available. There's also a review of PageMaker's Story Editor, including the spell-checking and Find and Change options.

Project 3   A Quick Invitation Using Paragraph Rules and PageMaker Graphics

A simple invitation makes good use of a powerful feature: specifying rules as a paragraph attribute. The project also gives you the opportunity to create a graphic with PageMaker's drawing tools and to manipulate objects using the Control Palette. And you'll learn to print multiple copies of an undersize document on a single letter-size sheet.

Project 4   Creating a Template for a Three-Column Self-Mailing Newsletter

This project introduces the use of master pages and templates for a publication that is produced repeatedly. There's also an in-depth look at style sheets and at the behavior of threaded text. And you'll learn to rotate text, place graphics, and export PageMaker text to a word-processor file.

Project 5   All About Tabs and Tables

This project is actually a series of exercises to help you master PageMaker's Indents/Tabs window. In addition to specifying and editing tabs, you'll work with leadered tabs, bulleted and numbered lists, and hanging indents in a variety of formats.

Project 6   Newsletter Variations Using Additional PageMaker Techniques

Working with a copy of the newsletter from Project 4, you'll work with inline graphics, create drop caps, rotate and skew text and graphics, and use a leading grid. You'll also see quite a few variations on the layout grid used in Project 4.

Project 7   A Tabloid Ad with Photographs and Display Typography

This project begins with a primer on digital halftones. You'll learn to work with photos in PageMaker, practice refining display typography, and learn to use the manual tiling option to print oversize pages.

Project 8   Using PageMaker to Draw, Manipulate, and Manage Graphics

The application doesn't purport to be a drawing program—and it isn't. But you can create some simple (and not so simple) graphics in PageMaker, and in doing so you'll master some important techniques. Try your hand at a truck or a skyline, a map or a floor plan, a pie chart or a pattern created from a Zapf Dingbats character. You'll also learn how to customize a graphic boundary for text wrap, to group PageMaker elements, and to use the Library Palette to store frequently used text and graphics.

Project 9   Working with Color in PageMaker

This project provides an overview of the production issues involved when you prepare and separate color files in PageMaker. You'll practice creating both spot and process colors, work with overlapping and butting colors, specify both object-level and ink-level overprinting, and print test separations directly on your desktop printer. Also included is a discussion of the various prepress options available when you work with color in PageMaker.

Structure of the Projects

The instructions for each project are self-contained: All the information you need to complete any of the designs is included in the instructions for that project. The projects are organized so that numbered, boldface instructions describe the general steps (specify the page setup, define the image area, draw the banner, and so on). Bulleted paragraphs within each numbered instruction detail the specific procedures and techniques required to execute that step. Generally, unbulleted paragraphs explain and amplify the techniques. Because the information is organized in this way, you should be able to move as quickly or as slowly through the projects as suits your needs and level of experience.

Tips in the margins highlight shortcuts as well as procedures that are important for a fundamental understanding and control of PageMaker's sometimes quirky personality. Most tips are placed adjacent to a step within the project to which that tip can be applied. You'll find additional tips in the margins of the Basics section and in the Glossary. The Glossary also includes keyboard sequences for many PageMaker commands, so you can refer to that section when you can't remember how to bring up the grabber hand, type an em dash, interrupt Autoflow, and so on.

Screen details with captions provide additional tips throughout the Projects section. Note, however, that the distortion in letterspacing and word spacing that sometimes occurs on-screen is exacerbated when screen images are reduced in size, as they generally are in this book.

In addition, throughout the projects you'll find sidebars that focus on PageMaker functions in a context that is both specific to the project at hand and more general as well. These sidebars cover the fundamental concepts and procedures needed to use PageMaker efficiently. They are highlighted with a gray tint to make them easy to find.

Macintosh or PC?

The mechanics of working in the Macintosh and PC versions of Page-Maker are virtually identical. In fact, with the release of PageMaker 5.0, Aldus ships the same manual with the software for both platforms. For the most part, the differences that do exist have to do with system configuration and font installation. The basics of system configuration are beyond the scope of this book; you'll need to consult your computer manual, your hardware dealer, or whatever technical support is available to you in order to get your system up and running to the point at which you can open PageMaker and print.

Once you are up and running, however, you should be able to complete the projects regardless of which computer you use. The projects and instructions were created on a Macintosh and then tested on a PC. With a few exceptions that are noted in the instructions, all procedures work both on the Mac and on the PC. Most of the screen details for menus and dialog boxes were taken from the Mac, but the differences in those screens on a PC are minimal—the text is a little different, and occasionally an option is in a different position in the dialog box. Keyboard shortcuts vary from one platform to another. You will generally find the Macintosh shortcut first and the PC equivalent immediately following.

Capitalization and Italics

The full names of all menu commands, dialog boxes, and dialog box options are capitalized in these instructions, even if part of a name is not capitalized in PageMaker. For example, whereas the PageMaker menu reads "Page setup," our instructions will tell you to choose the Page Setup command or to specify information in the Page Setup dialog box. On the other hand, if we are speaking generally about page setup, the phrase is not capitalized.

Specific words or values that you are instructed to type in dialog boxes are italicized. If the words should actually be italicized in the publication, that will be stated explicitly in the type specifications.

Typefaces Used in the Projects

In designing the projects, we've used fonts that come with most laser printers. If you don't have one of the fonts that we specify, by all means substitute something else. Your document won't look exactly like ours, and you'll probably get different line lengths and line breaks. Consider this a challenge rather than an obstacle.

If you need to substitute a font for the one we've used, look at the document facing the opening page of the project, study the typeface, and try to find the typeface on your system that most closely matches what we've used. To do this, type a few lines from our document in several typefaces that you have, using the same type specs and column width specified in the project. Then compare your printout to the type in the document. Look at the shapes of the letters, at whether your lines are longer or shorter than ours, at whether there is relatively more or less space between your lines of type than there is between the lines in the typeface we used. This is the way you learn about type and about the typefaces available on your computer.

If your type doesn't fit exactly the way ours does, explore the type and paragraph-formatting options to get it as close as possible. The point is for you to learn the PageMaker options that help you make documents that look the way you want them to look. The design of our documents is only a jumping-off point.

Fractional Measurements

In keeping with both traditional usage and PageMaker's menus, fractions of inches are expressed as decimals, fractions of picas are expressed as points, and fractions of points are expressed as decimals. Thus, you'll find measurements expressed as follows:

> 8.5 by 11 inches
> 7 picas 6 points (noted in PageMaker as 7p6)
> 9.5 points (noted in PageMaker as 0p9.5)

If you are not familiar with picas and points (the measurement system traditionally used in graphic design) see pages 33 and 210.

PROJECT 1

A SIMPLE CERTIFICATE FOR PAGEMAKER NOVICES

This project is intended for readers with little or no experience using PageMaker. The instructions are detailed enough that even if you've never used a mouse or selected a menu command, you won't feel lost. Later projects assume you're familiar with these Macintosh and Windows basics but not with the PageMaker options introduced in those projects.

The hands-on instructions will guide you through most of the basic procedures used to create and move around a page, format text with the Control Palette, and work with the tools in PageMaker's Toolbox. Whether you've come to desktop publishing never having been able to draw a straight line or having spent too many hours trying to master the exacting skill of inking, you'll be thrilled by the first dozen or so perfect circles and squares that you create—effortlessly—with PageMaker's tools.

If you want to produce a quick certificate without so much hands-on instruction, you should be able to move quickly through the boldface and bulleted instructions. Tips and paragraphs without bullets explain the techniques and PageMaker basics in more detail than you might want if you already have a little experience with the program.

Throughout this and other projects, we've highlighted sidebars to call your attention to an overview of some aspect of the program or to a particularly powerful, or perhaps quirky, feature. The sidebars are easy to find—they're boxed, with a light gray tint.

PAGEMAKER TECHNIQUES YOU WILL LEARN

▶ Change page setup specifications

▶ Display the rulers

▶ Bring in ruler guides

▶ Draw lines, rectangles, and circles with PageMaker's graphics tools

▶ Select and change line weights

▶ Use scroll bars and the grabber hand to move around the screen

▶ Type text in PageMaker

▶ Use the Control Palette to specify text attributes

▶ Define space between paragraphs

▶ Move PageMaker graphics

▶ Add shades to PageMaker graphics

A horizontal, or landscape, page orientation with equal margins on all sides is typical of certificates and diplomas.

ENROLLMENT CERTIFICATE

THE DESKTOP PUBLISHING SCHOOL
ADMITS

TO
THE HANDS-ON DESIGN COURSE

DTP

Times Roman has a utilitarian elegance appropriate for a design course.

The triple rule is the most official-looking one on PageMaker's menu. It gives this simple certificate an air of legitimacy.

BLUEPRINT FOR THE CERTIFICATE

GETTING SET UP

If you are not already in PageMaker and are using a Macintosh, open your Aldus PageMaker folder and double-click on the application icon.

If you are using an IBM PC or compatible, type *WIN PM* at the MS-DOS prompt, or start Windows, open the Program Manager window, open the Aldus folder, and double-click on the PageMaker application icon.

1. Choose New from the File menu.

- Move the pointer to the File menu, hold down the mouse button, drag the pointer down to highlight the word "New," and release the mouse button. This brings the Page Setup dialog box to the screen.

2. Specify the page setup details.

- Make any necessary changes in the Page Setup dialog box so that it conforms to the following specifications:

  Page Dimensions: 11 by 8.5 inches

  Orientation: Wide

  Start Page #: 1   # of pages: 1

  Click off Double-sided. (The Facing Pages option will automatically turn gray.)

  Restart Page Numbering should also be turned off. (This is used in multidocument publications.)

  Margin in inches: 1 for all four margins.

- The next two options in the Page Setup dialog box give PageMaker information about the printer you'll be using for your final output.

  Compose to Printer (Windows only): Hold down the mouse button on the arrow next to this box and scroll the submenu to select the

> **TIP**
>
> Windows users note: In the Page Setup box, for the Compose to Printer option, you specify the printer that you'll use for final output. In the Print dialog box, you specify the printer you're using to proof the document.

▶ ▶ ▶

The Page Setup dialog box for this project. To change the value in any text box, position the pointer in that box, double-click or drag to highlight the existing value, and then type the new value. To turn an option (such as Tall, Wide, or Double-sided) on or off, click on the appropriate button, box, or name for that option. In the Compose to Printer box (PC Page-Maker only), it's very important to specify the printer that you'll use for final output.

Page setup

Page: Letter ⬇   OK   Cancel

Page dimensions: 11 x 8.5 inches

Orientation: ○ Tall ● Wide   Numbers...

Start page #: 1   Number of pages: 1

Options: ☐ Double-sided   ☐ Facing pages
         ☐ Restart page numbering

Margin in inches:
   Left 1   Right 1
   Top 1   Bottom 1

Compose to printer: Apple LaserWriter II NTX on COM1 ⬇

Target printer resolution: 300 ⬇ dpi

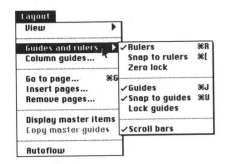

▲ ▲ ▲

*Some of PageMaker's most useful tools are hidden on **submenus**. To turn on Rulers, for example, hold down the mouse button as you scroll down the Layout menu to highlight the Guides and Rulers command. When the submenu drops into view, keep holding down the mouse button and drag the pointer over the Rulers option. When the desired option is highlighted, release the mouse button.*

target printer—the one you'll use to print the final version of your document. For this certificate, you'd probably use the same desktop printer that you use to proof documents. But when you use one printer to proof documents and another for your final camera-ready output, you must specify the printer you'll use for final output in order for your files to print correctly. (See page 229 for more information.) If the printer you'll be using isn't listed on the submenu, you'll need to install the driver for it. (See page 209 for how "To Add Files After You've Installed PageMaker.")

Target Printer Resolution: Type a value for the number of dots per inch (dpi) you'll use for the final printing. Or hold down the mouse button on the arrow next to the text field, and select the number from the pull-down menu. For this certificate, you're probably printing to a 300- or 600-dpi desktop printer. See page 372 for using this option when sizing bit-mapped images.

- After you have specified your page setup, click OK.

3. Display the Rulers.

- If the rulers are not visible, press Command-R on a Mac, Ctrl-R on a PC, to bring them into view. Or scroll the Layout menu to access the Guides and Rulers submenu, and choose Rulers.

Keep in mind these principles regarding PageMaker's rulers:

- All measurements (including those in the Control Palette) are relative to the zero point, which you can move around the page. (See the screen details, below.)

- As you move the mouse, hairline markers on the rulers indicate the position of the mouse on the screen.

In this project, all measurements are given in inches. This is PageMaker's default setting for measurements, so unless you've changed your defaults, you won't need to make any adjustments.

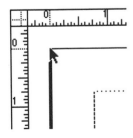

▲ ▲ ▲

*For single-page documents, the default position for the **zero point** is the upper left corner of the page. In this screen detail, hairline markers on the rulers indicate the position of the mouse at the zero point.*

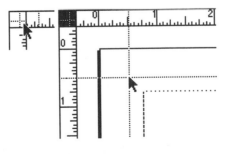

▲ ▲ ▲

***To move the zero point,** drag the intersecting hairlines at the corner where the horizontal and vertical rulers meet (above left). As you drag (above right), that corner is highlighted and the pointer is followed by dotted cross hairs representing the x-y axes.*

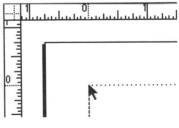

▲ ▲ ▲

Here we've moved the zero point to the upper left corner of the page margins.

4. Select a page view that enables you to see the entire document.

The View submenu (on the Layout menu) gives you options for eight different page views. If you're not familiar with these options, take a moment to click on each one and observe how the publication window changes from one view to another. How much of the page you see in each view depends on the size of the page and the size of your monitor. Note also how the ruler tick marks change as you increase and decrease the magnification.

Because different readers work with different monitors, we generally do not specify an optimal page view. You'll undoubtedly need to change views as you work on this or any other document. Learning the keyboard shortcuts for toggling between different page views (see pages 212–14) can speed up your work a lot.

5. Bring in ruler guides to help position the elements you'll create in later steps.

- On the Layout menu, scroll the Guides and Rulers submenu and choose Snap to Rulers.

- Position the pointer anywhere on the left ruler, press the mouse button to reveal a double-headed arrow, and drag a dotted vertical guideline to the 5.5-inch mark on the top ruler. This marks the center of the page on a vertical axis.

- From the top ruler, bring in horizontal ruler guides to the 2.5-, 4.5-, and 6.25-inch marks on the left ruler.

TIP

The **Snap to Rulers** command pulls ruler guides, text, and graphics to the nearest tick mark on each of the rulers. With Snap to Rulers on, you get the same accuracy at the 50% page view as you do at 200%.

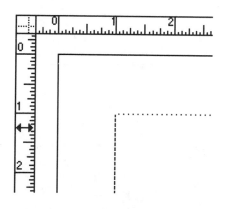

▲ ▲ ▲

To drag in ruler guides, *move the pointer into either ruler. When you hold down the mouse button, you'll see a double-headed arrow. As you drag that arrow into the page, you'll see a dotted ruler guide if you're working in black and white or a colored guide if you're working in color.*

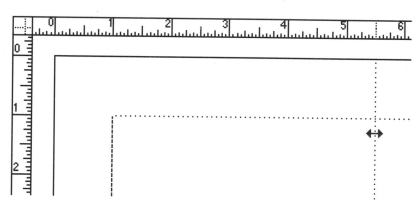

▲ ▲ ▲

Here we've dragged a vertical ruler guide to the 5.5-inch mark on the horizontal ruler. **To move a ruler guide,** *point to that guide with the pointer tool and drag the guide to the desired location.* **To delete a guide,** *drag it outside the page frame. Any tool turns into the pointer arrow when you move it into one of the rulers, so you don't have to change tools to bring in ruler guides.*

HOW TO MOVE AROUND THE PAGEMAKER SCREEN

Often when you're working in PageMaker, some of the page is hidden from view. You can move around the screen in three ways to display different parts of the page as well as the pasteboard beyond the page.

Use the scroll bars.

This is the slowest method, but it's also the easiest for beginners to remember. (Try to learn the other methods as soon as possible!) Use the gray bar on the right side of the window to move vertically; use the bottom bar to move horizontally. Click on the arrows at the ends of the scroll bars to move a short distance; click in the gray bar itself to move a greater distance. The position of the small box inside each scroll bar indicates the position of the screen image relative to the entire pasteboard area outside the page; you can also move around the screen by dragging one of these boxes to a point that is approximately where you want to be in the publication window.

Use the grabber hand.

The grabber hand provides more control over where you're moving than the scroll bars, and it's faster too. To invoke the grabber hand, hold down the Option key on a Mac, the Alt key on a PC, and then press the mouse button. As you drag the mouse, the hand pushes the page in any direction that you drag, including diagonally. (After you see the hand, you can release the Option or Alt key.) If you want to constrain the movement to a horizontal or vertical direction, hold down the Shift key in addition to Option or Alt.

Zoom in and out.

To display the zoom tool, press Command-Spacebar on the Mac, Ctrl-Spacebar on the PC, while you hold down the mouse button. Click the magnifier at the part of the page you want center-screen at the next largest page view. With this technique, you can enlarge up to 800%. To reduce the page view, add the Option key on a Mac, the Alt key on a PC. See pages 212–13 for other zooming techniques.

CREATING THE CERTIFICATE

1. Create a border.

- Move the pointer to the Element menu, choose Line, and, still holding down the mouse button, scroll the Line submenu to select the 6-point triple rule.

- Click on the rectangle tool in the Toolbox. Note that when you move the pointer back into the page frame, the icon turns into a crossbar.

- Place the crossbar at the upper left corner of the margin guides. Hold down the mouse button, drag the crossbar to the lower right margin guide, and release the mouse button.

Note: If you're working at a reduced page view, the border will look like a solid or double line. To see the line as it will print, choose Actual Size from the View submenu (on the Layout menu). At that size you may need to move around the screen to find the line. (See box, above.)

◄ ◄ ◄

To display the Toolbox, select Toolbox from the Window menu. **To hide the Toolbox,** click on the box in the upper left corner. **Keyboard shortcut:** Press Command-6 on a Mac, Ctrl-6 on a PC.

To select a tool, click on its icon in the Toolbox. The pointer changes to reflect the tool you've selected. (See page 193 for a description of all the tools.)

To move the Toolbox, point to its title bar and drag it to a new location.

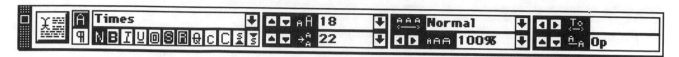

▲ ▲ ▲

*When you display the Control Palette
and select the text tool, the Palette
displays **character-formatting
options**. To move the Control
Palette to a different location on
the screen, position the pointer
in the vertical panel on the left
edge of the Control Palette
window, hold down the mouse
button, and drag the window
to a new location.*

2. Display the Control Palette for text formatting.

• Choose Control Palette from the Window menu. Or press Command-apostrophe on a Mac, Ctrl-apostrophe on a PC.

The Control Palette has different views that enable you to format text and manipulate objects. The view it displays depends on which tool is active and what you have selected at the time. In this project, we'll use it to format the text. But before doing that, note that with the pointer tool active and nothing selected, the Palette displays only x-y coordinates. As you move the pointer around the screen, the x-y coordinates change.

• Click on the text tool in the Toolbox.

When you select the text tool, the Control Palette displays character-formatting attributes, such as typeface, size, and type styles. See the sidebars on pages 258–59 for a review of these options.

3. Specify the text attributes.

• Specify the **font** as Times Roman. To display a list of fonts installed on your computer, move the pointer over the arrow next to the Control Palette's font field and hold down the mouse button. The currently selected font is under-lined, highlighted, or checked. Still holding down the mouse button, scroll the font list to select the one you want. When you re-lease the mouse button, the name will be displayed in the font field. (The arrows on the font list shown indicate a further submenu of fonts in the family; to organize and streamline your fonts in this way, you need a font utility. We use Adobe Type Reunion.)

Chicago
Courier
Geneva
Helvetica ▸
Helvetica Condensed ▸
Monaco
Palatino ▸
Symbol
Times ▸
Zapf Dingbats

▲ ▲ ▲

*Type numbers in the text fields to
specify the **type size** (top) and
leading (bottom). The arrows to
the left of those text fields are
nudge buttons. Clicking a nudge
button increases or decreases the
value by 0.1 point, depending on
whether you click an up or down
arrow. Holding down the Command
key (Mac) or Ctrl key (PC) while you
click a nudge button increases or
decreases the value by 1 point. The
arrows to the right of the text fields
display lists of sizes and leadings.*

• Specify the **size** as 18 points. Select the number in the type size field (by dragging over it or double-clicking on it) and type *18*. Press Tab, which advances to the next field in the Palette (the leading field).

• Specify the **leading** as 22 points. With the leading field selected, type *22*. This defines the amount of space between lines of text. For a de-tailed description of leading, see pages 22 and 34 in Chapter 2.

• Specify the **case** as all caps. Use the row of icons under the font field to specify type-style options such as bold, italic, and underline as well as small caps, large caps, subscript, and superscript. For all caps, click on the large-C button. Notice that the button turns black, indicating that it is selected. If you wanted to undo this formatting and specify normal uppercase and lowercase instead of all caps, you'd just click on that same but-ton to turn the option off.

- Click the **Apply** button.

When you type a value for an option, you must apply the change by clicking the Apply button, located on the left side of the Control Palette. You can also press Tab, or Return or Enter, to apply the changes. When you click a button or select an option from a menu list, PageMaker applies that attribute automatically.

4. Type the text.

- Click the I-beam on the 2.5-inch horizontal ruler guide. Type

ENROLLMENT CERTIFICATE [Return]

THE DESKTOP PUBLISHING SCHOOL [Return]

ADMITS [Return]

TO [Return]

THE HANDS-ON DESIGN COURSE

5. Specify centered alignment for the text.

The Control Palette has two different views for formatting text. In step 3, you used the character view, which displays attributes that apply to selected characters. To display attributes that apply to whole paragraphs, such as alignment or indents, you need to see the Control Palette in paragraph view.

- Click the ¶ button in the Control Palette to display paragraph attributes. Or press Command-Shift-accent grave (`) on the Mac, Ctrl-Shift-accent grave (`) on the PC.

- Drag over all the text you just typed to select it. Or use the Select All keyboard shortcut: Click the text cursor anywhere in that text, and press Command-A on a Mac, Ctrl-A on a PC.

- The alignment options are directly to the right of the ¶ button. They visually depict how the text will look: aligned at the left margin, aligned at the right margin, centered, and so on. Click on the centered alignment icon, and PageMaker highlights it, as in the screen detail above.

Note: When you change a Control Palette setting by selecting a menu option or a Control Palette icon, PageMaker applies the change immediately to the selected text.

▲ ▲ ▲

*The **text tool cursor** is an I-beam with a short horizontal crossbar two-thirds of the way from the top. You tell PageMaker where you want to begin typing by positioning this cursor and clicking to set an insertion point. You select existing text by dragging over it with this cursor.*

*If you click the ¶ button, the Control Palette displays **paragraph-formatting options,** such as alignment, indents, and space before and after paragraphs.*

▼ ▼ ▼

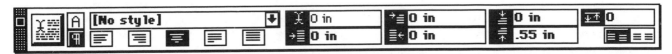

▲ ▲ ▲

View buttons *Click the* [A] *button on the Control Palette to display the character-formatting view. Click the* [¶] *button to display the paragraph-formatting view. To toggle between the two views, press Command-Shift-accent grave (`) on the Mac, Ctrl-Shift-accent grave (`) on the PC. (Accent grave is the unshifted character above the Tab key on most keyboards.)*

6. Style the headline.

- With the text tool, select the first line of text. You can drag over it, or you can triple-click on it. (Triple-clicking with the text tool selects an entire paragraph.)

- Click the [A] button in the Control Palette to display the character view.

- In the type size field, specify *36*.

- Click the Apply button, or press Tab or Return or Enter.

  The tops of the letters may appear to be clipped off. They'll print fine, and they'll also display correctly as soon as you refresh your screen. To refresh the screen, use the keyboard shortcut for whatever page view you are currently working in. (See page 213.) This is a bug that plagues display type, especially when the type is much larger than the leading.

7. Adjust the vertical spacing in the text.

- With the text tool, select the first line of text.

- Display the Control Palette in paragraph view.

- For the Space After, type *.55* and click the Apply button.

  The icon for specifying space after a paragraph is in the bottom row of the Palette, toward the right, with an up arrow pointing to the bottom of the text block. As the icon suggests, the value you enter in this field adds space below a paragraph, known in PageMaker language as the Space After.

	0 in
	.55 in

- With the text tool, select the word "Admits."

- Specify *.85* for the Space After option, and click the Apply button.

8. Add the line for a signature.

- Click on the perpendicular line tool ([⊢]) in the Toolbox. The pointer turns into a crossbar.

  Note that as you move the crossbar around the screen, the Control Palette displays the *x*- and *y*-coordinates. This enables you to draw and manipulate objects with mathematical precision. But for this project, it's more important to get the feel of working with the tools and rulers, so just hide the Control Palette by clicking on the little close box in the upper left window.

- Move the pointer into the left ruler and bring in vertical ruler guides at 3 inches and 8 inches to define the start and end points of the line.

- Position the crossbar at the intersection of the 4.5-inch horizontal ruler guide and the 3-inch vertical ruler guide. Drag the crossbar along the horizontal guide to the vertical guide at 8 inches.

  That's a very thick line. (It's the same triple rule you selected earlier for the border.)

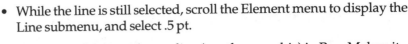

TIP

When you select a line weight and then draw a graphic, as you did when you created the border for this certificate, that line weight becomes the default for the publication. Any PageMaker graphics that you subsequently draw will use that line weight unless you specify otherwise. But when you change the line weight of a graphic you've already drawn, the line weight applies to that graphic only. The same principle holds when you specify a Fill.

- While the line is still selected, scroll the Element menu to display the Line submenu, and select .5 pt.

  Note that when you draw a line (or other graphic) in PageMaker, it remains selected until you click elsewhere on the page. You know it's selected by the square selection handles at each end of the line.

  When you changed the weight of the line, did the line disappear? If so, it's probably behind the ruler guides. From the File menu, select Preferences. In the Preferences dialog box, locate the section labeled Guides, click on Back, and then click OK to close the dialog box. PageMaker layers all the elements on a page. If you click on Back, all guidelines are positioned in the bottom (or back) layer. (For more about the way PageMaker layers elements on the page, see page 218.)

9. Create a seal.

- Choose the circle tool, and move the crossbar to the 3-inch mark on the horizontal ruler and the 5-inch mark on the vertical ruler.

- Hold down the Shift key and drag the crossbar on a diagonal to the 4.5-inch mark on the horizontal ruler and the 6.5-inch mark on the vertical ruler. Release the mouse button before you release the Shift key. (It's the Shift key that restrains the graphic in a circular rather than an oval shape.) The circle will have the same triple rule as the border does.

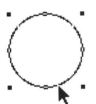 

▲ ▲ ▲

When you select a graphic with the pointer, the graphic is surrounded by eight small rectangles, or selection handles. **To move a graphic** *drawn with one of PageMaker's tools, point directly on the outline of the selected graphic; press the mouse button and, when you see a four-headed arrow, drag the graphic to the new position. If you point to a handle and drag, you will resize the graphic. If you resize a graphic by mistake, choose Undo from the Edit menu, or remove the selected graphic (press the Delete or Backspace key) and then redraw it.*

- Click on the pointer tool and position its tip anywhere directly on the circumference of the circle. Hold down the mouse button, and when you see the four-headed arrow, drag the circle and center it over the intersection of the vertical ruler guide that runs through the center of the page and the horizontal guide at 6.25 inches.

- With the circle still selected, scroll the Element menu to the Fill options and choose 10%.

- Select the text tool, and then display the Control Palette (from the Window menu, or press Command-apostrophe on a Mac and Ctrl-apostrophe on a PC). Click the Palette's ⊞ button to display the paragraph view, and specify centered alignment. Then click inside the circle on the 6.25-inch horizontal guide and type *DTP* in all caps. (We italicize anything you type on the page or in a text box. If the type style is also italic, we'll state that in the type specs.) Don't worry about the exact position yet.

- Drag the I-beam across the type to select it, click the Ⓐ button to display the character view of the Control Palette, and change the attributes to 36/36 bold. Check to see that Times Roman is still selected. Then click Apply.

  To specify boldface, click the B button in the row below the font field. The B will remain highlighted, indicating that bold is the currently specified type style.

FINISHING THE JOB

1. Choose Save from the File menu.

The Save and Save As commands in PageMaker are similar to those functions in other applications. In a more complex document, we'd certainly have saved several times before finishing the job. Get in the habit of saving your work every 15 minutes, or whenever you've done something to the layout that you'd hate to redo.

TIP

One of the most useful keyboard commands is the one that saves your current document: Command-S on a Mac, Ctrl-S on a PC.

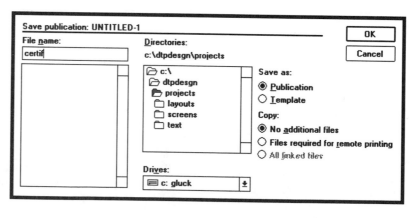

▲ ▲ ▲

On the Mac, type the name of the file you are saving in the text box at the bottom of the Save As dialog box. The folder you are saving to should be the one named at the top of the dialog box. Frequently you'll need to navigate through your hard drive to find the folder you want to save to. To move upward in the hierarchy, hold down the mouse button on the active folder at the top of the dialog box, and scroll to select the folder you want to go to. To choose a folder within the currently active folder, double-click on the name of that folder in the list box; the folder you click on becomes the active folder at the top of the dialog box.

TIP

In dialog boxes that save to your hard drive or access files from it you can use the up and down arrow keys to move through a list of filenames.

▲ ▲ ▲

In Windows, type a name of up to eight characters in the File Name text box at the top of the Save As dialog box. PageMaker adds a PM5 extension to the name after you save. To select the directory you want to save to, navigate through the Directories box under the path (in this screen, the path is c:\dtpdesgn\projects). When you find the directory you want, double-click on it. Its name will then appear in the path, and other PageMaker files inside it will appear in the list box under File Name.

2. Review your work.

Check to make sure everything is centered. Change the page view to Actual Size, and scroll around to check spelling, line weights (the border and the seal should be the same), and placements. If you want to reposition anything, select it with the pointer tool, and then drag the selected object to the new position.

3. Choose Print from the File menu.

The Print dialog box options are fairly complex, and they vary a little depending on the printer you've selected. Selecting one of the buttons on the right changes the options displayed. (You'll use these other options in later projects.) For this simple certificate, most of the default settings will be fine. For a detailed review of the Print dialog box, see pages 234–37.

- **Print To** If you work on a Mac, this option displays the name of the printer that you selected in the Chooser. It should be the printer you are currently using. If it isn't, select the Chooser under the Apple menu, click on the PSPrinter icon (if you are using a PostScript printer), and in the Printer list, select the name of your printer.

  If you work on a PC, this field displays the name of the printer you selected using the Printers option in the Windows Control Panel. It should be the printer you are currently using. If it isn't, you can change it in PageMaker's Print dialog box: Position the pointer over the arrow to the right of the text box, hold down the mouse button, and select your printer from the pull-down list.

- **Type** (PostScript printers only) Scroll the pull-down list to select the PPD (PostScript printer description) file for the printer specified for Print To. This generally has a version number following the name of the printer.

- Specify 1 copy, All pages, and wide orientation. (The icon for wide is the one with the little figure on its side.)

- To okay the settings in the dialog box, click Print or just press Return or Enter.

4. Sign your name and consider yourself enrolled.

THE CONTROL PALETTE'S TEXT VIEW...

Many text-formatting attributes can be specified either in the Control Palette or in menus and dialog boxes that you access from the Type menu. Beginners generally find it easier to leave the Control Palette on-screen and do as much formatting as possible through the Palette. But if you have a small screen, you may find it easier to bring up dialog boxes as needed. And when you create style sheets to define collections of type attributes (as you'll do in Project 4), you must do

that through dialog boxes rather than through the Control Palette.

The important thing is to be aware that you have different ways of working and to adopt the approach you find most comfortable. With a few exceptions, the options are essentially the same, whether you use the Control Palette or the Type menu.

For a description of each option labeled in the Control Palette, see the explanation on the facing page.

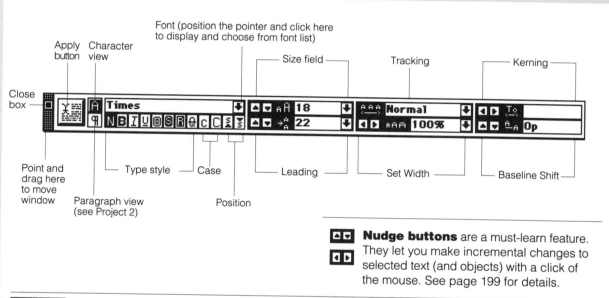

Font (position the pointer and click here to display and choose from font list)

Apply button   Character view

Size field   Tracking   Kerning

Close box

Point and drag here to move window

Type style   Case   Leading   Set Width   Baseline Shift

Paragraph view (see Project 2)   Position

Nudge buttons are a must-learn feature. They let you make incremental changes to selected text (and objects) with a click of the mouse. See page 199 for details.

TIPS

If you specify type attributes when there is no text insertion point, those specs become the new default for that publication. All text that you subsequently type will take on those attributes unless you specify otherwise.

If you select the text tool, set an insertion point, and then specify type attributes, the specs will apply only to the text you type next. If you move the insertion point before typing, the type specs revert to the publication default.

When you select text with the text tool and then you specify type attributes, the attributes apply only to the selected text.

A check mark on a submenu indicates the attribute of the selected text or, if no text is selected, of the default.

When there's no check mark on a submenu or when a type attribute box is blank, it means that the selected text contains mixed attributes. In this situation, if you want to determine a specific attribute, narrow your text selection to a single word or, if necessary, a single letter.

Two options (outline and shadow) are available only on the Macintosh. Some options, such as custom sizes and Set Width, are available only on printers that use scalable fonts, such as PostScript and PCL-V series printers; with other printers, what you see on the screen may not print accurately. Some printers, such as early Hewlett-Packard LaserJet models, do not print reversed type. Type manager utilities (such as Adobe Type Manager) can overcome some type-styling limitations in some printers.

. . . AND THE TYPE MENU

The type attributes described here are available in the Control Palette, the Type Specs dialog box (accessed from the Type menu), and the Type menu's pull-down lists. Exceptions: See notes at bottom of page.

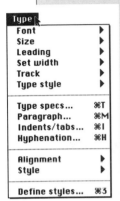

Font Hold down the mouse button to display and select from a list of the typefaces installed on your system.

Size Type size is measured in points. (See page 20.) You can choose from a pull-down list of standard sizes, but it's faster just to type the size you want in the Size box, which can be any number from 4 to 650, in one-tenth-of-a-point increments.

Leading Leading, the vertical space above and below a line of type, is also measured in points. You can choose from a pull-down list of values, but as with type size, it's easier to type the value—from 0 to 1300 in one-tenth-of-a-point increments. If you choose Auto Leading, PageMaker calculates the leading as 120% of the text size. (See page 34 for more information about leading methods.)

Set Width You can condense or expand the width of individual characters by specifying a percentage of the normal width from 5% to 250%. This is called horizontal scaling. (See pages 20 and 405.)

Color[†] Any colors that you've defined in your publication will appear on the Color pull-down menu in the Type Specs dialog box and can be applied to selected text. (See Project 9.)

Type Style As used here, "style" refers to Normal (regular roman type), bold, italic, underline, strikethrough (used to indicate text that has been deleted), reverse, and, on the Macintosh, outline and shadow. PageMaker also uses the word "Style," at the bottom of the Type menu, to refer to a collection of type-formatting attributes applied to a paragraph; see Project 4 for a discussion of this feature.

Position This option specifies the position of the text relative to the baseline of the rest of the line. In the Control Palette, click on the ⬚ to specify super-script and on the ⬚ to specify subscript. To return to Normal, click the highlighted button again. In

the Type Specs dialog box, choose those same options from the Position pull-down menu.

Case In the Control Palette, click on the ⬚ to specify small caps and on the ⬚ to specify large caps. To return to Normal, click again on the highlighted button. In the Type Specs dialog box, choose those same options from the Case pull-down menu.

Track You can adjust the space between letters and words by choosing one of six settings ranging from Very Loose to Very Tight. No Track, the default, is slightly tighter than Normal. (See page 42.)

No Break/Break[†] If you select text and then turn on the No Break option, PageMaker will not allow a line break within the selected text.

Options[†] This button brings up the Type Options dialog box, in which you can specify the size of small caps (as a percentage of the specified point size), the size and position of superscript and sub-script characters (as a percentage of the point size), and the Baseline Shift (in tenth-of-a-point increments above or below the normal baseline).

MM Fonts[†] (Mac only) This button displays a dialog box with options for adjusting Adobe's Multiple Master fonts. The button is active only if you have Multiple Master fonts installed on your system and only if the selected font is an MM font.

Kerning[*] This Control Palette field is used to adjust space between letter pairs, primarily in display type. See page 40 for details regarding this feature.

For a review of the Control Palette's paragraph view and the Paragraph Specifications dialog box, see pages 274–75.

---

[*] Indicates that an option is available in the Control Palette but not on the Type menu or in the Type Specs dialog box.

[†] Indicates that the option is available only from the Type Specs dialog box.

PLACING AND COPYFITTING TEXT IN A SMALL SPACE AD

This small space ad is designed to run in the classified section of a Sunday newspaper. For the purposes of this exercise, let's assume that the ad has been written by a very fussy personnel director, and your job is to lay it out in PageMaker. You are given 150 words of copy and told "Make it fit." No matter that almost any piece of writing will benefit from the editing required by copyfitting. Your job here is to make those 150 words fit.

You must also follow a format that the company uses for all ads of this type. The margins, headline, and company identification must follow the company style, but you have some flexibility with the typeface, size, and paragraph formatting.

The ease with which you can test different type specs for layout fit in a situation like this is one of the great economies of electronic page layout. Art directors and designers who have lived through the tedium of estimating manuscript copy, knowing that the typesetter will deliver galleys that are still too long or too short, will especially appreciate the magic of electronic trial and error.

For the copy in this ad, we suggest that you type the body text word for word as it appears on the facing page. It won't take you very long—the text has fewer than 150 words. By using the same text we used as you try the various formatting options, you'll see on-screen the results that we discuss in the text.

You can type the text in a word-processing program, or you can use PageMaker's Story Editor, which is discussed in detail at the end of this project. Don't overlook this powerful feature, not only for utilities such as the spell checker and the Find and Change commands, but also for the increased speed it offers for writing and editing text.

PAGEMAKER TECHNIQUES YOU WILL LEARN

▶ Break apart text blocks

▶ Place text from a word-processing program

▶ Use the manual text-flow mode

▶ Set up a two-column format

▶ Use baseline leading

▶ Copy, paste, and move PageMaker rules

▶ Toggle back and forth between the pointer and text tools

▶ Specify paragraph attributes

▶ Force-justify a headline

▶ Kern a headline

▶ Print with crop marks

▶ Review Story Editor options

▶ Use the spell checker

▶ Use the Find and Change options

Bookman is used for all the type (with the exception of the boldface Helvetica in the bottom line). With its strong thick and thin strokes and sturdy serifs, Bookman reproduces well on newsprint.

The 6-point horizontal rules provide a strong alternative to borders, which are overused in classified ads. The rules also work with the headline to play off the old Western "Wanted" posters.

The Force Justify alignment option makes the "Wanted" headline completely fill the space between the margins.

Opening up space between paragraphs and insetting one paragraph creates contrast within a simple text block.

WANTED
A Good Copywriter

Do you have experience writing promotion brochures and catalogs? Would you like to work with a young, fast-growing company with tremendous growth potential? If so, read on.

East-West MultiMedia is seeking an experienced copywriter to create direct mail pieces, catalogs, package copy, and space ads for a growing library of multimedia titles. You will need to create and develop concepts, plan production schedules, and traffic jobs.

> Qualifications: Two years commercial copywriting experience, excellent grammar and proofreading skills, knowledge of Mac and IBM computers, an ability to handle infinite details and to thrive under tight deadlines.

We have steady freelance work and a possible staff position within the next 12 months.

Send resume and cover letter with samples of your work to Copywriter, East-West MultiMedia, 3262 Sagebrush Road, Tucson, Arizona 35860. No phone calls accepted.

Join a Growing Organization
EAST-WEST MULTIMEDIA

BLUEPRINT FOR THE AD

SETUP

1. Prepare the text file.

If you have a word processor Type the body text (but not any of the headline text) in the ad above. For the formatting, specify 9/11 Times Roman. By originating the text in a word processor, you'll be able to get some hands-on practice using PageMaker's Place command.

If you don't have a word processor You can type the text directly on the page or, better yet, use PageMaker's Story Editor. If you're using Page-Maker for word processing as well as layout, you'll certainly want to master this feature, which is described in detail beginning on page 276.

TIP

Press the Tab key **to move from one text field to another in a dialog box** such as Page Setup. Press Return or Enter **to okay a dialog box**. Both of these keyboard shortcuts can be used so frequently that they are worth remembering early on.

2. Open a 1-page document with the following page setup:

- Page Dimensions: 4.25 by 6 inches

  Note that when you type the values in the size boxes, the Page submenu automatically changes from Letter to Custom. On the other hand, if you want to change from Letter size to Legal or Tabloid or one of the other page sizes listed on the Page submenu, you can select the name of the paper size from the list, and PageMaker will automatically insert the values for you.

- Orientation: Tall

- Options: Single-sided (click off Double-sided)

- Margins: Left and Right: 0.25 inches

  Top and Bottom: 0.35 inches

- Compose to Printer: From the pull-down menu, select the name of the printer that will be used for the final camera-ready pages. This may be different from the printer used to produce proofs (which you select in the Print dialog box). See page 229.

- Target Printer Resolution: Type, or select from the pull-down menu, the number of dots per inch of the target printer.

3. Change the unit of measure from inches to picas.

The unit of measure (inches, picas, and so on) is specified in the Preferences dialog box. Although you can override the specified measure when typing values in option boxes (see page 210), you want the rulers to be displayed in the measurement system you'll use most frequently in a given project; for most designers, that's generally picas.

- Choose Preferences from the File menu. The Preferences dialog box comes on-screen.

- Select picas from the pull-down menus for both Measurement System and Vertical Ruler.

  It's a nuisance to have to change both rulers, but you'll see the value of the vertical ruler when we work with leading grids in Project 6.

4. Define the image area.

- To turn on Snap to Rulers, scroll the Layout menu to select Guides and Rulers, and from that submenu, select Snap to Rulers. Or press Command-[on a Mac, Shift-Ctrl-Y on a PC.

- Bring in horizontal ruler guides at 6p, 7p9, 8p6, 10p, 31p6, and 33p.

DISPLAY TYPE

1. Add the horizontal rules.

- Select the perpendicular line tool (▭), and then choose the 6-point rule from the Line submenu (under Element). Draw a horizontal rule from the left margin to the right margin, with the top of the rule aligned at the top margin.

- With the rule still selected, copy it and then paste it.

  The Copy and Paste commands (as well as the Cut command) are on the Edit menu, as in most programs for the Macintosh and Windows.

  PageMaker pastes the copy so it is offset slightly below and to the right of the original, making it easier to find. (If you've scrolled to a different part of the page, PageMaker pastes the copy center screen.)

- With the pointer tool, drag the copy so that its top is aligned on the 8p6 horizontal guide. The sides of the rule align with the right and left margins.

- Paste again (the previous copy will still be in the Clipboard's memory, so you don't need to copy it again), and drag this copy so that the bottom of the rule sits on the bottom margin.

2. Type the display text.

With several lines of display type, as in this ad, we generally type all the copy at once, and then break the text into individual lines to style and position them by eye.

- With the text tool, click anywhere in the center of the page. Note that PageMaker automatically sets the insertion point at the left margin. Type the following:

  Wanted [Return]
  A Good Copywriter [Return]
  Join a Growing Organization [Return]
  East-West MultiMedia

- Display the Control Palette from the Window menu (or press Command-apostrophe on a Mac, Ctrl-apostrophe on a PC).

- With the text tool, select all four lines of text.

- In the Control Palette Font box, drag over the current selection and type *Bookman*.

  If you have another font installed that starts with a B and precedes Bookman alphabetically, PageMaker will display that font name, but as you keep typing, PageMaker will keep cycling through the options and match Bookman before you finish. Or you can select the name you want from the Font pull-down menu.

- Press Tab twice to move to the type size value, and type *12*. Press Tab again to select the leading value, and type *14*. Then press Tab, or Return or Enter, to apply the formatting.

TIP

When you type values in the Control Palette, you must press Tab, or Return or Enter, or click the Apply button on the Palette to apply the formatting. (The Tab key advances the active field to the next option at the same time.) When you click on an option to select it, or choose it from a menu list, PageMaker applies the formatting automatically.

- Display the Control Palette's paragraph view by clicking on the ¶ icon or pressing Command-Shift-accent grave (`) on a Mac, Ctrl-Shift-accent grave (`) on a PC.

- With the text still selected, click on the centered alignment icon (▤).

- Change the leading method from proportional to baseline.

  To do this, with the text still selected choose Paragraph from the Type menu. In the Paragraph Specs dialog box, choose Spacing. In the Spacing dialog box, note that Proportional leading is on by default. Click on Baseline to change to that method of leading. Click OK to close the Spacing dialog box, and then click OK again to close the Paragraph dialog box. To understand why baseline leading is preferable, read the sidebar on the facing page.

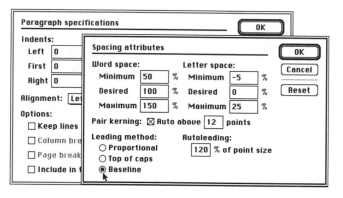

3. Style and position the display type.

In this step, you're going to use the text tool to style, cut, and paste each line individually. Then you'll switch to the pointer tool for precise positioning. If you're not familiar with text blocks and windowshade handles, refer to the sidebar on page 266. Because you'll be repeating many of the same actions with each line, it's a good opportunity to learn the keyboard shortcuts described in the tip at left.

- Turn on Snap to Guides (on the Guides and Rulers submenu under Layout).

- Display the Control Palette in character view.

- With the text tool, select the word "Wanted." Specify 48/36 Bookman. Then specify Bold and All Caps by clicking on the respective icons below the Font box. (See page 258 for a summary of character-formatting options in the Control Palette.)

  With the word still selected, cut it, set an insertion point between the 6-point rules at the top of the page, and then paste.

  With the pointer tool, select that line again, hold down the Shift key, and drag the text so that its baseline is on the 6p horizontal guideline. (By holding down the Shift key, you'll constrain the movement to a vertical direction, ensuring that the centered alignment is not upset.)

- With the text tool, select the second line and change the type specs to 18/15 Bookman.

TIP

Save time by learning these keyboard shortcuts for tasks in step 3:

Cut: Command-X on a Mac, or Ctrl-X on a PC.
Paste: Command-V on a Mac, or Ctrl-V on a PC.
Alignment: Command-Shift on a Mac or Ctrl-Shift on a PC plus the first letter of the desired alignment—L(eft), R(ight), C(entered), and so on.
Activate the **pointer tool:** Shift-F1.
Activate the **text tool:** Shift-F4.
Toggle between the pointer tool and the tool you're currently working with: Command-Spacebar on a Mac, F9 on a PC.

USE BASELINE LEADING FOR EASY ALIGNMENTS

When you work with display type, you generally want to position the baseline of the type relative to other elements on the page. It's easier to do this if the bottom of the text slug—the black selection bar when you select the text with the text tool, or the bottom windowshade handle when you select the text with the pointer tool—is the baseline of the text.

But by default, PageMaker uses proportional leading, which puts two-thirds of the leading above the baseline and one-third below. So if your headline is, for example, 48/48, you'll have 16 points (one-third of the leading) between the baseline of the headline and the bottom windowshade handle when you move the type. With baseline leading, the bottom windowshade handle will be aligned exactly at the baseline, and you can snap that windowshade handle right to a guideline or ruler tick mark.

The leading method is a paragraph-level attribute, and it's very easy to change it. Select the text—in this case, all four lines of the display text—and choose Paragraph from the Type menu. In the Paragraph dialog box, choose Spacing, and in the Spacing dialog box, click on Baseline under Leading Method.

With **baseline leading,** all the leading is above the baseline, and you can easily snap the bottom windowshade handle to a guideline or ruler tick mark.

▼ ▼ ▼

With **proportional leading,** one-third of the leading is below the baseline, so you can't take advantage of Snap To commands to align the baseline of the text at a guideline or ruler tick mark.

▼ ▼ ▼

Another advantage of baseline leading is that you can specify tighter leading for large type sizes, which means that the windowshade handles will be tighter to the text and thus less likely to interfere with other elements on the page. In the detail below, the type is 48/36.

▼ ▼ ▼

If you tighten the leading using proportional leading, part of the text extends above the line slug; whenever you cut and paste text, the text gets clipped off at the top edge of the slug. The text will print correctly, but in order for it to display correctly you have to force the screen to redraw.

▼ ▼ ▼

THE POINTER TOOL OR THE TEXT TOOL? GOOD QUESTION.

There are two fundamental ways of working with text in a PageMaker layout. When you type, edit, or apply type and paragraph formatting, you are working with text as characters, and you use the text tool in the same way you'd use the cursor in a word-processing program.

But you can also manipulate blocks of text similarly to the way you manipulate graphics. Using the pointer tool, you can stretch or shrink the width of a text block, drag it to a different position on the page, rotate it, and so on.

A text block is simply any unit of text that you can select at one time with the pointer tool. It can be as small as a single character or as long as the PageMaker window, including the paste-board. The four lines of display copy that you typed for this ad started out as one text block. When you broke them apart into individual lines, they became four different text blocks.

You can use either tool to cut, copy, or paste text, but with different results. When you cut (or copy) and paste with the pointer tool, the pasted copy retains the margins of the original. When you cut (or copy) and paste with the text tool, the pasted copy conforms to the margins of the insertion point. If you want to cut or copy only part of a text block, drag over that text with the text tool; using the pointer tool, you'd have to select the entire text block.

We'll look more at the behavior of text blocks in the sidebar that begins on page 336.

*When you select a text block with the **pointer tool,** two windowshade handles define the boundaries of the text.*

*Use the **text tool** to drag over selected text when you want to edit text or change the character or paragraph attributes.*

▲ ▲ ▲
To move a text block, *click on the text with the pointer tool. Then position the pointer inside the windowshade handles, hold down the mouse button, and when you see the four-headed arrow, drag the text to the new position. The dashed box displayed around the text as you drag defines the top, bottom, and side margins of the text. If you drag before the four-headed arrow appears, you'll see the bounding box around the text as you drag, but you won't see the text itself until you release the mouse button.*

▲ ▲ ▲
To change the width of a text block, *position the pointer on the end of a windowshade handle and drag. You can make the text narrower, as in the example above, or you can stretch the width, as we do with the body text later in this project.*

With the text still selected, cut and paste this second line under the word "Wanted."

With the pointer tool, select that line again, hold down the Shift key, and position the baseline on the 7p9 horizontal guide.

- With the text tool, select the third line and specify right alignment. (Learning the keyboard shortcuts for alignment options will save you a lot of toggling between character and paragraph views in the Control Palette.) Then cut and paste the line anywhere toward the bottom of the page.

With the pointer tool, select and position that line so that its baseline is on the 31p6 horizontal guide.

- With the text tool, select the last line and change the type specs to 14/14 Helvetica Bold, All Caps. With the text still selected, specify right alignment.

Select that last line with the pointer tool. Is there a big gap between the top and bottom windowshade handles? That gap represents the paragraph returns from the previous three lines, which weren't deleted when you cut each line. Gaps between windowshade handles can interfere when you try to select other objects on the page. So before you move this line of text, select the text tool, set an insertion point before the word "East," and drag up as far as you can. Then press Delete or Backspace to delete those extra paragraph returns.

After removing the extra carriage returns, select the line again with the pointer, and position its baseline on the 33p horizontal guide

BODY TEXT

1. Define the columns.

- Choose Column Guides from the Layout menu.
- In the Column Guides dialog box, specify 2 columns with a 1p space in between. Click OK. Note that changing the number of columns does not affect type that's already in position on the page.

2. Place the text.

For this first exercise in placing text, let's take a close look at the procedure in the sidebar on the following spread.

3. Format the text.

- To select all the text, click the text tool anywhere in the text block to set an insertion point. Then choose Select All from the Edit menu.
- Check to be sure that the type is specified as Times Roman 9/11.

HOW TO PLACE TEXT IN PAGEMAKER

The ability to bring text and graphics from other programs into a page layout program is the heart of electronic page layout. And in PageMaker, it's the Place command that enables you to do this.

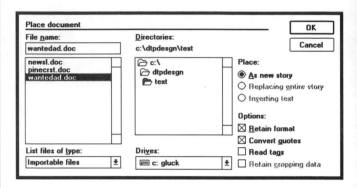

- Choose Place from the File menu (Command-D on a Mac, Ctrl-D on a PC).

  File selection dialog boxes—like Place and Save As—look quite different on the Mac and on the PC. For more detail on how to navigate through the PC screen shown here, or the Mac screen (not shown), see the description of the Save As dialog box on page 256.

- In the Place dialog box, scroll through your folders (Mac) or directories (PC) to select the name of the file you want to place.

  The dialog box displays the names of only those text, graphics, spreadsheet, and database documents that PageMaker can read directly from the selected folder or directory on the current disk.

- Choose from among the available Place options described below.

- Click OK, or press Return or Enter.

  PageMaker loads the pointer with a copy of the text file you've selected. (The original remains unchanged as a word-processing file.) When the dialog box closes, you'll see a loaded text icon.

  Note: Depending on your word processor and the format you use for saving text files, PageMaker may display a special dialog box in which you can specify how the text should be imported. If this happens (the words "import filter" will be included in the dialog box title), see page 329.

- Check that Snap to Guides is turned on. (It's on the Guides and Rulers submenu under Layout.) This ensures that PageMaker will align the text between the column guides when you click the loaded text icon on the page. In this project, you want to align the loaded text icon at the intersection of the left margin and the 10p ruler guide.

- Position the loaded text icon where you want the text to begin flowing, and click the mouse button.

  In the manual mode, the text flow stops at the end of each column or when something gets in

its way (such as a graphic or text that is already positioned at the bottom of the page).

If you're working on a small monitor, the text may be displayed as gray bars. This is called greeked text. You can control the size at which PageMaker displays greeked text through the Preferences command (on the File menu).

- Reload the text icon.

  The arrow (⊌) in the bottom windowshade indicates that there is more text to place. When you click on the arrow, PageMaker reloads the text icon. Click on the arrow now.

- Select an insertion point for the next text block.

  In manual text-flow mode, you have to click the loaded text icon to tell PageMaker where to continue flowing the text. In this project, position the text icon in the second column, aligned at the same horizontal guide as the first column of text, and click.

  The empty loop (⊔) in the bottom windowshade indicates that there is no more text to place.

Place Options

The various options in the Place dialog box tell PageMaker how—and in some cases where—to place the file you select.

As New Story (Mac) or **As New Item** (PC) PageMaker will load the text icon with the file you select, and you choose where in the layout you want the text to begin by clicking the icon at that position.

Text-Flow Modes

 Manual text-flow mode is PageMaker's default. It's selected when the Autoflow command on the Layout menu is turned off. When using this mode, PageMaker displays a loaded text icon, like the one at left. When you click the icon, text flows to the bottom of the column, stops, and waits for you to reload the icon. This is the mode to use for small amounts of text, as in this project.

*With the **Autoflow** command turned on, the text icon looks like this. When you click the icon, PageMaker flows text continuously, adding pages if necessary, until all the text is placed. This is the fastest mode to use when placing long text files.*

You can toggle back and forth between manual and autoflow modes: Whichever mode is selected, pressing Command on a Mac or Ctrl on a PC invokes the other.

*In **semi-automatic** mode, text flow stops at the bottom of each column. If there is more text to place, PageMaker automatically reloads the text icon but doesn't continue flowing the text until you click the text icon again. You maintain control over where the text is placed, but you don't have to take time to keep loading the text icon at the bottom of each column. Be sure to try this mode in some of your real-life work. It's faster than manual text flow but gives you just as much control over where you flow text.*

You can invoke semi-automatic mode by holding down the Shift key when either of the other two modes is active.

Replacing Entire Story or Replacing Selected Text

Use these options when you want to replace existing text with new text from a word-processor file. The action you take *before choosing Place* determines which option is displayed: Set an insertion point anywhere in the story (if you want to replace the entire story) or select text (if you want to replace that part of a story), and choose the Replacing option. The new story you place flows into the document in place of the entire story or the selected text. When you use these options, you lose any text and formatting changes you made to the original story in PageMaker.

Inserting Text Use this option when you need to add new text from a word-processor file to an existing story in the layout. *Before choosing Place,* set an insertion point where you want the new text to flow, and then choose this option in the Place dialog box. PageMaker inserts the new file in the existing one at the insertion point.

Retain Format Choose this box when you want PageMaker to retain text formatting from your word-processing program.

Convert Quotes Choose this option so that Page-Maker will convert typewriter-style quotation marks (" ") and apostrophes (') to the typographic characters designed for the typeface you are using (" " and '). (Inch marks and foot marks following numbers are not converted.) With this option selected, double hyphens will also be converted to em dashes.

Read Tags Choose this if, in your word processor, you format text with style name tags surrounded by angle brackets (< >). For a discussion of styles, see Project 4.

Retain Cropping Data This option is used with graphics files. See page 332.

TIPS

To place text, press Command-D on a Mac, Ctrl-D on a PC.

Turn on Snap to Guides when you place text. This ensures that, even if the text icon isn't positioned exactly on the margin guides, the text that flows in will observe those guides. Otherwise, the text has a tendency to flow to the edge of the page or even across the pasteboard. Then you have to reflow it or scroll to the edge of the text block and shorten the window-shade handles.

You can easily **postpone a place operation.** After the loaded text icon appears, you sometimes need to perform another operation, such as bringing in a ruler guide, changing pages, checking the text-flow mode, turning on Snap to Guides, and so on. Don't panic. When you move the text icon into the menu bar, the rulers, or the scroll bars, the cursor temporarily turns back into the arrow so that you can perform these operations. When you move the cursor back into the image area, the text icon reappears.

When you do want to **cancel a place operation,** click on the text icon in the Toolbox, and whichever tool you click on will be activated.

For additional tips on placing text, see Project 4.

TIP

For the repetitive actions in this copyfitting exercise, use these timesavers:

Select all text: Set an insertion point, and press Command-A on a Mac, Ctrl-A on a PC.

Toggle between character and paragraph views: Press Command-Shift-accent grave (`) on a Mac, Ctrl-Shift-accent grave (`) on a PC.

Use the Tab key to move from one value box to another.

4. Fit the copy.

The text is quite a bit shorter than the space it needs to fill. This is a good opportunity to practice using different formatting options, and to see how they affect the length of text.

Remember, with Preferences set to picas, values for paragraph attributes are specified in picas and points, with 12 points to a pica. Half a pica is specified as 0p6, 15 points is specified as 1p3, and so on.

- Specify a 2-pica paragraph indent.

  With the text tool, select all the text, and display the Control Palette's paragraph view. To indent the first line of each paragraph, type the desired value in the box next to the first-line indent icon (⭲≣2p). Here, that's 2 picas, so type 2. The Space After box (⯯0p) should specify 0. Press Tab to apply.

- To fill space, try a typeface with a larger x-height.

  Display the Control Palette in character view. While the text is still selected, change the typeface to Bookman, which doesn't get as many characters per line as Times Roman. Press Tab to apply. This helps fill the space, but not nearly enough.

- Increase the type size and leading.

  With all the text still selected, specify 10/12. Now the text is too long. And the type doesn't really look good. The ragged right margin is too uneven, with stairstepping and other bad holes. The problem

MORE COPYFITTING TIPS

The techniques for cutting and adding text to fit are flip sides of the same coin. So we've divided this list into global and micro changes. Most of the global changes can also be made on a micro level, which is generally called "cheating." Cheating can save the day, but it can also make your pages look like the work of an amateur. Be sure to check the printouts for overall evenness and readability of type. Even the global changes should not be made without balancing the visual effect with the copy requirements.

Global Changes Throughout a Document or Story

Typeface When you need to save space, use a typeface with a small x-height or a condensed typeface to get more characters per line. To fill space, use a typeface with a larger x-height. See the discussion of the relative efficiency of type on page 30.

Type size and leading We list these together because generally, if you change one, you should at least review the other. With tenth-of-a-point increments in both type size and leading, PageMaker lets you inch your way toward making the copy fit.

Tracking The Track command on the Type menu has six preset values for adjusting space between letters and words, ranging from Very Loose to Very Tight. The tighter the track, the more words per line. If you change the track for body text, make the change universal for all the text. If you mix tracks in text that should look alike, you'll see the difference in the overall color of the type, with some text darker than the rest.

Spacing You can also control the space between letters and words through the Spacing Attributes dialog box (accessed through the Spacing button in the Paragraph Specs dialog box). Every font design builds in values for the space occupied by every letter and by the space between words. The values you specify as spacing attributes are percentages of those built-in values. Tightening word spacing to around 80% and letter spacing to around –4% may is that the type is too large to set evenly in this relatively narrow column. Let's try a single column, and maybe justified type as well.

- Widen the text measure.

With the pointer tool, select the left column and drag the handle on the right side of either windowshade handle all the way to the right margin. Hold down the Shift key while you drag, constraining the movement to the horizontal direction so that you don't change the vertical position of the text.

This fits pretty well. You get more words in one wide column than in two narrow ones because you pick up the space between the columns and lose less space to the end-of-line rag. But let's try a few more options.

- Justify the text.

Display the Control Palette in paragraph view and click on the icon for justified text. Now the text is too short. In order to set a justified right margin, PageMaker adjusts the space between letters and words. In the process, you often "lose" short lines at the end of paragraphs, as we did here. Note, also, that you have to check justified text for uneven color in loose and tight lines, but that tends to be less of a problem in wider columns such as this.

- Now we need to fill space again. So try adding some space between the paragraphs.

make the type look better as well as pick up some space. But this depends very much on the typeface and type size, and you must check printouts.

Hyphenation You can turn hyphenation on and off through the Hyphenation command on the Type menu. You'll get more words per line with hyphenation turned on. The Hyphenation Zone, specified in the bottom of the Hyphenation dialog box, determines how close to the end of a line PageMaker can insert a hyphen. The smaller your Hyphenation Zone, the closer to the end of the line PageMaker can insert a hyphen, and the tighter your lines will be.

Space around headlines If you've specified space before or after headlines, making the value a little larger or smaller may solve your problem.

Paragraph indents and spaces A wide indent can force an extra line in some paragraphs. Adding space between paragraphs can fill space overall.

Micro Changes in Individual Paragraphs or Lines

Scan the last lines of paragraphs. To save space, you can often pull up a short line at the end of a paragraph through minor editing or by altering the word or letter spacing or the Hyphenation Zone in that paragraph. To fill space, applying the same techniques will often force an additional line break in a last line that is already long.

In ragged right text, look for lines that fall far short of the right margin. Again, minor editing and changes in spacing attributes and hyphenation can often save or create lines. In justified text, select Show Loose/Tight Lines in the Preferences dialog box. PageMaker will highlight all lines that set tighter or looser than the specified spacing parameters. Editing, changing the spacing specs, or even kerning may solve typographic and copyfitting problems at the same time.

You can **kern a range of text** by selecting that text and using the various kerning key combinations. For more on range kerning, see page 41.

▲ ▲ ▲

__To inset a paragraph__ from the margins, specify both a left and a right indent. With justified text, make the value for both indents the same. With flush left, rag right text, make the value for the right indent a few points less than the value for the left indent.

Select all the text. In the Control Palette box for Space After, type *0p6*, and then press Tab. This creates a half-line space between paragraphs. With this paragraph spacing you won't need to indent the first paragraph, so change First Indent back to 0.

- That looks pretty good. But let's say, for the purposes of this exercise, that you want to highlight the third paragraph in some way. Boldface would be too heavy-handed, and it prints badly on newsprint. Try indenting both the left and right margins so that the paragraph is inset from the rest of the text.

  Click the cursor anywhere in the third paragraph. In the Control Palette, type *1p6* in the box for the left indent, press Tab, type *1p6* in the box for the right indent, and press Tab again.

- That gained one line, and now the last line of the body copy is too close to the display type at the bottom of the page. We can steal enough space from between the paragraphs to make it work. With all the type still selected, change the paragraph Space After from 0p6 to 0p4. And use the pointer tool to select the text block and move it up a couple of points. That does it.

FINISHING THE JOB

1. Fine-tune the headline.

The headline's okay. But it's always worthwhile to spend the time to tweak an okay headline into one with more impact. The centered text is a little bland, and the letterspacing is uneven. We know this is supposed to be the company's format, but here's how we'd improve it.

- Select the word "Wanted" with the text tool, and with the Control Palette in paragraph view, click on the alignment icon for force justification (▤). This spaces out the letters so that the word is forced to fill out the line. (You can do this when there is more than one word on a line too.) It's a very effective technique with headlines, and in this case, it reinforces the play on "Wanted" posters.

- There's too much space between the "W" and the "A" and not quite enough between the "A" and the "N." We can fix this by kerning, the process of adding or removing small increments of space between two characters.

  With the Control Palette in character view, you can adjust letterspacing by using the nudge buttons at the upper right. Set an insertion point between the "W" and the "A." That space is pretty exaggerated, so let's try what's called a power nudge. Hold down the Command key on a Mac, the Ctrl key on a PC, and click the left nudge button once. Note that as you click, PageMaker displays the amount of space removed between the letters, in this case –0.1 em.

  To open up space between the "A" and the "N," set an insertion point. Click the right nudge button until the space looks sufficient. Four times seems about right. The value should read 0.04.

For a more detailed discussion of kerning, see pages 39–41, 407, and 409.

TIP

When you kern type, use the **magnifier icon** to enlarge the view up to 800%. Press Command-Spacebar on a Mac, Ctrl-Spacebar on a PC, to display the magnifier, and then use it to draw a selection box around the text you're working on. Even at this enlarged view, the 72-dpi screen resolution doesn't provide accurate enough information for the small increments used in kerning; you almost always have to make further adjustments after checking the printout.

THE ANATOMY OF A HEADLINE

Almost every headline can benefit from some fine-tuning. Here's a detailed look at the process in this project.

The headline's satisfactory, but a little bland. And the space around the "A" is uneven.

▼ ▼ ▼

When you specify Force Justify, the headline takes on the punch of an old "Wanted" poster. But the gap in the letter pair "WA" is even more pronounced than before.

▼ ▼ ▼

By kerning, you can manually adjust the space in the letter pairs "WA" and "AN" to even out the letterspacing across the word.

▼ ▼ ▼

WANTED
A Good Copywriter

WANTED
A Good Copywriter

WANTED
A Good Copywriter

▲ ▲ ▲

To kern a pair of letters, set an insertion point between the characters and click the nudge buttons in the upper right of the Control Palette. Clicking the left-pointing arrow removes 0.01 em; clicking the right arrow adds 0.01 em. Holding down the Command or Ctrl key while you click is called a power nudge because it increases the increments to 0.1 em. You can also enter values in the kerning field next to the nudge buttons.

The space between the "W" and the "A" was kerned –0.1 (one power nudge). The space between the "A" and the "N" was kerned 0.04, four regular nudges.

Note that the shapes of these letters makes it impossible to have equal space between the tops of both letter pairs or equal space between the bottoms of both letter pairs. The goal is equal overall space between the letters. Imagine that if you could fill each of those spaces with sand, the amount of sand would be the same between each letter pair.

▶ ▶ ▶

WAN

Before kerning

After kerning

WAN

Kerning values for "WA"

Kerning values for "AN"

2. Print.

- Choose Print from the File menu.

- In the Print dialog box, click the Options button, and in the Options dialog box, turn on Printer's Marks. Then click Print.

  If the page size of your document is smaller than the paper in your printer, PageMaker centers the document on the paper when printing. So you need to print crop marks, fine lines at the edge of the image area that mark where the paper should be trimmed to match the page size of your document. Crop marks are just one of several printer's marks that PageMaker prints.

THE CONTROL PALETTE'S PARAGRAPH VIEW . . .

Many paragraph-formatting attributes can be specified in either the Control Palette or the Paragraph Specs dialog box, accessed from the Type menu. Some people rely mostly on the Control Palette, some prefer to go in and out of dialog boxes, and others combine both approaches. And, of course, some use keyboard shortcuts as much as possible. With a few exceptions, the options are essentially the same, and you'll surely develop your own working style.

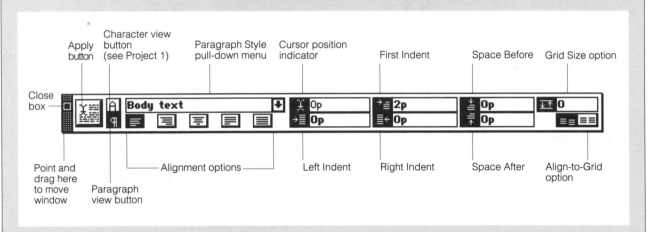

Paragraph Style pull-down menu * When you use style sheets, all the styles that you've defined are listed on this menu. To apply a style to selected paragraphs, choose a style from this list. **Keyboard shortcut:** Type the name of the style in the edit box, and then press Tab, or Return or Enter; the style name appears in the edit box as soon as you've typed enough letters that are unique to any style name. See Project 4 for a full description of creating and using style sheets.

Alignment In the Control Palette, click on any of the five icons. In the Paragraph dialog box, hold down the mouse button on the Alignment box to display a pull-down list of options. **Keyboard shortcuts:** Press Command-Shift (on a Mac) or Ctrl-Shift (on a PC) plus the first letter of the option (L for left, R for right, C for centered, J for justified, and F for force-justified). In the Control Palette, if you use the Tab key to move to the alignment options, you can use the arrow keys to move from one alignment icon to another, and then press the Spacebar to select the active icon.

Cursor position indicator * This tracks the position of the cursor on the page. You can't use it to reposition the cursor, but you can use the information it provides when you set indents. Position the cursor in the text where you want the indent to be, and note the value that's displayed in the position field; then type that number in the indent field, and press Apply, or Return or Enter.

Indents To indent the first line of a paragraph, type the value you want in the First Indent box. (This replaces the typewriter habit of using the Spacebar or Tab key to create indents.) To indent the left or right margin of a text block relative to the column margins, type the values in the respective boxes.

Space Before and **Space After** Another typewriter habit that you need to break is inserting an extra carriage return or two to create space between paragraphs. For precise control over the space between paragraphs and around headlines, type the values you want for Space Before or Space After. Don't worry if you don't know exactly what you want. You can quickly test different spaces.

---

* Indicates an option that is available in the Control Palette but not through the Paragraph Specs dialog box.

† Indicates an option that is available through the Paragraph dialog box but not in the Control Palette.

. . . AND THE PARAGRAPH SPECIFICATIONS DIALOG BOX

Paragraph specifications

Indents:		Paragraph space:	**OK**
Left `0` picas		Before `0` picas	**Cancel**
First `0` picas		After `0` picas	**Rules...**
Right `0` picas			**Spacing...**

Alignment: `Left` Dictionary: `US English`

Options:
- ☐ Keep lines together ☐ Keep with next `0` lines
- ☐ Column break before ☐ Widow control `0` lines
- ☐ Page break before ☐ Orphan control `0` lines
- ☐ Include in table of contents

Grid Size option and **Align-to-Grid option** These options are used to force the baselines of text in adjacent columns to align. When you turn on the Align-to-Grid option, PageMaker adds space after the selected paragraph so that the *next* paragraph aligns with the leading grid. The leading grid is determined by the value you type in the Grid-Size field; it's usually the same as the leading for your body text. (Note: To access these options through the Paragraph Specs dialog box, click the Rules button, and then in the Paragraph Rules dialog box, click the Options button.) For a detailed description of leading grids, see page 383.

Dictionary † If you use foreign-language or specialized dictionaries, use this pull-down menu to select which dictionary you want for hyphenation and spelling checks. To change the default dictionary, choose a dictionary when no publication is open. For more about dictionaries, see page 281.

Options † These control attributes such as the way paragraphs relate to one another. Some word-processing programs have these same options.

Keep Lines Together When you don't want a paragraph (such as one that includes a name and address) to be split at a column or page break, select the paragraph and check this option.

Keep with Next When you want to ensure, for example, that a headline remains with at least a few lines of the text that follows, check this option. You can specify up to 3 lines in the value box.

Column Break Before and **Page Break Before** If you want a paragraph, such as a headline or subhead, to begin at the top of a column or page, check the appropriate option.

Widow Control If you don't want to see one, two, or three lines of a new paragraph fall at the bottom of a column or page, specify the number here. If you specify 2, for example, and a situation arises in which the first two lines of a paragraph would fall at the bottom of a column, PageMaker will push those lines to the top of the next column, leaving the preceding column short.

Orphan Control To avoid having only the last line (or two or three) of a paragraph fall at the top of a column, specify the minimum number here. PageMaker will push additional lines from the preceding column forward to satisfy your minimum requirement.

Include in Table of Contents When you use PageMaker to generate a table of contents, you can specify the headings to be included by selecting them (or the style applied to them) and checking this box.

Note: Sometimes PageMaker has to choose between your specs for various paragraph options (such as "Keeps," Widows, and Orphans) and other rules for how it composes text. Fortunately, you can ask the program to alert you to these instances. Take a minute to bring up the Preferences dialog box (from the File menu). On the left side, under Show Layout Problems, there's an option named Show "Keeps" Violations. If you check that box, PageMaker will highlight any text that violates your settings for any of these paragraph options.

Rules † Click this button to display the Paragraph Rules dialog box when you want to define a rule above or below the selected paragraph. See page 292 for a description of this feature.

Spacing † Click this button to display the Spacing Attributes dialog box, in which you can alter the word spacing and letterspacing in selected paragraphs, change the value for automatic pair kerning, change the leading methods, and change the value for Auto Leading. See pages 34, 39, and 43–44.

For a review of the Control Palette's character view and the Type Specifications dialog box, see page 258.

PAGEMAKER'S STORY EDITOR

The Story Editor is PageMaker's built-in word processor. Although you can type and edit text in the page layout view, when you have extensive copy changes or need to write more than a paragraph or two from scratch, it's much faster to use the Story Editor. You work in one, continuous story window (as in a word-processing program), so you don't have to move from page to page or change page views, and the limited text formatting speeds up the screen redraw.

The Story Editor also provides a number of automated text-editing features, such as a spell checker and Find and Change options, that aren't available in the layout view.

Just as these mechanical features speed up text editing, so does the mind-set you bring to the Story Editor. It frees you from thinking about how the text looks so that you can focus on what it says. Electronic publishing tools have generated so much emphasis on visual options that the content often gets short shrift. If you find yourself falling into that trap, learn to use the Story Editor more.

What the Story Editor Looks Like

Essentially, you have two different views of every publication. In the layout view, you see all the elements of a page or spread—the various text blocks, graphics, rules, and so on—as they will look when printed. In the story view, you see only the text threaded together in any given story. You can see the layout view behind the story window, but there will be a gray box marking the position of the text that's in the active story window.

Text in the story window is displayed in whatever typeface and size is specified in the Preferences dialog box. The default is 12-point Geneva on the Mac, 12-point Times on the PC. You can change that, if you want, through the Preferences command on the File menu. But remember, when you're in the Story Editor, you're concerned with the words themselves, not the typography. You will see type styles (boldface, italic, and so on), and you'll see a suggestion of your paragraph formatting (Space After and indents), which helps you to see relationships between paragraphs. But you won't see the actual line breaks (text wraps to the width of the story window) or custom tab settings.

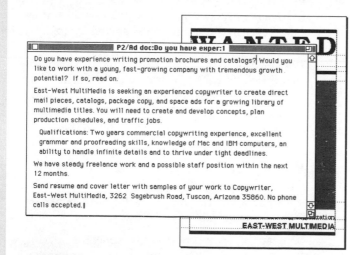

In the Story Editor, text is displayed in the typeface and size specified in the Preferences dialog box and wraps to the width of the window, regardless of text formatting. The layout view of the active story window is grayed out.

The layout view of the same page.

The windows themselves are as flexible as any other windows. To move a story window, drag the title bar. To resize, drag from the lower right corner.

You can have as many story windows open as your computer's memory will allow. The first few words of each story appear as a name in the title bar of that story's window, and the "titles" of all open story windows are displayed on the Window menu, which generally provides the easiest way to move back and forth between different story windows.

When you're working in the Story Editor, some of the menu names and dialog box options are different from those in the layout view.

Moving Between the Layout and Story Views

There are lots of different ways to move between the layout and story views, depending on what you're doing at the time and what you want to do next.

The easiest method to remember is Command-E on the Mac, Ctrl-E on the PC. (Think E as in Editor.) If you're in the layout view, this keyboard command takes you to the story view, and if you're in the story view, the same command returns you to the layout.

The advantage of learning other methods is that they provide control over the cursor position when you move from one view to the other. And that saves time. See item 4, page 278.

What You Can Do in the Story Editor

As you read the following options, remember that a story consists only of text threaded together. A story can span many text blocks across numerous pages, or it can be a single word or even a single character. (For more on threaded text, see pages 336–41.)

1. Edit an existing story.

Editing text in the Story Editor is just like editing in the layout view (only much faster) or in a word processor. You drag over existing text to correct it, set an insertion point to type new text, and so on. You can also use the Place command, including the Inserting Text and Replacing Text options available in layout view. You can format text in the Story Editor, but many of the changes won't be displayed until you return to layout view.

2. Type a new story.

If you're in the layout view and want to open a new, untitled story window, first be sure there is no insertion point in an existing text block. Then choose Edit Story from the Edit menu (or press Command-E on a Mac, Ctrl-E on a PC).

If you're already in the Story Editor and want to open a new, untitled window, choose New Story from the Story menu.

After you've typed the text in the story window, there are several ways to tell PageMaker you want to place this new story in the layout:

- Press Command-E on a Mac, Ctrl-E on a PC. This is the fastest method because PageMaker automatically loads the text icon with the story and returns to the layout view. If you decide you want to work more on the story before placing it, just press Command-E or Ctrl-E again to return to the story window.

- Click on the box in the upper left corner. (On the Mac, it's called the close box; on the PC, it's called the Control menu box, and you have to double-click on it.)

- Or you can choose Close Story from the Story menu (Command-W on a Mac, Ctrl-Shift-E on a PC).

With the last two methods, PageMaker displays a message box that lets you choose Place, Discard, or Cancel.

- If you choose Place, PageMaker closes the story window and displays the loaded text icon, which you click in the layout view just as you would if you were placing a story from a word processor.

- If you choose Cancel, PageMaker returns to the story window.

- If you choose Discard, PageMaker deletes the window for that story. Take the word "discard" very literally because that story will be gone forever. See item 7 on page 279 for how to save a story window to a word processor before discarding it.

Continues on following page

STORY EDITOR (continued)

To return to the layout without placing a new story, click anywhere in the publication window outside the story window. The new story will be listed on the Window menu as Untitled.

3. Import text files (from a word processor or from another PageMaker document) into a story window.

When you're working in the Story Editor, choose Place from the File menu (Command-D on a Mac, Ctrl-D on a PC) to display the Import to Story Editor dialog box. This offers the same options as the Place dialog box in layout view (see page 268), but the text is imported into a story window rather than into the layout.

Why import text into a story window? Two main reasons. You can apply styles much more quickly in the story window than in the layout. And if you know a text file needs to be stripped of extra carriage returns, tabs, and other characters before you can format it, you can use the Story Editor's Find/Change option for the cleanup.

4. Control the position of the cursor when you move between layout and story views.

PageMaker really does have a consistent way of responding to what you do, but sometimes it's hard to figure out what that consistency is.

When you move from layout view to story view

- To open the story window with the text insertion point at the same location as in the layout view: Choose Edit Story from the Edit menu or press Command-E or Ctrl-E.

- To open the story window with the insertion point at the beginning of the text block: With the pointer tool, triple-click on the text block.

When you move from story view to layout view

- To return to the layout view at the cursor position currently active in the story window: Choose Edit Layout from the Edit menu (Command-E or Ctrl-E). The story window remains open, behind the layout.

- To close a story window and return to your *previous* position in the layout: Press Command-W on a Mac, Ctrl-Shift-E on a PC. Or choose Close Story from the Story menu. Mac

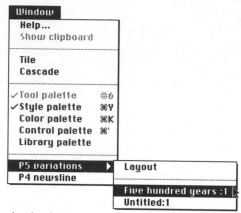

Moving between the layout view and various open story windows: *The bottom of the Window menu lists all open PageMaker files—in this case, P5 and P4. An arrow to the right of the filename indicates a pull-down list of open story windows for that file. Story windows are identified by the first 18 characters of the text. Stories that originated in the Story Editor and have not yet been placed in the layout are designated Untitled:1, Untitled:2, and so on. For tips on organizing multiple windows on the screen, see page 365.*

users can also click on the close box, and PC users can double-click on the Control menu box. (Both boxes are in the upper left corner of the window.)

- To return to your previous position in the layout without closing the active story window: Click in the layout window behind the story window. Or choose Layout from the submenu at the bottom of the Window menu. The story window will then be behind the layout window. To display it, choose the story name from the publication submenu at the bottom of the Window menu.

5. Apply styles.

We'll look at defining and applying styles in Project 4. (See especially page 318.) For now, be aware that you can apply styles in the Story Editor, and that the ability to do so is a vastly underused feature that can save you a lot of time.

You don't see the style formatting in the story window; that's part of why you can apply the styles so quickly. But you can see style names in a column to the left of the text if you turn on the Display Style Names option on the Story menu.

6. Import inline graphics.

This works much the same as it does when you place an inline graphic in the layout: Set an insertion point in the story window where the graphic is to be inserted, and choose Place. But in the story view, PageMaker displays a graphics marker (■). You can't resize or crop the graphic until you return to layout view. For more about inline graphics, see pages 374–377.

7. Export selected text to a word-processing file.

Say you're working in the Story Editor and are about to delete a section of text that you want to use elsewhere. Before you make the cut, select that text, and choose Export from the File menu to bring up a directory where you can name and file the selection on your disk, just as you would if you were saving. (See page 335 for more information about exporting text from PageMaker to a word processor.)

8. View "invisible" characters.

Choose Display ¶ from the Options menu to display "invisible" characters such as paragraph returns, tabs, and word spaces. If you're constantly pasting text on the wrong side of a word space, try editing with this feature turned on.

Displaying hidden characters can also help you diagnose problems when text won't do what you tell it to do. For example, you may find that the reason your tabbed text doesn't align is that in one place you've inserted two tab characters instead of one. Likewise, an extra carriage return can throw off the space between paragraphs. Seeing the invisible characters reveals how two lines or paragraphs that you think are similarly formatted are, in fact, not.

9. Create index entries.

You can create index entries in the Story Editor just as you do in the layout view. When you complete an index entry, PageMaker places an index marker (◊) before the entry, and that marker is visible in the story view.

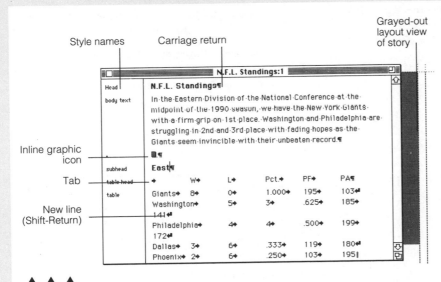

Style names   Carriage return   Grayed-out layout view of story

Head
body text
Inline graphic icon
subhead
Tab   table head
table

N.F.L. Standings:1

N.F.L. Standings¶
In the·Eastern·Division·of·the·National·Conference·at·the· midpoint·of·the·1990·season,·we·have·the·New·York·Giants· with·a·firm·grip·on·1st·place.·Washington·and·Philadelphia·are· struggling·in·2nd·and·3rd·place·with·fading·hopes·as·the· Giants·seem·invincible·with·their·unbeaten·record.¶

■.¶
East¶

◆	W◆	L◆	Pct.◆	PF◆	PA¶
Giants◆	8◆	0◆	1.000◆	195◆	103◄┘
Washington◆	5◆	3◆	.625◆	185◆	
141◄┘					
Philadelphia◆	4◆	4◆	.500◆	199◆	
172◄┘					
Dallas◆	3◆	6◆	.333◆	119◆	180◄┘
Phoenix◆	2◆	6◆	.250◆	103◆	195

New line (Shift-Return)

▲ ▲ ▲
A story window with the Display ¶ command turned on. When you can't figure out why text won't do what you tell it to do, this view often helps you diagnose the problem.

N.F.L. STANDINGS
In the Eastern Division of the National Conference at the midpoint of the 1990 season, we have the New York Giants with a firm grip on 1st place. Washington and Philadelphia are struggling in 2nd and 3rd place with fading hopes as the Giants seem invincible with their unbeaten record.

EAST

	W	L	Pct.	PF	PA
Giants	8	0	1.000	195	103
Washington	5	3	.625	185	141
Philadelphia	4	4	.500	199	172
Dallas	3	6	.333	119	180
Phoenix	2	6	.250	103	195

▲ ▲ ▲
The layout view of the same story. The only change made in the layout after closing the story window was resizing the football, an inline graphic.

Turn the page for more Story Editor features.

THE SPELL CHECKER

The spell checker is available only in the story view. From any active story window, choose Spelling from the Utilities menu (Command-L on a Mac, Ctrl-L on a PC). PageMaker displays the Spelling dialog box, which is actually a movable window. The Spelling window gives you these choices:

Options Both of these options are turned on by default. They slow down the spell check, but it's generally worthwhile.

> *Alternate Spellings* Turned on by default so that PageMaker provides suggested spellings of words it doesn't recognize.

> *Show Duplicates* Turned on by default so that PageMaker questions duplicate words.

Search Document Click the appropriate button to specify whether you want to check the spelling in the Current Publication (that is, the active publication) or in All Publications (when you have more than one PageMaker document open).

Search Story Click the appropriate button to specify whether you want to check spelling in the Selected Text, the Current Story, or All Stories. This last option is a blessing in documents that have multiple stories (such as this book, in which every tip and caption is an individual story) because it enables you to check the spelling throughout the publication without having to open each story individually.

Using the Spell Checker

When you click the Start button, PageMaker scans the text and stops on any word that it can't find in its dictionary or in the customized user dictionary. PageMaker also checks for duplicate words (if that option is turned on) and for capitalization errors, such as a lowercase letter that follows a period.

When PageMaker stops on a possible error, the unknown word is highlighted in the story window visible behind the Spelling dialog box, enabling you to see the word in context. You can move the Spelling window if it obstructs the highlighted words.

To correct a misspelling You can correct the spelling in the Change To box (the incorrect spelling is displayed there), and then click Replace. PageMaker makes the change and then continues checking the

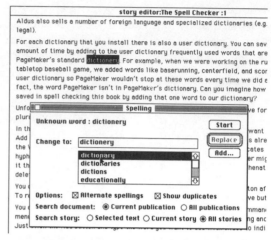

▲ ▲ ▲

When PageMaker finds an unknown word, that word is highlighted in the story window behind the Spelling dialog box. If the word is misspelled, you can edit the spelling in the Change To box or scroll the list of suggestions and double-click on the correct spelling.

text. Or you can scroll the list of suggested replacements and double-click on the correct spelling if it appears; again, PageMaker makes the replacement and continues checking the text.

Sometimes you have to go back to the story window to make a correction. Inadvertent spaces in the text require this. If you typed "graduates t his year," for example, PageMaker will stop at the "t." To make the correction, click in the story window, delete the space between "t" and "his," and then click in the Spelling window and press Start to continue the check.

To bypass a word PageMaker doesn't recognize If the unknown word is correct—which is often the case with proper names, abbreviations and codes, and words that are correct but are not included in Page-Maker's dictionary—click Ignore, and PageMaker will continue scanning the text.

After you tell PageMaker to ignore a word it doesn't recognize, it remembers that spelling and will ignore it for the remainder of the current spell check. On subsequent spell checks of the same text file, however, it will not recognize the word.

Duplicate words When PageMaker finds a duplicate word, the second instance of the word is highlighted in the story window behind the Spelling window. The Change To box is empty. To delete that second instance of the word, click Replace. In effect, you're replacing a word with the absence of a word (indicated by the empty Change To text box).

Capitalization errors When PageMaker finds a lower-case letter after a period, it capitalizes the letter in the alternate spelling list under the Change To box. To request a correction, double-click on that capital letter. To continue the search without making a change, click Ignore, or press Return or Enter.

PageMaker's Dictionaries

PageMaker's English dictionary is from Merriam-Webster and includes about 80,000 words. Aldus also sells a number of foreign-language and specialized dictionaries (such as medical and legal).

For each dictionary that you install there is also a user dictionary. You can save a tremendous amount of time by adding to the user dictionary frequently used words that aren't in PageMaker's standard dictionary. For example, the word "PageMaker" isn't in PageMaker's dictionary. Can you imagine how much time we saved in spell checking this book by adding that one word to our dictionary?

To add a word to the user dictionary In the Spelling window, when PageMaker flags an unknown word that you want to add, click the Add button, which brings up another dialog box where the unknown word is already entered in the Word text box. You can continue adding words, one after another, by clicking the Add button after each entry. To remove a word from the dictionary, type that word and click the Remove button.

Unfortunately, the spell checker isn't smart enough to recognize derivative forms (such as the plural and past tense) of words that you add. You must add each derivative word separately.

PageMaker also comes with a Dictionary Editor, through which you can import and export word lists to and from your user dictionary and create new dictionaries. You should close PageMaker before opening this utility, which is buried in a nest of

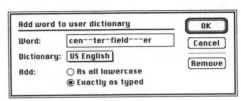

▲ ▲ ▲

To add a word to the user dictionary, click the Add button in either the Spelling dialog box (story view) or the Hyphenation dialog box (layout view). To indicate the desired hyphenation, type a tilde (~). One tilde indicates the most desired hyphenation point, three tildes the least desired.

folders. On the Mac, open the following folders to locate it: System/Aldus/Utilities. After the Dictionary Editor is open, from the File menu you can open your user dictionary (named Aldeng.udc) by this route: System/Aldus/Proximity/USEnglsh.

On the PC, first open the File Manager, and from there, open the following directories: Aldus\usenglsh\utility. The filename is de.exe. (not deapp.exe). After the Dictionary Editor is open, from the File menu you can open your user dictionary (named aldusn.udc) by this path: Aldus/usenglsh.

For more on user dictionaries, see the online help file in the same folder as the Dictionary Editor. On the Mac, it's named DictED and you can open it from within PageMaker. On the PC, it's named dicted.wri, and you open it through the File Manager.

Note: If you use foreign-language or specialized dictionaries, be aware that dictionaries are paragraph-specific, which means that there's an option in the Paragraph dialog box that lets you specify which dictionary you want PageMaker to use when checking any particular paragraph. This also means that you can specify a dictionary as part of a style definition, which can automate switching between different dictionaries.

US English is the default dictionary. To change the default for the current publication, bring up the Paragraph dialog box (Command-M or Ctrl-M), and choose another dictionary from the Dictionary submenu. To change the application default, follow that same procedure when no publication is open.

Turn the page for more Story Editor features.

THE FIND/CHANGE DIALOG BOX

In the Story Editor, you can use the Find and Change commands on the Utilities menu to search for text, text formats (such as font or style), or special characters (such as tabs and paragraph returns). You have the same search options as in the Spelling dialog box (searching the currently active publication or all open publications; searching selected text, all text in the current story, or all stories in the publication).

As you might expect, the Find and Change commands are much the same, except that the Find command simply finds, whereas the Change command finds and changes. But they function similarly, and both are best described by example.

To use these powerful word-processing features, you must have a story window active.

You need to make a correction in the Abominable Snowman story, and you don't know which page of the 60-page file it begins on. Choose Find from the Utilities menu (Command-8 on a Mac, Ctrl-8 on a PC). In the Find What dialog box, type *abominable snowman*. Turn on the Search All Stories option and also the Whole Word option (which will prevent PageMaker from stopping at the words "snow," "man," or "snowman" without the modifier "abominable"). PageMaker will find any reference to "abominable snowman" in the file. If the first reference it finds is, for example, in the introduction rather than in the story you need to edit, click on Find Next to continue the search.

You need to replace a graphic, and you don't remember what page it's on. You can't search for graphics, but if the graphic has a caption and you remember a key word from the caption, you can search for that.

Important: When PageMaker displays the story window with the reference you're looking for, you want to return to the layout page at that same cursor position. To do this, choose Edit Layout from the Edit menu, or press Command-E or Ctrl-E.

You need to search for a word that you aren't sure how to spell. There are two different techniques to choose from, depending on how close you can get to the correct spelling.

Say you need to find a reference to someone named Litwin, but you're not sure if there are one or two "t"s in the name. In the Find What text box, type *Lit*.

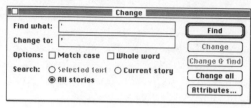

You can search for double word spaces, incorrect apostrophes and quote marks, and other typographic elements, as well as for text.

Turn off the Whole Word option so that PageMaker will look for any instance of the characters "lit." Turn on the Match Case option so that PageMaker will stop only when the "L" is capitalized. You may get some misses (PageMaker will stop at Little, Litchfield, and so on), but in a long file the chances are pretty good that PageMaker will still find Litwin, however it is spelled, faster than you will.

Say you're not sure whether the name is spelled Litwin or Litwyn. Type caret-question mark (^-?) as a wildcard in place of the uncertain letter. (To create the caret character, ^, press Shift-6). So if you type *Litw^?n* in the Find What text box, PageMaker will find either spelling.

You need to change the spelling of "theatre" to "theater" throughout the document. Choose Change from the Edit menu to bring up the Change dialog box. In the Find What text box, type *theatre*. In the Change To text box, type *theater*. Click Change All, and PageMaker will scan the specified range of text (Selected Text, Current Story, or All Stories) and make the changes.

You want to check for and correct inch marks (" ") that should be typeset quotation marks (" "). You can't use the Change All technique as in the previous example because in some cases, you need to change to an open quote while in others, you need to change to a close quote. Here's how to do it:

- Bring up the Change dialog box, and in the Find What text box, type the inch mark (") that you habitually insert for quote marks.

- In the Change To text box, press Option-[on a Mac, ^{ on a PC, to get a typographic open quote mark ("). Click Find.

- When PageMaker stops on the first open quote, click Change and Find. PageMaker makes the correction and finds the next inch mark. This will probably be at the close of the quotation, but you don't want to change that one yet (because the close-quote mark is a different character), so click Find Next. This should take you to the next open quote, where you click Change and Find. Repeat this process until you've changed all the open quotes.

- Now you need to change all the remaining inch marks to close-quote marks. Assuming there aren't any real inch marks in the publication, this time you can use the Change All approach. Leave the inch mark in the Find What text box. In the Change To text box, type a close quote (") by pressing Option-Shift-[on a Mac, ^} on a PC. Choose Change All.

Tedious, but it's a lot easier than trying to catch the wrong marks by eye.

You have a text file from someone who inserted extra carriage returns and tabs for spacing. You can search for those and delete them. The key combination you type to search for special characters is often different from the key combination you type to insert that same character in the text.

For example, say you have a file from someone who created space between paragraphs by pressing Return twice. You need to replace each instance of a double Return with a single Return. Here's how:

- Bring up the Change dialog box. In the Find What text box, type ^p ^p. Note: ^p is the code for a Return or an Enter character. You want PageMaker to find all instances of two such characters in a row, so you type the code twice.

- In the Change To dialog box, type ^p.

- You can click Change All, or, to make the corrections one at a time, click Change and Find so that you see each instance (highlighted in the active story window behind the Change window) before making the change. We usually do the first few instances one at a time, which gives us time to think about whether there are some instances that we might not want to change.

Special Characters

When you need to find or change special characters or insert them in the Index Formatting dialog box, you must often type a special key combination, which is different from the key combination you type when you want to insert that same special character in text.

For example, when you want to search for a tab character, you don't set an insertion point in the Find What text box and press the Tab key; you type the key combination ^t (no space, no hyphen, unless specifically indicated).

Note, on the other hand, that in the following list of special characters, when a key combination includes a hyphen, the same combination is used to type that character in text and in dialog boxes.

	Mac	PC
bullet	Opt-8	^8
caret	^^	^^
computer-inserted hyphen	^c	^5
copyright symbol	Opt-g	^2
discretionary hyphen	^-	^-
em dash	^_	^_
em space	^m	^m
en dash	^=	^=
en space	^>	^>
index entry marker	^;	^;
inline graphic marker	^g	^g
new line (Shift-Return)	^n	^n
nonbreaking hyphen	^~	^~
nonbreaking slash	^/	^/
nonbreaking space	^s	^s
page-number marker	^# or ^3	^3
paragraph return	^p	^p
paragraph symbol (¶)	Opt-7	^7
registration symbol (®)	Opt-r	^r
section symbol (§)	Opt-6	^6
tab	^t	^t
thin space	^<	^<
trademark symbol (™)	Opt-2	Alt-0153
typographic open quote	Opt-[	^{
typographic close quote	Opt-Sh-[	^}
typog. single open quote	Opt-]	^[
typog. single close quote	Opt-Sh-]	^]
wildcard	^?	^?

Continues on following page

THE FIND/CHANGE DIALOG BOX *(continued)*

If someone has inserted varying numbers of carriage returns to create space between sections, you may have to go through this process a few times. For example, if there are three returns in a row, PageMaker will replace one pair with one return, which still leaves two in a row.

Searching by Attributes

This feature seems pretty esoteric at first, but the longer we work with the Story Editor, the more useful we find this option. You can search for text that's tagged with any of the paragraph styles defined in your style sheet, as well as for text that has any specified font, size, or type style (bold, italic, and so on, including all caps, small caps, subscript, and superscript).

Here are some examples.

You used italic for emphasis, and you decided to change it to boldface. In the Change dialog box, be sure the Find and Change text boxes are empty, because you want to search only for attributes. Click the Attributes button. The Attributes dialog box has a Find section and a Change section. For the Type Style to find, specify Italic ; for the Type Style to change to, specify Bold. Click OK, and in the Change window, click Find.

When PageMaker finds the first instance of italic text, click Change and Find if you do indeed want to make the change. If you don't want to make a change (if, for example, the italicized word is a book title or a foreign-language word rather than a word or phrase styled for emphasis), click Find Next. Continue until PageMaker tells you that the search is complete.

You need to insert a Zapf Dingbat character at the beginning of every caption. When you bring up the Find window, drag it by the title bar so that it hangs beyond the active story window. This makes it easier to move back and forth between story windows and the Find window. Also, be sure the Find What text box is empty and that you've selected Search All Stories.

Click the Attributes button, and in the Find Attributes dialog box, scroll the Paragraph Style pull-down menu to select the *caption* style. Click

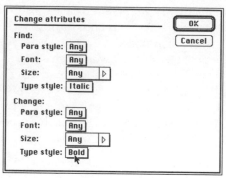

You can search text for a single type attribute, a combination of attributes, or a combination of text and type attributes.

OK (or press Return or Enter), and in the Find window, click Find (or press Return or Enter). When PageMaker finds the first caption, click in the story window, and add the Dingbat. Then click in the Find window, and press Find Next. Continue until PageMaker tells you that the search is complete.

Your font checker lists fonts you didn't think were in the document, and you need to find and change them. When you send a file to a service bureau for high-resolution output, you have to list all the fonts included in the publication. Failure to list one of the fonts can result in an incorrectly printed file.

To avoid this problem, you can use the Display Pub Info Addition or a font-checking utility that scans the file for fonts. (See page 233.) Sometimes this check reveals fonts that shouldn't be in the document, often left over from some formatting that you abandoned. Sometimes the error is even an invisible character, such as a word or paragraph space, that didn't get deleted when you cut some other text that the character belonged to. Not to worry. You can use the Find option to search your file by attribute.

Turn on the All Stories option so that PageMaker will scan all the text in the document (even text that may be on the pasteboard). Leave the Find What text box empty. Select the Attributes option, and in the Attributes dialog box, specify the font you want to find. Click OK to return to the Find window, and then click Find. When PageMaker finds the font, you can see whether it's an invisible character that can be deleted. If it is, click in the story window, make the deletion, and then return to the Change box and click Find Next to continue checking.

If the incorrectly formatted text is a visible character, you don't know what type formatting you do want until you find the text and see the adjacent formatting. Again, you'll have to move from the Find window (to find what you've specified), to the story window (to check the formatting of the adjacent text and make the appropriate change), and then back to the Find window to continue the search. If it sounds complicated, it is, a little. You just have to put your mind in a straitjacket while you methodically go through the process.

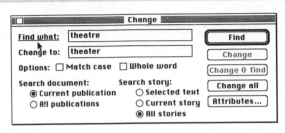

▲ ▲ ▲

If Find What or Change To is underlined, *it means you have specified one or more text attributes in the Attributes dialog box. Your search will be restricted both to the words you type and to the attributes specified. To reset all Attribute options to Any, hold down the Option key (on a Mac) or the Alt key (on a PC) while you click Attributes.*

More Story Editor Tips

Positioning windows If you have a small screen, try changing the size of the story window and repositioning the windows so that the story and the utility window (Spelling, Find, or Change) are adjacent to one another. Even on a larger screen, it's a good idea to move the utility window so that it hangs beyond the story window. That way, you can move between the two windows simply by clicking on one or the other.

When you're running a spell check on a long document, you can save time and wrist movement if you understand that pressing Return or Enter is the same as clicking the active button, only faster. Here's what happens when you

Choose a spelling from the suggestion list: Double-click on your choice; PageMaker makes the change and continues checking.

Correct the spelling in the Change To box: Replace becomes the active button. Press Return or Enter; PageMaker makes the change and continues checking.

Accept the word as spelled: Until you take some action in the spelling window, Ignore is the active button. Press Return or Enter to continue the check without making a change.

Open Stories is an Aldus Addition that will open up to 15 story windows on the Mac and up to 10 on the PC. Note: You must be in the layout view to choose this command.

To close all open Story Editor windows in a publication: Hold down the Option key on a Mac or the

Shift key on a PC, and choose Close All Stories from the Story menu.

To open the **Spelling dialog box:** Press Command-L on a Mac, Ctrl-L on a PC.

To open the **Change dialog box:** Press Command-9 on a Mac, Ctrl-9 on a PC.

▲ ▲ ▲

To change the defaults for the Story Editor *In the Preferences dialog box, choose Other. In the Other Preferences dialog box, you specify the font and size displayed in the Story Editor, and you turn the Display Style Names and the Display ¶ options on and off. To change defaults for all new publications, specify Preferences when no publication is open.*

PROJECT 3

A QUICK INVITATION USING PARAGRAPH RULES AND PAGEMAKER GRAPHICS

PAGEMAKER TECHNIQUES

▶ Use the Control Palette to track the pointer's movement and to size and position graphics

▶ Change the reference point in the Control Palette Proxy

▶ Define type margins by drawing a bounding box

▶ Create paragraph rules

▶ Use the Multiple Paste option

▶ Mask graphics with "invisible" boxes

▶ Use the Control Palette to align objects mathematically

▶ Use the nudge buttons

▶ Select multiple objects

▶ Use PageMaker's "power-paste" feature

*T*his is a fun project. It has a "cheap tricks" component—creating a simple graphic right within PageMaker. And it introduces some advanced options that are relatively easy to use but that many people tend to overlook.

One such feature is the ability to specify rules above or below a paragraph. Automating a relatively simple task like this saves time and also ensures that, in the case of repeated rules such as the ones used here, you'll have consistent space between each rule and the text that follows. And you don't even have to use the ruler.

In this project, we also introduce the Control Palette's object view, which enables you to track and manipulate objects with mathematical precision. There are many documents that don't require this kind of precision, and many people will continue to rely on the drag-it-with-the-pointer approach that made PageMaker so popular to begin with. But it's great to have the choice between the on-the-fly technique and the numeric options in the Control Palette. And after you become familiar with using the Control Palette to manipulate objects, you'll find that it saves you time even when you don't need mathematical precision.

The invitation measures 5.5 by 4.25 inches, and you can print four cards on a single 8.5- by 11-inch sheet (a technique used in printing business cards, as well). See the instructions for "How to Print Four Up," at the end of this project. Of course, you could also print one card per sheet, with crop marks, but you'd waste a lot of paper.

If you're printing the invitations yourself, you'll want to a get a 20-pound card stock with matching envelopes. The heavier stock will have to be hand-fed. To minimize paper jams, press against the leading edge of the paper (the side that enters the printer first) with a burnisher or the curved side of a plastic pen. Even when you do this, allow for about 15% paper waste due to jams and poor alignment.

The invitation is created in the upper left quadrant of an 8.5- by 11-inch sheet and then copied and pasted three times to **print four up** on a single page.

Avant Garde is a good contemporary face for an informal invitation, and its O's, which are perfect circles, echo the sunset theme. The headline is 12/36, all caps. The body type is 10/36.

The horizontal rules can be generated using PageMaker's Paragraph Rules option.

The sunset motif is created using PageMaker's circle tool with a white rectangle masking the lower part of each circle. See step 8, "Create the Sunset."

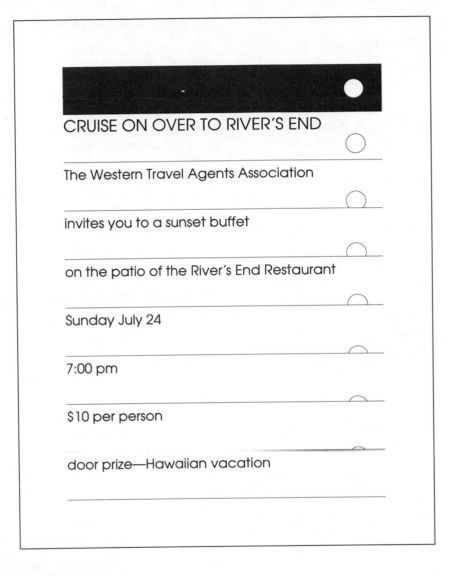

CRUISE ON OVER TO RIVER'S END

The Western Travel Agents Association

invites you to a sunset buffet

on the patio of the River's End Restaurant

Sunday July 24

7:00 pm

$10 per person

door prize—Hawaiian vacation

BLUEPRINT FOR THE INVITATION

1. Open a 1-page document with the following page setup:

- Page Dimensions: 8.5 by 11 inches or 51 by 66 picas

- Orientation: Tall

- Margins: 0 all around

- Compose to Printer: From the pull-down menu, select the name of the target printer that will be used for the final camera-ready pages. This may be different from the printer used to proof pages (which you select in the Print dialog box). See page 229.

- Target Printer Resolution: Type, or select from the pull-down menu, the number of dots per inch printed by the target printer.

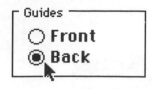

▲ ▲ ▲

We like our ruler guides to be in the back layer, but PageMaker puts them in front by default. **To change the default** *so that the guides will be in the back for every new publication you create, choose Preferences when no publication is open, and choose Back for the Guides option.*

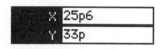

▲ ▲ ▲

Position field *As you drag in ruler guides or position objects on the page, the Control Palette numerically tracks the position of the pointer, much as the dotted lines on the ruler do. The* x *value corresponds to the position on the horizontal ruler, and the* y *value corresponds to the position on the vertical ruler. By watching the values for the x- and y-coordinates as you drag, you can position and size objects with mathematical precision.*

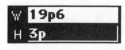

▲ ▲ ▲

Size field *To specify the height or width of a selected graphic, such as the banner at the top of this invitation, select the object, double-click on the value you want to specify, and then type the dimension you want.*

2. Specify Preferences (on the File menu).

- Specify picas for both the Measurement System and the Vertical Ruler.

- Set Guides to the back.

  PageMaker's publication window consists of overlapping layers of text, graphics, and nonprinting guides. Positioning the ruler guides in back enables you to select an item positioned on top of a guide and also prevents you from inadvertently moving a guide when you move other elements on the page. In later projects, we won't specify the position of the guides. Be aware that you have the option to move them from back to front, and vice versa, through the Preferences dialog box.

  For more information on PageMaker's layers, see page 218.

3. Divide the page into four quadrants.

- Display the Control Palette from the Window menu (or press Command-apostrophe on a Mac, Ctrl-apostrophe on a PC).

- Turn on Snap to Rulers (on the Guides and Rulers submenu under Layout). Or press Command-[on a Mac, Ctrl-Shift-Y on a PC.

- Bring in ruler guides to bisect the page horizontally (at 33p) and vertically (at 25p6), creating a space for four vertical cards of equal size. You'll work in the upper left quadrant of the page to create the master card.

4. Define the image area.

- Bring in horizontal ruler guides at 3p and 30p to define the top and bottom margins of the master card.

- Bring in vertical guides at 3p and 22p6 to define the side margins of the master card.

5. Create the banner.

- Check to be sure Snap to Guides is turned on. (It's on the Guides and Rulers submenu under Layout.)

- With the rectangle tool, draw a 3p-deep box beginning at the top margin and extending from the vertical guides that define the side margins. Note, on the PC, that as you drag the crossbar to draw the box, the *H*(eight) value changes in the Control Palette. Don't worry if you stop a little long or short of 3p for that value. With the rectangle selected, double-click on the *H* value, type 3, and then click Apply, or press Return or Enter. PageMaker will resize the box so that it is exactly 3 picas deep.

- With the rectangle you just drew still selected, choose Solid from the Fill submenu (under Element).

THE CONTROL PALETTE'S OBJECT VIEW

When you use any tool other than the text tool, the Control Palette displays numerical options for tracking the cursor and manipulating objects. Aldus calls this the layout view, but we think it's more descriptive to call it the object view.

In this project, you'll work with the size and position options. For a list of hands-on-the-Control-Palette exercises, see page 208.

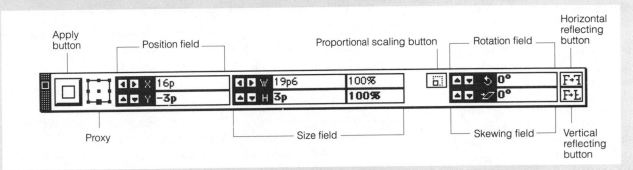

The first thing to remember is that when you want to manipulate an object using the numerical options in the Control Palette, you must first select the object.

The Proxy represents the selected object. The handles on the Proxy correspond to the corners, edges, and center of that selected object. The highlighted handle is the **reference point.** You can change the reference point by clicking on any handle. You can also use the arrows on the keyboard to move around the Proxy when it is active.

The *x*- and *y*-coordinates in the **position field** correspond to the reference point for whatever object is selected (see the screen details, at right).

The *x* and *y* values are always relative to the zero point. If you move the zero point, the position coordinates change. Positive values indicate a position to the right or below the zero point, negative values a position to the left or above the zero point.

In the **size field,** the *W* value corresponds to the width and the *H* value corresponds to the height of the selected object or to the object you are drawing when you use one of PageMaker's drawing tools.

When you change the size or position of an object using the Control Palette, the reference point determines how PageMaker applies the changes. This is the trickiest part of working with the Control Palette, and we'll come back to it many times in this and later projects.

Changing the Reference Point

You can change the reference point by clicking on any handle in the Proxy. It's real important to get familiar with reading the reference point, so take time to follow these steps using the mouse and keyboard.

1. Select the banner.

2. Click once in the upper left corner of the Proxy to set the reference point. The x- and y-coordinates correspond to the upper left corner of the banner.

3. Now click once in the lower left corner of the Proxy. The x- and y-coordinates change to correspond to the lower left corner of the banner.

4. Continue clicking on each reference point and watch the x- and y-coordinates change.

Note: The center reference point gives you the coordinates of the center point of the selected object.

For a complete discussion of the object view, see pages 203–8.

▲ ▲ ▲

When you haven't defined text columns or when you want to override columns that you have defined, you can draw what's called a **bounding box** *to define the left and right margins of text you're about to type. With the text tool, set an insertion point where you want the left margin to be, and drag diagonally to where you want the right margin to be. The depth isn't important. You'll see a rectangle as you drag; it disappears when you release the mouse, but PageMaker will remember its boundaries while you type the text (unless you click somewhere else before typing).*

6. Add the text.

- With the text tool, draw a bounding box to define the left and right margins of the text. To do this, position the text tool on the 3p vertical guide, about a pica below the black banner. Hold down the mouse button, and drag the I-beam diagonally to the vertical guide at 22p6. (The depth isn't important.)

- In the Control Palette, specify 10/36 Avant Garde.

  To avoid stumbling over something as seemingly straightforward as specifying type attributes, remember these two rules:

  If you change attributes in the Control Palette by typing a name or number, you must click Apply, or press Return or Enter, for your changes to take effect.

  If you set a new text insertion point after specifying the type attributes, PageMaker reverts to the default type specs instead of the ones you specified. The moral: Set your insertion point, specify the type attributes, and begin typing before clicking elsewhere on the page. (Or type your text, select it, and then specify the type attributes.)

- Type the headline and body text in 10/36 Avant Garde. Don't worry about the vertical position of the text block just yet.

  Remember, if the Control Palette is in your way, just move it. You don't have to switch from the text tool to the pointer to do this. As soon as you move the text tool within the left edge of the Control Palette, the on-screen icon turns into the pointer. Just point there and drag the Palette to a new position on the screen.

- With the text tool, select the first line, which will be the headline. Specify 12/36 Avant Garde, All Caps.

- Bring in a horizontal ruler guide at 7p1 to align the baseline for the headline.

  Did the *y* value in the Control Palette move from 7 to 7p3 without stopping at 7p1? See the Tip at left.

- Turn off Snap to Rulers and Snap to Guides.

  With proportional leading (PageMaker's default method for assigning space between lines of type), one third of the leading hangs below the baseline. So when you want to position text relative to the baseline, the Snap To commands are actually a hindrance because they pull the text block (as defined by the top or bottom windowshade handle) toward a guide or ruler mark. (See pages 34 and 265 for more on different leading methods.)

- With the pointer tool, select the text, hold down the Shift key, and drag the text block vertically so that the baseline of the headline is on the 7p1 ruler guide, just below the black banner.

  Note: When you want to move a text block (or any other object) in one direction only, hold down the Shift key before you drag. When you begin to drag, the four-headed arrow turns into a double-headed arrow, pointing either vertically or horizontally, depending

TIP

With Snap to Rulers on, the Control Palette displays only values for tick marks visible on the rulers in the page view you are using. To **display finer ruler increments,** you can work at a larger page view. Or if you turn off Snap to Rulers, the Control Palette will track in 1-point increments, even if those increments are finer than the tick marks visible on the rulers. It's very difficult to remember nuances such as these at first, but once mastered, they're extremely powerful.

on the direction in which you are dragging. (If you move the text block too quickly, before the arrows appear, a box that defines the text block, rather than the text itself, will move and you won't be able to see the baseline to position it.)

7. Add the horizontal rules.

- With the text tool, select all the text except the headline.

- Choose Paragraph from the Type menu to bring up the Paragraph Specifications dialog box.

This is one of PageMaker's multilevel dialog boxes. You can format many of the most frequently used options—indents and Space Before and Space After—using the Control Palette, as you did in Project 2. Other options are available only in this dialog box.

The Rules and Spacing buttons bring up additional boxes, and there are further levels beyond that. Don't be intimidated if you find yourself three levels deep in dialog boxes; it's just PageMaker's way of organizing options so that you don't have to sort through too many possibilities at once.

Here we'll work with the Rules option. The following steps take you quickly through the rule specifications for the invitation. For a closer look at the hows and whys of this feature, see the sidebars on the next two pages.

- Select Rules. This brings up the Paragraph Rules dialog box.

- Click on Rule Above Paragraph.

For Line Style, scroll the pull-down menu to select Hairline. (See the caption at left for instructions.) Or, if you work on a PC, you can type the name or value of the rule in the Line Style text box.

For Line Width, click on Width of Column.

Leave all the other default settings.

- Click the Options button to bring up the Paragraph Rules Options dialog box. The values you specify here determine where Page-Maker positions the rule relative to the baseline of the first line of text (for a Top rule, or a Rule Above the paragraph) or the last line of text (for a Bottom rule, or a Rule Below the paragraph).

For the Top rule, type *1p1* in the value box for the measurement above the baseline.

- Hold down the Option key on a Mac, the Shift key on a PC, and then click OK.

You'll come to love this Option-OK, Shift-OK combination. It closes all the levels of nested dialog boxes, so you don't have to okay each one separately. You can use the same technique to cancel too.

- To add a rule below the last line of text, set an insertion point after the word "vacation," press Return to create a new paragraph, and then press Tab or Spacebar to create a blank character in the paragraph. At that point, you'll see the rule.

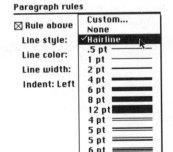

▲ ▲ ▲

*To display the **Line Style pull-down menu** in the Paragraph Rules dialog box: On a Mac, position the pointer over the Line Style box and hold down the mouse button; on a PC, position the pointer over the arrow next to the Line Style box and hold down the mouse button. If you select Custom, PageMaker displays a dialog box where you can specify any line weight from 0 to 800 points in tenth-of-a-point increments.*

PARAGRAPH RULES

To specify a rule before or after a paragraph, select the Rules button in the Paragraph Specs dialog box. Unlike rules created with PageMaker's line tools, which have a fixed position on the page, paragraph rules are part of the formatting for the paragraph, and they move with the paragraph when changes cause the text to reflow. Keep in mind:

- A paragraph is any text between two carriage returns. The single lines in this project and headlines, also, can be created as paragraphs.

- You can't select a paragraph rule with the pointer tool. Paragraph rules are created and altered as text, through the Paragraph command on the Type menu, not as graphics, through the Element menu.

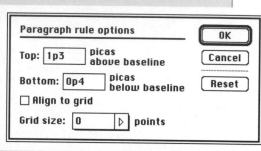

Line Style and **Line Color** These submenus make available the line options found on the Element menu and the colors defined for your publication.

Line Width You can specify Width of Text or Width of Column, but when you add these options to the Indent options, you have a lot of flexibility in rule width. See the examples on the facing page. You can also stretch (or shrink) a Column Width rule by dragging on the selection handles of the text block.

Options Select the Options button to bring up the Paragraph Rule Options dialog box. Here you specify the vertical position of paragraph rules relative to the text, and this gets a little tricky.

The **vertical position** for Rules Above (called Top in the Paragraph Rule Options dialog box) is measured up from the baseline of the first line in the paragraph. The position for Rules Below (called Bottom) is measured down from the baseline of the last line of the paragraph.

We generally stay away from the default position setting of Auto. It can cause Rules Above to print over the tops of capital letters and ascenders, and Rules Below to print over the bottoms of descenders. Watch out for these problems when checking your own settings for rule positions.

The space between the rule and the text is also affected by the line weight you specify. To see how this works: Create a line with a Paragraph Rule Above and gradually increase the weight of the rule, leaving its position value the same. The rule grows down toward the text, as you can see in the examples above. Paragraph Rules Below grow up toward the text.

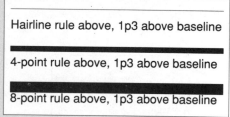

Paragraph rules extend the paragraph slug (the amount of space highlighted when you drag over a paragraph with the text tool) unless you use the Auto setting for the position of the rule. We'll examine in some detail the effect of paragraph rules on spacing when we work with leading grids in Project 6. We'll also explore the Align to Grid option in that project. See the sidebar "Working with a Leading Grid," beginning on page 383.

When you first begin working with paragraph rules, you'll go through a lot of trial and error specifying the value above or below the baseline. In the process, you may discover some interesting effects, and after a while, it won't take so long to get the look you want.

BY WAY OF EXAMPLE . . .

EUREKA!

Lorem ipsum dolor si amet,
consectetuer adipiscing elit,
sed diam nonummy nibh

▲ ▲ ▲

A Column Width rule is exactly the width of the margins for that text block. This is a 1-point Rule Above, positioned 1p6 above baseline.

EUREKA!

Lorem ipsum dolor sit et
amet, et consectetuer diam
adipiscing elit, nonummy

nibh euismod tincidunt ut
laoreet dolore magna zzril
aliquam erat volutpat. Ut

▲ ▲ ▲

This Rule Above has the same specs as the one to its left, except this one has a Right Indent of –12p. A negative indent extends a Column Width rule beyond the column margins, enabling you to run a single rule across two columns of text. A positive indent insets the rule from the column margins.

BULBS

▲ ▲ ▲

You can have two rules for the same paragraph. Here, the Rule Above is 1 point, Width of Column, positioned 1p6 above baseline. The Rule Below is 6 point, Width of Text, positioned 1p below baseline.

BULBS

▲ ▲ ▲

Use custom rule weights to set reverse type headlines in black or color paragraph rules. The easiest way to center type vertically in a rule is to set the type solid (with the leading the same value as the type size), use baseline leading for the paragraph (in the Spacing Attributes dialog box), and use the Auto setting for the position of the rule (an exception to our practice of not using Auto settings). This 18/18 type has a Rule Above with a custom Line Style of 22 points, Width of Column, Position Auto. The type has baseline leading, centered alignment, and the color set to Paper.

SPRING FEVER

▲ ▲ ▲

This one is full of tricks. It's actually two paragraphs. The 1-point rule is part of a blank paragraph with the Type Specs set for 1-point leading, even though there's no type, and the Paragraph option Keep with Next specified for 1 line. It's a Rule Below, positioned 0p below the baseline; it's defined as Width of Column, but its length is extended by dragging the text selection handles (an alternative to specifying a negative indent). The 6-point rule is a Rule Above the "Spring Fever" line, Width of Text, positioned 1p9 above the baseline, with a Right Indent of –0p2. Why the right indent? Italic text extends slightly beyond its own right margin; the negative indent extends the rule beyond the margin so that it visually aligns with the text.

▶ ▶ ▶

A custom text wrap around the art forces the text and paragraph rules away from the art. (See page 421 for an explanation of customized text wrap.) Paragraph rules behave a little strangely in the presence of a graphic boundary. If the leading for a line with a paragraph rule crosses the graphic boundary, the rule will be repelled, even if the rule itself doesn't cross the boundary. The paragraph rules here are Width of Column, positioned 1p4 above the baseline. The bottom rule has a Right Indent of –1p6.

CRUISE ON OVER TO RIVER'S END

Western Travel Agents Association

invites you to a sunset buffet

on the good ship Pacifica

Sunday, July 24 at 7 P.M.

door prize—Hawaiian vacation

For additional uses of paragraph rules, see pages 309 and 394.

A hairline-rule circle...

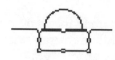

partially covered by a rectangle...

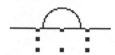

with the Line set to None and the Fill set to Paper...

makes a setting sun.

8. Create the sunset.

You can create a sunset motif by using a white rectangle to mask more and more of each subsequent circle, thus suggesting the sun sinking below the horizon line.

For maximum flexibility in working with small graphics, you'll want to work at a large page view and turn off both Snap To commands. Here's the fastest way to zoom in on your work area at 200%: On a Mac, press Command-Option-Shift while you click the mouse button on the point you want to be at the center of the screen; on a PC, press Shift while you click the right mouse button on that point. To move around the screen without changing page views, use the grabber hand: Hold down the Option key (Mac) or the Alt key (PC) while you press the mouse button and drag.

Now, on to the sunset.

- Hold down the Shift key and use the circle tool to create a circle about 1p3 in diameter. Position the top of the circle about 1p9 above the first paragraph rule. Set the Line to Hairline and the Fill to None.

  Note: In the following step, you can use the manual technique described below to copy, paste, and position the circles, or you can use the automated technique described on the facing page.

- With the circle still selected, copy it (Command-C or Ctrl-C), paste it (Command-V or Ctrl-V), and position the copy a little lower on its horizon line than the original.

  Paste and position five more copies, again positioning each one lower on the horizon than the preceding one.

  To move a circle, point anywhere on the circumference before you drag. If you point inside the circle, you'll deselect it. If you point to a handle and drag, you'll stretch the circle; if that happens, immediately select Undo from the top of the Edit menu (Command-Z on a Mac, Alt-Backspace on a PC).

  If you move the text when you're trying to move a circle, use the Undo command; then, with the text still selected, choose Send to Back from the Element menu (Command-B on a Mac, Ctrl-B on a PC). For more information about the Front/Back commands, see pages 218–19.

- Paste one more circle in the black banner. After you move it into position, you won't see the circle, but you will see the selection handles around it (selection handles automatically reverse out against black). While the circle is still selected, change the Fill to Paper.

  If you do "lose" the circle behind the banner, use the pointer tool to draw a selection box around the banner. Then deselect the banner by clicking anywhere inside the banner but outside the selection handles of the circle. Change the circle's Fill to Paper, and it will reverse out of the banner. If you lose the circle after changing its Fill to Paper, select the banner with the pointer and send it to the back.

ADVANCED TECHNIQUE: USING MULTIPLE PASTE TO POSITION THE SUN

Using the Multiple Paste command on the Edit menu, you can paste a copy of an object at a specified position relative to the original object and other copies. And although you don't have to use this mathematically precise technique to create an effective sunset in this invitation, it's a good opportunity to learn how.

First you have to do a little math.

1. **Determine the distance** the sun has to travel from above the first horizon line (the one under the banner) to the last (the one where even the sun's top is invisible, below the last line of type). Using the technique described below, we can quickly determine that distance to be 22p9.

Quick Measuring Technique

CRUISE ON OVER TO RIVER'S END

The Western Travel Agents Association

invites you to a sunset buffet

on the patio of the River's End Restaurant

Sunday July 24

7:00 pm

$10 per person

door prize—Hawaiian vacation

Measuring box

▲ ▲ ▲
Use the rectangle tool to draw a box over the distance you want to measure.

◀ ▶ W **3p11.6**
▲ ▼ H **22p9**

▲ ▲ ▲
While the box is selected, the values in the Control Palette's size field equal the dimensions in the box. In this example, the H(eight) value is the distance we want to measure. So the distance the sun has to travel is 22p9.

2. **Determine the number of units** among which the distance to be traveled is divided.

There are eight horizon lines in the invitation, including the last one, below which the sun has set. So the total distance is divided into seven units.

3. **Determine the distance per unit.**

Divide the space the sun has to travel (22p9) by the number of units (7).

With 12 points to a pica, $22p9 = (22 \times 12) + 9 = 273$ points. And $273 \div 7 = 39$.

Each copy of the circle must be 39 points below the preceding one. Now comes the easy part.

4. **Multiple Paste.**

In the language of the Multiple Paste dialog box, the distance between each of the circles—39 points—is the vertical offset. And you'll need to specify the value in picas; so $39 \text{ points} \div 12 = 3p3$.

Select the circle above the first horizon line and copy it (Command-C or Ctrl-C).

Choose Multiple Paste from the Edit menu.

In the Multiple Paste dialog box, specify *7* for the number of copies. For the Horizontal Offset, specify *0* (because all the copies should have the same horizontal alignment). For the Vertical Offset, specify *3p3*. Click OK, or press Return or Enter.

Multiple paste		OK
Paste **7** copies		Cancel
Horizontal offset: **0**	picas	
Vertical offset: **3p3**	picas	

TIPS

If you type positive numbers for offset values, the copies are offset to the right and bottom of the original. If you type negative values, copies are offset to the left and top.

Here's another way to paste an object repeatedly with the same offset: Copy the object, press Command-Option-V (Mac) or Ctrl-Shift-P (PC) to paste the first copy directly on top of the original. Then drag that copy to the new position. Press the key combination again for each duplicate that you want, and PageMaker pastes them using the offset defined by the distance that you dragged.

- Check to be sure all the circles are aligned at their right edges.

  (If you use the Multiple Paste technique, the alignment will already be even. But there's a good lesson here, so read on.)

  There are two ways to align objects. The manual technique is to bring in a vertical ruler guide at the right edge of the circles and use the pointer to move elements that aren't aligned at that guideline.

  The second technique is to use the Control Palette to create the alignment mathematically. See the sidebar below.

ALIGNING OBJECTS WITH THE CONTROL PALETTE

It would be great if you could select multiple objects and align them by typing a single value in the Control Palette. Alas, it isn't that easy. You have to type the value individually for each object. But doing so ensures precise alignment, and you can work quickly even at small page views. Here's how.

1. Determine the alignment you want. We decided that we wanted the circles to be right-aligned at 21p6 on the horizontal ruler. (Remember, that number is relative to the zero point, and ours was in the upper left corner of the page.)

2. Select the first circle.

3. In the Control Palette, click once on any handle on the right side of the Proxy.

4. For the *x*-coordinate, type *21p6*. Click Apply.

5. Repeat steps 2 and 4 for each of the circles. (The reference point you selected in step 3 remains selected until you select another reference point.)

With the reference point in the upper right corner of the Proxy, if you type 21p6 *for the x-coordinate, PageMaker moves the selected circle so that its rightmost point is aligned at 21p6.*

And More on Reference Points

In working with the Control Palette, have you seen a double-headed arrow rather than a box at the reference point? That's because there are two kinds of reference points. In this project, we've worked with reference points that tell PageMaker you want to move the selected object. But there are also reference points that tell PageMaker you want to resize the selected object. We'll come back to this later in more detail, but for now, be aware that the Proxy is even more complex than we've let on.

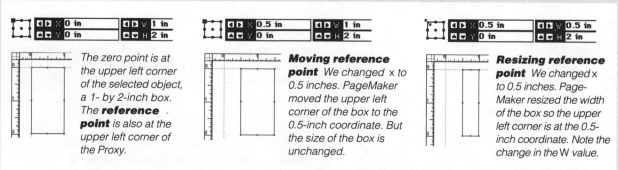

The zero point is at the upper left corner of the selected object, a 1- by 2-inch box. The **reference point** is also at the upper left corner of the Proxy.

Moving reference point We changed x to 0.5 inches. PageMaker moved the upper left corner of the box to the 0.5-inch coordinate. But the size of the box is unchanged.

Resizing reference point We changed x to 0.5 inches. PageMaker resized the width of the box so the upper left corner is at the 0.5-inch coordinate. Note the change in the W value.

Tip To change from one type of reference point to another, click on the reference point.

• To cover the part of each circle below the horizon, draw a hairline-rule rectangle and butt it to the horizontal rule. Change the rectangle's Line to None and Fill to Paper. Adjust the position of this "invisible" box until the horizon line is unbroken and the portion of the circle below it is completely masked. If you have trouble achieving this alignment, use the Control Palette's nudge button to move the box down in very small increments. See the sidebar below.

THE CONTROL PALETTE'S NUDGE BUTTONS

In this invitation, using white boxes to mask the bottom part of the setting sun presents a tricky alignment problem. You want the hairline rule representing the horizon line to be visible above the white box, but you want the portion of the circle below that line to be totally masked by the white box.

This kind of precise alignment is much easier to achieve with the nudge buttons than with the pointer tool. And it's a good demonstration of the accuracy of the Control Palette; it's about five times more accurate than the rulers.

Nudge buttons are the little up, down, and side-pointing arrows next to many of the Control Palette options. They're called nudge buttons because you can use them to move or resize an object in very small increments. Here's how to use them to align the white boxes at the horizon lines.

1. With the top of the white box positioned just above the horizon line, select the box.

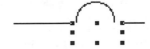

2. Click once on any top handle in the Proxy. This tells 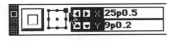 PageMaker you want to move the selected object (the white box) from the top. If you click an up nudge button, the top of the box moves up. If you click a down nudge button, the top of the box moves down.

3. Click once on the down arrow to the left of the *y*-coordinate. Click again, and again, until the top of the white box is just below the horizon line.

Note that as you click, only the *y* value changes. The amount that it changes is the amount specified in the Preferences dialog box. If the amount isn't small enough—that is, if some of the circle below the horizon line shows as soon as the top of the white box clears the horizon line—you need to specify a smaller amount for the nudge value.

To change the nudge value, choose Preferences from the File menu, and in the Preferences dialog box, type a smaller value for Vertical Nudge. You can type values as small as one-tenth of a point (0.01).

```
┌─ Control palette ──────────────────────┐
│                                        │
│  Horizontal nudge:  │ 0p0.1 │  │ Picas ││
│                                        │
│  Vertical nudge:    │ 0p0.1 │  │ Picas ││
│                                        │
│  ☐ Use "Snap to" constraints           │
└────────────────────────────────────────┘
```

4. When you return to layout view, you'll need to select the white rectangle again. Click the vertical nudge button—either up or down, depending on whether the top of the white box is above or below the horizon line. That should do it. You can see that the nudge values you can specify are many times finer than those you can work with manually.

For more hands-on practice with the Control Palette's object view, see the list on page 208.

HOW TO PRINT FOUR UP

Invitations, business cards, name tags, and other documents with a small trim size can be printed efficiently with multiple copies of the document on one sheet of paper. Simply create a master of the document, copy it, and then repeatedly paste the copy to fill the page, using ruler guides to align the tops and edges of the copies.

The following instructions for printing the invitation four to a page can be adapted easily for other dimensions.

1. Check all the alignments on your master. Print a copy and proofread for spelling, accuracy of information, alignments, and so on.

2. Be sure Snap to Guides (on the Guides and Rulers submenu, under Layout) is turned on.

3. With the rectangle tool, draw a temporary page frame around the master, from the upper left corner to the midpoint of the 8.5- by 11-inch page (where the 25p6 vertical guide and the 33p horizontal guide intersect). When you move the copies of the master in steps 6–8, you'll appreciate the aid of this page frame.

    Note that the ruler guides bisecting the page, which you brought in to define the trim of the master, also define the trim for the other units.

4. Select the entire master using one of the techniques described in the first Tip at left.

5. Copy the master and use the power-paste technique described in the second Tip to paste the copy directly on top of the original. The copy will be full of handles, which is fine, as you'll see in the next step.

6. With all the pieces of the copy still selected (as long as all those handles are showing, you know that all the pieces of your copy are selected), hold down the Shift key, position the arrow on any side of the temporary page frame, and drag the copy into position in the upper right quadrant. Do not point on a handle, or you'll stretch the frame. (If you do inadvertently stretch that or any other element, choose Undo from the Edit menu; all the pieces of the copy will remain selected after the mistake is undone.)

    When the duplicate card is in the correct position, deselect all the elements by clicking in a blank part of the page.

7. Choose Select All, copy, and power-paste again. This time, you'll have two copies directly on top of the first two cards.

8. Hold down the Shift key, and drag the new copies into position in the bottom half of the page. Deselect everything by clicking on the pasteboard.

9. To remove the temporary page frames around the invitations, select the first one with the pointer, hold down the Shift key while you select the other three, and then press the Backspace key.

10. Optional electronic trimming guide: If you plan to print and trim the cards yourself, you may want to add little tick marks to guide your trim. It sounds ridiculous, but we've found that 8-point Helvetica

▶ ▶ ▶

Copy and paste the master unit to print multiple invitations on the same sheet. Use a temporary page frame (already removed here) to facilitate alignment along the ruler guides that mark the trim for each copy.

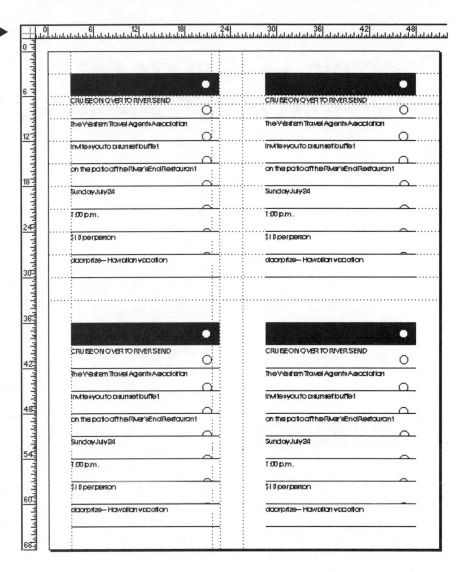

To see the page on-screen as it will print, **hide all the guidelines** by choosing Guides from the Guides and Rulers submenu, under Layout. The Guides command is one of several toggle switches on PageMaker's menus: The feature is on when it's checked and off when it's not checked. You can quickly turn the guides on and off with the keyboard short-cuts—Command-J on a Mac, Ctrl-J on a PC. When you turn on the guides after having hidden them, they re-appear in their previous position on the screen.

periods, being 1 pixel high, provide a sufficient guide and virtually disappear in trimming. Along the horizontal ruler guide separating the top and bottom cards, place a period at each corner of the image area. Along the vertical ruler guide separating the left and right cards, place periods to align with the tops of the banners and the last horizontal rules. You should have four periods along each guide.

Old-fashioned trimming guide: Use a ruler and a pencil to mark the cuts, and erase the pencil marks after trimming.

11. If you are printing the invitations on a laser printer, the 20-pound card stock must be hand-fed. To specify Manual Feed: In the Print dialog box, select the Paper button to display the Paper dialog box. In the Paper Source box near the top, type *M* (for manual feed), or select that option from the pull-down menu.

If your cards will be commercially printed, you will need to paste your camera-ready page onto a piece of art board and draw crop marks outside the live area to indicate the outside trim for each card.

CREATING A TEMPLATE FOR A THREE-COLUMN SELF-MAILING NEWSLETTER

This project introduces some of PageMaker's most powerful features. You'll use master pages and style sheets and create a template for a publication that is produced repeatedly. Master pages are the blueprints on which individual pages of the publication are built. By setting up column and ruler guides on the master pages, you establish a format that you can follow on all the pages of the publication. It's much faster than having to reinvent the wheel on every page, and it also ensures consistency from one page to the next.

A style sheet defines the formatting for text elements such as headlines, body text, captions, and so on. After you define a style, you can apply that formatting to selected text simply by clicking on the style name, rather than having to specify half a dozen different attributes. In addition to saving you time, style sheets are another tool for maintaining consistency. When you apply the subhead style, for example, you can be sure that all the subheads will look exactly alike.

If you know how to define type attributes, you already know a good deal of what there is to know about styles. Some of the rest is full of subtleties, but once mastered, those nuances provide powerful flexibility. We hope that the introduction to styles in this project will make you want to master the finer points, because the value of styles can't be overemphasized.

A template extends the blueprint concept to the entire publication. Whenever you create a publication repeatedly—anything from a one-page memo to a simple newsletter to the chapters in a book—create a prototype and save that file as a template. When you open the template to create a new document, PageMaker opens a copy of the original, so you always have the prototype intact.

This project contains a great deal of information that is essential to working effectively in PageMaker. The instructions assume familiarity with procedures used in earlier projects, but if you missed some important steps along the way or need to review them, you'll find cross-references to earlier projects throughout.

A primary design objective in developing the format for this project was that the newsletter be fast and efficient to produce. It shouldn't require much fine-tuning after you pour the text. In Project 6, we'll use a copy of this newsletter to look at some design variations that explore additional PageMaker techniques but add some production complexities to the basic format presented here. And you'll work with another copy of this newsletter in Project 9, when we look at PageMaker's color capabilities.

PAGEMAKER TECHNIQUES

▶ Create and use a template

▶ Work with master pages

▶ Customize column guides

▶ Use the Control Palette to size a graphic

▶ Use automatic page numbering

▶ Work with style sheets

▶ Create spacing guides

▶ Use arithmetic in the Control Palette

▶ Rotate text

▶ Format text in a word processor

▶ Use semi-automatic text flow

▶ Place graphics

▶ Export text to a word processor

▶ Examine the flexibility of threaded text

The Employee Newsletter of Southside Corporation

NEWSLINE

Oct 15, 1991

Captions for art are set 10/14 Helvetica bold. They extend 12p6 into the column rather than the full 18p column width.

Headline goes here in 14/15 Helvetica bold

Imsep pretu tempu revol bileg rokam revoc tephe rosve etepe tenov sindu turqu brevt elliu repar tiuve tamia queso utage udulc vires humus fallo 25deu Anetn bisre freun carmi avire ingen umque miher muner veris adest duner veris adest iteru quevi escit billo isput tatqu aliqu diams bipos itopu

50sta Isant oscul bifid mquec cumen berra etmii pyren nsomn anoct reern oncit quqar anofe ventm hipec oramo uetfu orets nitus sacer tusag teliu ipsev 75tvi Eonei elaur plica oscri eseli sipse enitu ammih mensl quidi aptat rinar uacae ierqu vagas ubesc rpore ibere perqu umbra perqu antra erorp netra 100at mihif napat ntint riora intui urque nimus otoqu cagat rolym oecfu iunto ulosa tarac ecame suidt mande onatd stent spiri usore idpar thaec abies

125sa Imsep pretu tempu revol bileg rokam revoc tephe rosve etepe tenov sindu turqu brevt

225at mihif napat ntint riora intui urque nimus otoqu cagat rolym oecfu iunto ulosa tarac ecame suidt mande onatd stent spiri usore idpar thaec abies 250sa Imsep pretu tempu revol bileg rokam revoc tephe rosve etepe tenov sindu turqu brevt elliu repar tiuve tamia queso utage udulc vires humus fallo 275eu Anetn bisre freun carmi avire ingen umque miher muner veris adest duner veris adest iteru quevi escit billo isput tatqu aliqu diams bipos itopu

Headline for second story in Newsline

300ta Isant oscul bifid mquec cumen berra etmii pyren nsomn anoct reern oncit quqar anofe ventm hipec oramo uetfu orets nitus sacer tusag teliu ipsev

325vi Eonei elaur plica oscri eseli sipse enitu ammih mensl quidi aptat rinar uacae ierqu vagas ubesc rpore ibere perqu umbra perqu antra erorp netra 350at mihif napat ntint riora intui urque nimus otoqu cagat rolym

FORECAS

Forecasts are 10/14 Helvetica b space after each paragraph.

Lorem ipsum dolor sit amet, co adipiscing elit, sed diam nonun euismod tincidunt ut laoreet do

Aliquam erat volutpat. Ut wisi minim

Veniam, quis nostrud exerci tat ullamcorper suscipit lobortis n ex ea commodo consequat. Du

NEWSLINE

The Employee Newsletter of Southside Corporation

Southside Corporation
12 Kramer Avenue, Chicago, IL 60600

FIRST CLASS
U.S. POSTAGE
PAID
CHICAGO, IL
PERMIT NO. 1234

Left sample page

This is a placeholder for the 14/14 Helvetica bold breakout

Oct 15, 1991 / Page 2

NEWSBRIEFS

Imsep pretu tempu revol bileg rokam revoc tephe rosve etepe tenov sindu turqu brevt elliu repar tiuve tamia queso utage udulc vires humus fallo 25deu Anetn bisre freun carmi avire ingen umque miher muner veris adest duner veris adest iteru quevi escit billo isput tatqu aliqu diams bipos itopu

❖ ❖ ❖

50sta Isant oscul bifid mquec cumen berra etmii pyren nsomn anoct reern oncit quqar anofe ventm hipec oramo uetfu orets nitus sacer tusag teliu ipsev 75tvi Eonei elaur plica oscri eseli sipse enitu ammih mensl quidi aptat rinar uacae ierqu vagas ubesc rpore ibere perqu umbra perqu antra erorp netra 100at mihif napat ntint riora intui urque nimus otoqu cagat rolym oecfu iunto ulosa tarac ecame suidt mande onatd stent spiri usore idpar thaec abies

❖ ❖ ❖

125sa Imsep pretu tempu revol bileg rokam revoc tephe rosve etepe tenov sindu turqu brevt elliu repar tiuve tamia queso utage udulc vires humus fallo

❖ ❖ ❖

150eu Anetn bisre freun carmi avire ingen umque miher muner veris adest duner veris adest iteru quevi escit billo isput tatqu aliqu diams bipos itopu 175ta Isant oscul bifid mquec cumen berra etmii pyren nsomn anoct reern oncit quqar anofe ventm hipec oramo uetfu orets nitus sacer tusag teliu ipsev 200vi Eonei elaur plica oscri eseli sipse enitu ammih mensl quidi aptat rinar uacae ierqu vagas ubesc rpore ibere perqu umbra perqu antra erorp netra mihif napat ntint riora intui urque nimus otoqu tamia queso utage udulc vires humus fallo

Eonei elaur plica oscri eseli sipse enitu ammih mensl quidi aptat rinar uacae ierqu vagas ubesc rpore ibere perqu umbra perqu antra erorp netra 475at mihif napat ntint riora intui urque nimus otoqu cagat rolym oecfu iunto ulosa tarac ecame suidt mande onatd stent spiri usore idpar thaec abies

Headlines can run on three or even on four lines if you want to write long heads

500sa Imsep pretu tempu revol bileg rokam revoc tephe rosve etepe tenov sindu turqu brevt elliu repar tiuve tamia queso utage udulc vires humus fallo 525eu Anetn bisre freun carmi avire ingen umque miher muner veris adest duner veris adest iteru quevi escit billo isput tatqu aliqu diams bipos itopu 550sta Isant oscul bifid mquec cumen berra etmii pyren nsomn anoct reern oncit quqar anofe ventm hipec oramo uetfu orets nitus sacer tusag teliu ipsev 575vi Eonei elaur plica oscri eseli sipse enitu ammih mensl quidi aptat rinar uacae ierqu vagas ubesc rpore ibere perqu umbra perqu antra erorp netra

Subhead is 10/14 Helvetica bold on one or two lines

600at mihif napat ntint riora intui urque nimus otoqu cagat rolym oecfu iunto ulosa tarac ecame suidt mande onatd stent spiri usore idpar thaec abies 625sa Imsep pretu tempu revol bileg rokam revoc tephe rosve etepe tenov sindu turqu brevt elliu repar tiuve tamia queso utage udulc vires humus fallo 650eu Anetn bisre freun carmi avire ingen umque miher muner veris

adest duner veris adest iteru quevi escit billo isput tatqu aliqu diams bipos itopu 675ta Isant oscul bifid mquec anoct reern oncit quqar anofe ventm hipec oramo uetfu orets nitus sacer tusag teliu ipsev 700vi Eonei elaur plica oscri eseli sipse enitu ammih mensl quidi aptat rinar uacae ierqu vagas ubesc rpore ibere perqu umbra perqu antra erorp netra 725at mihif napat green wood intui urque nimus otoqu cagat rolym oecfu iunto ulosa tarac ecame suidt mande onatd stent spiri usore idpar thaec abies

Subhead goes here

750sa Imsep pretu tempu revol bileg rokam revoc tephe rosve etepe tenov sindu turqu brevt elliu repar tiuve tamia queso utage udulc vires humus fallo 775eu Anetn bisre freun carmi avire ingen umque miher muner veris adest duner veris adest iteru quevi escit billo isput tatqu aliqu diams bipos itopu 800ta Isant oscul bifid mquec cumen berra etmii pyren nsomn anoct reern oncit quqar anofe ventm hipec oramo uetfu orets nitus sacer tusag teliu ipsev 825vi Eonei elaur plica oscri eseli sipse enitu ammih mensl quidi aptat rinar uacae ierqu vagas ubesc rpore ibere perqu umbra perqu antra erorp netra 850at mihif napat ntint riora intui urque nimus otoqu cagat rolym oecfu iunto ulosa tarac ecame suidt mande onatd stent spiri usore idpar thaec abies 875sa Imsep pretu tempu revol bileg rokam revoc tephe rosve etepe tenov sindu turqu brevt elliu repar tiuve tamia queso utage udulc vires humus fallo 900eu Anetn bisre freun carmi avire ingen umque miher muner

Right sample page

This is a placeholder for the 14/14 Helvetica bold breakout

Oct 15, 1991 / Page 3

PEOPLE

Caption for people shots can be one line or several, set to a 12p6 measure.

Caption for people shots can be one line or several, set to a 12p6 measure.

Caption for people shots can be one line or several, set to a 12p6 measure.

veris adest duner veris adest iteru quevi escit billo isput tatqu aliqu diams bipos itopu 925ta Isant oscul bifid mquec cumen berra etmii pyren nsomn anoct reern oncit quqar anofe ventm hipec oramo uetfu orets nitus sacer tusag teliu ipsev

Headline for another story

950vi Eonei elaur plica oscri eseli sipse enitu ammih mensl quidi aptat rinar uacae ierqu vagas ubesc rpore ibere perqu umbra perqu antra erorp netra 975at mihif napat ntint riora intui urque nimus otoqu cagat rolym oecfu iunto ulosa tarac ecame suidt mande onatd stent spiri usore idpar thaec abies 1000a Imsep pretu tempu revol bileg rokam revoc tephe rosve etepe tenov sindu turqu brevt elliu repar tiuve tamia queso utage udulc vires humus fallo 1025u Anetn bisre freun carmi avire ingen umque miher muner veris adest duner veris adest iteru quevi escit billo isput tatqu aliqu diams bipos itopu 1050a Isant oscul bifid mquec cumen berra etmii pyren nsomn anoct reern oncit quqar anofe ventm hipec oramo uetfu orets nitus sacer tusag teliu ipsev 1075i Eonei elaur plica oscri eseli sipse enitu ammih mensl quidi aptat rinar uacae ierqu vagas ubesc rpore ibere perqu umbra perqu antra erorp netra 1100a Isant oscul bifid mquec cumen berra etmii pyren nsomn anoct reern oncit quqar anofe ventm hipec oramo uetfu orets nitus sacer tusag teliu ipsev 1125i Eonei elaur plica oscri eseli sipse enitu ammih mensl quidi aptat rinar uacae ierqu vagas ubesc rpore ibere perqu umbra perqu antra erorp netra

1150t mihif napat ntint riora intui urque nimus otoqu cagat rolym oecfu iunto ulosa tarac ecame suidt mande onatd stent spiri usore idpar thaec abies 1175a Imsep pretu tempu revol bileg rokam revoc tephe rosve etepe tenov sindu turqu brevt elliu repar tiuve tamia queso utage udulc vires humus fallo 1200t mihif napat ntint riora intui urque nimus otoqu cagat rolym oecfu iunto ulosa tarac ecame suidt mande onatd stent spiri usore idpar thaec abies 1225a Imsep pretu tempu revol bileg rokam revoc tephe rosve etepe tenov sindu turqu brevt elliu repar tiuve tamia queso utage udulc vires humus fallo 2250u Anetn bisre freun carmi avire ingen umque miher muner veris adest duner veris adest iteru quevi escit billo isput tatqu aliqu diams bipos itopu

Headline for last story

1275a Isant oscul bifid mquec cumen berra etmii pyren nsomn anoct reern oncit quqar anofe ventm hipec oramo uetfu orets nitus sacer tusag teliu ipsev 1300i Eonei elaur plica oscri eseli sipse enitu ammih mensl quidi aptat rinar uacae ierqu vagas ubesc rpore ibere perqu umbra perqu antra erorp netra 1325t mihif napat ntint riora intui urque nimus otoqu cagat rolym oecfu iunto ulosa tarac ecame suidt mande onatd stent spiri usore idpar thaec abies 1350a Imsep pretu tempu revol bileg rokam revoc tephe rosve etepe tenov sindu turqu brevt elliu repar tiuve tamia queso utage udulc vires humus fallo 1375u Anetn bisre freun carmi avire ingen umque miher muner veris adest duner veris adest iteru quevi escit billo isput tatqu aliqu

Grid / master page

Newsline te

Oct 15, 1991 / Page RM

The grid created on the master page (left) uses two 12p6 columns for running text and a wider, 18p column for art and special departments. The wide column adds visual interest to a relatively simple format, gives you flexibility in sizing and cropping art, and forces you to leave some white space on the page.

PageMaker's Next Style option lets you automate formatting of paragraphs that always follow one another, such as the story heads, the flush left first paragraph following each story head, and the indented second paragraph of each story in the pages shown above.

The Zapf Dingbats dividers in the "Newsbriefs" column (above, far left) are also automated with styles. All you have to do is type *vvv* and apply the style; PageMaker applies the typeface, size, centered align-ment, and spacing before and after.

BLUEPRINT FOR NEWSLINE

PAGE SETUP

Page Dimensions: 8.5 by 11 inches or 51 by 66 picas

Orientation: Tall

Start Page #: 1 of 4

Options: Turn off Double-sided, Facing Pages

Margins: Left , 3p   Right, 3p

       Top, 9p6   Bottom, 3p9

Don't forget to specify Compose to Printer (Windows only) and the Target Printer Resolution (Mac and Windows). See page 229 for details.

In the interest of fast, efficient production, we've set up the file as single-sided pages, even though it is in fact a double-sided publication with facing pages. This saves you time in two ways: You have to set up only one master page instead of two; and when you turn pages, the screen redraw will be faster than it would be for facing pages. You'll still be able to print on both sides of the paper.

In order to use this time-saving approach, the grids for the right and left pages must be exactly the same, which they are in this newsletter. Also, the design must be straightforward enough that you don't need to view facing pages as a spread. If you use this grid for a more modular format—running some stories across two or three columns—or if you have a lot of art in your pages, the relationship of elements on facing pages becomes important, and a publication incorporating those variations would be better set up as double-sided facing pages.

TIP

Remember that you can **override the unit of measure** by typing abbreviations. Thus, if your preferences are set to inches, you can still type *3p*, *3p*, *9p6*, and *3p9* for the margins. The measurements throughout the project are given in picas, however, so when you've finished with the page setup, change the unit of measure through the Preferences command on the File menu.

HOW TO DETERMINE MARGINS

We've done the preliminary work of figuring out what the margins should be, and all you have to do is plug the numbers into the dialog box. In real life, the page margins evolve as you determine the type size, leading, number of columns, and so on. See Chapter 3, "Creating a Grid," for a detailed look at page structure and layout grids.

For efficient production, define the top and bottom margins at the points where body text begins and ends on most pages. You can position running heads, folios, and other elements outside the margins.

First, determine your type specs and create a sample page with text filling as many columns as you plan to have. Select a full column of text with the pointer tool to display the windowshade handles. Bring in one ruler guide to align exactly with the top handle; bring in another guide to align with the bottom handle. The distances of these guides from the top and bottom of the page are the measurements you want for the top and bottom margins.

When you place text, you position the loaded text icon at the top margin, and PageMaker flows the text to the bottom margin.

A common mistake is to define the bottom margin at the baseline of the last line of text. But with proportional leading (PageMaker's default method for assigning space between lines), one-third of the leading for each line is below the baseline; if there isn't room for the leading, the line is pushed to the next column. So for 10/12 body text, as in this newsletter, the bottom margin is 4 points below the baseline of the last line of text.

MASTER PAGE

In multipage documents, you'll save a lot of time if you set up your layout grid on master pages. The elements you position on master pages—both nonprinting guidelines and printing elements, such as rules and page-number markers—will appear on every page of the publication.

The following instructions tell you how to set up the master page for this newsletter. For a more detailed overview of master pages, see the sidebar that begins on page 306.

1. Click on the icon labeled R at the lower left of the screen.

In single-sided publications, the master-page icon is identified as a right-hand page. In double-sided publications, there are icons labeled *R* and *L* for right and left master pages.

2. Create customized column guides.

For the column guides to appear on every page of the publication, you must specify those guides on the master pages. If a regular page is displayed when you specify the column guides, the specs will apply to only that page.

- Choose Column Guides from the Layout menu.

- In the Column Guides dialog box, specify 3 columns with a 1p space between.

Note that PageMaker positions the leftmost column guide over the left margin and the rightmost column guide over the right margin.

You can move either of the outer column guides individually, although it isn't necessary to do so in this project. The other column guides move only as pairs (see the caption at left) and the space between columns—often called the alley—remains constant, unless you change the setting in the Column Guides dialog box. You'll move the guides in a minute.

- Turn on Snap to Rulers (Guides and Rulers submenu under Layout).

- Move the first pair of column guides to 21p and 22p, and move the second pair of column guides to 34p6 and 35p6. You should have one wide column on the left, measuring 18p, and two narrower columns on the right, each measuring 12p6.

- Bring in a vertical ruler guide at 15p6.

This guideline creates a 12p6 column within the 18p column. When you place art in this column, you can size it either to the 12p6 measure or to the full 18p width. Captions run to the 12p6 measure. This flexibility has several benefits: It makes the pages more interesting visually; it gives you two choices when cropping and sizing art; and it forces you to leave some white space on the page.

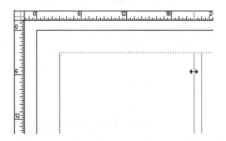

▲ ▲ ▲

To move column guides, *drag them with the pointer tool. You can move the outer column guides individually. Other column guides move as pairs—the right margin of one column moves with the left margin of the adjacent column—and the space between the columns remains constant. Note that when you move the guides, the hairline marker on the horizontal ruler aligns with whichever guide you are pointing to. If the Control Palette is active, the x-coordinate displays the position of the guide you are pointing to.*

TIPS

To insert a **page-number marker,** press Command-Option-P on a Mac, Ctrl-Shift-3 on a PC.

PageMaker begins numbering each file with the **starting page number** specified in the Page Setup dialog box. If you have a 200-page report divided into two files between pages 109 and 110, the Start Page # for the second file would be 110 and the first page icon on the bottom of the screen would be 110.

The default **numbering style** for page numbers is Arabic, but you can specify Roman or alphabetic numbering through the Numbers option in the Page Setup dialog box.

For right-aligned page numbers, be sure to apply the right alignment electronically so that the alignment will be maintained for two- and three-digit numbers. If you use the pointer tool to manually position the page-number marker at the right margin, longer numbers will overhang the margin.

3. Add ruler guides.

- Turn on Snap to Guides (Guides and Rulers submenu under Layout).
- Bring in vertical ruler guides over the left and right page margins.
- Bring in horizontal ruler guides at the following positions:

  4p: to mark the top of the gray banner

  6p: to mark the baseline for text that runs in the gray banner on pages 2 and 3

4. Add printing items.

- Draw the banner at the top of the page.

  Draw a 3p6-deep rectangle, with the top aligned at the 4p horizontal guide and the sides aligned at the left and right margins. (For Control Palette practice, see the sidebar below.)

  With the rectangle still selected, specify the Line as None and the Fill as 40%.

- Type the date and the page-number marker.

  A page-number marker is simply a key combination that tells Page-Maker to automatically insert page numbers. In this newsletter, we've typed the page number in the same text block as the issue date.

  With the text tool, set an insertion point on the left margin, just below the gray banner, and drag diagonally to the first vertical ruler guide to define a bounding box for the text. Type the date, followed by a Spacebar character, a slash, another Spacebar character, the word *Page*, and another Spacebar character. Then, for the page-number marker, press Command-Option-P on a Mac, Ctrl-Shift-3 on a PC.

Blueprint continues on page 308.

SIZING THE BANNER: OPTIONAL CONTROL PALETTE EXERCISE

After you become adept at using the Control Palette, you'll be able to create boxes to precise measurements in a flash.

Quickly draw a box from one margin to another, with the top aligned at the 4p horizontal ruler guide. Don't worry about the depth. With the rectangle still selected, click twice on any bottom handle in the Proxy. You should see a double-headed arrow, which represents a resizing reference point and tells PageMaker that you want to resize the graphic as if you had pulled on that handle.

For the *H*(eight) value in the Control Palette, type *3p6.* Then click Apply, or press Return or Enter. The top and sides of the rectangle are still aligned at the top and side margins, and the depth is exactly what you want.

When you set a **resizing reference point** (indicated by the double-headed arrow), changes you type in the Control Palette are applied as if you had dragged the corresponding handle on the selected object.

MASTER PAGES

Master pages provide the blueprints on which the individual pages of a publication can be built. Anything you put on a master page is displayed and printed on every regular page, unless you choose to turn off the master-page elements on a given page. Master pages can include the following:

- A nonprinting layout grid, which, in addition to the margin guides, includes column guides and vertical and horizontal ruler guides.

- Text and graphics that will appear on most pages of the document. These include page frames, rules between columns, report or issue dates, headline banners, markers for automatic page numbering, and so on.

Keep these points in mind:

- Master pages are not selected automatically.

  When you open a new document, PageMaker displays the first regular page or spread. If you want to create master pages, you have to remember to click on the L or R icon to the left of the numbered page icons at the bottom of the screen. One of the most frustrating moments in electronic pasteup is when you realize that you've just spent two hours setting up a layout grid on pages 1 and 2 instead of on the master pages.

  Similarly, after you've finished setting up the master pages, don't forget to turn to an actual page of the document before proceeding.

- Take time with your master pages. Care and precision will be reflected on every page of your document.

- If your left and right master pages have many of the same printing elements in the same positions—page frames, page-number markers, rules between columns, and so forth—create those elements on one page, choose the Select All command, and then copy and paste them onto the other master page. Then add the elements that are unique to each page. Nonprinting ruler guides and customized column guides cannot be copied from one page to another; you have to create them on both master pages.

- Printing items on the master pages cannot be edited, moved, or copied on an individual page.

If you have a graphic that you will use repeatedly, such as a black banner into which you will drop headlines, put a master unit on the pasteboard of your master pages. That master unit will then appear on the pasteboard of all regular pages of the publication and can be copied, moved into position, and edited as needed.

Or use the Library Palette (see page 422).

- Text-wrap specifications on a master page carry over to regular pages. So when you place text using autoflow, you can use the Text Wrap command to keep text from flowing into certain columns (such as the narrow left-hand columns on the pages of this book). On the master page, create a no-line rule at the top of the column and apply the column-break text-wrap icon (◼) to the rule. If you want to add text to that column after autoflowing the main text, remove the rule from the master page. (Text that you've already placed won't be affected.) Similarly, if you want to reserve space for a breakout on every page, create a white box on the master page and apply the wrap-all-sides icon (◼) to the box.

- You cannot print a master page directly, but if you turn to a numbered page within the publication, the printing elements from the master page will be displayed there, and you can print that page as you would any other page. If you want to print the layout grid, draw rules over the guidelines on a regular page, and use the Custom option on the Line submenu to specify a 0.5-point dotted rule. (The default dotted rule is 4 point, which is too heavy for this purpose.)

Customizing Individual Pages

Frequently, you need **to customize nonprinting column and ruler guides on individual pages.** Simply use the pointer tool to move the guides on that page manually or change the specifications in the Column Guides dialog box. If you change your mind and want to go back to the master guides, choose Copy Master Guides (Layout menu). This command affects only the page or spread currently displayed.

If you want **to eliminate all the master-page printing items on an individual page,** choose Display Master

Items (Layout menu) to turn off the master items. This command is an all-or-nothing choice: You can display and print all master items, or you can hide them all. The problem is that sometimes you want to display some, but not all, of them.

You can choose one of two techniques when you want **to selectively remove master-page printing items from an individual page.**

When you have just one or two master items to hide, the on-the-fly technique of masking works well. Cover the master item you want to eliminate with a white box, which is simply a rectangle with the Fill specified as Paper and the Line as None. When you click on one of these invisible boxes with the pointer, you will see handles around the box's edges but nothing else. These boxes are called masks because they mask the printing items underneath. They can be very handy, but they can also end up in the wrong place, masking something you intended to print.

When you want to eliminate several master-page printing items from an individual page, use the safer, "cleaner," power-paste method. Display the page you want to customize and turn off Display Master Items. Turn to the master page, set the page view to Fit in Window, and Shift-click to select and copy the items you want to print on the page you're customizing. Return to that custom page, display at Fit in Window, and press Command-Shift-V on a Mac, Ctrl-Shift-P on a PC, to "power paste" the items in the exact position in which they appeared on the master page from which you copied them.

Modifying Master Pages

The rules governing the modification of master pages so exemplify the trade-offs inherent in many aspects of electronic pasteup that the following information could be cast as a good news/bad news script. The rules are perfectly logical, if difficult to remember at first, and something that seems a nuisance in one situation can be used to advantage in another.

- If you return to the master pages and change any printing or nonprinting items there, those changes will be reflected on all of the corresponding regular pages except those that you have customized.

- A customized page is any page on which you have changed the column guides or have brought in ruler guides that aren't on the master pages. If you frequently bring in ruler guides on individual pages, as we do, you'll have a great many customized pages. To have the changes made on the master pages appear on a customized page, display that page and then choose Copy Master Guides from the Layout menu.

- When you copy master guides onto a page, however, you lose all your customized guides. This might not be a problem if your customized guides were temporary ones used to check alignment and to position loose odds and ends. The position of text and graphics already on the page will not change—only the guidelines.

- If your individual pages are a mess of customized ruler guides, you can quickly eliminate the guides simply by choosing the Copy Master Guides command. This is much faster than dragging every ruler guide off the page. You'll keep all your master guides and all the text and graphics added to that individual page, but you won't have a lot of extraneous ruler guides on the screen. And you don't have to display the master-page printing items to use the Copy Master Guides command.

- If you want to remove all the ruler guides on a page or spread, including the ones from the master pages, hold down the Shift key as you choose Guides from the Guides and Rulers submenu.

Copying Master Pages

You cannot directly copy master-page items from one document to another. But if you do want to reuse the master guides from an existing document, you can open a copy of that document, delete all the regular pages from the file (using the Remove Pages command from the Layout menu), and then add new pages (using the Insert Pages command, also on the Layout menu).

If you know you want to reuse the layout grid from a set of master pages, choose Template in the Save As dialog box after creating the master pages but before creating the document. Whenever you open that template in the future, PageMaker automatically opens an untitled copy.

TIP

After you determine the weight of the rules you want to use for a publication, use the pointer tool to select that weight from the Line menu (under Element) when nothing on the page is selected. That weight becomes the publication default and will automatically be used for every rule, box, and circle that you draw. Otherwise, you'll have to specify the line weight for each individual element.

PageMaker will insert the characters "RM," which stand for "right master," where you typed the page-number marker. On each page of the publication, the actual page number will be displayed in this position. (In a double-sided publication, the page-number marker on the left-hand page would read "LM.")

Select this line with the text tool, and format the type as 10/12 Helvetica. With the pointer tool, select the line and reposition it so that its baseline is at 8p6. It should remain flush with the left margin. (You might want to bring in a ruler guide at 8p6 and turn off the Snap To constraints when you move the text.)

- With the perpendicular line tool, draw a 0.5-point horizontal rule from the left to the right margin, between the issue date line and the top margin (at 9p on the vertical ruler).

- Turn off Snap to Guides, and draw a 0.5-point vertical rule in the alley between the first two columns, from the top to the bottom margin. Be sure it is exactly centered in the space between the columns.

- Copy that rule, and set the page view to Fit in Window. To paste the copy directly on top of the original, press Command-Option-V on a Mac, Ctrl-Shift-P on a PC. Then, holding down the Shift key, drag the copy to the right until it is centered between the next pair of column guides. (For another method, see the advanced technique described below.)

5. Change the default typeface.

- Being sure that there is no insertion point and that nothing is selected, specify 10/12 Helvetica in either the Control Palette or the Type Specs dialog box.

When you change type specifications and there is no text insertion point (and no text selected), those specs become the default for that

COLUMN RULES: ADVANCED TECHNIQUE

You want the vertical rules between columns to be in exactly the middle of the alley. And if you have three or more columns, you want the rules between each pair to be exactly alike. Here's how to do this with mathematical precision.

Move the zero point to the left margin of the alley between the columns. The alley is 1p wide, so when you position the rule between columns, the x-coordinate in the Control Palette should read 0p6. To reset the zero point back to the upper left corner of the page, double-click on the zero-point marker between the two rulers.

When you have the rule exactly centered in the space between the first and second columns and exactly aligned at the top and bottom margins, copy the rule and use the Multiple Paste command to ensure the same placement of the copy in the alley between the second and third columns.

In the Multiple Paste dialog box, specify 1 copy, Horizontal Offset 13p6 (the narrow columns are 12p6 + 1 pica in between, so you want to move the copy of the rule a total of 13p6), Vertical Offset 0. Press Return or Enter, and PageMaker positions the copy of the rule exactly where it should be.

document. Any new text you type will have the default specifications. It's helpful to set your default typeface to whatever face you'll be using for assorted odds and ends, and in this newsletter that's Helvetica.

6. Save as a template.

In the Save As dialog box, PageMaker gives you the option of saving the file as a publication or as a template. If you choose Template, when you open the file in the future, PageMaker will automatically open an untitled copy instead of the original. This enables you to reuse the original template each time you lay out the publication.

If you want to open the original template to make corrections, in the Open dialog box click the Original button. If you forget and open an untitled copy, you can do a Save As using the same filename as the original. PageMaker will ask whether you want to replace the original; respond Yes.

Windows users: When you save a document as a template, PageMaker adds a pt5 extension to the filename.

Save as:
○ **Publication**
◉ **Template**

▲ ▲ ▲

For documents that you create repeatedly, such as newsletters, select the Template option in the Save As dialog box.

DEFINE STYLES

If you are not familiar with PageMaker's style sheets, see the step-by-step instructions in the sidebar beginning on page 311. Use those instructions to learn how to define styles, and then return to this section to finish defining the style sheet for this project.

If you are familiar with PageMaker's style sheets, use the Define Styles dialog box (Command-3 or Ctrl-3) to define the following styles for the newsletter. Before creating the style sheet, we removed all of PageMaker's default styles, and we suggest that you do the same. Also, rather than listing the styles alphabetically, as they appear in the Style Palette, we've chosen an order that allows you to define them most efficiently, taking advantage of the Based On style feature. Still, a little back and forth between styles is inevitable. (See the tip at left.)

The style definitions include some attributes that we haven't worked with in earlier projects. See the notes following a style definition for explanations.

body text Next Style: same style; Type: 10/12 Palatino; Paragraph: First Indent 0p10, Widow Control 2, Orphan Control 2; Hyphenation: Limit consecutive hyphens to 2.

> By specifying 2 lines for both **widow and orphan control,** you tell PageMaker that you want at least two lines of a new paragraph at the bottom of a column and at least two lines at the end of a paragraph that falls at the top of a column. If necessary, PageMaker will force text from one column or page to the next in order to adhere to these specs, leaving some columns shorter than others. Note this timesaver: You don't have to click the Widow (or Orphan) box before you type a setting; just type the number, and the box will automatically be selected.

> Make conscious decisions about **hyphenation** (a Type menu command), which you can specify as part of a style definition by selecting the Hyphenation button in the Edit Style dialog box. We usually limit

TIP

To incorporate the **Based On** and **Next Style** options into a style definition, you sometimes have to return to one style definition after you've created others. For example, in the *news divider* style, you can't specify the Next Style as *news text* until you've defined the *news text* style; and in the *news text* style, you can't specify the Next Style as *news divider* until you've defined the *news divider* style.

consecutive hyphens to 2, and we turn hyphenation off in headlines and other display text. For captions, we specified Manual Only hyphenation. Manual Only means PageMaker won't automatically hyphenate any words, but if you really need a hyphen to make the copy fit, you can insert a "soft" hyphen by pressing Command-hyphen or Ctrl-hyphen; PageMaker will include the hyphen only if a line break occurs at that point.

body first Based On: *body text*; Next Style: *body text*; Paragraph: First Indent 0.

news text Based On: *body text*; Next Style: *news divider.*

news divider Next Style: *news text*; Type: 14/14 Zapf Dingbats; Paragraph: Alignment Centered, Space Before 0p6, Space After 0p4; Spacing: Desired Letterspacing 200%.

To set the **Desired Letterspacing,** click the Spacing button in the Paragraph dialog box to bring up the Spacing Attributes dialog box. The value specified for Desired Letterspacing must be between the values specified for maximum and minimum. So in order to set Desired Letterspacing to 200%, you must first change the Maximum Letterspacing to 200%. For more information about Spacing Attributes, see page 43.

caption Type: 10/14 Helvetica Bold; Hyphenation: Manual Only.

forecast text Based On: *caption*; Next Style: same style; Paragraph: Space After 0p7.

story head Next Style: *body first*; Type: 14/15 Helvetica Bold; Paragraph: Space Before 0p9, Space After 0p4, Keep Lines Together, Keep with Next 3 Lines; Rule Above 6 point, Width of Column with Right Indent 7p and (using the Options button) 1p10 above baseline; Hyphenation off.

For headline styles, specify **Keep Lines Together** (to avoid any column or page breaks in the middle of a headline) and **Keep with Next 3 Lines** (to avoid separating a headline from the first 3 lines of the story that follows). As with widow and orphan control, if necessary PageMaker will force text from one column or page to the next in order to adhere to these specs.

dept head Next Style: *forecast text*; Type: 18/18 Helvetica Bold Italic reverse, Case All Caps, Track Very Loose; Paragraph: Alignment Centered; Rule Above: 30 point, Width of Column and (using the Options button) 1p9 above baseline.

subhead Based On: *story head*; Next Style: *body first*; Type: 10/13; Paragraph: Space Before 0p6, Space After 0p3, Keep with Next 2 Lines; minus top rule.

breakout Based On: *subhead*; Type: 14/14; Paragraph: Alignment Centered, Space Before 0; Hyphenation off.

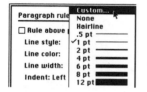

▲ ▲ ▲

Paragraph rules *can be any weight you want. To specify a weight other than those listed on the pull-down menu: In the Paragraph Rules dialog box, choose Custom from the Line Style menu....*

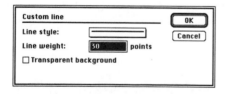

▲ ▲ ▲

...When the **Custom Line** *dialog box appears, specify the Line Weight in points (for example, for the department head rule you specify 30 points, not 2p6).*

Blueprint instructions continue on page 320, following the "Styles" sidebar.

HOW TO CREATE AND USE A STYLE SHEET IN PAGEMAKER

Learning how to use style sheets can save you more time than any other feature in PageMaker. And the good news is that if you know how to format text using the Control Palette or the various commands on the Type menu, you already know a great deal about how to define a style. The difference is that instead of specifying half a dozen attributes (font, size, leading, indents, and so on) for a single unit of selected text, you give that collection of attributes a name. The name is the style; the attributes are the style definition.

Once you've defined the style, you can apply all its attributes to selected text just by clicking on the name of the style, instead of having to specify each attribute individually. One click, instead of many. When you apply a style to a paragraph, the paragraph is said to be "tagged" with that style.

Using styles has two other fundamental advantages. One is that styles ensure consistency among similar text elements throughout a publication. Whenever you have a caption, for example, just apply the caption style to it and all your captions will look alike.

You don't have to remember all the type attributes of a caption, you just have to remember what element you consider a caption. (With long, complex documents, remembering the style names for various elements is not as trivial as this example suggests.)

A second advantage is that you can easily change the formatting in an entire document. You want to change all the headlines from Helvetica to Futura? No problem. It will take only a minute to change the style definition; PageMaker then automatically changes all the paragraphs tagged with that style.

Applying Styles

Before we look at defining styles, let's look at how easy it is to apply them. Actually, there are four techniques, described below. The first three techniques can be used in layout or story view. Whichever method you choose, you must first use the text tool to set an insertion point in the paragraph to which you want to apply a style or to select several paragraphs if you want to apply the same style to them all.

How to Apply a Style

Technique 1. Type the name *of the style you want to apply in the Control Palette's paragraph style text field. Then click Apply, or press Return or Enter.*

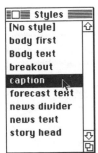

Technique 2. In the Style Palette, *click on the name of the style that you want to apply.*

The Style Palette lists, in alphabetic order, all the styles defined for a publication. You can bring the Palette on- and off-screen through the Style Palette command on the Window menu or by pressing Command-Y or Ctrl-Y. You can resize the Style Palette and move it around the screen as you would any other window.

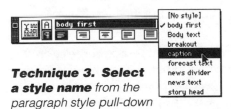

Technique 3. Select a style name *from the paragraph style pull-down menu, in the Control Palette. The style currently applied is indicated by a check mark and will be replaced by the style you now select.*

Technique 4. Use keyboard shortcuts. *(Mac layout view only.)*

To apply the first 12 styles listed in the style sheet, press Command plus F1 through F12. To apply the next 12 styles, press Command-Shift plus F1 through F12. Note: No Style is always F1. So for the style sheet shown here, body first would be F2, body text would be F3, and so on.

To make it easier to remember, include the number in the style name (for example, "2 body first," "3 body text," and so on). Using numbers in the names also enables you to place frequently used styles at the top of the list, even if their alphabetic position would otherwise place them farther down on the list.

Continues on following page

STYLES *(continued)*

Defining a Style by Example

It's remarkably easy to create a style based on text you've already formatted. All you have to do is set an insertion point in the formatted text and then type the new style name in the Control Palette's paragraph style text field. It really is that simple!

For practice, type one or two lines of text in one of the 12p6 columns in the newsletter template and give it the attributes of the *Newsline* story headline, listed below. (To simplify this first exercise, we've left out some of the attributes for this style; when you've finished with this sidebar, see page 309 for the complete style definition.)

Type: 14/15 Helvetica Bold.

Paragraph: Space Before 0p9, Space After 0p4, and (using the Rules button in the Paragraph dialog box) Rule Above 6 point, Width of Column with Right Indent 7p and (using the Options button to define the position of the rule) 1p10 above baseline. (For more on paragraph rules, see page 292.)

- Follow the steps in the box below to define a *story head* style based on the formatted text. PageMaker adds the story head style to the style sheet.

- Now set an insertion point somewhere else on the page and type another one- or two-line headline. With the insertion point anywhere in that new headline, select the paragraph style text field in the Control Palette, type *story head*, and

click Apply; or choose that style from the pull-down menu, and watch PageMaker apply all the attributes of the first headline to the new one. Pretty terrific, isn't it? It gets even better when you add the Next Style option, which we'll do a little later.

The Define Styles Dialog Box

Now that you've seen how simple it can be to define and apply a style, let's look at the full power of this feature in the Define Styles dialog box. To display this dialog box, choose Define Styles from the Type menu, or press Command-3 on a Mac or Ctrl-3 on a PC. Do that now. But to keep things simple, first set an insertion point outside of any existing text block.

The Define Styles dialog box is a sort of home base, with buttons for four actions you might want to take regarding styles: Create **New** styles, **Edit** existing styles, **Remove** existing styles from the style sheet, and **Copy** a style sheet from another publication. The alphabetic list on the left side of the dialog box includes all the styles created for the current publication. (There are six default styles for every new publication.) When you click on a style name, the attributes of that style are displayed below the list.

What this dialog box does, essentially, is allow you to create and edit one style after another, without returning to the layout. In the process, you'll move through a whole chain of dialog boxes, and although it may be confusing at first, you'll soon see that many of the options are familiar ones.

Defining a Style by Example

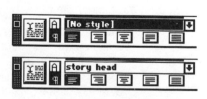

1. Format some text with the desired type and paragraph attributes. With the text insertion point set in that paragraph . . .

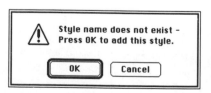

2. . . . Select the paragraph style field in the Control Palette (top) and type the name of the new style (bottom). You should choose a name that isn't already on the style sheet. Click Apply.

3. You'll see a message box asking whether you want to add the new style to the style sheet. Click OK, or press Return or Enter.

Defining a New Style

You've seen how to define a new style by example, without using any dialog box at all. Now let's use the Define Styles command to create a new style for the news dividers used on page 2 of *Newsline*.

- In the Define Styles dialog box, click on New. This brings up the Edit Style dialog box.

- In the Edit Style dialog box, the buttons on the right give you access to the type- and paragraph-formatting options that you've been working with in previous projects. When you define styles, instead of using the Control Palette to choose those options, you use dialog boxes. (For a review of the options in those dialog boxes, see pages 259 and 275.)

  But first, in the Name text box, type *news divider*.

- Click the Type button, and in the Type Specs dialog box, specify 14/14 Zapf Dingbats. Click OK, or press Return or Enter, to close the dialog box. PageMaker returns to the Edit Style dialog box.

- Now click on the Paragraph button. (It's abbreviated "Para..." on-screen, but we'll write it out for ease of reading.) Specify Alignment Centered, Space Before 0p6, Space After 0p4.

- Still in the Paragraph dialog box, click the Spacing button. This displays the Spacing Attributes dialog box, in which you can alter the spacing between letters and words. We want the Zapf Dingbats set open, so for the Desired Letterspacing, specify 200%.

  Note: The value for the desired spacing must be between the values specified for maximum and minimum. So you must also change the Maximum Letterspacing to 200%.

- Click OK in the Spacing Attributes dialog box . . . and OK in the Paragraph dialog box . . . and you're back in the Edit Style dialog box. In a chain of dialog boxes such as this, you can okay and close all of them at once by holding down the Option key (Mac) or the Shift key (PC) and clicking OK. Do that now to return to the layout.

- To test the style, set an insertion point anywhere on the page and type *vvv* ("v" is the keyboard

Using the Define Styles Dialog Box to Define Several Styles

Use the Define Styles command on the Type menu to define or edit several styles one after the other without returning to the layout. From this dialog box, you can also remove styles and copy style sheets from other PageMaker publications.

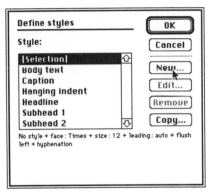

To define a new style, *click on the New button. If the name of an existing style is highlighted when you click New, the New style will be based on that highlighted style. See "Basing One Style on Another" on page 315.*

To edit an existing style, *select the name of the style you want to edit, and click the Edit button.*

Choosing New or Edit in the Define Styles dialog box (top) brings up the Edit Style dialog box. The Type, Paragraph, Tabs, and Hyphenation buttons take you to the same dialog boxes displayed when you choose one of those commands from the Type menu.

Continues on following page

STYLES *(continued)*

character for the Dingbat ❖ used in the newsletter). In the Control Palette, type *news divider* in the paragraph style text box. Actually, because it's the only style beginning with N, you only have to type the first letter and click Apply. Set an insertion point and do the same thing again. Are you convinced that styles can save you time?

Editing or Redefining a Style

By way of example, let's redefine PageMaker's default style for *body text* so that it defines the body text style used in the newsletter in this project.

- In the Define Styles dialog box, click on *body text* in the Styles list, and then click Edit.

The Style Palette or the Control Palette?

Do you really need to learn two or three or more ways to do the same thing? When it comes to working with styles, yes, there are definite advantages to mastering both the Control Palette and the Style Palette.

We've always relied a lot on the Style Palette. On our large 24-inch monitor, there's plenty of room to leave the Palette on-screen, displaying even a long style list. So we can quickly click on any style name, either to apply the style or to edit it.

With the Control Palette, on the other hand, you may first have to change from the character view to the paragraph view to get to the style list. And although you can type the name in the paragraph style text field, new users are more likely to scroll the list, and that takes time.

Even with our overall preference for the Style Palette, there are three Control Palette techniques that we highly recommend: defining a new style by example (page 312); redefining a style by example (described on this page); and typing the name of the style you want to apply (technique 1 on page 311). Of course, you can only type the name of a style if you remember what you named it. Did you name it *news divider* or *dingbat divider*? *Bullets flush left* or *flush left bullets*? With complex style sheets, it can be difficult to remember.

- In the Edit Style dialog box, note the definition for the default *body text* style at the bottom of the dialog box. The phrasing is different from the way we usually describe type, but it's essentially 12/Auto Times Roman, First Indent 2.

- Click the Type button, and in the Type Specs dialog box, specify 10/12 Palatino. Click OK to return to the Edit Style dialog box.

- Click the Paragraph button, and in the Paragraph Specs dialog box, change the First Indent to 0p10, and type 2 in each of the text boxes for widow and orphan control. Click OK. In the Edit Style dialog box, note the new definition of *body text*. Press Option-OK or Shift-OK to close the two remaining dialog boxes.

- Now type a few lines of text, and apply the *body text* style to that paragraph.

Redefining a Style by Example

You can redefine a style by example too.

- Type a few lines of text and give it the attributes of the captions used in *Newsline*: 10/14 Helvetica Bold.

- In the Control Palette's paragraph view, select the Styles field and type the name of the style you want to redefine. (In this example, type *caption*.)

Shortcut to the Edit Style Dialog Box

When you want to work on a single style, you can bypass the Define Styles dialog box by using either the Style Palette or the paragraph style pull-down list in the Control Palette.

Hold down the Command or Ctrl key while you click on the name of the style you want to edit. This displays the Edit Style dialog box for the style that you clicked on.

You can use this technique to define a new style too. Hold down the Command or Ctrl key while you click on No Style. This displays the Edit Style dialog box with the Style name field empty. Name the new style, define the attributes, and then return to the layout.

- Press Command-Shift or Ctrl-Shift and click on the style name you just typed. PageMaker displays a prompt asking whether you want to update the style. Click OK, or press Return or Enter, and it's done.

Another method is to set the insertion point in the formatted paragraph, press Command or Ctrl, and click on No Style in the Style Palette; then, in the Edit Style Name box, type the name of the style that you are redefining by example. The disadvantage of this method is that when you return to the layout, No Style is still highlighted in the style list, indicating that the style you just edited has not been applied to the formatted paragraph you used to edit it. You still have to apply the style to the sample text.

Basing One Style on Another Style

The Based On option tells PageMaker to base a new style on one that you've already defined. For this example, we'll define a style for the first paragraph of the newsletter stories. The formatting is identical to the *body text* style except that in the first paragraph following a headline, the first line is not indented. (In general, paragraphs following a headline, subhead, or clearly marked section break don't require a paragraph indent.)

- In the Style Palette, select the style you want to base the new style on (in this case, *body text*).

- Hold down Command or Ctrl, and click on No Style in the Style Palette or the Control Palette.

When the Edit Style dialog box comes on-screen, note that the Based On option specifies *body text*.

General Principle: The fact that you click on No Style in the Palette tells PageMaker you want to define a new style. But the style name that is highlighted *when* you click on No Style tells PageMaker which style you want to base the new style on. If you don't highlight a style in the Palette before clicking on No Style, the Based On box will specify No Style. To change the Based On style after you're in the Edit Style dialog box, scroll the Based On pull-down list to choose another style name.

Basing One Style on Another

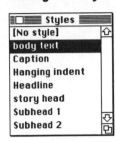 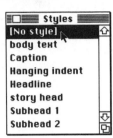

1. In the Style Palette or on the Control Palette paragraph style list, highlight the style you want to base the new style on (left), and then hold down the Command or Ctrl key and click once on No Style (right).

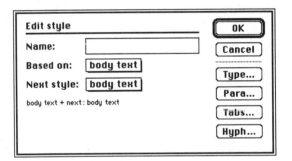

2. PageMaker displays the Edit Style dialog box for an unnamed style. The Based On option specifies body text, *the style that was selected when you clicked on No Style.*

3. Use the buttons on the right to specify the attributes that are unique to this new style, and then name the style. Here, we removed the first-line indent. Note that the style definition at the bottom of the dialog box lists only those attributes that differ from the base style.

Continues on following page

STYLES *(continued)*

- In the Edit Style dialog box, name the new style (in this case, we called it *body first*), and use the Paragraph option to specify the First Indent as 0. Click OK. Note the definition of the style at the bottom of the dialog box: Body Text + First Indent: 0. When you base one style on another, PageMaker's style definition lists only those attributes that differ from the base style.

   Click OK to return to the layout.

The main advantage of basing one style on another is that if you change the formatting of the base style, those changes carry over to any style based on it. For example, if you decide to change the *body text* style to Times Roman, all you have to do is change the font for the *body text* style; PageMaker automatically changes the font for the *body first* style because it is based on *body text*. And of course it will apply those changes to all the text throughout the document to which you've applied either of those two styles.

Using the Next Style Option

The Next Style option adds another level of automation by enabling you to specify that one style is always followed by another. It's a wonderfully elegant option.

In the newsletter in this project, for example, the headline is always followed by the *body first* style, which is always followed by the *body text* style. If you set that up with the Next Style option, here's what happens when you type a headline and apply the *story head* style: When you press Return or Enter and start typing a new paragraph, the new paragraph will automatically be in the *body first* style, and when you press Return and start typing again, that new paragraph will automatically be in the *body text* style.

Take a minute to test this for yourself, and you will forever be convinced of the value of styles.

- Command-click or Ctrl-click on *story head* in the Style Palette. In the Edit Style dialog box, scroll the Next Style pull-down menu and select *body first*. Click OK.

- Command-click or Ctrl-click on *body first* in the Style Palette. In the Edit Style dialog box, select *body text* from the Next Style menu. Click OK.

- Now type one or two lines and apply the *story head* style.

- Press Return or Enter to begin a new paragraph, and type a couple more lines. You don't need to click on the *body first* style: It's automatically

Specifying the Next Style

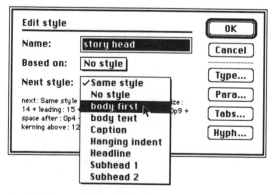

1. In this newsletter, the story head is always followed by a paragraph with the body first *style. So in the Edit Style box for* story head, *scroll the Next Style pull-down list and select* body first *from the list.*

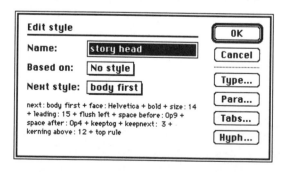

2. The Next Style becomes part of the style definition. Any time you tag a paragraph with the story head *style and then press Return and begin typing, the new paragraph will automatically have the* body first *style applied to it.*

highlighted in the Style Palette, and the text is already properly formatted.

- Press Return or Enter to start another paragraph, type a few more lines, and note that, again, PageMaker has already formatted this paragraph in the *body text* style. Because the Next Style for *body text* is *same style*, all subsequent paragraphs that you type will be in the *body text* style until you specify otherwise.

Removing a Style

To delete a style, bring up the Define Styles dialog box. Click on the name of the style that you want to delete, and then click Remove.

In the newsletter, we won't be using the *hanging indent, headline, subhead 1*, and *subhead 2* styles, so click on each name and remove it. This is more a matter of good housekeeping than of necessity, but it's helpful to keep the style list short.

WARNING: Be careful when you remove styles. After you close the Define Styles dialog box, you can't undo the remove. Clicking Cancel, however, cancels any changes you've made since you opened the dialog box.

Copying Styles from Another Document

- When you want the current publication to use the same style sheet as some other publication, select the Copy button in the Define Styles dialog box.

- This displays a Copy Styles dialog box that lets you scroll through your directories and folders to select the name of the file containing the style sheet you want to copy. In this dialog box, you can move forward and backward in the hierarchy just as you do in the Save As, Open, and Place dialog boxes.

- If the two documents have any style names in common, PageMaker displays a message box asking whether you want to "Copy over existing styles?" If you click OK, the definitions from the style sheet you are copying will replace the definitions in the current document.

Note: You can't copy selective styles in this dialog box—you have to copy the whole style sheet. But if you do want to copy selective styles, there are several workarounds. When you copy text from one PageMaker document to another—either through the Clipboard or by using the pointer tool to drag text from one publication window to another—any styles associated with the text are copied as well. Also, you can place text that includes the styles you want from one PageMaker document into another (See page 319.)

Overriding a Style

A style applies to an entire paragraph. You can't have a second style for selected text within the same paragraph, but you can override the style for selected text by applying different specs—italic, boldface, indents, and so on—to that text. Whenever you select a paragraph that includes a style override, you'll see a plus sign (+) following the name in the style list.

Type Style options (available in the Control Palette and the Type Specs dialog box), such as italic or boldface, with the exception of reverse, are permanent overrides. Even if you apply a different style to that paragraph, the type-style override remains. **To remove the type-style override,** select the text and change the Type Style option. Or select the paragraph and press Command-Shift-Spacebar on a Mac, Ctrl-Shift-Spacebar on a PC.

All other overrides, such as typeface, size, indents, tabs, and space before and after, are temporary; if you apply a different style to the paragraph, the style override is removed.

To preserve a temporary override when you change the style of a paragraph, hold down the Shift key when you select the new style name.

To incorporate an override into the style definition, select the text with the style and override applied, and then press Command-Shift or Ctrl-Shift and click on the style name in the Palette. This feature isn't nearly as useful as being able to mix styles in the same paragraph (for that, we'll have to wait for PageMaker 6 or 7). But it can be useful.

In this book, for example, we frequently use Helvetica Condensed Black leadins for the Palatino body text. Incorporating the Helvetica override as

Continues on following page

STYLES *(continued)*

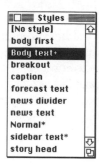

A + after a style name *indicates that the selected text has a style override, such as an indent not specified as part of the style or an italicized phrase within a paragraph whose text style is roman.*
An * after a style name *indicates that the style was imported with text from another application and is not part of the original PageMaker style sheet.*

part of the body text style doesn't eliminate the need to format the leadin manually; but it does eliminate the asterisk from the style list when a paragraph with that override is selected (so that you aren't left wondering what you did to that paragraph); and if you reapply *body text* to a paragraph with one of these leadins, the leadin won't be removed.

Importing Styles from Word-Processor Files

If you define and apply styles in a word-processor file and PageMaker has an import filter for that program, you can import the word-processor's style sheet when you place the text. Just be sure the Retain Format option is selected in the Place dialog box, which it is by default. (If you define styles using bracketed style name tags at the beginning of paragraphs, select the Read Tags option in the Place dialog box.)

If a style name used in the word-processor file is identical to a style name in the PageMaker file, but the definitions of the styles are different, the PageMaker style definition will override the word-processor definition.

If a style name used in the word-processor file is not included in the PageMaker style sheet, PageMaker adds that style name to its own style sheet. In the Style Palette, these imported styles are denoted by an asterisk following the name. Note, though, that PageMaker imports only styles that have actually been applied to text in the word-processor file; if you defined a style there but didn't actually use it, the style isn't imported into PageMaker.

Be aware that you may lose some formatting from the word-processor styles, depending on the compatibility of the word processor's style sheet with PageMaker's. And formatting that does not have an equivalent in PageMaker, such as a box around a paragraph, will not be imported. For a list of formatting elements that PageMaker does and does not import, see Online Help (from the Window menu on the Mac or the Help menu on the PC). For more on using Online Help, see page 194.

Applying Styles in the Story Editor

One of the satisfying things about applying styles is seeing all that formatting just happen. You don't get that thrill in the Story Editor (most formatting isn't displayed), but you do get lightning speed.

When you place a word-processor file that doesn't already have styles applied (or doesn't have the correct styles applied), import the file directly into the Story Editor (see page 277). To apply the styles, you can use the Style Palette or the Control Palette, just as you do in layout view. But you don't have to move from page to page and you don't have to wait for the screen to redraw when you apply the styles. When you place the story window in the layout, the text will be formatted according to the styles you've defined.

Printing a Style Sheet

You can't print a style sheet in PageMaker, but you can print one from some word processors. Here's how we print ours in Microsoft Word on a Mac.

- Export the styled text from PageMaker to Word. (See the sidebar "Using PageMaker's Export Feature" on page 335.) The styles applied to the exported text will be exported as well.

- Open the file in Word and choose Define Styles from the Format menu. While the dialog box is open, choose Print from the File menu.

If you use Microsoft Word for Windows, export the styled text from PageMaker to Word. Open the exported file in Word, and choose Print from the File menu. In the Print dialog box, click on the arrow to the right of the Print text box, and choose Styles from the pull-down list.

Word will print the style sheet in whatever typeface is defined as Normal for that publication. Style attributes that are unavailable in the word processor (such as reverse type and paragraph rules) and some style overrides (such as initial caps) will not be exported; you'll need to note those by hand on the printout.

Styles defined in the PageMaker document but not included in the exported or copied story won't be exported.

For a document with many different stories, use this technique to combine the stories and their styles into one story that you can export: Open a new PageMaker document. Choose Place, and select the name of the PageMaker document that contains the style list you want to export. In the Place PageMaker Stories dialog box, which lists all the stories in the document, choose Select All, and then press Return. PageMaker imports all the stories from the placed document as a single story. Export that single story and proceed as described above.

The Display Pub Info and List Styles Used options (from the Additions pull-down list on the Utilities menu) sound as if they should enable you to print style sheets, but in fact they are of limited use because they don't include the definitions of the styles on the list.

To display and hide the Style Palette: Press Command-Y on a Mac, Ctrl-Y on a PC.

To bring the Define Styles dialog box on-screen: Press Command-3 on a Mac, Ctrl-3 on a PC.

To OK (or Cancel) and close out of a nest of style dialog boxes: Hold down the Option key on a Mac, the Shift key on a PC, and click OK (or press Return). This is a great timesaver, well worth remembering.

To select the paragraph style field in the Control Palette, triple-click on that field (Mac only).

A style is not defined until you click OK in the Edit Style dialog box. If you click Cancel after defining or editing a style, that style will not be recorded.

Once you OK the Define Styles dialog box, you can't undo actions taken there with the Undo command.

Styles are a paragraph attribute. When you want to apply a style to a single paragraph, just set an insertion point anywhere in the paragraph and click on the style name. You don't have to drag over the entire paragraph.

Create a style for each type of page element. If you think two of those elements will have the same formatting, create two identical styles with different names, and apply each style to the appropriate element. This may seem fussy, but consider the following situation. When you first design the document, you think the story heads and sidebar heads should be identical. But you later decide to change the formatting of the sidebar heads. If you initially defined and applied identical styles with different names, all you have to do to make the change is edit the definition of sidebar heads. But if you applied the same style to both story and sidebar heads, in order to make the change, you have to define a new style and search through the document to apply that style to all the sidebar heads.

This one is very quirky. If you apply local formatting, such as boldface, to text, and then later apply a style that includes that same local formatting, the local formatting will be removed. It's as though the redundancy cancels out the specification. To restore the local formatting, select that text, and reapply the formatting.

To change PageMaker's default styles, or to remove them in order to start with a blank style sheet each time you open a new document, choose Define Styles when there is no publication open and make the desired changes.

Convert all styles imported with a word-processing file into PageMaker styles. In the Define Styles dialog box, select any style with an asterisk (which denotes an imported style), and click Edit; in the Edit Style dialog box, click OK. When you return to the Define Styles dialog box, the asterisk has been deleted from the style name, indicating that it is now a PageMaker style. Repeat for all imported styles. This is simple to do and can prevent problems that result when style definitions get confused, which can happen when you import multiple word-processing documents with overlapping style names.

When you finish reading this sidebar, return to page 309 to define the rest of the styles for this project.

COVER TEMPLATE

As you create the elements for each page of the template, refer to the sample document on pages 301–2.

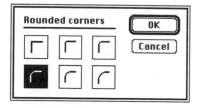

▲ ▲ ▲

To create a box with rounded corners, draw a rectangle. With the rectangle selected, choose Rounded Corners from the Element menu, and click on one of the corner options.

TIP

To select multiple items, use the pointer tool to drag a selection box around the items. If the items are not adjacent, use this alternative method: Select one item, hold down the Shift key, and select the next item; continue selecting items with the Shift key pressed.

1. Click on the page 1 icon in the lower right corner of the screen.

Note that the items you created on the master page are displayed on the regular pages of the publication.

2. On the Layout menu, turn off Display Master Items.

On the cover, the banner, date, and column rules are in different positions than on the inside pages, so you will create them specifically for this page rather than using the ones you created on the master page.

3. Create the elements that will appear on the cover of every issue of the newsletter.

Banner: Depth is 5p, beginning at the 4p horizontal ruler guide; Line is None, Fill is 40%.

Logotype: Type is 52/46 Helvetica Bold outline, all caps, flush left at the second column. Baseline is at 10p6.

PC users note: There is no outline style, so just use Helvetica Bold, or a heavier typeface if you have one.

Overline: Type is 18/18 Helvetica Bold, aligned right with the logotype; baseline is at 6p.

"S" in upper left: Type is 30-point Aachen Bold reverse, which creates a really fat outline shape. You can substitute 36-point Helvetica Bold reverse; note how thin it looks in comparison to the Aachen (see page 301). The box was created with the rectangle tool, with a Line of None and a Fill of 60%. To make rounded corners on the box, see the caption at left.

Issue date: Type is 10/12 Helvetica, positioned just below the banner. (Now wouldn't it have been nice to have defined an issue date style when you created the issue date on the master page and be able to use that style here?)

Forecasts head: Type the headline in the left column, about two-thirds of the way down the column. (The exact vertical position will be determined by the depth of the "Forecasts" text in each issue because the last line of text should be aligned with the bottom margin.) With the text cursor in the headline, apply the *dept head* style from either the Style Palette or the Control Palette (paragraph view).

Forecasts text: With the insertion point still in the "Forecasts" headline, specify the Paragraph Space After as 2p3. Press Return or Enter to begin a new paragraph and type several lines of dummy text. The text should automatically be formatted in the *forecast text* style because that is defined as the Next Style for *dept head*.

Horizontal ruler guide at 12p6: This marks the top of any photos and text blocks on the cover. When you place text, you'll position the top of the loaded text icon at this ruler guide.

Horizontal rule at 11p6: Line weight is 0.5 point, width is 45p from the left to the right margin.

Vertical column rules: Line weight is 0.5 point, length is 49p9 from the 12p6 horizontal guide to the bottom margin. Use the Multiple Paste command, as you did for the master-page rules (page 308), and specify a horizontal offset of 13p6.

PAGE 2 TEMPLATE

1. Turn to page 2.

Click on the page 2 icon. Or press Command-Tab on a Mac, F12 on a PC.

2. Create the "Newsbriefs" column.

- In the left column, type the word *Newsbriefs*, and apply the *dept head* style to it.

- Reposition the headline so that the top of the rule is aligned at the top margin (9p6).

- Bring in a horizontal ruler guide at 15p to mark the top of the "Newsbriefs" text.

> **TIP**
>
> **To move to the next page,** press Command-Tab on a Mac, F12 on a PC. To move to **the previous page,** press Command-Shift-Tab on a Mac, F11 on a PC.

3. Create a text placeholder for the breakout.

A placeholder is simply an item that you create to define the position for either text or graphics that you'll place on the page each time you produce the publication. You can't create text placeholders on the master page because you can't type over master-page text on regular pages. So you have to create them on the individual pages.

- In the gray banner at the top of the page, use the text tool to draw a bounding box from the left edge to the right edge.

- Type a single line of dummy text and apply the *breakout* style.

- With the pointer tool, adjust the position of the breakout so that its baseline is on the 6p horizontal ruler guide.

4. Copy the breakout and the "Newsbriefs" banner and headline.

You'll be able to paste them directly into position on page 3.

PAGE 3 TEMPLATE

1. Turn to page 3.

2. Power-paste the items that you copied from page 2.

Press Command-Option-V on a Mac, Ctrl-Shift-P on a PC. The items you copied on page 2 will be pasted into the same positions on page 3. Then double-click on the word "Newsbriefs" to select it, and type *People*.

3. Create a picture placeholder.

Create a box to serve as a placeholder for the first photo. The top of the box should be 15 points below the bottom of the banner. (For an advanced positioning technique, see the sidebar below.)

4. Create spacing guides to maintain a consistent distance between photos and captions.

In this project, the distance from the bottom of a photo to the top window-shade handle of the caption below should be 6 points. The distance from the baseline of the last line of a caption to the top of the next photo should be 20 points. How do you ensure that those spaces are always consistent?

There are two basic techniques. Using arithmetic in the Control Palette (described below and on page 334) gives you precision, but you have to remember the distance you want to measure. Spacing guides are a little slower, but they don't rely on memory. A spacing guide is simply a short line of text that has the same leading as the desired distance. You'll create spacing guides here, as part of the template, and learn how to use them on page 334, when you create an actual issue of the newsletter.

- Type one line of text that says *photo to caption,* and make the type specs 10/6 Helvetica.

- Set a new insertion point, type another line that says *caption to photo,* and specify 10/20 Helvetica. In both cases, the critical spec is the leading. But it's a good idea to use a typeface that's already in the document, just to keep things simple.

USING ARITHMETIC IN THE CONTROL PALETTE: ADVANCED TECHNIQUE

You can use arithmetic in the Control Palette to define the position of one object relative to another. (If you have trouble following these instructions, see page 206 for a complete description of the Proxy and reference points.)

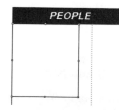

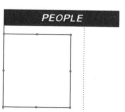

1. Position the rectangle so that the top is aligned with the bottom of the "People" headline. Leave the rectangle selected.

2. In the Control Palette, click once on any of the handles at the top of the Proxy. That tells PageMaker you want to move the selected object from the top. After the y value in the Position field, type +1p3. You can use the numeric keypad or the main keyboard. Then press Return or Enter.

3. PageMaker adds 1p3 to the y value, which moves the rectangle down 15 points.

PAGE 4 TEMPLATE

1. Turn to page 4.

2. On the Layout menu, turn off Display Master Items.

3. Bring in a horizontal ruler guide at 33p.

This bisects the page and indicates where the newsletter will be folded for mailing. The bottom part of the page carries the mailing information; the top part of the page becomes the mailing cover.

4. Create the mailing side, using the following specs.

Banner: Top is 2p6 from fold guide; depth is 5p9; width is across left and center columns; Line is None; Fill is 40%.

Mailing permit: Depth of box is same as banner; width is 7p aligned at right margin; Type is 9/11 Helvetica, centered, inset about 6 points from the edge of the box on both sides. When you do self-mailers, be sure to check the specs for your mailing permit with the Postal Service.

Logotype: Type is 42/42 Helvetica Bold outline on a Mac, or 48/48 Helvetica Bold on a PC; All Caps; the middle arm of the E is aligned with the bottom of the banner; the right margin of type is about 1p in from the edge of the banner.

Subhead: Type is 10/12 Helvetica, left-aligned with the logo; baseline is 1p6 below logo.

Return address: Type is same as subhead; baseline of first line is 2p3 below subhead.

Rule: Weight is 0.5 point; width is same as banner; position is centered between subhead and return address.

Cap S: Copy the type and box from the cover and paste it into position on the banner here.

5. Create a template for the mailing cover.

The camera-ready art for page 4 should look like the art shown on the next page, with the top half of the page—the mailing cover—rotated 180°. Because you'll be rotating the text, it's easiest to set it up as a single text block, using paragraph-formatting options to specify the various indents and the space between paragraphs. If you work on the fly—breaking apart text blocks and visually determining the alignments and spacing—things can get muddled when you rotate all those different text blocks.

There's another advantage to setting up the rotated text as a single text block. If you revise the copy from one issue to the next, you can edit the rotated text in the Story Editor, and the space between elements will not be altered. (You can edit rotated text in PageMaker, but when the text is upside down, it's a lot easier to work in the Story Editor!)

TIP

When you want to format new text (in this case, the return address) like existing text (in this case, the subhead) but don't want to clutter your style list with an infrequently used style, try this: Copy a few characters of the existing text, paste them, and type over them. The new text will have the same attributes as the text you copied. Here, you may have trouble copying the subhead with the text tool because the leading of the logotype overhangs the leading of the subhead. So use the pointer tool. Click to select the "Newsline" head. Then hold down the Command or Ctrl key while you click again, which will select the layer behind the "Newsline" head, which is the subhead.

- Use the Column Guides command to specify 1 column.

- Set an insertion point just below the top margin, and type the cover copy using the default type style.

- Select lines of text as indicated, and specify the following attributes:

  Headline: 30/15 Helvetica Bold Italic, All Caps, Left Indent 0p6.

  Line 2: 14/14 Palatino Bold, Left Indent 0p8, Space After 1p6.

  Note: The roman type in line 2 is indented a couple of points from the left margin of the italic type directly above it so that the two are visually aligned. The exact amount of the indent to achieve this effect depends on the typeface and size.

  Lines 3–5: 18/20 Helvetica Bold, Left Indent 5p6.

  Line 6: 12/14 Palatino, Left Indent 5p6, Space Before 1p, Space After 1p, Paragraph Rule Above: 4 point, Column Width with 5p6 Right Indent, positioned 1p6 above baseline.

  Lines 7–11: 12/18 Helvetica, Left Indent 19p.

  Last line: 12/14 Palatino, Left Indent 5p6, Space Before 1p3, Paragraph Rule Below 0.5 point, Width of Column, positioned 1p below baseline.

6. Rotate the text on the mailing cover.

- With the pointer tool, select the entire text block.

The top of page 4 is the mailing cover, which should be oriented upside down on the camera-ready art.

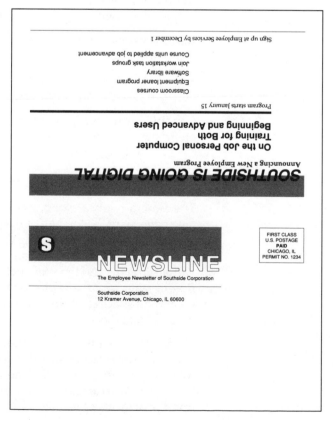

- Activate the Control Palette.

  Note that when you select text with the pointer tool, the Control Palette displays the object view, and you can manipulate the text in some of the same ways that you can manipulate graphics.

- In the Proxy, click on the center handle to make it the active reference point.

- Highlight the Control Palette rotation field, and type *180*.

  When you rotate an object, the reference point remains stationary.

  If one of the top handles were the reference point, when you rotated the object, the top of the text block would remain stationary and the bottom would be moved up to the pasteboard. If one of the bottom handles were the reference point, the bottom of the text block would remain stationary and the top would be on the wrong side of the mailing label. The easiest way to understand this is to experiment, selecting one reference point, rotating the text, observing what happens, pressing Undo (Command-Z on a Mac, Ctrl-Z on a PC), and then trying another reference point. But before you experiment, save your document so that if you get confused and think you've messed everything up, you can revert to this point in the instructions. (For information about the Revert command, see page 364.)

  When the text is rotated, the top of the headline might be clipped off and might not display even when you refresh the screen. But it will print correctly.

- With the pointer tool, position the text so that the rule below the last line is on the 3p6 horizontal guide.

- Turn on Display Master Items, and draw a box the same size as the gray banner now displayed at the top of the page. Then turn off Display Master Items. Specify a Line of None and a Fill of 40% for the rectangle.

- With the pointer tool, drag the gray box down into position behind the mailing cover headline. Because you can't see the top of the headline on the screen, you might have to go through a few printouts to get a tidy alignment of the banner and the type. We like the way it looks when the banner aligns with the arms of the G's in the words "Going Digital."

IMPORTANT: Each time you reposition an object, PageMaker moves that object to the top layer. So when you adjust the position of the gray banner, be sure to send it to the back layer; otherwise, it will cover up part of the headline instead of printing behind it.

7. Save and close the template.

The template now has all the elements needed to produce the newsletter.

▲ ▲ ▲

*To turn text, or any other object, upside down without changing its position on the page: Select the text with the pointer tool, and in the Control Palette, specify a **center handle as the reference point** (above left) so that the center of the object remains stationary when the object is rotated. In the rotation text field (above right), type 180.*

TIP

Gray fills in PageMaker are opaque. If you want type to print over a gray graphic, send the graphic to the back (Command-B on a Mac, Ctrl-B on a PC).

Blueprint continues on page 328, following the sidebar "Formatting Text in a Word Processor."

FORMATTING TEXT IN A WORD PROCESSOR

If you're starting electronic page layout with version 5.0 of PageMaker, you might think that the powerful text-editing capabilities of its Story Editor have eliminated the need for a word processor. And if you're on a tight budget, you can indeed get by with only the Story Editor. But a good word processor is still a key player if you do publication work in any volume or if you work in an organization where one person or group writes the copy and another does page layout.

The following information is intended to help you build the most efficient bridges between your word-processing program and PageMaker.

One Text File or Many?

The first rule of thumb is that stories that will run one after another in the page layout (such as the stories in columns 2 and 3 of the newsletter in this project) should be created and placed as a single file. This way, they will be threaded together in the page layout, and if you add or delete text from one story, PageMaker adjusts the other stories accordingly. If each story were placed as a separate file, copy changes in one story would force you to manually adjust the position of all the other stories.

If the various stories are written in separate files (which would be the case if different people write different stories), you should either combine the stories in a single word-processor file before placing them in PageMaker or thread them together when you do place them. (See the section on threaded text at the end of this project, and especially "Threading Unlinked Text" on page 340.)

The second rule of thumb is to create a separate text file for any copy that is self-contained, such as departments (the "Newsbriefs" column in this project) or sidebars. You don't want self-contained text to be affected by changes in the main stories, so you don't want it threaded together in a file with any other copy. (See "Unthreading Text," on page 340.)

Small amounts of text, such as the "Forecasts" on the opening page and the captions, could originate in a word processor or in PageMaker.

"Clean" Word-Processor Files

Most people bring old typewriter habits to computers, inserting extra characters (paragraph returns, tabs, Spacebar characters) in order to create divisions between sections or align indented text in their word-processor files. The problem is that when you style typography in PageMaker, or at least when you style it correctly, those extra characters get in the way, and you have to remove them.

The general principle is this: Never use a keyboard character when you can create the same result using commands on the Format menu of most word processors. (The catch, of course, is that you must learn to use the options on the Format menu.)

- Never insert more than one carriage return.

  If you want space between paragraphs, use the paragraph command in your word processor to define a "space after" of 6 to 12 points.

- Do not insert tab or Spacebar characters to indent the first line of a new paragraph.

  If you want to indent the first line, use the paragraph command to define a first-line indent.

- At the end of a sentence, press the Spacebar only once, never twice.

  PageMaker's typographic capabilities will distinguish between a word space and a space between sentences.

- Do not insert multiple tab and Spacebar characters to force alignments.

  If you don't know how to specify tabs and indents in your word processor, insert a single tab after the appropriate text, and leave the copy without proper alignments.

- Do not type anything in all caps. This includes AM, PM, and acronyms that generally appear in capital letters.

  If you type something in all caps, and the designer wants to style that text in boldface, upper- and lowercase, the designer will have to retype the text. And any time text is retyped is an opportunity for error.

If you want a headline or phrase in uppercase letters, type it in lowercase (with initial caps where grammatically correct), and use character-formatting options to specify All Caps. The designer can then "undo" the all caps formatting without retyping.

Acronyms, including AM and PM, are generally styled in small caps so that they don't stand out disproportionately in the text. If you type them in all caps, they will have to be retyped in lowercase in order to style them as small caps.

- Be aware of typographic characters.

  There are special typographic characters for quotation marks, apostrophes, and dashes. It isn't essential that you create these in your word processor. (If you check Convert Quotes in the Place dialog box, PageMaker automatically converts inch and foot marks into typeset apostrophes and quote marks, and double hyphens into em dashes.) But if you type two hyphens when you want a dash, do not insert a space character on either side of the hyphens. That space character would have to be removed manually.

Using Style Sheets in Your Word Processor

If your word processor has style sheets, you can tag each paragraph with the style name used in the PageMaker file. You don't have to do this; but even a minimum amount of formatting adds to the clarity of the words and helps the writer "see" some hierarchical structure in the text.

It doesn't matter what the style definition is in the word processor. When you place the text file in PageMaker, if the text file contains a style that has the exact same name as a style defined in the PageMaker style sheet, the PageMaker style definition overrides the word-processor style definition. So you can format your body text in a font that is easy to read on-screen in the word processor (where you don't have the advantage of 200% page view), apply the *body text* style to it, and when you place the word document in the PageMaker layout, PageMaker applies the attributes of the *body text* style defined in PageMaker.

For example, the *body text* style in this book is 10/12 Palatino, which is difficult to read on screen at actual

size. So in Microsoft Word, we define the *body text* style as 12/14, and when we place it in the layout, PageMaker automatically converts it to 10/12 because that is the *body text* style in the layout file.

The writer or the person preparing the text file doesn't even need to know what the PageMaker formatting is; he or she just needs to know which paragraphs are headlines, subheads, body text, and so on. And generally, the writer knows that better than anyone else.

If you don't assign styles in the text file, you can do it in PageMaker, either in the layout (see page 311) or, more quickly, in the Story Editor (see page 278).

If your word processor does not have style sheets, you can still tag paragraphs with style names to match the PageMaker styles. At the beginning of each paragraph, type the style name in angle brackets (<>). The tags must be at the beginning of the paragraph; any paragraph without a tag is formatted with the style of the previous paragraph. When you place a document that is marked with bracketed tags, be sure to check the Read Tags option in PageMaker's Place dialog box.

PC Filename Extensions

If you work on a PC, or if you work on a Mac and need to place files created in a PC program, the filenames must have the correct filename extensions for PageMaker to recognize them: for example, wp5 for WordPerfect 5.0 and 5.1, doc for Word for Windows, rtf for Microsoft Rich Text Format, dca for programs that create Document Content Architecture files, and txt for ASCII files. When you place a file with a nonstandard filename, a dialog box will prompt you to specify the file type.

Import Filters

PageMaker has import filters that it uses to place files from many word processors. If you're having trouble importing text from your word processor, or if the formatting is lost when you place the text, see "Trouble Placing Text or Graphic Files?" on page 331.

USING THE NEWSLINE TEMPLATE

1. Open a copy of the template.

Scroll through your folders or directories to locate the newsletter template that you saved earlier. When you open a file that you've saved as a template, PageMaker opens an untitled copy of the original. It's a good habit to save the file right away under whatever name you'll be using, such as Newsline 10/94 (or Nws10-94 if you are using a PC).

If you want to open the template itself, to make changes, click the Original button in the Open dialog box.

2. Change the issue date.

On the master page and the cover, type the current issue date over the placeholder. It's easy to forget this, so do it first thing each issue.

3. Place the body text from your word-processor file.

For practice purposes, use any text file on your hard drive. For an introduction to placing text, see the sidebar on page 268 in Project 2.

- Choose Place from the File menu (Command-D on a Mac, Ctrl-D on a PC). When the Place dialog box comes on-screen, scroll through your folders or directories to select the text file you want to place.

  Note: After you select the file to place, PageMaker may display a special Import Filter dialog box, as described on the following page.

  You may also see a dialog box with the curious name Panose Font Matching Results. This is a warning that one or more fonts included in the file you are placing are not currently installed on your system. See page 222.

- Be sure Snap to Guides is turned on so that the text will be placed within column guides.

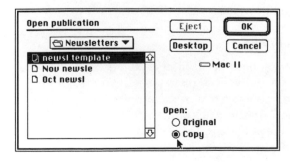

▲ ▲ ▲

On the Macintosh, files that you've saved as templates have a different icon than publication files.

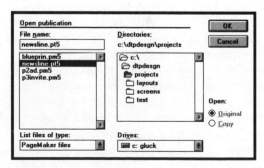

▲ ▲ ▲

On the PC, files that you've saved as templates have a pt5 extension. Publication files have a pm5 extension.

▲ ▲ ▲
*When you see the manual text-flow icon (left), hold down the Shift key to invoke the **semi-automatic text-flow** mode (right). When the text flow stops at the end of the column, PageMaker automatically reloads the text icon. To continue in the semi-automatic mode, press the Shift key before clicking the loaded text icon in each subsequent column.*

• When the loaded text icon appears, hold down the Shift key to invoke the semi-automatic text-flow mode. The timesaving advantage of the semi-automatic mode is that when the text flow stops at the bottom of a column, PageMaker automatically reloads the text icon; all you have to do is click where you want to continue placing text. (See page 269 for more on the three text-flow modes.)

• Position the loaded text icon in the center column on page 1 at the 12p6 horizontal guide and click. When PageMaker loads the text icon, hold down the Shift key again and click the text icon in the right-hand column on page 1. Continue placing text in the center and right columns on pages 2 and 3.

4. Style the body text.

• Select all the text (set an insertion point anywhere in the text on page 1 and press Command-A on a Mac, Ctrl-A on a PC).

When you use the Select All command or keyboard shortcut to select text that you want to reformat, the entire text file is selected—even text that has not yet been placed on the page.

• Apply the *body text* style using one of the techniques on page 311.

IMPORT FILTER DIALOG BOXES

If you import a text-only file, PageMaker displays the Text-Only Import Filter dialog box, which has options for the automatic removal of extra carriage returns and Spacebar characters.

When you import files from Microsoft Word, Word for Windows, or WordPerfect, holding down the Shift key while you select the name of the file to be imported prompts PageMaker to display a special dialog box for that import filter. The dialog box shown is for Microsoft Word on the Mac; the options in the dialog box vary depending on the filter. You can specify options for converting some word-processing formatting into comparable formatting in PageMaker.

If, after you choose the file you want to place, Page-Maker displays the Do Not Know How to Place dialog box, it means that the file doesn't have the extension that the import filter is specified to look for, or that the appropriate filter hasn't been installed. See page 331, "Trouble Placing Text or Graphic Files?" for suggestions on what to do in this situation.

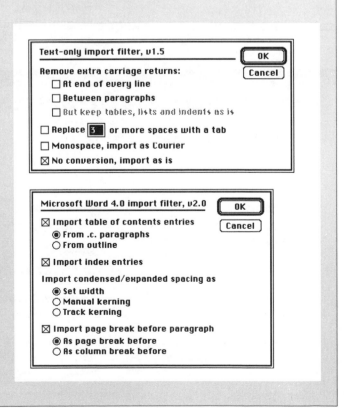

TIP

As you add headlines, watch how the additional lines force text from the bottom of the column you're typing in to the top of the next column. For a detailed look at the behavior of **threaded text,** see the sidebar beginning on page 336.

5. Add and style the headlines and subheads.

In the real world, the headlines probably would have been part of the text file. But it's not uncommon to add headlines to the PageMaker layout, and here's how you do it.

- Set an insertion point at the beginning of the line that you want the headline to precede. Type the headline, and then insert a carriage return. Use the up arrow key to move the insertion point back to headline (if you don't have arrow keys, use the mouse), and apply the *story head* style.

- Continue inserting headlines every column and a half or so, and apply the *story head* style. Try adding a headline toward the bottom of a column, and watch how the "Keeps" option that you specified as part of the headline style forces the headline to the next column.

- Add a subhead or two, and apply the *subhead* style. Again, note how the "Keeps" option forces column breaks.

6. Style the first paragraph following a headline or subhead.

- Set an insertion point in each paragraph following a story head or subhead, and apply the *body first* style.

- Continue this throughout the newsletter.

You may wonder why you have to go through this step if you've defined *body first* as the Next Style for heads and subheads. The Next Style option works only when you type text directly in PageMaker, which you did if you worked through the sidebar on style sheets that begins on page 311. But when you style existing text, as in steps 4–6, PageMaker can't apply the Next Style retroactively.

USING THE NEW-LINE CHARACTER IN HEADLINES

When you want to force a line break without creating a new paragraph and all the formatting that comes with it, insert a new-line character. The example here demonstrates its usefulness in headlines. It's also useful in tabular copy and in forcing line breaks for better type color in general.

About the move to 35 Miller Avenue

The line breaks in headlines are important, for both editorial clarity and visual balance. For example, you wouldn't want a line break between the street number and street name in the headline above.

About the move to

35 Miller Avenue

If you press Return or Enter to force a line break, you'll create a new paragraph, which will have all the formatting associated with the previous paragraph (or with the Next Style if one is defined).

About the move to 35 Miller Avenue

If you insert a new-line character (Shift-Return or Shift-Enter), the new line is part of the same paragraph as the previous line, so you avoid repeating the paragraph formatting or changing to the Next Style.

7. Add the art on the first page.

The wide column on page 1 is an ideal place for art—a photo, a chart, or any other visual. The art can be sized to any width within the column. The caption width, however, extends only 12p6 (to the 15p6 vertical guideline), forcing you to have some white space in the column. If you don't have any art, you could start the text in the left-hand column or leave the column blank above the "Forecasts" box.

8. Place the "Newsbriefs" text on page 2.

Presumably, the "Newsbriefs" have been written in a separate word-processor file, so they won't be threaded to the rest of the stories. Again, for this example, use any text file that you have on your hard drive.

TROUBLE PLACING TEXT OR GRAPHIC FILES?

When you're having trouble importing files, the reason is often failure to install the appropriate filter, incorrect filename extensions, or a file format that PageMaker doesn't recognize. Here's what to do for these and other common problems.

1. Check to see that the appropriate filter is installed.

    On the Mac, hold down the Command key and choose About PageMaker from the Apple menu; on a PC, hold down the Ctrl key and choose About PageMaker from the Help menu. In the dialog box, scroll the list past the Aldus Additions to a series of "installed import filters." If your word processor isn't listed, install its filter using the Installer program on the Mac or the Setup program on the PC.

2. (PC only) If the file you want to place isn't listed in PageMaker's Place dialog box and you know that the file is in the active directory, type *.* in the File Name box and press Enter; PageMaker will list all files in the directory regardless of type. When you place the file, you will probably see an error message that says "Don't know how to place this file," which means that PageMaker doesn't recognize the filename extension. In the error message box, scroll the File Type list to select a format, or see step 3.

3. Open the file in the program used to create it, and save it in a format PageMaker does recognize.

    Many word-processing programs let you choose from a scrollable list of file types when you save

a document. Try saving in a different format; be sure to choose a format for which you have installed the filter. (See step 1.)

To save graphics in a format that PageMaker recognizes, you often have to use a command other than the standard Save option. For example, PageMaker doesn't recognize the native file format used by drawing programs such as FreeHand or Illustrator. But if you open the original illustration file and use the Export command, you can save the file in EPS format, which PageMaker does recognize. Similarly, in image-manipulation programs such as Photoshop and Image Studio, use the Save As Other command to save files in Page-Maker-compatible TIFF format.

For a list of graphic file extensions that Page-Maker recognizes, see the Online Help topic "Graphics Filters."

4. Try other methods of importing the file into PageMaker. See pages 217–18 for a description of other options.

5. (Mac only) If you get a system crash when you import a file from Microsoft Word, turn off the Fast Saves option in the Preferences dialog box.

6. If you lose formatting when you import an Excel spreadsheet, bring it in as a graphic rather than using the import filter. This will maintain vertical alignments, graphic elements within the spreadsheet, and some other Excel 4.0 features that aren't supported by the Excel import filter.

TIP

Use the **arrow keys** to save time. After you insert a carriage return to separate the news divider from the news text, press the up arrow key to move the cursor back to the news divider line so that you can apply the *news divider* style.

- Click the loaded text icon at the 15p horizontal guide to place the text.

- Select all the text and apply the *news text* style.

- At the beginning of each news item except the first one, type *vvv* and insert a paragraph return. Apply the *news divider* style to each "vvv" paragraph and watch the text format itself perfectly.

Note: A style applies to an entire paragraph, and you can't have two styles in the same paragraph. So if you apply the *news divider* style to the "vvv" characters before inserting a carriage return, you'll turn the entire paragraph, including the news text, into Zapf Dingbats. You can't undo a style change with the Undo command, but it's easy enough to fix: Insert the carriage return after the characters that are supposed to be Dingbats, and reapply the *news text* style to the newly created paragraph.

HOW TO PLACE GRAPHICS IN PAGEMAKER

Placing graphics is very similar to placing text (described in Project 2).

- Choose Place from the File menu (Command-D on a Mac, Ctrl-D on a PC).

- In the Place dialog box, scroll through your folders or directories to select the name of the file you want to place.

  Choose from among the available options in the dialog box (described below).

- Click OK, or press Return or Enter, to close the dialog box.

- Click the loaded graphic icon on the page; PageMaker will position the top left corner of the graphic wherever you click. Note: The appearance of the loaded icon varies depending on the kind of graphic file that you've selected.

The options available for placing graphics vary depending on factors such as the file you select to place and whether you've selected an object or set a text insertion point before opening the Place dialog box.

As Independent Graphic PageMaker adds the graphic to the publication as an independent element, unconnected to anything else on the page. (Compare "As Inline Graphic," at right.)

Replacing Entire Graphic If you select a graphic in the PageMaker layout before choosing Place and then choose this option in the Place dialog box, PageMaker will replace the existing graphic with

the one being placed. This is a very useful technique, especially if you don't want to learn the ins and outs of the Links commands. You can use the Replacing Graphic option to place a revision of art that is already in the layout or to replace a box that indicates the position of art with the actual art.

Note: When you use this option, the new graphic keeps the size and proportions of the art it is replacing. If that distorts the art, simply hold down the Shift key and drag slightly on any selection handle. The new graphic also keeps any text wrap, rotation, skewing, or reflecting applied in PageMaker to the graphic it is replacing.

As Inline Graphic If you set an insertion point with the text tool before choosing Place, this option is selected by default and PageMaker places the graphic at the insertion point. The graphic will be embedded in the text, so if the text moves, the graphic moves with it. For more on inline graphics, see page 374.

Retain Cropping Data When using the Replacing Entire Graphic option, select this option if you want the cropping of the graphic you're replacing to apply to the new graphic.

To Size the Graphic as You Place: "Drag-Place"

You can drag a bounding box to define the size of a graphic you're about to place, just as you do with text. This technique is a real timesaver with large graphics because it allows you to keep the placed image within the page view. Here's how to do it.

9. Create the "People" column on page 3.

- If you have scanned photos in your files that you can use in this project, place them now. See the sidebar "How to Place Graphics in PageMaker" on these two pages.

  The photos can be sized to any width within the column. If all the pictures are single portraits, it's generally best to size them all the same. But you could run a single portrait to a 10p width, a shot of two people to a 12p6 width, and a larger group shot to the full 18p measure. If you do size pictures differently, make the difference between sizes at least 2 or 3 picas so that the difference looks intentional. (See pages 402-3 for an explanation of sizing and cropping graphics.)

- If you don't have any scanned photos, proceed as if the printer were stripping in conventional halftones: Create boxes on the page, called keylines, to indicate the size and position of each photo. On your

Position the loaded graphic icon where you want the upper left corner of the graphic to begin, press the mouse button, and drag the cursor diagonally to get the desired size. When you release the mouse button, PageMaker places the graphic in the area you defined. Very often this distorts the original proportions of the graphic, but again, you can undo the distortion by selecting the graphic, holding down the Shift key, and dragging slightly on any handle. Or use the proportional scaling option in the Control Palette (page 205).

How to Place an Image from the Scrapbook (Macintosh Only)

In the Place dialog box, scroll to the Systems folder and select Scrapbook File. When you click OK, the loaded graphic icon displays a number that indicates the number of items in the Scrapbook. The last item pasted into the Scrapbook will be the first item placed. After you place the first item, the loaded icon reappears. If you don't want to place another item, click the pointer anywhere in the Toolbox to cancel the place operation.

TIPS

If the graphic you want to place isn't listed in its folder or directory in the Place dialog box, the graphic is in a file format that PageMaker doesn't recognize. See page 331 for what to do.

If the graphic you place is larger than 256 KB, PageMaker displays a message box alerting you to the size and asking whether you want to "Include complete copy in the publication anyway?" If you choose No, PageMaker places a low-resolution screen image in the publication and links it to the original graphic file. This keeps your PageMaker file smaller, but requires that the original graphic file be available for printing. (See page 227 for more details.) If you choose Yes, PageMaker places the actual graphic in the publication, and you have a much larger and perhaps slower file. To change the default file size for this prompt,

choose Preferences from the File menu, choose Other to bring up a second-level dialog box, and specify the file size desired for Alert When Storing Graphics Over.

When you can't freely move a placed graphic with the pointer tool, you've inadvertently placed an inline graphic. This happens to us more often than we'd like to admit. The reason? You don't notice that there's an active text insertion point when you go to place a graphic; you race through the dialog box at a speed-demon pace and don't notice that the inline graphic option is selected, so you end up with an inline instead of an independent graphic. It's a nuisance, but it's easy enough to fix: Select the graphic with the pointer tool, cut it to the Clipboard, be sure there's no insertion point in the text, and paste. The graphic will be pasted as an independent graphic.

TIP

You can select and edit rotated text with the text tool, but when the text is upside down, editing becomes a bit of a puzzle. An easier approach: Use the pointer tool to triple-click on the rotated text. PageMaker displays the text, right side up, in a story window, where you can alter the text as needed. When you return to layout view, the text will be rotated as before.

camera-ready art, you would need to indicate whether the box rules print around the photo.

- Type the caption for each photo, and apply the *caption* style.

- Use one of the techniques described below to position the captions relative to the photos.

10. Update the mailing cover.

- Turn to page 4.

- With the pointer tool, triple-click on the rotated text to open that text in a story window.

- Use the Story Editor to make text changes to the mailing cover. For example, drag over the second line and type *Don't forget to sign up*. When you finish, press Command-E on a Mac, Ctrl-E on a PC.

- PageMaker returns to layout view. The text is in the rotated position with the changes you made in the Story Editor.

MAINTAINING CONSISTENT SPACE BETWEEN PHOTOS AND CAPTIONS

Technique 1: Spacing Guides

Earlier (page 322), we gave instructions for creating lines of text with leading equal to the space you want to measure. Here's how to use them.

1. The line *photo to caption* has a leading of 6 points, the distance you want between a photo and caption. When you select that line of text with the pointer tool, the distance between the windowshade handles is equal to that leading. Align the top of the spacing guide with the bottom of the photo, bring in a ruler guide at the bottom windowshade handle, and align the top of the caption at the ruler guide.

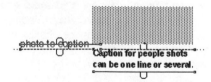

2. Use the same technique to measure the distance from one caption to the next photo, with a spacing guide that says *caption to photo* and has a leading value of 20 points.

Technique 2: Control Palette Arithmetic

You can tell PageMaker to move an object up or down by typing an arithmetic expression after the y value in the Control Palette.

1. Position the caption so that the top windowshade handle aligns exactly with the bottom of the photo.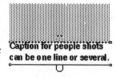

2. In the Control Palette, set a moving reference point at the top of the Proxy, which corresponds to the top of the selected text block. After the current position for the y-coordinate, type *+0p6* (the distance you want between photos and captions in this project).

   Click Apply, or press Return or Enter.

   PageMaker moves the caption down the specified distance (0p6).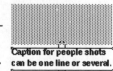

3. Repeat steps 1 and 2 for each caption. Use the same technique to control the 20-point space between a caption and the next photo.

USING PAGEMAKER'S EXPORT FEATURE

When you place a text file in PageMaker, the original document remains intact. Changes, additions, and deletions that you make in the layout are not incorporated into the original word-processor file. This can be very reassuring, especially to beginners: If you mess up the text while assembling the pages, you can place the original source file again and start over.

But there are times when you want the changes made in PageMaker to be incorporated into the original file or to be saved as a new text file. Perhaps you've made some editorial changes in PageMaker, and you need to send the copy back to a writer or client for further work. Or perhaps you've written captions in the layout that you'd like to incorporate into a presentation. Or you might want to archive the final text from the page layout as a word-processor file.

In these situations, use the Export command to save the text as a word-processor or text-only document. Exporting text is the reverse of placing: You send the layout text to a word-processor file.

To export an entire story, set an insertion point anywhere in the story, choose Export from the File menu, and when the Export dialog box comes onscreen, click the Entire Story option. (An "entire story" is a series of threaded text blocks. For more information about threaded text blocks, see the sidebar beginning on the following page.)

To export part of a story, use the text tool to select the text that you want to export, and click the Selected Text Only option in the Export dialog box.

Scroll the File Format box to select the name of your word-processing program. The exported document will retain any local and style formatting applied in PageMaker that your word processor recognizes. You'll lose formatting such as reverse type, letterspacing and word spacing, tracking, and paragraph rules, which have no counterparts in your word processor. But if you place the exported file back in the same PageMaker document—with the full style definitions—the lost formatting will be restored. If you place the exported file in a new PageMaker document without the full style definitions, you won't regain the lost formatting. And in both cases you'll lose typographic refinements such as kerning.

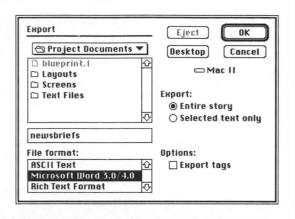

If there's **no export filter for your word processor** and your word processor can accept RTF (rich text format), select that; it will enable you to preserve some formatting. If you don't know which word processor is being used by the person who will work on the exported file, select the Text Only filter in the File Format box. The file will be readable by most word processors, but the formatting will be lost.

If you're **exporting to a word processor that doesn't support styles,** select the Export Tags option. PageMaker will export the styles as bracketed tags embedded in the text, and there's a good chance that the style formatting will be retained when you place the document back in PageMaker. But you might lose local formatting such as italic and boldface.

If the **filename field** in the Export dialog box already contains a name when the dialog box opens, that means the text you're exporting is linked to an external word-processing file. If you click OK, the original file is replaced with the text that you export. If you don't want to replace that original file, type a new name in the name field. (For more about linked files, see page 223.)

To combine unthreaded stories so that you can export them as a single file: Open a new PageMaker file, choose Place, and in the Place dialog box, select the publication that contains the stories you want to combine. This brings up the Place PageMaker Stories dialog box. To combine all the stories in the publication, choose Select All; to combine selected stories, hold down the Shift key while clicking on the stories you want to combine. After you place the stories in PageMaker, you can use the Export Entire Story option described earlier.

DEMYSTIFYING THREADED TEXT

The apparent eccentricities of threaded text are at first both baffling and frustrating. Until you understand the mechanics of this feature, text seems to move around a page and within a document as if it had a mind of its own.

What Is Threaded Text?

When you place a word-processor file, flowing text as you move from one column and page to another, every text block in that story is threaded to the one before and the one following it. When you edit text within the threaded file, causing lines to rebreak and adding or deleting lines, the changes "ripple" through to the other text blocks in the story.

Stop a minute at this distinction between a text block and a story. The individual text block is all the text contained between two windowshade handles when you select text with the pointer tool. The story is the collection of all the text blocks that are threaded together.

There are different ways you can see this relationship between a story and its threaded text blocks.

1. Look at the symbols in the selection handles.

An open box in the top windowshade handle ⬚ indicates the beginning of a story.

An arrow in the bottom handle ▽ indicates that there is more of the story to be placed.

A plus sign in the top handle ⊞ indicates that the text is threaded to another text block before this one.

A plus sign in the bottom handle ⊞ indicates that the text is threaded to another text block after this one.

An empty loop in the bottom handle ⊔ indicates the end of the story.

2. Use the Select All command.

Set an insertion point in the text and choose Select All from the Edit menu (or press Command-A or Ctrl-A). All the threaded text within that story will be highlighted.

3. Use the Story Editor.

Set an insertion point anywhere in the story and choose Edit Story from the Edit menu (Command-E or Ctrl-E). PageMaker displays a word-processor–style window with the entire story; scroll up and down the window to read or edit the story. (For a detailed look at the Story Editor, see Project 2.)

If you get confused about the order of threaded text blocks—and it can happen—there are several Aldus Additions (on the Utilities menu) that can help you sort things out. For a description of these options, see page 341 at the end of this sidebar. But first, let's take a close look at how threaded text behaves and how to manipulate it most efficiently.

Adding Lines to a Text Block

To see what happens when you add lines to one text block in a threaded story, look at this paragraph from Lewis Carroll that we've placed as a single story running across three columns. When we add text to the first column, note the ripple effect in the other two columns.

1. We created this paragraph as a single story placed in three columns. Each column is threaded to the others.

2. Adding text to the first column pushes an equivalent amount of text from the bottom of the first column to the top of the second, and from the bottom of the second column to the top of the third. The arrow in the bottom windowshade handle of the third column indicates that there is more text to be placed: The last two lines in that column have in effect been pushed forward into PageMaker's memory. You can restore them to the page either by pulling down that last windowshade handle or by clicking on the arrow and placing the text elsewhere on the page.

In the newsletter in this project, we recommended that you place the stories that run continuously on pages 1–3 from a single word-processor file so that the text in those six columns would be threaded.

And we recommended that you create the text for "Newsbriefs" in a separate word-processor file so that when you placed that file in PageMaker it would not be threaded to the other stories. If you were to add four lines to the text in the third column on page 1, the last four lines in that column would be pushed back to the second column on page 2 because that's where the thread leads. The ripple would not affect the first column on page 2, where the "Newsbriefs" story has been placed, because the text in those two columns isn't threaded.

Deleting Lines from a Text Block

When you delete copy from threaded text, the principle is the same as when you add text, but lines are pulled back instead of pushed forward.

> Alice was beginning to get very tired of sitting by her sister on the bank, and of having nothing to | do: once or twice she had peeped into the book her sister was reading, but it had no pictures or con- | versations in it, "and what is the use of a book,' thought Alice, "without pictures or conversations."

1. Again, we have a single story placed in three columns.

> Alice was beginning to get very tired of having nothing to do: once or twice she had peeped | into the book her sister was reading, but it had no pictures or conversations in it, "and what is the use | of a book," thought Alice, "without pictures or conversations."

2. This time, we deleted text from the first column, so an equivalent amount of text is pulled back from the second column to the first, and from the third column to the second.

Changing the Depth of a Text Block

Let's say you've already placed text on a page and you want to make room at the top of one column for a graphic. Simply select the text in that column with the pointer tool and drag the top windowshade handle down to the position where you want the text to begin. You won't have to adjust the bottom of the column; the text that no longer fits will be forced to the beginning of the next threaded column, and so on throughout the story.

Similarly, if you want to make room at the bottom of a page for some other element, select the text and raise the bottom windowshade handle.

> Alice was beginning to get very tired of sitting by her sister on the bank, and of having nothing to do: once or twice she had peeped into the book her sister was reading, but it had no pictures or con- versations in it, "and what is the use of a book,' | thought Alice, "without pictures or conversations." So she was consider- ing in her own mind (as well as she could, for the hot day made her feel very sleepy and stupid), whether the pleasure of making a daisy-chain would be worth the | trouble of getting up and picking the daisies, when suddenly a White Rabbit with pink eyes ran close by her. There was nothing so very remarkable in that, nor did Alice think it so very much out of the way to hear the Rabbit say to

1. Let's say you've poured a long text file and find that you have room for art on several of the pages. How do you change the depth of a text block to open up room for the art without repouring the entire story? Let's look first at creating space at the top of a column—say, the center column in the example shown above.

> Alice was beginning to get very tired of sitting by her sister on the bank, and of having nothing to do: once or twice she had peeped into the book her sister was reading, but it had no pictures or con- versations in it, "and what is the use of a book,' | thought Alice, "without pictures or conversations." So she was consider- ing in her own mind (as well as she could, for the hot day made her feel very sleepy and stupid), whether the pleasure of making a daisy-chain would be worth the | trouble of getting up and picking the daisies, when suddenly a White Rabbit with pink eyes ran close by her. There was nothing so very remarkable in that, nor did Alice think it so very much out of the way to hear the Rabbit say to

2. Select the column in which you want to place the art, and drag the top windowshade handle down...

> Alice was beginning to get very tired of sitting by her sister on the bank, and of having nothing to do: once or twice she had peeped into the book her sister was reading, but it | thought Alice, "without pictures or conversations." So she was consider- ing in her own mind (as well as she could, for the | hot day made her feel very sleepy and stupid), whether the pleasure of making a daisy-chain would be worth the trouble of getting up and picking the daisies, when suddenly a White Rabbit with pink eyes ran close by here.

3. The top of the text block in that column is pulled down, leaving a hole...

> Alice was beginning to get very tired of sitting by her sister on the bank, and of having nothing to do: once or twice she had peeped into the book her sister was reading, but it | thought Alice, "without pictures or conversations." So she was consider- ing in her own mind (as well as she could, for the | hot day made her feel very sleepy and stupid), whether the pleasure of making a daisy-chain would be worth the trouble of getting up and picking the daisies, when suddenly a White Rabbit with pink eyes ran close by her.

4. And you can insert the graphic in the space you've opened up.

Continues on following page

THREADED TEXT *(continued)*

Breaking a Text Block Apart

Now suppose you want to add a graphic in the middle of one of the columns. You can easily open up space for the graphic by breaking the text block apart so that there are two text blocks in the column, with a space between them for the art.

1. To make room for a graphic in the middle of a column of text: Drag the bottom windowshade handle up to where you want the last line of text before the art.

2. Click on the plus sign in the bottom handle of the text block that you just shortened.

3. Click the loaded text icon where you want the text to begin below the art.

4. Insert the art. The thread now runs from the text block above the art, to the text block below the art, to the top of the next column. If you add copy to the text above the art, lines from that text block will be pushed forward to the text block below.

If you need to change the space for the picture, simply change the depth of a surrounding text block by dragging the windowshade handle up or down.

Eliminating a Text Block Without Deleting Text

You say you want to open up an entire column for a graphic or a sidebar? Piece of cake.

1. To open up an entire column within a threaded story—for a graphic or a sidebar or any other element—drag the bottom windowshade handle in that column up to the top handle.

2. All the text in that column will be forced to the next column, and the text in every subsequent column will be similarly pushed forward.

3. Insert the graphic.

Note that this procedure is quite different from selecting the text block and choosing Cut, Delete, or Clear, any of which would eliminate the text from the layout, rather than force it to the next text block.

Recombining Text Blocks

Let's look again at the example of art in the middle of a column of text. What if you want to delete the graphic and fill in that hole with text? No problem, as you'll see in the following example.

1. To delete a graphic and recombine the text blocks above and below it into a single text block…

2. Eliminate the bottom text block by dragging the bottom windowshade handle up until it touches the top one…

3. Extend the top text block by dragging its bottom windowshade handle down…

4. The text will fill the column.

Note: If you expand the top text block before eliminating the bottom one, you'll end up with a mess of overlapping text blocks. You can still eliminate the bottom text block at that point, but it's more difficult to determine which handles belong to which text block when, in effect, there's a double exposure on-screen.

Adding Threaded Text Between Existing Text Blocks

Sometimes a column opens up in the middle of a story, and you need to fill the column with already placed text from that threaded story. Here's how:

1. Say you want to remove a graphic from the center column and fill that column with text from the threaded story. First, delete the graphic.

2. Then select the text in the column that precedes the deleted graphic, and click on the bottom windowshade handle…

3. When the loaded text icon appears, click in the empty column.

4. The text from the column following the deleted graphic fills in the hole, and text from subsequent columns is pulled back accordingly.

Continues on following page

THREADED TEXT (continued)

Understanding the principle at work when you fill in a column in this way will keep you from panicking if a loaded text icon appears on-screen when you aren't trying to place text. You've inadvertently clicked on the bottom windowshade handle of a text block, and PageMaker thinks you want to place existing text in a new position. Cancel the place by clicking on any tool in the Toolbox.

Unthreading Text

To unthread text from a story, use the text tool to select the text you want to unthread, cut it, set an insertion point anywhere *outside* the threaded file, and paste the text that you cut.

For example, say you decide to cut a sentence from a story and use it as a photo caption at the bottom of a column. Select the text, cut it, and then paste it in the bottom of the column under the space reserved for the photo. Because this text was pasted outside the threaded file, the caption will not be affected by changes you make to the threaded text. Obviously, this is desirable because you don't want the caption bouncing around the page and you don't want text from the main story popping up, midsentence, where a caption should be.

You can use this technique for longer text elements too, such as a self-contained sidebar or department, like the "Newsbriefs" text in this project. If that self-contained element is created as part of the word-processor file for another story, just use the text tool to cut it from the main story, and paste it elsewhere in the document.

Here's another situation: In creating the files for this book, we generally typed the tips in the same word-processor file as the instructions. When we placed the text in PageMaker, we'd see the tip in the wide column, delete it with the text tool, and paste it in the narrow column adjacent to the procedure it referred to.

Or consider a publication with numerous art credits that are to run on the page with the art. The person responsible for generating the text file for the credits could create a single word-processor file. The person responsible for the layout could place that credits file on the pasteboard, and cut and paste each

credit into the appropriate position. The original file doesn't even appear in the document; all its elements have been cut and pasted as individual text blocks, unconnected to each other or to any other text block in the PageMaker file.

The key in each of these situations is that when you paste the text you want to unthread, you set the insertion point outside of any other text block.

Threading Unlinked Text

Layout and editorial changes often require that loose text, such as a caption or a tip, be incorporated into the main story. In these situations, cut the text that you want to thread, set an insertion point in the threaded file, and paste.

When you want to place new text in the thread of an existing PageMaker story, set an insertion point where you want the new text inserted, choose Place, and in the Place dialog box select the Inserting Text option.

Moving Threaded Text from One Page to Another

To move a text block from one page or spread to another without breaking the thread to the preceding and following text, use the pointer tool to select the text block you want to move, drag it to the pasteboard, change pages, and drag the text into position on the new page. If, instead, you cut the text block to the Clipboard and paste it onto the new page, the text that you cut and paste will lose its thread to other text in the story. To see what we mean, select any text block that has a plus in the top and bottom windowshade handles. Select it with the pointer tool, cut it to the Clipboard, and paste it. When you select the text block you just pasted, the top and bottom windowshade handles are empty, signifying that there's no text before or after.

To better understand the behavior of threaded text, open a new PageMaker document and define three or four columns. Place any file that's handy, and then play with the windowshade handles. Raise them, lower them, add text, delete text, break text blocks apart, and watch how the changes ripple through the threaded blocks. It may help to number each paragraph. If you get confused, close the file and try again later. You really will get the hang of it.

Using Aldus Additions to Manage Threaded Text

There are several utilities on the Aldus Additions menu that can be helpful for managing and navigating through threaded text. You'll find these useful in complex documents, in which a story may continue for many pages and skip over columns or whole pages, and when you want information about the length of stories or text blocks.

Traverse Text Blocks This Addition is particularly useful because it enables you to move from one text block to the next when you don't know what page the next text block is on.

With the pointer tool, select a text block and choose Traverse Text Blocks from the Aldus Additions submenu, under Layout. (On some monitors, Additions that come at the end of the alphabet are listed on the More submenu at the top of the Additions list.) Select the text block you want to move to—First, Previous, Next, or Last—and click OK. PageMaker moves to that page in the layout, with the text block that you specified selected.

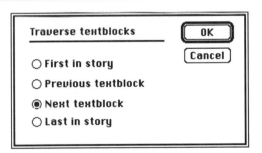

Find Overset Text Overset text is any part of a story that hasn't yet been placed on a page. Maybe the story didn't fit on the number of available pages, and you intended to make room for it later. Or perhaps in editing you added more text than there was originally.

The overset text is indicated by a down arrow in the bottom windowshade handle of the last text block, but you may not know it's there unless you happen to select that text block. So it's a good practice to use this utility before printing, to be sure that no text is inadvertently omitted.

Choose Find Overset Text from the Aldus Additions submenu (under Layout). PageMaker displays the first occurrence of unplaced text, with a down arrow in the bottom windowshade handle. Place the text as you normally would, and then continue running this Addition to locate other overset text until PageMaker displays a message box telling you there is no more overset text.

Display Text Block Info and **Display Story Info** These Additions are similar: One gives you information about the currently selected text block, and the other gives you information about the story of which the currently selected text block is a part. They are particularly useful if you write text to fit.

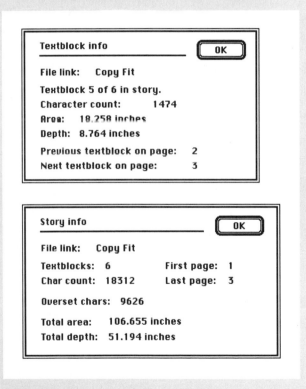

These Additions may not provide accurate information when the selected text block has been rotated.

ALL ABOUT TABS AND TABLES

There are two skills and one personality trait involved in typesetting tabular material. The first skill is being able to visualize what kinds of alignments—left, right, centered, or decimal—will create a neat, easy-to-read format for the tabular text. The second skill is knowing how to use PageMaker's Indents/Tabs window to create the alignments you want. And the personality trait is patience.

There's just no getting around the fact that typesetting tabular material is tedious work, requiring planning as well as trial and error. Every situation is different, and every situation requires much more fine-tuning than would typesetting a comparable amount of body text. Fortunately, PageMaker's Indents/Tabs window makes it relatively easy to experiment with different tab settings until you get the combination that works for a particular set of figures or text elements in a particular layout. All you need is the patience to stay with it and the assurance that the time required is inherent in working with tabular text, rather than any shortcoming on your—or PageMaker's—part.

Because each table you set presents a new layout problem, we've structured this project as a series of small exercises rather than as a single document. In order to get some hands-on practice, you'll need to use the column widths and type specs indicated with each exercise. Even so, be aware that the same typeface from different vendors can set differently. If your type sets slightly wider than ours, the text may not fit within the spaces between tabs. If that happens, see "How to Change a Tab You've Already Set," on page 348.

A great many people have an almost phobic reaction to working with tabs. The irony is that once you understand the basic mechanics of tabs, they give you tremendous control over type. And their usefulness is by no means limited to financial tables and other data-heavy pages.

To help overcome the *sturm und drang* that tabs evoke, the following exercises guide you from the most elementary aspects of the Indents/Tabs window to some of the subtler features. Spend an hour or two with this project; come back to it in a few days or a week to review the techniques. You really can learn how to set tabs, and once you do, you'll use them more than you ever thought possible.

PAGEMAKER TECHNIQUES

▶ Specify paragraph indents using the Indents/Tabs window

▶ Specify and edit tabs

▶ Create leadered tabs

▶ Customize leadered tabs

▶ Create bulleted and numbered lists

▶ Create hanging indents

THREE IMPORTANT TIPS AND ONE INVIOLATE RULE

First of all, understand that **the Indents/Tabs dialog box is actually a moveable window with a ruler.** What makes it so much easier to use than many people realize is that this ruler appears directly above the selected text, with the zero point on the ruler aligned at the left edge of the selected text block. So when you set a tab or an indent, you can actually see the position on the ruler relative to the text below. See the screen shot at the bottom of this page.

The Indents/Tabs ruler is displayed in whatever measurement system is specified in the Preferences dialog box. As with the ruler in the layout window, the increments in the Indents/Tabs ruler become finer as you enlarge the page view. A terrific new feature of PageMaker 5.0 is that regardless of your page view or the size of your monitor, the tabs ruler expands to measure the full width of the visible page. So regardless of how wide a table you have to typeset, you can see the ruler above its entire width.

Second, understand the name literally: **The Indents/Tabs window can be used to set indents as well as tabs.** The indents—first-line, left, and right—are the same indents that you set in the Control Palette and the Paragraph Specifications dialog box. Often when you set tabular text, you need to adjust the indents in conjunction with the tabs, and it's useful to be able to do all this in one window.

Third, always remember that **specifying tabs involves two separate functions:** In the Indents/Tabs window, you specify the position of the tab. And in the layout, you insert the tab character. If you stumbled over the second part: When you press the Tab key, you insert a tab character, which, instead of being visible like a letter or a number, is more of an instruction that tells PageMaker to push the text following the tab character to the position specified on the tabs ruler. When PageMaker doesn't produce the result you expect, the problem is often that you didn't insert the tab character. Or that you inserted too many tab characters.

Which brings us to the one inviolate rule for setting tabular material: **never insert multiple tab characters (or space characters)** in an attempt to align the text the way you would on a typewriter. If you break this rule, almost every change you make in your tabular material will require that you manually realign the elements. See page 349 for a detailed look at why this is so.

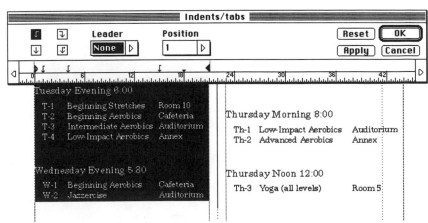

PageMaker displays the Indents/Tabs ruler directly above the selected text if there's enough room above that text for the ruler to fit. Note that the zero point of the tabs ruler is aligned with the left margin of the selected text. To take advantage of this visual relationship on a small screen, you'll need to position the selected text in the lower left area of the screen. On larger screens, you have more flexibility.

THE INDENTS/TABS WINDOW

Learning how to use this dialog box is the key to overcoming fear of tabs. These two pages will give you an overview of the options. The following pages provide lots of examples and hands-on practice.

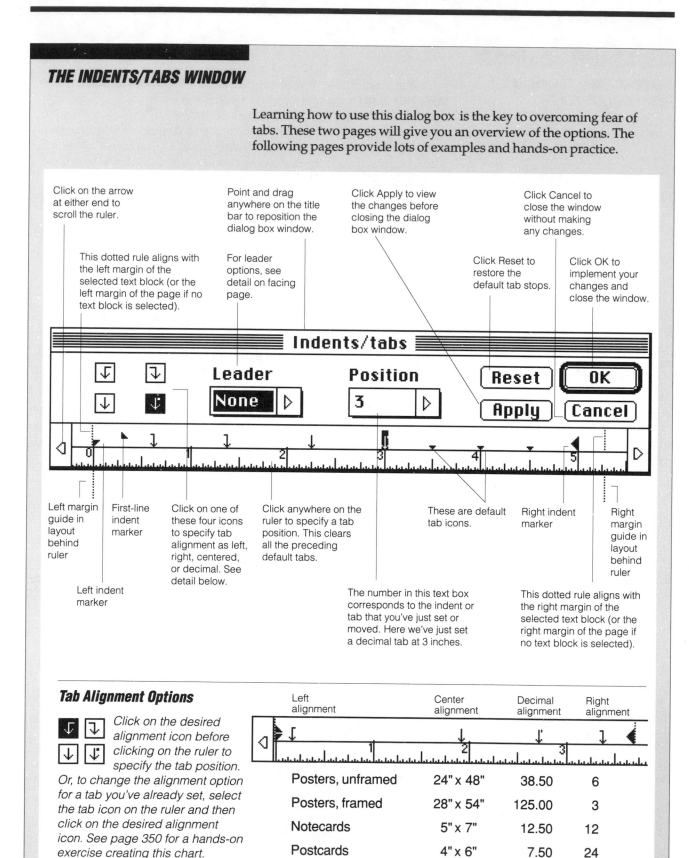

Click on the arrow at either end to scroll the ruler.

This dotted rule aligns with the left margin of the selected text block (or the left margin of the page if no text block is selected).

Point and drag anywhere on the title bar to reposition the dialog box window.

For leader options, see detail on facing page.

Click Apply to view the changes before closing the dialog box window.

Click Cancel to close the window without making any changes.

Click Reset to restore the default tab stops.

Click OK to implement your changes and close the window.

Left margin guide in layout behind ruler

First-line indent marker

Left indent marker

Click on one of these four icons to specify tab alignment as left, right, centered, or decimal. See detail below.

Click anywhere on the ruler to specify a tab position. This clears all the preceding default tabs.

These are default tab icons.

Right indent marker

Right margin guide in layout behind ruler

The number in this text box corresponds to the indent or tab that you've just set or moved. Here we've just set a decimal tab at 3 inches.

This dotted rule aligns with the right margin of the selected text block (or the right margin of the page if no text block is selected).

Tab Alignment Options

Click on the desired alignment icon before clicking on the ruler to specify the tab position. Or, to change the alignment option for a tab you've already set, select the tab icon on the ruler and then click on the desired alignment icon. See page 350 for a hands-on exercise creating this chart.

	Left alignment	Center alignment	Decimal alignment	Right alignment
Posters, unframed	24" x 48"		38.50	6
Posters, framed	28" x 54"		125.00	3
Notecards	5" x 7"		12.50	12
Postcards	4" x 6"		7.50	24

The Indent Markers

The first-line and left indent markers seem to have a mind of their own until you learn the correct way to move them. The right indent marker is more straightforward, as you'll see in the hands-on exercises on the next two pages.

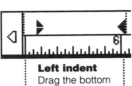

Left indent
Drag the bottom triangle to move both triangles together and indent the text from the left margin.

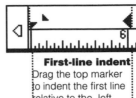

First-line indent
Drag the top marker to indent the first line relative to the left margin.

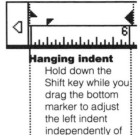

Hanging indent
Hold down the Shift key while you drag the bottom marker to adjust the left indent independently of the first-line indent.

Leadered Tabs

To insert a row of dots, dashes, or other characters between items in a table, specify a tab leader style. You can choose from the default styles on the Leader pull-down menu, or you can specify custom characters by typing any two characters in the Leader text box. See pages 353–56 for hands-on practice.

If you choose a leader style when no tab is highlighted on the tabs ruler, the leader applies to all subsequent tabs that you set. To add a leader to a tab you've already set, select that tab icon on the ruler and specify the leader. The leader will apply only to the selected tab. To change the leader style for a tab you've already set, select that tab icon and specify the new leader style. (With multiple tabs, you have to change the leader style for each one individually.)

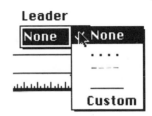

To display the Leader and Position menus

On a Mac, position the pointer over the arrow next to the text box, and hold down the mouse button.

On a PC, position the pointer directly over the word "Leader" or "Position" and hold down the mouse button. To close the menu, click anywhere else in the Indents/Tabs window.

Position Menu

We usually position and move tabs by clicking and dragging on the ruler.

But if you are working at a small page view (which you often are on small monitors), the Position pull-down menu enables you to set tabs at smaller increments than your ruler displays. Position a tab, or select a tab that you want to move. Type the numeric position in the text box. Then select Move Tab from the submenu. If you choose an action before typing the numeric position, there will be no effect.

Using this technique, you can specify tab positions in 1-point increments even if your ruler display is no finer than 3- or 6-point increments. The Position menu is also useful when you need to position two tabs within a point or two of each other.

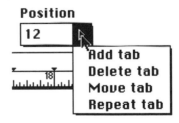

To set tabs at regular intervals, use the Repeat Tab command. If you set a tab at 3p3 on the tabs ruler and choose Repeat Tab, PageMaker will set tabs at 3p3 intervals. If you set one tab at 2p, set another at 6p, and then choose Repeat Tab, PageMaker will set tabs at 4p intervals following the 6p tab.

EXERCISE 1: SETTING INDENTS

Even though you already know how to specify indents using the Paragraph Specifications dialog box, you need to be able to set those same indents in the Indents/Tabs window. This set of exercises provides some hands-on practice.

1. Type some text.

- Type three short paragraphs of text.

  The text in our example is 9/12.5 Helvetica in a 9p7 column, but you don't need to match our example precisely in this exercise. The numbers in the first example, below, show where our paragraphs begin; we deleted the numbers before applying indents.

- Select all three paragraphs with the text tool.

- Choose Indents/Tabs from the Type menu (Command-I on the Mac, Ctrl-I on the PC).

- The split triangle on the left corresponds to the First and Left Indents; the solid triangle on the right corresponds to the Right Indent. Since there are no indents specified, the indent markers align with the left and right margins of the text. (The little down-pointing triangles are default tab settings. Don't worry about them now.)

- Click Cancel.

- With the text still selected, open the Paragraph Specifications dialog box (Command-M on a Mac, Ctrl-M on a PC). The values for the Left, First, and Right Indents are all zero and correspond to the position of the markers in the Indents/Tabs window.

- Make three copies of the text to work with in the next steps.

Paragraph specifications

Indents:

Left	0	picas
First	0	picas
Right	0	picas

(1) Virtually Baseball is an action and strategy game that translates the official rules of baseball to tabletop play.
(2) It's a game of skill, luck, and imagination, played on a 36" by 36" surface, accurately scaled to replicate a typical major league ballpark.
(3) The pitcher uses the pitching arm to slide the puck across home plate, where the batter tries to hit the ball with the small wooden bat.

TIP

Indents and tabs are paragraph-level attributes. If you want to set indents or tabs for just one paragraph, set a text insertion point anywhere in that paragraph before opening the Indents/Tabs window. (You needn't select the whole paragraph.) If you want to set indents or tabs for several paragraphs, you must drag the text tool over some part of all those paragraphs.

[Apply]

▲ ▲ ▲

The Apply button is one of the most user-friendly features to be added to PageMaker in recent years. It enables you to preview changes you make in the Indents/Tabs ruler before you close the window. If what you see isn't quite right—and often it isn't until you've fiddled a bit—adjust the indent or tab markers and press Apply again. And keep at it until you get it right. What if you make things worse than they were before you started? Just press Cancel, and PageMaker restores the settings that existed before you opened the Indents/Tabs window.

2. Set a first-line indent.

- In a copy of the text, select all three paragraphs with the text tool.

- Display the Indents/Tabs ruler, and drag the top triangle on the left to the position you want for the first-line indent of each paragraph.

- Click Apply to see the changes, and make adjustments if you want before closing the dialog box.

- Click OK, or press Return or Enter, to close the Indents/Tabs window.

- With the text still selected, open the Paragraph Specs dialog box (Command-M or Ctrl-M). Note that the value for the First Indent is the same value that you set in the Indents/Tabs window.

3. Inset a paragraph.

- In a copy of the text, click the text tool in paragraph 2.

- Display the Indents/Tabs ruler, and drag the bottom triangle on the left over 9–12 points. Note that when you drag from the bottom, the two triangles move as a pair.

- Click Apply. PageMaker indents the left margin of this paragraph to align with the left indent marker.

- Now drag the larger triangle on the right over 9–12 points.

- Click Apply. PageMaker indents the right margin of the text to align with this right indent marker.

- Click OK to close the window.

- With the insertion point still set, open the Paragraph Specs dialog box. The values for the Left and Right Indents are the same values you set in the Indents/Tabs window.

4. Set a hanging indent.

- In a copy of the text, select all three paragraphs with the text tool.

- Display the Indents/Tabs ruler. Hold down the Shift key and drag the bottom triangle on the left over 12–15 points. With the Shift key pressed, you can drag the left indent marker (the bottom triangle) independently of the first-line indent marker (the top triangle).

- Click Apply. PageMaker indents the left margin of this paragraph to align with the marker. The first line is not indented, so the left indent "hangs" inside the first line. We'll work a lot more with hanging indents later in this project.

- Click OK to close the window.

- With the text still selected, open the Paragraph Specs dialog box. Note that the First Indent value is the negative of the Left Indent value.

Paragraph specifications

Indents:
Left	0	picas
First	1p6	picas
Right	0	picas

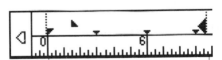

Virtually Baseball is an action and strategy game that translates the official rules of baseball to tabletop play.

It's a game of skill, luck, and imagination, played on a 36" by 36" surface, accurately scaled to replicate a typical major league ballpark.

The pitcher uses the pitching arm to slide the puck across home plate, where the batter tries to hit the ball with the small wooden bat.

Paragraph specifications

Indents:
Left	0p10	picas
First	0	picas
Right	0p10	picas

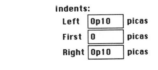

Virtually Baseball is an action and strategy game that translates the official rules of baseball to tabletop play.

It's a game of skill, luck, and imagination, played on a 36" by 36" surface, accurately scaled to replicate a typical major league ballpark.

The pitcher uses the pitching arm to slide the puck across home plate, where the batter tries to hit the ball with the

Paragraph specifications

Indents:
Left	1p3	picas
First	-1p3	picas
Right	0	picas

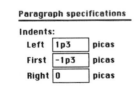

Virtually Baseball is an action and strategy game that translates the official rules of baseball to tabletop play.
It's a game of skill, luck, and imagination, played on a 36" by 36" surface, accurately scaled to replicate a typical major league ballpark.
The pitcher uses the pitching arm to slide the puck across home plate, where the batter tries to hit the ball with the small wooden bat.

EXERCISE 2: A SIMPLE TABLE

This simple price list uses only left-aligned tabs. It's a good place to start learning how—and how not—to typeset tables.

Type specs: 9/13 Helvetica
Column width: 12p5
Measurements: picas

Species	Size	Price
Autumn Olive	24"	$25
White Dogwood	48"	$60
Lilac	30"	$18

1. Type the text.

- Insert one tab character after each item except the last one in the line. Insert a paragraph return at the end of each line.
- PageMaker will use its default tab settings to align the text. Don't worry that the columns aren't properly aligned or spaced. (See the facing page for a more persuasive argument on this point.)

2. Specify the tabs for the data.

- Select all the text with the text tool.
- Display the Indents/Tabs window (Command-I or Ctrl-I).
- Click on the left-alignment tab icon.
- Click on the ruler at 7p4.

  PageMaker inserts a left-aligned tab exactly where you click on the ruler. The Position box displays the numerical position of that tab. If you need to adjust the position, see the sidebar below.
- Click Apply.

  PageMaker applies the new tab setting to the first tab on the line.
- Click on the ruler at 10p5.

  PageMaker inserts another left-aligned tab where you click.
- Click Apply.
- Press Return or Enter to close the Indents/Tabs window.

TIP

When you type data that includes inch and foot marks, remember to turn off Typographer's Quotes (in the Preferences/Other dialog box from the File menu). Otherwise, you'll get curly or slanted quote marks for inches (24") instead of the straight-up-and-down inch marks (24"). And when you finish typing the data, remember to turn Typographer's Quotes back on, or you'll get inch marks when you want curly typographer's quotes!

HOW TO CHANGE A TAB YOU'VE ALREADY SET

To move a tab, select that tab icon on the ruler and drag it to a new position. Or use the Position box, described below right. **To delete a tab,** select that tab icon on the ruler and drag downward, below the ruler. (If you delete the right-most custom tab, default tabs may reappear in the ruler.) **To change the alignment of an existing tab,** select the tab and click on the alignment icon you want to change to.

Before moving or deleting a tab, remember to select the paragraph(s) for which you want to adjust the tab before displaying the Indents/Tabs window. Then you must select that tab by clicking on its icon on the tabs ruler before moving or deleting the tab. When a tab icon is selected, it's highlighted, just like text.

Here we selected the tab at 10p6, typed a new position, 12p, in the Position box, and selected Move Tab from the Position menu. If you select Move Tab before typing a new position, there will be no effect.

HOW TABS WORK (AND WHY THEY SOMETIMES DON'T)

It's important to understand the distinction between tab characters and tab settings. When you press the Tab key while typing text, you insert a tab character. When you work in the Indents/Tabs window, you specify tab settings, which tell PageMaker where to move the tab characters. But before you ever open the Indents/Tabs window, there are default tab settings. Here's a closer look.

Layout View

When you press the Tab key as you type text, PageMaker applies its default tab settings. Because of the variable lengths of different items, text that should be in the same column may not hang off the same default tab setting. The whole point of custom tabs is to control the space between tabs so that items in the same column do hang off the same tab.

▼ ▼ ▼

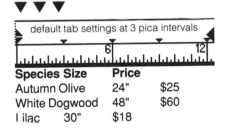

If you insert more than one tab character, trying to align the columns the way you would on a typewriter, you'd get something like this—better, but the Size column is too close to the Species column.

▼ ▼ ▼

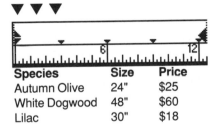

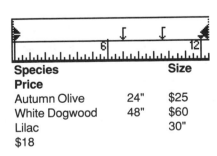

Story View

Tabs are actually characters, much like letters and numbers, except they're generally invisible. If you view the text in the Story Editor, with the Display ¶ option turned on, the tab characters are represented by right-pointing arrows.

▼ ▼ ▼

When you press the Tab key twice, you see two consecutive arrows.

▼ ▼ ▼

◄ ◄ ◄

Now if you use the Indents/Tabs ruler to adjust the space between columns, those extra tab characters are still there. If you open the layout detail at left in the Story Editor, it will look identical to the window above right. You've changed the tab positions, but where you inserted two tab characters (e.g., after "Species"), PageMaker still reads two tabs; so the word "Size" still jumps to the second tab character, even though now you want it to be aligned at the first tab character, and the word "Price" is forced to the next line. Note the same problem after the word "Lilac." To delete a tab character, set an insertion point to the right of the tab character, and press Delete.

EXERCISE 3: A TABLE WITH FOUR DIFFERENT KINDS OF TABS

This table uses all four tab alignments. To set each tab, select the icon with the appropriate alignment, click on the ruler where you want the tab to be, and then click outside the ruler to deselect the tab you just set—*before* selecting the alignment icon for the next tab you want to set.

Type specs: 10/15 Helvetica
Column width: 26p4
Measurements: picas

24	Posters, unframed	24" x 48"	38.50	6
36	Posters, framed	28" x 54"	125.00	3
18	Notecards	5" x 7"	12.50	12
19	Postcards	4" x 6"	7.50	24

1. Type the text.

When you type the text, insert a tab character after each item except the last one in each line. Insert a paragraph return at the end of each line. PageMaker will use its default tab settings (at half-inch, or 3-pica, intervals) to align the text. Don't worry that it doesn't look good!

▶ ▶ ▶

This is how the text will look with PageMaker's default tab settings.

Item #	Item	Size	Cost	Min. Order	
24	Posters, unframed		24" x 48"	38.50	6
36	Posters, framed	28" x 54"		125.00	3
18	Notecards	5" x 7"	12.50	12	
19	Postcards	4" x 6"	7.50	24	

2. Specify the tabs for the data.

- Select all the text except the headline.
- Display the Indents/Tabs window (Command-I or Ctrl-I).
- Click on the left-alignment tab icon.
- Click on the ruler at 3p9.

  PageMaker inserts a left-aligned tab exactly where you click on the ruler. The Position box displays the numerical position of that tab. You can adjust the position by sliding the tab icon along the ruler, or you can type a new value in the Position box.

- Click Apply.

  PageMaker applies the new tab setting to the first tab on the line.

- Deselect the tab you just set by clicking above the ruler, anywhere in the Indents/Tabs window.
- Click on the centered-alignment tab icon.
- Click on the ruler at 14p3.

  Note that PageMaker inserts a center-aligned tab where you click. Adjust the position if necessary.

- Click Apply to view the changes.
- Deselect the tab you just set by clicking above the ruler.
- Click on the decimal-alignment tab icon.

> **TIP**
>
> **When setting tabs with different alignments,** you must first deselect the tab you just set before choosing an alignment icon for the tab you're going to set next. To do so, click above the Indents/Tabs ruler, anywhere in the window. If you overlook this step, the tab you just set will still be selected when you click on a new alignment icon, and PageMaker will think you want to change the alignment for the tab you just set.

To copy tabs from one paragraph to adjacent paragraphs, select the paragraph with the tabs you want to copy and continue dragging to select the paragraphs you want to copy the tabs to. Bring up the Tabs window, which will display the settings for the paragraph you selected first. When you click OK, PageMaker applies the tabs to all the paragraphs in the selected range.

- Click on the ruler at 19p6.
- Click Apply to view the changes.
- Deselect the tab you just set by clicking above the ruler.
- Click on the right-alignment tab icon.
- Click on the ruler at 24p6.
- Click Apply.

Looks the way a table's supposed to look, doesn't it? Press Return or Enter to okay all the changes and close the Indents/Tabs window.

3. Specify the tabs for the column heads.

We recommend styling the column heads after styling the table itself. In other words, make the data look right and work the headline solution around that, rather than let the headlines dictate the column width in the table. In this exercise, for example, the statistical information requires a mix of left-, right-, center-, and decimal-aligned tabs, and the headlines look best centered over the data. (Exception: The first column head generally looks best flush left, even if the other heads are centered.) Often, too, the headlines are longer than the data in their respective columns—in which case, you can stack the headlines on more than one line, set them at an angle, or set them in condensed type.

- With the text tool, select the line of column heads.
- Display the Indents/Tabs window.

Because the column heads still adhere to PageMaker's default tab settings, the text should resemble what you see below.

▶ ▶ ▶

The column heads with PageMaker's default tab settings.

Item #	Item	Size	Cost	Min. Order		
24	Posters, unframed	24" x 48"		38.50	6
36	Posters, framed	28" x 54"		125.00	3
18	Notecards	5" x 7"		12.50	12
19	Postcards	4" x 6"		7.50	24

- Click on the center-alignment tab icon to select it.
- Using the previously styled columns of data as a visual guide, click on the ruler at what you think is the center point of each column.
- Click Apply to preview your settings. If you need to make adjustments, drag the tab along the ruler, or use the Position box (see the description on page 345).

▶ ▶ ▶

The column heads with center-aligned tabs at 6p6, 14p3, 19p6, and 24p3.

Item #	Item	Size	Cost	Min. Order
24	Posters, unframed	24" x 48"	38.50	6
36	Posters, framed	28" x 54"	125.00	3
18	Notecards	5" x 7"	12.50	12
19	Postcards	4" x 6"	7.50	24

EXERCISE 4: FINANCIAL STATEMENTS

Now that you know how to set tabs, we'll look at a few examples that throw curves in the process, which in truth is rarely as straightforward as the previous exercises would have you believe. We'll give you some formatting tips for each example and the type and tab specs used in our settings.

The ruler shows the settings for lines 4–9, which are indented from the left margin. The other lines have the same tabs but no left indent.

Type specs: 10/15 Helvetica
Column width: 18p6
Decimal tab: 17p3
Right tab: 17p7 (for line 7 footnote)
Left indent: 1p
Superscript: size, 58.3% (of point size)
                  position, 45% (of size)

Cash Flow Report

Net Income	8,588,000
Changes in Assets and Liabilities	
Accounts receivable	(440,000)
Inventories	(6,152,000)
Other assets	480,000
Accounts payable	736,000[3]
Accrued liabilities	846,000
Income taxes payable/refundable	2,284,000
Net Cash Flow from Operations	8,487,000

Losses and other negative numbers in parentheses

To properly align numbers so that parentheses overhang the column, use decimal tabs for the entire column. If you use right-aligned tabs, the close parenthesis mark will align with the right margin of the other figures, throwing off the visual relationship between the numbers in each row.

Footnotes in tables

To create a footnote, simply type the number, select it with the text tool, and specify Superscript in the Position pull-down menu (in the Type Specs dialog box). You'll also need to adjust the size and position of the superscript. (Select Options in the Type Specs dialog box to access these settings.)

Aligning the footnote is trickier than setting it because PageMaker doesn't know to hang the superscripted character beyond the tab setting for the figures. The easiest solution is to insert a tab character after the last number before the footnote. Specify this as a right-aligned tab a few points beyond the decimal tab setting for the figures. Because these two tabs will be so close together, you may need to use the Position box to specify the position of the second tab (the one for the footnote). See page 345 for how to do that.

Changing an indent doesn't affect the tab setting

Lines 4–9 in the table above have a left indent of 1p. The tab setting for those lines is the same as the tab setting for line 2, which has no indent. The principle here is that when you click a tab position on the ruler, that position is relative to the column margins of the text and is not affected by indents. Exception: If the indent you specify is sufficiently large to force the tabbed text beyond the tab position, PageMaker pushes the tabbed text to the next tab setting on the ruler.

EXERCISE 5: LEADERED TABS

We think dotted leaders are generally overused. Too often they add visual noise to the data, rather than clarity. Still, it's useful to know how to set them, which is fairly straightforward, and how to control their formatting, which is a little quirky.

The trick in the simple Contents listing on this page is to style the chapter heads and page numbers in bold, but have the leadered tabs be light (Normal, in PageMaker parlance). And the reason it's tricky is that you can't change the formatting of a tab leader. (Actually, you can select the leader, and you can specify new formatting, but doing so doesn't have any effect.)

1. Type the text and specify the leadered tab.

- When you type the text, insert a tab character between the chapter number and the page number.
- Select all the text and specify New Century Schoolbook 10/14. Specify the Type Style as Bold.
- With the text still selected, display the Indents/Tabs window.
- Click on the right-alignment tab icon, and click on the ruler just to the left of the right margin. (You can't set a tab directly on the margin.)
- Point to the Leader box, hold down the mouse button to display the Leader menu, and select the dotted rule.
- Click Apply. Then press Return or Enter to close the window.

2. Reformat the leaders using the manual method.

Because the tab leader adopts the formatting of the preceding character, you have to insert a space character and format that character with the type attributes you want for the tab leader. We usually use a thin space (equal to ¼ em) for this purpose.

- Set an insertion point before the first tab character, and then press Command-Shift-T on a Mac, Ctrl-Shift-T on a PC. PageMaker inserts a thin space between the chapter head and the tab.
- Select the space you just inserted and specify the Type Style as Normal. (If you have trouble selecting the space, try this: Put the cursor after the space, hold down the Shift key, and press the left arrow key. Doing this selects the character to the left of the cursor—in this case, the thin space.)
- Repeat the previous two steps for the next item in this list. Then stop.

> **TIP**
>
> A tab leader always adopts the formatting of the preceding character. So to control the formatting of the tab leader independent of the text that precedes it, insert a space character before the tab and give the space character the type attributes you want for the tab leader.

▲ ▲ ▲

The text and leaders are New Century Schoolbook Bold.

▲ ▲ ▲

The first two leaders have been changed to New Century Schoolbook Normal, using the manual method in step 2.

▲ ▲ ▲

All the leaders have been changed to New Century Schoolbook Normal, using the automated method in step 3.

TIPS

To delete a leader without deleting the tab: Select the paragraph, display the Indents/Tabs window, select the tab icon the leader is attached to, and from the Leader menu choose None. Similarly, if you want to add a leader to an existing tab or change the leader style, remember to first select the tab icon on the ruler and then change the leader specification.

3. Reformat the leaders using the automated method.

In a short list such as the one in this exercise, it's no big deal to manually format the tab leaders in this way. But with a long list, you can save a lot of time by automating the process.

This is a two-step process, which is done in the Story Editor's Change dialog box. (For more detail on the Story Editor, see page 276.) First you tell PageMaker to replace all the tab characters with a tab followed by a thin space. Then you tell PageMaker to change all the thin spaces from Bold to Normal.

Add the thin spaces.

- Use the text tool to select all the text that you didn't reformat in step 2 of this exercise.

- Press Command-E or Ctrl-E to open the selected text in a Story Editor window. Turn on the Display ¶ command (Story menu) so you can see the "invisible" characters such as tabs and spaces.

- Press Command-9 or Ctrl-9 to open the Change window.

- In the Find box, type ^t. (That's the code for a tab character in dialog boxes. And if you've never needed to type a "^" before, it's above the 6 key; press Shift-6.)

- In the Change To box, type ^<^t. (^< is the code character for thin space.)

- Turn on the Search Selected Text option.

- Click Change All.

Change the formatting of the thin spaces.

- The text should still be selected behind the Change window.

- In the Find box, type ^< (to search for all the thin space characters).

- In the Change To box, delete the characters that you previously typed there, and leave the box blank.

- Click the Attributes button, and in the Attributes dialog box, in the Change section, specify the Type Style as Normal.

- Click OK to return to the Change window, and click Change All.

WHEN TABBED TEXT DOESN'T ALIGN AND TAB LEADERS SEEM INVISIBLE

Does the last number in your list refuse to align with the numbers above it, even though they all hang off the same right-aligned tab? If so, set an insertion point after that last number and press Return. That should correct the alignment. This is one of those quirks about which we don't bother to ask, we're just glad to know how to fix it!

▼ ▼ ▼

Chapter 1 5
Chapter 2 27
Chapter 3 49
Chapter 4 63

If you specify your tab settings and leaders after setting a text insertion point but before typing the text, be aware that you won't see the leader until you type the text that follows it. Similarly, if you create a custom leader rule, such as the diamond border on page 356, you won't see the rule until you press the Return or Enter key. The principle is this: When you insert tab leaders, you don't see the leader until you type a character following the tab. In the case of the diamond border, the Return key is that character.

PageMaker changes the formatting of all thin spaces from New Century Schoolbook Bold to New Century Schoolbook Normal. Because the thin spaces precede the tab characters, all the tab leaders take on New Century Schoolbook Normal formatting.

- Note that when you change type attributes, PageMaker leaves those Attribute settings when you close the dialog box. To start with a clean slate the next time you open the dialog box, reset the Attributes to Any. The fast way to do this is to hold down the Option key (Mac) or Alt key (PC) and click the Attributes button.
- Press Command-E or Ctrl-E to return to the layout view.

Creating Custom Leaders

To create a custom leader, you can type up to two characters in the Leader text box. Don't forget—on the Indents/Tabs ruler—to set or select the tab icon to which you want to attach the custom leader.

How to change the default dotted leader to a custom dotted leader

You can't specify different line weights for tab leaders (dotted, dashed, or solid) the way you can for paragraph rules or for rules that you create with the drawing tools. But you can use the custom leader option to work around that limitation.

- With the text tool, select all the text and display the Indents/Tabs window.
- Select the tab icon that you previously set on the ruler. (If it's partially hidden behind the right indent marker, just click on the marker to get at it.)
- In the Leader text box, type a period and then press the Spacebar. Click Apply to view the changes—you should see a more open dotted rule than the one on the Leader menu list. Press Return or Enter to close the Indents/Tabs window.

Once you've set a custom tab leader, you can change the formatting of that leader. By specifying lighter or darker typefaces and larger or smaller point sizes, you can get a wide variety of dotted rules.

- Select the thin space character in the first line and change its type size to 7 point. The tab leader will adopt this 7-point formatting.
- Copy the space character you just reformatted, and paste it over the space character in the next line to change the formatting of that line. Continue pasting onto each line.

Instead of the dotted leader from the menu, here we created a custom leader by typing a period and pressing the Spacebar in the Leader text box. We specified the space before the tab as 7-point Times Roman.

◆ ◆ ◆ ◆ ◆ ◆ ◆ ◆ ◆ ◆ ◆ ◆ ◆ ◆ ◆ ◆ ◆

You can use custom lead-ered tabs to create decora-tive borders that set off breakouts or other display type and then automate the formatting using paragraph styles. See the instructions at right for how to do this.

◆ ◆ ◆ ◆ ◆ ◆ ◆ ◆ ◆ ◆ ◆ ◆ ◆ ◆ ◆ ◆ ◆

How to create decorative custom leadered rules

You can use the principle of leadered tabs to create decorative borders from Zapf Dingbats or characters from other symbol fonts. The border above and below the text at left is a leadered tab.

- Type the text that you want to appear between the rules. (The text in our example is 13/16 Bodoni.)

- Set a text insertion point before the first character of the text and press Return. This creates a new paragraph above the text in which to create the leadered tab.

- Press the up arrow key to move the text insertion point back to the beginning of the blank paragraph.

- Display the Indents/Tabs window. Set a right-aligned tab as close to the right margin as you can, and in the Leader text box, type *u* and then press the Spacebar. Click OK.

- In the layout, with the text insertion point still blinking, press the Tab key. You'll see a line of u's.

- Select the line of u's and specify 7/7 Zapf Dingbats. Copy that line and paste it in a new paragraph at the end of the text. Then press Re-turn. (When you insert tab leaders, you don't see the leader until you type a character following the tab. In this case, the Return key is that character.)

And voilà!

Well, not quite. Depending on the shape and size of the Dingbats, the leader characters might not align flush with the right and left margins of the text.

- To make the Dingbat leaders extend the full width of the text, stretch the text block handles beyond where you want the text margins to be. Specify left and right indents for the text paragraph but not for the tab leader paragraphs. It takes a bit of trial and error to determine the width of the text block so that the leaders will fill out the line. But once you've worked it out, you can create a style for the leadered rule. Read on.

How to use paragraph styles to automate custom leadered rules

Say you want to have breakouts throughout a publication that look like the example on this page. Here's how to automate the formatting using paragraph styles:

- Set up a sample text block using the techniques described above.

- Using the technique for defining a style by example (see page 312), de-fine one style for the leadered rule and another style for the breakout. For the leadered rule style, specify the Next Style as breakout. For the breakout style, specify the Next Style as leadered rule.

- Whenever you need to create a breakout in the document, set an inser-tion point, apply the leadered rule style, press Tab, and then press Return. Type the breakout text. Press Return, Tab, and Return again. Everything should be perfectly formatted, and you don't even have to remember the character to type for the custom leader.

EXERCISE 6: BULLETS AND NUMBERS (with a little help from PageMaker)

PageMaker has two built-in options that automate the formatting of numbered and bulleted lists. One is the Bullets and Numbering Addition and the other is a default style called Hanging Indent. These features can be useful, but there are also several ways that they can trip you up if you don't understand how they work.

We could rig these exercises so that the automated features work seamlessly to produce the intended effect, the way they do at trade show demonstrations. But the steps you'll go through are closer to what happens in real life. And although this approach may be a little more confusing initially, it will give you a better understanding of what to expect in real-world document production.

We'll also explain how to set up the same effects yourself, without using the automated options. And we encourage you to become familiar with both techniques. When you need to format a list, especially a long list, that was typed without bullets or numbers, the Bullets and Numbering Addition can save you time. But when you're typing a relatively short list and you know you want bullets or numbers, it's faster to add them yourself when you type.

Bullets and Numbering Dialog Boxes

To use the Bullets and Numbering Addition, you must be in layout view and you must have text selected with the text tool.

▶ ▶ ▶

Choose one of five bullet styles to insert in the selected text. If you want numbers instead of bullets, click the Numbers button.

▶ ▶ ▶

After you click the Numbers button, select a numbering style, scroll the Separator pull-down list to select the character that follows the number, specify the starting number, and specify the range of text in which to insert the numbers.

▶ ▶ ▶

To define a custom bullet, click on one of the default bullet options, and then click on Edit. In the Edit Bullet dialog box, specify the font and size, and then choose the desired bullet character from the character map.

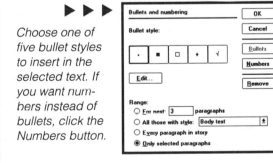

1. Type the list.

Type the text below in 9/11 Helvetica, in a 12p6 column, with no paragraph indents and no space before or after paragraphs. Press Return or Enter when you see the ¶ symbol. Before continuing with the next step, use the pointer tool to copy and paste the text block several times so that you'll be able to start over without retyping.

Bulleted text looks neat and organized. ¶
Bulleted text is easy to read. ¶
Bulleted text has become a desktop-publishing cliché. ¶
Bulleted text is still useful. ¶

2. Apply bullets.

Select one copy of the text with the text tool. Choose Bullets and Numbering from the Aldus Additions list (on the Utilities menu). Choose the first bullet style (a round bullet, the equivalent of pressing Option-8 on a Mac, Ctrl-Shift-8 on a PC). For the Range, click on Only Selected Paragraph.

-      Bulleted text looks neat and organized.
-      Bulleted text is easy to read.
-      Bulleted text has become a desktop-publishing cliché.
-      Bulleted text is still useful.

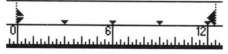

▲ ▲ ▲

PageMaker adds a bullet at the beginning of each selected line, inserts a tab character after the bullet, and applies the default tab setting at 3p to the tab character.

3. Apply the Hanging Indent style.

With the text still selected, apply the Hanging Indent style (from the Control Palette or from the Style Palette).

Note: The type specs for the default Hanging Indent style are 12/Auto Times Roman. So although applying this style aligns the text properly, it has the undesired effect of changing your type specs. You need to redefine the type specs or redefine the style for the hanging indent to reformat the text as 9/11 Helvetica.

- Bulleted text is neat and organized.
- Bulleted text is easy to read.
- Bulleted text has become a desktop-publishing cliché.
- Bulleted text is still useful.

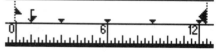

▲ ▲ ▲

PageMaker sets a custom tab at 1p and specifies the left indent at 1p so the run-over lines align with the tabbed text above. **This alignment of the tab and the left indent is the essence of what makes hanging indents work.**

4. Specify a custom bullet.

With the text tool, select a copy of the text from step 1. In the Bullets and Numbering dialog box, click on any bullet style, and then click on Edit. In the Edit Bullet box, specify the Font as Zapf Dingbats, the Size as 12 points, and select an arrow from the character map. Click OK. Before proceeding, make an extra copy of the text block.

➪   Bulleted text looks neat and organized.
➪   Bulleted text is easy to read.
➪   Bulleted text has become a desktop-publishing cliché.
➪   Bulleted text is still useful.

5. Apply the Hanging Indent style.

Note: Now applying the style not only changes the text formatting, it messes up the custom bullet, which suggests the following options: Apply the Hanging Indent style before running the Bullets and Numbering Addition, or create your own hanging indent, which is what we'll do in step 6.

Ì   Bulleted text looks neat and organized.
Ì   Bulleted text is easy to read.
Ì   Bulleted text has become a desktop-publishing cliché.
Ì   Bulleted text is still useful.

6. Create your own hanging indent.

Select the copy of the text from step 4. Display the tabs ruler. Specify a left-aligned tab at 1p. Hold down the Shift key and drag the left indent marker (the bottom triangle) to align with the tab at 1p. Click OK. Pretty easy to do it yourself, isn't it? You can create a hanging indent as part of any paragraph style by defining the tab and left indent as part of the style.

➪ Bulleted text looks neat and organized.
➪ Bulleted text is easy to read.
➪ Bulleted text has become a desktop-publishing cliché.
➪ Bulleted text is still useful.

7. Apply numbering.

Select another copy of the text from step 1. In the Bullets and Numbering dialog box, click on Numbers. For the Numbering Style, specify Arabic. Scroll the Separator list to select the period. The Start At text field should read 1.

1.   Bulleted text looks neat and organized.
2.   Bulleted text is easy to read.
3.   Bulleted text has become a desktop-publishing cliché.
4.   Bulleted text is still useful.

8. Create your own hanging indent.

Follow the same procedure as in step 6: With the text selected, specify a left tab at 1p and the left indent at 1p.

1. Bulleted text looks neat and organized.
2. Bulleted text is easy to read.
3. Bulleted text has become a desktop-publishing cliché.
4. Bulleted text is still useful.

9. Align double-digit numbers.

For a list with ten or more numbers, the periods and text following the double-digit numbers won't align with those following single-digit numbers if you use the default Hanging Indent style. Turn the page to see how to fix this.

8. Bulleted text looks neat and organized.
9. Bulleted text is easy to read.
10.   Bulleted text has become a desktop-publishing cliché.
11.Bulleted text is still useful.
12.   Bulleted lists are....

Creating Bulleted and Numbered Lists Without the Bullets and Numbering Addition

If you want to add bullets or numbers to an existing list, especially a long list, it makes sense to use the Addition even if you have to do some reformatting. But if you know you want bullets or numbers when you type the list, and you're a reasonably good typist, and the list isn't all that long, it's faster to create the formattting yourself. Here's how.

Bulleted lists and numbered lists with nine or fewer items

- Type the bullet character (the one used here is Option-8 on a Mac, Ctrl-Shift-8 on a PC) or the number and a period

- Press the Tab key.

- Type the text, and then press Return or Enter.

- Type the next bullet or number, and repeat the subsequent steps until you have the whole list typed.

- Select all the text, and specify a left-aligned tab where you want the text following the bullet to begin.

- If you want a hanging indent, specify the left indent to align with the left-aligned tab.

TIPS

If you want **to change the bullet character** or change from a bulleted to a numbered list (or vice versa), select the text, choose Bullets and Numbering, and click Remove. After PageMaker removes the bullets or numbers, run the Addition again, and specify the new bullet or number character. If you don't remove the existing character first, PageMaker will add the new character that you specify to the existing one.

You can specify the indents and tabs for bulleted and numbered lists as part of a **paragraph style.** But you still have to insert the bullets or numbers, and the tab characters, in the text to which you apply that style.

When you want to put **a box around a list,** you need to inset the left margin 9 to 12 points and the right margin 6 to 9 points from the edge of the box in flush left text. (For justified text, the left and right indents should be the same). If you decide to add the box after you've set up the text, you'll need to adjust all your indents—and tabs—accordingly.

Lists with ten or more numbers

The following list is used again in the tabloid ad you'll create in Project 7. So save the document you're working in, and you'll have a head start on that project.

Type specs: 10/13 Helvetica
Column width: 14p2
Space After: 0p7
Decimal tab: 1p3
Left tab: 2p3
Left indent: 2p3

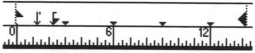

Paragraph specifications

Indents:

Left [2p3] picas
First [-2p3] picas
Right [0] picas

1. Carpool.

2. Recycle paper, glass, and aluminum. Buy products in recyclable containers.

3. Buy the most fuel-efficient car you can. (Aim for 35 miles per gallon.)

4. Eat fewer animal products.

5. Install water-efficient showerheads and toilets.

6. Weather proof your house.

7. Buy phosphate free biodegradable soaps.

8. Repair rather than replace.

9. Plant trees.

10. Join the Pinecrest Environmental Coalition.

- Press the Tab key at the *beginning* of the line.
- Type the number and the period.
- Press Tab again.
- Type the text, and then press Return or Enter.
- Repeat these steps for each numbered item on the list.
- Select all the text, and set a decimal-aligned tab at 1p3. (This specifies where the periods following the numbers align.)
- Specify a left-aligned tab at 2p3. (This specifies where the text following each number begins.)
- Hold down the Shift key and drag the left indent marker to 2p3. (This specifies that runover lines will align with the beginning of the text following each number.)
- Click Apply to check your work, and then click OK.

Note: If you open the Paragraph Specs dialog box with the text still selected, you'll see that the First Indent value is the negative of the Left Indent value. This takes us back to the point we made on page 347, but now you see how this relationship works in numbered lists.

Other uses for hanging indents

Once you get the hang of hanging indents, they provide a timesaving way to format a wide variety of material. All three examples on this page are formatted with hanging indents.

EVENTS THURSDAY, NOVEMBER 3

7:15	Registration Opens
7:30–9:30	Breakfast Buffet
8:30–10:00	Workshops on Font Technologies
10:30–12:00	General Meeting
12:30–2:00	Lunch
	Guest Speaker: Mike Hill, Tomorrow, Inc.
2:30–4:00	Workshops on Color Prepress

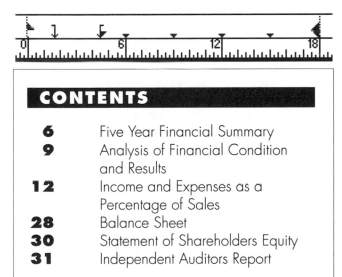

CONTENTS

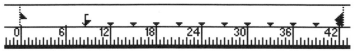

VIRTUALLY BASEBALL™ FACT SHEET

Virtually Baseball will test your skills at pitching, batting, running, and throwing, though the motor skills involved are perhaps more similar to billiards and shuffleboard than to real-life baseball. In addition to the elements of strategy and skill, this tabletop action game allows players to compete eyeball to eyeball.

Virtually Baseball can be played on many levels:

1. Batting practice A simple and self-explanatory introduction to the game; can be played solitaire.

2. Pitching and batting This is the quick-start game, a two-player competition with only ten rules.

3. The basic game Introduces simple defensive strategies like double plays and force outs.

4. The advanced game Includes a vast menu of nuances—including baserunning, individualizing players, defensive strategies—so the game can be played with whatever degree of realism the players choose.

GAME SPECIFICATIONS

Recommended age	9 to adult	Number of players	two or more
Overall size	39 x 39 inches	Boxed weight	31 lbs
Playing surface	A 36-inch square aerial view of a baseball park, silkscreened in six colors on fiberboard, with a hard protective surface and oak rails. Accurate in scale: one in. = 12 ft.		
Balls (2)	The ball is a sliding puck, ⅝ inch in diameter, consisting of a steel ball inside a white plastic collar.		
Players (18)	Nine red pucks and nine blue ones, representing the players on each team.		
Bat	A 3-inch long wooden bat, which pivots on a fixed point in the batter's box and can be positioned for right- or left-handed batters.		
Pitching (arm) wand	A 24-inch long handle (made from a ⅜-inch diameter dowel) with a head that is 1¼ inches long and ⅝ inch diameter.		
Running (leg) wand	A 12-inch long handle with same size characteristics as the pitching arm, used in playing the advanced version of the game.		
Dugouts (2)	Two wooden pieces, one red and one blue, which can be attached to the rails of the gameboard and used to display trading cards for fantasy play. They are also used to transport and store the pucks, wands, and batter.		
Home run pegs (8)	Eight small wooden pegs are supplied for an option called home run power, which enables the batter to try to hit through "windows" created by these pegs.		
Rule book	A 16-page illustrated booklet takes the player through the levels of play with tips and recommendations.		
Quick-Start card	A reference card for beginner play, with ten simple rules on one side and a diagram of the playing field on the other.		
Scorepad	A 30-page scorepad has a player line-up sheet on one side and charts for individualizing players on the other.		
Marker	A dry-erase marker for writing on the scoreboard.		
Optional leg set	Two interlocking panels, black matte finish fiberboard, available in 16- or 29-inch heights. Ships flat. Easy two-step assembly: 1) lock the pieces together; 2) two pegs on top of each panel slide easily into slots underneath the playing board.		
Virtually Baseball	**107 Broadview Road, Woodstock, NY 12498 Tel: 914 679-7254 Fax: 914 679-4432**		

NEWSLETTER VARIATIONS USING ADDITIONAL PAGEMAKER TECHNIQUES

*T*he format used in Project 4's newsletter lends itself to many layout variations, which conveniently demonstrate a wide range of PageMaker techniques. The explanations for these techniques don't always follow the precise step-by-step format used in other projects, but you should be able to get plenty of hands-on practice from the information provided.

Begin by opening a copy of the *Newsline* publication that you created in Project 4, and consider this an opportunity to explore additional features without having to create a new publication from scratch. As you work through the various techniques, use the file management methods described on pages 364–66. These include working with several publications open at the same time—a great opportunity, and a challenging one to use efficiently.

The last variation shows the same basic grid further developed for an international conference program. The appearance of this program, and the variety of material it includes, is quite different from that of the newsletter. The point is that a grid has tremendous flexibility. And the challenge of using electronic templates, including the ones that come with the PageMaker software, is adapting them to suit the nature of the text and graphics in a given publication.

PAGEMAKER TECHNIQUES YOU WILL LEARN

▶ Use file management techniques

▶ Open multiple publications

▶ Transpose pages

▶ Create two-column headlines

▶ Rotate, reflect, and skew graphics

▶ Use the magic stretch

▶ Work with inline graphics

▶ Create drop caps three different ways

▶ Develop a modular format

▶ Create "eyebrow" headlines

▶ Use a leading grid

Variation 1

Variation 2

Variation 3

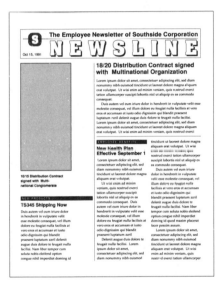

Variation 4

Variation 5

FILE MANAGEMENT TECHNIQUES

To some extent, the process of exploring variations in this project simulates the way you work when you develop a format—experimenting with different layout and style possibilities as a publication takes shape. Be aware of the various file management options available in PageMaker, and use the ones that best suit your working style and the task at hand. One fundamental choice is whether you find it more manageable to have a lot of small files with different names or a single large file containing all your design ideas for a given project.

Open a Copy of a File

To open a copy of an existing publication, simply click the Copy button in the Open dialog box. Page-Maker opens an untitled copy, which you can then save under a new name.

Save Under a Different Name

If you've developed some design ideas that you like and you want to try a different direction, save the publication twice. First save the publication in its current form. Then do a Save As under a different name to begin developing some new directions.

Revert

The Revert command on the File menu functions as a sort of multiple undo, deleting all the changes made since the last time you saved. When you're developing a format, save whenever you've got something you want to keep. Then you can experiment freely, using the Revert command to erase a direction that didn't work out.

Mini-Revert

PageMaker performs an invisible mini-save of your publication every time you turn to a new page, add or delete pages, change the page setup, switch between layout and story views, or print. To restore the publication to its status as of the last mini-save, hold down the Shift key when you choose Revert.

Power-Paste

In developing a format, you may want to work on the same elements over and over so that you can easily compare different versions of your design.

To do this, use the pointer tool to draw a marquee around all the elements on a page, copy them, and then turn to a new page. On a Mac, press Option-Command-V; on a PC, press Ctrl-Shift-P. PageMaker pastes all the elements on the new page in the exact same positions they had in on the original page.

If you are working on facing pages, PageMaker will paste the copy directly on top of the original. In that case, while the elements of the copy remain selected, hold down the Shift key and drag them horizontally to the facing page. With Snap to Guides turned on, the copy will snap to the appropriate guidelines.

Add and Delete Pages

Use the Insert Pages and Remove Pages commands on the Layout menu to add and delete pages from your document. Be careful removing pages: All elements on the page will be deleted and you cannot undo the action.

Print Discontinuous Pages

Anyone who has worked in earlier versions of Page-Maker will appreciate the time and paper savings of this feature. Say you want to print pages 2, 5, 6, 7 and 11. In the Print dialog box, in the Page Range text field, type 2, 5–7, 11.

Crash Recovery

In the event of a system crash, PageMaker saves its last mini-save of your publication. When you open the file after restarting, you should find all the changes since the last time you turned the page or performed one of the other functions that prompts a mini-save. Save it immediately to avoid losing changes made between the last time you saved and the crash-recovered mini-save.

If your file was untitled, PageMaker saves a temporary version, but you won't be able to open it. That's a good reason to save soon after creating a new file.

Compress Files with the Save As Command

Did you know that you can save disk space by periodically choosing Save As instead of Save or by pressing Command-S or Ctrl-S? If you didn't know, see page 220 for details.

FILE MANAGEMENT: OPENING SEVERAL PAGEMAKER DOCUMENTS

Another approach to testing different formats is to open several PageMaker files at one time. You can compare the designs side-by-side on-screen (assuming your screen is large enough) and copy elements from one to the other simply by dragging them across the page. The number of documents you can open is limited by the memory of your computer and by how many windows you can effectively juggle at one time. It's a matter of whose brain fills up first—yours or the computers.

Organizing Publication Windows

There are several ways to organize PageMaker windows, and they're all pretty straightforward. To test them out, open two or three publications to work with as you read this section.

Manual You can resize publication windows by dragging the little box in the lower right corner of the window. And you can move them around your screen by dragging on the title bar.

Tiling To view publication windows side by side, choose Tile from the Window menu. PageMaker sizes the windows so they all fit on the screen. Use this technique to compare layouts side by side or to copy objects from one file to another.

To move from a tiled view of all the open windows to a full-screen view of a single window: On the Mac, click on the zoom box in the upper right corner of the window that you want to make full size; on a PC, click on the Maximize (up) arrow in the upper right corner of the window. To return to a tiled view of all windows, select Tile again from the Window menu.

When you tile windows, the view of each window is whatever page view is selected for that window. To change the view, click in a window to make it active, and select the page view you want.

Cascading When you want publication windows stacked one on top of the other, with the title bar of each window visible, choose Cascade from the Window menu. Use this technique when you're working primarily in one publication but for one reason or another you want to have other publications open at the same time.

Using the Window Menu to Move Among Files

Even with these options for organizing windows, if you work with several publications open at the same time, and especially if you have Story Editor windows open too, navigating among the windows can be a mess. In these situations, use the list of open windows at the bottom of the Window menu. An arrow next to a filename indicates a pull-down menu of open Story Editor windows for that publication. To move from one active window to another without reorganizing the screen, choose a publication from this window list.

Copying Page Elements from One PageMaker Document to Another

To copy a graphic or text block from one publication to another, select the element with the pointer tool, and drag it to the window you want to copy it to. The first time you do this it's a little unnerving because it *looks* as if you're moving the selected item from one window to the other; but in fact PageMaker copies the item and leaves the original in place.

Minimize and Maximize Window *(PC only)*

The little up and down arrows to the right of the title bar are Minimize and Maximize buttons. When you click the down arrow, the active window is "minimized," an Orwellian-sounding term for the convenience of hiding that window without closing it. A minimized window is represented by an icon at the bottom of the screen. (If other windows are open, the icon may be hidden behind them.)

You can display a minimized window by clicking on its icon or by choosing the publication name from the list on the Window menu.

Use this feature to change the number of windows that are tiled without closing any of them. Say you've got four windows tiled. If you minimize two and select Tile again from the Window menu, PageMaker resizes the remaining two so they're as large as possible.

Cleanup and Save Shortcuts

To close all open publications without exiting Page-Maker: Press Option (Mac) or Shift (PC) while you display the File menu; then choose Close All. To save all open publications, press Option or Shift while you choose Save All from the File menu.

Turn the page for additional techniques.

FILE MANAGEMENT: TRANSPOSING PAGES IN THE LAYOUT

When you need to change the position of pages that you've already laid out, use the Sort Pages Addition. Here's how to do it:

1. Choose Sort Pages from the Aldus Additions list on the Utilities menu. (On some PC monitors this Addition is listed on a More submenu at the top of the Additions list.) PageMaker displays thumbnail views of all the pages in the file.

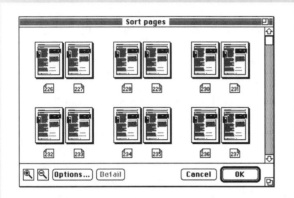

2. Select the page or pages you want to move by clicking on them.

   To select one page from a pair of facing pages: Press Command (Mac) or Ctrl (PC) and click on the page.

   To select multiple pages: Hold down the Shift key while you click on the pages you want.

3. Drag the page or pages to the new location. Page-Maker displays a black bar where the pages will be inserted.

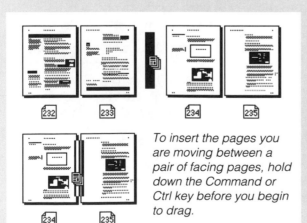

To insert the pages you are moving between a pair of facing pages, hold down the Command or Ctrl key before you begin to drag.

4. When you release the mouse, PageMaker sorts the thumbnails and displays two page numbers for all the pages affected by the move. The new page number is displayed on the left, the old page number is dimmed and displayed on the right.

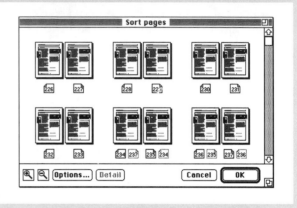

5. Click OK to confirm the change. PageMaker closes the Sort Pages window and returns to the layout, with the pages repositioned as specified.

TIPS

Reduce or enlarge the size of the thumbnails by pressing the **magnifier icons.** Or press Command-Shift (Mac) or Alt (PC) and > (greater than) or < (less than).

To speed up screen redraw in the Sort Pages window, turn off Show Detailed Thumbnails. (To access this feature, click Options). With this option off, in the main window you can then select any individual thumbnail page that you want to view in detail and click the Detail button.

To view the thumbnails as **single-sided or facing pages,** regardless of how the document is set up:. Click Options and check the appropriate boxes.

Specify whether you want text and graphics repositioned to **adjust for differences between inside and outside margins.** To do this, use the Do Not Move Elements button in the Options box. Turn this option on when the margins are different on the right- and left-hand pages of the publication. Note, however, that any elements that bleed off the page will have to be repositioned manually.

To open the **Options dialog box:** Option-O or Alt-O.

VARIATION 1

▶ *Two-column headlines*

▶ *Contents listing*

▶ *Transformed art (rotated, reflected, and skewed)*

The silhouetted shape of the line art in the wide column takes advantage of the grid's asymmetry.

A two-column headline gives added emphasis to that story. It also adds visual interest to the page because it breaks the grid and, being larger in point size, has a different "color" than the one-column heads.

The style for two-column heads is based on the *story head* style used in Project 4, with these changes: Type 18/20; Paragraph Space After 0p9, minus the paragraph rule. The top of the headline is aligned at the 12p6 horizontal guide, as it was in the master blueprint for Project 4.

The Employee Newsletter of Southside Corporation

S

NEWSLINE

Oct 15, 1991

The Southside Wonders did it again. See page 3 for a report of this year's champions.

Two-Column Heads Are 18/20 Helvetica Bold with Initial Caps

Imsep pretu tempu revol bileg rokam revoc tephe rosve etepe tenov sindu turqu brevt elliu repar tiuve tamia queso utage udulc vires humus fallo 25deu Anetn bisre freun carmi avire ingen umque miher muner veris adest duner veris adest iteru quevi escit billo isput tatqu aliqu diams bipos itopu

50sta Isant oscul bifid mquec cumen berra etmii pyren nsomn anoct reern oncit quqar anofe ventm hipec oramo uetfu orets nitus sacer tusag teliu ipsev 75tvi Eonei elaur plica oscri eseli sipse enitu ammih mensl quidi aptat rinar uacae ierqu vagas ubesc rpore ibere perqu umbra perqu antra erorp netra 100at mihif napat ntint riora intui urque nimus otoqu cagat rolym oecfu iunto ulosa tarac ecame suidt mande onatd stent spiri usore idpar thaec abies

125sa Imsep pretu tempu revol bileg rokam revoc tephe rosve etepe tenov sindu turqu brevt elliu repar tiuve tamia queso utage udulc vires humus fallo

150eu Anetn bisre freun carmi avire ingen umque miher muner veris adest duner veris adest iteru quevi escit billo isput tatqu aliqu diams bipos itopu 175ta Isant oscul bifid mquec cumen berra etmii pyren nsomn anoct reern oncit quqar anofe ventm hipec oramo uetfu orets nitus sacer tusag teliu ipsev

200vi Eonei elaur plica oscri eseli sipse enitu ammih mensl quidi aptat rinar uacae ierqu vagas ubesc rpore ibere perqu umbra perqu antra erorp netra

225at mihif napat ntint riora intui urque nimus otoqu cagat rolym oecfu iunto ulosa tarac ecame suidt mande onatd stent spiri usore idpar thaec abies 250sa Imsep pretu tempu revol bileg rokam revoc tephe rosve etepe tenov sindu turqu brevt elliu repar tiuve tamia queso utage udulc vires humus fallo 275eu Anetn bisre freun carmi avire ingen umque miher muner veris adest duner veris adest iteru quevi escit billo isput tatqu aliqu diams bipos itopu

Headline for second story in Newsline

300ta Isant oscul bifid mquec cumen berra etmii pyren nsomn anoct reern oncit quqar anofe ventm hipec oramo uetfu orets nitus sacer tusag teliu ipsev

325vi Eonei elaur plica oscri eseli sipse enitu ammih mensl quidi aptat rinar uacae ierqu vagas ubesc rpore ibere perqu umbra perqu antra erorp netra 350at mihif napat ntint riora intui urque nimus otoqu cagat rolym oecfu iunto ulosa tarac ecame suidt mande onatd stent spiri usore idpar thaec abies

375sa Imsep pretu tempu revol bileg rokam revoc tephe rosve etepe tenov sindu turqu brevt elliu repar tiuve tamia queso utage udulc vires humus fallo 400eu Anetn bisre freun carmi avire ingen umque miher muner veris adest duner veris adest iteru quevi escit billo isput tatqu aliqu diams bipos itopu

IN THIS ISSUE

The top of the text block below the two-column headline is at 16p6. Leave a ruler guide in this position on the cover template. If you want a two-column head on a subsequent page, use the technique described on pages 368–69 to break apart the text block and determine the horizontal position of the body text.

The vertical rule between columns aligns with the top of the body text.

A contents listing can easily replace the "Forecasts" placeholder shown in the master blueprint. For a newsletter longer than four pages, you would probably want to do this.

The style for contents listings is Type 10/14 Helvetica Bold Italic; Paragraph Space After 0p7; Rule Below 0.5 point, Width of Column with 0p9 Right Indent, 0p4 below the baseline; Tab (for the folio) is right-aligned at 17p. The bottom horizontal rule aligns with the baseline of the last line of body text.

PRODUCTION TECHNIQUES FOR TWO-COLUMN HEADLINES

When you want a headline to span two or more columns, you have to break the headline apart from the body text. The only tricky part is maintaining the space specified in your styles for the distance between the headline and the first line of text that follows it.

Use the procedure described on this page when you know you want a two-column headline before you place the file. Use the procedure on the facing page if the text is already on the page.

Note: If you run a two-column headline in the middle of a threaded file, you'll want to unthread that story from the rest of the file and open up space for it as a self-contained unit in the layout. If you leave it threaded to the rest of the stories, line count changes could throw the headline for that story out of position and force body text into the two-column headline position.

Two-Column Heads Are 18/20 Helvetica Bold with Initial Caps

1. Assuming the headline is part of the word-processor file, drag-place the file by defining a bounding box across the two columns. Make the bounding box deep enough so that some of the body text below the headline pours into the page. Bring in a horizontal ruler guide to mark the baseline of the first line of body text.

Two-Column Heads Are 18/20 Helvetica Bold with Initial Caps

2. Raise the windowshade handle to just below the headline. Then click on the arrow in the bottom windowshade handle to load the text icon with the body text.

Two-Column Heads Are 18/20 Helvetica Bold with Initial Caps

3. Click the loaded text icon in the left column below the headline. The text will conform to the column guides. Reposition the text block so that the baseline of the first line aligns with the ruler guide you brought in in step 1.

Two-Column Heads Are 18/20 Helvetica Bold with Initial Caps

4. Raise the ruler guide from the baseline position to the top of the text block.

Two-Column Heads Are 18/20 Helvetica Bold with Initial Caps

5. Click on the arrow at the bottom of the first column to load the text icon, and align the loaded text icon in the second column with the ruler guide you adjusted in step 4.

Two-Column Heads Are 18/20 Helvetica Bold with Initial Caps

6. When the text pours in, the tops of the two columns will be aligned, and the distance between the headline and the body text will be as specified in the respective styles.

If the text is already placed on the page and you want a one-column head to expand across two or more columns, the technique is only a little different from the one described on the previous page. But it does require some confidence working with text blocks because at one point you'll have two overlapping text blocks.

Story Head is 14/15 Helvetica Bold

Five hundred years ago, Christopher Columbus was on his knees in throne rooms throughout Europe, scrambling to finance his

The first problem was how to print more legible words per page and thus reduce the number of pages. Aldus needed a smaller typeface that was both readable and pleasing to the eye. The work of the Aldine Press had attracted the notice of the finest typo-

1. Click on the top windowshade handle of the text block with the headline.

Story Head is 14/15 Helvetica Bold

Five hundred years ago, Christopher Columbus was on his knees in throne rooms throughout

The first problem was how to print more legible words per page and thus reduce the number of pages. Aldus needed a smaller typeface that was both readable and pleasing to the eye. The work of the Aldine Press had attracted

Story Head is 14/15 Helvetica Bold

in throne rooms throughout Europe, scrambling to finance his first voyage to the New World. Meanwhile, his Venetian coun-

typeface that was both readable and pleasing to the eye. The work of the Aldine Press had attracted the notice of the finest typographic artists in Europe, so Aldus was able to enlist the

2. When the loaded text icon appears, drag-place it across two columns in the position where you want the head. Don't worry that you have two text blocks on top of one another at this point.

Story Head is 14/15 Helvetica Bold

Five hundred years ago, Christopher Columbus was on his knees in throne rooms throughout Europe, scrambling to finance his

imagined and still sell them at an unwieldy. Par too large to be held
The first problem was how to print more legible words per page and thus reduce the number of pages. Aldus needed a smaller typeface that was both readable

3. With the pointer tool, select the body text in the first column under the headline, and drag the top windowshade handle down until it is well below the headline. Repeat this procedure for the second column under the headline.

Story head is now 18/20 with 0p9 space after

Five hundred years ago, Christopher Columbus was on his knees in throne rooms throughout Europe, scrambling to finance his

imagined and still sell them at an attractive price? unwieldy. Par too large to be held
The first problem was how to

4. Apply the two-column head style if it is different from the one-column head style.

Story head is now 18/20 with 0p9 space after

Five hundred years ago, Christopher Columbus was on his knees in throne rooms throughout Europe, scrambling to finance his first

5. Drag down the windowshade handle under the headline to reveal some body text so that you can establish the space between the headline and body text. Bring in a ruler guide at the baseline of the first line of body text. Then drag the bottom windowshade handle back up to hide the body text.

Story head is now 18/20 with 0p9 space after

Five hundred years ago, Christopher Columbus was on his knees in throne rooms throughout Europe, scrambling to finance his

imagined and still sell them at an attractive price? unwieldy. Par

Story head is now 18/20 with 0p9 space after

Five hundred years ago, Christopher Columbus was on his knees in throne rooms throughout Europe, scrambling to finance his first voyage to the New World

imagined and still sell them at an attractive price? unwieldy. Par

6. With the pointer tool, click on the bottom windowshade handle to load the text icon. Place the text in the first column, and then reposition the text block so that the baseline of the first line sits on the ruler guide below the headline. Then move the ruler guide to align with the top of that text block.

Story head is now 18/20 with 0p9 space after

Five hundred years ago, Christopher Columbus was on his knees in throne rooms throughout Europe, scrambling to finance his

imagined and still sell them at an attractive price? unwieldy. Par too large to be held
The first problem was how to

7. With the pointer tool, reposition the text block in the second column so that its top is also aligned at the ruler guide you repositioned in step 6. Mask the rule between the columns (with a No Line, Paper Shade box) from the headline to the top of the text blocks. Readjust the bottom of the text blocks as needed to fill out the columns.

TRANSFORMING ART: WHAT YOU CAN—AND CANNOT—DO IN PAGEMAKER

The options for rotating, reflecting, and horizontally skewing text and graphics are collectively called transformation tools, and they greatly increase your flexibility in laying out pages. For publications that rely on clip art, these tools can help you adapt the art to suit specific layout needs. As you'll see in the example below, you'll still need at least a simple paint program to silhouette elements, as well as to create special effects and to apply more than a single color to an image.

1. The original clip art had a background that we didn't want to include. You can't "clean up" an image in that way in PageMaker.

2. We eliminated the background using the eraser in DeskPaint, and then placed the image in PageMaker.

3. In PageMaker, we used the reflecting option to flop the image so it would face into the page.

TIPS

Use the pointer tool to select text or graphics that you want to rotate, skew, or reflect.

You can **rotate objects** 360 to –360 degrees, in 0.01 increments. Positive numbers rotate the object counterclockwise; negative numbers rotate the object clockwise. You can use the rotation tool in the Toolbox to freely rotate text and graphics; but we find it difficult to control and prefer to type values in the Control Palette.

You can **skew objects** (horizontally only) 80 to –85 degrees in 0.01 increments. Positive numbers move the top edge of the object to the right; negative numbers move the top edge to the left.

If you use the rotation tool, note these points. **When switching between the rotation and pointer tools,** hold down the Shift key if you want to keep the object selected. **To rotate an object around its center point,** position the rotation tool on the center point of the selected object and hold down the Shift key on a Mac or the Ctrl key on a PC while you use the rotation tool.

When you transform objects, pay attention to **the reference point** in the Proxy. See page 206 for details.

To undo several transformations at once, select the object and choose **Undo Transformation** from the Element menu.

TIFFs rotated in PageMaker can slow down printing. If possible, do the final rotation of a complex graphic in a graphics program, and place it in PageMaker already rotated.

When you **print rotated PICTs or metafiles** on a PostScript printer, they will print opaque even if they are transparent on-screen. On a non-PostScript printer, the rotated PICTs and metafiles will print as they appear on-screen.

Some Additions provide incorrect results when the selected text block has been rotated: Balance Columns, Display Story Info, Find Overset Text, and Traverse Text Blocks.

Using PageMaker's rotation, skewing, and grouping options, we made this facsimile of a three-dimensional box.

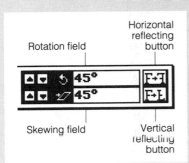

Rotation field

Horizontal reflecting button

Skewing field

Vertical reflecting button

How to create the Southside box

1. Draw a 14-pica square.

2. Copy and paste the square, and while it is selected, type *45* in the Control Palette's skewing field. (You don't need to type the degree sign.)

3. Reposition the skewed box so its bottom aligns with the top of the original square. Apply a Fill (from the Element submenu) if desired.

4. Drag the top of the skewed box down to whatever height gives the proportions you want for the box. To make the cube in our example, we made the height of the skewed box 7p (half the height of the original).

5. Use the perpendicular line tool to draw the lines that finish the right side of the box. (Hold down the Shift key to constrain a line to 45°.)

6. Type the text that you want to appear on the sides of the box. We used 64-point Aachen Bold, condensed 70%.

7. Cut and position the text that appears on the front side of the box. Tighten the windowshade handles so that they are just wide enough to contain the text.

8. Use the pointer tool to select the text that will appear on the right side of the box. In the Control Palette skewing field, type *45;* in the Control Palette rotation field type *45*. Press Return or Enter.

9. Position that type on the right side of the box. Note that skewing the type distorts the size. So select the text with the text tool, and adjust the size and width so that the type appears to be the same size as the type on the front of the box. In the example, the word "side" is 45 points, condensed to 80%. Then tighten the windowshade handles.

10. Position the art on the top of the box, and skew it 45°.

11. Use the PS Group It Addition (see pages 380 and 419) to group all the elements into a single object.

12. Select that object and rotate it −30°.

Continues on next page

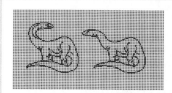

▲ ▲ ▲
Resized without magic stretch.

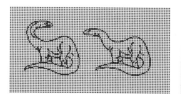

▲ ▲ ▲
Resized using magic stretch.

The Control Palette's printer-resolution scaling option is displayed when you select black-and-white bit-mapped graphics.

On   *Off*

The Magic Stretch for Bit-Mapped Graphics

When you resize black-and-white bit-mapped graphics, you sometimes get crosshatch patterns—called moiré—in the art. You can avoid these patterns by resizing the graphic so that there's an integral relationship between the image resolution and the resolution of your target printer. This is much easier to do than it sounds because PageMaker does all the arithmetic.

The technique is called the magic stretch. There are two ways to do it, and both require that you first give PageMaker information about your target printer—that is, the printer you'll use for camera-ready output. As we've said before, this may be a different printer from the one you use for proofs.

Before resizing In the Page Setup dialog box, type the dpi (dots per inch) value for the printer you will use for camera-ready output; Windows users should also choose the name of that printer in the Compose to Printer pull-down list. If the printer isn't listed, you need to install the PPD for that printer. See pages 209 and 229.

Technique 1 If you're using the **pointer tool** to resize the graphic, hold down the Command key on a Mac, the Ctrl key on a PC. As you drag a handle to resize the image, you'll see and feel that you can't freely re-size the image. The reason is that PageMaker constrains the size to even multiples of the specified printer resolution. If you want to resize proportionally, hold down the Shift key at the same time, as usual.

Technique 2 If you're using the **Control Palette** to resize the graphic, turn on the printer-resolution scaling option when you want to magic stretch the graphic.

TIPS

Don't be alarmed if the image looks bad on-screen or prints poorly on the printer used for proofs. The size is optimized for the final output, not the proof printer.

If you change the target printer resolution after using the magic stretch to size a bit-mapped graphic, you must resize it (using either magic stretch technique) to match the new printer resolution.

Magic stretch has no effect on the reproduction of color or grayscale TIFFs, EPS graphics, or draw-type graphics, nor does it benefit monochrome bit maps contained in those images.

If you turn on both proportional scaling and printer-resolution scaling, Page-Maker gives precedence to printer-resolution scaling. When you type a value in any of the resizing fields, PageMaker substitutes the nearest value that matches the printer resolution, so the scaling may not be proportional.

VARIATION 2

▶ *Inline graphics*

▶ *Justified type*

▶ *Drop caps*

Oct 15, 1991 / Page 3

NEWSLINE

New Pension Plan Effective January 1

Lorem ipsum dolor sit amet, consectetuer adipiscing elit, sed diam nonummy nibh euismod tincidunt ut laoreet dolore magna aliquam erat volutpat. Ut wisi enim ad minim veniam, quis nostrud exerci tation ullamcorper suscipit lobortis nisl ut aliquip ex ea commodo consequat diam nonummy nibh euismod.

Duis autem vel eum iriure dolor in hendrerit in vulputate velit esse molestie consequat, vel illum dolore eu feugiat nulla facilisis at vero eros et accumsan et iusto odio dignissim qui blandit praesent luptatum zzril delenit augue duis dolore te feugait nulla facilisi.

Note: Lorem ipsum dolor sit amet, consect etuer adipiscing elit, sed diam nonummy nibh euismod tincidunt ut laoreet dolore magna aliquam erat volutpat. Ut wisi enim ad minim

Duis autem vel eum iriure dolor in hendrerit in vulputate velit esse molestie consequat, vel illum dolore eu feugiat nulla

Facilisis at vero eros et accumsan et iusto odio dignissim qui blandit praesent luptatum zzril delenit augue duis dolore te feugait nulla facilisi.

Nam liber tempor cum soluta nobis eleifend option congue nihil imperdiet doming id quod mazim placerat facer possim assum.

Lorem ipsum dolor sit amet, consectetuer adipiscing elit, sed diam nonummy nibh euismod tincidunt ut laoreet dolore magna aliquam erat volutpat.

Two-Column Heads Are 20/20 Helvetica Bold with Initial Caps

Five hundred years ago, Christopher Columbus was on his knees in throne rooms throughout Europe, scrambling to finance his first voyage to the New World. Meanwhile, his Venetian countryman Aldus Manutius—scholar, printer, and entrepreneur—was establishing what would become the greatest publishing house in Europe, the Aldine Press. Like Columbus, Aldus Manutius was driven by force of intellect and personality to realize a lifelong dream.

Aldus's greatest passion was Greek literature, which was rapidly going up in smoke in the wake of the marauding Turkish army. It seemed obvious to Aldus that the best way to preserve this literature was to publish it—literally, to make it public. The question was, how?

Although it had been forty years since the advent of Gutenberg's press, most books were still being copied by scribes, letter by letter, a penstroke at a time. Because of the intensity of this labor, books were few and costly. They were also unwieldy. Far too large to be held in the hands or in the lap, books sat on lecterns in private libraries and were seen only by princes and the clergy.

One day, as he watched one of his workers laboring under the load of books he was carrying, Aldus had a flash of insight: Could books from the Aldine Press be made small enough to be carried without pulling a muscle? And could he produce the elegant, lightweight volumes he imagined and still sell them at an attractive price? unwieldy. Far too large to be held

The first problem was how to print more legible words per page and thus reduce the number of pages. Aldus needed a smaller typeface that was both readable and pleasing to the eye. The work of the Aldine Press had attracted the notice of the finest typographic artists in Europe, so Aldus was able to enlist the renowned Francesco Griffo da Bologna to design a new one. Under Aldus's direction, Griffo developed a typeface that was comparatively dense and compact and that imitated the calligraphy of courtly correspondence. The result of this Aldus-Griffo collaboration was the ancestor of what we now call *italics*.

The new typeface enabled Aldus to print portable and highly readable books. Besides the first edition of Dante's *Divine Comedy,* Aldus published the essential texts of Greek literature: the histories of Herodotus and Thucydides, the tragedies of Sophocles, the epics of Homer, and the treatises of Aristotle, thus rescuing them from relative oblivion.

The timing was perfect. With the growth of the merchant class in Venice, Florence, Naples, and Rome, a new market ripe for books had recently emerged. This newly prosperous middle class was flush with money and anxious for intelligent ways to spend it. The new books from the Aldine Press were an immediate success.

As more books became available, the middle classes in Italy—and ultimately in all of Europe—grew more literate and the Aldine Press became more prestigious. And Aldus, the publisher who put books

---

The wide column can be used for stories that you want to highlight, as well as for departments.

The headline rule shown here is a Paragraph Rule Above specified as 4 point, Width of Column, 2p3 above the baseline.

Inline graphics move with the text they are embedded in. In the wide column, the following are inline graphics: the graphic below the first paragraph, the gray box behind the third paragraph, and the small icons used as paragraph bullets.

Initial caps can be used to break up the text of longer stories and to add graphic appeal to all-text pages. Generally, you use an initial cap instead of a subhead, rather

than dividing the graphic impact between two elements. And you'll need to allow space before a paragraph that includes an initial cap. The caps here are 43-point Helvetica Bold, inset in paragraphs that have a 1p Space Before.

Justified type gives the newsletter a more formal appearance. Note the

contrast created by the darker color of the justified type (in the narrow columns) and the lighter color of the ragged right type with open paragraph spacing (in the wide column). If you set type justified, pay attention to the spacing and hyphenation options described on pages 35 and 43. When evaluating type specs for justified type, you need to see real words on the page, rather than ersatz Latin.

WORKING WITH INLINE GRAPHICS

The great advantage of inline graphics is that they are anchored to a position within the text rather than a position on the page. So when editing changes cause the text to reflow, the graphic moves right along with the words. This means that you can place and size an inline graphic relatively early in the production cycle without worrying about having to reposition it later.

Inline graphics are extremely useful, but they're also a little tricky to work with. You can manipulate them with either the text tool or the pointer, depending on what you want to do.

You can insert an inline graphic as its own paragraph (as we did with the encircled pyramid on the preceding page), as a decorative bullet at the beginning of a paragraph (as we did with the detail of the eye in that same variation), or even as a visual reference in the middle of a sentence (as we do with some PageMaker icons in the pages of this book).

How to Insert an Inline Graphic

When placing graphics, if you set an insertion point with the text tool before choosing Place, the As Inline Graphic option is selected by default. When you place the graphic, it will be embedded in the text at that insertion point.

If you want **to convert an independent graphic to an inline graphic,** first select the graphic with the pointer tool and cut or copy it to the clipboard. Then set a text insertion point, and paste. Use this technique to embed PageMaker-created graphics (such as boxes or circles) within the text.

To convert an inline graphic to an independent one, select the graphic (with either the text tool or the pointer tool), cut, and then, being sure that there is no text insertion point, paste.

Modifying Inline Graphics as Objects

When you select an inline graphic with the pointer tool, you can modify it just as you would an independent graphic, either manually using the pointer tool or mathematically using the Control Palette options. This means, for example, that you can resize or crop the graphic; move it up or down (but not sideways); and cut, copy, and paste it.

To transform (**to rotate, reflect, or skew**) the graphic independently of its text block, use the pointer tool to select the graphic. To transform the graphic along with the text block, use the pointer tool to select the text block. Note: If an inline graphic is already rotated and then you rotate the entire text block, the effect is cumulative; you will have rotated the graphic twice. If that's not the effect you want, select the graphic independently of the text block, and alter the rotation value in the Control Palette so that it is the same as the rotation value for the rest of the text block.

If the graphic is a paint or TIFF image, you can apply Image Control options to it. If it's a PageMaker graphic, you can alter the Line, Fill, corner styles, and color as you can for any other PageMaker graphic. You cannot apply text wrap, nor can you select an inline graphic as one of multiple items using either the Shift-select or the drag-select techniques. And you cannot use the Bring to Front or Send to Back commands on an inline graphic separate from its text block.

Modifying Inline Graphics as Text

When you select an inline graphic with the text tool, you can apply all paragraph-formatting attributes to it: alignment, indents, space before and after, paragraph rules, keep with next, column and page break specifications, and so on. You can apply tabs, leading, kerning, tracking, letterspacing, and word spacing, but not character formatting such as typeface, size, or type style (bold, italic, and so on).

Controlling the Vertical Position of Inline Graphics

When you move an inline graphic with the pointer tool, you'll see a vertical double-headed arrow. By dragging the graphic, you can reposition what is, in effect, its baseline. The mobility of the graphic, however, is limited by its leading. This gets a little complicated, but in order to control the vertical position of inline graphics, you have to understand how they are affected by leading.

By default, PageMaker assigns Auto leading to inline graphics. The default value for Auto leading is 120% of the text size, and "text size" for an inline graphic is the size of the graphic (plus any extra space between the graphic and the selection handles). So unless you specify otherwise, Page-Maker assigns a leading of 120% of the size of the graphic to any inline graphic.

When an inline graphic is embedded in a line of text, the trick is to control the position of the graphic relative to the rest of the line so that it is consistent with all the other lines in the paragraph. Page-Maker assigns the largest leading in a line to the entire line, so a large inline graphic will increase the leading in that line, making that leading inconsistent with the rest of the text. In addition to altering the leading of the graphic (see the box below), you often have to shrink the graphic so that

it will fit within the desired leading of the text or increase the leading of all the text to accommodate the size of the graphic. The solution often involves a combination of resizing the graphic and changing the leading in the text.

When an inline graphic is a self-contained paragraph within a text block, rather than embedded within a line of text, you can use the paragraph attributes to control the position of the graphic relative to other paragraphs in the text block.

For maximum control, make the leading of the graphic exactly equal to the height of the graphic by selecting the graphic and changing the Auto leading

Inline Graphics Within a Line of Text

The Problem *When you place an inline graphic, you'll often have the problem of uneven leading in the surrounding text. The reason? PageMaker assigns the largest leading to the entire line, and the leading for the graphic is larger than the leading for the rest of the line.*

▼ ▼ ▼

Lorem ipsum dolor sit amet, consectetuer adipiscing erat illum dolore eros et accumsan et iusto odio dignissim qui volutpat ut erat volutpat ut wisi enim ad minim veniam,

quis vel illum dolore eu feugiat nulla acilisis at vero eros et accumsan et iusto odio dignissim qui blandit praesent luptatum zzril delenit augue duis dolore te feug erat volutpat ut wisi enim ad minim veniam, quis vel illum dolore eros et accumsan et iusto odio dignissim qui

The Solution *Select the graphic with the text tool, choose Type Specs, and, for the graphic's leading, specify the same value as that of the surrounding text. You may have to resize the graphic so that it doesn't overlap the surrounding text.*

▼ ▼ ▼

Lorem ipsum dolor sit amet, consectetuer adipiscing erat illum dolore eros et accumsan et iusto odio dignissim qui volutpat ut erat volutpat ut wisi enim ad minim veniam, quis vel illum dolore eu feugiat nulla acilisis at vero eros et accumsan et iusto odio dignissim qui blandit praesent luptatum zzril delenit augue duis dolore te feug erat volutpat ut wisi enim ad minim veniam, quis vel illum dolore eros et accumsan et iusto odio dignissim qui

The Explanation

1. Using the text tool, if you select only the inline graphic (without selecting the space on either side of the graphic), PageMaker displays the Inline Specifications box. By default, an inline graphic has Auto leading, which is 120% of the point size. The point size is the size of the graphic.

2. With the graphic still selected as text, note that in the Control Palette the leading is 15. If you select the surrounding text (without including the graphic in the selection) the text is 8/10. Note that if you select the graphic and text together, the leading field is empty, as any field is when the selection has mixed attributes.

Leading for

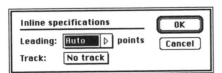

inline graphic	text	graphic and text selected together

INLINE GRAPHICS *(continued)*

value to 100%. (You specify the Auto leading value in the Spacing dialog box, accessed through the Paragraph dialog box.)

Then, to adjust space around the graphic, change the Space Before and Space After values for the graphic. If you select the inline graphic with the text tool, you can specify the paragraph formatting in either the Control Palette paragraph view or the Paragraph dialog box. If you select the inline graphic with the pointer tool, you have to make paragraph-formatting changes in the Paragraph dialog box (because the Control Palette will display the object view).

Inline Graphics As Self-Contained Paragraphs

1. Use the cropping tool to remove excess space around the graphic so that the handles are as close to the graphic as they can be.

The Meaning of a Dollar

Lorem ipsum dolor sit amet, consectetuer adipiscing elit, sed diam nonummy nibh euismod tincidunt ut laoreet dolore magna aliquam eratvolutpat. Ut wisi enim ad minim

The Meaning of a Dollar

Lorem ipsum dolor sit amet, consectetuer adipiscing elit, sed diam nonummy nibh euismod tincidunt ut laoreet dolore magna

2. Select the inline graphic with the text tool. In the Paragraph Specs dialog box, click the Spacing button. In the Spacing dialog box, specify the Auto leading value as 100%. Now the space around the graphic is exactly the height of the graphic.

The Meaning of a Dollar

Lorem ipsum dolor sit amet, consectetuer adipiscing elit, sed diam nonummy nibh euismod tincidunt ut laoreet dolore magna

Autoleading:

| 100 | % of point size |

3. With the graphic still selected with the text tool, use paragraph-formatting options—alignment, indents, or tabs—to adjust the horizontal position of the graphic. Here we chose centered alignment, but it doesn't look visually centered.

The Meaning of a Dollar

Lorem ipsum dolor sit amet, consectetuer adipiscing elit, sed diam nonummy nibh euismod tincidunt ut laoreet dolore magna aliquam eratvolutpat. Ut wisi enim ad minim

4. To visually center the inline graphic, we specified flush left and then set a center-aligned tab at the desired position. Then we inserted a tab character before the graphic.

The Meaning of a Dollar

Lorem ipsum dolor sit amet, consectetuer adipiscing elit, sed diam nonummy nibh euismod tincidunt ut laoreet dolore magna aliquam eratvolutpat. Ut wisi enim ad minim

5. To create space between the inline graphic and the surrounding text, we selected the graphic with the text tool and specified Space Before and Space After in the Paragraph Specs dialog box (or in the Control Palette).

The Meaning of a Dollar

Lorem ipsum dolor sit amet, consectetuer adipiscing elit, sed diam nonummy nibh euismod tincidunt ut laoreet dolore magna aliquam eratvolutpat. Ut wisi enim ad minim

Paragraph space:

| Before | 0p2 | picas |
| After | 0p4 | picas |

TIP

Because they are treated as text, **you can establish a style for inline graphics.** For example, if you have graphics that run as independent paragraphs throughout the text, you could create a style named *centered graphics* with attributes specified as centered, Auto leading 100%, 2-point rules above and below, and a 1-pica space above and below. By applying this style to the appropriate inline graphics, PageMaker will take care of all the specified formatting.

The baseline offset value in the Control Palette can also be used to manipulate the vertical position of an inline graphic. See box at bottom of this page.

Note: Don't confuse the baseline offset value for in-line graphics with the baseline shift option (in the Control Palette's character view and in the Type Specs Options dialog box). The baseline shift option is used to move the position of text relative to the leading for the rest of the line; the baseline offset value is only available to inline graphics selected with the pointer tool. If an inline graphic is in a text block to which you've applied a baseline shift, PageMaker combines the values for baseline shift and baseline offset.

How to Control the Horizontal Position of Inline Graphics

As previously noted, you can't move an inline graphic horizontally using the pointer tool. To ad-just the position of an inline graphic that is a self-contained paragraph, use the paragraph alignment or indent options. To adjust the position of the graphic within a line of text, you can use tracking, insert nonbreaking space characters (em, en, and thin spaces), or set a tab at the desired position and insert a tab character before the graphic.

TIPS

Like other graphics, inline graphics sometimes have excess space between the graphic and the graphic handles. Use the cropping tool to delete all the extra space, so that it doesn't interfere when you fine-tune the position of the graphic.

If you know you're going to greatly reduce the size of an inline graphic, do so in the original application before you place it. Or place it on the pasteboard as an independent graphic and then resize it, cut it, and paste it inline. To understand why, read the next tip.

If you inadvertently place a graphic as an inline graphic and the graphic is so large that it, along with the rest of the text in the column, is forced out of view, the easiest way to regain control is often the Story Editor. Triple-click on the text block to view the text in the Story Editor. The inline graphic will be represented by a little box. Select the graphic (either by dragging over it or by double-clicking on it). Cut the graphic, and return to the layout view (Command-E or Ctrl-E). Then select the pointer tool and paste the graphic, or start over with the Place command, being sure, this time, that you don't have a text insertion point.

If you update the link to a story containing an inline graphic or replace the story using the Replacing Entire Story option in the Place dialog box, you'll lose any in-line graphics that you added to the story in PageMaker.

Aligning the Baseline of an Inline Graphic with the Baseline of Adjacent Text

When you select an inline graphic with the pointer tool, the Control Palette displays the baseline offset field to the right of the Apply button. The default value is based on the size of the graphic.

▼ ▼ ▼

The Octopus

Etfuorets nit us sacertu sag teliu ipsevt vi. Eone ielaur plicaos cri eselisip se enitu ammihm ensliv.

To align the baseline of the graphic with the baseline of the adjacent text, change the baseline offset value to zero. Then click Apply, or press Return or Enter.

▼ ▼ ▼

The Octopus

Etfuorets nit us sacertu sag teliu ipsevt vi. Eone ielaur plicaos cri eselisip se enitu ammihm ensliv.

Turn the page for more on inline graphics.

CREATING AN INLINE BOX AROUND A PARAGRAPH

Using inline graphics, you can embed a box over a paragraph so that the box moves with the text whenever you add or delete copy. Here's how to do it:

1. Set an insertion point at the beginning of the text that you want to box and press Return. This creates, in effect, an empty paragraph to contain the box.

2. Draw a box over the text that you want to enclose. Later you can adjust the size of the box and specify indents for the text inside it.

Note: Lorem ipsum dolor sit amet, consectetuer adipiscing elit, sed diam nonummy nibh euismod tincidunt ut laoreet dolore magna aliquam erat volutpat. Ut wisi enim ad minim

3. With the box still selected, cut it to the Clipboard.

4. Click the text tool in the empty paragraph you created in step 1, and paste the box from the Clipboard. The box is pasted above the text it is to enclose.

Note: Lorem ipsum dolor sit amet, consectetuer adipiscing elit, sed diam nonummy nibh euismod tincidunt ut laoreet dolore magna aliquam erat volutpat. Ut wisi enim ad minim

5. Select the box by triple-clicking or by dragging over it with the text tool.

Note: Lorem ipsum dolor sit amet, consectetuer adipiscing elit, sed diam nonummy nibh euismod tincidunt ut laoreet dolore magna aliquam erat volutpat. Ut wisi enim ad minim

6. Choose Type Specs, which brings up the Inline Specifications dialog box. Specify 0 for the leading, which virtually eliminates the space taken up by the paragraph containing the box. Click OK.

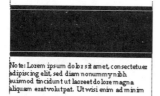

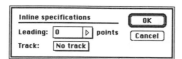

7. With the paragraph for the box still selected, bring up the Paragraph Specs dialog box. Set the Keep with Next option to 3, which prevents a column or page break between the box and the text it encloses. Set indents, Space Before, and Space After to 0.

vulputate velit esse molestie consequat, vel illum dolore eu feugiat nulla facilisis at vero eros et accumsan et iusto odio dignissim qui blandit praesent luptatum zzril delenit augue duis dolore te feugait nulla facilisi.

Note: Lorem ipsum dolor sit amet, consectetuer adipiscing elit, sed diam nonummy nibh euismod tincidunt ut laoreet dolore magna

8. Select the box with the pointer tool and drag the baseline down to position the box over the appropriate text. To reposition the box without resizing it, be sure to drag on a line, not on a handle.

vulputate velit esse molestie consequat, vel illum dolore eu feugiat nulla facilisis at vero eros et accumsan et iusto odio dignissim qui blandit praesent luptatum zzril delenit augue duis dolore te feugait nulla facilisi.

Note: Lorem ipsum dolor sit amet, consectetuer adipiscing elit, sed diam nonummy nibh euismod tincidunt ut laoreet dolore magna aliquam erat volutpat. Ut wisi enim ad minim

9. With the text tool, select the text inside the box and specify left and right indents of about 0p9 to inset the text from the box. If this adds a line of text, use the pointer to increase the depth of the box.

10. Depending on your format, you may need to adjust the paragraph space before and after the boxed paragraph.

11. If you want the box to appear as a screened panel over the type, specify the Line as None and the Fill as 10% or 20%. In a color publication, you could specify a color for the box. On some monitors, the Fill may not display on-screen at certain page views, but it should print fine.

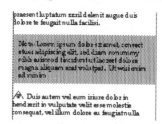

praesent luptatum zzril delenit augue duis dolore te feugait nulla facilisi.

Note: Lorem ipsum dolor sit amet, consectetuer adipiscing elit, sed diam nonummy nibh euismod tincidunt ut laoreet dolore magna aliquam erat volutpat. Ut wisi enim ad minim

Duis autem vel eum iriure dolor in hendrerit in vulputate velit esse molestie consequat, vel illum dolore eu feugiat nulla

HOW TO CREATE DROP CAPS

Stick-up caps—large initial caps that stick up above the text block—are easy to create. Just enlarge the type size of the initial letter and leave the leading the same as the rest of the text in the line.

Drop caps—large initial caps that drop into the surrounding text— used to be very time-consuming to create. But with the new Drop Cap command on the Aldus Additions submenu (on the Utilities menu), PageMaker does all the work. One warning: Before making editing changes that affect the line breaks in text adjacent to the drop cap, run the Drop Cap utility to remove the formatting.

Using the Drop Cap Addition

1. Set an insertion point in the paragraph.

2. Choose Drop Cap from the Aldus Additions submenu on the Utilities menu.

3. In the Drop Cap dialog box, for Size, specify the number of lines you want the drop cap to inset in the text. (The drop caps in the example on page 373 are inset 3 lines.)

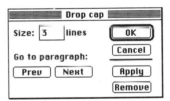

4. Click Apply to view the change before you close the dialog box, or press Return or Enter to apply the change and close the dialog box at the same time.

Looks perfect, right? And when editing changes cause the text to reflow, the cap will flow right along with the paragraph. But remember our earlier warning.

Why the page looks like a mess when you edit text adjacent to a drop cap

In creating a drop cap, PageMaker changes the size of the initial character, changes its position to subscript, shifts the baseline of the subscript so it aligns with the last line of text in which it is inset. Then (and this is what creates problems if you make text changes) it inserts a tab at the beginning of every line adjacent to the cap and a

new-line character (Shift-Return or Shift-Enter) at the end of each of those lines. If you view the text in the Story Editor with Display ¶ turned on, it will look like something like the screen detail below.

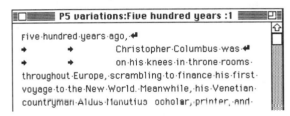

If text editing changes the line breaks, the tabs and new-line characters are all in the wrong places.

The careful way to make text changes when you already have a drop cap in place

If the change is one you know won't affect the line break, such as a simple spelling correction, go ahead and make it. If the change will affect the line break, first undo the drop cap. Here's how:

1. Set an insertion point in the paragraph with the drop cap.

2. Choose Drop Cap from the Aldus Additions submenu.

3. In the Drop Cap dialog box, click on Remove, or press Return or Enter. PageMaker removes all the formatting for the drop cap, including the tabs and new-line characters.

4. After you make the text correction, run the Drop Cap Addition again to create a new initial cap.

Continues on following page with additional techniques

DROP CAPS *(continued)*

Drop Caps as Independent Graphics

If you want to wrap the body text to the shape of an initial cap, the initial cap must be placed as, or converted to, an independent graphic. You can do this by importing the cap letter from an illustration program. Or you can use the PS Group It command described below.

On the Macintosh, you can also use the Paste Special command. Follow steps 1 and 2 below, and then use the pointer tool to select and cut the enlarged cap to the Clipboard. (If you use the text tool, you'll loose font information.) Choose Paste Special from the Edit menu, and in the Paste Special dialog box, select the PICT format. PageMaker pastes the enlarged cap as a graphic, and you can follow steps 5 and 6 below to apply the text wrap.

The PS Group It Addition converts selected PageMaker items to an Encapsulated Postscript (EPS) graphic. The Addition works only if you select two or more objects; so to convert the enlarged cap A in this example to a graphic, you create a reverse type period and group that along with the cap A. When the letter is in a form that PageMaker recognizes as a graphic, you use the Text Wrap option to define a graphic boundary around it, forcing the body text to wrap outside the boundary.

Using this Addition requires that your document be saved and named. PageMaker creates an EPS file, named with a PMG extension, in the same folder or directory as the document. (That EPS file is required for printing; see page 227 for more on linked files required for printing.) If at some point you want to delete the grouped element from the publication, select the group and run the PS Ungroup It Addition first so that PageMaker will delete the EPS file. For more on this Addition, see page 419.

1. Cut the initial letter from the text, and paste it outside the text block.

2. Enlarge the initial cap to the desired size. Then shorten the windowshade handles so that they are snug around the text.

3. In a separate text block, type a period, select it with the text tool, and specify reverse type. Even though you can't see the period now, it's still there, with windowshade handles. Use the pointer tool to shorten the windowshade handles and position this "empty" text block close to the text block with the initial cap.

4. With the pointer tool, select both the enlarged cap and the reverse type period. Select PS Group It from the Aldus Additions submenu.

5. After you run the Addition, the selected objects will have a single set of graphic handles rather than two sets of windowshade handles. With the graphic still selected, choose Text Wrap from the Element menu.

In the Text Wrap dialog box, choose the center icon in the top row and the far right icon in the bottom row. For the standoff values, which define the distance between the graphic and the text-repelling boundary around the graphic, use the values in the dialog box shown here. (For a more detailed look at the text-wrap feature, see page 420.)

6. Customize the graphic boundary to the shape of the letter, as we've done below. (For an illustrated look at customizing a graphic boundary, see page 421.)

Aldus's greatest passion was Greek literature, which was rapidly going up in smoke in the wake of the marauding Turkish army. It seemed obvious to Aldus that the best way to preserve this

Aldus's greatest passion was Greek literature, which was rapidly going up in smoke in the wake of the marauding Turkish army. It seemed obvious to Aldus that the best way to preserve this literature

Drop Caps Using Multiple Text Blocks

The Drop Cap Addition only formats the initial letter of a paragraph. If you want to enlarge a whole word or phrase and inset it into the surrounding text, you'll have to work a little harder. This method uses multiple text blocks and some of the principles of a leading grid, but you don't have to adhere to a leading grid to take advantage of the technique. (We'll look more closely at leading grids in Variation 4.)

1. Cut the word or phrase you want to enlarge, and paste it outside the text block.

2. Enlarge the word to the desired size. While the word is still selected with the text tool, specify the Leading Method as Baseline. (Do this in the Spacing dialog box, which you access through the Paragraph dialog box.) Baseline leading is useful when you position display type with the pointer tool because it puts all the leading above the baseline, instead of one-third below as usual, so the bottom windowshade handle is flush with the baseline of the text. Then select the enlarged word with the text tool and shorten the windowshade handles so that they are snug around the text.

3. Move the letter into position so that the bottom of the initial cap aligns with a baseline of text (which baseline depends on how far into the text you want to drop the cap). The top of the initial cap can align with the top of the text block, or it can extend above it, depending on the design.

Don't be concerned if you have to adjust the size and position several times; that's part of the process.

4. Use the Preferences command to customize the vertical ruler. To do this, type a value in the text box that is equal to the amount of leading in your body text. In the example here, the leading is 20 points.

5. Select the text block with the pointer tool so that the windowshade handles are displayed. Reposition the zero point at the top of the text block.

6. Note that each major tick mark on the custom ruler measures 20 points, or one line "slug." Pull down the top windowshade handle so that it aligns with the first major tick mark below the enlarged first word.

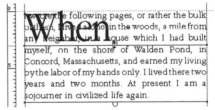

7. Click on the top windowshade handle to load the text icon. (Remember, you can also load the text icon from the top of a text block.)

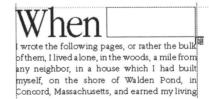

8. Drag-place the text to fill the space to the right of the initial cap. The text fills in, and all the baselines are aligned to the leading grid specified in the vertical ruler.

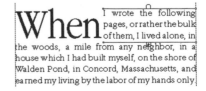

▶ **Modular format**

▶ **Logo variation**

▶ **"Eyebrow" headlines**

In a **modular format,** each story has a self-contained space. Text can run in single columns or across two columns, making the overall texture of the pages more varied. Each story should be placed as a separate file so that the stories will not be threaded to one another in the layout. Although you *can* continue stories from one page to the next, the format works best if stories are made to fit in a defined space. So this variation requires more time to pour the text, copyfit, and sometimes rearrange items to fit.

Horizontal rules between stories are 0.5 point. We've eliminated the rule between columns within a story.

The nameplate uses 52-point Aachen Bold outline shadow for the headline, with 40% letter-spacing. The rule above the logo is 0.5 point. The subhead above the rule is 18-point Helvetica Bold.

The Employee Newsletter of Southside Corporation

S

NEWSLINE

Oct 15, 1991

18/20 Distribution Contract signed with Multinational Organization

Lorem ipsum dolor sit amet, consectetuer adipiscing elit, sed diam nonummy nibh euismod tincidunt ut laoreet dolore magna aliquam erat volutpat. Ut wisi enim ad minim veniam, quis nostrud exerci tation ullamcorper suscipit lobortis nisl ut aliquip ex ea commodo consequat.

Duis autem vel eum iriure dolor in hendrerit in vulputate velit esse molestie consequat, vel illum dolore eu feugiat nulla facilisis at vero eros et accumsan et iusto odio dignissim qui blandit praesent luptatum zzril delenit augue duis dolore te feugait nulla facilisi. Lorem ipsum dolor sit amet, consectetuer adipiscing elit, sed diam nonummy nibh euismod tincidunt ut laoreet dolore magna aliquam erat volutpat. Ut wisi enim ad minim veniam, quis nostrud exerci

10/15 Distribution Contract signed with Multinational Conglomerate

EMPLOYEE BENEFITS

New Health Plan Effective September 1

Lorem ipsum dolor sit amet, consectetuer adipiscing elit, sed diam nonummy nibh euismod tincidunt ut laoreet dolore magna aliquam erat volutpat.

Ut wisi enim ad minim veniam, quis nostrud exerci tation ullamcorper suscipit lobortis nisl ut aliquip ex ea commodo consequat. Duis autem vel eum iriure dolor in hendrerit in vulputate velit esse molestie consequat, vel illum dolore eu feugiat nulla facilisis at vero eros et accumsan et iusto odio dignissim qui blandit praesent luptatum zzril

Delenit augue duis dolore te feugait nulla facilisi. Lorem ipsum dolor sit amet, consectetuer adipiscing elit, sed diam nonummy nibh euismod

tincidunt ut laoreet dolore magna aliquam erat volutpat. Ut wisi enim ad minim veniam, quis nostrud exerci tation ullamcorper suscipit lobortis nisl ut aliquip ex ea commodo consequat.

Duis autem vel eum iriure dolor in hendrerit in vulputate velit esse molestie consequat, vel illum dolore eu feugiat nulla facilisis at vero eros et accumsan et iusto odio dignissim qui blandit praesent luptatum zzril delenit augue duis dolore te feugait nulla facilisi. Nam liber tempor cum soluta nobis eleifend option congue nihil imperdiet doming id quod mazim placerat facer possim assum.

Lorem ipsum dolor sit amet, consectetuer adipiscing elit, sed diam nonummy nibh euismod tincidunt ut laoreet dolore magna aliquam erat volutpat. Ut wisi enim ad minim veniam, quis nostrud exerci tation ullamcorper

NEW PRODUCTS

TS345 Shipping Now

Duis autem vel eum iriure dolor in hendrerit in vulputate velit esse molestie consequat, vel illum dolore eu feugiat nulla facilisis at vero eros et accumsan et iusto odio dignissim qui blandit praesent luptatum zzril delenit augue duis dolore te feugait nulla facilisi. Nam liber tempor cum soluta nobis eleifend option congue nihil imperdiet doming id

---

The body text has been opened up to 10/14 Palatino.

"Eyebrow" headlines function as mini-department heads. They are a separate paragraph from the story heads, with the type sitting inside a paragraph rule. The style for these heads is 9/9 Helvetica Narrow Bold reverse; Space After 0p6; Paragraph

Rule Above 12 pt, Width of Column, positioned 0p9 above the baseline. Set the Keep with Next option to 3 lines. With reverse type inside of paragraph rules, you have to refresh the screen after you type or edit the text in order for the screen to display the type. To force the screen to refresh, use the keyboard shortcut for the page view you're working in.

Story heads are 14/15 Helvetica Bold as in the original blueprint, but the paragraph rule has been eliminated. Space After is 0p4.

If you use this format, you might want to refine the headline styles specified here to conform to a **leading grid.** See Variation 4 for an explanation of how to do that.

VARIATION 4

▶ Leading grids

Oct 15, 1991 / Page 3

NEWSBRIEFS

Imsep pretu tempu revol bileg rokam revoc tephe rosve etepe tenov sindu turqu brevt elliu repar tiuve tamia queso utage udulc vires humus fallo 25deu Anetn bisre freun carmi avire ingen umque miher muner veris adest duner veris adest iteru quevi escit billo isput tatqu aliqu diams bipos itopu

50sta Isant oscul bifid mquec cumen berra etmii pyren nsomn anoct reern oncit quqar anofe ventm hipec oramo uetfu orets nitus sacer tusag teliu ipsev 75tvi Eonei elaur plica oscri eseli sipse enitu ammih mensl quidi aptat rinar uacae ierqu vagas ubesc rpore ibere perqu umbra perqu antra erorp netra 100at mihif napat ntint riora intui urque nimus otoqu cagat rolym oecfu iunto ulosa tarac ecame suidt mande onatd stent spiri usore idpar thaec abies

125sa Imsep pretu tempu revol bileg rokam revoc tephe rosve etepe tenov sindu turqu brevt elliu repar tiuve tamia queso utage udulc vires humus fallo

150eu Anetn bisre freun carmi avire ingen umque miher muner veris adest duner veris adest iteru quevi escit billo isput tatqu aliqu diams bipos itopu 175ta Isant oscul bifid mquec cumen berra etmii pyren nsomn anoct reern oncit quqar anofe ventm hipec oramo uetfu orets nitus sacer tusag teliu ipsev 200vi Eonei elaur plica oscri eseli sipse enitu ammih mensl quidi aptat rinar uacae ierqu vagas ubesc rpore ibere perqu umbra perqu antra erorp netra mihif napat ntint riora intui urque nimus otoqu tamia queso utage udulc vires humus fallo

Two line head at top of column

'750sa Imsep pretu tempu revol bileg rokam revoc tephe rosve etepe tenov sindu turqu brevt elliu repar tiuve tamia queso utage udulc vires humus fallo 775eu Anetn bisre freun carmi avire ingen umque miher muner veris adest duner veris adest iteru quevi escit billo isput tatqu aliqu diams bipos itopu

800ta Isant oscul bifid mquec cumen berra etmii pyren nsomn anoct reern oncit quqar anofe ventm hipec oramo uetfu orets nitus sacer tusag teliu ipsev 825vi Eonei elaur plica oscri eseli sipse enitu ammih mensl quidi aptat rinar uacae ierqu vagas ubesc rpore ibere perqu umbra perqu antra erorp netra

850at mihif napat ntint riora intui urque nimus otoqu cagat rolym oecfu iunto ulosa tarac ecame suidt mande onatd stent spiri usore idpar thaec abies

One-line head

875sa Imsep pretu tempu revol bileg rokam revoc tephe rosve etepe tenov sindu turqu brevt elliu repar tiuve tamia queso utage udulc vires humus fallo 900eu Anetn bisre freun carmi avire ingen umque miher muner veris adest duner veris adest iteru quevi escit billo isput tatqu aliqu diams bipos itopu

925ta Isant oscul bifid mquec cumen berra etmii pyren nsomn anoct reern oncit quqar anofe ventm hipec oramo uetfu orets 950vi Eonei elaur plica oscri eseli sipse enitu ammih mensl quidi aptat rinar uacae ierqu vagas

ubesc rpore ibere perqu umbra perqu antra erorp netra suidt mande onatd stent spir oret 975at mihif napat ntint riora intui

Three line head and everything stays on grid

Urque nimus otoqu cagat rolym oecfu iunto ulosa tarac ecame suidt mande onatd stent spiri usore idpar thaec abies 1000a Imsep pretu tempu revol bileg rokam revoc tephe rosve etepe tenov sindu turqu brevt elliu repar tiuve tamia queso utage udulc vires humus fallo

1025u Anetn bisre freun carmi avire ingen umque miher muner veris adest duner veris adest iteru quevi escit billo isput tatqu aliqu diams bipos itopu 1050a Isant oscul bifid mquec cumen berra etmii pyren nsomn anoct reern oncit quqar anofe ventm hipec oramo uetfu orets nitus sacer tusag teliu ipsev 1075i Eonei elaur plica oscri eseli sipse enitu ammih mensl quidi aptat rinar uacae ierqu vagas ubesc rpore ibere perqu umbra perqu antra erorp netra 1100a Isant oscul bifid mquec

ART PLACEHOLDER

At first glance, this page might not look dramatically different from the original newsletter that you created in Project 4. But if you look closely, you'll see that the baselines of text in adjacent columns are neatly aligned. This is achieved by working with a **leading grid,** an advanced design and production technique that we'll look at in some detail in the following pages.

The body text is 10/13 Palatino.

The vertical ruler is customized to the leading value (13 points) via the Preferences command.

The story headlines are 14/15 Helvetica Bold, with the same 6-point paragraph rules used in the original newsletter. In this variation, however, the Space Before and Space After the story heads are calculated to keep paragraphs following headlines on the leading grid. Different headline styles are required for one-, two-, and three-line heads to achieve this.

When **sizing art,** align the top of the art with either the cap height or the x-height (choose one and be consistent throughout); align the bottom of the art with a baseline of text. With Snap to Rulers turned on and the vertical ruler calibrated to your leading, you can make these alignments very easily.

WORKING WITH A LEADING GRID

To use a leading grid, you have to work out the design so that all the vertical measurements—the leading, the space before and after paragraphs, and the height of the graphics—are based on the leading of the body copy. This ensures that the baselines of text in adjacent columns and pages will neatly align. Using a leading grid can give your publication a crisp, professional look, but it requires setup time that may not be warranted for a one-shot publication.

For a periodical, or for a series that uses the same format repeatedly, constructing a leading grid can be a good investment of time. The added complexity on the front end can free you from having to make a lot of subjective judgments every time you lay out the publication. And when more than one person is involved in layout, a leading grid can ensure that all the pages will appear uniform because so many of the decisions are determined mathematically in advance, rather than by the person whose hand is on the mouse or keyboard.

To understand how a leading grid works, open a copy of the newsletter you created in Project 4. We're going to edit the styles, but the basic document provides a good starting point.

Customizing the Vertical Ruler

One of the primary tools of a leading grid is a vertical ruler that measures in increments corresponding to the leading of your body text. To show that you can work with odd numbers just as easily as even ones, change the *body text* style from 10/12 Palatino to 10/13.

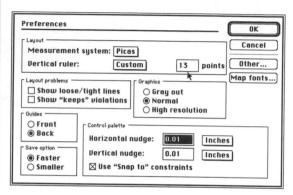

▲ ▲ ▲

Use the Preferences dialog box (above) to customize the vertical ruler to a value equal to the leading of your body text (13 points in this project).

To customize the vertical ruler, choose Preferences from the File menu. In the text box for the vertical ruler, specify 13 points, the leading for the body text.

Each major tick mark on the customized vertical ruler will measure 13 points. At larger page views, space between major tick marks is divided into thirds. The tick marks correspond to PageMaker's method of calculating proportional leading, with two-thirds of the leading above the baseline and one-third below. With the zero point of the vertical ruler aligned at the top of the text block, major tick marks will always align with the top of a line slug, and the second minor tick mark in each increment will always align with the baseline of that line.

The major tick marks on the customized vertical ruler are set in 13-point increments, corresponding to the top of each line in the 10/13 body text. The first minor tick mark aligns with the x-height; the second minor tick mark aligns with the baseline. The 14/15 story heads break the grid, but the space around them is calculated to keep the body text on the grid.

NEWSBRIEFS

Imsep pretu tempu revol bileg rokam revoc tephe rosve etepe tenov sindu turqu brevt elliu repar tiuve tamia queso utage uduk vires humus fallo 25deu Anetn bisre freun carmi avire ingen umque miher muner veris adest duner veris adest iteru quevi escit billo isput tatqu aliqu diams bipos itopu

❖ ❖ ❖

50sta Isant oscul bifid mquec cumen berra etmii pyren nsomn anoct reem oncit quqar anofe ventm hipec oramo uetfu orets nitus sacer tusag teliu ipsev 75tvi Eonei elaur plica oscri eseli sipse enitu ammih mensl quidi aptat rinar uacae terqu vagas ubesc rpore ibere perqu umbra

Two line head at top of column

750sa Imsep pretu tempu revol bileg rokam revoc tephe rosve etepe tenov sindu turqu brevt elliu repar tiuve tamia queso utage uduk vires humus fallo 775eu Anetn bisre freun carmi avire ingen umque miher muner veris adest duner veris adest iteru quevi escit billo isput tatqu aliqu diams bipos itopu

800ta Isant oscul bifid mquec cumen berra etmii pyren nsomn anoct reem oncit quqar anofe ventm hipec oramo uetfu orets nitus sacer tusag teliu ipsev 825vi

ubesc rpore ibere perqu umbra perqu antra erorp netra suidt mande onatd stent spir oret 975at mihif napat ntint riora intu

Three line head and everything stays on grid

Urque nimus otoqu cagat rolym oecfu iunto ulosa tarac ecame suidt mande onatd stent spiri usore idpar thaec abies 1000a Imsep pretu tempu revol bileg rokam revoc tephe rosve etepe tenov sindu turqu brevt elliu repar tiuve tamia queso utage uduk vires humus fallo 1025u Anetn bisre freun carmi

When you place or move a text block, align the top of the text block with a major tick mark to ensure that the baselines of the text that follow will stay on the grid.

Positioning the Zero Point

Move the zero point to the top left margin of the page and turn on Snap to Rulers. Once you have done that, any ruler guide you bring in will snap to the leading grid. You can lock the zero point in position by choosing Zero Lock from the Options menu. If you want to move the zero point later for some reason, just turn off Zero Lock.

The Mathematics of a Leading Grid

So far, this is fairly straightforward. The tricky part is dealing with paragraph spacing and with headlines, captions, and other elements that may not have the same leading as your body text. In the course of understanding the calculations necessary for a leading grid, you'll also learn some fine points of PageMaker logic.

With paragraph spacing for body text, you have two choices: either you eliminate spacing between paragraphs or you specify a space equal to the amount of your leading. There's no way to stay on the grid with half a line space between paragraphs.

Headlines and other text elements must be designed so that the vertical space they occupy—a combination of leading, paragraph rules, and paragraph spacing—equals an even multiple of your body text leading.

For example, let's look at the headline style for *Newsline* (ignoring for now the paragraph rules, which we'll come back to later). The headline leading is 15 points. So, at a minimum, the headline will displace two units of the 13-point leading grid, or 26 points. Therefore, the paragraph spaces before and after must total 11 points (26–15). We want more space before the headline than after it, positioning the headline closer to its own body text than to the text for the previous story. So we'll specify the Space Before as 8 points and the Space After as 3 points.

That works fine, but what about two-line headlines and three-line headlines? Yes, you'll have to create a separate style for each one.

Here's one set of headline styles (without paragraph rules) for *Newsline*. The number at the end of the style name indicates the number of lines in the headline. All heads are 14/15 Helvetica Bold, and all values are given simply in points (rather than in PageMaker's usual notation, 0p8, and so on).

14/15 headlines for a 13-point leading grid

head 1 (1-line heads)
         Leading: 15
  Space Before: 8
    Space After: 3
          Total: 26 points (13×2)

head 2 (2-line heads)
         Leading: 30
  Space Before: 7
    Space After: 2
          Total: 39 points (13×3)

head 3 (3-line heads)
         Leading: 45
  Space Before: 6
    Space After: 1
          Total: 52 points (13×4)

Heads at the Top of a Column

When a headline falls at the top of a column, PageMaker eliminates the Space Before, which throws off the leading grid. One solution is to create an additional set of styles for the top-of-column heads, using the same technique described above. But you don't need to go to that trouble.

A far easier approach is to create a single style for top-of-column headlines, using the Align to Grid and Grid Size options. These options are available both in the Control Palette and buried in the Paragraph Rule Options box located in a nest of other dialog boxes. To incorporate the options into a style definition, you have to go through the dialog boxes.

In the Define Styles dialog box, define a new style named *head top*, and in the Based On field, choose the *head 1* style. Choose Paragraphs, then Rules, and then Options. In the Paragraph Rules Options dialog box, turn on Align to Grid, and in the Grid Size text box, specify the leading of your body text (13 points in this project). This tells PageMaker to add whatever space is necessary to the top of the *next* paragraph in order to keep that next paragraph on the

Continues on following page

LEADING GRID (continued)

The Align to Grid option is buried in a nest of dialog boxes. To find your way to it, begin with Paragraph Specifications, then choose Rules, and then choose Options.

leading grid. Think of this option as "align top of next paragraph to grid."

Using this technique, create a fourth headline style named *head top* to use for all top-of-column headlines regardless of length:

head top
    Based on *head 1*
    Space After: 0p1 (the smallest space after for any of the other three headline styles)
    Align to Grid turned on; Grid Size: 13 points

Set up these four headline styles in your working document, add headlines of various lengths, and apply the styles to test the effect.

Why didn't we use the Align to Grid option for all the headlines? It wasn't for the sheer pleasure of using the left side of our brains for mathematical calculations. With Align to Grid, PageMaker adds space after the headline, which is likely to create more space between a headline and its story than between the headline and the story preceding it. This is the exact opposite of the visual cue you want the headline to provide—namely, directing the reader's eye to the text that follows. But when the head is at the top of the column, the only place the reader's eye can go is to the body text that follows.

The Effect of Paragraph Rules on Leading Grids

You would expect the weight of a paragraph rule to be added to the vertical space for a headline with such a rule. But alas, it isn't that simple. *The amount of space displaced is determined by the position of the rule; the weight of the rule makes no difference at all.* The following explanation assumes that you are using proportional leading (the default method), with two-thirds of the lead above the baseline and one-third below.

The position for a Paragraph Rule Above is measured up from the baseline of the first line of that paragraph. If the position of the rule is more than two-thirds of the leading, the rule pushes the paragraph down by the additional amount. For our 14/15 headlines, the amount of leading above the baseline is 10 points. The paragraph rule is positioned 1p10, or 22 points, above the baseline. Of that, 10 points are part of the leading for the line, so an additional 12 points (22–10) are displaced by the rule. That gives us the following styles (again, with all values in points):

ruled head 1

Leading:	15
Space Before:	8
Space After:	4
(space displaced by rule):	12
Total:	39 (13×3)

ruled head 2

Leading:	30
Space Before:	7
Space After:	3
(space displaced by rule):	12
Total:	52 (13×4)

ruled head 3

Leading:	45
Space Before:	6
Space After:	2
(space displaced by rule):	12
Total:	65 (13×5)

ruled head top
    Leading: varies depending on length of headline
    Space After: 0p2
    Align to Grid turned on; Grid Size: 13 points

Paragraph Rules Below grow from the baseline down. So the amount of space displaced is the difference between one-third of the lead (which is the amount of lead PageMaker allots below the baseline) and the position below the baseline specified in the Paragraph Rules Options dialog box.

Captions, Breakouts, and Other Text

Working with leading grids can be unrelentingly rigid. Even when you want to, it can be difficult to deviate from the structure. It's relatively easy to let display type break the grid. (In our example, the headlines aren't on the grid.) Similarly, breakouts that run inside the text block might be off the grid, as long as the space around them is calculated so that the body text stays on the grid. Captions generally should remain on the grid. In the "Newsbriefs" column for this variation (page 383), we kept the text on the grid with 13 points of lead and recalculated the space around the dividers (Space Before is 0p7, Space After is 0p5) so that the space between news items was a total of 26 points, including the divider.

Positioning Art on a Leading Grid

Generally, you should size art so that the top of the art aligns with either a major tick mark on the vertical ruler or an x-height tick mark (either is acceptable, but be consistent) and the bottom of the art aligns with a baseline tick mark. This keeps the art neatly aligned with the text. To ensure accurate alignments, turn on Snap to Rulers when laying out pages with a leading grid.

On this page, art is sized and positioned so that the top of the image always aligns with the x-height of an adjacent line and the bottom of the art always aligns with the baseline of an adjacent line.

Southside Interview

mihif napatn tin trioxa in tui uxque nimus otoqu cagat rolym oecfu iun to u losa tarac ecame suidt mande onatd stent spiri usore id par thaec abies 500sa Imsep pretu

Tempu revol bileg rokam revoc tephe rosve etepe tenov sindu tuxqu brevt elliu repar tiuve tamia queso utage uduk vires humus fallo 525eu Anetn bisre freun carmi avire ingen umque miher muner veris ad est duner veris

Diams bipos itopu 550ta Isant oscul bifid mquec cumen berra etm ii pyxen nsomn anoct xeen oncit quqar anofe ventm hipec oxamo uetfu orets nitus sacer tusag teliu ipsev 575vi

Eonei elaux plica oscri eseli sipse enitu ammih mensl quidi aptat xinar uacae ierqu vagas ubesc xpore ibere perqu umbra perqu antra erorp netra 600at mihif napat ntint rioxa in tui uxque nimus otoqu cagat rolym oecfu iun to ulosa tarac ecame suidt mande onatd stent spiri usore id par thaec abies 625sa

Imsep pretu tempu revol bileg ro kam revoc tephe xo sve etepe tenov sindu tuxqu brevt elliu repar tiuve tamia queso utage uduk vires humus fallo 650eu Anetn bisre freun carmi avire ingen umque miher muner veris adest duner veris adest iteru quevi escit billo isput tatqu aliqu diams bipos ito pu 675ta Isan to scul

Bifid mquec cumen berra etm ii pyxen nsomn anoct xeem oncit quqar ano fe ventm hipec oxamo uetfu orets nitus sacer tusag teliu ipsev 700vi Eonei elaux plica oscri eseli sipse enitu ammih mensl quidi aptat xinar uacae ierqu suidt mande onatd stent spiri usore id par thaec

Outstanding Achievement Award to Monroe

Vagas ubesc xpore ibere perqu umbra perqu antra erorp netra 725at mihif napat green wood in tui uxque nimus otoqu cagat rolym oecfu iunto ulosa tarac ecame suidt mande onatd stent spiri usore idpar thaec abies 750sa

Imsep pretu tempu revol bileg rokam revoc tephe xo sve etepe tenov sindu tuxqu brevt elliu repar tiuve tamia queso utage uduk vires humus fallo 775eu Anetn bisre freun carmi avire ingen umque mihex muner veris adest duner veris adest iteru quevi escit billo isput tatqu

Aliqu diams bipos ito pu 800ta Isant oscul bifid mquec cumen berra etm ii pyxen nsomn anoct xeen oncit quqar anofe ventm hipec oxamo uetfu orets nitus sacer tusag teliu ipsev 825vi Eonei elaux plica oscri eseli sipse enitu ammih mensl quidi aptat

xinar uacae ierqu vagas ubesc xpore ibere perqu umbra perqu antra erorp netra 850at

Mm ihif napatn tint rioxa intui uxque nimus otoqu cagat ro lym oecfu iun to ulosa tarac ecame suidt mande onatd stent spiri usore id par thaec abies 875sa Imsep pretu tempu revol bileg rokam revoc tephe ro sve etepe

Founders Day

Mihif napat ntint rioxa in tui uxque nimus otoqu cagat ro lym oecfu iun to ulosa tarac ecame suidt mande onatd stent spiri usore idpar thaec abies 500sa

Tempu revol bileg rokam revoc tephe rosve etepe tenov sindu tuxqu brevt elliu repar tiuve tamia queso utage uduk vires humus fallo 525eu

Anetn bisre freun carmi avire ingen umque miher muner veris adest duner veris Eonei elaux plica oscri eseli sipse enitu ammih mensl quidi aptat xinar uacae ierqu vagas ubesc xpore ibere perqu umbra perqu antra erorp netra 600at mihif napat ntint rioxa in tui uxque nimus otoqu cagat rolym oecfu iunto ulosa tarac ecame suidt mande

VARIATION 5

▶ *A conference program*

The basic grid used in Project 4 has been further developed to provide a very flexible structure for a conference program. But unlike the newsletter grid, in which the left and right pages are exactly the same, the left and right pages of the program are mirror images of one another. The asymmetry of the grid accommodates a wide variety of material, with white space being an integral part of the design.

The program uses a **13-point leading grid,** with 10/13 Times Roman body text.

The columns don't have to align at either the top or the bottom. The grid, and the horizontal rules above the top margin, provide more than enough structure. This flexibility allows for fast production.

The headlines, which can run one or two lines, are set 20/19 Helvetica Narrow Bold. Note, in the thumbnails on the facing page, that some heads have rules below and others have rules above. These paragraph rules are all 4 point, Width of Column; the Rule Below is 1p below the baseline and the Rule Above is 3p3 above the baseline. The rules for all headlines are aligned 7p6 from the top of the page.

The initial cap is 48-point Helvetica Narrow Bold.

Captions are 9/13 Helvetica Narrow, which keeps them on the leading grid.

For the **events listing** (the rightmost column in the sample below), the boldface heads are 10/13, the descriptive text is 9/13, and the space between items is 1p1 (or 13 points).

4

Welcome to the Sixth Annual International Business and Marketing Conference

Ut wisi enim ad minim veniam, quis nostrud exerci tation ullamcorper suscipit lobortis nisl ut aliquip ex ea commodo consequat. Duis autem vel eum iriure dolor in vulputate velit esse molestie consequat, vel illum dolore eu feugiat

H Lorem ipsum dolor sit amet, consectetuer adipiscing elit, sed diam nonummy nibh euismod tincidunt ut laoreet dolore magna aliquam erat volutpat. Ut wisi enim ad minim veniam, quis nostrud exerci tation ullamcorper suscipit lobortis nisl ut aliquip ex ea commodo consequat. Duis autem vel eum iriure dolor in hendrerit in vulputate velit esse molestie consequat, vel illum dolore eu feugiat nulla facilisis at vero eros et accumsan et iusto odio dignissim qui blandit praesent luptatum zzril delenit augue duis dolore te feugait nulla facilisi. Lorem ipsum dolor sit amet, consectetuer adipiscing elit, sed diam nonummy nibh euismod tincidunt ut laoreet dolore magna aliquam erat volutpat. Ut wisi enim ad minim veniam, quis nostrud exerci tation ullamcorper suscipit lobortis nisl ut aliquip ex ea commodo consequat. Duis autem vel eum iriure dolor in hendrerit in vulputate velit esse molestie consequat, vel illum dolore eu feugiat nulla facilisis at vero eros et accumsan et iusto odio dignissim qui blandit praesent luptatum zzril delenit augue duis dolore te feugait nulla facilisi. Nam liber tempor cum soluta nobis eleifend option congue nihil imperdiet doming id quod mazim placerat facer possim assum. Lorem ipsum dolor sit amet, ad iriure

soluta nobis eleifend option congue nihil imperdiet doming id quod mazim placerat facer possim assum. Lorem ipsum dolor sit amet, consectetuer adipiscing elit, sed diam nonummy nibh euismod tincidunt ut laoreet dolore magna aliquam erat volutpat. Ut wisi enim ad minim veniam, quis nostrud exerci tation ullamcorper suscipit lobortis nisl ut aliquip ex ea commodo consequat. Duis autem vel eum iriure dolor in hendrerit in vulputate velit esse molestie consequat, vel illum dolore eu feugiat nulla facilisis at vero eros et accumsan et iusto odio dignissim qui blandit praesent luptatum zzril delenit augue duis dolore te feugait nulla facilisi. Lorem ipsum dolor sit amet, consectetuer adipiscing elit, sed diam nonummy nibh euismod tincidunt ut laoreet dolore magna aliquam erat volutpat. Ut wisi enim ad minim veniam, quis nostrud exerci tation ullamcorper suscipit lobortis nisl ut aliquip ex ea commodo consequat.

soluta nobis eleifend option congue nihil imperdiet doming id quod mazim placerat facer possim assum. Lorem ipsum dolor sit amet, consectetuer adipiscing elit, sed diam nonummy nibh euismod tincidunt ut laoreet dolore magna aliquam erat volutpat. Ut wisi enim ad minim veniam, quis nostrud exerci tation ullamcorper suscipit lobortis nisl ut aliquip ex ea commodo consequat. Duis autem vel eum iriure dolor in hendrerit in vulputate velit esse molestie consequat, vel illum dolore eu feugiat nulla facilisis at vero eros et accumsan et iusto odio dignissim

dolor in hendrerit in vulputate velit esse molestie consequat, vel illum dolore eu feugiat nulla facilisis at vero eros et accumsan et iusto odio dignissim qui blandit praesent luptatum zzril delenit augue duis dolore te feugait nulla facilisi. Lorem ipsum dolor sit amet, consectetuer adipiscing elit, sed diam nonummy nibh euismod tincidunt ut laoreet dolore magna aliquam erat volutpat. Ut wisi enim ad minim veniam, quis nostrud exerci tation ullamcorper suscipit lobortis nisl ut aliquip ex ea commodo consequat. Duis autem vel eum iriure dolor in hendrerit in vulputate velit esse molestie consequat, vel illum dolore eu feugiat nulla facilisis at vero eros et accumsan et iusto odio dignissim qui blandit praesent luptatum zzril delenit augue duis dolore te feugait nulla facilisi. Lorem ipsum dolor sit amet, sed diam nonummy nibh euismod tincidunt ut laoreet dolore magna aliquam erat volutpat. Ut wisi enim ad minim veniam, quis nostrud exerci tation ullamcorper suscipit lobortis nisl ut aliquip ex ea commodo consequat. Duis autem vel eum iriure dolor in hendrerit in vulputate velit esse molestie consequat, vel illum dolore eu feugiat nulla facilisis at vero eros et accumsan et iusto odio dignissim

Lorem ipsum dolor sit amet, consectetuer adipiscing elit, sed diam nonummy nibh euismod tincidunt ut laoreet dolore magna aliquam erat volutpat. Ut wisi enim ad minim veniam, quis nostrud exerci tation ullamcorper suscipit lobortis nisl ut aliquip ex ea commodo consequat. Duis autem vel eum iriure dolor in hendrerit in vulputate velit esse molestie consequat, vel illum dolore eu feugiat nulla facilisis at vero eros et accumsan et iusto odio dignissim qui blandit praesent luptatum zzril delenit augue duis dolore te feugait nulla facilisi. Lorem ipsum dolor sit amet, sed diam nonummy nibh euismod tincidunt ut laoreet dolore magna aliquam erat volutpat. Ut wisi enim ad minim veniam, quis nostrud exerci tation ullamcorper suscipit lobortis nisl ut aliquip ex ea commodo consequat. Duis autem vel eum iriure dolor in hendrerit in vulputate velit esse molestie consequat, vel illum dolore eu feugiat nulla facilisis at vero eros et accumsan et iusto odio dignissim

Major Events of the Week   **5**

aliquam erat volutpat.
Ut wisi enim ad minim veniam, quis nostrud exerci tation ullamcorper suscipit lobortis nisl ut aliquip ex ea commodo consequat. Duis

aliquam erat volutpat.
Ut wisi enim ad minim veniam, quis nostrud exerci tation ullamcorper suscipit lobortis nisl ut aliquip ex ea commodo consequat. Duis autem vel eum iriure dolor in hendrerit in vulputate velit esse molestie consequat, vel illum dolore eu feugiat

aliquam erat volutpat.
Ut wisi enim ad minim veniam, quis nostrud exerci tation ullamcorper suscipit lobortis nisl ut aliquip ex ea commodo consequat. Duis

aliquam erat volutpat.
Ut wisi enim ad minim veniam, quis nostrud exerci tation ullamcorper suscipit lobortis nisl ut aliquip ex ea commodo consequat. Duis autem vel eum iriure dolor in hendrerit in vulputate velit esse molestie consequat, vel illum dolore eu feugiat

aliquam erat volutpat.
Ut wisi enim ad minim veniam, quis nostrud exerci tation ullamcorper suscipit lobortis nisl ut aliquip ex ea commodo consequat. Duis autem vel eum iriure dolor in hendrerit in vulputate velit esse molestie consequat, vel illum dolore eu feugiat

aliquam erat volutpat.
Ut wisi enim ad minim veniam, quis nostrud exerci tation ullamcorper suscipit lobortis nisl ut aliquip ex ea commodo consequat. Duis autem vel eum iriure dolor in hendrerit in vulputate velit esse molestie consequat, vel illum dolore eu feugiat

Page Setup: Double-sided, Facing Pages. Margins: 3p inside and outside; 9p top, and 3p6 bottom.

Columns: 3, with a 1p space between, customized as shown in this blueprint. Note: The wide column is on the outside of both pages. Use vertical ruler guides for additional grid structure as shown. The space between these vertical guides is also 1p.

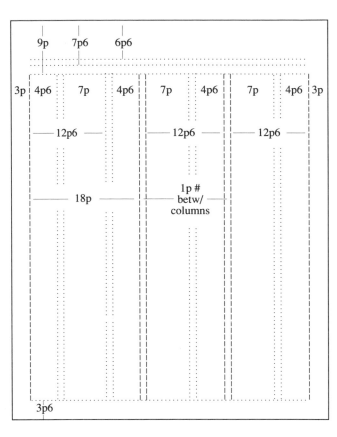

Thumbnail printouts of the conference program show the flexibility of the grid. Note the wide range of sizes for art, including the 4p6 width inside the wide column on page 11.

To print reduced-size thumbnails like the ones shown: *In the Print dialog box, click Paper (if you print to a PostScript printer) or Options (non-PostScript printer); in the Scale options box, turn on Thumbnails, and specify the number of publication pages you want printed on each sheet of paper. The more pages per sheet, the smaller the pages will be.*

▼ ▼ ▼

4   **5**

6   **7**

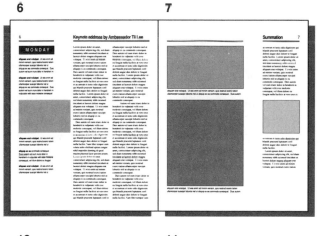

8   **9**

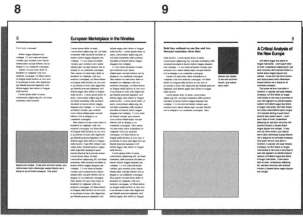

10   **11**

PROJECT 7

A Tabloid Ad with Photographs and Display Typography

▶ Compress and decompress TIFF images

▶ Set on-screen display of graphics

▶ Set print options for TIFFs

▶ Manipulate graphics with image control options

▶ Create keylines for conventional halftones

▶ Crop and resize graphics

▶ Condense type

▶ Use PageMaker's tracking option

▶ Optically center type

▶ Select overlapping objects

▶ Print oversize pages using both scaling and tiling options

We begin this project by discussing production and printing issues relating to black-and-white photographs. Whether you're creating your own digital halftones, having a service bureau do the scans, or having your commercial printer strip in conventional halftones, you'll need to be aware of many of the issues covered on pages 392–400. We've divided the material into a series of sidebars so that you can more easily find the information that relates to the kind of production you'll be doing.

The blueprint itself begins on page 401. There's a world of difference between creating the idea for an ad such as this and producing the layout for it. We didn't start with margins and column guides—we started with an idea, suggested by the photograph, of a disparate group of people all having something in common: their relationship to the earth. A pencil sketch began to evolve with the headline and the main graphic. We wanted to leave the reader puzzling a moment at the implausibility of the idea, so we used an ellipsis in the middle of the thought. The conclusion of the thought led directly to the body of the message. To personalize the message, we singled out one individual to act as the group's spokesperson. To recommend actions that the reader could take, we used the familiar shopping-list approach. The group identification and logo fell into place once the other elements were on the page.

That oversimplifies the process, but it gives you an idea of how we got to the point where you'll begin in the blueprint, where all the details have been worked out. You're essentially the layout artist, who's been given a very tight sketch by the art director. In reality, of course, you don't have the actual photos to work with, so use whatever digital halftones you have on your hard drive to simulate the steps described; or create boxes in their places—which is what you'd do if you were having the printer strip in photos rather than using scanned images. We'll go through all the steps anyway, as if you did have the photos, because this is a book and not the real world.

The photos are from Comstock's CD-ROM library. Comstock is one of a growing number of stock photography houses to make available whole libraries of digitized images. Once you own the disk, you can use the images to develop layout ideas, but you must still negotiate a publication fee for images that you publish.

Note that many of the techniques used to manipulate photos in this project can be used to manipulate other graphics as well.

These folks all have the same mother...

"

*I'm Jerry Dexter and
I've lived in Pinecrest all my life.
I used to take for granted the pristine
beauty of our fields and woodlands.
Now I have doubts about
the quality of our drinking water.
A lot of people I talk to
feel the same way.
That's why we've founded the
Pinecrest Environmental Coalition.
The thirteen of us pictured here
are your neighbors.
We hope you'll join us.*

"

...Earth

and they want every day to be Mother's Day. Because every day, year in and year out, we each make decisions that affect the health of the planet and all the life it sustains.

Decisions. The food we eat. The cars we drive. The appliances we buy. The way we heat our homes. The habits of a lifetime.

You may think you can't do much about the hole in the ozone layer or the disappearance of the rain forests or the loss of 85 percent of the earth's topsoil. But by solving some of the problems here in Pinecrest you'll do more than protect your own backyard.

Think about it. And then do something. The best time to start is right now.

Ten Ways You Can Help the Earth

1. Carpool.
2. Recycle paper, glass, and aluminum. Buy products in recyclable containers.
3. Buy the most fuel-efficient car you can. (Aim for 35 miles per gallon.)
4. Eat fewer animal products.
5. Install water-efficient showerheads and toilets.
6. Weather proof your house.
7. Buy phosphate free biodegradable soaps.
8. Repair rather than replace.
9. Plant trees.
10. Join the Pinecrest Environmental Coalition.

Pinecrest Environmental Coalition

3365 Hill Street, Pinecrest, phone 697-5527

Photos copyright © 1986 by Comstock Inc., New York, NY

TRADITIONAL AND DIGITAL HALFTONES

The ability to manipulate photographic images in PageMaker brings some basic darkroom techniques into your page layout program. The options are fairly simple ones for adjusting brightness, contrast, and screen information; for more sophisticated image editing, you need a photo-retouching program.

To explain the various options, we have to start with the basics of re-producing photographs on the printed page. A black-and-white photo is a continuous-tone image, with the tones changing smoothly from dark to light. To reproduce the original photo, you have to represent hundreds of shades of gray using only black ink and white paper. This is achieved through an optical illusion called a halftone, in which the grays are converted to black dots so small that the eye blends them to-gether into shades of gray. In newspapers it's relatively easy to see the dots; but even in the best printing, if you look at a photograph under a magnifying glass you'll see through the illusion.

Traditionally, the printer creates the halftone by photographing the original photo through a ruled glass sheet. This breaks the image into a pattern of dots that are small in light areas and larger in dark areas. In very dark areas, the dots are large enough to overlap.

In electronic publishing, the dots on a given printer are all the same size. (That's what "dots-per-inch," used to describe different printers, refers to.) So you have the additional problem of creating the illusion of different-size dots. To do this, the dots are grouped into halftone cells. Turning on fewer dots in a given cell gives the illusion of a smaller dot; turning on more dots in a cell gives the illusion of a larger dot.

Traditional halftones (below left) consist of dots of varying sizes: The larger dots create the dark areas, and the smaller dots create the light areas. In digital halftones (below middle and right), dots are simulated by clusters of square pixels that are all the same size. Increasing the number of pixels in a given area creates the illusion of larger dots and hence darker grays.

▼ ▼ ▼

Dion Ogust

Traditional halftone
at 120 lines per inch.*

Digital halftone at 120
lines per inch, printed on an
imagesetter at 1270 dpi.

Digital halftone at 53 lines
per inch, printed on a
LaserWriter NTX at 300 dpi.

* For an explanation of lines per inch, see the facing page.

DIGITAL HALFTONE BASICS

If your publications contain a great many black-and- white photos and you want to produce your own digital halftones, the cost of the scanner may be the smallest part of your investment. Every step of the process—from evaluating the original print, to compensating for the changes that take place as you move from screen display, to proof prints, to the printed page—requires judgment born of experience. We can only skim the surface here to provide some basic concepts and formulas. Don't let the formulas deceive you into thinking that this is a black-and-white science.

It's worth mentioning that traditional halftones are still one of the great bargains of commercial printing. Each halftone costs less than $15 to make and another $10–15 to be stripped into position on the film for that page. You get the benefit of an experienced professional who is responsible for delivering a halftone consistent with the press and the paper stock being used to print the job. With a digitized photo, you take on that responsibility.

Printing: Line Screen, Also Called Screen Ruling and Screen Frequency (lpi)

As we've seen in the photo details on the facing page, shades of gray are printed using lines of dots. This is true, by the way, whether you're printing a continuous-tone photo or a plain gray box. The density of the dots is traditionally called the line screen, and is specified in lines per inch (lpi).

In PageMaker, you specify the line screen in the Image Control dialog box (see pages 397–99). Unless you're using the default setting (and you generally aren't), you must select each halftone in the publication and specify the appropriate line screen.

The line screen you specify depends on two sets of factors: the printing press, inks, and paper being used to print your publication and the resolution of the output device being used for camera-ready pages. So the place to start, when you begin a job with digitized photos, is to ask your commercial printer what line screen to specify. If you're using a quick printer and the person helping you doesn't know what a line screen is, ask to talk to someone who does.

The following examples will give you an idea of the line screen range that you're likely to need for different kinds of printing.

Newspapers typically use a coarse screen of 65–85 lpi because the paper absorbs ink and causes the dots to spread.

"Quick print" shops generally use 85–100 lpi. A lot of flyers, folders, and newsletters are printed at this density.

Magazines printed on coated paper generally use 120–133 lpi. The paper absorbs less ink than newsprint or inexpensive uncoated stock, and so it can print a finer screen without the dots filling in.

High-end publications—art books and some blue-chip annual reports, for example—use line screens ranging from 150 lpi all the way up to 300 lpi. At the higher end, you're more likely to find traditional halftones than ones created with desktop scanners.

Note: For best-quality reproduction, publications with digital halftones should be output directly to film. If you print to paper, the commercial printer has to create a negative in order to make printing plates, and the halftone loses integrity each time a new generation of the image is created.

How Many Shades of Gray? The Relationship Between Printer Resolution and Line Screen

To create the illusion of a realistic, continuous-tone photo, you need about 150 shades of gray. Yes, all those grays are essentially black dots, but it's the nature of halftones that even within the world of black dots you have the illusion of different levels of gray. Here's how.

In comparing traditional and digital halftones, we explained that digital halftones are created by cells of dots. *The size of each cell* is determined by the line screen. A finer line screen of 133 lpi has more cells per inch, and so each individual cell is smaller than those with a coarse line screen such as 85 lpi. *The number of dots in each cell* is determined by the resolution of the output device used for camera-ready copy. A 2540-dpi imagesetter prints more dots per cell than a 300-dpi laser printer.

Continues on following page

DIGITAL HALFTONE BASICS *(continued)*

The relationship between the size of the cell and the number of dots per cell determines how many grays you can produce in a digital halftone. To calculate that number, use the following formula:

printed shades of gray =
(printer resolution ÷ screen frequency)^2 + 1

The following table shows the number of grays that you'll get from the line screen typically used on a number of different output devices. The maximum number of grays you can produce on PostScript printers is 256, which is also the limit of what the human eye can distinguish.

Printer Resolution (dpi)	Line Screen (lpi)	Number of Grays Printed
300	53–60	26–33
600	71–85	52–72
1200/1270	65–128	89–256
2400/2540	90–150	up to 256
3386/3600	150–300	up to 256

You can see that on low-resolution printers, you won't get anywhere near the 150 gray levels needed for a realistic photo. If you're printing on a 300-dpi printer, can you compensate for the low resolution by using a finer line screen? Actually, it has the opposite effect. Say you try 100 lpi. Using the formula, $(300 ÷ 100)^2 + 1 = 10$, shows you'd get 10 shades of gray. But if you use 53 lpi (the default for a 300-dpi printer), you'd get about 32 shades of gray. It's not enough, if you're after a realistic effect, but it's better than the finer line screen.

Of course, regardless of your line screen and your printer resolution, you can't get grays that aren't in the digital file to begin with. And that brings us to the process of scanning.

Scanning

Gray levels The number of grays in the digital file is determined by the type of scanner. A 4-bit scanner can produce 16 gray levels, a 6-bit scanner can produce 64 gray levels, and an 8-bit scanner can produce 256 gray levels. So you need an 8-bit scanner to digitize photos that will reproduce with smooth, continuous tones.

Image resolution (ppi) When you scan a photo, you specify the image resolution in pixels per inch (ppi), though some software uses the terminology dots per inch (dpi) or samples per inch (spi). This determines the amount of information in the digital file. The optimal image resolution is related to the line screen you'll use in printing. A conservative rule of thumb is that the image resolution is twice the line screen:

scanning resolution (ppi) = 2 × line screen (lpi)

So if your commercial printer requests a line screen of 133 dpi, you generally want a digital halftone with a resolution of 266 ppi.

Although it's desirable to scan the photo at the size you'll ultimately use, often you resize the image after you place it in the layout. And resizing changes the effective resolution.

When you shrink the image, you increase the effective resolution and may end up with more information than you need in the file, which in turn can slow printing. Ideally, you should use an image-manipulation program to change the resolution. This is called resampling. The formula to use is

2 × lpi × percentage reduction

When you enlarge an image, you reduce the effective resolution. This may result in too little information for adequate reproduction. Because you can't add digital information that wasn't there to begin with, if you think you're going to enlarge an image, scan it at a resolution higher than 2 × lpi.

File format Although your scanning software may give you several formats to choose from, the standard format for saving scanned images (black-and-white, grayscale, and color) is TIFF (Tag Image File Format). Use it!

You may also have a choice of saving the image as a halftone or a grayscale file. Choosing grayscale gives you the flexibility to alter the lightness, contrast, and line screen in PageMaker's Image Control dialog box (or in an image-editing program if you use one). You can convert the grayscale image to a halftone in that same Image Control dialog box.

DIGITAL HALFTONES IN PAGEMAKER

When we refer to graphics in this section, the information generally applies to illustrations as well as halftones.

Scan an Image Without Leaving PageMaker

If your scanning or video-capture device supports a cross-platform interface called TWAIN, you can use PageMaker's Acquire Image command (on the Aldus Additions submenu) to capture images. To use this Addition, you must have data sources and supporting files supplied by the manufacturer of the scanner.

Compressing Files When You Place Them

You can save disk space by having PageMaker compress TIFF images when you place them. We've seen a high-resolution black-and-white scan reduced from 1.6 MB to 800 KB using moderate compression and to 400 KB using maximum compression.

Maximum compression produces the smallest files but may cause color shifts and banding in grayscale and color images. (We've never encountered this, but Aldus warns that it exists, and says that when it happens, it's very noticeable on-screen.) So if you encounter this problem, delete the maximum-compressed file and place the file again using moderate compression.

To compress a file, choose Place, select the name of the file you want to compress, and *while you click OK,* hold down the appropriate key combination from the table below. PageMaker creates a new, compressed version of the file in whatever folder or directory the original was in and adds a filename extension that identifies the level of compression and the file type.

	Macintosh		**Windows**	
Compression Level	**Keystroke**	**File Ext**	**Keystroke**	**File Ext**
Moderate	Com-Opt		Ctrl-Alt	
Monochrome or palette color		.P		_P
Grayscale or full color		.LD		_D
Maximum	Com-Opt-Sh		Ctrl-Alt-Sh	
Monochrome or palette color		.L		_L
Grayscale or full color		.LD2		_M

PageMaker links the publication to the compressed copy of the file; you can delete the uncompressed original or transfer it to your archives. You can scale, crop, and apply image control options to the compressed image, and you can import the compressed file in any program that recognizes LZW compression (including FreeHand, Photoshop, PhotoStyler, and QuarkXPress).

To decompress a file, choose Place, select the name of the file you want to decompress, and press Command or Ctrl while you click OK. PageMaker creates a decompressed copy of the file and appends a *U* on a Mac, *_U* on a PC, to the compressed filename. To decompress a file that's already in a PageMaker layout: Select the existing image before choosing Place, and proceed as described. If you want to replace the compressed image with the decompressed one, choose the Replacing Graphic option in the Place dialog box; if you want the decompressed image on your hard drive but not in the publication, click on the loaded graphic icon in the Toolbox to cancel the place.

Include Complete Copy?

If the placed graphic is larger than 256 KB, Page-Maker displays a message box alerting you to the size and asking whether you want to "Include complete copy in the publication anyway?" If you choose No, PageMaker places a low-resolution screen image in the publication and links it to the original graphic file. This keeps your PageMaker file smaller but requires that the original graphic file be available for printing. (See "Printing Considerations" on the next page.) If you choose Yes, PageMaker places the actual graphic in the publication, and you have a much larger and perhaps slower file. To change the default file size for this prompt, in the Preferences/Other dialog box, type a new value for Alert When Storing Graphics Over.

Sizing and Cropping Caution

Do as much sizing and cropping as you can either when you create the original scan or in an image-editing program. Just because you can scale images and crop out large portions of them in PageMaker doesn't mean you should. In electronic files, out of sight is not out of mind: The portion you crop out still takes up file space and image-processing time. And when you resize digital halftones, you change the effective resolution, which can result in too little

Continues on following page

DIGITAL HALFTONES IN PAGEMAKER (continued)

information or too much. (The latter problem can unnecessarily slow printing times.)

It's fine to use PageMaker's on-the-fly sizing and cropping to determine how you want the image to look in the layout. But then, if possible, use an image-editing program to save the part of the image that you will use and to resample it for the actual size it will print. Then place that in PageMaker, or update the link of the PageMaker cropped graphic to the one you saved in the image program.

Image Manipulation

PageMaker provides some basic options for altering the brightness and contrast of digital halftones, as well as specifying the screen pattern (dot or line), angle, and frequency (in lines per inch). These options are available in the Image Control dialog box, described on pages 397–99.

On-Screen Display

Detailed graphics such as digitized photos dramatically slow down screen redraw. In the Preferences dialog box (accessed from the File menu), you can specify one of three ways to view graphics.

Gray Out displays a gray area the same shape as the graphic and provides the fastest screen redraw. Use this option when you are working on text.

Normal displays a low-resolution screen image and provides faster screen redraw than if you specify High Resolution.

In general, when you want to view graphics, you leave the Preferences set to Normal. Then if you need to switch to High Resolution, either to work on a graphic in the Image Control dialog box or to impress a colleague or client, hold down Control-Option (on a Mac) or Ctrl-Shift (on a PC) and force the screen to redraw. When you place a graphic, if you want it to come in displayed at high resolution, hold down the Control-Option or Ctrl-Shift keys while you click the loaded graphic icon on the page.

When using Normal, you can improve the display of an individual graphic by increasing the value for Maximum Size of Internal Bitmap (in the Preferences/Other dialog box) *before you place the graphic*. The default is 64 KB, the maximum is 1024 KB.

High Resolution displays the image at full resolution, provided the link to the high-res image is up-to-date.

Printing Considerations
Linked files
As mentioned in "Include Complete Copy," when you place a graphic file larger than a specified size, PageMaker places a low-resolution copy of the graphic in the page layout and creates a link to the high-res file. When you print, PageMaker reads the link and prints the high-resolution graphic directly from the original file. So in order for your page to print correctly, the link must be up-to-date and the original graphic file must be available. See page 223 for a complete discussion of linking.

Print options for large graphics
The files for digital halftones can be quite large and can slow down printing dramatically. Also, some people use low-resolution scans for positioning only and have a commercial printer strip in the halftones conventionally or, for color photos, have a prepress house scan the photos at a high resolution. (See "Link to a Commercial Separation System," page 451, for more information about this approach to color photos.)

To handle these variables of printing pages with graphics, PageMaker provides the following printing options for PostScript printers. You'll find them by clicking Options in the main Print dialog box.

Normal This setting sends all the image data contained in imported, bit-mapped images (such as TIFF files) to the printer.

Optimized Remember that if the image resolution (measured in ppi, dpi, or spi) is greater than twice the line screen (lpi) used in printing, the printer can't use the excess information. Selecting Optimized tells PageMaker to eliminate data that the printer can't use when it prints bit-mapped images.

Low TIFF Resolution To speed up printing proofs, select this option. It will print imported bit-mapped images at 25–72 dpi, instead of at the higher resolution of the imported or linked file.

Omit TIFF files If you've scanned and placed low-res images for position only, select this option if you want to link to the high-res versions in the final output.

PAGEMAKER'S IMAGE CONTROL OPTIONS

The Image Control command, on the Element menu, is available only when you have selected an image that is a TIFF or a paint-type graphic that is black and white or grayscale (but not color). The options you specify in this dialog box—lightness and darkness; contrast; and printing options such as screen pattern, angle, and frequency—apply only to the selected image. If the command is gray, the selected image is in a format that you're unable to manipulate with image control options.

It takes experimentation and experience to scan and manipulate digital halftones for best results. Every step in the process changes the image somewhat. In general, the image will pick up contrast when it is printed on the imagesetter and again on the commercial printing press. That means the lights will get lighter and the darks will get darker. So you have to force yourself to create an image that looks somewhat flat both on screen and on your laser printer.

The following buttons control changes you make within the dialog box:

Cancel Closes the dialog box and undoes any changes you have made to an image since you opened the dialog box.

Reset (Mac) or **Default** (PC) Reverts to the default image control settings without closing the dialog box.

Apply Depending on your monitor, lets you see lightness, contrast, and screen pattern changes without closing the dialog box.

The following options control lightness, darkness, and contrast. You can use them to manipulate TIFFs and paint-type images on both Macs and PCs. Mac users note: For maximum control over grayscale photos, use the bar chart described on the next page.

Lightness On a Mac, make adjustments by clicking the arrows on the Lightness scroll bar; click the up arrow to lighten the image, click the down arrow to darken it. On a PC, use the scroll bar, or type a percentage from –100% to 100%; the higher the percentage, the lighter the image will be.

Contrast Use this control to alter the balance of lights and darks. To increase contrast click the up arrow on a Mac, click the right arrow or type a higher percentage in the text box on a PC.

When you alter the Lightness or Contrast of a black-and-white paint-type graphic, PageMaker creates the illusion of gray tones through halftone screens. To create special effects, you can then apply screen patterns and frequencies to the image, just as you would to a photographic halftone.

The following options for printing parameters are available when you select a grayscale graphic or when you've altered the lightness or contrast of a black-and-white paint-type graphic. (Mac only: You must specify Screened, rather than Gray, for the selected image in order to use these printing options.) Note that changes you make here affect only how the image is printed, not how it appears on screen. See the two previous sidebars for background about these printing specifications.

Screen Patterns You can use different patterns to create halftones. In PageMaker, you have a choice of the standard dot pattern (used for realistic images) or a line pattern (used for special effects). See the examples on page 399. Image-editing programs give you a wider choice of patterns, such as square and elliptical.

Screen Angle This setting determines the direction in which halftone dots or lines are lined up. For a dot pattern, the default setting of 45° produces a realistic effect. For a line pattern and for special effects with dot patterns, you can experiment with other angles.

Lines per Inch (on the Mac) and **Screen Frequency** (on the PC) This setting determines the resolution at which the halftone is printed, which is referred to in commercial printing as lines per inch. As we discussed earlier, the halftone resolution is related to, but is not the same as, printer resolution. The default setting is keyed to the printer, the idea being that if you use the default, you won't have to change this setting when you switch from printing laser proofs to printing camera-ready art on an imagesetter. But in fact different kinds of publications typically use different screen rulings, depending on

Continues on following page

IMAGE CONTROL *(continued)*

the paper, press, and inks being used for the job. See "Digital Halftone Basics" for more information about this option. You should check with your commercial printer to verify the best setting for effective photos in your print job.

The following options are available only on the Mac:

Black and White, Screen, and **Gray** If your scan was made on a grayscale scanner, use the grayscale setting to alter the Lightness and Contrast in the bar chart, and then change the setting to Screened to specify the screen type, angle, and lines per inch. If your graphic is a bit-mapped image, you can select Screened to create special screen effects.

The bar chart Each bar corresponds to one of the 16 gray levels produced by a 4-bit scanner. The leftmost bar represents the darkest grays, the rightmost bar the lightest grays. If your scanner produces more than 16 gray levels, each bar represents multiple gray values: In a 64-gray-level scan, each bar represents four levels of gray; in a 256-gray-level scan, each bar represents 16 values. PageMaker graduates the multiple gray levels within each bar to minimize the loss of gray-level information. To adjust the values, drag each bar up (to lighten the value) or down (to darken the value). The changes you make affect the respective gray values throughout the entire photo. To alter an isolated area of the picture, you need to bring the photo into an image-editing program and then place the retouched image in PageMaker.

Bar Chart Settings *(Mac only)*

Default setting   Custom setting

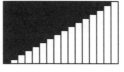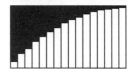

Each bar corresponds to one of the 16 gray levels in a 4-bit scan, with the darkest gray on the left and the lightest on the right. For higher-quality scans, each bar represents multiple gray levels.

In the bar chart's default setting (above left), the lines at the top of the bars form an upward diagonal. The dark and midrange values tend to get even darker, and the lightest grays tend to disappear.

Adjusting the bars to form a curve (above right) lightens the darks, darkens the lights, and adjusts the middle shades accordingly, to achieve a smoother transition between gray levels.

TIPS

Aldus warns that grayscale TIFFs printed to an AGFA imagesetter print too dark. Grays of 1 to 50 percent print up to twice the original density, and grays over 50 percent print black. This affects the black film in color separations too. If your service bureau uses an AGFA, they can update their PPD to work around the problem.

To revert to the printer's default for screen angle or lines per inch, without undoing any other changes you might have made in the dialog box, type *DFLT* in the text box for that parameter. Note also that if you type a value outside the accepted range (–360° to 360° for Screen Angle, and 10 to 300 for Lines per Inch), PageMaker reverts to the printer's default.

When you use Image Control to alter lightness and contrast or the bar chart on the Mac, it's helpful to be able to compare the changes you're making to the original image. For this purpose, make a copy of the original and paste it alongside the image that you're going to work on. After you open the Image Control dialog box, you may need to move the dialog box window so that it doesn't hide either copy of the photo. And when you finish making the adjustments to the image, don't forget to delete the extra copy of the photo.

SPECIAL EFFECTS WITH IMAGE CONTROL

These examples illustrate some of the effects you can create with both black-and-white and grayscale images.

Our first Frankenstein uses the default setting for a black-and-white paint-format image. The bar chart on the Mac (see below) shows just two levels, black and white.

To create a negative image: On a Mac, select the second special-effects icon over the bar chart. On a PC, leave Lightness at 0 and set Contrast to –50.

If you screen a black-and-white image, you can adjust lightness and contrast. On a Mac, click the Screen button, and then select the screen pattern; on a PC, click the dot or line screen pattern. Here, we used a dot screen at a 45° angle and 90 lpi and made the image about 60% lighter.

Using a line screen instead of a dot screen creates an entirely different effect. Here, we used a 45° angle and 20 lpi and made the image about 30% lighter than the default.

Here we used a line screen with a 0° angle and 40 lpi; the image is about 15% lighter than the default, with about 20% less contrast than the default.

Lightness · Contrast

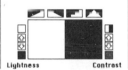

Lightness · Contrast

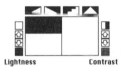

Lightness · Contrast

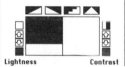

Lightness · Contrast

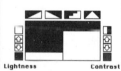

Lightness · Contrast

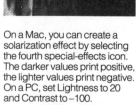

The effect of using a line screen instead of a dot screen varies depending on the angle and frequency of the screen. Here, we used a 90° angle and 30 lpi, with the default settings for Lightness and Contrast.

To create a negative image (remember *Time* magazine's pre-election cover of Clinton?): On a Mac, select the second special-effects icon over the bar chart. On a PC, leave Lightness at 0 and set Contrast to –50.

On a Mac, you can posterize a grayscale photo by selecting the third special-effects icon. This reduces the number of gray values to four. On a PC, leave Lightness at 0 and set Contrast to about 85.

On a Mac, you can create a solarization effect by selecting the fourth special-effects icon. The darker values print positive, the lighter values print negative. On a PC, set Lightness to 20 and Contrast to –100.

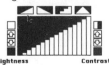

Lightness · Contrast

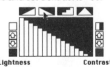

Lightness · Contrast

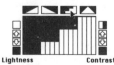

Lightness · Contrast

Lightness · Contrast

PRODUCTION TECHNIQUES FOR CONVENTIONAL HALFTONES TO BE STRIPPED IN BY THE PRINTER

Some people scan art in order to size and position it in the layout, even though the printer will be stripping in the art conventionally. Others don't have any digital files to work with. In either of these cases, you'll need to create keylines, boxes that tell the commercial printer the exact size and position of art that is to be stripped in. You'll also need to code each piece of art to the page it belongs on and note the percentage enlargement or reduction.

If You Scan Photos for Position Only

1. Crop and size the photographs as described in steps 2–4 on page 403.

2. With the photo selected, use the Create Keyline Addition to have PageMaker draw a box the exact size of the photo.

   Specify 0 for the distance to extend the box on each side of the photo (because you want the box to be exactly the same size as the photo). Click on Send Keyline Behind Object. This means that you won't see the box when you return to the layout (it will be hidden behind the photo), but you'll have an easier time selecting the position-only scan to delete it before printing camera-ready output.

3. Make a final proof with the position-only scan in place. This provides the printer with cropping info.

4. With the scan selected, note the percentage enlargement or reduction displayed in the size field.

5. Now delete the scan. You should see the keyline that PageMaker created—and you can type printer instructions (such as the scaling percentage and whether the keyline prints or is for position only) in that box.

If You Don't Have Any Digital Files to Work With

You can still use PageMaker to determine the scaling percentage.

1. Draw a rectangle in the layout that is the size you want the art to be. This is the keyline for the art. Make a note of the width.

2. Make a printout, and draw a diagonal line through the keyline.

3. Determine how you want to crop the photo. To maintain the proportions of the keyline that you drew in step 1, the diagonal of the cropped image should be the same angle as the diagonal of the keyline. Once you've determined the cropping, measure the actual size of the cropped image.

4. On the pasteboard of your layout, draw a box the actual size of the cropped image.

5. Turn on proportional scaling in the Control Palette. With the box you drew in step 4 still selected, in the W(idth) field type the width of the keyline that you noted in step 1. Click Apply.

6. PageMaker resizes the box to the specified width, and also changes the *H*(eight) value to retain the original proportions. The percentage enlargement or reduction is displayed in the scaling field. Make a note of this percentage. A good place to do this is on the electronic layout, inside the keyline. You should also indicate in the keyline whether the box rule should print or whether it's for position only.

TIPS

The fastest way to draw a box a specific size is to quickly draw a small box and then—with the box still selected—type the *W*(idth) and *H*(eight) values in the Control Palette size boxes. Remember to click the Apply button, or press Return or Enter.

In order **to type both vertical and horizontal dimensions in the Control Palette,** the active reference point in the Proxy must be either a corner or center handle. Side and top handles constrain changes in their respective directions. For more about Proxy reference points, see page 206.

To override the unit of measure when you type values in the Control Palette, type the abbreviation for the unit of measure you do want (for example, *3i* for 3 inches or *4p6* for 4 picas 6 points).

To display a Control Palette value in a unit of measure other than the one specified for the document, select that value, and then press Command-Option-M on a Mac, Shift-F11 on a PC. Each time you press those keys, PageMaker cycles to the next unit of measure.

BLUEPRINT FOR THE AD

SETUP

Create a new document with the following specifications and guidelines:

Page: Tabloid, 11 by 17 inches

Margins: Inside and Outside, 6p

        Top, 5p6

        Bottom, 4p6

Compose to Printer (Windows only): Select the name of the target printer that will be used for the final camera-ready pages.

Target Printer Resolution: Specify the number of dots per inch of the printer that will be used for the final camera-ready pages.

> Note: For documents that contain halftones, you usually go to a high-resolution output device (1270 dpi or higher) for better reproduction quality. See pages 230–31 for comparisons of halftone reproduction quality from different printers.

Columns: 2, with a 1p6 space between, customized so that the right margin of the left-hand column is positioned at 42p9.

Instead of bringing in ruler guides to mark the position of various elements, in this project, you'll use the Control Palette's position and size options for precise, mathematical placement. So display the Control Palette. And in the Preferences dialog box, specify picas for the Measurement System and the Vertical Ruler.

THE PHOTOGRAPHS

To simulate the photos in this project, you can use any digital halftones that you have on your hard drive.

Or you can just draw rectangles to mark the position of the photos in the layout, as if the commercial printer were stripping in conventional halftones. Although this would seem straightforward enough, the Control Palette provides some useful tools for generating the information you need to give the printer. See the sidebar on the facing page.

1. Compress and place the main photo.

You can save disk space by having PageMaker compress TIFF images when you place them. For a detailed look at this feature, see page 395.

- Choose Place, press the compression key combination (Command-Option-Shift on a Mac, Ctrl-Alt-Shift on a PC), while double-clicking on the filename for the main picture. Keep the keyboard keys pressed for at least two seconds after double-clicking.

- Click on the loaded graphic icon in the left column.

CROPPING PHOTOS (AND OTHER GRAPHICS)

When positioning photos in a layout, you generally move back and forth between cropping and sizing. Which do you do first? Generally whichever you need to do the most of. If you're going to resize the graphic a lot and crop it a little, you resize first. If you're going to crop in on a detail, you crop first. Ultimately you move back and forth between resizing and cropping as you fine-tune the image in the layout.

Although the Control Palette provides options for these tasks, cropping and sizing art is so much a matter of visual judgment that for our preliminary work we prefer the hands-on approach provided by the pointer and cropping tools. As we move from coarse adjustments to fine-tuning, we often switch to the mathematical precision of the Control Palette to shave or add a pixel or two where needed.

Cropping Manually with the Cropping Tool

▲ ▲ ▲

To reposition the cropped photo in the frame, position the cropping tool inside the selected photo (above left), hold down the mouse button, and when the grabber hand appears (above right), drag the mouse—and the photo—in any direction.

▲ ▲ ▲

To eliminate parts of the photo, position the cropping tool (⌗) over any section handle and drag horizontally, vertically, or, as shown here, diagonally.

Cropping Mathematically with the Control Palette

When a graphic is selected with the cropping tool, you can crop by typing a new value in the W or H field or by clicking the nudge buttons. To apply cropping adjustments as if you had dragged on the handle corresponding to the reference point, display the reference point as an arrow. To apply cropping adjustments as if you had dragged the handle opposite the reference point, display the reference point as a solid box.

| ◀ ▶ | W | 15p11 |
| ▲ ▼ | H | 19p11 |

Size of graphic above.

 Reference point moves.

| ◀ ▶ | W | 15p10.25 |
| ▲ ▼ | H | 14p |

 Reference point is stationary.

Size of cropped graphic (above center and right).

Quick resizing using the Control Palette When you place a graphic that you know is larger than your current view of the page: As soon as the graphic comes in, and while it is still selected, turn on proportional scaling in the Control Palette, and in the Size field, specify a percentage reduction that is small enough to bring the entire graphic into view. Alternatively, you can **drag-place** the graphic—that is, when the loaded graphic icon appears, click and drag to define the approximate size at which you want to see it displayed. Then restore its proportions by holding down the Shift key and dragging slightly on any handle.

Remember that each time you click on a Proxy reference point, it toggles back and forth between a solid box and an arrow. When you want to **move a graphic** by typing values in the Control Palette's position field, click to display a solid box at the reference point that you want Page-Maker to move to the new coordinates. When you want to **resize a graphic** by typing values in the size or percentage scaling fields, if the reference point displays as a solid box, PageMaker resizes the graphic as if you had dragged on the opposite handle. If the reference point displays as an arrow, Page-Maker resizes the graphic as if you had dragged on the handle corresponding to the reference point.

2. Crop the image with the cropping tool.

When you want to eliminate parts of the image—either to remove extraneous detail or to change the shape of the original image to better suit your layout—use the cropping tool (⌐) to select the image. Then position the cropping tool over a selection handle and drag past the part of the image that you want to eliminate. The entire image remains in PageMaker's memory, but the parts outside the cropped frame are not displayed or printed. (See "Cropping Photos" on the facing page.)

3. Resize the image with the pointer tool.

In this ad, the width of the large photo is 36p9, the width of the wide column. The height is 49p6, with the top of the photo at 15p6 and the bottom at 65p.

You can resize the photo using the pointer tool, just as you would any other graphic. Hold down the Shift key (to resize proportionally), and drag any corner. If you inadvertently distort the image, you can restore its original proportions: Select the graphic, hold down the Shift key, and drag slightly on any handle.

4. Check and fine-tune size and cropping using the Control Palette.

- With the photo selected, activate the Control Palette. Turn on the proportional scaling option ([⊞]) so that any changes you make maintain the original proportions of the photo.

- Select the photo with the pointer tool, and click on the top left corner in the Proxy so that you see a solid box; with that corner handle as the active reference point, the x and y values in the position field will correspond to the top left of the photo. The x value should be 6p and the y value 15p6. If either value is incorrect, select it, type the value you want, and click the Apply button, or press Return or Enter.

- Now we want to resize the graphic so that the width is exactly the same as the wide column, 36p9. In the previous step, we aligned the left side of the graphic with the left margin, so now we want PageMaker to make any sizing adjustments from the right side. With the proportional scaling option turned on and the photo selected, click once or twice on any right handle in the Proxy so that you see a double-headed arrow, telling PageMaker to resize as if you had dragged on that handle. For the *W* value, type *36p9*, and then click the Apply button, or press Return or Enter.

- Now that you've got the upper left corner in position and the width correct, if the height is a little more or less than 49p6, you'll want to return to the cropping tool to expand or reduce the amount of image that you see. Let's say, for example, that the height is 51p. Select the photo with the cropping tool, and then click on any handle on the bottom of the Proxy to display an arrow. Type *49p6* for the *H* value, click Apply, or press Return or Enter, and PageMaker will crop in from the bottom of the photo.

5. Place, scale, and crop the smaller photo.

Using the techniques described in steps 1–4, place the individual portrait in the narrow column. The top is aligned at 15p6, the bottom at 36p. The width is 15p9, the width of the narrow column.

6. Use the Image Control options to edit the photographs.

See the "Image Control" sidebar beginning on page 397.

7. Change the Preferences setting for graphics display.

It's great to be able to see images and text together on screen, but graphics slow down screen redraw. When you're working with text in the next section of this project, you don't need to actually see the graphics. In the Preferences dialog box (from the File menu), find the Graphics section, and choose Gray Out. See page 396 for more details on screen display options.

THE HEADLINE

1. Type the headline.

- Before typing, use the text tool to drag a selection box at the top margin across the two columns. Be sure to start and end at the left and right margins so that the type will be centered.

- Specify the type as 65/55 Times Roman Bold. Alignment is centered.

- Type the headline. For the ellipsis character at the end of the headline, type Option-semicolon on a Mac, Alt-0133 on a PC. PC users note: You must type the numbers on the numeric keypad.

- Adjust the position of the headline so that the baseline of the second line is at 13p6.

> **TIP**
>
> **If you print to a non-PostScript printer,** for the ellipsis character, type three periods without any space between them. Then adjust the space by following the kerning instructions in step 4 on page 407.

2. Refine the headline.

Every headline requires fine-tuning that is unique to the particular set of words in a specific layout. The following steps detail what we did; the captions on the facing page explain why.

- Rebreak the lines.

  Force a line break (without a paragraph break) between "have" and "the" by pressing Shift-Return on the Mac, Shift-Enter on the PC.

- Condense the type.

  When you condense (or expand) type, you adjust the horizontal shape of the characters. This option, which PageMaker calls Set Width, is available in the Type Specs dialog box and in the Control Palette's character view.

  Select the headline with the text tool and specify a width of 85, which means that the type is condensed 15% on the horizontal axis;

the vertical axis doesn't change. You can condense and expand type in one-tenth-of-a-percent increments.

- "Hang" the punctuation to optically center the headline.

  Insert an em space (Command-Shift-M on a Mac, Ctrl-Shift-M on a PC) before the first letter in the second line to shift the line to the right. (An em space equals the type size.) If you use the Spacebar, there might be a discrepancy between the screen display and the printout or between laser and high-resolution printouts.

- Track the headline.

  Select the text with the text tool, and specify Normal on the Track submenu (available in the Control Palette's character view and on the Type menu). At large type sizes, Normal is tighter than Page-Maker's default of No Track and looser than Tight.

You can further fine-tune the spacing through the Spacing option in the Paragraph dialog box or manually kern space between individual letter pairs as needed. Spacing and kerning adjustments are added on top of the tracking specified for the selected text. Normally we would kern the headline at this point, but we know that the treatment of the headline and the word "Earth" in the text below the large photo are interdependent. So before making the final adjustments to the headline, we'll proceed with the main text block.

This is the **headline as typed,** electronically centered and without any spacing adjustments.

These folks all have the same mother…

Force line breaks for editorial and visual impact.

These folks all have the same mother…

Condense the type to 85%. This gives Times Roman Bold—which is rather clunky at large sizes—a more distinctive and slightly elongated look with the same visual proportions as the tall thin tabloid page.

These folks all have the same mother…

Punctuation at the end of a line doesn't occupy the same visual space as letters do. So to avoid visual holes between the punc-tuation and the x-height of the rest of the line, **hang the punctuation** beyond the line. To do that here, we inserted an em space at the beginning of line 2.

These folks all have the same mother…

The **tracking** option provides five preset levels for increasing or decreasing spacing uniformly across a range of selected text. Here we tightened the track from No Track to Normal, which almost always makes headlines look smarter.

These folks all have the same mother…

THE MAIN TEXT

1. Specify typographer's quotes.

To ensure that all apostrophes and quotation marks are typeset characters, rather than inch and foot marks, choose Preferences from the File menu, click Other, and in the Other Preferences dialog box, turn on Use Typographer's Quotes. It's a good idea to set this as the application default (by turning on this option when no publication is open).

2. Type the main text under the large photo.

The type specs are 16/20 Times Roman.

The first-line indent is 5p except for the first paragraph, which, as the continuation of the headline, has a first-line indent of 0. Alignment is justified.

The baseline of the first line is at 70p.

Remember that the ellipsis character used in the headline is Option-semicolon on a Mac, Alt-0133 on a PC. (If you work on a non-PostScript printer, see the tip on page 404.)

3. Create visual continuity with the headline.

If the word "Earth" were in the body text type, the headline would leave readers dangling. Giving that word and the ellipsis that precedes it the same upsized, boldface treatment as the headline leads the reader's eye from the headline to the main message.

- Select the ellipsis and the word "Earth," and change the type specs to 65/20; Type Style: Bold; Set Width: 85%; Track: Normal. Note that you keep the same leading as the body text so that the leading will be consistent throughout that text block.

Because the type for "…Earth" is so much larger than the leading, the type will appear scrambled or clipped off when you first change the size. To correct the on-screen display, force the screen to redraw by clicking on the zoom box on the Mac or the maximize arrow on the PC (both in the upper right corner of the publication window).

> **TIP**
>
> Don't be alarmed if your line breaks differ from the ones described in the instructions. The same font often varies from one vendor to another, both in the width of the letters and even the character forms themselves. Also, if the position of your column guides varies even slightly from ours, your line breaks could be different. So read the text to understand the effect we are after in this project, and use the techniques you've learned so far to achieve that effect.

A CLOSE LOOK AT SOME TYPOGRAPHIC PROBLEMS

The first dot in the ellipsis appears to be inset from the "D" in the line below. Punctuation at the beginning or end of a line generally leaves a small visual hole such as this.

In justified text, watch for spacing that is too loose (as this is) or too tight relative to the rest of the text.

In advertising copy, and in display type in general, avoid a line break in the middle of a key phrase.

…Earth and they want every day to be Mother's Day. Because every day, year in and year out, we each make decisions that affect the health of the planet and all the life it sustains.

We have three problems. First, we don't want a line break in the middle of the phrase "Mother's Day." In advertising and promotion copy, try to avoid a line break in the middle of a key phrase or slogan; this one is especially troublesome because the headline relies on an extended metaphor (Mother Earth/Earth Day/Mother's Day).

The second problem is that the word spacing in the line is more open than in the rest of the text block. In justified text, PageMaker often has to add or delete space between words or letters in order to align the type at the right margin. It's usually more of a problem in narrow columns than in wide ones, but it's something you should always check.

The third problem is that the ellipsis isn't quite aligned with the left margin. This is similar to the problem we had with the ellipsis in the headline, only here the visual hole is at the beginning of the line.

We'll correct these problems in the next step.

4. Refine the type.

- Select the ellipsis character and replace it with three periods, without any spaces between them. To manually open up space between the periods, select all three periods, and in the Control Palette's character view, click on the right arrow in the kerning field to open up space in increments of 0.01 em. We clicked eight times. Kerning more than two characters at a time like this is called range kerning.

- Moving the first period in the ellipsis to the left, to align it visually with the left margin, is a little tricky. You might think that you could set an insertion point before the character and use one of the manual kerning techniques to move that character into the margin.

  But when you kern letter pairs in PageMaker, the changes affect the space *after* the letter. In order to move the first character of a line to the left, you have to insert a fixed space before that letter and kern between the fixed space and the first visible character. What you're doing, essentially, is kerning the space after an invisible character preceding the character you want to affect!

  To insert a fixed space, press Option-Spacebar on the Mac, Ctrl-Shift-H on the PC.

  With the insertion point between the fixed space and the first period, you can use the kerning arrows in the Control Palette to move the period to the left. Because you want to remove a lot of space, press Command on the Mac, Ctrl on the PC, while you click the left kern arrow twice. (Note the value in the kern field is −0.2.) Now release the Command or Ctrl key, and click on the left kern arrow five times. (Note the value in the kern field is −0.25.) That looks about right.

- Select "…Earth" and change the type size to 61 points.

*There are **two kerning increments** available in the Control Palette. Each time you click on the left or right kern arrow, PageMaker expands or tightens the space between the characters by ¹⁄₁₀₀th of an em (top). If you hold down the Command or Ctrl key while you click on the kern arrows, the increment is ¹⁄₁₀th of em (bottom). See pages 39–41 for a detailed discussion of kerning.*

▼ ▼ ▼

*To **hang punctuation** beyond the left margin so that it appears visually aligned with the text below: Insert a fixed space before the punctuation (Option-Spacebar or Ctrl-Shift-H), and kern between the space character and the punctuation. Note that the curved strokes of letters— such as the bottoms of the "a" and the "t"—hang below the baseline.*

USING THE CURSOR POSITION INDICATOR TO DETERMINE INDENTS

When the Control Palette is in paragraph view, the field just above the left indent field tracks the position of the text cursor. You can't alter this value, but the information it provides can save you time. Here's how we used the cursor position indicator in this situation.

We set the insertion point where we want the text indented to, in this case just before the letter E.

▼ ▼ ▼

...Earth and they want every day Because every day, year in and year out, we each affect the health of the planet and all the life it sus Decisions. The food we eat. The cars w ances we buy. The way we heat our homes. The h You may think you can't do much about t

The cursor position display tells us that the cursor is at 3p6.5. The stem of the E is a little past the cursor position, so after we select the last three paragraphs, we type 3p8 in the First Indent box. (Don't forget to click Apply, or press Return or Enter.)

▼ ▼ ▼

Cursor position   First-line indent

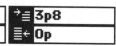

5. Adjust the first-line indent of the subsequent paragraphs.

We want to align the paragraph indent of the body text with the "E" in the word "Earth." The reason for doing this is purely visual.

See the technique described above for a really neat way to determine the size of an indent. Then select the last three paragraphs and specify that indent.

...Earth and they w. Because every day, year in and year affect the health of the planet and all Decisions. The food we ea ances we buy. The way we heat our 1 You may think you can't do layer of the disappearance of the rair of the earth's topsoil. But by solvin Pinecrest, you'll do more than prote Think about it. And then do is right now.

▲ ▲ ▲

The stem of the "E" in the word "Earth" creates a strong vertical that isn't quite aligned with the first-line indent of subsequent paragraphs.

...Earth and they w Because every day, year in and year affect the health of the planet and all Decisions. The food we eat. T we buy. The way we heat our homes You may think you can't do r layer of the disappearance of the rair of the earth's topsoil. But by solvir Pinecrest, you'll do more than prote Think about it. And then do so right now.

▲ ▲ ▲

With the alignment adjusted, the type looks neat and intentional.

THE HEADLINE, AGAIN

Changes we've made in the display type for the word "Earth" require similar adjustments in the headline, so the type treatment for the two blocks of display type will be identical.

1. Change the type size.

Select the headline, and change the size to 61 points to be consistent with the word "Earth."

2. Correct the ellipsis.

You can do this quickly by copying and pasting the ellipsis created from three kerned periods preceding the word "Earth."

3. Recenter the two lines.

Because the three periods, kerned, are not as wide as the ellipsis character, the second line is no longer optically centered. Drag over the em space you inserted at the beginning of the line, and change it to an en space (by pressing Command-Shift-N on a Mac, Ctrl-Shift-N on a PC). An en space is half as wide as an em space.

4. Kern the headline.

You'll find some letter combinations are noticeably too far apart ("ave" in the word "have," for example) while others are more subtly too close together ("ese" in the word "these"). We'll leave the solution here to your own visual judgment. Refer back to pages 39–41 and page 273 for a review of kerning goals and techniques.

THE QUOTATION

1. Type the text for the quotation.

The type is 13/16 Times Roman Italic. Alignment is centered.

2. Optically center the text.

In refining the headline, we looked at the need to optically center large type. With longer passages of centered text, such as the quotation in this ad, the type can be a visual element on the page, an interesting shape in itself. To date, computers haven't been able to deliver that as a default setting. So when you use centered type, do so deliberately. Manually break the lines to control the contrast between short and long lines, but pay attention to the sentence structure and the cadence of the words at the same time. Be careful of going too far, though, unless your intention is genuinely poetic. Turn the page for a visual comparison of the default and custom settings.

In the electronically centered text at near right, the lines are almost all the same length. In the setting at far right, the line breaks have been manually controlled to create an interesting silhouette and to make the copy easier to read as well. When forcing line breaks, use a new-line character (Shift-Return or Shift-Enter) rather than a normal paragraph return.

▶ ▶ ▶

I'm Jerry Dexter and I've lived in Pinecrest all my life. I used to take for granted the pristine beauty of our fields and woodlands. Now I have doubts about the quality of our drinking water. A lot of people I talk to feel the same way. That's why we've founded the Pinecrest Environmental Coalition. The thirteen of us pictured here are your neighbors. We hope you'll join us.

I'm Jerry Dexter and I've lived in Pinecrest all my life. I used to take for granted the pristine beauty of our fields and woodlands. Now I have doubts about the quality of our drinking water. A lot of people I talk to feel the same way. That's why we've founded the Pinecrest Environmental Coalition. The thirteen of us pictured here are your neighbors. We hope you'll join us.

When optically centering type, remember that you can use the whole arsenal of spacing adjustments that you'd use in refining any type. In the quotation here, in order to fit the word "pristine" on the third line, we used range kerning: We selected all the words we wanted to fit on that line and clicked on the left kern arrow in the Control Palette, closing up enough space to pull up the word "pristine." You could also cheat the column measure a little by dragging the text handles slightly beyond the margins.

3. Add the quotation marks.

- Before typing, drag a short bounding box just outside the text area to define the text width for the quote marks. Specify 60/60 Times Roman Bold; type the open and close quotes as separate text blocks.

  Note: If the Preferences dialog box specifies Use Typographer's Quotes (which we recommended earlier), you won't be able to type a close-quote mark in a text block by itself. To do so, you have to type the close-quote character, Option-Shift-[on a Mac, Ctrl-Shift-] on a PC.

  Also, the quote marks are going to be a nuisance to work with. They're designed typographically to sit above the baseline, so regardless of which leading method you specify, the text handles will overlap the space below. And anytime you have overlapping text handles, you're bound to trip over them. It drives you wild unless you understand, typographically and technologically, why it happens. And even then it drives you wild, but at least you know what's going on.

- Bring in a vertical guide at the center of the column. A quick way to bisect any area is to draw a rectangle the width of the area and drag the ruler guide over the center handles. (If you select the text with the pointer tool and click on the center point in the Proxy, the x value in the position field is the center of the text column. But because you have to drag ruler guides rather than type a position for their placement and because the value here—52p1.5—is difficult to hit by manually dragging a guide, we recommend the box technique.)

- Move the quotes into position, centered over the vertical guideline you just brought in. The quotes should be positioned closer to the text than to the graphic elements above or below so that they clearly belong to the text. In our layout, the top of the top quote mark is at 37p6, and the bottom of the bottom quote is at 59p.

THE "TEN WAYS" LIST

1. Draw the border.

- Using a double-rule line weight, draw a box in the narrow column from 60p6 to 92p.

To use the Control Palette to check the size of your box:

- Click on a top handle in the Proxy to specify a moving reference point (indicated by a rectangular box). The y-coordinate, which corresponds to the top of the box, should read 60p6. If it doesn't, type that value, and press Return or Enter. PageMaker repositions the box so that the top rule is at 60p6.

- Click twice on a bottom handle in the Proxy to specify a resizing reference point (indicated by a double-headed arrow). Now the y-coordinate corresponds to the bottom of the box and should read 92p. If it doesn't, type that value for the y-coordinate, and press Return or Enter. PageMaker will resize the height of the box so that the y-coordinate is at 92p.

Note that when you specify a moving reference point, PageMaker *moves* the object as if you had dragged the handle corresponding to the active reference point. When you specify a resizing reference point, PageMaker *resizes* the object as if you had dragged the handle corresponding to the active reference point.

2. Create the banner.

- Draw a 4p-deep solid banner from the inside top of the box. The *H*(eight) value in the Control Palette should read 4p. Alignment with the inside of the double rule on three sides is critical. Use the Control Palette to be sure that you have precise mathematical alignment. (See pages 296 and 297 for aligning objects with the Control Palette.)

- Type the headline, forcing a line break (by pressing Shift-Return or Shift-Enter) after the word "You."

The type specs are 20/22 Helvetica Bold reverse. The alignment is centered.

- The headline is a little tight to the edge of the banner. We have three options: We can reduce the type size; we can tighten the spacing (through either the Tracking option or the Spacing option); or we can condense the type on the horizontal axis, as we did with the headline. We chose the third option.

With the text still selected, change the Set Width to 90. You can do this in the Control Palette character view or in the Type Specs dialog box.

TIP

If you have trouble typing the banner headline to the full width of the column, the handles of some other element on the page are probably obstructing it. With the pointer tool active, choose Select All from the Edit menu (Command-A on a Mac, Ctrl-A on a PC), and you'll see what's in the way. In this case, it's probably the text handles for the quote marks above the box. With the pointer tool, drag the window-shade handles of the banner headline to the full width of the column.

TIP

If your text doesn't fit in the space of the box, move the left indent marker and the left-aligned tab from 3p6 to 3p. Or range kern the text. You should be able to pull up runover lines with either technique.

3. Type the list.

The list for this ad was used in Project 5. If you didn't do that project, see page 360 for how to format this list.

If you did that project and saved the document as suggested there, open that document now.

- With both documents open, choose Tile from the Window menu. PageMaker sizes both open windows to position them side by side.

- With the pointer tool, select the list from the Project 5 document, and then drag it over to the document with the ad. This is called "drag and drop": PageMaker copies the text you drag and pastes a copy with the same formatting and margins in the document you drag to. The original remains in place.

- After you've copied the list, close the Project 5 document. To expand the publication window for the current document to full-screen: On a Mac, click on the zoom box in the upper right corner of the window; on a PC, click on the maximize (up) arrow (also in the upper right corner of the window).

- Use the pointer tool to position the list inside the border you drew earlier. The list should be centered vertically between the bottom of the banner and the bottom of the box.

THE ORGANIZATION'S ID

1. Type the text.

Type both lines using 14/22 Helvetica. Then select the first line and change its specs to 24-point Helvetica Bold.

2. Shorten the text handles.

Select the text with the pointer tool, and drag one of the right window-shade handles so that the handles are only a little bit wider than the text itself. This keeps the handles from hanging out beyond the text and interfering with the logo, which you'll create shortly.

3. Position the type by eye.

With the text still selected, drag the text block so that the last line aligns at the bottom margin, and hang the word "Coalition" over into the right-hand column to break the rigidity of the grid.

4. Add the logo.

- In the Preferences dialog box, specify Normal for the Graphics option.

- Place and size the logo art. The tree we've used is a piece of clip art in EPS (Encapsulated PostScript) format, which is transparent. To opaque the corner of the box over which it prints, you have to create a mask, as described in the illustrations and captions on the facing page.

MASKING RULES AND ALIGNING CIRCLES

When you position a transparent graphic over a box, you have to mask the box rules so that they don't print behind the graphic. When the graphic is a circle, you have the additional challenge of aligning the mask exactly with the circle. Here's how to accomplish both tasks.

Here's how to use the Control Palette to **draw and align identical circles.**

- Crop in on the graphic so that the selection handles are flush with the circle.

- With the graphic still selected, click on a center handle in the Proxy.

- Note the *x* and *y* values and the *H* and *W* values. (The *H* and *W* values should be the same if you've cropped exactly on the circumference of the circle.)

- Draw a circle with the circle tool.

- With that circle still selected, specify the *x*, *y*, *W*, and *H* values that you noted earlier.

- When you click Apply, or press Return or Enter, the circle should be resized and repositioned to align exactly with the circle in the graphic.

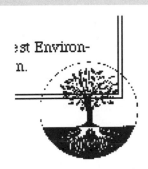

1. The double rules of the box are visible behind the transparent EPS graphic.

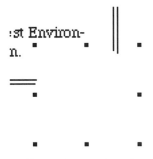

2. To mask the rules, draw a circle the same size as the logo. See the tip at left for how to draw and align the PageMaker circle so that it exactly covers the circle in the graphic. Specify the Line as None and the Fill as Paper.

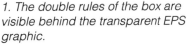

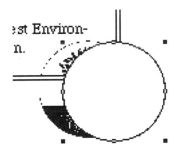

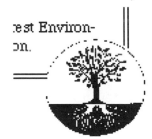

3. Text and graphics are layered in the PageMaker file—like sheets of paper, one on top of the other—in the order in which they are created.

The white circle (which, in the illustration above left, has been pulled to the side for the purpose of this explanation) is on top; the tree is next, the text is below that, and the box rules are on the bottom. If you select the top element and choose Send to Back, the element goes to the bottom of the stack. In this situation, that would put the mask behind the box rules, which would defeat the purpose of the mask. So you have to select the tree and bring it to the front.

How do you select an element that is totally hidden behind another element? First, select the top element (the white circle); then hold down the Command key on a Mac (Ctrl on a PC), and click again where the two elements overlap. This selects the element on the next layer down—in this case, the tree. Choose Bring to Front from the Element menu (Command-F on a Mac, Ctrl-F on a PC).

PRINTING OVERSIZE PAGES

When you print an 11- by 17-inch page on a laser printer, you can print the page on a single sheet at a reduced size, or you can use the Tiling option to print the page full size in sections that you then paste together. In the course of producing any oversize publication, you'll probably use both methods. The reduced image is fine for proofreading all but very small type and for checking the overall layout. But a full-size, tiled proof is essential for checking type specifications and kerning and for fine-tuning the layout.

If the camera-ready pages are to be output from an imagesetter, you won't need to worry about tiling or pasting the final art. Imagesetters can handle 12-inch rolls of paper, with unlimited depth, so a tabloid page with crop marks will fit on a single sheet.

Scaling

- In the Print dialog box, if you print to a PostScript printer, click the Paper button; for a non-PostScript printer, click the Options button. In both cases, you'll then be able to choose Reduce to Fit from the Scaling options. PageMaker will print the reduced image centered on the sheet.

- If you also want crop marks, click Options (all printers) to turn on Printer's Marks. The page will print smaller because PageMaker has to make room for crop marks. (Note: You'll also get registration marks and color density bars, which are included with crops whenever you select Printer's Marks.)

Tiling

When you print oversize pages in sections at full size, the sections must be manually pasted together to form a full page. If the laser printer pages are to be used for proofing only, the cut lines aren't so important. But if the laser printer pages are to be used for camera-ready art or for formal presentation, the cut lines are critical. The goal is to avoid cut lines through the art or through individual letters. You can control this by using the Manual Tiling option and moving the zero point before printing each section.

- To print the pages in sections at full size, position the zero point about a half inch above and to the left of the upper left corner of the page. This allows room for the crop marks to print.

- In the Print dialog box, for a PostScript printer, click the Paper button; for a non-PostScript printer, click the Options button. In both cases, you'll then be able to turn on the Tile option. Also turn on Manual, which instructs PageMaker to print the first section with the zero point in the upper left corner of the page.

- To print crop marks, turn on Printer's Marks (in the Print/Options dialog box).

- To print each subsequent section, move the zero point about a half inch above and to the left of the desired cut line.

▶ ▶ ▶

To manually tile this page, you want to print four sections, labeled AA through DD, that will avoid cut lines through the art and text. In order to avoid a cut line through the headline, you'll need to print a fifth section, EE, with just the headline. To print section AA, position the zero point about a half inch above and to the left of the upper left corner of the page. To print subsequent sections (including the headline), position the zero point about a half inch above and to the left of the desired cut line (in effect creating a margin that allows the full image of each section to print, with crop marks). Be sure to turn on Manual Tiling and Printer's Marks.

EE   AA | BB

These folks all have the same mother...

EE

"

*I'm Jerry Dexter and
I've lived in Pinecrest all my life.
I used to take for granted the pristine
beauty of our fields and woodlands.
Now I have doubts about
the quality of our drinking water.
A lot of people I talk to
feel the same way.
That's why we've founded the
Pinecrest Environmental Coalition.
The thirteen of us pictured here
are your neighbors.
We hope you'll join us.*

"

AA

CC

...Earth and they want every day to be Mother's Day.

Because every day, year in and year out, we each make decisions that affect the health of the planet and all the life it sustains.

Decisions. The food we eat. The cars we drive. The appliances we buy. The way we heat our homes. The habits of a lifetime.

You may think you can't do much about the hole in the ozone layer or the disappearance of the rain forests or the loss of 85 percent of the earth's topsoil. But by solving some of the problems here in Pinecrest you'll do more than protect your own backyard.

Think about it. And then do something. The best time to start is right now.

Ten Ways You Can Help the Earth

BB

DD

1. Carpool.
2. Recycle paper, glass, and aluminum. Buy products in recyclable containers.
3. Buy the most fuel-efficient car you can. (Aim for 35 miles per gallon.)
4. Eat fewer animal products.
5. Install water-efficient showerheads and toilets.
6. Weather proof your house.
7. Buy phosphate free biodegradable soaps.
8. Repair rather than replace.
9. Plant trees.
10. Join the Pinecrest Environmental Coalition.

Pinecrest Environmental Coalition

3365 Hill Street, Pinecrest, phone 697-5527

CC | DD

PROJECT 8

USING PAGEMAKER TO DRAW, MANIPULATE, AND MANAGE GRAPHICS

PageMaker's drawing tools, although limited to lines and ovals and rectangles, can be used to create more varied and complex graphics than you might think possible. Of course, you don't have the range or sophistication in PageMaker that you have working in a full-fledged drawing program. But for simple schematics, maps, and geometric drawings, you may find PageMaker's tools quite adequate.

And if desktop publishing is your introduction to computers, as it is for many people, the prospect of learning PageMaker and a word-processing program and a drawing program can seem quite daunting. As long as you're doing your layout in PageMaker, why not see how far you can push the graphics tools? In the process, you'll master subtleties of the program that will enhance your layout abilities. When you're ready to move on to a real drawing program, the challenge won't seem quite so formidable.

The examples in this project are intended to inspire your exploration of PageMaker's graphics capabilities. There's a truck and a skyline, a map and a floor plan, a pie chart, some rules, and a pattern created from a Zapf Dingbats character. The instructions for executing most of the examples are more general than those in other projects. The point here is not so much to have you duplicate any of our efforts but to show you the possibilities and the features used to create them.

You can manipulate PageMaker graphics in many of the same ways that you manipulate graphics imported from other programs: You can resize, rotate, reflect, and skew them, and you can group them and then manipulate them as a group. The ability to group items greatly expands the usefulness of PageMaker's drawing tools, and it enables you to do things with PageMaker-drawn graphics that you couldn't do otherwise, such as wrap text around a composite image. You can also create libraries of images directly in PageMaker and display the library as a palette of miniature images that can be dragged onto the page. We'll explore all those features in this project.

PAGEMAKER TECHNIQUES

▶ Use the Front/Back commands

▶ Draw concentric circles

▶ Group PageMaker elements

▶ Wrap text around a graphic

▶ Customize a graphic boundary

▶ Use the Library Palette

▶ Create patterns

CREATING A PAGEMAKER TRUCK

If you want to master the way PageMaker layers elements on the page, try drawing the truck used in this brochure. You can make your truck simpler or more complex than the one shown, but try to keep the outline roughly the same if you want to follow the text-wrap exercise later in the project.

For information about manipulating objects using the Control Palette, refer to pages 197–99 and 203–8.

Keep the following general tips in mind.

Set the default line weight to 2 point. (Note: When you group elements in PageMaker and then reduce the size of the grouped object, you'll be reducing the weight of all the lines.)

As you create the truck, treat the shapes you draw with the rectangle and ellipse tools as building blocks. Draw the big shapes first, shade them, and then add smaller shapes inside the large ones, using contrasting shades for detail. In addition to various shades of gray and textures on the Fill submenu (under the Element menu), there's a whole library of gray shades available through the Define Colors command. (See page 449 for more information about color libraries.)

Draw the wheels last, using the techniques described on the following page.

How to navigate through PageMaker's layers

As you work, keep in mind that PageMaker layers text blocks, graphics, and ruler guides. It's as though the objects were stacked one on top of another on the screen. The object you draw first is on the bottom; the object you draw last is on top. Whenever you move an element, that element moves to the top layer.

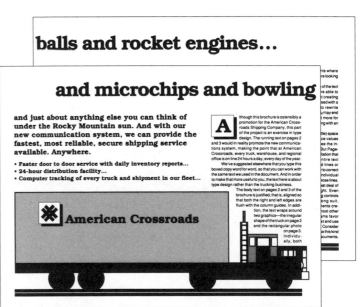

▲ ▲ ▲

To select an item hidden below the top layer, hold down the Command or Ctrl key while you click the pointer tool on the top element; still holding down the Command or Ctrl key, click again to select the element on the second layer; click again for the element on the third layer; and so on. You'll see only the handles of the lower object (screen detail, above left); when you choose Bring to Front, you'll see the object itself (above right).

When you turn on proportional scaling in the Control Palette, it remains on until you turn it off. And when you select a reference point in the Proxy, that reference point remains selected until you specify another reference point.

You can change the stacking order by selecting an object and choosing Bring to Front or Send to Back from the Element menu. Use the keyboard shortcuts for these—Command-F and Command-B on the Mac, Ctrl-F and Ctrl-B on a PC—whenever you have to work with overlapping elements.

As you build the truck, you might lose a piece of it behind a new layer. The Bring to Front/Send to Back keyboard shortcuts should enable you to retrieve pieces that are lower in the stack. If all else fails and you really can't find a piece you know you've drawn, redraw it on top. (We admit to having done this once or twice.)

Use the Control Palette for precise alignments.

Unlike page layout, in which you can begin with rough positioning and refine placements later, with graphics you need accuracy as you work. Work at a large page view, and use the Control Palette's numerical precision for alignments.

The wheels: an exercise in drawing concentric circles

The Control Palette makes it incredibly easy to draw concentric circles. Here's how:

- Hold down the Shift key, and use the ellipse tool to draw the largest circle.

- Copy the circle and power-paste it (Command-Shift-V on a Mac, Ctrl-Shift-P on a PC) so that the copy is placed directly on top of the original.

- With the circle selected, choose the center reference point in the Control Palette Proxy. Turn on the proportional scaling option, and specify a percentage for either the *W* or the *H* value. (We specified 85% for this second circle.) Press Return or Enter.

- Power-paste again. (The original circle is still on the clipboard.)

- Specify the percentage for either scaling field. (We specified 55% for the third circle.) Press Return or Enter.

- Power-paste and specify the percentage for the fourth circle. (We specified 40%.) Press Return or Enter.

When you are satisfied with the shape of the concentric rings of the wheel, add the shades. Again, start from the largest circle, which is on the bottom layer, and move toward the center. If you work in this order, you shouldn't have to fuss with the stacking.

When you've got one wheel drawn to your satisfaction, use one of the techniques described on the next page to group the four circles into a single element.

Copy the grouped element and paste and position three copies. If you use the power-paste technique and hold down the Shift key while you drag each copy of the wheel into position, you'll ensure the horizontal alignment of all four wheels without any further work on your part.

GROUPING GRAPHIC ELEMENTS

When you use PageMaker's graphics tools to create art such as the truck, you end up with a graphic made of many smaller elements. Our truck, for example, has more than 35 shapes, and each shape has 8 handles. All those handles represent potential havoc on a page. There are several ways to group elements in PageMaker. In addition to cleaning up all the extra handles, grouping enables you to manipulate the elements as a single unit.

The Group It Addition

To use this technique, select two or more elements with the pointer tool and choose PS Group It from the Aldus Additions list (on the Utilities menu). PageMaker actually creates a new Encapsulated PostScript (EPS) file of the composite graphic and replaces the original elements on the page with that new EPS graphic. The new file is located in the same folder or directory as the publication, and it is automatically given the publication name plus a PMG extension. The PMG file is linked to the PageMaker publication and is required in order to print the file correctly. (See page 227 for more on links required for printing.)

TIP

In order to use the **Group It Addition,** you must first name the document that contains the elements you want to group. And even if the document is already named, be aware that using this Addition **forces PageMaker to save** the file in its current form (although there's no indication that this is happening). So be sure you want to keep any changes you've made before using this Addition.

If at some point you need to modify an element within the group, select the grouped item with the pointer tool, and choose PS Ungroup It from the Aldus Additions list. (If for some reason you've deleted the PMG file, you won't be able to ungroup the elements.) PageMaker replaces the EPS graphic with the individual items. Any transformations made to the group—scaling, rotation, skewing, and so on—are undone when you ungroup. When you ungroup an element, the PMG file is deleted. But if you delete a grouped unit without ungrouping it first, the PMG file is not deleted and just adds to the clutter on your hard drive.

When you use the Group It Addition, PostScript fonts are not downloaded. This also means that if you're using TrueType fonts and are targeting a PostScript printer, the grouped item won't contain the TrueType font information. If you need to group PageMaker elements and have fonts downloaded, move the elements to a page by themselves and make an EPS file of that page. (See the center tip at left.)

TIP

To convert an entire Page-Maker page to a graphic, use the PostScript printing feature, in the Print Options dialog box, to create an EPS file of the page. We've used that technique for the sample documents throughout this book. See page 238 for details.

If you use the Group It Addition with a keyline or with color elements, see pages 441 and 453 respectively.

Paste Special (Macintosh only)

This is more of an on-the-fly technique. It's a little faster and doesn't create a linked file, but you can't ungroup the object at a later time. And if elements in the group have color applied, it's safer to use the Group It Addition than this method.

TIP

You can **place the PMG file** created using the Group It Addition in other PageMaker documents and in other programs that recognize EPS graphics, but you can ungroup the elements only in PageMaker.

Use the pointer tool to select the elements you want to group. Copy or cut them to the Clipboard, and then choose Paste Special from the Edit menu. The Paste Special dialog box displays a list of the available formats. Choose PICT. Note that PICTs with text may not display accurate line lengths on-screen. Check the printout though; it should be fine. Note also that if you use the text tool to select text when using Paste Special, you'll loose the font information.

PAGEMAKER'S TEXT WRAP

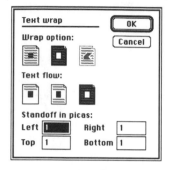

▲ ▲ ▲

The Text Wrap dialog box, on the Element menu, defines the way text wraps around a selected graphic.

In commercial typesetting, wrapping text around a graphic can require one round of galleys after another before the line breaks and spacing are even and crisp. The time and expense can be prohibitive. PageMaker's Text Wrap option facilitates the process, although it still requires patience and precision.

To create a text wrap:

1. Select the graphic that you want the text to wrap around.

2. Choose Text Wrap from the Element menu.

3. Specify a Wrap option.

 Text flows over the graphic.

 Text jumps over or flows around the graphic; to specify the wrap behavior, choose one of the Text Flow icons described below.

4. Specify the Text Flow.

 Column-break: Text stops at graphic and continues in next column.

 Jump-over: Text stops at graphic and continues below it.

 Wrap-all-sides: Text flows around graphic on all sides. Choose this icon to customize a graphic boundary.

5. Specify the Standoff.

The Standoff defines the distance between the graphic and the boundary around the graphic beyond which text cannot flow. To adjust the Standoff, select the graphic and type a new value, or drag the line of the graphic boundary closer to or farther from the graphic.

The dotted line defines a graphic boundary around the truck, beyond which text cannot flow. The distance from the boundary to the graphic is determined by the Standoff value in the Text Wrap dialog box.

Diamond-shaped handles on the graphic boundary can be added, deleted, and moved to change the shape of the boundary.

The square handles are the selection handles.

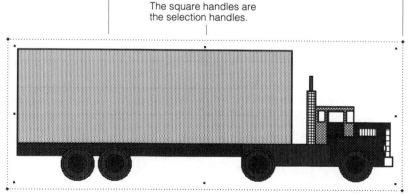

▲ ▲ ▲

When you define text wrap around a graphic, PageMaker displays a rectangular graphic boundary around the object.

▲ ▲ ▲

To customize the boundary so that the text wrap will follow the shape of the art, follow the procedure described on the next page.

HOW TO CUSTOMIZE A GRAPHIC BOUNDARY

To change the shape of the boundary so that it follows the outline of the truck, divide the boundary into smaller line segments by adding and dragging additional handles. For each line segment you want to create, you add two handles; the distance between the handles defines the length of the new segment.

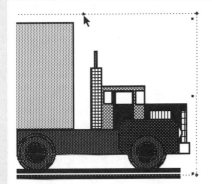
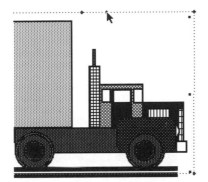
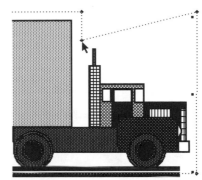

1. Click on the graphic boundary to add a handle where you want to make the first turn, about two picas in front of the trailer.

2. and 3. Add a second handle (above left), and drag it directly below the first one (above right), a pica or two above the exhaust pipe.

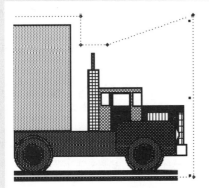
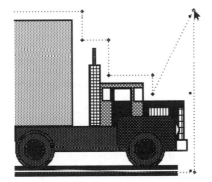
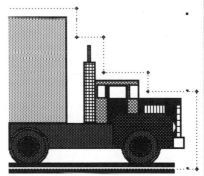

4. Add a third handle, and drag it down parallel to the second one.

5. and 6. Continue adding and dragging three more handles to define the shape over the cab and hood, and then drag the existing handle from the upper right corner to define the right edge of the shape around the hood.

TIPS

Graphic boundaries are extremely elastic. Drag handles to change the direction or length of a line; drag whole lines to change the distance between the boundary and the graphic.

When customizing a graphic boundary, begin by creating the rough shape you want, and then fine-tune the placement of individual handles and lines.

You can edit a graphic boundary after the text wraps around it. Hold down the Spacebar while you adjust the boundary if you want PageMaker to delay reflowing the text.

To delete a handle on a graphic boundary, drag that handle on top of another handle.

Hold down the Shift key to constrain movement of a handle.

Check to be sure each segment of the boundary is straight.

THE LIBRARY PALETTE

The Library Palette is an intelligent scrapbook in which you can collect text and graphic elements that you use frequently. You can create and save different libraries; you can identify each item in a library by name, date, creator, and keywords; and if your libraries get big, you can search for items by name, creator, and keywords.

To create a new library or open an existing one Choose Library Palette from the Window menu. On the Mac, PageMaker displays the Open Library dialog box, in which you can click New (to create a new library) or scroll through your folders to open an existing library. On the PC, if PageMaker can't find an existing library (which will be the case the first time you use this feature), the New Library dialog box is displayed; type a name for the library (with the file extension DB), and choose a location on your hard drive.

If PageMaker can find an existing library (on both the Mac and the PC), it will open that library when you choose Library from the Window menu. The Library window has its own Options menu, from which you can choose New Library or Open Library. Choosing either of those options displays a dialog box in which you can navigate through your folders and directories to choose an existing library or name and save a new one.

You can open only one library at a time. When you open a new library, PageMaker automatically closes the currently open library.

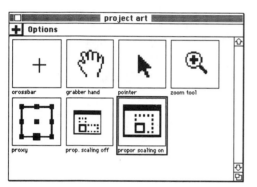

▲ ▲ ▲

In this library, we've collected screen images of PageMaker icons used in this book. You can resize or move the window just as you would any other window.

To add an object to a library Use the pointer tool to select the object in the PageMaker document, and then click on the + icon in the upper left corner of the Library window. PageMaker adds the selected object to the Library, and you'll see a thumbnail of that image inside a box.

To place a library object on a page Select the object in the library and drag it onto the page! It's that simple.

To delete an object from the library Select the object in the Library window, and from the Library's Options menu, choose Remove Item.

To catalog library items Double-click on the item in the Library window to display an Item Information dialog box, in which you can enter or edit the title, author, date, keywords, and description. To have this box displayed automatically when you add an item to the library (or to ensure that it doesn't display automatically), use the Edit Items After Adding option. On the Mac, you access this option through the Preference command on the Library Options menu. On the PC, the command is on the Library Palette's Options menu.

To search for library objects Choose Search Library from the Library Options menu, and fill in the appropriate fields in the dialog box. You can have two keyword entries connected by "And," "Or," or "But not." The Library will then display only those items that satisfy the search criteria. To display the entire Library again, choose Show All Items from the Library Options menu.

To import items from Aldus Fetch If you use Aldus Fetch to catalog image libraries, you can import the Fetch items into a PageMaker library. From within Fetch, open the catalog, select the items you want to import, and choose Copy References from the Fetch Edit menu. Also select Include Thumbnails. Then, from the PageMaker library window, choose Import Fetch Items from the Options menu.

▲ ▲ ▲

The Library Palette has its own Options menu.

PATTERNS AND MORE

Patterns require planning and precision, but the results can be well worth the effort. The basic procedure is fairly straightforward, although there are many different ways to execute the following steps.

1. Determine the design motif of the pattern.

2. Determine the density of the pattern on the page.

3. Establish the grid for the pattern by dividing the page size by the number of pattern units.

4. Use the Multiple Paste Command (on the Edit menu) to specify the number of copies and the offset from the original. (See pages 295 and 308 for details about Multiple Paste.)

In this invitation, we created the pattern from an 18-point Zapf Dingbats character. (The keystroke is Shift-9.)

To space the characters at equal intervals, we inserted a tab between each character in the line. We set the first custom tab at 4p9 and selected Repeat Tab from the Position menu.

Then we copied the first line and used the Multiple Paste command to specify 8 copies with a vertical offset of 4p1.5. To horizontally offset every other row, we selected those rows with the pointer tool and specified +2p5 for the Control Palette x-coordinate. It takes a little time to figure out the math, but the result sure is precise.

The airplane flying toward the top of the page is a 48-point character rotated 70°. Note how shifting the axis and the size of one element creates a dramatic focal point in an otherwise static background.

Turn the page for more examples.

You don't need drafting skills or a CAD program to create a working floor plan. This design studio is drawn at ⅛ scale (⅛ inch equals 1 foot), using the Control Palette for precise measurements.

Walls that are broken by doors and windows are created as solid 4-point rules and then partially masked with white boxes as needed. That way, you don't have to worry about aligning a series of short rules.

The door swings and the chairs are created by masking parts of circular graphics. For example, the chairs are made from two concentric circles, with a 12-point white rule over part of the arcs and a 0.5-point rule positioned where the mask and the circles butt. You should create elements that require masks outside the area of the main drawing and move them into position last.

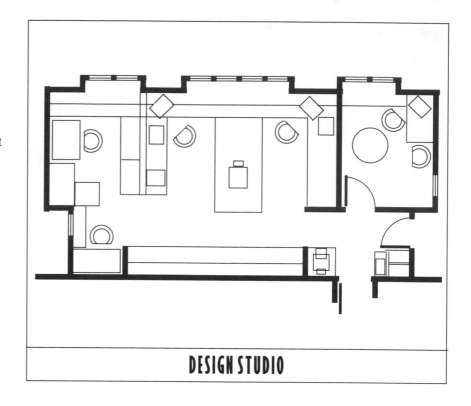

DESIGN STUDIO

If the truck was too easy for you, try incorporating the dimensionality of a skyline. Ours was created through a playful, trial-and-error approach (and a great many printouts) until a satisfying effect was achieved.

You can overlap shapes, change their height and width, and play with different shades for the fill. To create angular, postmodern lines, you can skew rectangles and use white (reverse) diagonal lines.

As the skyline develops, use the Send to Back/Bring to Front commands to create a sense of depth. All the shadows on the sides of the buildings are 80%, and those on the ground are solid black.

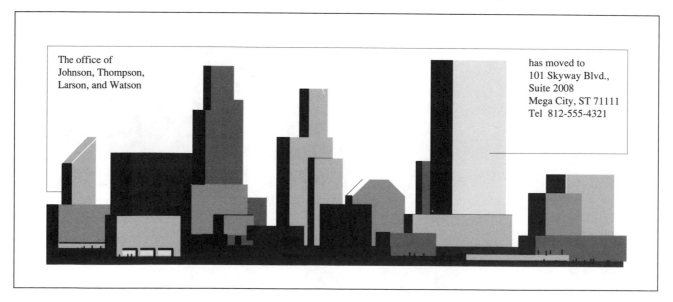

The office of
Johnson, Thompson,
Larson, and Watson

has moved to
101 Skyway Blvd.,
Suite 2008
Mega City, ST 71111
Tel 812-555-4321

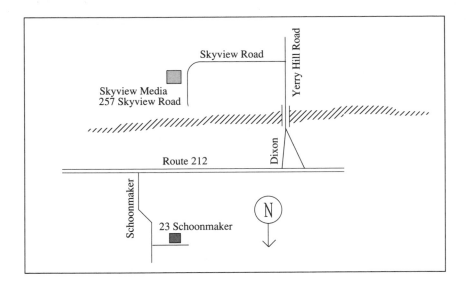

For simple area maps, use Page-Maker's double line for main arteries and a single line for side streets. To indicate a curve in the road, draw a box and, while it is selected, use the Rounded Corners option on the Element menu to specify the arc; then mask any part of the box that you don't want to see. To create the freeform edge of a river or lake, draw a series of rounded-corner boxes, and specify the Line as None and the Fill as the most open of PageMaker's patterns.

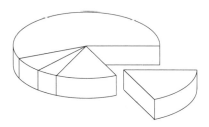

To create a pie chart, divide an ellipse into quadrants by bringing in ruler guides over the selection handles. Use these guides to estimate the line positions that define the size of each segment. You'll need a mess of masks to cover up parts of the ellipse. To remove a piece of the pie, copy the lines for that piece, paste them on the side, and use the Group It Addition to turn it into a single graphic. Then mask over the lines of that piece in the pie itself, and use the Group It Addition to turn the pie into a single graphic. Finally, move the isolated piece of pie into position.

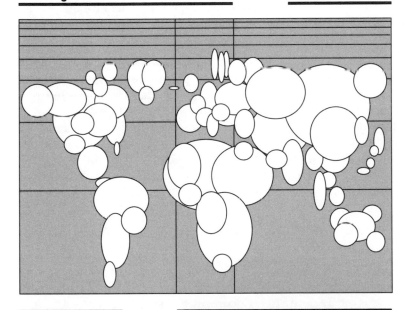

The Sixth Annual International Business and Marketing Conference   **January 11-15, 1992**

Pompidou Centre Paris, France   **EPICENTERS for the NINETIES**

A stylized map doesn't have to be geographically accurate. This one is created entirely with PageMaker's circle/oval tool. You can use this sort of representational graphic for quantitative comparisons, whether you're analyzing population centers, wheat production, or pollution.

PROJECT 9

WORKING WITH COLOR IN PAGEMAKER

With the release of version 5.0, PageMaker offers full color capability. You can bring color photos and illustrations into PageMaker layouts, add spot and process color to type and graphics in the layout, and provide plate-ready film separations to the specifications of your commercial printer. We hasten to add that producing quality color pages—from PageMaker or from any other desktop application—requires a steep learning curve.

Color is the most complex dimension of graphic design. The aesthetics of color—what colors you choose, how you combine them, how they are perceived, the subtleties in a color photograph—make the nuances of typography look simple by comparison. And the use of color on the printed page is inextricably bound to the way color is prepared for the printer and created on press, to such a degree that in order to use color at all, you have to understand some fundamental principles of color printing.

But color is glorious too and great fun to work with. And the ability to do color prepress work on desktop computers has the potential to make color affordable for publications that would otherwise be limited to basic black. Just be aware, if you aren't painfully so already, that when you work with desktop color, you take on responsibility that has traditionally been handled by highly trained craftspeople. And because color is the frontier of electronic publishing, you're investing time and money in a technology that is still evolving. You're advised to approach desktop color cautiously, beginning with simple uses of color and gaining experience and confidence before proceeding with more ambitious projects.

That's the approach we take in this project. We start with the simplest use of a spot color, move on to four-color process printing, and then review the tricky issues of overprinting, knockouts, and trapping.

In order to keep the emphasis on color, we haven't given step-by-step instructions for creating a new document. Some of the samples shown adapt the newsletter created in Project 4, and you can also just create PageMaker shapes for hands-on experience in applying color and dealing with color overlaps.

If you are new to color work, we urge you to scout the design section of bookstores (or the book section of art supply stores) and give yourself a course in color theory. As with so much of design, there are also lessons everywhere you look. Keep a file of color combinations that you like—a piece of fabric can be as useful as another publication. And study master colorists—Matisse, Klee, and contemporary poster artists such as Folon. You won't be able to match their pigments exactly, but you'll have a great deal of fun trying, and you'll develop your own eye for color in the process.

PAGEMAKER TECHNIQUES

▶ Create spot and process colors

▶ Apply colors to PageMaker graphics and type

▶ Incorporate color as part of a style definition

▶ Apply color to imported graphics

▶ Create a tint of a color

▶ Convert spot colors to four-color process colors

▶ Create traps for overlapping and adjoining colors

▶ Specify object-level and ink-level overprinting

▶ Edit the Color Palette

▶ Understand limitations of color monitors

▶ Work with color libraries

▶ Review color prepress options

▶ Print color composites and separations in PageMaker

SPOT AND PROCESS COLOR

▲ ▲ ▲

The illustration above was created in Aldus FreeHand with two spot colors—Pantone 3272 and Pantone 123—plus process black. The Pantone colors are printed with premixed inks. When you print color separations, all the blue-green elements print on one piece of film, all the orange on another, and all the black on a third.

All the colors in the illustration at right were created by specifying different percentages of the four process colors—cyan, magenta, yellow, and black (shown below). When you print separations, each color that you define is separated into its component process colors. So you have only four pieces of film, even though you see many more than four colors.

▼ ▼ ▼

Most color publications are printed using one of two methods—spot color or process color.

Spot colors are premixed inks. If you want one or two or three colors in your publication, or if you need to match a specific color such as a corporate logo, you generally use spot colors. The most frequently used spot colors come from the Pantone Matching System (PMS), a trademark system of over 700 colors, coded by number, that are available not only in printing inks but in colored markers and paper as well.

There are only four process colors—cyan, magenta, yellow, and black. (They are often referred to as CMYK, with black denoted by the letter K.) When combined in various percentages, these four inks create the entire spectrum of colors that you see in printed pages, including the subtle hues in color photographs. Publications with color photos or illustrations that use more than three colors are printed using process colors. You might define a dozen or more colors for the artwork in your publications, but they will all be printed using combinations of those same four process colors.

You can create both spot and process colors in PageMaker. In either case, you should choose the colors from printed samples, called swatch books or color matching systems, rather than from the colors displayed on the monitor. This is one of the few inviolate rules about design in this book. (The exception is if you're creating something that will be viewed on a monitor, such as a slide presentation.) See page 448 for more on this subject.

COLOR PRINTING

Color printing requires a separate printing plate for each process color and each spot color used on a page. If you have blue, yellow, and black in your publication, the printer will make three plates, and the pages will require three printing impressions, with the lighter color laid down first, followed by the darker color and then the black, which always prints last.

The plates are made from film negatives, one negative for each color. Traditionally, the printer—or, for very high-quality color work, the color separator—made the negatives by photographing color art through different filters. It's now possible to make these color separations directly from PageMaker and to print the separations directly to film on a high-resolution imagesetter.

If you stack the pieces of film on top of one another, you'll see a black-and-white composite of what the printed page will look like. But if the film isn't stacked exactly right, the elements will be aligned improperly. This alignment of color film is called registration, and it's facilitated by printing registration marks—cross-hair lines over a circle—outside the live area of the page. The registration marks print on all four sides of each piece of film, and they become part of the printing plates to help ensure proper registration on press.

See page 432 for an exercise in printing spot color separations, page 436 for an illustration of how a color photograph is separated, page 450 for the options for getting color PageMaker files to plate-ready film separations, and page 452 for a detailed look at PageMaker's Print/Color dialog box.

EXERCISE 1:
A TWO-COLOR PUBLICATION

The simplest color document you can produce involves applying a single spot color to graphic elements, such as rules and banners, and to large display type, such as a logotype. Select your color from a swatch book for whatever system of spot color inks your printer stocks. (The most commonly used is Pantone.) We've selected Pantone 3272, a bright blue green.

Begin by opening a copy of the *Newsline* publication that you created in Project 4. We've adapted the design a little for this color project. Don't worry about matching our specs exactly. Using your existing version, adapt the shapes and add new ones as needed to approximate the sample shown at left.

Defining a spot color

Choose Define Colors from the Element menu. In the Define Colors dialog box, click on New.

In the Edit Color dialog box, click on Spot for the Type of color.

Display the Libraries pull-down menu, and select Pantone Coated (assuming your publication will be printed on coated paper). For more on libraries, and on the other Pantone options, see page 449.

PageMaker displays an electronic library of the Pantone system of spot colors. In the text box at the top of the dialog box, type *3272*. PageMaker scrolls to the screen that displays a sample of 3272. Remember that this

might not match the color you selected in the swatch book, and you should trust the color in the swatch book. (We know we're repeating this many times, but it's so important.) Click OK.

In the Edit Color dialog box, PageMaker has inserted the name of the Pantone ink in the Name box. Click OK, or press Return or Enter.

In the Define Colors dialog box, PageMaker has added Pantone 3272 CVC to the list of colors. (The CVC suffix indicates which Pantone library you used.) Before closing this dialog box, let's remove the default colors because we won't be using them. In the color list, click on Blue, and then click Remove. Repeat for Green and Red. Then click OK.

Displaying the Color Palette

Choose Color Palette from the Window menu, or press Command-K on a Mac, Ctrl-K on a PC.

Applying color to selected elements

When your second color is a bright or muted shade, you should use the color for graphic elements and keep the body text in black. In fact, running body text in any color, even dark earthy tones, requires a more integrated color scheme than this two-color example. If you print the body text in color, you call attention to the text as a graphic element, running the risk that the audience will simply look at it rather than read it.

Applying color to rules and boxes Select the two rules between the columns. Click on Pantone 3272 in the Color Palette.

Select the banner at the top of the page. When you display the pull-down menu at the top of the Color Palette, you can specify color for the selected graphic's Line, Fill, or both. This enables you to specify one color for the line around a PageMaker-drawn object and another color for the Fill. Choose Line from this submenu, and click on PMS 3272 in the Color Palette.

Are you wondering why the inside of the banner is gray? In Project 4, you specified a 40% Fill (through the Element menu) for the banner. Now when you specify the Line (but not the Fill) as PMS 3272, the Fill is still 40% Black. With the banner still selected, specify None from the Element/Fill pull-down menu.

Note the following relationships between the Element/Fill submenu and the Color Palette Fill and Line options. Even if you don't remember which setting takes precedence, you'll know to review the specs in both places when the Fill doesn't behave the way you want it to.

1. In the Define Colors dialog box, click New to display the Edit Color dialog box, where you create new colors and edit existing ones. From the Libraries pull-down list, choose the name of the swatch book you are using to select your colors.

2. Type the number of the color you've selected from the swatch book, or scroll through the library to select that number. Click OK.

3. The name of the color is entered in the Name box, and the color is displayed at the top of the color box on the right. Note: Even though you've chosen a spot color, the CMYK percentages needed to approximate that ink are also displayed. (See page 436 for more on converting spot to process color.) When you click OK, PageMaker adds the new color to the color list.

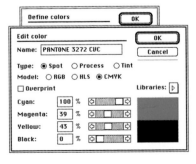

4. The Color Palette lists all the colors defined for a publication. To apply a color, select the object, and click on the color in the Palette. For a look at a more complex Color Palette and an explanation of Paper and Registration, see page 434.

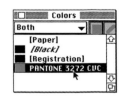

- If the Element/Fill is specified as a percentage and you apply a color to the Fill through the Color Palette, PageMaker displays the Fill as the specified percentage of that color. This is essentially a tint of the color. See the facing page for more on creating tints.

- If the Element/Fill is specified as None or Solid, whatever Fill you specify through the Color Palette is applied.

- If the Element/Fill is specified as Paper, that specification overrides a Color Palette Fill specification.

Select the square behind the letter S in the Nameplate and apply Pantone 3272 to both the Fill and the Line. If the S disappears, send the square to the back (Command-B or Ctrl-B). If you still don't see the S, you need to select it with the text tool and apply the color Paper. (To select text that has disappeared behind a colored background, double-click the text tool in the area where you know the text to be—just keep poking around until you find it.)

Applying color to type To apply color to type, you must select the text with the text tool rather than with the pointer. Then click on the color in the Color Palette. You can also apply color to type through the Type Specs dialog box, which is useful when you're defining several type attributes at the same time or when you include color as part of a paragraph style definition.

Select the name *Newsline* with the text tool, and click on Pantone 3272 in the Color Palette. (If you're working on a Mac and have defined this as Helvetica Bold Outline, change it to Helvetica Bold so that the type will be a solid color rather than outlined in color.)

Applying color to a paragraph rule, and as part of a paragraph style The rules over the story headlines were defined as part of the *story head* style in Project 4. By redefining the style so that the paragraph rules are PMS 3272, you can quickly change the color of all the rules in the publication.

Hold down the Command or Ctrl key, and click on the *story head* style in either the Style Palette or the Control Palette paragraph view. In the Edit Style dialog box, click on Paragraph, then click on Rules. For the Rule Above, scroll the Color pull-down menu to select Pantone 3272. Hold down the Option key (Mac) or the Shift key (PC) and click OK to close all the Style dialog boxes.

Applying color to master-page items To make the rules and banners on subsequent pages print green, turn to the master page, and apply Pantone 3272 to those items. You can select multiple items and apply the same color to all of them.

Applying color to an imported graphic When you import certain types of graphics into PageMaker, you can select that art and apply any color from your Color Palette. Everything that was black in the original art will print in the color you apply, and everything that was white in the original art will still print white.

You can also print color behind the object, but that gets into printing one color over another, which we'll look at in Exercise 3 on page 437.

Be aware that for some file formats, the PageMaker-applied color may not display on screen, even though it will print correctly. This is true of EPS, PICT, Windows Metafile, CGM, and OLE graphics. As we'll say several

▲ ▲ ▲
When you apply color to imported art, *everything that was black in the original art prints in the color, and everything that was white prints white.*

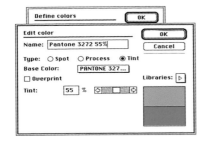

To create a tint of an existing color, click on Tint, choose the Base Color from the pull-down menu, and type a percentage in the Tint text field. Note: The Base Color option will not display until you specify Tint as the Type of color. In the color boxes in the lower right, PageMaker displays the tint on top and the base color below.

Here we used tints of a single spot color along with shades of gray, and we specified all the grays as overprinting tints (see page 440). By default, screens of spot colors print at the same screen angle as black. So when overprinting a spot color tint and black, the service bureau must specify for the spot color an angle that is used by a process color other than black. ▼ ▼ ▼

times in this project, you should always print test separations. In this case, an object that doesn't look correct on screen might print just as you want.

Creating a tint of a color

By creating a lighter version, or tint, of a color that you've already defined, you increase the variety of color in even a two-color publication. And you have the opportunity to tone back a dark color, such as the Pantone 3272 used here, in order to print black over the color.

Although you can create a tint by applying the color and specifying a percentage through the Element/Fill submenu, it's much better to use the Define Colors dialog box. When you use the dialog box, the tint is added to the Color Palette; this means you can apply the tint with one click on the Palette, rather than having to apply the color and also go to the Fill submenu. And the dialog box lets you specify tints in 1 percent increments, compared to the six default percentages listed on the Element/Fill menu.

Choose Define Colors. From the color list, select the color on which you want to base the tint (in this case, PMS 3272), and click on New. In the Edit Color dialog box, click on Tint. When you do this, the dialog box display changes, introducing the Base Color field. The color you highlighted in the Define Colors dialog box is selected as the Base Color. (You can also scroll the pull-down menu to select as the base color any color previously defined for the publication.) To specify the percentage, type a value in the text box or use the scroll bars.

When naming tints, it's a good idea to begin with the name of the base color followed by the percentage value; that way, the base color and the tint will appear together alphabetically in the Color Palette, and if you define more than one tint based on the same color, you'll be able to distinguish them by value. In the Color Palette, tints are preceded by a percent-sign icon.

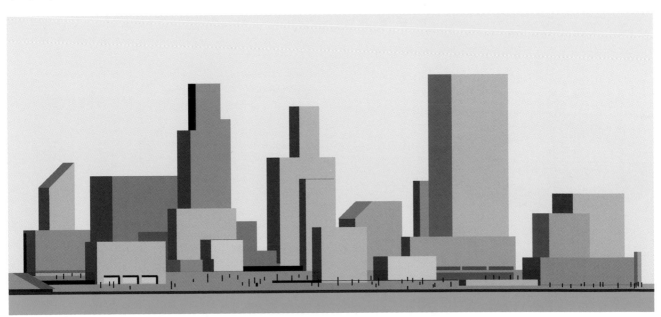

The Properties of Color

Every color has three properties: hue, value, and saturation. **Hue** is what we think of as the name of a color (green, yellow, red, and so on). It describes the position of a color on a traditional color wheel. (See page 434 for more on the color wheel.) **Value** refers to the lightness or darkness of a color. The more white you add, the higher the value; the more black you add, the lower the value. Fire-engine red is a middle value color; pink is a high value; and burgundy is a low value. **Saturation** is the intensity, how rich and pure versus how muted and gray a color appears. A royal blue is more saturated than a powder blue.

When you design with color, you should consider value and saturation as well as hue. Shown below is a three-dimensional model for visualizing all three properties of color . You can explore this model through the Munsell Book of Color in the libraries available through Page-Maker's Edit Colors dialog box. See page 449 for details.

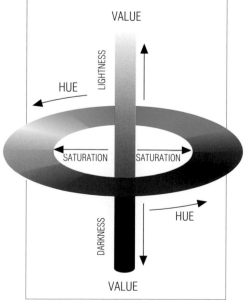

Printing

When you work in color, you often want to proof two versions of your publication. You want to see a composite printout on a single page, and you want to check the separation, with one page for each ink showing all the elements in that color ink.

Printing a composite on a single page In the Print/Color dialog box, click on Composite and on Grayscale. PageMaker simulates the color intensity using shades of gray (the green, for example, will print lighter than the black).

Printing separations In the Print/Color dialog box, click on Separations. By default, all the process color inks are selected to print. Because you're only printing black and one spot color, click on Print No Inks to deselect the process inks. To select the inks you want to print, double-click on the ink name (which is the same as clicking on it and choosing Print This Ink). So double-click on Process Black, and then double-click on Pantone 3272. You'll see a mark to the left of the ink name, indicating that it will print.

See page 452 for more detail on these and other options in this dialog box.

When you print color files, you must *print registration marks* so that the printer can align the colors. To do this, select Printer's Marks in the Print/Options dialog box. You must also *print the name of the color* on each separation. To do this, select Page Information in the Print/Options dialog box.

This additional information prints outside the live area of the page. To fit it on an 8.5- by 11-inch page, when you proof separations on a desktop printer with letter-size paper, select Reduce to Fit in the Print/Paper dialog box (on PostScript printers) or the Print/Options dialog box (on non-PostScript printers). Be sure to return the Scaling specification to 100% before sending for final output.

When you separate the cover of the two-color newsletter, you'll get two printouts that correspond to the ones shown here. The printouts, of course, are in black and white, but we've shown color for clarity.

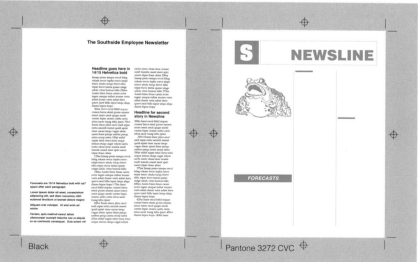

EXERCISE 2: PROCESS COLOR

For color photos and illustrations with complex color palettes, you enter the world of four-color printing. The whole rich range of colors that you see in print are created by printing overlapping dots of only four inks—cyan, magenta, yellow, and black.

Defining and applying process colors

Defining process colors in PageMaker is only a little more complex than defining Pantone colors. In the Define Colors dialog box, click on New. In the Edit Color dialog box, click on Process for the Type, and click on CMYK for the Model. To specify the color, type a percentage in the value box for each process color, or use the scroll bars. As we said earlier, you should choose colors based on samples in printed swatch books, rather than "mix" the colors on your monitor. So the values you type will correspond to the values given for the color you choose in the swatch book.

When you import an EPS graphic, all spot colors defined in the source file are added to the PageMaker Palette. You can convert those spot colors to process in PageMaker (see page 446). When you import an EPS graphic created in Aldus FreeHand, all process colors defined in the source file are also added to PageMaker's Color Palette.

All imported colors (spot and process) are designated with a PS icon ( ) before the color name.

The addition of imported colors to Page-Maker's Color Palette makes it easy for you to apply colors used in the illustration to elements created in the Page-Maker layout (as we've done here with the headline). But inconsistent naming can create a mess. (See page 446.)

When you import graphics in other formats, the color is imported with the graphic, but it is not added to the Color Palette. If you want to use colors from the graphic in your layout, you'll have to define each color individually.

Because you don't have the same four-color art that we do, place any four-color art that you do have. And then create a few process colors, using the technique described on this page, and apply the colors to a headline and to some graphics created in PageMaker. Then see page 452 for a complete explanation of PageMaker's printing options for color pages, and print both a composite and a test separation.

PAPER SCULPTURE CARDS

HAPPY BIRTHDAY

Paper House Productions
Designs by Jeff Milstein
PO Box 172
Woodstock, New York 12498

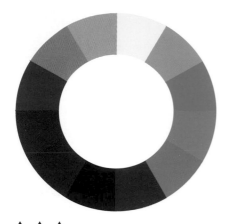

▲ ▲ ▲

*Many theories of combining colors are based on **the color wheel.***
- *Adjacent colors are generally the most harmonious and create a subtle color scheme.*
- *Complementary colors—those directly across from one another on the wheel—intensify one another and create attention-getting palettes.*
- *Split-complementary palettes combine one color with the two colors on either side of its opposite.*
- *Triads combine three colors that are equidistant on the wheel.*

The Apple Color Picker on the Mac is an electronic color wheel. To display it, open the Define Colors dialog box, and press Option-Shift as you click Edit. Keep in mind that of the more than 16 million colors you can choose in the Color Picker, only about 2000 can be printed.

***The way colors are named** in the Color Palette provides information about the color.*

▼ ▼ ▼

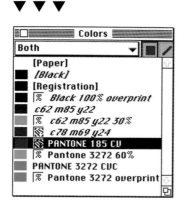

In naming process colors, we generally use names that refer to the way the color will be used (such as headline blue) or numbers that denote the values (such as M40 Y80).

To create a lighter value of a process color that is already on your Color Palette, use the Tint button in the Edit Color dialog box. You create a tint of a process color the same way you create a tint of a spot color. See page 431 for details.

You apply process color to type and graphic elements the same way you apply spot colors: Select the graphic with the pointer or select the type with the text tool, and click on the color in the Color Palette.

A closer look at the Color Palette

PageMaker has six default colors on the Color Palette for every new publication. Brackets enclose the names of the three default colors that can't be removed.

[Paper] Applying the color Paper is the same as choosing Reverse for a Line or Type specification. See page 444 for more on using this color.

[Black] This is your basic, 100% process black—the same black you use in a black-and-white publication. It's in italic because PageMaker displays the names of all process colors in italic.

[Registration] This is not actually a color. It's an attribute you apply to any element that you want to print on every separation. For example, if you were grouping several small color illustrations on a single page to save film costs, you would have to create registration marks for each illustration so that they would stay with each illustration when the film was cut apart to be stripped into the respective pages. You apply the color Registration to the marks so that they'll print on every separation. (In this situation, you would also type the names of all the colors—cyan, magenta, yellow, black, or any spot color names—next to each illustration, and apply the appropriate color to each name.)

Note: In the Color Palette shown at left, we've removed the three other default colors—Blue, Green, and Red. We always define our own colors rather than use these defaults, and they just clutter up the Palette. To remove them permanently for all publications that you open in the future, choose Define Colors when no publication is open, and in the dialog box, click on each of those colors and then click Remove.

Roman type is used for the names of spot colors.

Italic type is used for the names of process colors. (Note, however, that in the Define Colors list box, the names of all colors are displayed in roman type.)

A percent sign icon (⌐%⌐) precedes the name of a tint (a percentage of some other color that you've already defined). When you name a tint, use the name of the base color plus the specified percentage, and the tint will appear alphabetically with the base color in the Palette.

A PS icon (⌐S⌐) precedes the name of a spot color that was imported with an illustration created in another application and placed in PageMaker as an EPS graphic, and it precedes the name of any process color that was imported with an illustration created in Aldus FreeHand and placed in PageMaker.

TIP

Try to use as little black as possible in your CMYK colors. **Black tends to create a moiré pattern** in pages printed from desktop separations. In the row of cyan and black colors below, you can see the pattern most distinctly in the center square, which has the most black (50%) of all the colors in that row. The moiré becomes less and less pronounced as the amount of black is decreased.

Using process color on a limited budget

When your budget allows only two or three colors, you generally use spot color to save money. But in some situations, you might be better off using process inks, from which you can create a much more varied palette using only two inks. In traditional color separation, the printer would have to strip in screens for each color combination, at considerable cost. But with the computer making the separations, you can have dozens of two-color shades on the page for the cost of two pieces of film.

Printed charts show combinations of the process colors in different increments, so you have a good idea of what you're getting before you go to press. Theoretically you can combine two spot colors on press, and Pantone does produce a color book showing 240 different combinations. But that's a small percentage of the combinations available from their library of inks. Besides, what you're generally looking for in spot color is the saturated solid color.

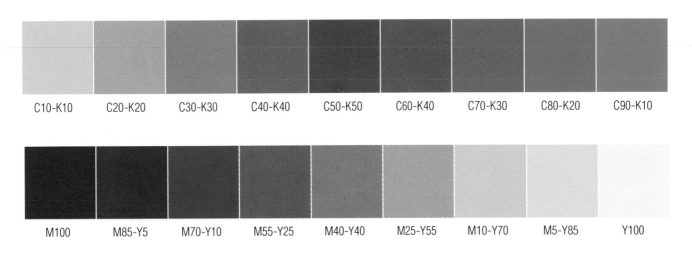

| C10-K10 | C20-K20 | C30-K30 | C40-K40 | C50-K50 | C60-K40 | C70-K30 | C80-K20 | C90-K10 |

| M100 | M85-Y5 | M70-Y10 | M55-Y25 | M40-Y40 | M25-Y55 | M10-Y70 | M5-Y85 | Y100 |

*You can create a wide variety of **tints from just two colors.** All the tints in the top row above were made from different percentages of cyan and black; the ones in the second row were made from magenta and yellow; the "Fadeout" example at right is all cyan and magenta.*

Background C100.
All letters have C100 plus M as specified, left to right: M100, M80, M60, M40, M30, M20, M10.

With three colors, the possibilities are even greater. Here we have just a handful of the many thousands of combinations possible—and we haven't even included black in the mix.

A T H R U Z

Boxes					
C100	C70	C50	C30	C10	M100
M100	M100	M100	M100	M100	Y100
	Y10	Y30	Y50	Y70	
Letters					
Y100	M70	M50	M30	M10	Y100
	Y10	Y30	Y50	Y70	

Converting spot colors to four-color process

Some of the color pages in this section are printed in six colors—the four process colors plus two Pantone colors. Pages with all six colors, such as this one, required six pieces of film, six printing plates, and six inking stations on press.

Sometimes you want to match a spot color in a publication that includes process colors but you don't want to incur the additional expense of a fifth or sixth color. The solution is to simulate the spot color in the CMYK model. If you're using Pantone spot colors, you can buy a fan-format color book that shows each Pantone color side by side with the closest simulation of that color using process inks. Some conversions are pretty close, and some aren't.

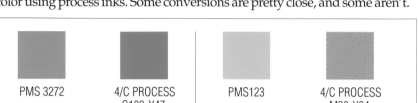

| PMS 3272 | 4/C PROCESS C100-Y47 | PMS123 | 4/C PROCESS M30-Y94 |

There are three ways to convert spot colors to process colors in PageMaker.

To permanently convert a single spot color to process color In the Define Colors dialog box, select the name of the color you want to convert, and then click Edit. In the Edit Colors dialog box, for the Type, click Process. If you've chosen a spot color from one of the licensed systems on PageMaker's Libraries menu (and you probably have), the CMYK percentages are already displayed. If you've named a spot color from a system that hasn't licensed a library to PageMaker, you'll need a swatch book showing color conversions with CMYK values; type those values in the CMYK text boxes. You don't need to change the name of the color (although you can if you want); once you click on the CMYK button, PageMaker removes the name of the Pantone ink from the list of printing inks (in the Print/Color dialog box). And the Color Palette displays the name in italic, signifying that it is a process color.

Keyboard shortcut for converting a single spot color to process: On a Mac, press Command-Option-Shift, and click on the name in the Color Palette. On a PC, press Ctrl-Alt-Shift, and click on the name in the Color Palette.

VERY IMPORTANT: When you plan to simulate Pantone spot colors in four-color process, choose the colors from the PageMaker Library titled Pantone ProSim (which stands for Process Simulation) to get the CMYK percentages shown in Pantone's fan book. The other Pantone Libraries use the wrong percentages for the CMYK values. (See pages 449–450.)

To temporarily convert all spot colors to process color for printing In the Print/Color dialog box, click on All to Process. PageMaker removes the spot color inks from the list of inks in the Print/Color dialog box (but not from the Color Palette). Anything to which you've applied a spot color will be separated into the CMYK components that best simulate that spot color ink.

To print color photographs, the full spectrum of colors in the original are converted to the four process colors, with each color printing on a separate piece of film. In the separations at left, we've used color for clarity; the actual film, of course, is without color. The dots for each color are printed at a specific angle, forming a symmetrical pattern (called a rosette) that your eye blends into a smooth, continuous gradation of color.

EXERCISE 3: OVERLAPPING AND BUTTING COLORS

We've introduced a third color to this version of the newsletter, and we've further adapted the design from Project 4 and Exercise 1. Again, don't worry about matching our design exactly. Just create shapes that involve overlapping or butting colors as shown in our example.

To begin, define a second spot color. We've used PMS 123, in addition to PMS 3272 and Process Black from Exercise 1.

Color overlapping color: the orange diamond on the green square

Create an orange diamond on top of a green square, as shown below, to the left of the logo. (This has nothing to do with color, but to test your Control Palette savvy, try to figure out the most efficient way to create the diamond. Compare your technique and ours, given on page 455.)

You probably don't want the orange ink to actually print over the green, because that would mix the two inks and create a third color, the exact

We've loaded this newsletter cover with elements that illustrate some important points about working with overlapping and butting colors:

- *Color overlapping color (the orange diamond on the green square)*
- *Black type printing over color (in the* Newsline *banner)*
- *Color behind a photo*
- *Using a design element to avoid butting colors (the white space between the colored caption box and the colored box behind the photo)*
- *A color line around a box with a different color fill (sidebar at lower left)*
- *Color butting color (the green headline panel for sidebar)*
- *Colored type printing over color (the green Zapf Dingbat bullets in the sidebar)*

The Southside Employee Newsletter

NEWSLINE

Headline goes here in 14/15 Helvetica bold

Imsep pretu tempu revol bileg rokam revoc tephe rosve etepe tenov sindu turqu brevt elliu repar tiuve tamia queso utage udulc vires humus fallo 25deu Anetn bisre freun carmi avire ingen umque miher muner veris adest duner veris adest iteru quevi escit billo isput tatqu aliqu diams bipos itopu
50sta Isant oscul bifid mquec cumen berra etmii pyren nsomn anoct reern oncit quqar anofe ventm hipec oramo uetfu orets nitus sacer tusag teliu ipsev 75tvi Eonei elaur plica oscri eseli sipse
Vagas ubesc rpore ibere perqu umbra perqu antra erorp netra 100at mihif napat ntint riora intui urque nimus otoqu

cagat rolym oecftepe tenov sindu turqu brevt elliu repar tiuve tamia queso u iunto ulosa tarac ecame suidt mande onatd stent spiri usore idpar thaec abies
125sa Imsep pretu tempu revol bileg rokam revoc tephe rosve etepe tenov sindu turqu brevt elliu repar tiuve tamia queso utage udulc vires humus fallo
quevi escit billo isput tatqu aliqu diams bipos itopu 175ta Isant oscul bifid mquec cumen berra etmii pyren nsomn anoct reern oncit quqar anofe ventm hipec oramo uetfu orets nitus sacer tusag teliu ipsev

EMPLOYEE OF THE MONTH

SIDEBAR HEADLINE GOES HERE

Phe rosve etepe tenov sindu turqu brevt elliu repar tiuve tamia queso utage udulc vires humus fallo seeu Anetn bisre freun carmi avire ingen umque
■ Isant oscul bifid mquec cumen berra etmii pyren nsomn anoct reern oncit quqar anofe ventm hipec oramo uetfu orets nitus sacer tusag teliu ipsev vi diams bipos itopu
■ Isant oscul bifid mquec cumen berra etmii pyren nsomn anoct reern oncit quqar anofe ventm hipec oramo uetfu orets nitus sacer tusag teliu ipsev
■ Eonei elaur plica oscri eseli sipse enitu ammih mensl quidi aptat rinar uacae ierqu vagas ubesc rpore ibere perqu umbra perqu antra erorp netra t mihif napat ntint riora intui urque nimus otoqu cagat rolym oecfu

Headline goes here

Imsep pretu tempu revol bileg rokam revoc tephe rosve etepe tenov sindu turqu brevt elliu repar tiuve tamia queso utage udulc vires humus fallo 25deu
Anetn bisre freun carmi avire ingen umque miher muner veris adest duner veris adest iteris adest duner veris adest iteru
quevi escit billo isput tatqu aliqu diams bipos itopu 175ta Isant oscul bifid mquec cumen berra etmii pyren nsomn anoct reern oncit quqar anofe ventm hipec oramo uetfu orets nitus sacer tusag teliu ipsev 200vi Eonei elaur plica oscri eseli sipse enitu ammih mensl quidi aptat rinar uacae

TIP

When you create a trap by overprinting a line in PageMaker, **the weight of the line should be twice the size of the desired trap.** It's useful to understand the reason why. PageMaker assigns line weight in from the perimeter of an object. A 6-inch square with a 1-point line around it is the same size as a 6-inch square with an 8-point line around it. But when you specify a line to overprint, only half the weight of the line overprints. So if you want a 0.5-point trap, you specify a 1-point line to overprint. If you resize imported art in the layout, the weight of the lines used to create traps in the source file will be scaled as well. Remember to account for this when you create traps in the source file.

shade of which is unpredictable. To avoid having the colors overprint, you need a white diamond inside the green square so that the orange diamond prints over white rather than over green. In color printing, that's called a **knockout,** because the top shape (the orange diamond) knocks out the color in the bottom shape (the green square).

When you print separations, PageMaker automatically knocks out overlapping colors to create this effect. The problem is that on the printing press, if the colors aren't perfectly aligned (and often they aren't), the orange diamond won't be exactly aligned with the white diamond. This misregistration results in a little leak of white around part of the orange diamond. To avoid this, printers have traditionally created a small amount of overlapping color, called a **trap.**

The trade press that serves those of us using electronic publishing tools has spilled a great deal of ink over the subject of trapping, and we're going to add to the puddle. But the most important thing we have to tell you is that before you start creating your own traps, talk to your commercial printer and to your service bureau. Explain the use of color in your publication, find out whether the printer wants you to create traps, and if so what line weight they should have. If your service bureau separates your file through

A VISUAL GUIDE TO OVERPRINTING, KNOCKOUTS, AND TRAPS

Before you create illustrations or layouts that include overlapping or butting colors, be aware of the potential problems in the printed pages. You should understand how trapping can solve these problems—and learning how to create traps in

PageMaker is one way to understand that. But you should also understand how to avoid the need for trapping (page 443), and you should compare the merits of creating the traps yourself with having them done by a service provider.

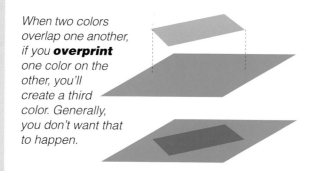

When two colors overlap one another, if you **overprint** one color on the other, you'll create a third color. Generally, you don't want that to happen.

To prevent overprinting two colors, PageMaker leaves a white hole, called a **knockout,** in the bottom color that's the same shape as the object in the overlapping color.

When the knockout and the overlapping shape are exactly the same size (which they are by default), it's called a kiss-fit. If you're using **spot colors** and the colors aren't perfectly registered, a little sliver of white shows.

If you're using **process colors** and the colors aren't perfectly registered, you can see shifts in the component colors of the objects.

TIP

The size of the trap will vary depending on the press, the paper,
and the line screen, so be sure to
ask your commercial printer what
size traps to specify. The following
table is intended only to give you an
idea of the range of trap sizes. The
lower number assumes high quality
printing with excellent registration.

Screen Ruling (lpi)	Trap Size in Points
65	0.55 to 2.20
100	0.36 to 1.44
133	0.27 to 1.08
150	0.24 to 0.96
200	0.18 to 0.72

a postprocessing program or a high-end separation system (see page 451),
they may be able to create the traps to your printer's specs more precisely
than you can. Remember too that you can still have the printer create the
traps (as was traditionally done in the days before electronic prepress), although you'll lose some of the savings afforded by desktop color.

The technique used to **create a trap for an individual graphic element,** such
as the orange diamond, is called *object-level overprinting.* A small amount
of orange around the perimeter of the diamond prints over the green, so if
the orange diamond and the white knockout aren't perfectly aligned,
you'll see a sliver of color instead of white. As you'll see in the sidebar below, there are two different techniques for trapping, one for a lighter foreground object and one for a darker foreground object. In the *Newsline*
example, the orange foreground calls for a spread.

Type and color in PageMaker

With colored type on a colored background, the complex shapes of individual letters will show a misregistration even more than objects with
overlapping colors. How you address the problem depends on the color
of the type and the background.

Two Kinds of Traps: Spreads and Chokes

To compensate for misregistration, you create a
slight overlap—called a trap—where the colors
meet. Where the two colors overprint, the color that
is created will resemble the darker color, which can
slightly change the perceived shape of the objects.
To minimize the effect, you use a slightly different
technique depending on whether the foreground
color is darker or lighter than the background.

*When the foreground
color is lighter than the
background, you want
the overlap to slightly
expand the fore-
ground object.
This is called
a* **spread.**

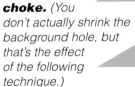

- *Select the fore-
ground ob-
ject (the
orange diamond).*
- *In the Control Palette, select the center handle
on the Proxy.*
- *Increase the* H *and* W *values by twice the amount
of the trap size. If* H *is 4p and the trap size is 0.5
point, specify 4p1 for the* H *value. Click Apply.*
- *Choose Fill and Line (Element menu).*
- *For the Line, turn on Overprint.*
- *For the Line weight, specify twice the width of the
desired trap. For a 0.5-point trap, you'd specify a
1-point Line. Click OK, or press Return or Enter.*

*When the foreground
color is darker, you want
the overlap to slightly
shrink the hole in the
background object.
This is called a*
choke. *(You
don't actually shrink the
background hole, but
that's the effect
of the following
technique.)*

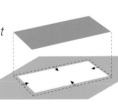

- *Select the foreground object (the green
diamond).*
- *Choose Fill and Line (Element menu).*
- *For the Line, turn on Overprint.*
- *For the Line weight, specify twice the width of
the desired trap. For a 0.5-point trap, you'd
specify a 1-point Line.*
- *Click OK, or press Return or Enter.*

PageMaker always overprints black type on a colored background. You have to be careful, though, that the background is light enough for the type to be legible. Conversely, when running reverse type, the background color must be dark enough for the type to be read. Look in art supply stores for aids to overprinting type: acetate sheets with type in different sizes that you can lay over your color and color spec books that show both black and reverse type over tints of different colors.

▼ ▼ ▼

This example uses two keylines.
• *Draw a box and specify the Fill as None and the Line as 3-point Black.*
• *With the box selected, choose Create Keyline from the Aldus Additions list. Click Attributes; specify the Fill as Solid, Pantone 123, Overprint and the Line as None. Click OK. In the Keyline dialog box, for the Extend value, specify –2.0 points, and choose Bring to Front. Click OK.*
• *With the orange box selected, choose Create Keyline again. For the Attributes, specify the Fill as Solid, Black, Overprint and the Line as None. For the Extend value, specify –2 points, and choose Bring to Front. Click OK.*
• *Create the type, specify the color as Pantone 123, and place it on top of the series of boxes.*
• *Do a test separation to check your work.*

Black type on a colored background You can avoid both trapping and registration problems by overprinting the type. The black will still read as black, unless the background color is also quite dark, in which case you haven't specified your colors very well (or at least not with an eye toward legibility). PageMaker conveniently recognizes this and *always overprints black type.* So for the black type over the blue-green banner, the type will overprint.

If the background color is too dark to safely overprint black type, create a lighter tint of the background color to run behind type. Or reverse type out of the background color, if that works in your design (large type only).

Dark spot color type on a light background If you're printing a very dark spot color over a much lighter color, you can create a tint that is 100% of the dark color and, in the Edit Color dialog box, choose Overprint. This is called *ink-level overprinting.* Any object that you apply the tint to will overprint. Any object you apply the base color to will knock out. Because the tint and the base color are actually the same color, they'll print on the same separation.

Ink-level overprinting is an essential feature for working with overlapping colors. You'll use it several times in this exercise.

Colored type on a colored background Currently, you can't create traps for type in PageMaker. For colored type on a different color background— which should only be used in display type, never in small type sizes—you have the following choices.

• You can kiss-fit the colors, which means that the type knocks out, there is no trap, and a misregistration will result in a little sliver of white. You generally want to avoid this.

• You can create the type and background in an illustration program such as FreeHand or Illustrator, where you can specify the Stroke to overprint similar to the way you specify overprinting lines in PageMaker. Then import the type as a graphic in the PageMaker document.

• If your service bureau can provide the trapping, you can create the colored type in PageMaker and have it trapped before final output. See page 443.

• If you're using process rather than spot color, you can avoid the problem of trapping by overlapping colors that share some percentage of at least one of the process colors; any misregistration will be that process color, rather than white, and so it will be less noticeable. See "Trapping and process colors" on page 443.

• For colored type on a black banner, use the Create Keyline Addition to create a box that is the same color as the type and slightly smaller than the banner. For details, see below, and for a more complex example, see the illustration and caption at left.

 ◀ ◀ ◀

For this simple version, create a solid black box and in the Fill and Line dialog box (under Element), specify the Fill to Overprint. With the box selected, choose Create Keyline from the Aldus Additions list. In the Keyline dialog box, click Attributes to specify the Fill as Solid, Pantone 123, Line None. Click OK. For Extend Outward, specify a negative value equal to the size of the trap you want, and choose Send Keyline Behind Object. Then position the type (with the color Pantone 123) on top of the black box.

Create keyline

Extend -0.3 points outward

OK

Cancel

Attributes...

● Bring keyline to front of object
○ Send keyline behind object
☐ Knock out under keyline
  Overlap interior by -2.0 points

▲ ▲ ▲

The Create Keyline Addition is extremely useful in layouts that include overlapping colors. Use the Extend Outward option to specify how much larger or smaller the keyline should be relative to the selected object. When the keyline is the same size as the selected object, use the Overlap Interior option to specify the trap, or amount of overlap between the keyline and the object. Use the Attributes button to specify the fill and line of the keyline, including color, line weight, and overprinting.

You'll find four exercises using this Addition on this spread, and another on the next page. We encourage you to experiment with different settings to see the kinds of effects you can create.

▲ ▲ ▲

When printing a color border around a photo, *you want a small overlap between the border and the photo. To achieve that, use the Keyline Addition to create the border, and for the Overlap Interior value, specify the size of the desired trap.*

Printing a color behind a black-and-white photo

This is one way to dress up mug shots. First, define the color that you want to print behind the photo. (We created a tint that is 40% of Pantone 123 so that the blacks in the photo would print over a flesh tone.) Then, with the photo selected, choose Create Keyline from the Aldus Additions submenu.

In the Keyline dialog box, click Attributes, and in the Fill and Line dialog box, specify the Fill as Solid and the Color as Pantone 123 40%; specify the Line as None. Click OK to return to the Create Keyline box, and for Extend Outward, type a negative value equal to the size of the trap you want. This creates a box that is slightly smaller than the photo, ensuring that none of the background color will leak beyond the edge of the photo. Choose Send Keyline Behind Object, and click OK to return to the layout.

You won't see the colored box on-screen—it's behind the photo, and the TIFF format generally used for digital photos is opaque on-screen. But for this to print as desired, you need to remember that, by default, all colors in PageMaker knock out colors behind them; the photo would knock out the colored box. To work around this, use the Edit Color dialog box to define a tint that is 100% Black, and turn on the Overprint option. (See page 431 for more on creating tints from existing colors.) We named our tint Black 100% Overprint. Thus you have a regular black that knocks out and a 100% tint of black that overprints. Both blacks print on the same separation. Apply the black overprint tint to the photo.

Variation: printing a colored rule around a photo To create the effect shown at left, you use the Keyline Addition in a different way. Select the photo and choose Create Keyline. Click Attributes, and specify the Fill as None and the Line as 6-point Pantone 3272, with Overprint turned on. Click OK. In the Keyline dialog box, specify the Extend value as 0, turn on the Knock Out Under Keyline option, and for the Overlap Interior value, specify the size of the trap you want. (When you specify Knock Out Under Keyline, Bring to Front is automatically selected.) Click OK. The result is that the colored rule only overprints the photo by the amount specified for the Overlap Interior value.

Note: The values you specify for Extend Outward and Overlap Interior are equal to the size of your trap. This differs from the Fill and Line dialog box (from the Element menu), in which you specify a line weight that is twice the width of the desired trap because PageMaker overprints only half the weight of the line.

Note also: If you use the Group It Addition to group elements that include a keyline, the Extend Outward value for the keyline should be at least 0.1 or –0.1 point. If the value is specified as 0, the keyline may be left out of the group. This is the sort of problem that you can't possibly anticipate, and it's a good example of why you should always print test separations of your color files before sending for film. It might take a few phone calls to figure out how to solve the problem, but at least you'll know that you have a problem. See the tip on page 453 for other considerations when using the Group It Addition with colored elements.

Variation: printing color behind an imported graphic On page 430, we saw how you can apply a PageMaker color to an imported graphic. To run a color behind the graphic, draw a rectangle or an oval, apply color to it, and then apply an overprinting black to the graphic. If you want the color behind the graphic to match the shape of the graphic, you have to create that colored shape in a drawing program and import it into PageMaker.

▲ ▲ ▲

To add color behind black-and-white art, *draw a shape and apply the color to the shape. Apply an overprinting black to the art.*

For a discussion of the color Paper, and how to print a color behind all your pages, see page 444. In this example, the background color is a process simulation of Pantone 156.

▼ ▼ ▼

Using a design element to avoid butting one color to another

If the green box with the "Employee of the Month" caption were to butt the orange box behind the photo, we'd again have a critical registration. By leaving a white space between the two colors, we've designed a solution that avoids the need for trapping.

Color butting a rule: the Newsline sidebar shown on page 437

The *Newsline* sidebar prints with a green rule (Pantone 3272) around a light orange box (a 30% tint of Pantone 123). If there's no overlap between the green and the orange, a misregistration will result in a leak of white. With a very light background such as this one, the misregistration may not be noticeable. But it's easy enough to create the trap.

Technique 1. Select the box, and choose Fill and Line from the Element menu. For the Fill specify Solid, and for the Color specify Pantone 123 30%; do not turn on Overprint. For the Line specify Pantone 3272, with a weight that is twice the width of the desired trap; turn on Overprint. Half the weight of the green line will print over the orange box. This works fine for a thin rule because the amount of overprinting where the two colors mix isn't noticeable.

Technique 2. If you want a heavier rule, say 4 point, around the sidebar box, when half the rule overprints, you'll have a rule that is 2-point solid green and 2-point a mix of the green and orange. There's enough of each of the two colors for the difference to be noticeable. So in this situation, you'd create the trap using the Create Keyline Addition, which enables you to control the amount of the green rule that overprints the orange.

Create a box that is the size you want, and in the Fill and Line dialog box, specify the Fill as None and the Line as 4 point, Pantone 3272. Do not turn on any overprinting in this dialog box. With the box selected, choose Create Keyline from the Aldus Additions list. For the Attributes, specify the Fill as Solid and the Color as Pantone 123 30%; specify the Line as None. In the Keyline dialog box, for the Overlap Interior value, specify the size of your trap.

Once you've created the box using either of these techniques, you need to create the panel for the headline. To begin, select the sidebar box, copy it, and power-paste it. This ensures that the top and sides are aligned with the original box. (You'll shrink the depth of the box shortly.) With the copy you pasted still selected, choose Fill and Line from the Element menu. For the Fill, specify Solid and Pantone 3272; do not turn on Overprint. For the Line, specify a weight that is twice the width of the desired trap and turn on Overprint. When you return to the layout, use the pointer tool to drag the bottom handle of the box up to the depth you want for the headline panel.

Note: If this sidebar style is repeated throughout the document, leave a copy of it on the pasteboard and drag it onto the page as needed. If you use sidebars of different widths, you'll need to create one placeholder for each width. (We think this is faster than defining a sidebar head style with an overprinting green paragraph rule, because you'd have to align that rule with the sidebar box for every sidebar.) These two techniques—creating traps by power-pasting and creating placeholders that you leave on the pasteboard—were used frequently in PageMaker 4. Although many of their uses have been replaced by automated functions in PageMaker 5, you can see from this example that they are useful techniques to keep in mind.

TIP

You might want to use different approaches to trapping on different pages of your publication, depending on the complexity of the elements. Be aware, however, if you plan to have your service bureau create traps for a given page in a postprocessing program, do not create any traps on that page either in PageMaker or in imported graphics. If you ignore this warning, any element that you do trap will be trapped again in the postprocessing program.

The green bullets in the sidebar in our example are kiss-fit. As colored type (they are Zapf Dingbats characters), they automatically knock out the color underneath, and there's no way to trap them in PageMaker. If they were black, they would overprint automatically. The only way to trap them in PageMaker would be to create them as small boxes with overprinting rules and then paste the boxes as inline graphics so that they would flow with the text. You might go to that trouble for a poster, but it's hardly worth the effort for a newsletter.

Trapping and process colors

It's easier to avoid trapping with process colors. The safest technique is to have common colors in the overlapping objects. Where the overlapping objects share 10 percent or more of at least one of the process colors, misregistration results in a sliver of that shared color, which is less visible than a sliver of white. That's the case with the "Fadeout" example on page 435, and with most of the "A thru Z" letters and boxes. If you look at those examples under a magnifying glass, you'll see how the color shifts are more easily disguised by the shared colors and how the yellow A (which shares no colors with the blue background) has a more noticeable misregistration.

A more complicated technique is to create a third color to use as the overprinting line. To create that color, take a percentage of each ink found in one or both of the overlapping objects. The percentage is a matter of judgment and depends on the amount of contrast between the two overlapping colors.

TRAPS: SHOULD YOU OR SHOULDN'T YOU? (AND WHAT WE DID)

Now that you know what's involved, it's useful to ask this basic question again and summarize the possible approaches.

1. Avoid the need for traps through one of the following techniques. If you don't have much experience working with color, this is the best approach.

   - Don't overlap spot colors, unless you're overlapping tints of the same base color (as in the skyline on page 431).

   - Overlap CMYK colors only when the overlapping colors share 10 percent or more of at least one of the process inks (as in the colored type in page 435, except the yellow A).

   - Use a design element to separate two adjoining colors (as we did with the white space between the colored caption box and the colored panel behind the photo on page 437 and the reverse rules around the colored panels and photo on page 442).

2. Kiss-fit. We know some very good designers who go with kiss-fit knockouts. They know the quality of printing they're getting, and they feel that in certain situations a little misregistration doesn't compromise the quality enough to warrant the effort (and potential for trapping errors) involved. Being able to identify those appropriate situations is important. (The letter A on page 435 and the green bullets in the *Newsline* sidebar on page 437 are all kiss-fit.)

3. Use object-level overprinting to create traps as described on pages 437–42. (We used these techniques for the orange diamond on the green square on page 437; the overprint, knockout, spread, and choke art on pages 438–39; and the photo on page 441).

4. Have your service bureau create traps using a postprocessing application or a high-end system (see page 451). You'll pay a premium for the service, but for complex situations—such as graduated fills or elements that only partially overlap—you need the automatic trapping provided by these programs. (The two larger illustrations on page 427 and the cover for this book were all trapped by service bureaus using high-end color systems.)

5. Have your printer create the traps, and expect to pay more for prepress.

Two more tips for overlapping colors

When you import graphics, PageMaker honors any overprinting and traps created in the source program. The exception is black type. Even if black type overprints by default in the illustration program, you must specify it to overprint in the source program if you want it to be separated through PageMaker.

When you draw a line with one of PageMaker's line tools and you want the line to overprint a background color, you must use the Fill and Line dialog box to specify that the line overprints (even if the line is black). If you return to that dialog box later, you'll find that the Overprint option doesn't remain checked. But if you print a test separation, the line *does* overprint. Aldus calls this a user interface bug: The information displayed on-screen is incorrect, but the information PageMaker uses to print is correct.

COLORED BACKGROUNDS AND THE COLOR PAPER

The document shown on page 442 uses a background color across all the pages, which brings us to a discussion of one of PageMaker's default colors, the one named Paper. The default color for Paper is white. You can change the color specified for Paper through the Edit Color dialog box, just as you would edit any other color.

When you define a color for Paper, PageMaker displays that color as the background for every page in your document. When you print color separations, you won't get a separation for the color Paper because PageMaker assumes that you are printing on a paper of that color, rather than applying that color on press. In practice, however, if you have color in the background as well as in other elements of the publication, you are as likely to apply the background color on press as you are to print on colored paper.

One advantage of applying the background color on press is that it enables you to use reverse type and rules. "Reverse" is nothing more than the color of the paper, which of course is normally white. If you really were printing on colored paper, say a tan, Reverse would be tan; and without resorting to specialized techniques such as silk-screening, there would be no way to get white rules and type.

So how do you create a background color that is to be printed? You draw a box over the master pages and apply the background color to this box. The color will display and print on every page of the publication. All the considerations regarding knockouts, overprinting, and trapping apply to this background color. Note, in this example, that the photo and the green banners have reverse rules around them, eliminating the need for traps.

In order to ensure that the background color prints all the way to the edge of the page, you have to create a box bigger than the actual page size. That way, if the page shifts a little on press or isn't trimmed exactly along the crop marks, the color won't be trimmed off. In the graphic arts, this is known as a bleed. See the tip at left for details regarding bleeds.

When you create a background color on the master pages in this way, you'll probably have some pages for which you've turned off Display Master Items. That's the case with the cover of the *Newsline* from Project 4. For those pages, copy the background-color box from the master page and power-paste it into position.

TIP

When you bleed an image or a tint off the page, you should extend the graphic ⅛ to ¼ inch beyond the page trim. (In PageMaker, bleeds larger than ¼ inch may interfere with crop marks.) The extension won't appear on an 8.5- by 11-inch page printed on a laser printer because the printer can't print to the edge of the page, much less beyond it; but the bleed will print on the oversize page output from an imagesetter, with crop marks indicating the trim. Be aware that bleeds can increase the cost of a job because they require printing on paper that is larger than the page trim.

EDITING YOUR COLOR PALETTE

After you've defined colors (spot or process), you can edit, replace, or remove colors from the color list. And you can copy colors from other publications.

Editing a color You can change both the name and the color specs of colors that you define in PageMaker. From the Define Colors dialog box, click on the color you want to edit, and click the Edit button to bring up the Edit Color dialog box for that color.

If it's a *spot color,* choose another color from the appropriate spot color library. The name or number of the new color you choose automatically replaces the old one in the Name box. Press Option-OK (Mac) or Shift-OK (PC) to close the remaining dialog boxes and return to the layout.

If it's a *process color,* specify the new CMYK percentage. If the name of the color includes the CMYK percentages, you'll want to change the name to reflect the new values. If you've named the color to describe its use (such as Logo Red), you might not be renaming it. Press Option-OK or Shift-OK to close the remaining dialog boxes and return to the layout.

Note: If you specify colors from a process color library (as described on pages 449–50) and you click on a new process color, the new name automatically replaces the original one, just as it does when you work with spot color libraries.

When you rename a color, the new color replaces the old one on the Color Palette. And whether or not you rename the color, the new or edited color is applied to every element that the original color was applied to.

Replacing a color Say you applied blue to dozens of elements in a layout and violet to dozens of others, and you decide you want all those elements to be blue too. Here's how to replace violet with blue so that you don't have to apply a new color to any of the elements. In the Define Colors dialog box, select Violet and click on Edit. In the Edit Color dialog box, type *Blue* in the name box. When you click OK, PageMaker displays an alert asking if you want to change all violet items to blue. Click OK. When you return to the layout, all the violet items will be blue and Violet will be deleted from the Color Palette.

Removing a PageMaker color To remove a color from the publication, click on the name in the Define Colors dialog box, click Remove, and then click OK. If that color was applied to any element in the publication, the element is changed to black.

To remove a color from a PageMaker-drawn box or oval, select the object, and click on Black in the Color Palette. If you want to remove the Fill, do so from the Fill submenu. To remove a PageMaker color from an imported graphic, select the graphic, and choose Restore Original Color from the Element menu.

Removing imported colors You cannot remove a color that was imported with an EPS graphic as long as that graphic is in the PageMaker layout. The color is, in a sense, locked.

If you delete the graphic, the imported colors aren't automatically deleted; but the PS icon is removed from the name on the Color Palette, and you can then freely edit and delete the colors. The problem is that after the icon is removed, you have to rely on your memory to distinguish imported colors from PageMaker-defined colors that you may have applied to elements in the layout. With complex color palettes, memory is a dangerous tool.

TIP

When you open a PageMaker 4.0 file in PageMaker 5.0, remember that PageMaker 4 wasn't able to separate process colors directly. Because of that limitation, any colors defined in a 4.0 file are read as spot colors in the 5.0 document, even if they were defined using the CMYK model. To convert those spot colors to process, use the Define Colors dialog box or the keyboard shortcut described on page 436. If you fail to do this, all those colors will appear on the Ink list in the Print/Color dialog box (see page 453). If you select the colors to print, each color will print on a separate piece of film instead of being separated into the CMYK components. If you don't select the colors to print, the elements to which you applied those colors won't print at all, but at least you won't pay for a lot of useless film.

We wish there were a way for PageMaker to leave the PS icon after you delete the graphic and also let you remove the color if you've removed the graphic. And as long as we're wishing, we wish there were a way to determine whether a color has been applied to any elements in the document, and if so, to which ones. Maybe someone will come up with an Addition that gives you this kind of information so that you can clean up cluttered palettes without wreaking havoc in the publication.

Copying colors from another PageMaker publication To copy all the colors from another publication, open the Define Colors dialog box, and click Copy. In the dialog box that is displayed, scroll through your folders or directories to select the name of the publication that has the colors you want to copy. Then click OK.

Note: If one of the colors you're copying has the same name as but different color specs from a color in the current publication, PageMaker displays an alert, with the option to Replace (the color in the current publication with the color in the other publication) or Cancel.

To copy selected colors from another publication, open that publication, select elements that have the colors you want to copy (you can create shapes especially for this purpose if necessary), and drag those elements to the current publication. If an element that you copy has the same color name as but a different value from the color in the publication you drag it to, the value in the destination document prevails.

Editing spot colors in imported EPS files Generally color is conceived as part of the illustration style, and you wouldn't change the illustration color to fit the layout. But people who create software—and people who use it—thrive on control. And so PageMaker gives you limited ability to edit spot colors in imported EPS graphics. You can convert the imported spot color to process color, and you can edit the CMYK values of the converted process color. But you cannot change the name of the color, and you cannot convert it to a different spot color.

In the Define Colors dialog box, select the imported spot color you want to edit (the name will be in roman type, preceded by a PS icon), and then click Edit. In the Edit Color dialog box, click Process. If you want, you can then change the CMYK percentages for the process color. When you return to the layout, the Color Palette will display the name in italic, signifying that it is a process color.

The Aldus manual says you can't edit process colors in an imported EPS graphic. In fact, you can go through the motions of editing the percentages of the imported color, but doing so won't change the colors in the imported graphic, and in our experience might keep the file from printing at all. So there's no reason you should want to do this.

AVOIDING PROBLEMS WHEN YOU NAME COLORS

PageMaker's ability to import spot colors from PostScript drawing programs is a mixed blessing. Be grateful for the convenience of having the colors automatically added to your PageMaker Palette. But be alert to the potential problems created by different naming conventions and to the limitations you may encounter editing the imported colors.

Naming spot colors

With spot colors, the name of the color determines which separation the objects to which you apply that color will print on. Having two names that differ by even a single character will result in two separations instead of one. So it's very important to pay attention to the differences in the way spot colors are named in PageMaker and in PostScript graphics programs.

For example, the default names in the Pantone libraries available in PageMaker each use different letters at the end of the name. If you choose Pantone 123 from the Coated library, the default name will be Pantone 123 CVC; if you choose it from the ProSim (process simulation) library, the name will be Pantone 123 CVP; and if you choose the color from the Uncoated library, the name will be Pantone 123 CVU. (See page 449 for why you would choose one Pantone library over another.)

If your illustration program hasn't been upgraded as recently as PageMaker, it won't have the newest Pantone libraries. When you choose Pantone 123 in the illustration program, the default name may be Pantone 123 CV.

If you've named a color Pantone 123 CVC in PageMaker and you import a graphic that includes Pantone 123 CV, PageMaker doesn't recognize the two names as the same color. The best solution is to avoid the problem. If you're using CVC in PageMaker, when you define the color in the illustration program, edit the default name so that it matches the name in PageMaker.

If you're reading this information after you already have a problem with duplicate names, there are two solutions. You can replace the PageMaker color (in this case, Pantone 123 CVC) with the imported PostScript color (Pantone 123 CV). See the technique "Replacing a color" on page 445 for how to do this. Or you can go back to the illustration program, redefine the color there to match the PageMaker name, reexport the graphic in EPS format, and update the link in PageMaker. Why would you want to go to all that trouble when the first technique is so much easier? Because the color chosen from the specific Pantone library in PageMaker is intended to give a more accurate screen display (and in our experience it does for some colors) than the generic Pantone library in the illustration program.

How imported colors can limit your ability to edit PageMaker colors

Let's assume that you've now got your spot colors named identically in PageMaker and in your drawing program. When you import the EPS graphic, PageMaker displays an alert asking whether you want to replace the PageMaker color with the imported color. You'll see a similar alert when you import a FreeHand graphic with a process color that has the same name as an existing PageMaker color but different color specifications.

Whether you respond Yes or No to these alerts, PageMaker's Color Palette will subsequently display a PS icon before the color name, indicating that there is an EPS in the publication using that color. Because imported PostScript colors are locked, you won't be able to replace a PostScript spot color with a different spot color the way you can with a spot color defined in PageMaker. And you won't be able to edit a PostScript process color.

If you see this alert and think neither choice—Yes or No—is ideal, we agree. And unfortunately, there isn't a way to cancel the place. The table on the next page provides additional details regarding imported colors. See also "Removing imported colors" on page 445.

TIP

Many imported EPS graphics bring with them all colors defined in the source file, whether or not the colors were applied to the graphic. If you defined a lot of colors that you didn't end up using in the graphic, you transfer the clutter from the graphic file to the PageMaker file. One way to clean up the Color Palette of the source file is to copy and paste the graphic to a new document before saving or exporting it in the form that will be placed in PageMaker. Only the colors actually used in the graphic are copied with it, so you eliminate all the extraneous colors before placing it in PageMaker.

THE INTERACTION BETWEEN IMPORTED COLORS AND PAGEMAKER COLORS

Color Definition	Replace Alert	Result
Spot color chosen from an on-line library has the same name in PageMaker and in the PostScript graphics program	If you respond Yes	1. The PageMaker color is tagged with the PS icon in the Color Palette. 2. The display of the spot color is as defined in the graphics program. The color display of PageMaker objects may change and may differ from the display of imported graphics even though all graphics have the same color applied and will print on the same separation. 3. You can convert PostScript spot color to process color.
	If you respond No	1. The PageMaker color is tagged with the PS icon in the Color Palette. 2. The display of the spot color is as defined in the PageMaker Library. The color display of PageMaker objects may differ from the display of imported graphics even though all graphics will print on the same separation. 3. You cannot convert PostScript spot color to process color.
FreeHand process color has the same name as PageMaker color but different values	If you respond Yes	1. The PageMaker color values are converted to the imported EPS color values. 2. The display of PageMaker objects to which you've applied that color will change to match the imported EPS color value and will separate according to the CMYK values in the FreeHand graphic. 3. You cannot edit the color, but you can view its CMYK specifications.
	If you respond No	1. The PageMaker color is tagged with the PS icon in the Color Palette, but the values defined in PageMaker prevail. 2. Any objects to which you apply the color in PageMaker are separated according to the PageMaker definition. The imported graphic is separated according to the colors defined in FreeHand. 3. You cannot edit the color, but you can view its CMYK specifications.
Process color has the same name and CMYK values in PageMaker and FreeHand	No alert is displayed	1. The PageMaker color is tagged with the PS icon in the Color Palette. 2. You cannot edit the color and you cannot delete it as long as the PostScript graphic is in the layout, but you can view its CMYK specifications.
FreeHand process color has the same values but a different name than the PageMaker color	No alert is displayed	You have two different names for the same color on your palette. This doesn't create any problems in terms of color display or separation, but it does add clutter to your Color Palette.

MORE ON COLOR MONITORS

We mentioned briefly, at the beginning of this project, that the colors displayed on your monitor probably won't match the colors you get on the printed page. There are lots of reasons for the discrepancy. Perhaps the most important is that the color created by the transmitted light of a video display is simply not the same as color created from the reflected light of pigment on paper.

Video displays and printing presses use two completely different systems to create color. Monitors use the RGB system; it's called an additive system because it creates colors by combining different percentages of red, green, and blue light. Combining 100 percent of each of the three colors produces white light. If you create slide presentations, computer software or games, or anything else that will be viewed on a video monitor, you use the RGB system. (That explains the RGB button in the Edit Color dialog box.)

The process colors used in four-color printing are a subtractive system. Each color—cyan, magenta, and yellow—is created by subtracting red, green, or blue from white light. Combining 100 percent of process cyan, magenta, and yellow theoretically creates black; but in fact it creates a muddy brown, so black ink is used to create a pure black and to deepen shadows.

Having to turn to a color swatch book to choose your colors instead of just experimenting with colors on-screen takes some of the magic away from a color monitor, but it's the only way to ensure that you get the results you want. If you're ever tempted to ignore this advice, remember that of the 16 million colors you can display on a 24-bit monitor, only a fraction can be printed.

If it drives you crazy to look at colors on-screen that are far from the printed result (and that can be the case), you can work backward. Create the publication with on-screen colors that are what you want; then use a swatch book to match those colors as closely as possible, and change the color definitions just before sending for final output. This can work well for publications with relatively simple color palettes, but with a complex use of color, it creates additional work and room for error.

If you do a lot of color work, you'll want to follow industry developments in color management. The current development is Color Management Systems (CMS), the goal of which is to make color consistent as data moves across a specified publishing system (from scanner to monitor to printer). We'll probably see CMS add-ons to PageMaker during the life of version 5; the problem, however, is that there is no single standard for these systems, and the investment of time and money you make early on is likely to require continued investment as these products (and ideally a standard) evolve.

COLOR LIBRARIES

Color work used to be a lot simpler for graphic designers. You had a Pantone swatch book for choosing spot color inks, and you had a book or a chart showing different combinations of process colors for four-color work. As electronic publishing expands the market for color printing, a whole new set of tools is created to meet the perceived need. And that's why PageMaker's Libraries menu, in the Edit Color dialog box, offers a choice of more than a dozen color systems. It's enough to confuse experienced designers, to say nothing of those who are entering publication work through desktop technology.

The most important thing to remember is that the libraries for spot colors—Pantone, DIC (Dainippon), and TOYO—refer to proprietary, premixed inks. You select colors from those libraries only if your commercial printer stocks that system of inks. The libraries for process colors—Focoltone, Munsell, Pantone, and Trumatch—all use combinations of cyan, magenta, yellow, and black. Process colors aren't proprietary and don't belong to any company in the way that spot colors do. What's unique about each process color library is the percentage increments used in combining colors and the way the color swatch books are organized.

Pantone has six libraries on the menu—four for spot colors and two for process. Each of the four spot color libraries adjusts the screen display to most closely approximate how that color will look when printed in different conditions: Pantone Coated is for printing on coated paper and gives the brightest display, Pantone Uncoated is for printing on uncoated paper and so gives a duller screen display, Pantone ProSim displays CMYK simulations of the colors, and Pantone ProSim Euro shows the European standard for the CMYK

TIP

To shorten your Libraries menu, you can delete libraries that you don't use. Library files have AFC or BFC extensions. On the Mac, open the following folders to find those files: System/Aldus/Color. On the PC, open Aldus/USEnglsh/Color.

TIP

If there are certain combinations of colors that you use repeatedly, you can **create your own color libraries.** First create a publication with the colors you want in the library. Then choose Create Color Library (from the Aldus Additions list on the Utilities menu), and give that collection of colors a name. PageMaker creates a library containing those colors, and it will appear on the Libraries pull-down list in the Edit Color dialog box.

simulations. (Ink standards are different in Europe and in the United States.) The two libraries for process colors correspond to the printed swatch books for the U.S. and the European standards. Even with all these options, you still have to refer to a swatch book to see the color you'll get in print!

Some printers will supply color charts for specifying process colors; and you'll find swatch books for spot and process colors in art supply stores. You'll also find vendor information for each on-line library if you click the About button when that library is displayed. (This *is* licensing, after all!)

You don't have to select a color from a PageMaker library when you use the swatch books. For spot colors, you can just type in a name or number, and for process colors, you can specify the CMYK percentages, using whatever names you want.

There are, however, advantages to selecting spot colors from a library. You'll have the standard name for the color on each separation (Pantone 3272 CV, say, instead of green), ensuring that your commercial printer knows exactly what ink you want. And you can easily convert spot colors to process, because the library includes the CMYK conversion values. If you're converting Pantone spot colors to process inks, be sure to use the Pantone ProSim library, which has the correct CMYK values specified by Pantone for the conversion. The Coated and Uncoated libraries that shipped with PageMaker 5 do not have the correct percentages; new libraries with the correct CMYK values should be available on the Aldus on-line forums.

The merits of choosing a color from one of the on-line process color libraries is more subjective. If you choose a color from a library, you'll get a name such as Trumatch 26-a2. The name doesn't mean much, but it's very easy to locate in the Trumatch swatch book, and there is a suggestion of the color in the Color Palette, next to the name. If you type the percentages for that same color from the swatch book—Y30 M6 C90 K12—and give it whatever name you want, you have the exact same color and the same separations. You have to decide which is method is faster and which name is more useful for you.

There are two other libraries—Grays and Crayon—that aren't licensed by anyone. If you like crayon colors, choose a color from the Crayon library, and PageMaker inserts the CMYK percentages. The Grays library displays grays in 1 percent increments, for both spot and process colors. (All the percentages of a spot gray will print on the same separation.) You can achieve the same effect by defining a percentage of black. But if you want to add a range to grays to your default Color Palette, see the bottom tip on page 449. Having a range of grays on your Color Palette is very useful; it expands the slim selection on the Fill submenu, and it makes the grays more accessible than those on the submenu.

COLOR PREPRESS OPTIONS

Now that you know how to create color pages in PageMaker, the question remains: How do you get your pages to plate-ready film separations? As we said at the beginning of this project, you can print separations directly from PageMaker, but that isn't the only option.

The evolution of desktop technology has introduced a variety of ways to prepare color pages for printing. Interestingly, many experienced designers have begun to pull back a bit and concede that they don't want the responsibility of scanning color photos and dealing with the technicalities

TIP

Graphic images sometimes combine different file formats. If you've imported an EPS graphic that has within it a **Desktop Color Separation (DCS) image**—such as the art on page 433, for example, which is a FreeHand EPS graphic that includes a DCS file imported into FreeHand from Photoshop—you need to use a special filter to correctly separate the file.

The recommended procedure is to move the default EPS import filter to the Alternate Filters folder or directory and to move the EPS Import Nested DCS Filter from the Alternate Filters folder or directory to the Filters folder or directory. The special filter must be active both when you place the file and when you print. If the graphic is already placed, switch the filters, restart PageMaker, and use the Replacing Graphic option to place the graphic again in the same size and position as the original graphic. Be sure to alert your service bureau to the presence of nested DCS files.

The special filter will read color information for all imported EPS graphics, but it's slower than the standard EPS filter. So switch back to the standard filter for jobs that don't include nested DCS images.

of color prepress. If that's your feeling too, you can still make good use of PageMaker's color capabilities in design and layout while relying on experienced color professionals to scan color photos and output files to the specifications of your commercial printer. For a publication created in PageMaker, there are four basic options and numerous ways to combine the different approaches.

1. Print separations directly from PageMaker.

Using the Print/Color dialog box options (described beginning on page 452), you can separate both spot and process color directly in PageMaker. For the best quality, send your PageMaker files to a service bureau for output directly to film. Designers who do a lot of color work and need to do it as inexpensively as possible generally use this method.

Even though you probably won't be printing the final output yourself, you need to understand the Print/Color options—to print composites for proofing, to print test separations before sending files to the service bureau, and to write instructions so that the service bureau outputs the files according to the specifications from your commercial printer.

2. Separate color files through a desktop postprocessing program.

Programs such as Aldus PrePrint, Adobe Separator, and Aldus TrapWise have more sophisticated options for color work than PageMaker has. Some let you balance, sharpen, and otherwise enhance color photographs for reproduction; others have capabilities for automatically trapping overlapping colors or for special printing requirements such as dot gain and ink coverage. After determining your separation requirements with your commercial printer, discuss your needs with the service bureau that will print your separations. They might recommend using one of these desktop programs, or they might recommend the approach described in method 3.

If your service bureau is going to separate the file using a program other than PageMaker, ask whether they want you to send the native PageMaker file or whether they want you to make a PostScript file for separations (in which case, see page 238).

3. Link to a high-end commercial separation system.

Designers who need to incorporate high quality color photos into electronic layouts often work with a service bureau or commercial printer using a method that links PageMaker to high-end color systems such as Hell ScriptMaster and Crosfield StudioLink. This is made possible through the Open Prepress Interface (OPI), an extension of PostScript that describes the way scanned images are used.

Typically, you send a color photo to a color separator or to a service bureau that specializes in color. They make two scans of your image—a high-resolution commercial scan and a low-res TIFF. They send you the low-res scan to position, scale, and crop in PageMaker. When you send the PageMaker file (or a PostScript version of it) back to the service bureau or color house, they link the low-res image with the high-res scan and print film separations. All the placement, sizing, and cropping you applied in PageMaker is retained.

This method gives you maximum layout control of all the elements on your page, saves the stripping costs incurred in traditional color prepress (see method 4), but leaves the responsibility for color in the hands of color professionals. It also saves disk space (high-res scans take up huge amounts of memory) and speeds up screen redraw time (because you're only working with the low-res images).

4. Combine PageMaker with conventional color separation.

You can lay out the page in PageMaker, place a scan or photostat for position only (FPO) to indicate the size and position of color art or photos, and let the printer separate the art and strip it into the PageMaker-created page. Using this method, you have two options if you want color in type or in PageMaker graphics such as rules and boxes. You can specify those colors in the PageMaker file and print separations into which the printer strips the art. Or you can specify color on a tissue overlay on the camera-ready pages, and the printer will create all the film separations. Using any variation of this method, the printer takes responsibility for the quality of the color separation and for the registration of the elements in the separations and charges you accordingly. If you want the highest quality reproduction for color photographs, or if desktop color seems too much on the pioneering edge for you, this is the route to take.

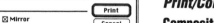

PRINTING COLOR PAGES FROM PAGEMAKER

In the course of printing color files—either composites for proofing or separations—you may need to select options in all four of PageMaker's Print dialog box displays. And you will need to include information about these options in the work order that accompanies your color files to the service bureau. We'll review the options that relate specifically to printing color files and include some early warnings from Aldus about known problems with separating color in PageMaker.

Print/Document Display

Type Be sure to specify the printer being used for final output (for example, your service bureau's imagesetter). This tells PageMaker which PPD to use (see page 229 for more on PPDs), and the PPD includes important information for color separations.

Proof If you have a lot of color art in your publication and you are printing pages to check text, you can speed up print time by checking this option. PageMaker prints a box with an X in the center in place of each graphic.

Print/Color

Composite Choose one of these options to print all the colors on a single page for proofing.

Grayscale or **Color** Choose Grayscale to proof your pages on a black-and-white printer. PageMaker simulates the color intensity using shades of gray. So a forest green will print darker than a sky blue, which will print darker than a soft pink. If you're printing to a color printer, the Grayscale option is replaced by a Color option, and you choose that.

Print Colors in Black Use this option for pages with two or fewer spot colors that will be separated by your commercial printer. All colors print as a percentage of black necessary to make a proper separation. Forest green, sky blue, and soft pink will all print as black; a 20% tint of any of those colors will print as 20% black; and so on.

TIP

With all the different graphic formats, it's not surprising that not all of them behave the same in PageMaker. For a useful guide to how some 30 different formats display and print (as composites and as color separations in PageMaker), print the **PM5 Post-Script Printing Chart.** On the Macintosh, the file is in the Page-Maker 5 applications folder, and you can open it through PageMaker. The chart is not available in Windows PageMaker, but it does include Windows graphic formats, so if you work in Windows, get a copy of the chart from a friend who works on a Mac.

TIP

If you use the Group It Addition with color elements, be aware of the following:

When you use the Addition, you must have a color PostScript PPD selected in the Print dialog box. If you don't, the colored elements will be separated as black and white.

If you redefine any process colors used in the grouped elements, the change is not reflected in the group. The grouped elements will separate according to the colors originally applied to them.

If you use Group It with a keyline, see the note on page 441.

Separations Choose this option to proof color separations on your desktop printer before sending for final output. You'll save a lot of money if you catch errors *before* you go to film.

Ink list box The scrollable box below the Separations option lists all four process color inks, any spot colors defined in your publication, and any spot colors imported with a color graphic. A mark next to the ink name indicates that PageMaker should print a separation for that ink. (On the Mac, you'll see a check mark, on the PC, an X.) To select (or deselect) an ink for printing, double-click on the name. Or highlight the name and choose Print This Ink.

Be sure to review the list carefully and select the inks you want to print. And include a list of inks to print in the work order.

Be aware that the Ink list box includes all spot colors defined in the publication, whether or not those colors are actually applied to elements on the page. Also, when you import EPS graphics from some applications, all the colors defined in the graphic file are imported and included on the Ink list, again whether or not the colors are used in the graphic. PageMaker will print a separation for every color (spot or process) selected in the Ink list, whether or not that color is actually applied to an element in the publication. If you defined numerous colors that you didn't use and you don't review the Ink list carefully, you can end up with a lot of blank pieces of film. Fortunately, only process colors are selected to print by default, so you have to make a conscious decision about which spot inks to print.

Print All Inks and **Print No Inks** These buttons do just what they say: They select, or deselect, all the inks on the list.

All to Process Click this button if you want to convert all the spot color inks defined in the publication to process colors. Remember that every spot color ink prints on a different separation. If you have a color photo and three spot colors, you'd have seven separations and a very expensive print job. When you click All to Process, PageMaker uses the CMYK conversions in whichever spot color library you selected the color from. To convert individual spot color inks to process, use the Define Colors dialog box (see page 436).

Note: Aldus warns that Adobe Photoshop duotones won't separate when you select All to Process in the Print dialog box. In this situation, you have to convert each spot color to process through the Define Colors dialog box.

Optimized Screen (PostScript printers only) The pull-down list displays the screen ruling and printer resolution combinations listed in the selected PPD file (the printer selected in the Type field in the Print/Document display). The line screen (lines per inch, or lpi) is the density of the dots used to print colors, tints, and halftones; it's determined by your commercial printer, based on the press and the paper that you're using. The printer resolution (measured in dots per inch, or dpi) should match the Target Printer Resolution specified in the Page Setup dialog box; you generally print film separations at 2540 dpi. Always discuss these settings with your commercial printer. (See pages 393–94 for a discussion of line screen and printer resolution.)

Angle and **Ruling** (PostScript printers only) In color printing, each color is printed as a pattern of dots called a halftone screen. This is essentially the same process used to print continuous-tone photos that we looked at in

TIP

If you import **Photo CD** images, PageMaker displays a special import filter dialog box in which you specify a color format and resolution. For Resolution, choosing Let Application Decide uses the resolution appropriate for the selected PPD. Be aware, also, that the Photo CD format stores color information in RGB format, which PageMaker can't separate directly. To work around this, use an image-editing program to convert the image to a CMYK TIFF or a DCS image.

Project 7 (see pages 392–94). But in color printing, the lines of dots for each process color are printed at a different angle. With the proper angles, the dots form a rosette pattern that the eye easily blends into different colors. When the angles are incorrect, the dots form a cross-hatching pattern, or moiré.

The setting selected from the Optimized Screen pull-down list includes the information for screen rulings and angles for process inks. These generally are not the same angles used in traditional color prepress, but they do produce the best results when you print PageMaker separations on PostScript imagesetters.

Note: The Ruling and Angle settings in the Print dialog box don't affect images to which you've applied screen ruling and angle settings through the Image Control command (on the Element menu).

Negative (PostScript printers only) Always ask your commercial printer how to print color separations. If film negatives are requested, check the Negative option; for film positives, leave that option unchecked.

Mirror (PostScript printers only) The Mirror setting determines whether the film will be right-reading or wrong-reading, emulsion side up or down. Use the following table to get the desired results in PageMaker. (Don't be led astray by information in the PageMaker User Manual that gives different settings. Aldus corrected this in the Read Me file on the application disks.)

	Right-Reading		Wrong-Reading	
Emulsion side	up	down	up	down
Set Mirror to	off	on	on	off

Preserve EPS Colors (PostScript printers only) Turn this option on if you've applied PageMaker colors to imported EPS graphics and want to print with the colors specified in the original source file.

Print/Options Display

Several settings in this dialog box are relevant to color files. In fact, the first two are essential.

Printer's Marks Turn this on to print crop marks (to trim the pages correctly), registration marks (to align the color separations on press), a density-control bar (to check press calibration), and a color-control bar (to check color accuracy on color proofs).

Page Information Turn this on to print the name of the process or spot color on each separation. (PageMaker also prints the filename, date, and page number.)

TIP

If you include **color screen captures** in PageMaker layouts, be aware that PageMaker will not separate them directly. The color captures will separate if you output your color pages through PrePrint or through some high-end systems (such as Scitex). But the black type will print as a four-color black, which always presents a registration problem. To work around that, the color captures in this book were converted to CMYK TIFFs in Photoshop, and the information in the CMY channels for the type was deleted.

Graphics (PostScript printers only) These options determine how TIFF images print.

   Normal Choose this when printing separations directly from PageMaker.

   Optimized Choose this if you want PageMaker to eliminate data that the printer can't use (if, for example, you scanned a photo at a higher resolution than you need given the resolution of the output device). See page 396 for details.

   Low TIFF Resolution Choose this to speed up printing proofs. Imported bit-mapped images print at 25–72 dpi, instead of at the higher resolution of the imported or linked file.

Omit TIFF Files Choose this if you are printing a PostScript file for a link to an OPI postprocessing system.

Write PostScript to File (PostScript printers only) Choose this if you are creating PostScript files for use with postprocessing software or an OPI-compatible system. See page 240 for details.

Print/Paper Display

Center Page in Print Area Some desktop color printers offset the printed page asymmetrically from the edge of the paper. Turn this option on to have the image centered.

Reduce to Fit Turn this option on to fit Printer's Marks and Page Information when you print test separations of 8.5- by 11-inch pages on desktop printers. Be sure to turn this option off before sending for final output.

PROOFING COLOR PAGES

Color pages require more proofing stages than black-and-white pages do. You'll use at least three or four of the following stages in the course of producing most color publications:

Black-and-white composites Use this throughout the publication cycle to check layout and text as you would in a black-and-white file. Page-Maker's default setting is to print Grayscale composites. See page 452.

Test separations from your desktop printer The less experience you have producing color pages, the more important it is to print test separations on your desktop printer. You can check that you've applied the right color to the right elements and that you're getting the knockouts and overprinting you want. In order to check your traps, you'll need to look at the separations on a light table, and even then it's difficult given the small size of the overprinting line generally used for traps.

Color comps from a desktop color printer The proofs provided by desktop color printers enable you to check the overall use of color in the design and whether the correct colors are applied to the correct elements. Many service bureaus can provide them, and they are very useful, but they are not an accurate guide to the color itself, nor do they reveal problems with trapping or moiré pattern.

Color proofs The best way to check your color pages is on a laminated color proof such as a Cromalin or Matchprint. They're created from the actual film separations (whereas color comps are created from the electronic file). The printed page won't match the color proof exactly, but it's as close as you can get before going on press, with a fairly accurate indication of trapping as well. Many service bureaus that provide film separations also provide these proofs. And of course so do printers who provide conventional color separations.

A less expensive proofing system is overlay proofs, in which each separation is printed on an acetate sheet the same color as one of the process inks. You can't use them to predict the final color of the printed page, but you can check overprinting, knockouts, and traps.

GLOSSARY

TIP

New Additions will periodically become available from both Aldus and third-party developers. You'll find information about them on the Aldus forum on CompuServe, in *Aldus Magazine,* and from user groups.

Additions Utilities that you install to perform special tasks while working in PageMaker, such as automatically inserting drop caps, grouping PageMaker elements into a single unit, and transposing pages in the layout. About 20 Additions are packaged with PageMaker 5.0 and can be installed as part of the program installation. Others are available from independent developers. See also *script.*

Aldus Additions A command on the Utilities menu that displays a list of installed Additions. See also *Additions.*

alignment The placement of type relative to the margins. See also *centered, flush left, flush right, force justify, justified, ragged right,* and *wraparound text.*

alley The space between two columns of text.

ascender The portion of a lowercase letter, such as "b" or "f," that rises above the x-height.

ASCII An acronym for American Standard Code for Information Interchange, the form in which text-only files are stored. These files include all characters, tabs, and carriage returns, but not character and paragraph formatting such as italic, boldface, hanging indents, and so on.

autoflow The fastest mode for text placement in PageMaker, in which text flows continuously from column to column and page to page until the entire file has been placed. To use this mode, select Autoflow from the Layout menu. Compare *manual text flow* and *semi-automatic text flow.*

Auto leading An amount of space between lines that is always proportional to the type size. The PageMaker default for Auto leading is 120% of the type size. So if your type is 10 point, Auto leading is 12; if the type is 14 point, Auto leading is 16.8. (PageMaker rounds off to the nearest tenth of a point.)

bad break A line break that is visually jarring, such as a page that begins with the suffix "ing" or a column that ends with a single word. See also *orphan* and *widow.*

baseline An imaginary line on which the letters in a line of type sit. The baseline aligns with the bottom of the x-height of the characters, and descenders of letters such as "g" and "p" drop below the baseline.

baseline leading A method of leading used in PageMaker that places all of the leading above the line. See also *proportional leading* and *slug.*

baseline shift Moving the baseline of selected text, as in superscripts and subscripts for fractions, footnotes, and some special typographic effects. The option is found in the Control Palette's character view and in the Type Specs/Options dialog box and can be specified in tenth-of-a-point increments.

bit-mapped The representation of a character or graphic as a series of square dots or pixels, which sometimes print with jagged edges. See also *paint-type graphics.*

bleed art Any photo, illustration, or tint that runs off the edge of the page.

blurb Text that summarizes an article, usually set smaller than the headline and larger than the running text. Sometimes used interchangeably with "breakout."

body text The main text, also called body copy or running text, usually set in 9- to 12-point type in continuous paragraphs.

bounding box A rectangular space defined in PageMaker by dragging the mouse diagonally to establish left and right margins between which to place or type text. See also *drag-place.*

TIP

When you specify **Auto leading,** you often need to know the value of that leading in order to determine other measurements on the page. You can calculate the value by multiplying the type size by 120%. Or keep a chart handy:

Type size	Auto leading	
6 point	1.0 point	6/7
7 point	1.5 point	7/8.5
8 point	1.5 point	8/9.5
9 point	2.0 point	9/11
10 point	2.0 point	10/12
11 point	2.0 point	11/13
12 point	2.5 point	12/14.5
13 point	2.5 point	13/15.5
14 point	3.0 point	14/17

TIP

To have different **column-guide** settings on the right and left pages, choose the Set Right and Left Pages Separately option in the Column Guides dialog box.

breakout A sentence excerpted from the body copy and set in large type, used to break up running text and draw the reader's attention to the page. Also called a pull quote or blurb.

bullet A typographic element used to designate items in a list. The keystroke for the commonly used round bullet is Option-8 on a Mac, Ctrl-Shift-8 on a PC.

byline The name of the author of an article.

callout A label that identifies an element in an illustration.

camera-ready Photographs, art, and complete pages in a form that the printer can photograph for making printing plates.

cap height The height of a capital letter in a given font and size.

center axis The imaginary center line through a page, a text block, or a piece of art.

centered Aligned along a center axis.

character An individual letter or symbol.

clip art Public-domain art, either in books or on disks, that you can use free of charge and without credit in a publication.

Clipboard An electronic holding place for the most recent cut or copy made from a document. Whatever is on the Clipboard can be pasted into the current document. When you shut down, whatever is on the Clipboard is lost.

CMYK An acronym for cyan, magenta, yellow, and black (the last denoted by K to avoid confusion with blue), the four process colors from which all other colors are made in four-color printing.

Color Palette A list of colors defined for a publication that you can display by choosing the Color Palette command from the Window menu or by pressing Command-K on a Mac, Ctrl-K on a PC.

column guides Nonprinting vertical rules in a PageMaker document that determine the left and right margins of text that you type or place. You can specify columns through the Column Guides command on the Layout menu and reposition them manually with the pointer tool.

column rules Thin vertical rules separating columns of type.

composite A printout in which you see all the colors on a single page rather than printed on individual separations. Compare *separation*.

condensed type Type in which the individual character is narrower than normal, giving you more characters per line. You can condense type in Page-Maker through the Set Width option in the Control Palette character view or in the Type Specs dialog box.

continued line A line of text indicating the page on which an article continues, or the carryover line on the subsequent page that identifies the story being continued. Also called a jumpline.

continuous tone The smooth gradation of tones from light to dark in a black-and-white or color photograph.

Control Palette A floating window with three different views: one for applying character formatting (such as font and type size), one for applying paragraph formatting (such as indents and space before and after paragraphs), and one for manipulating objects (such as position and size). To display and hide the Control Palette, press Command-apostrophe on a Mac or Ctrl-apostrophe on a PC, or choose the Control Palette command from the Window menu.

copy fitting Editing text to fit a specified space.

copyright Ownership of a work by the writer, artist, photographer, or publisher.

TIP

When you need **to estimate the number of words** that will fit in a column or a layout, place the Copy-fit file that is installed with PageMaker 5.0. It's a text file composed of five-letter nonwords, with a word-count every twenty-fifth word. The file looks terrible on the page (an unbroken stream of five-letter words gives type a very monotonous color), but it can provide the information you need. To place this file on the Mac, follow this path: System/Aldus/Utilities. On the PC, the path is Aldus/USEnglsh/Utility.

TIP

When you open a PageMaker 4 publication in PageMaker 5, be aware of the following:

- Line breaks may be different. PageMaker 5 calculates character width in ¹/₂₀th-of-a point units, whereas PageMaker 4 used information from the target printer's driver file. Hyphenation is calculated differently as well.

- You may need to relink imported EPS graphics even if the graphics aren't required for remote printing. The probable cause is that the new EPS filter in version 5 doesn't recognize the graphic stored in the publication until an up-to-date link is established.

- Gray tones may print darker on 300- and 600-dpi printers in version 5 than they did in version 4.

- All colors defined in PageMaker 4 files are read as spot colors in PageMaker 5. See page 446.

TIP

To deselect one item from a large group of selected items, hold down the Shift key and click on the item you want to deselect. Similarly, **to add an item to a group of selected items,** hold down the Shift key and click on the item you want to add.

counter The white space inside a closed letter such as "a," "e," or "p."

crop To trim a graphic to fit a space without reducing the size of the graphic.

crop marks Intersecting lines indicating where a page is to be trimmed. To print crop marks, turn on Printer's Marks in the Print/Options dialog box. Crop marks are also used to indicate the art that will be stripped in by the printer.

cropping tool The PageMaker tool used to trim graphics.

crossbar The shape of PageMaker's pointer when you select any of the drawing tools.

crossover Type or art that extends across the gutter between two pages. Alignment of crossover elements is critical.

cursor keys A set of four keys that can move the I-beam or a selected object in the directions indicated by the arrows on the keys: up, down, right, and left.

deck A line following the headline that gives more information about a newsletter, magazine, or newspaper story. Also called a tagline.

default A preset value or option that is used unless you specify otherwise.

descender The portion of a lowercase letter, such as "g" or "y," that drops below the baseline of the type.

deselect To turn off a command or an option by clicking on it when it is currently selected. Also, to cancel the selection of text and graphics in the publication window by clicking elsewhere on the page.

dialog box A box displayed on the screen that enables you to select or specify options and values.

digital halftone A photo that has been converted, through the scanning process, to a series of dots that can be stored and manipulated electronically and then printed as part of the electronically composed page. See also *halftone.*

dingbat A decorative or symbolic device used to separate items on a page or to highlight each item on a list.

discretionary hyphen A hyphen inserted manually by pressing Command-hyphen on a Mac, Ctrl-hyphen on a PC. A discretionary hyphen shows on-screen and on the printed page only if it is used to break a word at the end of a line.

display type Large type, often boldface, used for headlines, breakouts, and other attention-getting text.

dots per inch (dpi) The measurement of the resolution of a printer.

download To send printer fonts from your computer to your printer. You can let PageMaker automatically download a font each time you use it, or (to save time) you can manually download a font. Fonts that you download manually remain in the printer's memory until you turn off the printer.

downloadable fonts Individual fonts that you can buy and install in your desktop-publishing system.

drag To hold down the mouse button while you move the pointer to a new location on the screen.

drag-place To drag the mouse diagonally, defining the width of a graphic or text block before you place it. See also *bounding box.*

draw-type graphics See *object-oriented graphics.*

drop cap An enlarged initial letter that drops below the first line of body text. Compare *stick-up cap.*

dummy A term that can mean different things in different organizations: a rough preliminary sketch of a publication or story, an early proof with type and rough art in place, or a mock-up of an entire publication.

ellipsis Three dots (…) used to indicate an incomplete thought or a place where text has been deleted from a quote. You can create an ellipsis character by typing Option-semicolon on a Mac, Alt-0133 on a PC.

em dash A dash the width of an em space, inserted by pressing Option-Shift-hyphen on a Mac, Ctrl-Shift-equal sign on a PC.

em space A typographic unit equal to the point size of the type being used. For 10-point type, an em space would be 10 points. To insert an em space in PageMaker, press Command-Shift-M on a Mac, Ctrl-Shift-M on a PC.

Encapsulated PostScript A file format that enables you to print line art with smooth (rather than jagged) edges and to see and resize the graphic on-screen as it will print. EPS files can be created in graphics programs that produce PostScript code (such as Illustrator or FreeHand) or with the EPS option in PageMaker's PostScript Print/Options dialog box. EPS images do not print well on non-PostScript printers.

en dash A dash the width of an en space, inserted by pressing Option-hyphen on a Mac, Ctrl-equal sign on a PC.

en space A space half as wide as an em space, inserted by pressing Command-Shift-N on a Mac, Ctrl-Shift-N on a PC. In this glossary, the space between each term and its definition is an en space.

face A named type design, such as Times Roman or Helvetica.

fill A pattern or texture inside a rectangle or other closed shape. See the Fill submenu on the Element menu for fills available in PageMaker. Other art programs may have additional fills that can be used in imported graphics.

filter A file that transfers text or graphics in one application into a format that another application can recognize. When you install PageMaker, you install numerous text and graphic filters. In certain dialog boxes, you can choose a filter from a pull-down menu, but other than that choice, the work done by filters is invisible to you.

fixed space A space inserted between two characters by pressing Option-Spacebar on a Mac, Ctrl-Shift-H on a PC. A fixed space is the width of a regular word space, but PageMaker will not break a line on either side of a fixed space. Also called a nonbreaking space.

flush Aligned or even with, as in flush left or flush right text.

flush left Aligned along the left edge or margin.

flush right Aligned along the right edge or margin.

fold marks Dotted or dashed lines, printed outside the image area on camera-ready art, that indicate where to fold the printed piece.

folio The page number.

font In desktop publishing, sometimes used interchangeably with "face" to refer to the entire family of characters of a particular shape or design, such as Helvetica. In traditional typesetting, font refers to only one size and style of a given typeface, such as 10-point Helvetica roman or 12-point Helvetica Bold.

font substitution The way in which an application substitutes a font that is installed in your system for a font that is called for in the document but is not installed in your system.

footer See *running foot*.

force justify An alignment option that adds space between characters in order to force the line to fill to the right margin.

format The overall appearance of a publication, including page size, paper, binding, length, and page-design elements such as margins, number of columns, treatment of headlines, and so on.

> **TIP**
>
> **The size of a PageMaker-generated EPS graphic** is defined by the page size you create the graphic on, not by the graphic itself. Reducing the page size before you make the EPS file means you won't have to crop the image when you place it in another PageMaker document.

> **TIP**
>
> When you **force-justify headlines** with two or more words, you must insert a fixed space between the words (Option-Spacebar on a Mac, Ctrl-Shift-H on a PC). This tells PageMaker to add extra space between letters and between words. If you use a regular Spacebar character, PageMaker adds all the extra space between words.

TIP

Because **paragraph attributes** (such as indents and space before and after) apply to the entire paragraph rather than to selected characters, you don't have to drag through the entire paragraph. Simply set an insertion point anywhere in the paragraph, and the formatting you specify will apply to the entire paragraph.

formatting Type and paragraph specifications that are applied in a word-processing or page layout program.

for position only A low-resolution scan, or a photocopy or photostat of a piece of art pasted in place on the camera-ready page, indicating the position of the actual art that is to be stripped in by the printer. Usually written as FPO.

galley Traditionally, a proof of type before it is arranged on the page; used for proofreading and layout. (The term derives from the long, shallow metal trays used to hold metal type after it had been set.) In desktop publishing, you may still want to print galleys to the specified column width in your page layout program for proofreading.

gatefold A paper fold in which one or two sides of an oversize page fold in toward the middle of the sheet.

Gothic-style typefaces Sans serif typefaces.

grabber hand A PageMaker icon invoked by pressing the Option key on a Mac, the Alt key on a PC, and dragging the mouse; used to move around in the publication window.

graphic boundary A nonprinting dotted line around a graphic that determines how close text can come to the graphic. The distance between the graphic boundary and the graphic is called the standoff and is defined through the Text Wrap command on PageMaker's Element menu.

greeking The process of simulating text as gray bars in order to speed screen display (an option available through PageMaker's Preferences command). Also used to refer to Latin text in rough layouts and dummies.

grid A series of nonprinting vertical and horizontal rules used to determine placement of text and graphics on the page.

gutter The space between two facing pages. The term is sometimes used to refer to the space between two columns of text.

hairline rule A very thin typographic rule. In desktop publishing, the width of a hairline rule varies depending on the resolution of the printer.

halftone The representation of a continuous-tone photograph or illustration as a series of dots that look like gray tones when printed. Also called a screened halftone because traditionally the original image is photographed through a finely ruled screen, the density of which varies depending on the printer's capabilities. See also *digital halftone*.

handles Used in PageMaker to refer to the eight small, solid rectangles that surround a selected graphic. See also *windowshade handles*.

hanging indent A paragraph style in which the left margin of the first line extends beyond the left margin of subsequent lines.

hard return A line break that signals the end of a paragraph, created by pressing Return or Enter. See also *new-line character*.

header See *running head*.

hidden characters Characters that you insert but don't usually see, such as those created by pressing the Tab, Spacebar, Return, or Enter key. You can see these characters in story view if you turn on Display ¶ from the Story menu.

Hyphenation Zone An option in the Hyphenation dialog box that specifies how close to the end of a line PageMaker can insert a hyphen. The smaller the number, the closer to the end of a line words can be hyphenated and the more hyphenated words you'll have.

I-beam The shape PageMaker's pointer assumes when you select the text tool.

image area The area inside the page margins. Some page elements, such as page-number markers, are placed outside the image area.

TIP

Sometimes you want **to temporarily slide an item or group of items off the page** and onto the pasteboard. If you hold down the Shift key when you drag the items off and then back onto the page, you will be able to easily reposition them with the same horizontal alignment they had before you moved them. The same technique works for vertical movement as well.

imagesetter An output device, such as the Linotronic, that produces high-resolution pages from desktop-generated files.

initial cap A first letter set in enlarged and sometimes decorative type for graphic emphasis.

ink-level overprinting A specification that instructs PageMaker to print one color ink over another. To specify ink-level overprinting, use the Edit Color dialog box to create a tint of a color and turn on the overprint option. Compare *knockout* and *object-level overprinting*.

inline graphic A graphic that is anchored to a position within a text block. To insert an inline graphic, set an insertion point with the text tool before placing or pasting the graphic.

insertion point A blinking vertical bar indicating where the next text block will be typed or pasted. The position of the insertion point is set by clicking the I-beam on the page.

inside margin The space between the binding edge of the page and the text.

italic type Type designed with letters that slant toward the right, often used for display text and captions. Compare *oblique type*.

jaggies The stair-stepped appearance of bit-mapped art and type created by diagonal lines in a technology that is based on square pixels.

jumpline See *continued line*.

justified Type that is flush, or even, along both the right and left margins.

kerning The process of adjusting the space between letter pairs, used primarily in headlines and other display type. PageMaker offers three levels of kerning: $1/100$, $1/25$, and $1/10$ of an em increments. See also *range kerning*.

keyline Traditionally, an outline indicating the shape, size, and position of art to be stripped in by the commercial printer. In PageMaker, you can use the Create Keyline Addition to create rectangles that are the same size as, or a specified amount larger or smaller than, an image in the layout.

kicker A phrase preceding a headline that provides information about the story.

kiss-fit In overlapping colors, a white shape in the background color that is the same shape and size as the foreground object. See also *knockout;* compare *overprinting* and *trap*.

knockout The default setting in color separations by which PageMaker eliminates a background color so that it does not mix with an overlapping color.

landscape A horizontal orientation, wider than it is tall, for pages or photographs. Compare *portrait*.

layout The arrangement of text and graphics on a page.

layout view The default PageMaker mode, in which you create and manipulate elements as they appear on the page. See also *story view*.

leader A line or row of dots between two items in a table, specified through the Indents/Tabs dialog box. Also, a rule that moves the eye from a callout or label to the part of the illustration it describes.

leading The distance from the baseline of one line of text to the baseline of the next, measured in points.

leading grid An approach to page layout in which all vertical measurements take into account the leading of the body copy to ensure the alignment of baselines of text in adjacent columns and pages.

letterspacing The amount of space between letters. In PageMaker, you can control letterspacing through the Spacing option in the Paragraph Specs dialog box.

TIP

To visually align roman type with italic type directly above or below it, indent the left margin of the roman type a couple of points from the left margin of the italic type (the exact amount depends on the typeface and size).

line screen The resolution at which halftone art is printed. Also called screen ruling and screen frequency. See also *lines per inch (lpi)*.

line slug See *slug*.

lines per inch (lpi) The density of the lines of dots used to reproduce a continuous tone photograph, a tinted box, and gray or colored type. The density varies depending on the paper and printing press used.

Linotronic A high-resolution PostScript printer that outputs pages as paper or film at resolutions of up to 2540 dots per inch.

Links A set of PageMaker features that tracks changes made to the original source files of text and graphics placed in a publication.

logotype A company, product, or publication name designed as a distinctly recognizable unit.

magic stretch See *printer-resolution scaling*.

magnifier tool An icon that looks like a magnifying glass, which you click to enlarge or reduce the page view. To display the tool for enlarging the page view, press Command-Spacebar on the Mac, Ctrl-Spacebar on the PC. To display the tool for reducing the page view, press Command-Option-Spacebar on the Mac, Ctrl-Alt-Spacebar on the PC.

manual text flow A mode of placing text in PageMaker in which the text flow stops at the end of a column; you must click on the windowshade handle at the bottom of the text block to reload the text icon and continue placing text in the next column or page. Compare *autoflow* and *semi-automatic text flow*.

margin The distance from the edge of the paper to the image area occupied by text and graphics.

margin guide A nonprinting dotted rule that appears on every page of a PageMaker document, as specified in the Page Setup dialog box.

marquee See *selection box*.

master page The page, identified by an L (for left) or an R (for right) icon in the lower left of PageMaker's publication window, on which you create elements that will appear on all the actual pages of the document. Master-page items can be printing items (such as running heads) or nonprinting items (such as ruler and column guides).

masthead Traditionally, the listing of staff, ownership, and subscription information for a periodical. The term is sometimes used to refer to the typographic treatment of the publication name on the cover, although that is more accurately called a nameplate.

measure The length of a line of type, traditionally expressed in picas.

mechanical Traditionally, a piece of artboard with type galleys, line art, and for-position-only photostats in place and with tissue overlays marked for color. In electronic publishing, a mechanical is the final camera-ready page produced by either a laser printer or an imagesetter, with position-only stats keyed to flat art that is to be stripped in by the printer. Also called a pasteup or camera-ready page.

menu A list of commands that appears when you point to any of the items listed just above the publication window (File, Edit, Type, and so on).

menu bar The area at the top of the screen containing menu names.

mini-save An automatic save of a document, which PageMaker generates each time you click a page icon, change the page setup, insert or delete a page, or switch back and forth between story and layout views. You can revert to the last mini-save by holding down the Shift key when you select the Revert command on the File menu.

TIP

A late and undocumented addition to the **linking feature** is the upside-down question mark (¿) that appears to the right of the page number in the Links dialog box. This symbol indicates that the graphic will not print correctly at high resolution. To find out why, select the name of the graphic in the document list, and then review the details in the Status field at the bottom of the dialog box.

In PageMaker's **Open and Place dialog boxes,** you can use the up and down arrow keys to move through a list of filenames; when you reach the file you want, press Return or Enter. You can also type the first letter (or first few letters) of the filename and then press Return or Enter.

If your text is behaving peculiarly, try these troubleshooting techniques:

• **Global recompose:** To force PageMaker to recompose all the text in a publication, hold down the Option key on a Mac, the Shift key on a PC, while choosing Hyphenation from the Type menu. On the PC, PageMaker also re-composes the text any time you press OK in the Page Setup dialog box.

• **To repair a corrupted publication:** With the pointer tool active and nothing selected, hold down Option-Shift on a Mac, Ctrl-Shift on a PC, while choosing Hyphenation. If PageMaker finds no errors in the file, it beeps once. If it finds and corrects an error, it beeps twice; if it finds a problem but can't fix it, it beeps three times.

modular layout A format in which different elements on a page or spread are designed as self-contained units.

moiré A cross-hatching pattern that results from improperly aligned screens used in producing halftones and tints.

monospacing Letterspacing that is the same for all characters regardless of their shape or width. Traditional typewriter characters are monospaced. Compare *proportional spacing.*

Multiple Paste A command on the Edit menu through which you can dupli-cate an object that you just copied. You specify the number of copies that you want and the horizontal and vertical distance at which each copy should be pasted relative to the one before. In some applications, this function is called "step and repeat." To achieve the same effect manually, see *power-paste.*

nameplate The typographic design of a publication's name as it appears on the cover of the publication.

negative leading A type specification in which there is less space from baseline to baseline than the size of the type itself (for example, 40-point type with 38-point leading). Negative leading is often used with larger type sizes set in all caps in order to tighten up the text unit.

new-line character A character inserted by pressing Shift-Return on the Mac, Shift-Enter on the PC, that instructs PageMaker to begin a new line with-out applying the attributes of a new paragraph. Also called a soft return.

nonbreaking space A space that will not allow a line break on either side. See also *em space, en space, fixed space,* and *thin space.*

nudge buttons Small arrows in some Control Palette fields that you click to manipulate text or graphics in small increments. Click up- and right-pointing arrows to increase the value displayed, click down- and left-pointing arrows to decrease the value. For some options, you can specify the nudge amount through the Preferences dialog box. For others (such as kerning), the nudge amount is fixed.

object-level overprinting A specification that instructs PageMaker to print the fill or line of the selected object over any background object, rather than knocking out the background color. You specify object-level overprinting in the Fill and Line dialog box. See also *ink-level overprinting* and *knockout.*

object-oriented graphics Graphics created as a series of mathematically defined curves and lines. They can be resized without causing distortion or moiré patterns. Also called draw-type graphics.

oblique type A slanted version of a roman typeface. The letters maintain their original forms except for the slant, whereas italic letters have a different shape from their roman counterparts.

OLE Short for object linking and embedding, this is a new way of sharing data between programs.

orphan In PageMaker, defined as the last one, two, or three lines of a para-graph standing at the top of a column. You can instruct PageMaker to disallow orphans through the Paragraph Specs dialog box.

outside margin The space between the outside trim and the text.

overline A brief tag, over a headline, that categorizes a story. Also called a kicker or an eyebrow.

overprinting Printing one color over another. See also *ink-level overprinting, object-level overprinting,* and *knockout.*

page-number marker A key sequence (Command-Option-P on a Macin-tosh, Ctrl-Shift-3 on a PC), generally typed on the master pages, that instructs PageMaker to insert page numbers in the document.

TIP

If a pasteboard item over-laps a page in the document file, PageMaker reads that item as being on the page, and the item will not appear on the pasteboard of other pages in the file. The item will also print outside the image area if the paper size you print on is larger than the page size. So you'll want to remove these items or move them entirely onto the pasteboard before printing final output.

Page Setup The size, orientation, number of pages, and margins for a document; specified in PageMaker's Page Setup dialog box.

page view The amount of the page and surrounding pasteboard seen on the screen, which varies depending on the size of your monitor and the view selected through PageMaker's Layout menu.

paint-type graphics Graphics represented by square dots or pixels, which can be individually manipulated on-screen. These graphics may be distorted or lose resolution when resized. See also *bit-mapped.*

Pantone colors A standardized system of colors, available in printing inks, papers, markers, and other materials, that can be specified in PageMaker.

paragraph rules Rules specified through the Paragraph command, which are anchored to and move with the associated paragraph.

paragraph style See *style.*

pasteboard In a PageMaker document, the area surrounding the page on-screen in which you can leave master items, such as standing headline treatments or spacing guides, as well as any text or graphics, until you are ready to move them into position on the page. Items on the pasteboard appear on the pasteboard of every page of the publication.

pasteup Traditionally, the process of assembling mechanicals by pasting galleys and line art in place. In desktop publishing, traditional pasteup has largely been replaced by electronic page assembly. But pasteup is still a valuable skill for taking care of last-minute corrections.

perpendicular line tool The PageMaker tool used to draw vertical, horizontal, and diagonal lines in 45-degree increments.

perspective The representation on a flat plane of three-dimensional objects as they appear to the eye.

pica A traditional typographic measurement, composed of 12 points. A pica is actually equal to a little less than $1/6$ inch, but in desktop publishing, you will generally see it expressed as $1/6$ inch.

PICT format A Macintosh file format for saving object-oriented graphics.

picture window A rectangle that indicates the position and size of art to be stripped in by the printer.

pixel The smallest dot or unit on a computer screen. The clarity of screen resolution depends on the number of pixels per inch on the monitor.

Place A PageMaker command on the File menu that enables you to import text and graphics created and saved in other applications. You can also place text from another PageMaker document.

placeholder Text or graphics that you leave in place in an electronic template so that you can place, paste, or type new items over the placeholder and retain the same spacing relative to other elements on the page.

PMG The file extension given to the EPS file PageMaker makes when you use the Group It Addition to transform selected elements into a composite graphic.

point The basic measurement of type. There are 12 points to a pica, and 1 point equals about $1/72$ inch.

pointer The icon that moves on the screen as you move the mouse. The shape of the pointer depends on which tool is selected.

pointer tool The PageMaker tool that takes the shape of an arrow on the screen and is used for selecting graphics and text blocks. Other PageMaker tools turn into the pointer tool when you move them into the rulers, menu bars, Style Palette, or page icons.

TIP

When you use the **Group It Addition,** the EPS file that PageMaker makes of the composite graphic is not automatically stored in the publication. So even if that EPS file is smaller than 256 KB (the default limit for automatically storing graphics inside the publication), it is required for remote printing. If you want the composite graphic stored in the publication so that it won't be required for remote printing, select the graphic, choose Link Options from the Element menu, and specify Store Copy in Publication. See page 419 for more on the Group It Addition.

portrait A vertical orientation for pages or photographs. Compare *landscape*.

PostScript A page description language developed by Adobe Systems and used by many laser printers and high-resolution typesetters. It is as close to a standard as there is in desktop publishing at this writing.

power-nudge To increase the nudge amount by a factor of ten, which you can do by holding down the Command key on a Mac, the Ctrl key on a PC, while you click a nudge button. See also *nudge buttons*.

power-paste A key sequence that enables you to paste a copy directly on top of the original. Dragging that copy to a new position sets a spatial relationship that PageMaker will repeat if you continue to power-paste the same copy from the Clipboard. To power-paste, press Command-Shift-V on a Mac, Ctrl-Shift-P on a PC. See also *Multiple Paste*.

PPD Short for PostScript printer description, these files provide PageMaker with information about fonts, paper sizes, and resolution of specific printers. The information is provided by the printer manufacturer. If you use a PostScript printer for proofs or for camera-ready pages, you select a PPD from the Type pull-down menu in the Print/Document dialog box.

ppi Pixels per inch. A measurement of the amount of information in a digital image. Sometimes used interchangeably with dots per inch (dpi) or samples per inch (spi).

Preferences A command on PageMaker's File menu used to specify the unit of measure (inches, picas, millimeters, and so on), nudge increments, resolution for graphic display, typeface for story view text, and a few other options.

prepress Traditionally referred to the work done by a commercial printer after you delivered camera-ready art, work such as creating halftones, stripping art into place, and making color separations. A great deal of the savings afforded by desktop technology comes from the fact that you can do much of the prepress work yourself, supplying the printer with film separations of fully composed pages.

print driver A software file that specifies what kind of printer is connected to the computer.

printer font A mathematical description of every character in a font, which enables a printer to print characters in any size at the best resolution possible on that printer.

printer-resolution scaling Resizing an object to the match the resolution of the printer being used for final output. To use this option in PageMaker, specify the dots per inch value for the printer in the Page Setup dialog box, and then hold down the Command key on a Mac or the Ctrl key on a PC while you drag on a handle to resize. If you're using the Control Palette to resize a graphic, turn on the printer-resolution scaling option. Also called the magic stretch.

printing rule A rule that traps a screen or surrounds a piece of art.

process colors Cyan, magenta, yellow, and black, used to create all the other colors in four-color printing.

proofread To check typeset material for spelling, punctuation, alignment of elements, and other details and to be sure that corrections have been made properly. Standard proofreading marks can be found in many printing reference guides, style manuals, and dictionaries.

proportional leading The default method of leading used in PageMaker that places two-thirds of the specified leading above the text baseline and one-third below it.

TIP

To speed up printing when you want to proofread text and don't need to see graphics, click on the Proof Print option in the Print dialog box. PageMaker will print the text as usual and replace each graphic with a large X.

If you're **unable to select a field or a nudge button in the Control Palette,** you probably need to select a different reference point in the Proxy. When a corner handle is selected, you can change both horizontal and vertical values. When a center handle along the top or bottom edge is selected, you can change the *y*-coordinate (but not the *x*-coordinate) and the value and percentage for height (but not for width). When a center handle along the side edges is selected, you can change the *x*-coordinate (but not the *y*-coordinate) and the value and percentage for width (but not for height).

On a Macintosh, you can **improve PageMaker's performance** by increasing the amount of memory allocated to the application. You can do this only when PageMaker is not open. Click once on the application icon, and press Command-I to display the Get Info dialog box. In the Memory section at the bottom, you'll see that the suggested memory size is 2750 KB. You increase the value by typing a larger value for the Current Size. (We generally run PageMaker at 6000 KB.) More memory is particularly useful if you use a lot of Additions or display TIFFs at high resolution.

proportional scaling Resizing an object so that the height and width maintain the same proportions as the original. To resize proportionally when you use the pointer tool, hold down the Shift key while you drag. To resize proportionally when you specify the height, width, or percentage of original size in the Control Palette, turn on the proportional scaling icon in the Palette.

proportional spacing Letterspacing that is proportional to the shapes of the letters, with the "m" and the "w," for example, taking more space than the "i" and the "l." Compare *monospacing.*

Proxy An icon in the Control Palette's object view with handles that represent the handles of the selected object. The active handle represents the point you are manipulating in the selected object. See also *reference point.*

publication window The image that appears on-screen when a document is open, which includes one or two pages, the title bar, page icons, and—if displayed—rulers, scroll bars, toolbox, and palettes.

pull quote See *breakout.*

rag The shape created by the uneven line breaks in ragged right text.

ragged right Text alignment that is even or flush on the left margin and uneven on the right.

RAM An acronym for random access memory. This is where the computer stores information temporarily while you're working with it. If you lose power or shut down before saving, whatever is in RAM at the time is lost.

range kerning Kerning a selected range of text at one time, rather than manually kerning individual letter pairs. See also *kerning.*

recto The right-hand page.

reference point The active handle in the Control Palette Proxy, which represents the point you are manipulating in the selected object. Changes you specify in the Control Palette are applied as if you had dragged on the handle in the selected object corresponding to the reference point. The *x*- and *y*-coordinates displayed in the Control Palette are also determined by the reference point.

reflect To flip an object horizontally or vertically, which you can do through the reflecting icons in the Control Palette.

registration The alignment of two or more elements, such as a color tone within a box, so that they appear seamless.

registration marks A set of symbols, usually a circle with cross-hair lines through it, placed outside the live area of the page and used by the printer to accurately align overlays or separations in multicolor printing. To specify registration marks in PageMaker, turn on Printer's Marks in the Print/Options dialog box.

resolution The clarity or fineness of detail visible on-screen or in the final printout, expressed as dots per inch. In printed material, the resolution is dependent on the printer's capacity, which in the current desktop technology ranges from 300 dots per inch in most laser printers to 2540 dpi in Linotronic 300 imagesetters.

reverse White letters or rules against a black or color background.

Revert A sort of "multiple undo" command on PageMaker's File menu that lets you return to the last saved version of your document.

Roman-style typefaces Typefaces with serifs. Compare *Gothic-style typefaces;* see also *serif.*

roman type Vertical-style type, as opposed to italic or oblique. In PageMaker's Type Style options, roman type is called Normal; in some word-processing programs, it is called Plain.

TIP

If you have **trouble selecting an item on the page or setting an insertion point** with the text tool, choose the Select All command. This will reveal the handles around every text block and graphic on the page and enable you to spot where overly long windowshade handles or "invisibles" (such as reverse type and white masking boxes that you've lost) may be creating problems.

TIP

You can **place text from one PageMaker document in another.** In the Place dialog box, choose the publication you want to place text from. You'll then see the Place PageMaker Stories dialog box, which displays the first 40 characters of every story in the publication. Use the View button to view the entire text of the high-lighted story. When you select a story and click OK, PageMaker loads the text icon just as it does when you place text from a word processor. Note, however, that when you place PageMaker 4 stories in PageMaker 5, the Place PageMaker Stories dialog box reappears after you select the story you want to place and click OK. The second time you select and click OK, PageMaker loads the text icon.

rule In typography, a straight line, identified by its weight in points.

ruler guide A nonprinting dotted rule used to determine the alignment of text or graphics on the page. You drag guides in from either the vertical or the horizontal ruler, and they function as extensions of the tick marks on the ruler.

runaround text See *wraparound text.*

running foot A line at the bottom of the page with information similar to that in a running head.

running head A line at the top of the page that may include such informa-tion as title, author, chapter, issue date, and page number.

running text See *body text.*

sans serif A typeface without finishing strokes at the ends of the characters. (From the French *sans,* meaning "without.")

scale To enlarge or reduce a graphic so that it fits the space allotted for it.

scanner A hardware device that "reads" a photograph or other piece of art and transforms it into a collection of dots that can be stored as a bit-mapped file on a hard disk, manipulated in various software programs, and placed electronically in a page layout program.

screen A tint, a percentage of either black or a second color, behind text or art. Also called a tone.

screen angle The direction in which halftone dots are lined up.

screen capture A bit-mapped image of the screen, created by pressing Command-Shift-3 on a Mac, PrtSc or Alt-PrtSc on a PC.

screen font The character set that is displayed on-screen as pixels and that calls up the respective printer font when you print a publication.

script a simple set of instructions that automates a task. PageMaker comes with several scripts, including two for creating properly typeset fractions, that you access by choosing Run Script from the Aldus Additions list. You can also write your own scripts to work with PageMaker.

scroll bars The gray bars on the right and bottom sides of a publication window used to move horizontally or vertically around the page. PageMaker's Style and Color Palettes also have scroll bars.

select To indicate where the next action will take place by clicking the pointer on text or graphics or by dragging the cursor across the text.

selection box A box drawn by dragging the pointer tool to enclose and select more than one graphic or text block at a time so that the material can be copied, cut, or moved as a unit. An item must be completely within the selection box in order to be selected, which for text means that the window-shade handles, not visible when you draw the selection box, must be within the box. Also called a marquee.

self-mailer A printed piece designed to be mailed without an envelope. The area for the mailing label and postal indicia, if there are any, must be designed in accordance with postal regulations.

semi-automatic text flow A mode of placing text in PageMaker in which the text flow stops at the end of a column; the text icon is automatically re-loaded and begins flowing text when you click it into position. You invoke the semi-automatic mode by holding down the Shift key with either the autoflow or the manual flow selected. Compare *autoflow* and *manual text flow.*

separation A printout, on paper or film, that shows only one process or spot color used on the page. Compare *composite.*

serif A line or curve projecting from the end of a letter form. Typefaces with these additional strokes are called serif faces.

TIP

If you're unable to move a text block even though you see the four-way directional arrow when you select and drag, you might have extremely long windowshade handles that are blocked by the edge of the pasteboard. Similarly, when you use the Select All command and are unable to move selected items as far in one direction as you'd like, there's probably something on the pasteboard blocking the movement. In either case, choose Show Pasteboard to see the entire pasteboard so that you can shorten the handles or move the obstructing item.

set solid Type in which the leading is 100% of the point size—14/14 for example, or 32/32.

shade In PageMaker, a tone or a pattern chosen from the Fill submenu and used to fill a graphic, such as a banner.

show through Printing on one side of the paper that can be seen on the other; commonly found in lower-quality paper stock.

sidebar A smaller, self-contained story inside a larger one, usually boxed with its own headline to set it apart from the main text.

silhouette A photograph from which the background image has been removed, outlining a subject or group of subjects.

skew To distort an object by slanting it. The skew option in the Control Palette allows horizontal skewing (but not vertical) in 0.01-degree increments from –85 to 85 degrees.

slug In traditional typesetting, a line of type cast in hot metal was called a slug. The PageMaker equivalent is the black selection rectangle that appears when you drag over a line of type. The depth of the rectangle equals the leading of the line. Hence the phrase "line slug."

small caps Capital letters that are smaller than the standard uppercase characters for that typeface and size. You can specify small caps through the Case option in the Control Palette or in the Type Specs dialog box (or press Command-Shift-H on a Mac). The default size for small caps is 70% of the standard cap height; you can customize the size through the Options button in the Type Specs dialog box.

Snap to Guides A command on PageMaker's Guides and Rulers submenu (under Layout) that causes text and graphics being moved or placed to snap to the nearest ruler guide.

Snap to Rulers A command on PageMaker's Guides and Rulers submenu (under Layout) that causes ruler guides, text, and graphics being moved or placed to snap to the nearest ruler tick mark.

soft return See *new-line character*.

spacing guide An element sized to match a distance you need to measure frequently in a given publication, such as the space between pictures and captions.

spot color In PageMaker, a term used to refer to Pantone colors, as distinct from process colors.

spread Two facing pages in a publication.

rectangle tool The tool used to create squares and rectangles.

stacking order The order in which text and graphics overlap on-screen in a PageMaker file. The order can be manipulated through the Bring to Front and Send to Back commands on the Element menu.

standoff The distance between a graphic and the graphic boundary, defined in PageMaker's Text Wrap dialog box. See also *graphic boundary*.

stick-up cap An enlarged initial letter extending above the body text, used as a graphic element to draw attention to the beginning of a story or chapter. Compare *drop cap*.

story In PageMaker, all the text blocks that are part of a threaded text file.

Story Editor The word-processing features built into PageMaker as a separate mode for working in the program.

story view Windows that enable you to create and edit text using PageMaker's Story Editor. You can move back and forth between the layout view and the story view by pressing Command-E on a Mac, Ctrl-E on a PC. See also *layout view*.

TIP

If a keyboard combination doesn't work, ask yourself if that combination is preempted by some other utility installed in your system.

TIP

Be aware of this annoying but harmless **display problem:** When you cut and paste large type with the text tool, the very tops of the letters appear to stay in the old position and the type you paste appears slightly clipped off at the top. The type will print correctly, and it will also display correctly as soon as you refresh your screen. You can force the screen to refresh by using the keyboard shortcut for whatever page view you are currently working in.

TIP

If you ever see the error message, **"Cannot use these specifications. Not a valid measurement,"** you probably deleted a value in the dialog box and failed to specify another in its place. We do this all the time when our intention is to change the value back to 0.

stripping The assembling of all photographic negatives or positives necessary to create a printing plate of the entire page.

style This word has a multitude of meanings in electronic publishing. On Page-Maker's Type menu, style refers to weight, slant, and certain special typographic effects such as outline, shadow, and reverse; we refer to this as a type style. Style also refers to a collection of typographic attributes—such as typeface, size, and indents—specified in the Define Styles command, that can be applied to selected text by clicking on the appropriate name in the Style Palette; we refer to this as a paragraph style because the formatting applies to the entire paragraph. Traditionally, style refers to the broad characteristics of a typeface (such as serif or sans serif).

Style Palette A list of styles defined for a publication, which you can leave on-screen by selecting the Style Palette command on the Window menu, or by pressing Command-Y on a Mac, Ctrl-Y on a PC.

surprint To print one image over another, such as type over a graphic.

tabloid A large-format publication, usually half the size of a standard newspaper page.

target printer The printer on which the final output will be printed, which may be different from the printer used for proofing.

template An electronic prototype of a publication that provides the layout grid and style sheets for similar publications. PageMaker comes with a library of templates for many different kinds of documents. You can make your own templates by creating the prototype and selecting the Template option in the Save As dialog box.

text block In PageMaker, text that, when selected, is bound at the top and bottom by two windowshade handles with loops. See also *threaded text*.

text tool The tool used in PageMaker to select text for editing and changing type specifications. When the text tool is selected, the pointer looks like an I-beam.

Text Wrap The command on PageMaker's Element menu that enables you to specify the relationship of text to graphics. Text can wrap around a graphic, flow through a graphic, or jump over a graphic. See also *graphic boundary* and *standoff*.

thin space A fixed space half the width of an en space, inserted by pressing Command-Shift-T on a Mac, Ctrl-Shift-T on a PC. Compare *em space*, *en space*, and *fixed space*.

threaded text Text placed or typed as a single file, connected in Page-Maker's memory from one column to the next and from one page to the next. When you cut, add, or move copy in a threaded-text file, PageMaker automatically adjusts subsequent text across as many pages as needed to maintain the link between all the text blocks in the threaded file.

thumbnails Rough sketches of a page design; also miniature pages that you can print by selecting the Thumbnails option in the Print/Paper dialog box (if you use a PostScript printer) or in the Print/Options dialog box (if you use a non-PostScript printer).

tick marks Marks on rulers showing the increments of measure. The larger the page view in PageMaker, the finer the increments on the ruler.

TIFF Short for Tag Image File Format, a format for electronically storing and transmitting bit-mapped, gray-scale, and color images.

Tile A print option in PageMaker that enables you to print oversize pages in sections, or tiles. Each section is printed on a single sheet of paper; the various tiles are then pasted together to form a complete page. Tile is also an option on the Window menu that sizes all open publication windows so that they can be viewed simultaneously.

Try this **"fast-move" technique:** Select the text or graphic, hold down the mouse button, and drag immediately, before you see the directional arrows. You'll see a bounding box that defines the edges of the text block or graphic but not the element itself.

tint A percentage of black or a color. In PageMaker, you create tints through the Edit Color dialog box.

toggle command A command that you turn on and off by choosing that command from a menu, such as Rulers or the various palettes listed on the Window menu.

tone See *tint*.

Toolbox A small window containing PageMaker's text and graphics tools.

Track In PageMaker, the preset spacing values available through the Track submenu in the Control Palette and in the Type Specs dialog box.

transformation In PageMaker and some other applications, refers to manipulating an object by rotating, skewing, or reflecting.

trap An overlap of abutting colors that eliminates the possibility of white leaks between the colors if the printing plates are not properly aligned.

trim In PageMaker, the page size defined in the Page Setup dialog box. In commercial printing, the size of the page after it is cut during the binding process.

type style See *style*.

verso The left-hand page.

vignette A graphic in which the background fades gradually until it blends with the unprinted paper.

weight The density of letters, traditionally described as light, regular, bold, extra bold, and so on. Also, the thickness of a rule.

white space The areas of the page without text or graphics; used as a deliberate element in good graphic design.

widow In PageMaker, defined as the first 1, 2, or 3 lines of a paragraph standing at the end of a column. You can instruct PageMaker to disallow widows through the Paragraph Specs dialog box.

width The horizontal measure of letters, described as condensed, normal, or expanded. You can alter the width of characters through the Set Width option in the Control Palette or in the Type Specs dialog box.

windowshade handles The horizontal lines with loops in the center and square dots on either end that appear at the top and bottom of a text block selected with the pointer tool.

word spacing The amount of space between words. In PageMaker, you can control the word spacing through the Spacing option in the Paragraph Specs dialog box.

wraparound text Text that wraps around a graphic. Also called runaround text. See also *Text Wrap*.

WYSIWYG An acronym for "What You See Is What You Get." Pronounced "wizzy-wig," it refers to the representation on a computer screen of text and graphic elements as they will look on the printed page.

x-height The height of the main body of a lowercase letter, excluding ascenders or descenders.

zero point The point at which the 0 on the horizontal ruler intersects with the 0 on the vertical ruler.

zero-point marker Intersecting dotted lines where the horizontal and vertical rulers meet. Drag this marker to the point on the page where you want the zeros on the two rulers to meet. See also *zero point*.

Play is generally recognized as an important component of both learning and creativity. Just "playing around" in PageMaker can accelerate your learning curve and sharpen your graphic eye. When there's no end result at stake, no fear of making a mistake, no deadline to meet, you may find it easier to experiment and become comfortable with certain commands and functions.

INDEX

Note: Page numbers in italics refer to illustrations or captions.

CREDITS

Text files were written in Microsoft Word 5.1 and placed in electronic layouts created in Aldus PageMaker 4.2 and 5.0 on an Apple Macintosh. Body text is Palatino with display in Helvetica Condensed Black Oblique. Tips are Helvetica Light with Helvetica Black for emphasis; captions are Helvetica Light Oblique with Helvetica Black Oblique for emphasis.

Cover design and art by Don Wright.
Interior design by Don Wright, production by Ronnie Shushan.
Cover color separations by Color Control, Redmond, WA.
Interior color separations by ADMAC, Berkeley, CA. Printed to film on a Scitex Dolev at 2540 dpi with a 150-line screen.

All other interior pages output by Sprintout, New York, NY.
Printed at 1270 dpi on a Linotronic 300 with a 120-line screen.

Printed by Malloy Lithographic, Ann Arbor, MI.

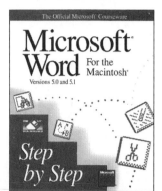